THE INDO-PAKISTANI CONFLICT

THE

INDO-PAKISTANI

CONFLICT

RUSSELL BRINES

PALL MALL PRESS

LONDON

Published by Pall Mall Press Ltd
77–79 Charlotte Street, London, W.1

FIRST PUBLISHED 1968

© 1968 RUSSELL BRINES

SBN 269.16232.1

PRINTED IN GREAT BRITAIN AT THE
CURWEN PRESS · PLAISTOW · E13

CONTENTS

FOREWORD

A brief but vicious war between India and Pakistan burst upon a surprised world in the autumn of 1965. In three weeks of major fighting and several more weeks of periodic skirmishing, the two largest of the emergent nations turned centuries of hostility against each other. They fought in one of the world's most sensitive areas, where the danger of setting off global conflict was perhaps greater than it has ever been in South Vietnam. Yet for various reasons the Indo-Pakistan War remains one of the most mysterious struggles of recent times. Even articulate Indians and Pakistanis seem unaware of all the forces which drove them into battle.

This is a case study of these forces, of the fighting and its aftermath. It shows how such wars are created, and therefore may have pertinence beyond the subcontinent. Many of the elements involved in this struggle are perceptible in other emergent areas, where the lessons of the conflict are applicable also.

The book is based upon available documentation, augmented by personal observation and the testimony of the necessarily anonymous sources available to the travelling journalist. The hostilities began during one of my several trips to the subcontinent, and I observed them from the Indian side. Plans to visit Pakistan at that time had to be cancelled, but subsequently I returned to both countries. My assessments have been weighed against thirty years' experience in covering Asia, as a foreign and war correspondent.

To the countless sources who aided my research, and particularly to those who read and criticised the manuscript, I would like to express sincere appreciation. As usual, this book would have been impossible without the patient and intelligent support of my wife, Barbara.

I

THE GLOBAL SETTING

THE GREAT flat plains of the Punjab sweep for hundreds of miles across north-western India and West Pakistan toward distant mountains. Occasionally, the land is broken by rivers and irrigation canals, by roads and clustered villages and cities. But otherwise the Punjab and its rich grainfields form a continuous tableland. From the air, it seems serene and empty, a countryside carefully laid out in brown and green mosaic. In fact, it is one of the most tumultuous regions of the subcontinent, and one of the most important.

For centuries, the Punjab has been invaded by conquering armies, plunging through the hot dust toward the loot of Delhi. They came by a historic north-western invasion route into India. The British built their fabled Grand Trunk Road along this pathway in an effort to protect their empire and to amalgamate it. When they dissolved the Indian Empire in 1947, the Punjab was divided between the newly independent nations of Pakistan and India. With few natural features to separate the new countries at this point, an arbitrary border was drawn on a map. Today, it cuts partly across fields where it is often difficult to locate. The British also tried to bind diverse peoples together by grafting British traditions and customs on to the past. The traditions still persist on both sides of the border, but so do ancient fears and enmities and the new apprehensions of modernity.

It was here, in September 1965, that the modern armies of India and Pakistan fought a major battle, involving hundreds of 45-ton tanks, heavy artillery and low-flying fighter planes. This was the climactic campaign in a brief but ferocious conflict between the two largest powers of the emergent world.

Hostilities began the previous month with sharp guerrilla action in the cool mountains of Kashmir, 200 miles to the north. A succession of counter-moves transferred the centre of action quickly and logically to the Punjab. Each army then fought to destroy the other's striking power.

The campaign in the Punjab was described as the 'biggest tank battle since World War II'. Perhaps it was, in terms of numbers, if not in tactics. But no outsider knew for certain. The world press and foreign officials were excluded from direct observation during the combat and were forced to rely largely upon second-hand reports. There is little doubt, however, that both sides fought with primitive ferocity. In the most reliable casualty estimate, the authoritative Institute for Strategic Studies of London reported that India lost between 4,000 and 6,000 in dead and wounded, and Pakistan between 3,000 and 5,000. According to the Institute, up to 300 Indian tanks and 50 aircraft were destroyed, while Pakistan lost more than 250 tanks and a maximum of 50 aircraft.[1] These figures approximated the independent estimates of United States officials. In late November 1965, the Indian government acknowledged 2,226 war dead and 7,870 wounded. It claimed 5,800 Pakistani dead.[2]

This toll resulted primarily from the fighting in the Punjab, which lasted exactly twenty-two days. For the men involved, the casualty rate approximated that of the Korean War. In three years of wide-ranging tank and aerial conflict in Korea, the total military dead and wounded for the two Korean armies reached an estimated 800,000, plus 151,449 for the United Nations' forces.[3] India and Pakistan committed to battle less than a fifth of these three Korean armies. But, on the basis of the Institute's minimum estimates, their military losses would have approached 400,000 men, if hostilities had continued for three years at approximately the same intensity.

The Punjabi campaign ended quickly and indecisively, however, after furious diplomatic activity, which probably was made effective by the mutual exhaustion of the two belligerents. The United Nations concluded a truce arrangement on September 22, 1965, fifty days after the first fighting erupted. Although both sides violated the truce, it became effective for all practical purposes by the end of 1965. On January 10, 1966, the Indian Prime Minister, Lal Bahadur Shastri, and President Ayub Khan of Pakistan agreed, at a

Soviet-sponsored meeting in Tashkent, to observe the second part of the United Nations' truce resolution by evacuating the territory each had seized in the fighting. A few hours later, Shastri died from his third heart attack—an indication, perhaps, of the severity of the secret political pressures applied against him.

The brief conflict was immensely significant for the world as well as for the subcontinent. It was fought in a highly sensitive area. Kashmir is encircled in the east by Chinese Sinkiang and Tibet; in the west, northern Kashmir is separated from the Soviet Union by a strip of Afghanistan some forty miles wide. The Punjab battlefield lies within 400 miles of the Russian border to the north and an equal distance from the nearest Chinese Communist military position in the north-east. This strategic situation aroused both Moscow and Peking and made the fighting a potential fuse in the enlarging Sino-Soviet struggle for influence in the subcontinent. Great Britain and the United States also had a major security interest in the hostilities, in addition to a financial stake of more than $10 billion. Therefore, the possibility of foreign involvement was great. Without prompt counter-action, the conflict could have become another war involving several great powers. As a result, Washington and Moscow followed parallel courses, in this instance, to restore peace, and their temporary co-operation made the truce possible. Feeble efforts by Peking to aid Pakistan and to enhance its own position by propaganda threats against eastern India were nullified largely by timely American warnings.

For the subcontinent, major hostilities between the two organised armies marked a dangerous new phase in an ancient ordeal. Centuries of bloody history had built up mutual fears and suspicions between the Hindus of India and the Muslims of Pakistan. Under British rule, communal religious riots flared periodically for more than a century into ugly spasms of murder. When the British prepared to grant independence in 1947, the compacted political and religious pressures forced the creation of a disjointed Muslim Pakistan out of portions of the Indian Empire. It consists of two parts, West and East Pakistan, divided by 1,000 miles of Indian territory. At independence, the subcontinent was swept by one of history's most passionate upheavals—a groundswell of killing, looting, arson and rape. More than half a million persons died. The holocaust, in essence, was a religious civil war. It ended indecisively.

It left festering doubts and more fears and suspicions. Hatreds moved from back alleys into the political policies of the two new nations. India and Pakistan waged a military conflict over Kashmir in 1947–48. They approached all-out war against each other on at least two other occasions. Each of these crises failed to decide any of the basic issues between the neighbours, and the failure made the next upheaval more likely, if not inevitable. In 1965, new compulsions and new apprehensions, springing from the long past, created warfare that neither side could afford. The conflict marked the first direct application of military power to the full range of problems dividing the two nations, with Pakistan seeking a solution through force. Again the effort was indecisive, and consequently a sequel may already be in incubation.

Whether the struggle of 1965 amounted to war depends largely upon definition. The Indians, in general, have avoided using this term to describe the action, although President Ayub of Pakistan bluntly told his people at the outset: 'We are at war'. The belligerents did not formally declare a state of hostility, and diplomatic relations were maintained during the height of the conflict. The fighting itself was confined to a relatively small section of north-western India and West Pakistan; the majority of the peoples in the two countries were not directly involved. Further, diplomats sometimes rely upon the traditional definition that only military operations designed to knock out the adversary constitute war: that lesser action does not properly amount to war. In this instance, there is no indication that either side had the capability or the intention of forcing the other to capitulate.

In a standard dictionary definition, however, war is 'hostile contention by means of armed forces, carried on between nations, states, or rulers, or between parties in the same nation or state'. This description is particularly suitable to current world circumstances. Modern geopolitics have produced the new strategy of limited war, the purpose of which is to use controlled military power to produce political changes within a hostile nation, rather than to seek capitulation. That was clearly Pakistan's original purpose. As a result, the Indo-Pakistan conflict became an armed interlude in a long-standing political war between the neighbours; it grew out of the political struggle and, when armed hostilities ended, the political fight continued. The resort to power was itself a most significant development which will undoubtedly have serious repercussions. In reality, then, the two nations fought a limited war that was precipitated by calculated attack under the modern disguise of guerrilla infiltration. It developed into the first open conflict between sovereign nations since the Anglo-French-Israeli attack on Suez in 1956. The campaigns in the Punjab constituted the most overt resort to organised conventional warfare since the Korean War of 1950.

Kashmir was the initial objective. The neighbours have quarrelled constantly since 1947 over this strange and remote state, which touches the rim of the world. The dispute involves the entire state of Jammu and Kashmir, a mismatched political entity of two parts. Kashmir sprawls in the foothills of the Himalaya Mountains. Its people, different from those of the rest of the subcontinent, are three-quarters Muslim, with minorities of Hindus and Buddhists. Jammu, which is predominately Hindu, lies mostly in the hot, flat plains of northern India. The whole state totals 84,471 miles, slightly larger than England and Scotland, with about 5 million inhabitants. This awkward amalgamation of extremely dissimilar peoples and regions is the result of ancient intrigue under the British Empire. In 1947, the heir to this intrigue, the last semi-independent Maharajah of Jammu and Kashmir, was given the standard choice, on the British withdrawal, of acceding to either of the two new Dominions or attempting to maintain an independence of doubtful durability. He vacillated, until his domain was invaded by tribesmen from Pakistan who were, the evidence suggests, supported by Pakistani officials. The Maharajah then acceded to India and called for help. At British suggestion, the new Indian government accepted accession with a clear pledge to hold a future plebiscite to determine the people's wishes. Indian troops then went into Kashmir and repelled the invaders. Hostilities widened, however, and the Pakistani regular army became openly involved in mid-1948. At the end of that year, an armistice ended a contained but relatively full-scale conflict for possession of the state. Since then, a cease-fire line supervised by United Nations observers has been maintained along positions held at the end of the fighting. India controls about two-thirds of Kashmir, and Pakistan the remainder.

The twenty-year military and diplomatic contest for control of the state centres around the Valley, or Vale, of Kashmir, the most populous area in the mountainous section and therefore its political centre. The Vale spreads green fields and crystal lakes across a high plateau 85 miles long and 20 miles wide, caught in the mighty grip of the distant Himalayas. Here lies Srinagar, the summer capital of Jammu and Kashmir, an ancient city of learning and a tumultuous city of modern intrigue. India firmly controls the Valley, although the population is estimated to be 90 per cent Muslim. Pakistan has sought through the years to enlist world support in ejecting India by a plebiscite. In a fair election, the Vale would be expected to vote for merger with Pakistan, carrying the rest of Kashmir with it. The Pakistanis argue that Kashmir logically belongs to them. All its roads, waterways and commerce flowed westward under the Empire. Moreover, it is contended that the creation of Pakistan as a separate religious state is incomplete as long as contiguous Muslim-dominated Kashmir is not included. This argument is based on the premise that circumstances have not changed sufficiently since the accession of October 1947 to justify Indian repudiation of the pledge to permit a plebiscite. The pledge was made officially at that time and reiterated publicly by Indian leaders for another decade. New Delhi claims, however, that circumstances have changed many times, often through Pakistani actions, and that the pledge is outdated. It contends, less convincingly, that irrevocable accession to India has been ratified by the independent actions of the State Assembly and endorsed through public elections.

Through the years of dispute, Kashmir has assumed increased significance for both sides. In 1947, it meant little to most Indians, and New Delhi appeared resigned to its annexation by Pakistan. Now, however, for reasons of national security, both nations are convinced they must maintain their present positions in Kashmir, and Pakistan has been compelled at great risk to continue pressing for control of the Indian sector. The state has become of primary strategic significance—particularly to India, menaced by the Communist Chinese foothold on the north-eastern rim of Kashmir. Swept by powerful divisive influences, India and Pakistan believe with good reason that yielding on Kashmir would so encourage separatism that their internal unity would be threatened. To the Pakistanis, Kashmir retains its deeply emotional religious significance; it is the 'soul' of Pakistan, and their Muslim 'brothers' must be rescued from Indian bondage. Although Hindus frequently speak of the sacredness of Himalayan mountains and rivers, they appear less emotionally moved on a religious level than the Pakistanis over the future of the state. Many Indians, however, believed that the creation of Pakistan was a rape of Mother India and that the loss of Kashmir would be a further unacceptable violation.

To the adversaries, these are reasons enough for their unremitting conflict over Kashmir itself. But Kashmir is only a backward, un-economic slice of snow and rocks, with one beautiful valley. Apart from strategic considerations, it is of major significance because of the symbolism that has been poured into it. The central issue between India and Pakistan is whether an Islamic state and a secular Hindu state can coexist in relative peace. Mohammed Ali Jinnah, the father of Pakistan, told his people nearly thirty years ago that the Hindus would never accept the existence of Pakistan and would attempt to eliminate it. This belief is the wellspring behind incessant claims from Rawalpindi, the Pakistani capital, that Hindu 'aggres-sion' threatens the country. Pakistan, with 100 million people, is constantly aware of the shadow cast by nearly 500 million in India. Moreover, Pakistan was so disfigured at birth, with its widely separate and vulnerable wings, that it was condemned to perpetual insecurity. Many Indians, on the other hand, believe the fiery proselytising speeches of more fundamentalist Pakistanis. They are convinced that Islamic forces will some day attempt to dominate India and destroy the relative religious tolerance practised there. As Jawaharlal Nehru, the Indian Prime Minister, said in 1951: '. . . it is not Kashmir, therefore, but rather a much deeper conflict that comes in the way of friendly relations between India and Pakistan and the situation is a grave one. We cannot give up the basic ideal [secularism] which we have held so long and on which the whole conception of our state is founded.'[4]

If the Kashmir problem could somehow be settled with satisfac-tion to both nations, the result would be a significant beginning toward resolving the principal issue between them; but the ideolo-gical conflict will persist as long as there are mutual fears and men to exploit them. Kashmir crystallises the fear, the mistrust and the bigotry that darken the subcontinent and provides a vehicle for enlarging them with modern political complications. The confronta-tion of Islam and Hinduism is an echo of the religious wars of the

Western past. It is, unfortunately, an indication of how rigidly history stood still during the generations of British rule and during the evolution of a westernised elite that has produced from India and Pakistan some of the world's most urbane diplomats. Yet, without continual agitation, it is quite possible that there would be no serious conflict between the two religions on a national level. Muslims and Hindus in both nations have learned to live peaceably together in local neighbourhoods, except when roused by agitators into flash floods of violence. National leaders took over the prejudices of the mob and incorporated them into international political policies; so that, for example, the legitimate security considerations of Kashmir have been complicated and distorted by the mistrust of back alleys. And behind these leaders, at nearly every level, men are ready and willing to whip up the masses, through fanaticism, through ignorance or political opportunism.

The war of 1965 resulted from the interplay of policies and events against this complex background. Its origins can easily be traced back to the partition of India and the horrors of the religious civil war. History had pointed the neighbours towards conflict, and the achievement of independence was not enough by itself to force either of them to change course. By following policies that, at times, were violently antipathetical to each other, the neighbours perpetuated an atmosphere of tension in which armed hostilities were probably inevitable at some point. But there have been periods of genuine peace and goodwill during the past two decades; moments when it appeared that a durable accommodation might be possible. Invariably, however, the spell was broken by some new policy or some new political statement, initiated by one of the nations without regard for the probable impact on the other. Because suspicion is so close to the surface, goodwill was instantly washed away. Each failure hardened the impasse. Thus it can be said that the persistent policies of the two governments made an armed interlude inescapable as an element of their hostility, but that these policies themselves were neither inevitable nor unalterable. During the past few years, each country has undertaken a number of highly significant initiatives, with fatal unconcern for the repercussions. The combination of these international policies and domestic events finally ignited the spark. But it was a war of misunderstanding, miscalculation and misapprehension. By Western standards, the stakes were not worth the sacrifice; from the point of view of the belligerents, they were very much worth while.

The military conflict actually began in the spring of 1965 with a test of strength in the improbable battle area of the Rann of Kutch. This is a deserted and apparently worthless stretch of sand and marsh grass, literally a salt waste, lying along the border between the north-western Indian state of Gujarat and the state of Sind, the southern part of West Pakistan. Probing actions between lightly manned rival police forces opened in January 1965. Impartial foreign diplomats say that Pakistan followed with a limited attack on April 9 which provoked sharp, controlled fighting until April 29. The campaign was obviously intended as a test of weapons and of the political climate, for the battle area was flooded, as usual, by monsoon rains in the autumn. Pakistan used American-supplied Patton tanks and other American arms for the first time, and apparently escaped any major reprisals from Washington for employing weapons that had been furnished solely as protection against aggression, particularly by communist forces. Pakistan also drew the Indians into an unfavourable battle position where it had a distinct logistical advantage, and made local gains. Hostilities ended with a political agreement hailed in Rawalpindi as a victory but bitterly condemned by Indian nationalists. Pakistan evidently concluded from all this that it was politically and militarily capable of attacking a somewhat bumbling giant neighbour to forestall or to reverse political developments which she considered dangerous to her security. The Pakistanis were not deterred by brief Indian counter-action in May, when Indian forces crossed the cease-fire line in northern Kashmir and occupied offensive positions in the mountain areas of Kargil. In August, all evidence shows, Pakistan launched a limited war against Kashmir, which quickly got out of hand.

The fighting opened with guerrilla skirmishing in Kashmir on August 5. India claims that Pakistan sent several thousand specially trained and equipped infiltrators across the cease-fire line into Indian Kashmir for the purpose of starting camouflaged war. Pakistan has vehemently denied there were any infiltrators. She contends that the Kashmiris themselves revolted against Indian rule and that neither soldiers nor Pakistanis were involved. The evidence, as most independent sources agree, generally supports the Indian

B

version of these conflicting stories and places the blame on Pakistan for initiating the hostilities. There is little reason to doubt that Pakistan had trained guerrillas for some time, with the encouragement if not the actual participation of Communist China, and sent a considerable number of them into Indian Kashmir. The United Nations Military Observer group officially reported infiltrations across the line from Pakistani territory but did not identify the infiltrators by nationality. The evident Pakistani purpose was to set off an anti-Indian revolution in the Kashmir section of Jammu and Kashmir which would either bring down the Indian-dominated state regime or would create a situation permitting active Pakistani intervention to aid the rebels. In fact, no revolution occurred, as observers on the scene agree, although it appears that attempts were made to start one. The guerrillas also failed to cripple the state and were eventually controlled by Indian forces.

The Indian army quickly responded by crossing the cease-fire line to the north and north-east, and capturing strategic positions a short distance inside Azad (Free) Kashmir, the Pakistan-held portion of the state. These moves were necessary in part, as the Indians contend, to close off main infiltration or invasion routes into Indian Kashmir; they also gave Indian forces a potential offensive position threatening Azad Kashmir. But no additional Indian advances were made. Pakistan contends that New Delhi invented the story of the infiltrators in order to justify the thrusts across the cease-fire line. Then, say the Pakistanis, they were faced with the possible loss of Azad Kashmir and a direct threat to Pakistan. In retaliation, Pakistani forces struck on September 1 at Chhamb, a point at the extreme south-western edge of the cease-fire line. This was the first Pakistani involvement in the conflict, Rawalpindi maintains.[5] The Chhamb attack was made by at least a brigade of regular troops, led by tanks. It created the possibility that Pakistan could block a vital road and seal off the entire Indian garrison of at least 100,000 men in Kashmir. Four days later, Indian tank-led units attacked West Pakistan in force across the international boundary in the Punjab, and the main conflict began. India insists, and Pakistan denies, that regular Pakistani forces first crossed an international border during the attack on Chhamb.

The Pakistanis, it appears, initiated hostilities for two main reasons. First, they wanted to block the further integration of

Kashmir into the Indian Union. For several years, New Delhi had moved slowly but inexorably towards the complete absorption of the state, and another important legal step in this process was taken in December 1964; so that the prospect grew stronger that, in a relatively short time, the Indians would succeed in removing Kashmir from legitimate international dispute. Secondly, Rawalpindi was visibly concerned by an independent rearmament programme pursued by India after the surprise Chinese Communist attack on Kashmir and eastern India in 1962. From abroad, Pakistani diplomats had predicted an armed showdown as early as the summer of 1965, because, they claimed, the build-up would give India an 8-1 numerical military supremacy over Pakistan— compared with the previous ratio of 5-1. Independent foreign observers said that the prospective equation, when the prolonged build-up was completed, would be nearer 6-1, or even 7-1, with many of the Indian forces pinned along the 1,800-mile Indo-Chinese border.[6] The Institute of Strategic Studies estimated that India would reach authorised ground strength probably in late 1967 or early 1968.[7] India had obtained limited quantities of non-offensive military equipment from Great Britain and the United States. The American share, valued at around $80 million, consisted entirely of communications and support equipment and light arms for the mountain divisions being formed as part of anti-Chinese defences. The Soviet Union had pledged assistance that, according to independent sources, would total at least $500 million. The Soviets had provided, by the outbreak of hostilities, twelve MIG-21 fighter planes, sought by India to offset Pakistan's American-supplied F-104 supersonic fighters. They had also furnished other equipment, including surface-to-air missiles for anti-aircraft defences, and were co-operating in a long-protracted project to build an Indian factory for the manufacture of MIG-designed fighters. Rawalpindi bitterly protested against 'massive' foreign arms aid to India, and President Ayub said after the start of hostilities in the Punjab: 'We always knew these arms would be raised against us.'[8]

In actual fact, India's newly imported arms played no important part in the war: but Pakistan had been almost entirely equipped by the United States as an anti-communist ally and used these weapons freely. Neither were there any indications in India during 1965 that

New Delhi was preparing for an aggressive attack, as constantly predicted by the controlled Pakistani press. Indian rearmament, apparently, was substantial if incomplete, but there is no convincing evidence that it was as large as Pakistan claimed or as threatening to it. In the atmosphere of the subcontinent, however, fear is sometimes more persuasive than fact. Indian authorities had levelled precisely the same charges in 1954, when the United States concluded a military assistance agreement with Pakistan. Although for eleven years Pakistan made no effort to turn its American weapons against India, the Indian fears remained strong and influential. In essence, the Americans created a sufficiently strong Pakistani army after 1954 to establish an acceptable military balance for the apprehensive Pakistanis. This balance persisted until the Indians upset it by attempting to enlarge their defences against a growing menace from Peking. The coupling of this development with the prospective disappearance of Kashmir as an international issue, with grave political and religious complications for Pakistani leaders, evidently triggered what was, essentially, a war of desperation.

If the initial guerrilla infiltrations were part of a carefully calculated plan, they were followed by an unusual mixture, on both sides, of opportunism, military hysteria and combat inefficiency. Action demanded counter-action, and the probable consequences do not appear to have been carefully considered. After the outbreak of guerrilla hostilities, each side could have pulled back from head-on conflict, although with some internal political risk: India by confining its initial response to the elimination of infiltrators within Indian Kashmir; Pakistan, by abandoning conflict after the failure of the 'revolution'. Instead, both nations turned to prompt enlargement of the conflict. This was unusually swift military escalation of the type which India, in particular, has vigorously criticised in other Asian wars. But Pakistan was desperate, and India was angry. The Indians fully believed that they were defending themselves against aggressive attack and that, therefore, no restraints were justified. They were convinced, for example, that they were right in attacking across the international boundary of the Punjab to prevent the isolation of the Kashmir garrison, even though the case for previous Pakistani violation of the international border was weak. This move was logical in military, if not diplomatic, terms, and it constituted a part of India's long-prepared war strategy. The action, however, was sharply criticised, and the Indians reacted with extreme bitterness. Yet Nehru had warned as early as 1952: '. . . if Pakistan by mistake invades Kashmir, we will not only meet them in Kashmir, but it will be a full-scale war between India and Pakistan.'[9]

This was a generals' war. President Ayub, a semi-dictatorial ruler, evidently assumed a dominant rule in military strategy. He did not need parliamentary sanction for his actions. Indeed, he was fully supported by the aroused people in West Pakistan, the country's political centre. In India, the Prime Minister, Shastri, left the military initiative to General J. N. Chaudhuri, Chief of Staff of the army. When Chaudhuri decided on the Punjab campaign, Shastri did not go to Parliament, but won quick informal approval from a secret meeting of the Chief Ministers or governing authorities of the states. Chaudhuri decided to advance the attack by one day, and there was no objection. In this atmosphere, military considerations were predominant. The conduct of the war does not appear to have been influenced by world diplomatic factors: internal politics alone dictated further warfare, after the initial outbreak, for all influential parties and factions strongly supported their respective governments. Restraints were practised, such as the avoidance of bombing attacks on crowded cities, but they were apparently determined by military, rather than political, circumstances. Neither side was willing to consider a truce until the first mutual military exhaustion in the tank battles of the Punjab.

Consequently, the world community discovered that it had failed after two decades of effort to erect effective barriers against war between implacable neighbours; even in the unusually strategic subcontinent. None of the restraints on which diplomats had relied proved applicable. The belligerent governments did not show any concern that local hostilities might invite foreign intervention, with the threat of nuclear attack. The impact of 'world opinion', on which Indian statesmen had placed so much emphasis in other circumstances, was negligible. India's operations were widely misunderstood, and she was virtually isolated diplomatically; yet this only increased Indian determination and defiance. Both nations initially defied the United Nations and its peace overtures with particular acrimony. They fought long beyond their financial capabilities, and to do so both severely penalised the economic development which they sorely needed. Neither poverty nor disapproval nor danger could influence the belligerents.

This factor illuminated the deep feelings behind the conflict—historic passions from the distant past which were partially submerged and partially controlled by the discipline of British colonialism. When that discipline was removed, the emotions rose to the surface and were exacerbated by the ordeal and the mistakes of creating modern nations out of unreconciled races and regions. The leaders embraced the past and perpetuated it, instead of submerging it beneath the great challenges of modernity. Into this mélange were infused the power politics of a divided world. Both India and Pakistan were influenced more than their people seem to realise by the global East-West struggle and by the attempts of their leaders to profit from it. The fusion of past and present has kept the neighbours in a tacit state of belligerence for years and now this has been prolonged. During their armed interlude, the belligerents discovered for themselves that the generalities of 'peace', long preached by diplomats, have no relevance when security or local ambitions are involved.

The same circumstances, as a generalisation, apply in varied degrees to most of the seventy-five-odd new nations created from the collapsed British, French and Dutch empires. The frozen past is alive again, and ancient enmities and ambitions are once more virile. 'Nations' have been created out of mismatched local entities, many of them unviable; borders have been carelessly drawn. All of these influences, and many more, have enormously complicated the stupendous task of building strong nations from peoples plagued by suspicion, illiteracy and economic want. While the leaders need time to solve their great problems, the demand is for speed: while they need peace, the pressure is towards war. Jawaharlal Nehru predicted that India could not create economic stability without peace and based his foreign policy on this premise. Apparently, he hoped that India by enlightened political efforts could escape the cycle of wars and imperialism which have dominated history and which characterised the growth of the older modern nations. Yet India has been attacked twice in the 1960s, and her ordeal appears far from over.

In 1963, an official United States assessment predicted that dangerous tensions would arise periodically throughout the foreseeable future in the non-communist world and, eventually, within the communist bloc. In the emergent countries, stated the report, local upheavals and anti-government movements could be expected from a variety of factions—communists of rival pro-Moscow, pro-Peking, and pro-Castro wings; nationalists and extreme rightists. These factional elements, in many instances, could be expected to create crises in order to involve the big powers on their side in local conflicts. Some would court both East and West to advance their own claims to power. The report maintained that Africa was drifting toward 'chaos' and Latin America faced a new series of anti-government upheavals; accidental hostilities threatened peace as directly as planned action; in time, communist countries might become equally unruly and could reach the point of open conflict between themselves.

This assessment was confirmed almost immediately by an expanding series of crises in Africa and by new tensions in Latin America. Violent internal unrest and upheaval have been historic features of nation-building. Africa, in particular, seemed to be embarked on the dismal succession of coups, palace revolutions and local aggressions which characterised Latin America for 150 years after its nations achieved independence from Spain and Portugal. African turmoil continued so strongly in the first part of 1966 that one seasoned observer, after touring the continent, predicted at least another five to ten years of turbulence.[10] In Africa, as elsewhere, the haste to telescope centuries of development into decades has added powerful disruptive pressures on a scale unknown when the European peoples gave tortured birth to their nation states. The modern process has also been vastly complicated by outside interference. Africa has become a new battleground for 'revolutionary' competition between Moscow and Peking. Soviet and Chinese Communist agents, trying to outdo each other, have been implicated in gun-running in every important part of the continent; they have been expelled from a number of African countries.

There is, unfortunately, no convincing evidence that the new non-communist nations will be any more successful in escaping the second historical concomitant of nation-building—the cycle of wars of ambition, fear and religious bigotry between national entities. Although Nehru and some like-minded leaders have vigorously attempted to avoid this bloody phase of development, they have been outnumbered by men more hobbled to the past. The cycle of international conflict began nearly twenty years ago with the Arab-Israeli war. It has expanded, slowly and cautiously, through further hostilities or hostile threats in the Middle East, through brief border conflicts and local imperialisms in Africa. The expansionism of President Sukarno of Indonesia nearly produced two more wars in embattled South-east Asia. The potentialities are great that this process will enlarge into a new and threatening aspect of modern turmoil. There are more nations than ever before. Their emergence has revived religious passion and tribal enmities as motives for armed conflict. Many, like India and Pakistan, have incorporated these ancient fears and enmities into national policies. The discipline under which the world has lived for more than 200 years has been suddenly removed, with nothing to replace it. The discipline was supplied by European military dominance. The big powers warred among themselves, with devastating results, but they kept the majority of the world's people at relative peace with each other. Now the big powers have declared a tacit truce between themselves for many reasons, including the fear of nuclear war. The initiative for conflict has passed to the majority of ill-assorted legal nations created from the wreckage of European colonialism.

The majority of new nations embraced non-alignment and used every possible political means to prevent the re-establishment of foreign military discipline. They were so successful that Western peace-keeping power has actually been used only sparingly in a vast, turbulent, emergent world. In the fierceness of independence, the desire to escape any form of foreign control is understandable and normal. But the new nations, in creating this situation, had only one hope of averting their own cycle of conflict and turmoil between national entities. The hope was that modern leaders would be wise enough to recognise the lessons of history and to avoid the mistakes of their European predecessors. But they have not done so.

It is possible, therefore, to foresee a number of military conflicts of varying intensity between non-communist national entities, in addition to all the other enormous internal and external pressures of the immediate future. Not only have the motivations for hostilities become stronger and more widespread; modern tactics have supplied new tools for low-cost combat. Guerrilla warfare, once solely a defensive strategy imposed on the weaker adversary, has become an offensive weapon for disguised aggression. It was used in this way by Sukarno in his 'confrontation' with the new state of Malaysia, beginning in 1963; it was attempted by Pakistan in Kashmir. Limited war, likewise, has become a method of political intervention in the affairs of another state. The potentialities range from small-scale tribal and border conflicts to major clashes between powerful armoured forces in the Middle East: and, perhaps, again in the subcontinent. The sensitivity of the modern world and its inter-dependence make each armed conflict a potential threat to peace. The situation clearly calls for fresh international peace-keeping techniques.

The Indo-Pakistan conflict was symptomatic of this accelerated global restlessness. The brief war was the largest military engage-ment between members of the emergent world, and the first major armed struggle between two sovereign powers which had been freed from colonialism. Consequently, it may provide the stimulus for a chain reaction accelerating pressures for conflict in other areas of the emergent world, as has happened in the past. The fighting on the subcontinent demonstrated a particularly significant point for ambitious or fanatical leaders elsewhere: it proved that local non-communist wars can be fought without effective international restraints, especially without immediate danger of foreign involve-ment and nuclear escalation.

Against this broad background, a case study of the Indo-Pakistan conflict may help to illuminate some of the tensions afflicting much of the world and some of the dangers hanging over it. The story properly begins with the pressures that subdivided the British Indian Empire.

2

THE PARTITION OF INDIA

THE PARTITION of the British Indian Empire into separate Hindu and Muslim nations in 1947 was a last-minute concession to rampant history. Pakistan was created from two sections of the Empire, roughly 1,000 miles apart, to give political autonomy to the Muslim minority. Hindu India, which lies between Pakistan's two wings, is four times as large and more than four times as populous. This subdivision was an awkward and tragic effort to end the religious war which had raked the subcontinent intermittently for centuries. Unseeing, men had been pushed towards it, or had driven themselves towards it, for at least thirty-seven years before independence. But partition did not become inevitable, or even widely accepted, until the gloomy day of August 16, 1946.

Early that dawn, small groups of men began slipping into the south-eastern city of Calcutta from the odorous slums on its fringes. Singly and in small bands, they dispersed through the broad streets of the Victorian city to await the rattle of steel shutters that would mark the opening of business for innumerable small shops. Mohammed Ali Jinnah, the dictatorial leader of India's Muslims, had declared a 'Direct Action Day' to emphasise, for the British and the Hindus, his determination to achieve the creation of Pakistan. The local Muslim government had proclaimed a holiday, so the men lurking in the early shadows knew that only Hindus would dare to open their shops. When they did, the waiting men pounced on them, beating, slashing, stabbing; looting the shops, then hurrying to find more victims. The attackers were *goondas*, professional toughs from the slums. They came well armed with *lathis*—long steel-tipped sticks—with knives, bicycle chains, broken bottles. They were mostly Muslims at the outset.

Throughout the early morning, the killing and torment of the helpless went on: frightened shopkeepers, old women and girls, cripples and ricksha men. At knife point, Hindus were obliged to renounce their faith; in some instances were even forced to kill one of the sacred cows roaming the streets. The enormity of this sacrilege is illustrated by the fact that the cows were untouched in 1943 when more than a million persons died in a Bengali famine. As the turmoil mounted, the Muslim police at first looked the other way, partly through religious prejudice and partly, it appears, because of orders. By mid-morning, Hindu and Sikh *goondas* were out in revenge, not to protect members of their own community or to risk their own lives, but to seek defenceless Muslims. They were equally ruthless. The thugs and the fanatics, who eventually joined the conflict, fought only one brief pitched battle; yet, when the spasm of murder ended three days later, 6,000 men, women and children were dead, and 20,000 had been injured.[1]

It was the worst communal riot in the 120 years during which records have been compiled on the informal man-to-man war between Hindus and Muslims and Sikhs. Shocked men talked at once of civil war, and they were right, for the conflict quickly spread to other parts of the empire. Conflict, murder and brutality created a constant undertone for the political negotiations that continued for almost another year about the kind of state to establish when British rule was removed. Although Jinnah, like other leaders, deplored the violence in Calcutta, it had reinforced his contention that the establishment of Pakistan was the only alternative to civil war. The pressures for partition, which Jinnah was leading and had helped to create, had been powerful but not irresistible up to that point. After the Calcutta explosion, there was no turning back and partition became inevitable.

This murderous episode erupted from the peculiar alchemy of the subcontinent. It sprang, first, from the inflammable nature of the men and their beliefs. Religious hatreds had been nurtured through generations of economic, social and political rivalry between religious communities, and manipulated continually by ignorant or unscrupulous leaders. Jinnah called for 'Direct Action' primarily in reaction to the unwise public comments of a man he hated, Jawaharlal Nehru. The day passed quietly elsewhere in the empire, but it is inconceivable that Jinnah did not expect some form of trouble.

In Calcutta, a local Muslim political leader was accused of arming, organising and setting loose the first wave of *goondas*, partly for his own advantage. Finally, the thugs were ready to exploit the situation.

The circumstances were not unusual or accidental. The mixture of naked force, ruthlessness, hysteria and cynical manipulation has been a constant factor in the life of the subcontinent for many generations. It has heavily influenced most of the major political decisions of recent times. It affects day-to-day living; for who can say how explosive religion would be, if there were no politicians or thugs to exploit it? The presence of these forces helps to explain why Muslim and Hindu leaders reacted with over-sensitivity in the forties to political statements and actions which on the surface appeared of secondary importance, as they still do today. It helps to explain how the two peoples could stumble into civil war in 1946 and into limited war in 1965. The mob, in many respects, is the unseen ruler of the subcontinent. It is always there, and its role in history cannot be ignored.

The faith of Islam was brought to India in the eighth century AD by Arab traders and, principally, by Turkish invaders knifing through the vulnerable north-west. For 1,000 years, the Hindus lived under despotic and often cruel Muslim rule. Even today, they cannot forget that their sacred land was violated by Muslim conquerors, and this underlies their fear of a strong and aggressive Pakistan. Neither can the Muslims of the subcontinent forget that their forefathers once dominated the Hindus and that, for many reasons, the Muslim community sank into a secondary position under British rule. Today's Muslims, in large measure, are the descendants of converted Hindus and therefore are indistinguishable from their Hindu neighbours, except in belief and in some externals. The Turkish conquerors converted partly by the sword but mainly by persuasion. They preached equality and thereby led an early revolution against the caste system, upon which Hinduism is based. The outcasts, who had no standing in traditional society, turned for relief to the new religion. They gave Indian Muhammadanism the forcefulness of social protest and the restlessness of the dispossessed.

Islam is a virile, disciplined faith. It exalts masculinity and some forms of war, yet emphasises strong communal controls. The Prophet Muhammad (AD 570–632) preached complete submission to the will of Allah and established a form of prayer symbolising this act. Islam means 'to surrender', and a Muslim is one who does this. Muhammad bound his first converts together in a religious blood brotherhood, and since then Muslims have formed tight communities and strongly religious states. He established strict injunctions on daily living, some for hygienic reasons, which became part of continuing religious belief. In this faith, the world is divided into two hostile camps; one is at peace because the true faith reigns, but the second, the 'abode of war', lies in the darkness of non-Islamic doctrine. Theoretically, all children are born Muslims, but the unbelievers have been diverted to other faiths by misguided parents. It is the duty of a ruler of an 'abode of Islam' to convert the unbelievers and bring them into the light. If they refuse to be converted peacefully, the Muslim duty in theory is to wage *jehad* or 'holy war', a concept preached often by modern propagandists but seldom implemented. The Koran, the holy book which Muhammad dictated, says that 'to fight for religion is better than the world' but it also contains this instruction: 'Fight in the way of Allah against those who fight against you, but begin not hostilities. Allah loveth not aggressors.' In general dogma, Muslims can be governed only by Muslims, and the unconverted are tolerated within a Muslim state, but often as second-class citizens. Each true believer is considered equal in the worship of the one true God; the rich and the poor kneel together in the communal prayer frequently characterising the faith. In practice, Islam has failed to achieve the political and social democracy often proclaimed for it, and in the reality of the subcontinent it is no longer a revolutionary force.

Orthodox Hinduism preaches the reverse of these fundamentals. Human beings are born with unequal capabilities and intellect, because of their actions (karma) in a previous existence. Their concern is to perform the duties assigned to them in this life in the hope of improving their spiritual and social position in the next life. This provides the religious justification for dividing society into numerous castes, each assigned a position and a function, with those outside of caste performing the unwelcome chores. These basic inequalities make it inconceivable, in the Hindu view, to expect men to worship the same God in the same way or to create a theocratic or religious state for this purpose. Rather, men should be permitted to worship diverse gods in different ways, and they should be left alone to do so. Since Hindus acquire religion by being born into it, freedom of worship means freedom to evolve their own religious creeds without interference. They are tolerant of others who wish to do the same, and in the past have adjusted themselves to them; but the Hindus are less tolerant of efforts to convert them away from their faith. The Hindu worships alone at temples which have been opened only recently to all castes but not to all religions. 'His human utopia', says one historian, 'is a state of philosophic anarchy; the Muslim's is the well-drilled regiment.'[2]

The two communities have other basic differences of great importance to the simple common man, easily influenced by the priest or politician he trusts. To Hindus, the cow is sacred and protected; more than 200 million of them roam through food-short modern India. Muslims eat beef but regard pork as unclean; the Hindus have no such taboo about pigs. Hindu temples are elaborately carved with figures of men and animals, but the Koran strictly forbids idols. The divergences extend further to dress and family customs. Neighbours in crowded cities can look like each other and speak the same language, yet still be divided by the chasm created by religion. They can work harmoniously together, yet be turned into madmen raging against each other by the slaughter of a cow or the desecration of a temple, or even by the intemperate words of fanatical priests and laymen belonging to both faiths.

Under British rule, the Muslims fell swiftly from proud overlordship to a muttering minority. Both communities faced the consequences of conquest by an alien power, but rather than join together in opposition, they contended with each other for influence. The Hindus profited economically. They lived near the seaports where trade was brisk. Hindu landlords were appointed when the British reorganised the land tenure system. Through the seaports, new ideas and education came into the country. The Hindus welcomed them, but the Muslims penalised themselves by refusing to accept the learning of infidels. By the middle of the nineteenth century, the Hindus had developed a large middle class of business and professional men. The Muslim middle class was small and generally uninfluential. In the Muslim south-eastern areas, now East Pakistan, Hindus supplied 90 per cent of the professional class, controlled 80 per cent of commerce and almost exclusively dominated money-lending. For a decade after the army mutiny against the British in

1857—the Indian Mutiny or the First War for Independence, depending on the point of view—the British discriminated against the Muslims, because they believed the outbreak was a Muslim plot to restore the Mogul dynasty.

In reaction to this situation and, in part, to the activities of Hindu political factions, Muslim communalism grew stronger. One result was a fundamentalist revival which sought to strip modern innovations and foreign influences from the Islamic faith. The movement, called Wahabiism, preached the slogan 'Back to the Koran!' and sought to restore the holy war. This created its own counter-action within the Muslim community, an attempt to restore prestige by modernising the faith. Sir Syed Ahmad Khan, the founder of Aligarh University, the great Muslim institution within what is now Hindu India, expressed the new modernism in this way: the two camps of Islam and War are conditions of the mind, and Islam is to be spread by example, not violence. The international Islamic state need not be political; it can be served by the actions of the faithful, who in turn can be loyal to many governments, including those controlled by non-Muslims.[3] But fundamentalism persisted. It is notable that modern Pakistani leaders talk in these terms, at least in propaganda, and speak of creating an international political state.

Throughout the last half of the nineteenth century, riots were frequent between the two communities. These arose, in part, from the incipient politico-religious conflict between the strengthened Muslim community and such organisations as the dogmatic Hindu Mahasabha. The Indian revolutionary organisation, the National Congress, which was founded in 1885, was led for long periods by religiously aggressive and sometimes dogmatic Hindus, such as Tilak, who alienated the Muslims. But communal bloodshed also resulted from more mundane quarrels: the clash of crowds at overlapping Hindu and Muslim festivals; exorbitant rents or interests levied by a member of one community on a tenant or debtor of the other; controversy over ownership of land or the right to erect a religious building; a false rumour in a bazaar.

The politico-economic conflict between the two communities widened quickly at the start of the twentieth century. In 1905, Lord Curzon, the able but imperious Viceroy, divided the south-eastern province of Bengal into two parts for administrative reasons. Eastern Bengal became a Muslim province, thus foreshadowing the creation of East Pakistan. Hindu Bengalis vigorously protested and, in the new anti-foreign nationalism of the times, their grievances became a nation-wide issue. Tilak coined the word *swaraj* (self-rule) which became the watchword for independence. Agitation, demonstrations and an anti-British economic boycott eventually forced annulment of the partition six years later. In the process, Congress was fashioned into a nation-wide party, instead of a collection of loose groups. Muslim leaders, fearing the prospective success of Hindu agitation, formed the Muslim League in 1906 to obtain greater political influence. In 1909, the Morley-Minto reforms granted Indians limited representation in provincial legislative councils. This first step towards home rule also established the system of providing separate electoral lists for minority groups, with a certain number of seats reserved for them. The purpose was to solve communal rivalry, but the result was to exacerbate it. The concept of 'communal representation' meant the recognition of the political separateness of Hindus and Muslims, a precedent of immense consequence. 'Behind the shadow of democracy', says a historian, 'had come the shadow of Pakistan.'[4] The principle was enlarged, not reduced, in two successive Indian constitutions granted by the British, in 1919 and 1935. It was poison in the bloodstream of politics.

For the next forty-eight years, until independence, the conflict between the Muslim League and Congress became the dominant undertone to the central Indian struggle for freedom. The two political groups co-operated for six years, after concluding the Lucknow Pact of 1916 by which the Hindu Congress agreed to a separate Muslim election list. Thereafter, they grew apart, and the break became auspicious in 1928. At that time, the late Pandit Motilal Nehru, father of Free India's first Prime Minister, drew up a proposed constitution for immediate dominion status for India. Although never adopted, the Nehru report frightened the Muslims, because it proposed a strong federal government and the elimination of separate electoral rolls and other mechanisms on which the Muslims depended to maintain a political foothold. 'This', says a noted Hindu, 'was the Congress principle of secularism, but, admirable though it might be in theory, it drove the Muslims away from the Congress.'[5] The report also brought together two divergent wings of the League behind a declaration of policy advocating a separate electorate and a loose federation which would practically assure self-government for Muslim provinces. These divergent positions were maintained afterwards by the two parties. In 1937, the conflict became so critical that some observers date partition from that time. During provincial elections that year, the Muslim League campaigned on a pledge to co-operate with Congress on a coalition basis, but had little success. Congress won intoxicating victories and, notably in the United Provinces, refused to share power; instead, it insisted that Muslims could be taken into the government only if they joined Congress. This was consistent with the position of Gandhi and other Congress leaders that their party represented all India and no others were necessary, but the purpose may have been to smother the League before it grew stronger.[6] The policy convinced Muslim leaders that they had been doublecrossed and turned them towards more bitter communalism.

Two significant factors appeared behind this reaction. One was the growth of strong and perhaps legitimate fear that the Hindus intended to swamp the Muslims politically under the democratic independence towards which the country was heading. The second was the burgeoning ambition of Mohammed Ali Jinnah, the gaunt, determined lawyer who became the *Qa'id'i 'Azam*, the 'Great Leader' of India's separatist Muslims and the father of Pakistan. The tides of popular feeling and the strong man's drive merged at this point and became inseparable.

Jinnah was a reed of a man, standing over six feet and weighing less than 140 pounds. The sharp bones of a determined face struck out over hollow cheeks; he suffered from chronic bronchitis and died from lung cancer. He was impeccable, aristocratic, and icy even in the worst heat, always wearing carefully tailored Savile Row suits and frequently sporting a monocle. Arrogant, yet honest; insulting, but sensitive to the slightest personal snub; a revolutionary who disdained the mob and its sweaty, violent protests—Jinnah still remains mysterious, for no one knows with certainty the source of the drive which shattered a continent. His grandfather was a Hindu and, although born in Karachi as a Muslim, Jinnah himself revealed no particular religious devotion. In 1892, at the age of sixteen, he began law studies in England and passed his examinations in the unusually short period of two years. Admitted to the bar at the age of twenty, he returned to practise in Bombay.

C

Ten years later, Jinnah joined the Congress Party and later the Muslim League. During this period and until 1928, he preached Hindu-Muslim unity and predicted that independence would not come until the two communities joined together.[7] Jinnah rose in the hierarchy of Congress until 1920, when Gandhi and his tactics of non-violent civil disobedience became popular. Jinnah is reported to have been dismayed and alienated when he attended one demonstration which turned violent. At the Nagpur party congress in December 1920, he pleaded for a return to constitutional methods to win freedom. He was jeered by impatient delegates, particularly by fellow Muslims, and soon resigned from the party. In addition to his feeling about Gandhi's strategy, Jinnah was apparently motivated, like many other Muslims, by apprehension that the Hindu Congress was jeopardising Muslim interests and must be opposed with a stronger organisation.[8] In 1934, Jinnah became President of the Muslim League under an apparent mandate to revitalise it with a strong hand. Within a year, the quickening political turmoil in India enabled him to establish dictatorial control, and he became the *Qa'id'i 'Azam*. In one Hindu version, Jinnah moved from Congress to the League primarily to lash back at Gandhi and the Congress delegates who had insulted him.[9]

But to establish and expand his power, Jinnah had to rule the forces upon which it was based. His growing intransigence over Muslim separatism was attuned to the prevailing emotions of the men around him as well as the Muslim masses from whom the leader himself held aloof. The Muslims, frightened by the strength of Hinduism in the anti-foreign nationalism sweeping the country, feared that their community and their faith would be eliminated under Hindu rule and that they would become socially and economically inferior. 'In my judgement,' said Jinnah, 'democracy can only mean Hindu raj [power] all over India; to this, Muslims will never submit.'[10] Political leaders kept the eyes of the common man on the communal problems and did little to plan economic and social improvements within the Muslim community. One consequence of their agitation was that communal riots were particularly violent throughout the 1920s and 1930s.

In general, the Muslim leaders feared the establishment of a Hindu state more than they abhorred the thought of continuing under British rule. They did not participate in civil disobedience against the British nor did the League or its Muslim members assume any other conspicuous role in the battle for independence. The nationalism preached by these leaders, consequently, was confined to narrow communal hatreds. It was not nationalism in the sense of opposing foreign rule, the force dominating the Hindus; and it was far from such sophisticated manifestations of nationalism as pride in race or country.

For their part, the Hindus and particularly their leaders were more preoccupied with the still unfinished campaign for independence and their incipient social revolution. This did not deter them from seeking political control over the Muslim minority, but it deeply coloured their attitudes. The Hindus had supplied the manpower and the energy for the agitation which seemed to be weakening the British but which had not yet brought freedom. Hindu leaders had gone to jail. In their eyes, the Muslims had simply stood by during this great campaign, and, worse, had complicated it by creating communal bloodshed. Experience had made the Hindu leaders obdurate and impatient. Few of them took Muslim separatism seriously, then or later. And, typically, the Hindus looked at communal problems in many diverse ways, not with the relative unity of the Muslim community. During this period, the Hindu Mahasabha contributed further to communal violence but it did not speak for the entire Hindu community or for the majority of its members. The Mahasabha attacked Congress for being too lenient toward the Muslims, but Congress retained its power.

The Congress decision to renounce a coalition with the League after the 1937 elections placed Jinnah in a dangerous position. This ambitious and implacable man and his political organisation were virtually forced out of national politics. Jinnah then had the choice of bowing to Congress or of turning towards communalism. His choice was predictable; he aroused the masses with the cry that Islam was in danger. Every slight and act of discrimination was magnified, and the charge that already Hindus were taking control over the government was emphasised. Two years later, Congress resigned from its ministries in protest against being committed by the British to the Second World War without consultation. Jinnah proclaimed December 22 as a 'Day of Deliverance', from Hindu rule, and it was commemorated every year until independence. This was a politician's trick, but it brought out the people in widespread observance. The mood had changed abruptly between 1937 and 1939, wrote one traveller, and 'Pakistan was in the air'. With the exaggeration that later became notable, the Muslim leaders also accused Congress of numerous atrocities. They recited a number of political and social complaints which were petitionable but hardly atrocious.   Chiefly, they protested against the expulsion of non-Congress Muslims from ministries and their replacement by party members whom the League considered renegades from Jinnah's organisation. Other 'atrocities' included insistence upon the Hindu rather than the Urdu version of Hindustani.

The word 'Pakistan' had first been put forward in 1933 as a religious concept by Indian Muslim undergraduates at Cambridge. Taken from the Persian, it means 'Land of the Pure'. When given a political sense later, Muslim separatists made Pakistan into an acrostic of the regions they envisaged in their homeland. The 'K', as often claimed, stood for Kashmir, but East Pakistan was not included.* The Muslim League first adopted the concept of a separate state in a resolution of 1940, but Pakistan was not mentioned by name. For several years, primary support for the idea came not from the Muslim-dominated regions which were to form the new state, but from inland areas where Muslims were in the minority and more fearful of their future. Muslim splinter parties outside the League were indifferent or opposed to the proposal, and at first it had only limited acceptance within the community. Jinnah and the League also failed to win support from Muslim countries outside India. The Arabs, in particular, held back because in their view Congress was fighting the same nationalist battle against imperialism that they were, and demands for partition threatened to perpetuate foreign control. Practical politics thus nullified the claim that all Muslims were religiously united by the urge to convert the world. Even the prospect of creating a new 'state of Islam' could not bring them together.

Within India, however, the pressures were mounting. By the end of the Second World War, it was clear that Britain intended to grant early independence, although some Hindus remained suspicious and doubtful. It should also have been clear that Jinnah alone spoke for the majority of the Muslims and would have a decisive voice in

* In the acrostic for Pakistan, P is for the Punjab, A for Afghans (Pathans), K for Kashmir, S for Sind, and 'stan' is Persian for country.

any political arrangement for an independent nation. As early as 1942, the League had endorsed his dictatorial power with a resolution stating: 'This meeting emphatically declares the Quaid-i-Azam Muhammad Ali Jinnah, President of the All-India Muslim League, alone represents and is entitled to speak on behalf of the Muslim nation.' Since then, his prestige and authority had increased greatly. The problem confronting the British and the Hindus, therefore, was how to create a viable new nation that would satisfy Jinnah. In one of history's most tragic misconceptions, the Hindu leaders universally ignored this reality and consistently underestimated Jinnah himself.

Jinnah based his demands for a separate Muslim state on the contention that the subcontinent was actually composed of two individual nations. 'Islam', he said, 'is not merely a religious doctrine, but a realistic and practical code of conduct—in terms of everything important in life; of our history, our heroes, our art, our architecture, our music, our laws, our jurisprudence. In all these things, our outlook is not only fundamentally different, but often radically antagonistic to the Hindus'. Our names, our clothes, our foods—they are all different; our economic life, our educational ideas, our treatment of women, our attitude to animals—we challenge each other at every point.'[11]

The concept of partition was anathema to Hindus. Religiously, it would mean the rape of Mother India, the far corners of which were sacred to a nature-worshipping people. Perhaps the tendency to discount the power of Muslim separatism arose first from the religious belief that nothing could disturb the pre-ordained wholeness of this land. As the late President Rajendra Prasad pointed out, the daily cleansing ritual performed by millions of Hindus obliges them to picture the entire country and renews their belief in the sacredness of its mountains and rivers. The water with which the Hindu washes himself comes from a number of holy rivers, including the Indus which, except for its headwaters, lies within modern Pakistan. Prasad added that this daily ritual has been observed faithfully under all dominations, including the Muslim and the British. 'It cannot be denied that, irrespective of who rules, and what were the administrative or political divisions of the country, the Hindus have never conceived of India as comprising anything less than what we regard as India today.'[12] This explanation was republished in 1946.

There were other grave practical disadvantages in the creation of Pakistan. Jinnah originally demanded six provinces of British India and eventually settled for a smaller area, but the liabilities of the proposed new state were inherent from the beginning. The spread of Islam had been irregular, so that the two most populous regions lay across the continent from each other. To place them under a single government meant establishing administrative control over two separate and dissimilar wings of what was to be a single nation. Today, West Pakistan, the political centre of the country, is separated from East Pakistan, the agricultural centre, by the heartland of Hindu India; the two sections of Pakistan are 750 miles apart at the closest point. This division disrupted the political and economic integration which had characterised British India. East Pakistan, for example, depends heavily upon the growing of jute, but in 1947 the processing plants were in Indian Calcutta.

From the military point of view, the division was potentially dangerous. The Japanese advance into the borders of India during the Second World War had demonstrated the new vulnerability of the eastern frontier. East Pakistan has an indefensible border with Burma and is entirely surrounded by India. From the beginning, therefore, it was a strategic liability for the new nation. The turbulent north-west, which was incorporated into Pakistan, the weaker of the two new nations, had been the traditional invasion route into India, and the British had based their strategy on containing the northern neighbour, an aggressive Russia. Moreover, the severance of the north-west revived historic hostility between that region, the 'sword arm' of the subcontinent, and the rest of India.

Politically and socially, the predictable consequences of partition were equally serious. It would not solve the communal problem. Jinnah's maximum demands would have given him the homeland of only 63 per cent of India's Muslims, along with 16 per cent of the non-Muslims. Some of the minorities which the Muslims proposed to assimilate were as hostile to them as they were to the Hindus. In the North West Frontier Province, a Muslim organisation known as the Red Shirts (Khuda-i-Khidmatgar, 'Servants of God') consistently opposed partition and won brief control of the province by defeating the Muslim League in the 1946 elections. Its leader, the venerable Abdul Ghaffar Khan, had been deeply influenced by Gandhi and had introduced his non-violent tactics among his Pathan followers in seeking independence from British India. In the Punjab, the bearded Sikhs, who were finally the chief losers, were unalterably opposed to partition. The East Pakistanis, who generally behaved more like their Hindu Bengali neighbours than the Muslims of the West, were lukewarm from the beginning. Finally, to build Pakistan, the Muslim leaders had to anticipate constructing a nation virtually from the bare ground, for their territory would contain few of the essentials for nationhood.

'These disadvantages', writes a historian, 'were so certain, so clearly pointed out, so much calculated to affect Muslims as well as Hindus, that they seemed to most foreign observers to forbid creation of Pakistan.'[13] They seemed, at least, to support the Hindu contention that, for all practical purposes, India was one nation and should be maintained as one nation. Except for religion, Jinnah described differences between the two communities which were no more unbridgeable than the distinctions of region, language and thought characterising the vast mass of India or such other fundamentally dissimilar peoples as those constituting China. He did not mention, of course, the ability of individual Muslims and Hindus, or even large groups of them, to live and work together—perhaps indefinitely, if not aroused by agitators. The question of reconciling the two religions, or of creating conditions for their coexistence, has long occupied philosophers, and throughout history several compromise beliefs have arisen. It is possible that, if the issue were solely religious, an adjustment would have been made long ago, but economic and political rivalry infinitely complicated the basic issues. While religion was the watchword of separatism, it was not the sole motive. And, while the power of separatism was undeniable, its logic is open to doubt. It can be argued that the revival of fundamentalist religious beliefs as justification for nationhood is incompatible with modern times.

None of these formidable obstacles deterred Jinnah. He preached his vision with cold determination and ruthless single-mindedness. He was impervious to argument and personal appeal from leading Hindus, and if his lawyer's mind saw the illogic in his scheme, he gave no public indication. Even today, Hindus are inclined to believe that he was influenced only by the thirst for personal power. The 'two nations' doctrine and the demand for partition probably 'began as mere political slogans advanced for tactical purposes', says one commentator, 'but they proved to have such fascination that, in the end, they dominated their author. Jinnah began to feel that he had the power to achieve partition, and power can be a great intoxicant. He thought that if he could do it, why should he not? The other Muslim politicians, for the most part, hitched their waggon to the rising star . . .'[14] Pandit Jawaharlal Nehru, who was to play such an important role in the drama, said bluntly that Jinnah used separatism and anti-Hinduism as a means of winning easy power and secular attention, not because he really believed in Islam and Pakistan. Leonard Mosley disagrees with this in his study of the period, *The Last Days of the British Raj*. 'This, I think,' he says, 'is an unfortunate misreading of Jinnah's state of mind . . . [Nehru] could not believe that Jinnah was sincere. Yet there was always one thing certain about Mohammed Ali Jinnah. He could be arrogantly, stupidly, infuriatingly wrong, but he was always honest and he was never insincere.'[15]

Whatever the case may have been there is reason to believe, as Mosley contends, that Jinnah did not expect to realise Pakistan, until partition was actually achieved. It was possible that, despite his public inflexibility, he was prepared to accept a compromise, after prolonged bargaining, at least until the Calcutta riots. But time was running out. The League had rapidly expanded its influence as the promoter of Pakistan during the war years, when London severely crippled Congress by imprisoning its leaders and disbanding its organisations. In the elections of 1945–6, the League almost completely swept the seats elected by the Muslim community, thus virtually eliminating the splinter parties which had won three-quarters of these in 1937. This meant that it spoke politically on behalf of the 90 million Muslims against some 250 million Hindus. With its new strength, the League demanded Pakistan as the non-negotiable basis for further consideration of the kind of constitution to frame for a freed subcontinent. The Indian Congress, which also had increased its strength, refused. But it softened its previous insistence upon a strong central government by the granting of greater local powers.

In this atmosphere, the British proposed a compromise. A three-man Cabinet Mission was sent to India in March 1946, by the newly elected Labour government, and canvassed opinion for three months.

In its report, the Mission rejected the outright establishment of Pakistan but recommended a rather cumbersome system which made concessions to separatism. A unitary government would be established but with control only over foreign affairs, defence and communications. The remaining authority would go to the provincial governments, thus giving Muslim-dominated areas extensive autonomy and protection against Hindu pressure. Further, the provinces would be free to form themselves into large groups, with the potentiality of creating a state within a state. Three rough groupings, two predominantly Muslim and the third Hindu, were to be established at once. They would have the right in ten years to band more tightly together or to secede from one group and join the other. An interim coalition government of the two main parties would be formed until a constituent assembly could frame a constitution.

To the surprise of the British, both the League and Congress accepted the plan in essentials. Jinnah, according to one account, acquiesced because he interpreted it as a route to Pakistan.[16] Congress was deeply influenced still by Gandhi, who endorsed the proposal after prolonged thought. Moreover, the Cabinet Mission plan closely paralleled a proposal made earlier by Maulana Abul Kalam Azad, the Muslim President of Congress and one of the distinguished non-League Muslims who opposed partition as a means of insuring the community's rights. Azad pointed out that the numbers and location of India's Muslims meant that:

> They are in quantity and quality a sufficiently important element in Indian life to influence decisively all questions of administration and policy . . . In such context, the demand for Pakistan loses all force. As a Muslim, I for one am not prepared for a moment to give up my right to treat the whole of India as my domain and to share in the shaping of its political and economic life. To me it seems a sure sign of cowardice to give up what is my patrimony and content myself with a mere fragment of it . . . I would say that in any case the nine crores [90 million] of Muslims constitute a factor which nobody can ignore and, whatever the circumstances, they are strong enough to safeguard their own destiny.[17]

Two months after announcement of the Cabinet Mission plan, Nehru succeeded Azad as President of the Congress. In his speech to the party congress and in a subsequent press conference, Nehru predicted that the grouping scheme would fail. The Hindus, he said, would not support it and anti-separatist forces would oppose it successfully in two key provinces, the North West Frontier and Assam. This prediction was only partially correct. But Nehru had implied that the provinces could refuse at once to join the initial groupings assigned to them by the plan, instead of waiting a decade. This was a position clearly contrary to the conditions under which the League had accepted the Mission proposal and was repudiated by the British.[18] Nehru's comments, therefore, could be interpreted as evidence that the new President intended using his influence to have Congress sabotage the plan before it became effective. At least, they revealed Nehru's own dissatisfaction with the proposed solution. Michael Brecher, Nehru's biographer, calls the speech 'one of the most fiery and provocative statements in his forty years of public life'. The episode was a 'serious tactical error', says Brecher, a sentiment echoed by modern Hindu commentators. 'Jinnah was given an incomparable wedge to press more openly for Pakistan on the grounds of Congress "tyranny".'[19] And this was the result.

If Jinnah had been disposed to compromise, the atmosphere created by mutual receptivity to the Cabinet Mission plan presented the last feasible opportunity to work out an arrangement short of partition. The plan itself appeared unworkable, and its tentative acceptance by both parties was more of a façade than solid agreement. Yet the proposal contained sufficient safeguards in answer to legitimate Muslim fears for it to have provided the basis for further negotiation, conducted secretly and removed from popular emotion. If Jinnah was not prepared to compromise and, instead, was fighting for Pakistan with a fanaticism undetected by the Hindus, then even at this date it was doubtless too late to hold the country together. The unfortunate fact is that the Hindu leaders never handled Jinnah either as a fanatic or as a political opportunist, but as a man of doubtful reality. And Jinnah, whatever his motives, took advantage of every Congress mistake with such skill and determination that he condemned the subcontinent to indefinite torment, of which the war of 1965 was a part.

In these delicate circumstances, it was an irony of history that the two chief protagonists, Nehru and Jinnah, were dissimilar men who spoke with open contempt of each other. Jinnah called Nehru 'an arrogant Brahmin who covers his Hindu trickiness with a veneer of Western education. When he makes promises, he leaves a loophole, and when he cannot find a loophole, he just lies.' To Nehru, the well-educated author and book-lover, Jinnah was a narrow-minded provincial. 'He had no real education', the Indian leader once said. 'He was not what you call an educated man. He had read law books and an occasional work of light fiction, but he never read any real book.'[20] Moreover, these two men and others around them allowed personal attitudes to colour the policies they were creating for great nations: a luxury that more seasoned statesmen have found too expensive to ask their people to bear. Yet personalities still weigh heavily in the political decisions of the subcontinent.

On June 27, the Muslim League formally withdrew its support for the Cabinet Mission plan. It also set aside August 16 as 'Direct Action Day' for Muslims to demonstrate their determination to partition India. Jinnah predictably had been incensed by Nehru's comments. Lord Wavell, the Viceroy, had attempted to bring the parties together and, at his insistence, Congress had passed a resolution reaffirming its confidence in the Cabinet plan and deprecating Nehru's remarks. But Jinnah refused to be placated. He also based his action on the contention that the British had violated an implied pledge to allow the League to form an interim government by itself, after Congress had at first declined to partici-pate—although manifestly the Muslims, outnumbered more than two to one, could not legitimately claim the right to rule the country. 'This day,' said Jinnah, 'we bid good-bye to constitutional methods . . . Today we have also forged a pistol and are in position to use it.' He had been given an opportunity to strike hard, and he seized it quickly. But it was a fatal step, too fatal to be justified by the circumstances.

Jinnah could hardly have been unaware of the consequences of his decision to turn to direct action. He had ridden the forces of com-munal passion and had helped to arouse them too long to be blind to their power and explosiveness. Riots had been almost continual throughout 1946 in Bihar and Bengal provinces. There is no concrete evidence that Jinnah planned or expected the holocaust of Calcutta, but he could hardly have been surprised by it. The mobs represented his ultimate weapon, and he was turning to it. Calcutta, India's largest city, is traditionally the most volatile. It was part of

Muslim-controlled Bengal province, administered at that time by the government of the Chief Minister Shaheed Suhrarwardy, a high-living political boss who travelled with a bodyguard of *goondas*. Suhrarwardy had his own dreams of empire, but he paid lip service to the concept of Pakistan to win favour with Jinnah and to prevent being displaced from office. He had made special preparations for an auspicious August 16. Eleven days earlier, he wrote a newspaper article under a nom de plume, saying: 'Bloodshed and disorder are not necessarily evil in themselves, if resorted to for a noble cause. Among Muslims today, no cause is dearer or nobler than Pakistan.' On 'Direct Action Day', the Muslim thugs who started the killing were suspiciously numerous, well-armed, and mysteriously supplied with such scarce essentials as transport and petrol for burning shops. They moved with precision, in the vacuum created by police inaction, to strike the final blow for Pakistan.

On that morning, 1,000 miles away in Bombay, Nehru undertook what must have been one of the most distasteful assignments of his career. He called on Jinnah to ask him to abandon direct action and join an interim government which was being formed under Nehru, with five places reserved for the Muslim League. Apart from their other differences, these two sensitive men epitomised the continuing psychological conflict of the subcontinent. Nehru, the revolutionary, had spent years of dreary imprisonment in the fight for independence; he was in a hurry to achieve it and to build a new state embodying his westernised idealism. He was disdainful of men with a lesser vision who battled for more limited goals. Jinnah also wanted independence, but he had suffered nothing in its cause. Rather, it was the vehicle for achieving religious separatism, a reactionary aspiration in terms of Nehru's revolution. Jinnah had marched step by step from one power position to another by using every force at his command. After each gain, he could be dislodged only by the use of superior power, in one form or another. He capitalised ruthlessly on each weakness of his adversary, and one of the exploitable weaknesses of this moment was time. The Hindus were impatient for freedom and authority, and events would soon foreshorten the time left for sane independence.

Nehru's mission, undertaken at the Viceroy's urging, was foredoomed, if for no other reason than the fact that Jinnah had all the power. They talked fruitlessly for eighty minutes, and while they talked the thugs of Calcutta were slaughtering the innocent. As Nehru left Jinnah's house, he could see the traditional black flags of protest flying over Bombay. The city was Hindu-controlled and remained quiet during that day, but the black flags were more symbolic than ever. The civil war had begun.

It flamed rapidly, and in a matter of weeks much of the country was involved. Hindus were blamed for a particularly violent upheaval in northern Bihar, and the Muslims replied with another massacre in East Bengal. In the Punjab, the effort of a non-League government to maintain order by arresting fanatical leaders and outlawing extremist organisations of both factions eventually failed when the League drove it out of office. In Noakhali, Bengal, where Muslims heavily outnumbered Hindus, Gandhi quieted the turmoil by walking through the region. Bombay and many other cities were plagued with riots. In September, Gandhi said: 'We are not yet in the midst of civil war, but we are nearing it.' Nehru was stoned and insulted during a visit to the North West Frontier in October.

The fighting spilled over into 1947, and its roar was a continuing undertone to political negotiations for an independent regime. The scope of hostilities also expanded. From the murder of one helpless man, they grew into hysterical and sometimes pre-planned clashes between rival groups and, finally, in the Punjab, into pitched battles between trained men operating with near-military precision. Arms were plentiful and so were private armies. The Hindu RSS (Rashtriya Swayamsevak Sangh) was a violent and growing organisation dedicated to Hindu domination over the subcontinent. The Muslim League National Guard, formed in 1937, had become a paramilitary force. Lesser organisations and individual fanatics of both groups helped to increase the turmoil.

In early 1947 and later in that year, a third great communal force, the Sikhs, fought some of the worst battles in the Punjab. Founded in the fifteenth century by Nanak Chand, Sikhism was originally a faith to bridge the enmities between Islam and Hinduism by crusading against fanaticism and preaching tolerance. In time, under a succession of ten *gurus* or teachers, it grew into a distinct community, with its own language, beliefs and literature. Most distinctively, male Sikhs observe the five K's: the hair and beard are allowed to grow (kesh); each man at all times carries a comb (kangha) in his hair, wears a particular type of shorts (kuchha), a steel bangle on the right wrist (kara), and always carries a genuine or symbolic sabre (kirpan). These obligations are mostly martial symbols, and the Sikhs have traditionally been among India's best fighters and have constituted the backbone of its modern armies. They believe in a single God; not a Being, but an abstract truth that can be realised by righteous living, without the worship of images or natural features. Most of the *gurus* were notable warriors who died while fighting oppression by the Muslims and Moguls. Their death spots, held sacred, are chiefly in northern India. One of the most famous is at Nankhana Sabib, in the area of western Punjab which Jinnah was coveting at that time. The centre of the religion, the great Golden Temple with its free kitchen and hotel for every destitute passer-by, is at Amritsar, on the invasion route into India through the Punjab.

In 1947, the Sikh community totalled 4½ million persons, concentrated mostly in the Punjab. There, it was outnumbered three to one by Muslims and nearly two to one by Hindus. But the unusually industrious Sikhs had developed the country's most fertile farms by using waters from a river irrigation system constructed by the British, and they also contributed its most skilled mechanics. As the talk of Pakistan grew, many Sikhs began to suspect that its creation could cost them the regions which they had developed so painstakingly in the western Punjab. Anger fired by agitators was mounting in the community, even while the Sikh leaders were displaying such complacency, in New Delhi negotiations, that their rights were seldom considered in the march towards partition. On the farms and in the narrow streets of Punjabi towns, nationalism also was rising, and demands for the creation of a separate Sikh state, Khalistan, created strong response. The Sikhs maintained well-trained para-military forces, once called the Shahidi Jathas after the *jathas* or guerrilla bands which roamed the north to escape Mogul persecution. When, it is said, one of their most implacable demagogues, Master Tara Singh, unsheathed his sword in the Golden Temple, the Sikhs embarked on their own holy war. The Punjab remained aflame for nearly a year until early 1948, and became the bloodiest battleground of the conflict.

The three faiths created the most violent communal problems, but India at this time faced other great challenges to its unity. The empire which was being dismantled had served to hold together an unparalleled collection of diverse peoples. In addition to the provinces for which Hindus and Muslims were wrangling, the country contained the domains of some 562 semi-independent princes. They ruled areas ranging from a few acres to large states under a system by which Britain handled their foreign affairs, guaranteed their defence and continuity of rule, and refrained from interfering in domestic affairs, except to eliminate flagrant corruption or ineptitude. The rulers themselves ranged from tottering and austere old men to playboys, from the proudly poor to the flamboyantly wealthy, and from enlightened leaders, in a few cases, to medieval despots. Hindu and Muslim politicians were manoeuvring to take over these territories when British rule ended, but some of the most powerful princes were planning to declare independence. Further separatist tendencies of varied strength came from many other sources. The Pathan tribesmen in the north-west and the Nagas in the south-east were pressing for independence, as were other unassimilated tribes. Sikh demands for a separate state of Khalistan were serious. South India, heir to Dravidian culture, was Hindu but fearful of the northern Hindus and anxious to create its own state. The Calcutta political leader, Suhrarwardy, eventually came out openly for his own independent domain in Bengal.

The Communist Party of India (CPI) was active, troublesome, and potentially dangerous at this period. Like the rest of the Soviet-dominated world movement, the Indian Communists had swung from condemnation of the Second World War to support for the Allies after Russian involvement. By further doctrinal readjustment, they supported the British defence of India against advancing Japan in 1942. Their leaders, accordingly, were released from jail, while anti-war Congress officials remained in prison. Growing rapidly to a claimed membership of 25,000, the CPI easily survived the rupture of its uneasy alliance with Congress in 1945 and two years later was ready to declare open warfare against Nehru and his government. Under strong direction from Moscow, the Indian Communists were prepared with apparently pre-arranged plans to exploit India's anticipated post-war turmoil. Internal differences, however, led them into a two-phased strategy. One wing followed the standard Soviet tactic of seeking power through violent urban insurrection. An influential Left faction advocated Mao Tse-tung's tactics of basing armed revolt on the peasantry and encircling the cities from the countryside. In this 'two-step' revolution, the first goal is to eliminate the strongest opponents—the 'agents of imperialism and feudalism'—in alliance with non-communist leftists. The party would take over power in a second step. Moscow had officially endorsed Mao's tactics, and therefore the double strategy was acceptable to it at the time. The diversity within Indian communism led eventually to the violent party split of the 1960s.[21]

The immediate result of this dualism was that bleeding India was the only newly-independent nation to come at the moment of freedom under the simultaneous attack of both types of communist strategy. Communist agitators were deeply involved in a brief mutiny within the Indian navy in February 1946, and in other incidents affecting the military services. Their influence was clear also behind a series of strikes and other disturbances sweeping industrial centres. In what is now the state of Kerala, on India's south-western tip, party leaders instigated an abortive insurrection in 1946 in which hundreds were killed. Two years later, the party's left wing staged a limited but full-scale Maoist 'peasant war' in Hyderabad, in the centre of India. The strategy of violent insurrection by which Stalin plunged South-east Asia into more than a decade of upheaval and guerrilla warfare—terminating in the Korean War—was hammered out at party conferences in Calcutta in February 1948. These incidents merely outline the activities of thousands of well-financed foreign-directed communists who grew exceedingly active and bold as the subcontinent's distress widened.

The CPI endorsed the creation of a separate Pakistan, as well as other 'autonomous' states in a severed India, and it supported the Muslim League in what proved to be a temporary alliance. Communist demonstrators participated in Jinnah's Direct Action Day. How influential they were in helping to spread communal violence is not clear, but no doubt they were as deeply involved as their numbers and influence would permit. Communists of both factions can be identified in the forefront of all the subsequent communal troubles of Hindu India, as well as political, economic and regional upheavals. Moscow's basic strategy towards India at this time and for several more years was to encourage all possible separatism, in the apparent hope of slicing the Asian giant into portions that could be easily attacked for party benefit.[22] It is by no means clear that current Soviet leaders have abandoned this strategy, although they have suspended it.

In any case, the communist threat was another significant factor in accelerating the pressures for a speedy settlement of the sub-continent's troubles in 1947. The British Labour government, for example, was advised that, without swift action, the Congress Party would break up, and the communists would assume power. This proved to be unnecessarily pessimistic, but it was not entirely invalid under prevailing circumstances. The subcontinent in 1947 was suffering from all the accumulated ills that the communists have consistently maintained will bring them to power, plus a number of others which party theoreticians had failed to mention.

Lord Louis Mountbatten was appointed Viceroy to succeed Lord Wavell and reached India in March 1947. Dynamic, persuasive and bold, Mountbatten plunged into a new effort to settle the constitutional crisis. His directive obliged him to seek a unitary government but gave him certain alternatives, if the impasse continued. Finding Jinnah obdurate and the Hindu leaders divided and with the civil war spreading, Mountbatten quickly decided that the Cabinet Mission plan would not work. He first proposed an alternative that would transfer power to the provincial governments which, if they chose, could later form a central government. The princely states would be free to conclude any arrangements they could make. This plan had been taken to London on May 2 and tentatively approved by the British cabinet, before Mountbatten, on a hunch, showed it to Nehru during a meeting at the mountain resort of Simla. The Indian leader immediately rejected it with heat and finality. In a subsequent memorandum, Nehru said: 'The inevitable consequence of the proposals would be to invite the Balkanisation of India . . .' This was a fear that would dominate his regime.

The ebullient Mountbatten was temporarily defeated and the work of weeks was washed away. He then turned to a solution which had been suggested earlier by his senior Indian adviser, V. P. Menon, and which had been ignored. Menon was one of the principal figures in this drama, although he worked in the anonymity of the civil service; his position was Reforms Commissioner and Constitutional Adviser to the Viceroy. Believing that the proposal of May 2 would lead to 'sheer anarchy', Menon had followed the Viceroy to Simla, on Lady Mountbatten's advice, to argue personally for his

D

ideas. He proposed partition of the country, including the disputed states of the Punjab, Bengal and Assam, and the establishment of two separate governments as the only means of assuring a peaceful transfer of power. India would then accept Dominion status, as Jinnah had already pledged for Pakistan. Previously, Nehru and other Hindu leaders had opposed the idea of becoming a Dominion on the grounds that the masses would believe they were receiving less than full independence. The Menon proposal had been approved tentatively and secretly by Sardar Vallabhbhai Patel, the strong man of the Congress Party whose support was necessary for any solution acceptable to the party.

When Menon presented his arguments in person at Simla, Mountbatten merely told him to convince Nehru and the partition plan could be held as 'a second string in our bow'. On the morning after Nehru's rejection of the Mountbatten proposals, however, the atmosphere was far different. Menon found Nehru too preoccupied to talk. 'Mountbatten also was in an unusual state of agitation', Menon recounts. 'He told me that he had shown the plan to Nehru, who had reacted violently against it; if he had put it before a full meeting of [Congress] party leaders the result would have been disastrous. I then argued that all was not lost; he could try my plan, which had a chance of success. Mountbatten agreed that that was the only way.'[23] Quick meetings were held, and Menon was given a single afternoon to prepare a written draft of his proposals. Nehru approved them before leaving Simla. From that encounter, the division of India along the lines now prevailing was decided. Mountbatten later wrote:

> Looking at the problem early in 1947, the first thing that struck me (and an opinion which I have not changed) was that the right answer would have been to have kept a united India.
>
> The ingenious Cabinet Mission plan in 1947 was accepted by every party in India at one time or another, although never by all parties at the same time. It was, in fact, one of those plans that could be made to work only by the active will and continuous co-operation of all parties.
>
> In March 1947, however, I soon realised that nothing I could do or say would deflect the Muslim League from its intention to make an issue of partition of the country. No other solution would

have been peacefully accepted by the Muslim League and so India was partitioned.[24]

Mountbatten obtained general approval of partition, in writing from Hindu and Sikh leaders, and from Jinnah by his usual curt nod. The Viceroy flew to London on May 18 to explain the swift change to a puzzled British government, which then endorsed partition. The final draft was accepted by subcontinent leaders and announced on June 3. The date for independence, originally set for June 1, 1948, was moved ahead to August 15, 1947. Then began the frenzied and gigantic task of meeting this deadline by partitioning the territory, dividing its assets, regrouping the army, forming governments, and attending to innumerable other details, while attempting to maintain order. Bengal and the Punjab were divided to form the foundation of Pakistan. Their final boundaries were decided when Sir Cyril Radcliffe, who had never seen India before, was obliged to draw a line on the map to end an impasse in two boundary commissions. The 'Radcliffe Award', decided in five weeks, cut through farms, irrigation districts and treasured homelands, and was unpopular in both countries. Some boundary questions remained unsettled for another thirteen years. In general India received 82·5 per cent of the assets and Pakistan 17·5 per cent, but some alterations were made.

Before the two young nations could proudly declare their independence on August 15, the civil war grew more violent and more atrocious. When it ended the following spring, at least half a million persons—perhaps more—had been killed violently and thousands more had died from heavy floods and hunger. The turmoil, the brutality and the uncertainty also created the greatest mass migration in history—the movement of between 12 million and 14 million fearful people from one country to the other. Most of the Sikhs and Hindus in West Pakistan fled at once, or were driven, to India, and the migration from East Pakistan still continues. Hundreds of thousands of Muslims fled or were driven to Pakistan: but a substantial minority remained in India; it numbered around 50 million in 1965. The horror of those days, the wanton brutality and the constant fear will not easily be erased from the national consciousness of both countries. The refugees, who still live hopelessly on the streets of main cities, have become a constant factor in the political life of Pakistan and India. So have the memories.

The hasty and bloody amputation of British India was accomplished before there were adequate arrangements to care for the two patients. No agency was capable of maintaining order, or of handling the millions of refugees. From the vantage point of hindsight, the speed and unpreparedness have been sharply criticised. Leonard Mosley suggests that Mountbatten advanced the date of independence by nearly ten months in order to meet his own schedule for returning to the British Navy. The critics, says V. P. Menon, 'are entirely ignorant of the situation, especially in North India, as it was then. If he [Mountbatten] had waited for ten months more, what guarantee was there that a bloody revolution would not have taken place and that there would have been no power left to be transferred? In the course of the last twelve years, since retirement, I have consulted both official and non-official friends of mine, some of whom were in the Punjab at the time. They all agree that, in the situation as it then was, delay would have been more dangerous than the early transfer of power.' Menon dismisses the argument that another struggle by the Congress to preserve the country's unity would have been successful. 'Civil Disobedience has validity only within a framework of law and order. In 1947 the British Government was no longer in a position to maintain law and order, and a struggle would have precipitated anarchy in the most literal and complete sense. Indeed, even as it was, on some occasions during 1947, we were not far from anarchy.'[25]

There was another powerful, more enduring factor behind this unfortunate haste. It was the single-minded, super-sensitive impatience to achieve instant independence; a powerful and lingering characteristic throughout the former colonial nations. Hindu leaders, in particular, were suspicious of every British move and hostile to any suggestion that might delay or curtail freedom. For instance, they had vetoed the idea of keeping British garrison forces in India as a peace force after independence at a time when this guarantee of British power might have been effective. In the summer of 1947, Pandit Nehru had said: 'I would rather see every village in India put to the flames than have to call in British troops to protect us.' In mid-August, he was so disturbed by the carnage he saw during a trip to the Punjab that he rushed among fighting Sikhs and Muslims and beat them with his fists. By then, it was too late. Nehru later told an interviewer:

The truth is that we were tired men, and we were getting on in years too. Few of us could stand the prospect of going to prison again—and if we had stood out for a united India as we wished it, prison obviously awaited us. We saw the fires burning in the Punjab and heard every day of the killings. The plan for partition offered a way out and we took it. But if Gandhi had told us not to, we would have gone to fighting and waiting. But we accepted. We expected that partition would be temporary, that Pakistan was bound to come back to us. None of us guessed how much the killings and the crisis in Kashmir would embitter relations.[26]

Partition had been approached circuitously, but in the end it was decided by the power of the mob in Calcutta.[27] Jinnah himself could not have retreated from division or violence thereafter. There is no sign that he wanted to do so, although he settled finally for a truncated version of Pakistan. By turning to direct action, he had set the subcontinent aflame and had released pressures that would remain strong two decades later. 'Jinnah', says one Western historian, 'must bear the responsibility for Direct Action Day in Calcutta and all that flowed from it.'[28] But there were other factors, as V. P. Menon explains, including the strong wave of emotionalism, what he calls 'sectarian nationalism', among the Muslim masses. 'That emotion, combined with Jinnah's strong and astute leadership, and the errors of the Congress—errors arising from an inability to grasp what was going on in the minds of the Muslims and of the British—are enough to explain what happened.'[29] Hindu fanatics and Sikh fanatics also contributed their ghoulish share.

Many of the Hindu leaders had been compelled by the bloodshed at Calcutta to accept the unpalatable idea of partition, and others would be persuaded by later violence. Some, like Nehru, were won over, in part, by the eloquence of Mountbatten.[30] But partition, for them, was unreal and temporary. At the beginning of March 1947, Congress itself leaned toward the theory of temporary partition. The Working Committee adopted a resolution recommending the division of the Punjab into Hindu and Muslim sections, with the Sikhs being allowed to choose the community in which they would live. The resolution was written by Sardar Patel, the practical politician who most certainly realised that it created a precedent for dividing the entire country. 'If the League insists on Pakistan,'

Patel wrote to a member of the working committee, 'the only alternative is the division of the Punjab and Bengal . . . I do not think that the British Government will agree to division. In the end, they will see the wisdom of handing over the reins of Government to the strongest party. Even if they do not, it will not matter. A strong Centre with the whole of India—except E. Bengal and part of the Punjab, Sind and Baluchistan—enjoying full autonomy under the Centre will be so powerful that the remaining portions will eventually come in.'[31] Patel also wanted to jettison the pre-dominantly Muslim areas before they drained Congress Party strength. During the first effort to maintain an interim coalition government, inter-community bickering had disrupted policy-making, and a Muslim finance minister had threatened Patel's party organisation by levying heavy taxes on its principal supporters, the Hindu millionaires.

Patel's resolution was adopted without consulting Mahatma Gandhi, one of several political moves made at this time behind his back. Gandhi was the last of the prominent Hindu leaders to hold out against the creation of Pakistan. Although still extremely influential, he was being pushed from practical political authority by the tide of events. Alarmed by the trend within Congress, he journeyed to New Delhi from Bengal in May to fight it. But he could not sway Patel or Nehru, nor could he persuade Mountbatten to insist upon a unitary government. The Viceroy said the matter was out of his hands and advised Gandhi to work on Jinnah. The two former associates did meet on May 6, for a three-hour session that availed Gandhi nothing. Afterwards Jinnah issued a statement saying that '. . . Mr Gandhi does not accept the principle of division. He thinks that division is not inevitable, whereas in my opinion not only is Pakistan inevitable but is the only practical solution of India's political problem.'[32] By June 1947, Gandhi himself was leaning toward this view. Saddened by political developments and horrified by the violence, he was on a peace mission in Bengal when India became independent.

Pakistan had become inevitable only through stubborn politics, particularly but not exclusively on the part of Jinnah and the Muslim League. For a decade before independence was achieved, Hindu and Muslim politicians had waged a ceaseless, if unequal, battle for power. The League, under Jinnah, had pressed steadily for advantage, as indeed a determined minority must do, and through implacability had overcome the disadvantage of the Hindu numerical superiority. Since 1940, the League had forced the men concerned with India's problems to think primarily of safeguarding the Muslims or of allaying their suspicions. Every proposal to accomplish this, short of partition, started with the premise that Hindu power should be weakened by reducing the authority of the central government in favour of autonomous states. Such a system, however, would have been an open invitation for all of the powerful separatist forces to tear the nation apart. It is probable that India would have degenerated into a number of small countries, satrapies and even kingdoms. A division limited to two large and strong nations was less threatening, as Nehru himself concluded.

The alternative, unfortunately, was never tried. Muslim and Hindu leaders made no attempt to adjust their differences or to reduce mutual apprehensions. They did not join together to plan a mutual future in a united nation, nor except for Gandhi did they make any united effort to allay communal passions. Since the end of their brief alliance in 1922, Congress and the League had found no issue and no pressure sufficiently strong to bring them together. Even the struggle for independence, great as it was, failed to create Hindu-Muslim unity. It is no wonder that some Indians say today: 'It would have been better if we had been forced to fight for our freedom.'

There were men who believed that communal passions could be controlled and eliminated. Maulana Abul Kalam Azad, the Muslim President of the Congress Party who opposed partition, wrote: '. . . I am one of those who consider the present chapter of communal bitterness and differences as a transient phase in Indian life. . . . When India attains her destiny, she will forget the present chapter of communal suspicion and conflict and face the problems of modern life from a modern point of view.'[33] During the worst phase of the civil war, following independence, Gandhi kept peace in turbulent Calcutta by persuading the ruthless but courageous Suhrarwardy to join him in a vigil to restrain the mobs. Gandhi had made Hindu-Muslim unity one of his three great lifetime objectives, and died for this ideal before the gun of a Hindu fanatic in 1948.

The political leaders, however, were prisoners of their time and of the great events swirling around them. Their behaviour was consistent with the mores and methods of the communities which they led. These communities were rooted in the past, and British rule had done little to bring them into the present, despite the veneer of Western civilisation and custom at the top. From the murderous *goonda* and the street agitator behind him to the urbane politicians who pursued power more avidly than peace, the struggle was a medieval power clash. It demonstrated the retarded level of nation-building which both factions had reached when British rule was removed. It pointed to the immense difficulties that lay ahead before India and Pakistan could build unified nations dedicated to the rule of law, not force, and based on viable economies. The circumstances required the most far-seeing statesmanship by both sides, not only from Jinnah and Nehru, but from the ranks of leaders behind them who reached into the masses. And there was no statesmanship.

What Jinnah had done by releasing violence, moreover, was to turn more sharply towards the past. He hobbled young India and young Pakistan to the ugliest of the passions which the massacre in Calcutta had set off. He created a new nation of two such dissimilar parts that some artificial cement was needed to bind together West and East Pakistan. Fear of 'aggressive' India became the cement. Finally, Jinnah founded a nation on a religious fundamentalism that was too archaic for the rest of the Muslim world to accept. Consequently, the immense problems of nation-building were complicated, from the outset, by violent new passions and hatreds and by the enormous repercussions of the civil war.

3

THE HERITAGE OF CIVIL WAR

THE GREAT civil war of 1946–8, one of the most horrible in history, solved none of the subcontinent's problems. It produced partition, but it did not consolidate the principle of partition, for many Hindus at the time were unconvinced of its reality. The fighting did not prove the justness of creating a religious state, nor the justness of preventing it. Neither did it demonstrate the martial superiority of either side. The armies were not involved, and the bloodshed did not reduce any community to impotency. It failed, most particularly, to re-establish justice. The Sikhs lost their lands, and millions of individual Muslims and Hindus survived only in irremediable poverty.

Like all civil conflicts, the war was fought with the most vicious ferocity that brother can turn against brother. But unlike most of its predecessors, it created no new mechanism to enforce peace. The state was divided, not unified. The balance of power, represented by the impotent British Indian Army, gave way to a more precarious new balance, the creation of separate armies. The passions underlying the upheaval were not suppressed either by superior power or by more persuasive morality. Instead, they were hardened by combat into greater implacability.

The new nations were born into this negativism while the fighting was still under way. Immediately and almost automatically, the sovereign governments plunged into the turmoil, instead of rising above it. With his goal achieved, Jinnah did not weaken, nor did he cry 'Enough!' As Governor-General of Pakistan, he preached the same anti-Hindu distrust as when he was a minority political leader without governmental responsibility. Hindu officials responded in kind. Although both sides attempted to establish order within their territories, there is no evidence that the governments sought any co-operative means of restoring peace. Yet the appearance of Nehru and Jinnah together in the blood-soaked Punjab might have saved thousands of lives. Instead, the governments took over the passions and hatreds of the masses and incorporated them into basic policies towards each other. The clash of the centuries, which had been maintained by individuals and groups, suddenly became a clash between two nations. The civil war, which had been started by politicians and *goondas*, imperceptibly became an international conflict, the 'War of Succession', as it has been called. And within eight months of independence, the rival armies were fighting each other in Kashmir.

This inability of the two governments and their leaders to rise above the frenzy around them was understandable. The institutions were new, and the men were unused to power. They had fought for their goals bitterly and often illegally over the years: the Hindus for independence of Britain and for a democratic nation, and the Muslims for independence of the Hindus and for a theocratic state. In the fight, the leaders acquired the quick-tempered sensitivity, the implacable dedication and the short-sightedness which characterise revolutionaries everywhere. If Gandhi and Nehru were too suspicious of the British to accept their forces for peace-keeping purposes, so Jinnah was too suspicious of the Hindus to regard their newly-established army with anything but the most vigorous mistrust. In their relations with each other, the rival leaders turned naturally to the revolutionaries' tactics of illegality, double-dealing and inflated bombast. Moreover, the new governments deliberately embraced the masses for support in building their respective states; the Hindus seeking instant democracy and the Muslims attempting to transform Islam into political nationalism. The mob acquired greater power.

But the failure of the new governments to act as responsible governments was a profound mistake of lasting significance. Under the best of circumstances, partition could work only in an atmosphere of inter-governmental trust and confidence. Jinnah and his successors had to be satisfied that misshapen Pakistan fulfilled their religious dreams and that it was secure. The Hindus had to accept the permanency of their unwelcome neighbour. These were difficult readjustments which the people could accept only over a period of time. The primary task of the governments, in the beginning, was to provide the atmosphere in which these readjustments could begin. Instead, both sides committed enough actions against each other to exacerbate and to prolong the tensions.

As one result, relations between the two countries have been coloured and often determined by two central concepts born in the turmoil of 1946–8. One is the Pakistani belief that the Hindus never accepted partition, that they will not for ever tolerate a separate Pakistan, and that some day they will take military measures to reincorporate it into India. The Hindus, in turn, fear that a strong Pakistan intends eventually to establish Muslim rule over all India by force. The evidence for both of these beliefs is unconvincing to a Westerner, but the fears nevertheless are strong. The second belief is religious. To Pakistanis, the creation of their nation through Islamic idealism will be incomplete as long as Muslim Kashmir, a neighbour, remains unabsorbed. To Hindus, no further concession can be made to the concept of an Islamic Pakistan without weakening Indian secularism. There is ample evidence to dispute the logic of these standpoints, but not their emotional appeal. From these primary factors spring the other considerations which have complicated Indo-Pakistani affairs. Essentially, however, the improvement of relations has been retarded by the frequent tendency of both sides, and particularly Pakistan, to look at today's events with the eyes of 1947.

In the absence of mutual trust, the creation of Pakistan was sufficient by itself to prolong and to enlarge the communal enmities and fears which had produced it. The outlines of the nation were determined by the wanderings of Muslim conquerors centuries ago. They entered India in force from the north-west and originally settled there. West Pakistan, accordingly, was built around the Muslim enclave in western Punjab and enlarged by the annexation of adjacent territories through plebiscite. It totals 310,403 square miles, about the size of France and Great Britain together, and had a population of 42,880,000 in 1947. The Muslim conquerors eventually travelled across the northern plains of India, the easiest route, to establish their second centre in the south-east, the area of eastern Bengal. The division of this province, with the accession of a district of Assam, produced East Pakistan, totalling 55,126 square miles. It had a population of 50,840,000 at partition; a density of 922 persons to the square mile, compared with 138 in the west.

Both wings of the disjoined country are so vulnerable strategically that the nation's existence, literally, depends upon India. In the north-west, the flat Punjab is open to invasion from both directions, as history has proved. East Pakistan is completely surrounded by Indian territory and is highly vulnerable to blockade or invasion. Normal communications between the two sections must cross India or circumvent it by a lengthy sea route. During conflict, military lines of supply between the wings would inevitably be tenuous and difficult, so the two parts of the country cannot support each other in any war situation in which India is not aligned with Pakistan. If India fought Pakistan or remained neutral while one section of Pakistan was under foreign attack, the disjoined country could operate in a military sense only as half a nation. This reality should have been apparent in 1947. It was proved in 1965 when East Pakistan was contained by a division or two of Indian troops and remained out of the war, for all practical military purposes. The inherent strategic liability placed Pakistan under a permanent cloud. It was bound to influence the thinking of Pakistani leaders for the foreseeable future. To quiet all fear, India and Pakistan must approach a relationship as solid as that which has existed for many years between Canada and the United States; a relationship of mutual trust along undefended borders. But Canadian-American trust did not exist when the two nations were young and impetuous. It had to be built up through the years.

The strategic situation raises the question of why Jinnah accepted such an awkward solution. If, as he claimed, the Muslims could not protect their rights as a minority within one nation, how could they defend themselves as an artificially weakened sovereign country? The very existence of this inconsistency has served to strengthen the arguments of Indians who maintain that Jinnah intended to consolidate and to expand his truncated nation by force against India. If this were his intention, however, his successors have avoided several major opportunities to implement it. Alternatively, it is probable that Jinnah himself was as impatient as his Hindu counterparts in 1947 and, like them, was swept along by the events he was instrumental in unleashing. He could have been as blind to the potentialities as everyone else. As the chief architect of Pakistan, however, Jinnah had the responsibility of examining it thoroughly before partition. For nearly a decade, every discussion of Pakistan centred around the sole concept of establishing a seriously divided new nation. Jinnah himself had demanded such a state. Yet he apparently realised the strategic liabilities, for once he requested an 800-mile connecting corridor through India. He dropped the idea, in face of strong Congress refusal. Is it possible that Jinnah accepted the final partition because he did not believe the Hindus were martial enough to threaten him and, therefore, he did not fear them as much as he claimed?

In any case, the strategic disadvantage of Pakistan constituted a built-in cause for continuing friction that could have been serious even without all the immense complications of the civil war and communalism. India after partition continued to throw a huge shadow: a population at least two and a half times larger and a land area (1,262,275 square miles) three and a half times greater than Pakistan. This was an unacceptable disadvantage for any proud young nation like Pakistan. Even under normal circumstances it probably would have resulted in strenuous efforts to even the balance through diplomacy, military power and, perhaps, even aggression. Jinnah had achieved Pakistan by maintaining relentless attack, and his successors were obliged, whenever possible, to continue the same tactics. The fact that the Muslims themselves had precipitated a solution that left them in such an international position did not nullify the pressures for remedial action which inevitably arose.

Pakistan had been created for religious ideals which, in the heat of political battle, had tended towards fundamentalism and rigidity. Islam was the only tie, moreover, between West and East Pakistanis who differed sharply from each other in customs, heritage and language. The new state emphasised religion as both an ideal and a unifying factor; but elsewhere in the world Islam had failed to become an adequate nationalism for diverse peoples—and in Pakistan it also failed. The nation was held together primarily by fear of 'aggressive' India. There was justification for this fear in 1946–8. But it is notable that Pakistani officials continued to emphasise it in later years, when India showed no signs of military aggressiveness.

The logistics of the situation, then, pointed toward a period of friction between the new neighbours. It would last at least until the leaders reached mutual understanding and trust. The communal conflict became an international conflict by progression and its scope was infinitely broadened; just as every attempted political solution since 1909 had widened communal differences, instead of diminishing them. The civil war left an indefinite pall over the subcontinent. Like all civil conflicts, the memories will die hard; the effects of the American Civil War linger a century later. The leaders, immersed in a multitude of great problems, had neither the time nor apparently the inclination to oppose these trends.

The first series of clashes between India and Pakistan were products and symbols of this underlying situation. The neighbours fought politically over the division of assets and the control of strategic resources; they fought militarily over Kashmir and quarrelled over economics. These conflicts exacerbated the tensions and fears and helped to prolong them. But they did not by themselves create the animosities which persisted twenty years later, as diplomats often contend.

The bloody civil strife in the Punjab, which started in August 1947, set the immediate scene for the beginning of Indo-Pakistan national antagonisms. The conflict began when the Sikhs finally realised that the Boundary Awards would deprive them of their lands in the western Punjab. With atrocities and wantonness on all sides, the loss of life was heavy in Muslim, Sikh and Hindu communities. To the Muslims, the carnage was a deliberate Hindu plot to nullify partition; Hindus believed that the Muslims intended to eliminate minorities within Pakistan through murder. In mid-September, Jinnah told Lord Ismay, his military Chief of Staff, that he had no faith in the Indian government's intentions and was 'beginning to feel that there was no alternative but to fight it out'.[1] At that time, the fledgling Pakistani army was too weak and ill-formed to fight. On September 15, Pakistan's first Prime Minister, Liaquat Ali Khan, told his people: 'Today, we, in Pakistan, are surrounded on all sides by forces which are out to destroy us.'[2] A few weeks later, Pakistan formally charged India before the United Nations with deliberate 'genocide' during the civil conflict. These three reactions to India, constituting a mixture of defiance and fear, became the hallmark of subsequent Pakistani policy.

The evidence is convincing, however, that the young Indian nation neither contemplated military aggression nor practised 'genocide', although it undertook a number of measures to weaken Pakistan in other ways. Independent investigation of the civil war disclosed no instances of planned Hindu genocide. In some areas, however, Hindu attacks were better prepared and were launched with better arms and organisation. Charges that high Hindu officials abetted the attacks have not been proved, but some state officials were implicated in certain regions.[3] Pakistan had repeated its charges of genocide so frequently and under such unlikely circumstances that there is good reason to believe it has now become primarily an established facet of internal propaganda, however sincerely it might have been believed in 1947.

Nevertheless, it was in this atmosphere of wartime mistrust that New Delhi applied other pressures against super-sensitive Pakistan. The most significant of these produced a protracted quarrel over the division of national assets. Pakistan demanded one-fourth of the national treasury of 4,000 million rupees and was awarded 750 million by an arbitration tribunal established to settle the impasse. Sardar Patel, the tough Hindu Home Minister and party leader, attempted to withhold any settlement until the Kashmir issue, then critical, was resolved; but he finally handed over 500 million rupees, after Gandhi undertook a protest fast. Pakistan also complained that India was withholding military equipment and undertaking other measures to keep her militarily weak. All of the British-built ordnance factories and most supply depots were located in Indian territory and remained there to serve a new Indian army which was three times larger than that of Pakistan. The Pakistanis protested to the United Nations that India had failed to carry out commitments to act as banker for her until the complicated process of building a Pakistan government was completed. India was accused also of withholding crucial supplies of water needed for irrigation in the Punjab through her control of key headworks. The two nations quarrelled bitterly over economic differences, precipitated in part by the separation of the raw materials in East Pakistan from processing plants in Indian Calcutta.

These controversies added a new political dimension to communal problems and the sense of vulnerability engendered in Pakistan by her military position. Although most of the issues disappeared in time, Pakistan claimed that India had again cut off vital water supplies as a result of the war of 1965. In any case, these early controversies expedited Pakistan's search for political and economic self-sufficiency, as well as military independence, to escape the Indian shadow.

Sardar Patel, whose influence is detectable behind most of these non-military pressures, was a master politician who controlled and responded to the deep currents in Hindu society which represented the conservative and traditional points of view. During the crucial years between independence and his death in late 1950, Patel shared power with Pandit Nehru from behind the scenes. Nehru, the articulate and polished world figure, typified the westernised idealism which had been superimposed upon Patel's world of Asian realism. Nehru, the aristocrat, drew his strength from many sources; Gandhi's support, his own revolutionary record and personal magnetism, and a philosophy that appealed to working men as well as intellectuals. Patel, who came from a Gujarat village and a devout Hindu family, was educated in India and remained plebeian. Lacking a reputation as a revolutionary leader, even within India, and without popular appeal, Patel could rely for strength only upon Hindu conservatives. But from this base, he won control over the practical affairs of the Congress Party, one of the world's most complex political organisations. Congress can be administered only with firmness and intrigue. Nehru disliked the plots and subterfuges of daily politics; Patel thrived on them.

At independence, Patel was seventy-two, a short, deliberate, hard-faced man who seldom revealed his feelings. Through his age and seniority, he expected the honours of power, but Gandhi intervened to make the 57-year-old Nehru the first Prime Minister of India. The choice was significant, for more reasons than Gandhi's explanation that the occasion required Nehru's Western training. Nehru was a socialist who gave the country its economic design, and a humanist who believed in equal rights for all religious groups. Patel was a strong capitalist and pragmatist. He 'never really trusted the Muslims and shared the extremist Hindu Mahasabha view on the "natural" right of the Hindus to rule India'.[4] Amid the riots of 1947, Patel publicly expressed doubt of the loyalty of Muslims remaining within India. Nehru, like Gandhi, defended them, and the Indian Muslims thereafter turned to him for support.

The two men had many political as well as personal differences. They were kept together by Gandhi, during his lifetime, and by his posthumous influence. The division of power between Patel and Nehru was never clear, for it depended upon peculiarly Indian circumstances; Patel, for instance, had the political strength to remove Nehru as Prime Minister, but never made the effort. Patel controlled the party machine and the key ministries of government and was instrumental in determining major internal policies. Nehru's prestige and popularity gave him command of the country as a whole and made him its unchallenged spokesman abroad. The combination of internationalist and practical politician was required by the times, and the duumvirate worked with less surface difficulty than might be expected. Michael Brecher, Nehru's biographer, concludes that there was rivalry between the two men, but that it has been exaggerated, and that they were co-equals in the nation's affairs. 'Nehru', he says, 'could have carried the country alone through this period of turmoil, though the attainment of stability would have been delayed.'[5]

The operation of the duumvirate helped to establish a lasting ambivalence in Indian policy. While Nehru won international fame by preaching a philosophy that, in many respects, reflected the highest aspirations of Western idealism, Patel consolidated India. He did it through the use of intrigue and power. Nehru very often described India as the law-abiding great democracy he hoped it would become; Patel dealt with it as a turbulent Asian society under constant threat of being torn apart by prejudice and individual ambition. The combination was fortunate for the country. It brought international prestige and internal stability more quickly than would have been possible otherwise. But the world often looked at India solely through Nehru's vision and frequently condemned her, sharply and unnecessarily, for failing to live up to the dream. The pattern had been set when Gandhi's concept of non-violence was widely accepted as the established format of Indian life, not as a tactic or an aspiration. Non-violence is part of ancient Indian philosophy, which Gandhi, like others before him, probably adopted precisely because his people were inclined toward such violence. But India became known for her 'non-violence' and later for her Nehruan 'peaceableness', and any contrary behaviour, however understandable or justified, automatically became suspect.

This bifocalism was particularly significant in colouring attitudes towards the long Indo-Pakistani conflict over Kashmir and two

E

other dissident princely states, left dangling by partition. With the independence of the Dominions, British paramountcy lapsed; that is, the system of loose alliances with the 562 semi-independent states on the subcontinent was eliminated without the substitution of any clear-cut alternative. The rulers were free to join either Dominion, and Mountbatten advised them to do so after respecting the wishes of their people. Technically, the princes also were free to seek independence. The vagueness of this arrangement was an open invitation for the two nations to exploit the vacuum. It was also a serious challenge for India, where most of the states were located, because the balkanisation which Nehru feared could be created as effectively by the existence of independent kingdoms as by autonomous Muslim states. New Delhi had both the means and the necessity to press for accession of the states within Indian territory, and did so with methods ranging from agitation to the use of force. But Pakistan also meddled deeply within India, with far less justification. In general, the Indians have been more severely condemned.

Nehru set the guidelines for the consolidation of India, and Patel carried them out. On June 15, 1947, Nehru told a Congress convention that the party would not recognise the independence of any states within India and added: 'Further, any recognition of such independence by any foreign power will be considered an unfriendly act.' Congress took the official position that the states had to accede to one of the Dominions and that India was obliged to assume responsibility for the defence and protection of those states failing to make the choice. Princes whose domains were contiguous to Pakistan could join her, but those within Indian territory could only accede to New Delhi. Finally, the Congress decided that the states within India would be asked to accede by August 15 on defence, foreign affairs and communications. The inference of these policies was that states in a geographic position to join Pakistan could do so without further Indian interference, but that others would be absorbed into India, whether they liked it or not.[6] This position was consistent with the Indian insistence upon creating a unified nation under strong central control, and it is difficult to see how India could have survived on any other basis. Jinnah promptly opposed the Congress stand and he said later in July that 'The Muslim League recognises the right of each state to choose its destiny'.[7] This also was consistent, but the Indians suspected that one of Jinnah's major purposes was to weaken India by helping to fragment it.

Only three of the princes held out. Within a year, the domains of the remainder were incorporated into India; an area totalling about half a million square miles, containing nearly 90 million people. Patel, working with the astute V. P. Menon, mixed cajolery, bribery and strong political pressure to win over the princes, sometimes under difficult circumstances. It was a bloodless revolution, the magnitude of which has sometimes been obscured by Patel's administrative skill. But the development of India depended upon this foundation; without it, the Indian social revolution could not have proceeded and India as a sovereign nation could have been destroyed. Patel accomplished what has been called his 'master achievement' with strictly pragmatic methods.

The first Indo-Pakistani dispute over accession involved the small state of Junagadh on the west coast of modern India. Entirely surrounded by Indian territory, the state was four-fifths Hindu but was ruled by a Muslim Nawab of unstable flamboyance. He acceded to Pakistan, but India refused to recognise the act and called for a plebiscite. For several weeks, Pakistan ignored the suggestion. Indian troops surrounded the enclave, then moved into it when disorders broke out. In February 1948, a plebiscite overwhelmingly opted for India, and the state is now a part of Gujarat. Junagadh, lying 240 miles by sea from the nearest point in Pakistan, would have been a liability to Jinnah, but he pressed its case, probably as an argument in his fight for Kashmir.[8] Pakistan has never recognised the accession to India.

Deep in the heart of modern India, a far more serious threat was created by the Nizam of Hyderabad, a stubborn and fabulously wealthy autocrat. Hyderabad was the largest of the princely states, totalling 82,313 square miles, with a population of nearly $16\frac{1}{2}$ million in 1941. The Nizam and the ruling class were Muslims, but 87 per cent of the population was non-Muslim, including 81 per cent Hindus. They lived on a level below the general average of the subcontinent. The regime was so archaic that a system of forced labour for the state was abolished only in 1947. The countryside was exploited by 1,100 feudal landowners. The state, occupying most of the Deccan plateau, was surrounded by Hindu territory and was landlocked.

The Nizam had been fighting since 1938 against attempts of the state Congress Party to modernise his regime, banning the party and jailing its leaders. The resultant vacuum permitted the growth of strong communal organisations and the establishment of a cohesive and aggressive Communist Party. The Hindu Mahasabha and a parallel organisation were opposed by the organised militancy of a fanatical Muslim group, known as the Razakar Volunteers, pledged to fight against Hindu rule over the state. The Razakars launched widespread violence against Hindus before independence. The communists, meanwhile, made the state into the base for what they hoped would be a spreading upheaval. They were particularly strong in eastern Hyderabad and an adjacent area of Madras, where they manipulated ancient land grievances and played on the regional nationalism of Telegu-speaking peoples. By 1943–4, they were able to lead a peasant revolt which spilled over to neighbouring parts of British India. The peasants refused to furnish forced labour or to pay taxes and successfully resisted retaliatory police action.

These forces strengthened while the Nizam embarked on tortuous negotiations to establish his independence and New Delhi insisted that he accede to India. Hyderabad was quickly involved in its own brutal communal conflict and, at the same time, in a communist agrarian 'revolution'. With their differences unresolved, India and Hyderabad signed a standstill agreement in November 1947, to freeze their relations as they then existed while further efforts were made to reach a settlement. New Delhi contended that the Nizam violated the agreement, however, by concluding a $62 million loan to Pakistan. Hyderabad claimed the loan had been negotiated before the agreement was signed. Meanwhile, the Razakars were conducting brutal attacks on Hindu villages within the state and were crossing the border into India proper. When New Delhi demanded suppression of these activities, the Nizam replied that the Razakars were necessary for internal control. He made no effort to carry out New Delhi's injunction to modernise his government.

In the countryside, the communists spread their influence through guerrilla action, terror, intimidation, and a propaganda campaign based upon the elimination of feudal landlordism. All the tactics and techniques which later became familiar in China and Vietnam were employed in Hyderabad, on a small scale, except that no puppet government was established. The communists, however, secured control of a large part of the state, holding 2,000 villages, and acted as the *de facto* government in that area. They collected taxes, assassinated or intimidated recalcitrants, and maintained a secure base in the rolling, forested countryside in the north-eastern part of the state. Guerrillas secured weapons by ambushing Hyderabad government forces sent against them. All of this had been accomplished while the party was officially banned by the Nizam's government. In May 1948, fearing an Indian invasion, the Nizam removed the restrictions. The communists then instructed the villagers in their domain to fight any Indian troops attempting to cross their territory. New Delhi also saw signs of a firmer alliance between the communists and the Razakars which could have intensified anti-Hindu violence within the state while complicating a solution of its status.

In mid-June the Nizam refused to sign an agreement with India which his negotiators had worked out in New Delhi. India then prepared to invade, and Hyderabad appealed to the United Nations Security Council. On September 13, before the appeal could be heard, Indian forces crossed the border at five different points in a police action to restore order. The state was subdued in a 'hundred-hour war' and taken over on September 18. The Nizam, left as ruler under an Indian administrator, eventually withdrew his complaint to the UN. The aftermath was bitter. The Razakars were disbanded and large numbers of Muslims evidently were killed in reprisal; Pakistan claimed that Indian troops were involved. The fight to smash the communist 'revolution' was prolonged but successful. The communists killed at least 2,000 persons during their rule. Hyderabad finally disappeared in an Indian reshuffle of state borders.

The incident precipitated a long debate over the legality of the Indian action. But the concept of legality would appear to be spurious in this connection and unnecessarily confusing. There is no precedent that fits the circumstances. More realistically, the central questions were whether India was justified in using force to consolidate its national territory and whether force was necessary at the time. While it is customary for diplomats to deplore the use of force under any circumstances, it is nevertheless a necessary part of every nation's policy under present world conditions. If India was justified in insisting upon the integration of all territories within its boundaries, then it was justified in employing all necessary force for that purpose. 'Whatever the legal rights and wrongs of specific acts in the Hyderabad controversy,' says a Western historian, 'India could not have tolerated the state's existence as a sovereign political entity. To do so would have jeopardised the economy, political structure and security of India itself.'[9]

The timing of the Hyderabad invasion would also appear justified. The Nizam was not only a stubborn old man who seemed determined to pursue independence as long as possible; he was also ineptly playing with forces which threatened territories outside his domain. Apart from the communal problems created by his penchant for releasing fanatics, the Nizam gave a potentially dangerous foothold to organised communism. The party capitalised its opportunity with sufficient skill to indicate the potentiality for launching a full-scale guerrilla war at a particularly inopportune moment for young India. Communist leaders in the city of Hyderabad insisted in 1965 that the guerrilla conflict, which lasted from 1946 to 1949, was started in full expectation of victory. One of them explained, 'it was expected that there would be a general revolution' in India, and Hyderabad would be one base for the expanding military conquest of the country.[10]

Much of the foreign criticism over the Hyderabad incident, it appears, resulted from the shock of witnessing the unexpected use of force by 'non-violent' India. Since then, Pakistan has consistently cited the Hyderabad and Junagadh episodes as proof of India's 'aggressiveness'. Far from supporting that claim, these two events demonstrated that India could move with resolute firmness when her security and national well-being were involved. She behaved very much like any other nation confronted with insoluble and pressing problems.

India responded in much the same way to the infinitely more complex challenge of Kashmir.

4

KASHMIR: THE FIRST WAR

KASHMIR is one of the corners of the world which has been consigned to subservience by geography and history. From its central valley, the land climbs in all directions towards the great broken masses of mountains that lead to the Himalayas. It fits like a piece of jigsaw puzzle into the rough corners of four nations: Tibet, on the east; China, north-east and north; Afghanistan, north-west, and Pakistan. At 10,000 feet, the mountains are foothills, and at 18,000 feet they are deserts of ice and stone. But they have been passable for centuries, and the recorded story of Kashmir contains few periods of independence. The strategic location of the land, its beauty and the peculiarities of its people have made Kashmir the plaything of kings and the pawn of generals.

The record of Kashmir's rule and misrule by conquerors of the past lives in the gray eyes, fair skins and unusual customs of many of its people. They are distinctive from the dark men of the hot plains in both Pakistan and India. In appearance, the Kashmiris resemble many of the wild tribesmen, also descended from invading soldiers, who live to the westward in Pakistan and Afghanistan; although, unlike them, the Kashmiris have long been tamed. In tradition, the articulate men of the Vale are bound together with pride in an ancient if troubled history. They remember, for instance, that Srinagar was once the seat of learning and culture in that part of the world. And Srinagar, the ancient capital, is unlike any other city in the subcontinent; a peeling, cluttered memento from the Persian past crowded along the swift Jhelum river and touching the sparkle of Lake Dal.

In the distance, surrounding Srinagar on all sides, the Himalayas rise in sculptured rock and snow, reaching to the deeply-ridged monarch, the 26,000 feet of Nanga Parbat. These mountains, grasping the sky, form an immense cathedral of the Infinite: it is easy to understand their influence on the men who live near them. Some devout Hindus still make the annual pilgrimage to the Cave of Armarnath, the Eternal Lord, deep in the ice-fields ninety miles from Srinagar. The Muslims of Pakistan, for whom the mountains have no religious significance, call to Kashmir in the name of Islam, and it is a persuasive call. But the Kashmiris remember long beyond the importation of both religions.

What they want and what they have always wanted, as far as can be discerned, is the right to be 'masters of their own destiny', as one of their leaders has put it. In 1965, the fluent lawyer, G. M. Karra, explained the problem quite directly in an interview with the author. Karra was one of the most articulate political leaders of a movement to detach Kashmir from India and to annex it to Pakistan.

'We would prefer independence,' said Karra, 'but we recognise that this is impossible.'

'Why is it impossible?' I asked.

'First, the United Nations has limited us to a choice between India and Pakistan. Then, most of us realise that Kashmir could not exist independently. It could not sustain itself economically. It would be under constant pressure and intrigue from India, Pakistan, China and Russia. They would not let us live in peace.'

Karra, then in his sixties, had been a revolutionary since student days and was a veteran of several periods of imprisonment for his activities. He sucked for a moment on his water-pipe, the *hookah*, coughed and added: 'So, you see, Pakistan is the only choice.'

The dream of independence has been a consistent thread through the political controversy over the status of Kashmir since 1947. If given a free plebiscite under responsible leaders, the people of the mountain portion of the state doubtless would vote that way, although the Hindu population of Jammu might vote for India. But independence is clearly impossible for Kashmir, as Karra pointed out, and it has not been seriously considered. The term 'self-determination', therefore, does not strictly apply to this situation, even though it is a slogan of such emotional appeal that it has been used constantly. Nor does there appear to have been a great outpouring of love for Pakistan, in either 1947 or 1965. Many Muslims of Srinagar in the latter year quite evidently wanted to escape from Indian rule, partly because of past injustices and current Indian mistakes. Pakistan was their only alternative, and this factor, rather than the pull of religion, seemed influential in forcing them to look westward.

To a considerable extent, history is repeating itself in modern dress in Kashmir. The territory has become involved in a power struggle between two neighbours, and, as in the past, the desires of the people are subordinate to the central conflict. They are resentful and sullenly defiant, even though India has proved to be a more benevolent overlord than any other Asian nation in history. The state is not as happy as India claims, nor as downtrodden and in need of rescue as Pakistan contends. Time has transformed it from a Himalayan outpost into one of the most important strategic areas of today's world.

The history of Kashmir is tarnished with an unusual measure of cruelty and avarice, even for Asia. Part of the territory was conquered by Alexander the Great during his invasion in the fourth century BC when the vastness and mystery of India turned him back. A century later, the city of Srinagar was founded near its present site by the great Indian Emperor Asoka. In the sixth century AD, the country was ruled from Kabul, Afghanistan, by a king remembered in history because he enjoyed hearing the trumpeting fear of a war elephant who plunged from a precipice, and had a hundred more of them killed in this way. Another in a succession of vicious monarchs, in a drunken frenzy ordered Srinagar to be burned down, but the city was saved by alert retainers who set fire to haystacks instead. Another king, in the ninth century, started the long and unfinished attempt to control the mighty rivers roaring through the country. In the mid-twelfth century, the Kashmiri historian, Kalhana, said that his people had become renowned for cowardice and boasting. A modern commentator has added: 'The Kashmiri is a loquacious person, but he rarely resorts to force, and the possibility of his blood being shed can readily instil terror into his heart.'[1]

Protected in part by its remoteness, Kashmir evaded the first aggressive wave of Muslim influence upon India, when in the tenth century the Turkish Mahmud of Ghazni, invading from Afghanistan, established himself on the throne at Delhi. Islam reached the mountains four centuries later, and then by a political quirk. An adventurer named Rainchan Shah, son of a Tibetan ruler, assumed power through murder, after the Hindu ruler had fled Kashmir before a Tartar invasion. Rainchan Shah was a Buddhist but, for political reasons, decided to change his faith. Caste prevented him from becoming a Hindu, so he turned to Islam.

It was in the early sixteenth century that Kashmir was conquered for the first time from the east. The attackers came from what is now Chinese Sinkiang province and crossed Ladakh, the eastern tip of Kashmir where Red China now has a foothold. From the south, the Indian Emperor Akbar conquered and annexed Kashmir in 1589, ending its isolation and linking it thereafter to the lands lying southward and westward. His son, Jahangir, built the first of the great Mogul gardens, with their rushing waters and giant *chenar* trees, around the lakes near Srinagar, and they still exist. Jahangir visited the mountains often, travelling across the hot plains in vast caravans, and left poetic descriptions. But his Kashmir governors were noted for their cruelty. When the Mogul empire began to weaken in the eighteenth century, Kashmir declared independence, along with other remote regions. This lasted only briefly, however, and the mountain territory was conquered by Admad Shah Durrani, ruler of Afghanistan, in 1752.

In despair over continued Afghan cruelty, the Kashmiris appealed for help to Ranjit Singh, the 'Lion of the Punjab', leader of the Sikhs in the plains. One of his generals, Gulab Singh, the Rajah of Jammu, conquered Kashmir in 1819 and ruled as governor until 1846. Conditions improved, but only slightly. The Sikhs regarded the Kashmiris with contempt, and the fine for killing one was: four rupees for a Hindu and two rupees for a Muslim. In 1846, after the Sikhs had been defeated in an unwise attack on the British, Gulab Singh bought central Kashmir from the victors for one million pounds, under the Treaty of Amritsar, and annexed it to Jammu. Gulab Singh was a devout Hindu of the Rajput warrior caste, who served the Sikhs with skilful opportunism. The British established him as a ruler of Kashmir in order to create a barrier against a revived Sikh nation and against the unruly tribes of the area.[2] He was the kind of man who, it was said, would pay attention to anyone in a crowd if he held up a rupee and shouted: 'Maharajah, a petition!'

The last semi-independent Maharajah of Jammu and Kashmir, Sir Hari Singh, was very little better. A one-time playboy who reputedly paid up to £50,000 for an imported dancing girl, he ruled the state for twenty-five years as a personal preserve, with little regard for the welfare of his subjects. Under the Treaty of Amritsar, he was sovereign and owned all the land. Collecting usurious land taxes and controlling a number of state enterprises, he built up a huge fortune and lived in splendour. But times were changing in the mountains. A young Muslim student named Sheikh Abdullah returned in 1930 from Aligarh University with a new sense of Muslim nationalism. He started agitation for greater Muslim representation in the government, and by the next year he 'was recognised as the first Kashmiri for many a day to have raised the standard of revolt against foreign domination'.[3] Arrested and then released, he fought for many years against the Maharajah with a combination of courage, ruthlessness and opportunism which would characterise his later career. In early 1932, his agitation created sufficient turmoil for British troops to be sent to Kashmir to pacify it. In 1946, he initiated a 'Quit Kashmir' movement to oust the Hindu ruler, and was sentenced to nine years' imprisonment when he presented his case by telegram to the British Cabinet Mission, then in New Delhi.

Sheikh Abdullah is one of the principal characters of the Kashmir story and, in some ways, the most enigmatic. He was born in a village near Srinagar in 1905, the son of a shawl weaver. From somewhere, he had inherited the charismatic appeal that is so important in Asia. He used it so effectively that he remains the dominant political figure in Kashmir, despite years of imprisonment and eclipse. An imposing man, who stands 6 feet 4 inches tall, he can attract and move audiences of thousands with his oratory. What he tells his people and the world is sometimes confusing and contradictory, but the central theme is independence and Kashmiri nationalism. In his fight against the Maharajah, he based his appeal primarily upon opposition to communalism and 'foreign rule'. His campaign brought him in sympathy with the Indian Congress, and he became a close personal friend of Pandit Nehru. Abdullah's basic position created sharp conflict with Jinnah and the Muslim

League, who were unconcerned by the relations between the princes and their subjects. The two men also competed politically for Muslim support in Kashmir, each claiming to represent the entire community. By 1939 rival Muslim political groups were simultaneously fighting the Maharajah and each other. Jinnah made no attempt to see Abdullah during a trip to the mountains in 1943. The Pakistanis built Abdullah into a martyr after another of his arrests in 1953, but before then they had labelled him a Quisling. The 'Lion of Kashmir', as the Sheikh is called, was placed under house arrest by Indian authorities in 1965, in an incident that may have been a contributing factor to the timing of the war.

In 1947, Sir Hari Singh was the last of the princes to hold out against accession to either Pakistan or India, because he could not make up his mind. The Hindu prince ruled a preserve of a little more than 4 million people, of whom over 3 million, or 77·11 per cent, were Muslims; 20·12 per cent Hindus and 1·64 per cent, Sikhs. The Muslim population in the Vale was 90 per cent; in Jammu it was 53 per cent, and decreasing owing to migrations from civil conflict. An enclave of some 50,000 Buddhists in Ladakh did not count then, but given the chance, they might have voted to join Tibet. The Maharajah would lose all his power by joining India and most of it by choosing Pakistan. Moreover, with bloody fighting under way in the Punjab, an open accession to Pakistan could have resulted, says one commentator, 'in the massacre and expulsion from the State of its Hindu and Sikh inhabitants'.[4] Sir Hari, accordingly, attempted to maintain independence.

The delay worried New Delhi. Nehru sent messages to the Maharajah, advising him to consider the alternatives carefully. Although he personally abhorred all the prince stood for, Nehru also discussed the possibility of visiting Kashmir to seek a decision. Nehru, a Kashmiri Brahmin by birth, loved Kashmir and visited it often. But Sir Hari had imprisoned Congress party leaders and had threatened to arrest Nehru if he reached Kashmir. The Indian leader had been jailed briefly, then escorted from the state when he hurried to help Sheikh Abdullah in his troubles of 1946, despite the pressing problems then facing him in New Delhi. In the end, Lord Mountbatten went to Srinagar to advise the Maharajah to accede to one of the Dominions by August 14. But the Viceroy apparently applied none of the pressure he had used in other circumstances during this period, and he left Kashmir without obtaining a decision.[5]

Through Sardar Patel, the prospective Indian rulers had assured the British they would not oppose the accession of Kashmir to Pakistan.[6] Mountbatten himself said later: 'Had he [the Maharajah] acceded to Pakistan before 15th August 1947, the future government of India had allowed me to give His Highness an assurance that no objection whatever would be raised by them. Had His Highness acceded to India by August 14th, Pakistan did not then exist and therefore could not have interfered. The only trouble that could have been raised was by non accession to either side, and this was unfortunately the very course followed by the Maharaja.'[7]

While the ruler temporised, armed rebellion broke out in July 1947, in the Sudhnuti tract of Poonch province, the west-central part of the state. It resulted from many factors, including heavy taxation and intense dissatisfaction among the numerous soldiers returning to the province from service in the Second World War. 'Essentially,' says one commentator, 'theirs [the Sudhans] was a straightforward peasant revolt, the religious beliefs of the participants being irrelevant; an uprising of the oppressed against ancient feudal tyrannies; the sort of thing that ought to have got sympathetic acknowledgement from someone of Mr Nehru's ideals.'[8] The Indians, instead, claimed that it was foreign-inspired and was part of a Pakistani assault on Kashmir.[9] By August, the revolt was accelerated. Its leaders proclaimed independence and established the first Azad (Free) Kashmir 'government'. Arms came from factories which had long been maintained by Pathan tribesmen across the border. By October, at the latest, the rebellion was receiving Pakistani support and weapons.[10]

In the far north-west of Kashmir, a territory administered by the British as the Gilgit Agency was nominally handed back to the Maharajah in late July. There were few ties between the remote mountain area and Srinagar, and revolt was swift. Muslim soldiers deserted, pro-Pakistani sentiment made its appearance, and the area was taken over quickly by forces sympathetic to Karachi. A week later, the Gilgitis occupied Baltistan, the area lying to the east, giving Pakistan control over a large slice of strategic mountain country in northern Kashmir. India, with the sharpened suspicions of the times, claimed that a British officer was instrumental in delivering Gilgit to Pakistan, but there is equal evidence that his actions saved many lives.[11] This rebellion appeared to have no connection with the Azad Kashmir movement in the Poonch area.

Meanwhile a vigorous anti-Muslim movement had begun in Jammu and Kashmir during August. Two months later, the state was heavily infiltrated by Hindu fanatics of the RSS, trained Sikh fighters and other elements. The agitation finally produced the slaughter of two crowded convoys of fleeing Muslims in November. Some 5 million Muslims fled the area, of whom 80 per cent sought refuge in the territory of Azad Kashmir. There was no doubt that the Maharajah and his officials were involved in this communal violence.[12]

These episodes and the continuing civil war within India proper aroused the border areas between Kashmir and newly-created Pakistan. They were inhabited by a number of Muslim tribes known for their fighting prowess. The British had been unable to control them. From this district and from a base somewhere within Pakistan proper, a tribal invasion of Kashmir began on October 19. In the first wave were at least 900 Mahsuds, the fiercest fighters of the region, and invaders from half a dozen other tribes soon followed. Riding in trucks, the raiders crossed the border on October 22, and headed south-eastward towards Srinagar on the main Jhelum Valley road. Two days later, they reached the sizable town of Baramula, a trade and communications centre thirty-five miles from Srinagar. There they halted, for murder, rapine and plunder, mostly against other Muslims. The attackers alerted the Maharajah to his danger by cutting power lines and plunging Srinagar into darkness during a palace reception. Having finished with Baramula, they moved onward and were expected to reach the capital by October 26.

With an inadequate state army, depleted by desertions and the expulsion of mistrusted Muslims, Sir Hari appealed to India for help on October 24. This set off a round of diplomatic and military activity in which V. P. Menon played a major role. In his book *The Story of the Integration of the Indian States*, Menon says that, upon receiving the Maharajah's appeal, Mountbatten immediately took up the position that it would be improper for Indian troops to enter an independent Kashmir and that the state must first accede to India. During the tense and hurried strategy meetings being held in New Delhi, the Viceroy also stressed his opinion that accession should be contingent upon a plebiscite to determine the people's desires after the raiders had been ejected. Nehru and other Indian Ministers 'readily agreed'.[13]

The Maharajah promptly accepted the terms. He signed the Instrument of Accession on the night of October 26, when Menon awoke him in the winter palace of Jammu to which he had fled. After a further meeting in New Delhi, the accession was accepted by the Indian government, subject again to the proviso that a plebiscite would be held. The Indian leaders decided to fly an infantry battalion to Srinagar the next day. Even then, British authorities, including the Chiefs of Staff of the three services, who held their commands on a temporary basis, gave warning of the dangers. Nehru replied that the alternative to military intervention would be worse: a massacre in Srinagar that could set off a major communal holocaust in India. He reminded the British that their countrymen in the Kashmiri capital would surely be murdered because no one could protect them.[14]

Beginning on October 27, the Indians mounted an airlift of surprising efficiency to Srinagar. The first contingents, arriving with the tribesmen only five miles away, barely saved the city. By early November, the Indians were attacking along the main invasion route, the road leading north-westward from Srinagar through Baramula to Uri. Using armour and superior tactics, Indian forces recaptured Uri on November 14. The tribesmen fled from the general area. An official Indian account of the hostilities states that the army had sufficient momentum at that time to capture Muzaffarabad, the rebel centre lying west of Uri. The army was halted, however, by blown bridges and shortages of petrol and other supplies.[15]

Meanwhile, Jinnah on October 27 had ordered General Sir Douglas Gracey, his temporary British Commander-in-Chief under the terms of partition, to send regular Pakistan troops into action. Gracey temporised and the next day, with Field Marshal Sir C. Auchinleck, the Supreme Commander, persuaded Jinnah reluctantly to withdraw his orders. While India had inherited its military forces virtually intact, Pakistan was forced to build its from less organised units, and it is doubtful whether Jinnah at that time could have mustered an effective force.[16]

The first phase of the initial war over Kashmir has left still unresolved the fundamental question of how the tribal raiders were organised, supplied and led. Pakistan continues to insist that she had no direct role in the invasion, although she has never denied that individual Pakistanis helped the rebels, some of them army officers granted generous leave. India has maintained that Pakistan controlled and directed the tribesmen, using them as a disguise for aggressive force. Actually, the preponderant evidence is that Pakistan permitted the tribal incursions of 1947 and probably instigated them. The first movement of Mahsuds was kept secret, even from British military and civilian advisers, whom the Pakistanis regarded as neutral or hostile to their desire to gain Kashmir. 'It seems clear', says one commentator, 'that Pakistani politicians and civilian officials must have connived at this, helping the tribesmen to get vehicles and petrol and supplies, and ensuring that preparations were being kept secret.'[17] Lord Birdwood, whose account of this period often supports Pakistan, reaches somewhat the same conclusion. He speculates that Pakistani officials feared the untamed border tribesmen and might have had difficulty in controlling them. But, he adds, Pakistan had aided the tribesmen previously and was unconvincing in her contention that every effort was taken to prevent the invasion. 'The general conclusion is that while there was no plan of control by the Pakistan government at the highest level, there was knowledge and tacit consent . . .' for the attack. And, Lord Birdwood continues, 'Pakistan's assistance was substantial.'[18]

Clearly, the motorised movement of any fighting force requires equipment and logistical support beyond the capacity of independent tribal units. Menon, presumably quoting from official Indian documents, claims the initial attacking force totalled an estimated 5,000 men, riding in between 200 and 300 trucks. He adds that the first Indian army units which contacted them at Baramula 'found them to be an organised body of men armed with light and medium machine-guns and mortars, and led by commanders who knew modern tactics and the use of ground.'[19] Yet the general interpretation of this initial campaign, shared by modern Indian officials, is that Srinagar escaped conquest only because the attackers lingered too long for loot in Baramula. This suggests that tribal indiscipline and primitiveness were mixed with whatever professional Pakistani guidance was provided. Most probably, Pakistani officers, operating as 'volunteers' with official sanction or, perhaps, under orders, tried to fight an efficient campaign but lacked the manpower and influence to control all their forces. Josef Korbel, a former United Nations observer, says that all the groups invading Kashmir were under the command of General Akbar Khan, who later became the Pakistani Chief of Staff and who was imprisoned for his part in a plot against the government in 1948. He was known as 'General Tariq', the name of a Moorish hero who had defended Islam in Spain more than 1,000 years earlier.[20] And V. P. Menon adds this testimony: During a meeting at Lahore between Mountbatten and Jinnah on November 1, the Pakistani leader proposed that both sides simultaneously withdraw at once from Kashmir. Mountbatten asked how the tribesmen could be forced to pull out. 'If you do this,' said Jinnah, 'I will call the whole thing off.'[21]

On the other hand, the evidence discounts the persistent Pakistani claim that the efficiency of the October 27 airlift proved that the Indians had prepared beforehand for an invasion of Kashmir and that the preceding events, including the Maharajah's clumsy intrigues, were designed to justify it. The British Chief of Staff of the Indian army, says Menon, first learned on October 24 of the capture of Muzaffarabad by the tribal forces two days earlier, and through this obtained initial news of the invasion. 'Prior to this date,' he says, 'no plans of any sort for sending Indian forces into Kashmir had been formulated or even considered.' The first moves came the next day when plans were hastily made and an infantry battalion was alerted for possible movement to Kashmir.[22] The airlift and subsequent military actions were handled swiftly but with considerable capability by the previously untested Indian military authorities.[23] During the campaign, Indian forces contributed a number of other unprecedented achievements. They brought armoured cars into action against the tribal invaders, after driving them 300 miles into Kashmir across the 9,000-foot Banihal Pass, at the southern entrance to the mountains. Later, they fought with light tanks for the first time across the ice-fields in the 11,000-foot Zoji Pass, north-east of Srinagar. The late General K. S. Thimmayya initiated military air travel to remote Leh, Ladakh, by making a pioneer flight over an uncharted area at 23,000 feet, without using oxygen.[24]

After the dispersal of the initial invasion force, action shifted to a new south-western front in Jammu, where other tribal forces had

F

found an area for fresh flank attacks. The nature of the conflict was different in this region. Local insurgents were more deeply involved in the struggle than had been the case in the Srinagar battle. As a result, rebel forces included dissidents from both sides of the border, tribal fighters from Pakistan and Pakistanis who involved themselves for various reasons. Militarily, the campaign was fought primarily for control over limited communications, rather than for major territorial expansion. Some of the bitterest hostilities of the first Indo-Pakistani conflict occurred in this sector, and it became equally important in the war of 1965. With Kashmir's main roads and rivers leading directly to Pakistan, the Indians were dependent upon a single, newly-built, narrow road for the movement of supplies through Jammu to the north-west front. The road ran through Akhnur, where a lone bridge was highly vulnerable to demolition. It continued northward to Naushera and then to Jhangar. At this point, the road forked. One arm turned westward towards Mirpur and the Pakistan border. The second continued northward to Uri.

Rebel forces fought through the winter and into the spring of 1948 to cut this Indian line of supply. The Indians had been rein-forced in November but were hard-pressed. As the battle intensified, some Indian commanders pushed on towards Mirpur, extending the fighting against the advice of the British Chief of Staff and, apparently, without control from New Delhi. The evident purpose was to gain local military advantage. There was no indication that the commanders intended to advance into Pakistan proper, but Karachi grew increasingly suspicious of Indian intentions. On February 6, rebel forces launched an attack on the key junction of Naushera. It became what the Indians term the biggest battle of the conflict. In fighting which ranged from hand-to-hand combat with Pathan swords to onslaughts with modern artillery, the Indians repulsed waves of attackers totalling an estimated 15,000 men.[25]

At this period, Lord Birdwood concludes from his investigations, Pakistani officers realised the Azad Kashmir forces could not hold the Indian army. They decided, therefore, to maintain the Pakistan Seventh Division in position behind the front. They also adopted a more lenient policy towards officers and non-commissioned officers who wished to take leave to join the rebels. On March 17, Pakistan mountain artillery, with a support force of regular army infantrymen, went into action in an unsuccessful attack on Poonch, to the north of Naushera.[26]

The Indians launched an offensive in the spring of 1948 after increasing their force to two divisions. One wing of the drive was aimed at Poonch, the key to the logistics campaign along the western front, where the Indian garrison had been besieged for a year. In a second thrust, the Indians sent one column towards Uri with a flanking movement over the mountains to the north. The flank attack under the colourful General Thimmayya was so successful that he captured Tithwal on May 23 and looked down on Muzaffarabad, only eighteen miles away. Muzaffarabad, now the capital of Azad Kashmir, was the political key to the campaign. The official Indian estimate reads: '. . . if the Indian army were allowed to reach Domel and Muzaffarabad, all would be lost for the cause of the raiders. Pakistan, which till then had helped the invaders covertly, now came out into the open and flung in more regular army battalions to stem the tide of the Indian Army's drive westward.' Indian forces advancing from Uri encountered regular Pakistani units four days later.[27] The threat to Muzaffarabad forced a Pakistani withdrawal from the entire northern sector, but the Indians stopped, apparently on their own volition, and a Pakistani brigade stabilised the situation.[28] In this account and in the guarded words of the official Indian military version of this northern campaign, there appears some confirmation for the general belief now held in New Delhi that the Indian advance was halted on Nehru's orders. 'If only', the Indians moan, 'he had allowed the campaign to continue for five more days, we would not have this trouble over Kashmir.' With the capture of Muzaffarabad, the Indians could have gone on to reclaim all of Kashmir.

Pakistan publicly acknowledged its commitment of regular forces in May and said the move was prompted by the threat of an invasion of Pakistan resulting from India's spring offensive. The Pakistanis launched their own offensive in the summer. The purpose, the Indians say, was to disperse Indian forces and to conquer as much territory as possible. In addition to the main fronts, fighting flared up in two other key sectors. Pakistani units in the Kargil sector in the north-central area at one point cut the road connecting Srinagar and Leh and threatened Leh itself. Tribal elements advanced toward Srinagar through the Zoji Pass, but were repulsed when the Indians brought up their tanks.[29]

Eventually, the Pakistani force in Kashmir matched the Indians' two divisions. By November, the Pakistanis had removed their screening force from around Lahore, thus exposing themselves to invasion through the Punjab. Despite the claims of Indian aggression and the popular fears they aroused, Pakistani authorities were evidently convinced that, in fact, there was at the time no threat of an assault along the most feasible route into Pakistan proper. The Indians had scrupulously avoided any attack into the Punjab, and as a consequence had forced their troops into the long and difficult campaign to keep open the Jammu-Jhangar supply road. New Delhi, as Lord Birdwood points out, had given Pakistan a 'privileged sanctuary' like that provided later for communist forces in Korea through Washington's decision to avoid bombing Manchuria.[30] But Pakistan did not appear to have sufficient strength, during that period, to force the Indians to grant a sanctuary by the threat of retaliatory power. Nevertheless, the Pakistanis insist that their forces could have captured all of Kashmir if the truce had not intervened and, like the Indians, bemoan the fact that the issue was not settled at that time.

The fighting was intermittent and eventually influenced by considerable diplomatic activity. India referred the dispute to the United Nations on December 31, 1947, seeking official condemnation of Pakistan 'aggression'. The international body never adopted this attitude, but it continued long afterwards to wrestle with Kashmir and its peculiar problems. On April 21, 1948, the second Security Council resolution on the question called upon both Indian troops and tribal forces to withdraw under a formula for establishing a coalition interim government. This was never implemented, and a truce was not concluded until a minute before midnight on December 31, 1948. The truce was arranged under UN auspices, but it was actually brought about by an exchange of telegrams between General Gracey and General Sir F. R. R. Bucher, the British Chiefs of Staff of Pakistan and India respectively. Fearing a full-scale inter-dominion war, the two generals, says Lord Birdwood, undertook the real initiative for peace, and the UN were 'comparatively inactive passengers'. Menon says India was so encouraged by a possible UN solution that she took the initiative in instructing General Bucher to inaugurate armistice efforts.[31]

On January 20, 1949, agreement was reached in Karachi on a cease-fire line drawn along the positions held by the two armies at the end of hostilities. The line, which quickly solidified into a *de facto* international boundary, follows an irregular course from Jammu across peaks and valleys to remote ice-fields in the far north-east. It cuts through some villages, even houses, and encircles others. Consequently, the line has inherent complications which have been exploited periodically by both sides. Prior to 1965, peace was enforced technically, when there was peace, by a United Nations Military Observer Group for India and Pakistan (UNMOGIP). It totalled forty-five officers and men from twenty countries. At great personal risk, these men lived in forward positions and investigated incidents of attack and counter-attack during the hundreds of military clashes between 1949 and 1965. Their only brief was to report to the United Nations in New York and to counsel caution through personal diplomacy in the field. Peace was actually enforced by the balance of power between India and Pakistan, by the political climate of the moment, and by the concern of both sides to save face internationally. Behind the lines, each nation has attempted to consolidate its hold over the territory under its control. Both term the other's area 'occupied Kashmir'.

The clearest impression obtained from this record is that, at the start of independence for the subcontinent, the Kashmiris were pushed back into their historic mould of subservience to the power around them. Neither India nor Pakistan fought solely on behalf of the Kashmiris; they fought for their own purposes. It is true that Indian troops, at great sacrifice, saved Srinagar from horrible destruction by primitive attackers. But as the campaign continued, the security and well-being of the newly-established Indian nation clearly became paramount.

> Personally, [says Menon] when I recommended to the Government of India the acceptance of the accession of the Maharajah of Kashmir, I had in mind one consideration and one consideration alone, viz., that the invasion of Kashmir by the raiders was a grave threat to the integrity of India. Ever since the time of Mahmud Ghazni, that is to say, for nearly eight centuries, with but a brief interval during the Moghul epoch, India had been subjected to periodical invasions from the north-west. Mahmud Ghazni had led no less than seventeen of these incursions in person. And within less than ten weeks of the establishment of the new State of Pakistan, its very act was to let loose a tribal invasion

through the north-west. Srinagar today, Delhi tomorrow. A nation that forgets its history or its geography does so at its peril.

We had no territorial ambitions in Kashmir. If the invasion by the raiders had not taken place, I can say in the face of any contradiction that the Government of India would have left Kashmir alone.[32]

Pakistan has less reason to claim that it fought for the welfare of the Kashmiris. If there was idealism behind involvement of Pakistanis in the Poonch revolt and the insurgency of Jammu, the campaign waged by tribal forces, and in many respects by the regular Pakistani army, was for conquest. The record is clear that, until the major raids began, India had made no move to enter Kashmir with military force. The Pakistanis, however, were involved in paramilitary action in July to capitalise upon the Gilgit upheaval and to annex Baltistan. This was a rather clear indication that Karachi would not tolerate an independent Kashmir, despite Jinnah's insistence that the princely rulers could adopt such a position. Gilgit was important strategically, for from it Pakistani-controlled forces later threatened both Srinagar and Leh. Thus, pro-Karachi forces were in a position to threaten or to assault Srinagar some weeks before the time when, Pakistan later claimed, the Indians were intriguing to win the state politically. In July, Sheikh Abdullah was in jail, Nehru was under threat of imprisonment if he visited the state, Congress leaders were in custody, and the Maharajah was still trying to hold on to his power.

Tactically, the Pakistani campaign reflected a consistent attempt to capture as much of Kashmir as possible and to maintain a foothold in the state at all costs. The initial tribal invasion, if successful, might have produced easy victory by occupying the capital and thereby giving Pakistani-controlled forces dominance over the state. When that failed, other tribal forces under apparent Karachi influence struck in confused Jammu in a clear effort to nullify Indian army capability by cutting communications and isolating units in the north. The parallel between this strategy and that of the 1965 war is striking. In early 1948, regular Pakistani forces, quite logically, were deployed behind Azad Kashmir troops to prevent possible Indian invasion from Jammu, while other units screened the Punjab. But when the Pakistani army entered the conflict and admitted doing so, in May, it fought far northward, around Uri. There was, as Karachi claimed, a possibility of Indian invasion into Pakistan proper through this difficult mountainous country. But it was minimal, in view of the fact that the Indian army, which was considerably the larger, had avoided striking Pakistan through the more accessible Punjab. Instead, Karachi apparently took the grave gamble of committing its regular forces in order to save Muzaffara-bad: a vital political position for a continued effort to conquer Kashmir but of purely secondary significance in the defence of Pakistan proper. In doing so, Pakistani forces illegally crossed the Kashmiri border. India's operations were covered by the clearly legal accession of the Maharajah, although Pakistan later contended, unconvincingly, that he had abdicated power by fleeing to Jammu. Finally, by November 1948, if not earlier, Pakistan was convinced that she was in no danger of direct Indian invasion, for Lahore was left poorly defended. Therefore subsequent operations, and those which had been planned until an armistice was enforced, were obviously intended solely to expand the attack on Kashmir.

Jinnah regarded Kashmir as economically and racially part of Pakistan, and most of his countrymen expected the automatic absorption of the state at partition. This was, however, a unilateral opinion which seemed to be nullified, in part, by the fact that Sheikh Abdullah became Kashmir's dominant political figure by preaching independence to his people. Distrusting the intentions of the Hindu Maharajah as well as those of New Delhi, Jinnah had first exerted pressure on Kashmir by hit-and-run border raids, an apparent economic blockade and a certain amount of political intrigue. Finally, he turned to the ruthlessness which he had used in calling for direct action in 1946. It is doubtful whether the tribal invasions would have been made or the necessary military equipment supplied without his approval. In December 1947, five months before Pakistan admitted involvement, India formally charged it with granting the raiders bases in Pakistan and transit through the country; as well as supplying food, some military training, trans-portation, and arms such as mortars, artillery and mines which the tribesmen did not possess.[33] In deciding on this action, Jinnah must have known that by it Muslim would slaughter Muslim, for the invasion route to Srinagar crossed an area dominated by his co-religionists.

The precipitate use of force, however, was another tragic blunder. It changed the entire geopolitical situation of the disturbed subcontinent and led to two wars, interspersed with abnormal tensions between the countries; while by waiting Jinnah might have obtained Kashmir easily and bloodlessly. There is no reason to reject V. P. Menon's testimony that India could and would have let Kashmir go to Pakistan before the start of the raids. Indian leaders had agreed upon it, and it had been endorsed by an earlier Congress Party position which would have minimised political opposition. Nehru, his compatriots and the Indian nation were far more idealistic then than later events permitted them to be. Pressures to acquire the state were comparatively feeble within an India preoccupied with other problems. Even after the outbreak of hostilities, many Indians in the indifferent south thought that Kashmir should be abandoned.[34] Devout Hindus believed that Kashmir was an irremovable part of Mother India just as fervently as Pakistanis believed in 'Muslim brotherhood', but they were less prepared to go to war for the concept; and despite Muslim suspicions and Nehru's affection for Kashmir, there is no clear evidence of Indian political manoeuvring to control the state before the fighting began. Sir Hàri's probable policies are less certain. He was, however, distinctly unwilling to accede to India until forced to do so. In time, the pressure of events could have turned him towards a favourable political deal with Pakistan.

In fact, the major armed assault altered the situation more completely and more quickly than perhaps many of the participants realised amid the pressures of the moment. First, it intensified the strong fears within India that Pakistan would use force to expand. Pakistan had struck first in the war of decision between the neighbours which many on both sides had predicted. Menon, in pointing out the significance of this factor in his own actions, suggests that the same thought occurred to other Indian leaders. Secondly, it transformed Kashmir from a theoretical into an active battle area. When the conflict was suspended at the end of 1948 without decision and with both sides under formidable arms, the possibility of a second Kashmiri war could never be excluded. The importance of this factor to India is confirmed by the circumstance that she kept sizable military force in Kashmir during what Indians regarded as a life-and-death attack by China in 1962. Thirdly, Pakistan's military offensive inevitably strengthened the anti-Muslim elements in north India and helped to widen the chasm between the country's idealists and what might be called its political pragmatists.

These factors were present or prospective when the Indian leaders accepted Mountbatten's suggestion to qualify the accession of Kashmir with a clear pledge to permit a future plebiscite. Lord Mountbatten wrote to the Maharajah that 'the question of accession should be decided in accordance with the wishes of the people of the state . . .'[35] The first of Nehru's many public promises on this point was made on November 2, 1947. There was general belief, at the time, that the vote would be restricted to a choice between India and Pakistan and the latter would win.

It can be argued, however, that in terms of political reality the pledge was too impractical to be valid. In essence, it committed the new government to use its young army to save a remote capital from medieval assault, to drive out the attackers, then to hand over the state to the power behind the attackers. This would have been an unprecedented act of sacrificial benevolence. Even if the purpose had been to protect Kashmiri independence, the Indians would have been undertaking an operation that has seldom been practised in history and never by Asians. Nearly twenty years later, many Asians, including Indians and Pakistanis, refused to believe that American troops and their foreign allies were fighting to save South Vietnam from the communists, not to conquer it, and that they were prepared to withdraw at the end of hostilities. These doubters could not find in their experience any basis upon which to accept the American pledge, despite the fact that United Nations troops, except for security forces, had withdrawn from South Korea at the end of the Korean War. In 1947, New Delhi pledged itself to a Western concept of international behaviour which was so advanced that neither Europe nor the United States had considered adopting it at that time. The idea was so alien to Asia that India encountered strong scepticism. Pakistan never believed her, and many Asians were convinced that Indian troops went into Kashmir solely to seize it.

There is no reason to doubt that the pledge was made in good faith by the Indian leaders and that Nehru, among others, was sincere in his promises to implement it. After all, the hard-headed members of the Congress Party had adopted the slightly less idealistic programme of promising to defend princely states, even if they avoided accession, on the grounds that they would also be defending India. But in the case of Kashmir there were complications at once. An international conflict had been started over a particularly sensitive territory, and strong security fears within India had to be quieted before the *status quo ante* was acceptable. It was quite possible that some Indian officials were prepared to accept an unqualified plebiscite before the attack, but that afterwards they would support a vote only if Pakistan gave more assurances than she was willing to do. This may have been the reaction of Sardar Patel, whose role in the whole affair is not clear. Moreover, as the fighting progressed, Nehru began to encounter the usual opposition from groups unwilling to abandon territory bought with their sons' blood, and from more fanatic forces. In 1949, while first UN negotiations were under way, Nehru came under strong domestic pressure for his handling of the crisis. The Hindu Mahasabha, in particular, attacked the government for planning to abandon part of 'Mother India', and its influence forced Nehru to say in a political speech in September that Kashmir is 'part of India'. The invasion, therefore, not only altered the situation radically but placed a definite time limit on the period during which an unqualified plebiscite would be acceptable in India's political climate. It was generally assumed within India that, after the war had been fought, all Nehru's tremendous prestige would have been necessary to persuade the country to carry out the pledge.

With their regular troops facing each other across a long cease-fire line in Kashmir and with UN efforts to solve that war faltering, Pakistan and India approached conflict with each other on two other occasions. The first crisis, in 1949–50, was precipitated by a trade war when Pakistan refused to follow other Commonwealth nations in devaluing its currency. Then the neighbours were enflamed by a two-way refugee tide created by the expulsion of Hindus from East Pakistan and a counter expulsion of indigent Muslims from Assam, where they had wandered in search of work. Communal riots broke out, and suspicions increased. When Sardar Patel went to Calcutta to put down communist agitation, he was accused of engineering a master plan to expel Muslims. Patel, with considerable popular support, had demanded the ejection of ten Muslims for every Hindu driven from East Pakistan, but Nehru publicly opposed him. Relations between the two men deteriorated sharply and continued to worsen. In February, the Pakistani Prime Minister, Liaquat Ali Khan, claimed that India was preparing for war and said, '. . . to me, it appears that what has happened in Kashmir and what is happening in East Bengal are interlinked and we cannot separate them.' The crisis was resolved by an international agreement establishing certain rights for refugees. 'We have stopped ourselves at the edge of the precipice and turned our back on it', Nehru told the Indian parliament.

In 1951, tensions again mounted over frustration with the Kashmir negotiations and a continuing series of incidents along the cease-fire line. Nehru said in March that in Pakistan '. . . during the past few months there has been constant and continuous talk of *jehad* or holy war against India'. In July, India reinforced its garrison in eastern Punjab, and Pakistan claimed that all Indian armoured units had been moved into an offensive position. Nehru denied the possibility of war, but said the Indian decision had been influenced by consistent anti-India propaganda within Pakistan. There appeared to be some concern in New Delhi that Pakistan planned to create trouble in Kashmir in order to press the United Nations to stronger action. In November, Nehru offered a non-aggression pact to Pakistan but specified that it would include Kashmir. The proposal sounded to an Indian commentator like a gentle hint that India would retaliate in the Punjab to any further trouble in Kashmir.[36] The crisis, which had produced sharply defiant anti-Indian statements in Pakistan, ended after a new UN initiative and the assassination of Liaquat Ali Khan. Meanwhile, the rivalry between Nehru and Sardar Patel had manifested itself openly in 1950 during a contest over the Congress Party presidency, which Patel's candidate won by a narrow margin. Their differences were not enough to split the party but were sharp enough to make the two men the symbols of the right and the left in the party and among the political masses. On Kashmir, the division of their authority was not clear, although some of Patel's supporters say Nehru had a free hand, as he had in foreign affairs. Other Indians in a position to know claim that Nehru wanted to carry out the pledge of a Kashmiri plebiscite but that he was prevented from doing so by Patel.[37] The duumvirate ended with Patel's death in late 1950, and Nehru won control of the party the following year. Politically, the right wing receded within Congress, but on the streets its influence remained strong.

It was against this background that UN negotiators attempted, during the early years, to solve the complex Kashmir question. They floundered, in essence, on the issue of providing a method of troop withdrawal, in advance of plebiscite, that would satisfy both sides. Throughout this period, Nehru clung to his promise of a plebiscite and indicated that it was not mere idealism by taking a stand against communalism that required considerable political courage. But clearly he could not abandon Kashmir amid India's newly-strengthened security fears. Pakistan, on the other hand, continued its defiance and took no initiative to strengthen Nehru's position. Instead, it often appeared that Pakistani officials attempted to use diplomacy to win by political means what they had lost by premature military attack.

5

KASHMIR: THE POLITICAL STRUGGLE

THE POLITICAL war over Kashmir has been relentless and deadly. It has been continual since 1947 on two major fronts: in the visible arena of international diplomacy, particularly at the United Nations, and in the half-hidden politics of the two portions of the severed state. The conflict has been conducted behind a smoke-screen of extraordinarily misleading propaganda from all participants, which has served to confuse and complicate the basic issues and to fool most of the spectators.

Both sides have manoeuvred continually to gain advantage in Kashmir. A façade of logic, morality and legality has been carefully maintained, but behind it each belligerent has pursued its goals with every exploitable method. Pakistan has consistently attempted to cancel out the military blunder of 1947–8 by enlisting the support of the world behind her 'moral' right to claim all of Kashmir. She has mixed power with subversion and political manipulation. The pressure of Kashmir, and the insecurity it symbolises, has forced Pakistan into becoming the only major power seeking decisive military support from both the United States and the Communist bloc. India has manoeuvred just as persistently behind the façade, since 1953 at the latest, to incorporate Indian Kashmir into the Indian Union by political means. The evident purpose is to eliminate all Pakistani claims to this territory. India also has made its own adjustments to the changing geopolitics of the subcontinent and, as one result, had reached a greater power position in 1965 than Pakistan desired or, apparently, contemplated.

The arguments presented by both sides before the United Nations are largely diversionary to the main effort and designed primarily to maintain the façade; since Pakistan, apparently, has abandoned hope that the UN will hand it Kashmir. The real struggle has been conducted for many years in strategic areas of the cease-fire line, in the back alleys of Srinagar where Kashmiri 'revolutionaries' gather, and in secret political conferences. These are the meaningful areas of conflict, and they always have been. Although the United Nations and international diplomacy have influenced the situation, their impact has never been decisive. From the beginning, the controversy involved the basic question of national security for both sides, a consideration that has intensified through the years. Each adversary has demonstrated that it would accept the edicts and the advice of the United Nations when favourable to its purposes but would reject them otherwise. The quest for security quite naturally is of over-riding significance for both countries, and all tactics necessary to achieve this goal are considered to be justified, as long as the façade of legality is preserved.

The first phase of the political war over Kashmir lasted roughly until the end of 1953. It was a period when Nehru talked most vigorously of permitting a plebiscite and when he made a number of persuasive gestures towards preparing for one. From the Indian point of view, these efforts were nullified by Pakistan's refusal to evacuate Azad Kashmir in advance of a vote. This created an impasse which has persisted, stultifying United Nations efforts to solve the problem. In late 1953, political developments within Kashmir led to greater control from New Delhi. Simultaneously, an atmosphere of hope that the Kashmir problem could be settled through bilateral Indo-Pakistani negotiations was dispelled by reports of a military pact between the United States and Pakistan, which was concluded the following year. Although the agreement probably postponed the Indo-Pakistani war by a decade, it nevertheless became either the cause or the justification for an intensified Indian effort to integrate Kashmir politically. The Soviet Union then became directly involved and, through clever manipulation, stiffened the Indian stand and convinced many Indians that Moscow was far more firmly behind them than it actually was. The third phase followed the Chinese Communist attack on India in 1962. By demonstrating the strategic importance of Kashmir in modern warfare, Peking made it impossible for India to give up the state under any conditions, and this position was solidified by

Pakistan's flirtation with Peking. By 1965, Indian implacability over Kashmir was fully demonstrated and, combined with other factors, it produced war.

Through these drastic historical changes, both principals have maintained consistent and relatively unchanging positions before the United Nations on Kashmir. With the war temporarily going against it, India referred the matter to the United Nations at the end of 1947 and charged Pakistan with 'an act of aggression against India'. In essence, the Indian case, as presented by Sir N. Gopalaswami Ayyangar, a former Prime Minister of Kashmir, was that Pakistan, having failed to subdue Kashmir by economic blockade, resorted to an increasing level of subversive armed combat, starting with the Poonch revolt and coming to a climax with its open support for the invading tribesmen. The Indians demanded that Pakistan be condemned and that forces under its control be expelled from areas they continued to hold in Kashmir. After that, the promised plebiscite could be held. India had defended Kashmir upon the legal accession of the state, but would have been obliged to do so without accession, because the Indian government succeeded to British suzerainty and responsibility in all areas which did not elect to join Pakistan.

Sir Mohammed Zafrullah Khan, the Pakistani representative, won initial support by subordinating the Kashmir affair to a general attack on what he claimed was a concerted Hindu plan of 'genocide' to exterminate Pakistan through the civil war. He demanded broad indemnities for that conflict, including Indian withdrawal from Junagadh. On Kashmir, Sir Zafrullah denied formal Pakistani support for the tribal invaders, although open support had been given since October. Kashmir belongs to Pakistan, he contended, because it is an economic part of the nation and because the people would vote that way in any free and overall election. Pakistan has maintained this basic position since then and has insisted that there has been no fundamental change in the Kashmir situation since the autumn of 1947, when all participants expected that it would become part of Pakistan.

This initial debate, at Lake Success, established a number of significant precedents. Kashmir was one of the first great issues of infinite complication to be placed before the young United Nations Organisation. It could have provided an opportunity for the United

Nations to establish itself as the supra-national judicial body which many of its early proponents envisaged: a solemn court of last resort, seeking the truth behind complex international situations through its own investigative facilities, weighing solid evidence and deciding each case on its merits, instead of choosing between rival propagandists, as all diplomats are under these circumstances. But the United Nations established the pattern so abused in subsequent years of behaving somewhat like an inferior local political club. The delegates not only tolerated rabble-rousing speeches unworthy of the consideration of an impartial international jury; they responded to them with emotion and prejudice. The voting was influenced more by backstage pressures and by the political bias of the delegate's home country than by sober consideration. Whatever other influences were at work, India was clearly at an initial disadvantage because she was so much larger than Pakistan and was therefore more easily portrayed as a bully threatening the smaller neighbour.

The debate further revealed the United Nations penchant for using uncritical slogans. The term 'self-determination' was freely applied to the Kashmir issue, and it has become such a hallmark of the controversy that it is used constantly today. But self-determination means the right of peoples freely to decide their own fate, including their political future. The ideal was formulated by the late President Woodrow Wilson of the United States and, like many ideals, has had both instant appeal and strict practical limitations. In Kashmir, the self-determination that might create an independent mountain nation has never been seriously considered, for a number of practical reasons. The United Nations itself paid little attention when Sheikh Abdullah pleaded before it for independence. Nevertheless, 'self-determination' has been used repeatedly in the international forum as the proper phrase to apply to the only alternatives ever given to the Kashmiris: the choice between one of two adjacent overlords, neither of whom has an enviable record. In its basic resolution on Kashmir of January 5, 1949, the United Nations formally ruled out independence and limited the Kashmiris to annexation by either India or Pakistan. This would be decided, the United Nations said, 'through the democratic method of a free and impartial plebiscite'. 'Self-determination' continues to dominate any debate over the issue.

This distinction would have been relatively unimportant, perhaps, had the Kashmir question not become so deeply involved in moral issues of doubtful significance. When international morality is questioned, however, there is a great difference between the choice actually given to Kashmir and the concept that India is denying its people self-determination. In the emotionalism following the withdrawal of Western European colonialism, 'self-determination of peoples' means the independence so cherished by newly-freed nations, an idea which Indian diplomats have helped to foster. As a result, no one at the United Nations today dares oppose the slogan, on Kashmir or any other issue to which it is applied. Consequently, the true division of world opinion over Kashmir is impossible to determine from UN debates, particularly the changes produced by the war of 1965. The United States, for example, strongly supported self-determination for Kashmir in 1947, partly through the necessity of upholding an American concept, and continued to do so for many years after, when it appeared to be a workable formula. Many Washington officials changed their opinion after the Pakistani attack of 1965. But the outcry from the emergent world can be readily imagined if an American spokesman were to tell the UN: 'Self-determination is a false slogan for Kashmir. Let's drop it and start over again.'

Similarly, India has helped to impale herself on the dilemma created by her plebiscite pledge at the time of the Maharajah's accession. That the pledge was given and reinforced by further public promises for many years and that no effort to implement it was made is undeniable. India has good reason to claim that Pakistan is responsible for making the plebiscite unacceptable in New Delhi. But this argument has won little response, and Pakistan has gained some diplomatic ground, though no tangible benefit, by repeatedly charging India with repudiating a solemn international undertaking. The Indians have been deeply embarrassed, and evidently their policies have been influenced accordingly. They have absorbed more international abuse for this one instance of what may have been impracticable idealism than Soviet Russia, for example, has received for violating dozens of solemn international commitments under far less controversial circumstances. No one has seen fit to credit India at the United Nations with adopting a moral position far ahead of the Asia of that time—or even of today. While insistence

G

upon adherence to international obligations is an important and necessary fundamental of diplomacy at the UN, the organisation failed, in this instance, to determine the validity of the undertaking.

The failure is due, in great measure, to the fundamental error made by the UN at the outset of the Kashmir issue. It refused to condemn Pakistani 'aggression', despite the evidence presented by India and despite the logic of the situation. In Indian eyes, the fact that the tribesmen invading Kashmir rode in trucks that they could not possibly have owned was *ipso facto* proof of the owner's guilt. Admittedly the situation was confused and the evidence only circumstantial. There was at that time, and far more strongly in later years, a disposition to condone or to applaud outside support for revolutions. But the failure even to censure Pakistan for a war situation in which she clearly was involved helped to open the way for much of the disguised aggression which has followed. To escape international blame and save face, the attacker needed only to confuse the issues, disguise his involvement, and insist upon his innocence. When first the UN, then individual nations, refused to recognise any form of unadmitted aggression, the pattern of turning guerrilla warfare into a subversive offensive weapon became standard. Instead of realising the implications of their rebuff in 1947, the Indians took a vigorous part in spreading this subterfuge. Nehru refused to condemn the North Koreans for their clumsy and open aggression in 1950, on the grounds that a nation with which future business is intended should not be condemned; a point later cited as proof that he had no intention of dealing with Pakistan. India, as chairman of the International Control Commission in South-east Asia, long overlooked the infiltration of North Vietnamese regulars into Laos and South Vietnam, as well as other truce violations, while continually criticising Pakistan for similar infractions. And in 1965, when Pakistan again attacked Kashmir with the same tactics as in 1947, India failed once more to convince the United Nations.

The United Nations began concerted attempts in 1948 to mediate in the Kashmir dispute. A five-member Commission on India and Pakistan (UNCIP) prepared and altered a number of plans which were finally accepted by both sides and incorporated into the key UN resolution of January 5, 1949. It provided for a cease-fire and truce agreement, under which the bulk of forces which had been introduced into the war were to be withdrawn. Under this section, a cease-fire line was stabilised. It provided for an area of about 5,000 square miles, with 700,000 inhabitants, under Pakistan control, as Azad Kashmir. The remainder of the state, covering about 81,000 square miles with $3\frac{1}{2}$ million residents, remained under Italian control. This area included the upper courses of the Jhelum and Chenab rivers, two of the waterways on which Pakistan depends. The resolution provided for further demilitarisation after the truce arrangements, with the UN Commission and a Plebiscite Administrator, to be appointed, determining the final disposition of military forces within Azad Kashmir. When this had been accomplished, the third step would be a plebiscite under UN supervision to determine whether the people wanted to join Pakistan or India. The plan settled into an impasse after completion of the truce details. It remained deadlocked, despite efforts of individual UN mediators which lasted until Dr Frank Graham reported failure in 1953 and recommended a settlement through direct Indo-Pakistan negotiations.[1]

While many points were raised during Indo-Pakistani debate over each step of the negotiations, the essential area of disagreement was Pakistan's insistence upon maintaining Azad Kashmir as an armed and viable state. From this flowed quarrels over the methods and scope of disbanding military forces and the nature of the local administration which would govern the entire state until a plebiscite had been completed. India wanted to eliminate Azad Kashmir as a separate entity, disbanding its forces, which Pakistan admitted were under control of the Pakistan army, and placing its administration under Sheikh Abdullah. The Sheikh, who had been released from jail during the period of accession and named Prime Minister in 1948, was then regarded by Pakistan as an Indian tool. The Pakistanis would not accept his control, nor would they relinquish the military symbol of Azad Kashmir's organised battalions. Since then, India has contended that Pakistan's refusal to withdraw the forces under her control voided the resolution by failing to carry out a necessary prelude to plebiscite. Pakistan contends that arrangements for a phased withdrawal were not completed, and India used the impasse as an excuse to proceed with the integration of Indian Kashmir.

There was deep mutual mistrust throughout these negotiations, which had been heightened by the crises of 1950 and 1951. Inevitably the mistrust would dominate the reactions of the two countries to proposals from foreign sources whose impartiality was often questioned. But, in retrospect, the controversy over Azad Kashmir seems to be much deeper. A certain amount of security was involved. During the war, Pakistani forces and those under their control had driven through the passes from Azad Kashmir to threaten Srinagar. The truce arrangement provided for maintenance of an Indian force in the Vale to maintain order, but the Indians opposed efforts to reduce it below the level they considered necessary to hold the passes and to prevent attack or the pressure of a military threat to the Vale. Despite the previous expectation of a pro-Pakistani vote by the Kashmiris, there was apparently an Indian belief that the atrocities practised by the tribal invaders might create sufficient pro-Indian sentiment to decide the election. Evidently, India did not want undue Pakistani pressure from Azad Kashmir to disrupt that possibility.

Beyond that, the constant but sensitive question of face was detectable. Pakistan had fought the big neighbour, and the conflict had aroused deep emotions in West Pakistan. To withdraw from the territory won by arms, while India still held the Vale, could have produced a severe loss of internal prestige. In the Pakistani view, it might also permit an armed Indian invasion to conquer the entire state. India, on the other hand, having successfully defended Kashmir, could not allow it to be assaulted again or captured, and still maintain face. The Indians could give up the state through plebiscite, but they could not be placed in the position of being forced out. New Delhi could not forget that the initial attacks had come largely from the area incorporated into Azad Kashmir.

In their own way, the Indians were fighting for the principle of denying an aggressor the fruits of conquest. Apart from face, the effort to eliminate Azad Kashmir was, in large measure, an attempt to roll back the advances made by Pakistani forces across the pre-war boundaries of Kashmir. Although the United Nations had failed to condemn Pakistan, one of its negotiators, Sir Owen Dixon, had given guarded support for the Indian position. In his final report, issued on September 15, 1950, he said: '. . . when the frontier of the State of Jammu and Kashmir was crossed on, I believe, October 20, 1947, by hostile elements, it was contrary to international law, and when in May 1948, as I believe, units of the regular Pakistan forces moved into the territory of the state, that, too, was inconsistent with international law.'[2]

Pakistan used Azad Kashmir as the beachhead for maintaining continual pressure on Indian Kashmir for the next sixteen years. It is possible that this was the major reason why she fought so stubbornly to preserve it and, in so doing, jeopardised the chance of still winning the state by plebiscite. By their strategy in the closing phases of the war, the Pakistanis had indicated their determination to maintain control over as much of Kashmir as possible, probably expecting a second round of politico-military conflict. The cessation of hostilities without a clear-cut decision was an invitation to continue the struggle until one was arrived at. Pakistan had fought for a Muslim nation primarily through power politics since Jinnah turned to direct action. Looking at Nehru from that standpoint, Karachi doubtless believed that he was waging the same kind of struggle, that promises of a plebiscite were only part of the trappings, and that Nehru, therefore, would yield only to superior force. But it may be that the Pakistanis misjudged Nehru's strong Western idealism. Up to the autumn of 1953, there is no proof that he was playing this double game; in fact, the evidence points more towards the conclusion that he intended a plebiscite but could not overcome Pakistani intransigence, which played into the hands of Hindu extremists. The Indian government maintains today that 'merely by withdrawing its troops from the state, Pakistan could have had a plebiscite at any time'[3] in Kashmir during the period of the quarrel over Azad Kashmir. While this is not irrefutable proof, it points to the possibility that Pakistan made another serious mistake in the 1949–53 period by failing to understand her adversary.

After solidification of the cease-fire line into a *de facto* international boundary, the severed portions of Kashmir developed their own peculiar internal structures. Azad Kashmir, for all practical purposes, quickly disappeared into Pakistan and conformed, on the surface at least, to the rest of the nation. The poverty-stricken area was, and remains, dependent economically on the central government. There is no sign of impressive economic development within the mountainous area; nor is there confirmation of persistent Indian claims that Azad Kashmiris are living under worse conditions than before. The Hindu population, which totalled about 12·5 per cent in 1947, has dwindled to some 2 per cent. Politically, the regime has given the appearance of stability, by contrast with the publicly explosive affairs of Indian Kashmir. This may be due in part to the fact that the region is sparsely settled, without major cities, and authority customarily rests with tribal chiefs. It may be due also to press censorship. In fact, Azad Kashmir had eight Presidents between 1947 and 1964, compared with four Prime Ministers in Indian Kashmir. One of Azad's ex-Presidents was jailed on official charges of corruption, but the real reason was said to be his support for proposals to reunify the state with a semi-independent status.[4]

Sheikh Abdullah quickly became the energetic and controversial dictator of Indian Kashmir. He dominated the National Conference, a party which he had founded, and it in turn so controlled the political life of the Kashmiri section of the state that few candidates opposed it during elections; and the Sheikh used his jails freely to silence other opponents. From this base, he vigorously promoted drastic political and economic programmes with little regard for the circumstances or the consequences.

Politically, the Sheikh drove towards the establishment of self-rule and the elimination of the monarchy, two goals which his party had long advocated. Despite the delicacy of UN negotiations over Kashmir, he demanded the election of a Constituent Assembly. The UN opposed the move in a resolution which India rejected. The election was held in the autumn of 1951, when Dr Graham was attempting to solve the Kashmiri impasse. The Conference won a virtually unanimous victory. Under the Sheikh's order to decide 'the state's future political affiliation', the Assembly quickly stripped major power from the Maharajah and affirmed Kashmir's autonomy over all matters except defence, foreign affairs and communications. In April 1952, the Sheikh repeated this point and declared in a speech that the constitution of India could not be applied to Kashmir. During July, he conferred with Nehru in New Delhi, and on July 24, the Indian leader announced in the Lok Sabha that Kashmir would have a special status different from any other Indian state. Kashmir could elect its own Chief of State and pursue certain social and economic programmes which otherwise conflicted with sections of the Indian constitution. Within Kashmir, the people would have special rights. Following this agreement, the Kashmir Assembly abolished hereditary rule, thus ending the overlordship of the hated Dogras from the plains. Sir Hari Singh agreed to abdicate and his son, the popular Karan Singh, was elected as a commoner to be the first Chief of State. Indian Kashmir also adopted its own flag.

In the view of some Indian commentators this adjustment was consistent with the basic philosophy of Indian-Kashmiri relations up to that point. The Indian constitution, which had been adopted on January 26, 1950, contained a special article (370) referring to Kashmir and detailing some temporary conditions applicable to it. This proviso was necessary, says an Indian constitutional lawyer, because of New Delhi's commitment to allow the people of Kashmir to decide whether they would remain in the Indian Union. Under this purely interim arrangement, the Indian constitution as a whole did not apply to Kashmir. Certain sections could become pertinent only upon the order of the Indian President, in consultation with the State Assembly. The legislative authority of the Indian parliament was limited to matters specified in the instrument of accession. 'The above interim arrangement will continue until the Constituent Assembly for Jammu and Kashmir makes its decision [on accession]. It will then communicate its recommendations to the President, who will either abrogate Article 370 or make such modifications as may be recommended by that Constituent Assembly.'[5]

Sheikh Abdullah's position in 1952 was consistent with the central theme of independence and anti-monarchism which had run through his revolutionary career. He also repeated another consistent point, that 'Kashmir's accession to India will have to be of a restricted nature so long as communalism has a footing on the soil of India'. But it was notable that he expressed other views on different occasions. In 1949, for example, he told Nehru in Srinagar: 'I want you to believe that Kashmir is yours. No power in the world can separate us.' On another occasion, he described Kashmir as the bridge for the reunion of India and Pakistan. In March 1952, he said: '. . . No country—neither India nor Pakistan—can put spokes in the wheel of our progress.'[6] With power, the Sheikh became more arrogant and, in Josef Korbel's eyes, more unstable. 'The story of Sheikh Abdullah is a sad and sorry one', the former UN official says. 'It is a story of the patriot, once passionately devoted to his people's welfare, but one whose patriotism was too shallow to reject the temptations of power. Once a fighter, he turned into an opportunist and, worse, a dictator who at the end found himself entangled in the web of his own methods and policy.'[7]

Economically, Abdullah pushed through a number of swift changes which created strong opposition and fear. He angered Kashmiri nationalists by accepting comparatively large loans from India to finance improved education, to make a start towards industrialisation and for other projects. He aroused the Hindus of eastern Jammu not only by his political speeches but by an extensive land reform programme which threatened their holdings; and he promoted a method of sovietised nationalisation and agrarian reform that raised suspicions abroad of his purposes. Abdullah as a socialist was not out of step with the India of this period, but his open importation of Soviet methods clearly was, although New Delhi overlooked the fact. In 1944, the Sheikh gave the National Conference a programme which pledged the party: 'to fight for the poor against those who exploit; for the toiling people of our beautiful homeland against the heartless ranks of the socially privileged. . . . In our time, Soviet Russia has demonstrated before our eyes, not merely theoretically but in her actual day-to-day life and development, that real freedom takes birth only from economic emancipation.'[8]

In implementing this pledge during the 1950s, Sheikh Abdullah and his government confiscated large tracts of land with delayed compensation to the owners. They established co-operatives and collective farms and manipulated affairs so that numerous peasants were obliged to join them. By March 1953, the state government claimed that it had transferred 188,755 acres to 153,399 tillers, but the transfers were unequal. State officials often received more than the official minimum of 20 acres; peasants less. In many instances, the land reverted to the government, and in other cases the new 'owners' of small plots were unable to make a living from them and therefore 'voluntarily' joined the collective farms. By this time, the government owned 87,500 acres. 'Exactly the same method', says Korbel, 'was applied in Communist Poland, Hungary, Bulgaria, and Yugoslavia.' And, it might be added, in Communist China and Cuba. 'It is unlikely', Korbel continues, 'that this could be coincidental nor does it seem unfounded to assume that the member of the Land Reform Committee, Ghulam Sadiq, got his inspiration for this policy from his fellow comrades.' Korbel identifies Sadiq as a communist leader in Kashmir during this period and as one of the leading 'front' men for the numerous subterfuges then being practised on the subcontinent by Soviet Russia.[9] Sadiq later became Chief Minister of Indian Kashmir and followed policies which, at least, identified him as an extreme leftist.

Opposition to the Sheikh's policies in Hindu Jammu created sufficiently turbulent demonstrations in early 1952 for troops to be called. The opposition was fanned by the Hindu party, Praja Parishad (People's Party), which has vigorously fought control from Srinagar. Supported by representatives from the Hindu Mahasabha and other rightist groups, the agitation grew into work stoppages and demonstrations on behalf of complete integration with India. Some dissatisfaction was evident also in remote Ladakh. The Buddhists at that time would probably have chosen union with India or Tibet in preference to second-class citizenship in an independent Kashmir government which had long been inattentive to their needs. Apart from the influence of outside agitators, the turbulence within the Jammu portion of the state illustrated one of the permanent political realities of mismatched Jammu and Kashmir. Sheikh Abdullah drew his support from the politically inarticulate Muslims of the mountain section. Although the Praja Parishad contested elections, it could not break the Sheikh's power nor divert his sovietisation. Abdullah and his supporters had won considerable world sympathy by opposing rule over them by the 'foreign' Hindus of New Delhi. Yet, with authority, they unhesitatingly applied equal 'foreign' rule to the Hindus of Jammu and to the Buddhists.

Finally, in August 1953, the Sheikh's cabinet split under suspicious circumstances, and the deputy Prime Minister, Bakshi Ghulam Mohammed, joined two Hindus in turning against him. The opponents had sufficient strength to persuade Karan Singh to remove Abdullah from office and to have him arrested at the mountain resort of Gulmarg, near Azad Kashmir. One Indian version of this episode, published many years later, is that the Bakshi and his associates learned that Abdullah went to Gulmarg to confer with Pakistani 'friends across the border', whereafter he intended to arrest his cabinet opponents and hold a press conference to proclaim the independence of Kashmir. This was to be followed by a request that India, but apparently not Pakistan, withdraw its troops from the state. Nehru was described as violently upset by the Sheikh's arrest, an action contrary to his desires.[10] At the time, the suspicion that Abdullah was removed at India's instigation was so strong that Nehru publicly denied it. Shortly before his downfall, the Sheikh had spoken openly of renouncing the accession to India. The Bakshi had visited New Delhi in July. In a broadcast explaining the arrest, the Bakshi claimed that Abdullah was removed because he sought to achieve independence in co-operation with a foreign 'imperialist power'.

Bakshi Ghulam Mohammed immediately inaugurated a regime of such corruption, cruelty and inefficiency that it was still regarded with extreme bitterness in Srinagar in 1965. He also quickly brought the state legally into India. The Constituent Assembly, still dominated by the government, ratified the state's accession to India on February 6, 1954. Two months later, the long-standing customs barrier between the two areas was eliminated. Kashmir's new position as part of the Indian Union was endorsed in an order issued by President Prasad on May 14, observing the legalities of Article 370. A state constitution was drafted and adopted on November 19, 1956. Under it, Kashmir became an integral part of India. The accession of the state was formalised by India on Independence Day, January 26, 1957, and the act was made 'irrevocable'. The initial process of integration was finalised three years later, when the Indian Supreme Court assumed jurisdiction over the state on January 20, 1960.

Meanwhile, Sheikh Abdullah remained in jail for five years without formal charges being placed against him. Released in 1958, he immediately attacked the Bakshi regime for allegedly mistreating Muslims and condemned India for failing to hold the plebiscite. He was arrested again after three months' liberty, and eventually charged with treason. He was brought to trial with fourteen others in 1961, and they were told some time later that they were charged with plotting to overthrow the government. In his defence, Abdullah once more demanded independence and the right of self-determination for Kashmir. He was released again by the ailing Nehru in 1964 in an apparent last-minute attempt to solve the Kashmir issue, but Abdullah embarked on a highly-suspicious diplomatic campaign which resulted in house arrest in 1965. This dreary record is not unfamiliar in Asia. It indicates, among other things, the type of government that the Kashmiris would obtain if by some means they achieved independence.

Pakistan immediately transformed Sheikh Abdullah into a hero and thereafter repeatedly invoked his image on behalf of its cause. The Pakistanis fought every step of the way to halt or to revoke the Indian process of legally integrating Kashmir. They used diplomacy, threats, constant indignation and frequent public demands for war. They held demonstrations in their own country and through sympathetic groups in Indian Kashmir. But, significantly, they did not go to war. The Pakistani campaign inflamed tensions and made Kashmir into a more volatile symbol than it had been before; but it had little tangible effect on the situation. The United Nations refused to involve itself as deeply again in mediation efforts, although it frequently considered Kashmir in subsequent years. Pakistan had no allies capable of helping it to achieve success. For all practical purposes, India succeeded in consolidating its hold over Indian Kashmir when the Constituent Assembly ratified accession in early 1954, and there was little prospect of dislodging it by political means.

India's position had changed sharply and with relative speed between the Nehru-Abdullah 'special status' pact of July 1952, and the Bakshi Assembly's ratification of accession less than two years later. Nehru and other Indian government officials later justified these and subsequent events by claiming with considerable logic that the Kashmir situation had been altered radically by conclusion of a military alliance between the United States and Pakistan. The alliance was designed specifically to arm Pakistan against possible communist aggression, and a large quantity of American weapons were supplied solely for that purpose. The Indians claimed that Pakistan intended to use its new firepower only against them. The military agreement was rumoured several times during the latter part of 1953 but was not announced officially until February 22, 1954. Actually, however, the Indian process of integrating Kashmir began in August 1953, with the removal of Sheikh Abdullah and his replacement by the ever co-operative Bakshi. Despite Nehru's denials, most historians believe that India was responsible for the cabinet upheaval and that Abdullah was removed because he was reluctant to lead Kashmir into the Indian Union.[11] While the process of integration may have been speeded by formalisation of the US-Pakistan pact, it had become virtually irreversible before the alliance was more than rumour. The Assembly vote on accession was taken sixteen days before the military agreement was announced and nearly three months before it was formally concluded in May 1954.

Integration was the logical and predictable political reaction by India to the impasse over Azad Kashmir. The circumstances indicate that it was a necessity recognised by some elements of the Indian government when Pakistan refused to disband its Azad forces and clearly evinced its intention of maintaining a foothold in Kashmir. If the presence of these forces constituted a security threat against which New Delhi felt obliged to prepare itself, all possible military and political measures to discourage a new attack were required. The Indian army had begun rebuilding. Politically, the possibility of attack could best be minimised by making the territory of Indian Kashmir unmistakably India, so that an assault would be clear aggression and would justify response in battle areas more suited to the Indian army. Defence would be far more difficult, as long as Kashmir's status remained ambiguous and undecided. The arming of Pakistan by the United States greatly augmented this problem, by strengthening Pakistani power, but it did not originate it.

This logic applied when Nehru concluded the 'special status' pact with Abdullah. There is no reason to discount the sincerity of the agreement, since it was unnecessary for the façade of legality. Nor is there reason to doubt that Nehru was willing to accept this arrangement for an indefinite period. It is logical to suppose, however, that Nehru was holding out at that time against government officials demanding more vigorous action in Kashmir, just as he had opposed Sardar Patel in earlier years. But Nehru could not tolerate an independent Kashmir or an independence-minded Kashmiri Prime Minister, any more than could Pakistan. The Sheikh's intransigence and unpredictability probably eliminated, in the end, the final chance for Nehru to implement his idealism by giving special treatment to Indian Kashmir. Nehru responded with passion to the American-Pakistan negotiations, because they involved Indian security of which he was acutely conscious, and because in his view they threatened his entire foreign policy of insulating the subcontinent from the cold war through non-alignment. The conclusion of the pact itself would have been sufficient pressure to force Nehru into radical policy changes on Kashmir.

If India's reaction to the impasse was logical and predictable, so was that of Pakistan. Having lost the first struggle for the state, largely through their own mistakes, the Pakistanis turned to the threat of greater force. They were bound to build up their inadequate military force, not only to continue the power struggle for Kashmir but to compensate for the security weaknesses of disjointed Pakistan in the total confrontation with India. This was a difficult decision, which produced strong opposition within Pakistan, for it meant abandoning some of the independence she cherished. It was indicative of the pressures under which she believed herself to be living that Pakistan became the first former colony not under direct communist attack to join a military alliance.

If they foresaw these developments, the leaders on both sides lamentably did nothing to prevent them. Instead, as in the conflict preceding partition, they mistrusted and misunderstood each other and pursued inflammatory policies without regard for the effect on the adversary. This was the more remarkable because during part of this period, Nehru and Mohammed Ali, the Pakistani Prime Minister, seemed to be in rather close rapport. After meeting at the Commonwealth Conference in June 1953, they began a correspondence to discuss mutual problems during which they exchanged twenty-five letters over the next fourteen months. In September, Mohammed Ali conferred with Nehru in New Delhi and they issued a communiqué saying: 'The Kashmir dispute . . . should be settled in accordance with the wishes of the people of the State . . . the most feasible method of ascertaining the wishes of the people was by fair and impartial plebiscite. . . .' This appeared to be an encouraging sign of progress through the bilateral negotiations which Dr Frank Graham had suggested after the failure of UN mediation. There is no evidence, however, that the two leaders reached agreement on the substantive issues of Kashmir. The atmosphere of accord was dissipated by the uproar over the United States-Pakistan pact. Subsequently, Mohammed Ali sought to reassure Nehru by pledging, in writing, that American arms would not be used against India. The Indians were never convinced and insisted that Pakistan would attack. The prediction came true, but only after eleven years of peace and many other disruptive incidents. During their long correspondence, the leaders never made any apparent effort to solve the deeper problems of how to quiet communal passions and how to relieve the legitimate anxieties of divided Pakistan. Instead, the Mohammed Ali-Nehru correspondence, in its early stages, became a façade behind which Pakistan moved towards a military alliance that she knew would infuriate India, while the Indians began the process of annexing Indian Kashmir, to violent Pakistani protest.

To hold Kashmir, the Indian leaders had tolerated Sheikh Abdullah's sovietisation, although many of them were alert to the dangers and had fought bitterly against Indian communism. Nehru for a decade accepted the dictatorial corruption of Bakshi Gulam Muhammed, although his regime violated every principle of democratic government which was being applied to India. The Indians had suffered what they regarded as grave international indignities on this issue, and in response they had insisted with increased sharpness that the Kashmiris voluntarily had joined India when the Bakshi Assembly took its various legal actions. The Pakistanis, in fighting for the state, had lost a war and had bartered away part of their independence to regain military strength. The government had built Kashmir into a symbol of Muslim brotherhood which served, in part, to hold the country together but which was also a noose around its own neck, limiting freedom of action on this issue. Clearly, by 1954, there was no turning back for either side without substantial concession from the other; and Kashmir had become too much a question of prestige to be able to expect concession.

Despite other arguments, the significance of Kashmir can be summarised by a broad conception of the security fears of the two protagonists. Militarily, it provides a point of tension as long as hostile armies face each other. In terms of conventional attack, it is a second front to the easier invasion route through the Punjab. But the new importance of subversive warfare and militarily enforced political pressure have made Kashmir particularly sensitive, especially to India. In the early years of the controversy, Pakistan's most convincing concern, perhaps, was the fact that, through Kashmir, India controlled its vital river waters. This placed Pakistan under unacceptable pressure from a distrusted neighbour. That this factor, despite its importance, was not decisive appeared to be indicated by the fact that a settlement of the problem, in large measure, under the Indus basin waters agreement of 1960 did not prevent war five years later. The religious and political complications of the Kashmir issue, moreover, stem from a basic security question. Pakistan was built from a vague concept into a nation by relentless pressure on the Hindu majority. Jinnah and his successors used every victory to press for a further expansion of the Muslim state. The Indians have frequently said, with justice, that they can never be sure where Pakistan will stop; the acquisition of a disputed Kashmir might lead to fresh pressure elsewhere. On the other hand, the Pakistanis may perpetually be unsure of themselves until their borders are readjusted and the state is by some means geographically united. In the meantime, Kashmir by 1954 had become for both nations a symbol of national unity which, if yielded, could threaten the disintegration of the home countries themselves.

These are some of the factors which made the struggle over Kashmir into an Asian power clash and nullified Western attempts to resolve it; but the struggle itself arose from the basic fear and mistrust of the two nations. If these were eliminated, Kashmir might assume its proper place as a secondary objective; if not, a solution of Kashmir would not settle the fundamental controversy. For this reason, the Indians have long contended that all of the subcontinent's problems should be attacked at once. The Pakistanis have merely raised more suspicion by frequently insisting that Kashmir is a separate and isolated question.

Throughout the controversy, India generally has been on the defensive and usually has been more sharply criticised than Pakistan for its actions in Kashmir. But the evidence is convincing that Pakistan would follow a parallel, perhaps more aggressive policy, if the situations were reversed and it had occupied a Hindu Vale in 1948. After events had worn down India's initial Western idealism towards the problem of Kashmir, the two sides fought an amoral struggle for an objective that had become vital to each of them.

6

THE COLD WAR

THE US-PAKISTAN military agreement established a distinct land-mark in the recent history of the subcontinent from which several significant trends can be traced. It quickly sharpened Indo-Pakistan tensions. It became a constant factor in the reaction and counter-action which characterised subsequent relations between the suspicious neighbours. In time, Pakistan used the American weapons acquired for defence against communism to strike at India. But the pact itself, contrary to its critics, was more of an influence for peace than for war.

Washington, as is well known, intended the alliance solely to strengthen defences protecting the subcontinent and the Middle East against the threat of aggressive Soviet communism. The fact that no Soviet attack was made has been cited as proof that none was intended, but this is not convincing. The evidence, although only circumstantial, is far more persuasive that the American presence in Pakistan saved India, as well as Pakistan, from a dangerous Soviet military threat. Under that protection, the neighbours continued their struggle for Kashmir and helped to broaden, rather than contain, Sino-Soviet influence. India and Pakistan avoided military hostilities for eleven years, primarily, it appears, because American arms assured Pakistan that it had relative security from India. War finally resulted from a series of reactions to the Chinese Communist attack on India in 1962, one of the most serious being a shift of the military balance to India's favour.

Nevertheless, it is often argued, particularly in India, that the US-Pakistan alliance was both wrong and unnecessary and that it involved India in the cold war against its will. Nehru made this contention in opposing the alliance, and many Indians still believe they could have avoided the international struggle if Pakistan had not aligned itself. These contentions reveal a widespread tendency to ignore the history of international communism up to comparatively recent years and to misinterpret the significance of the term 'cold war' as a label for the times. This oversight is certainly not limited to Asia, where it is pronounced; it is reflected rather sharply by Western confusion over recent events. Yet the significance of the US-Pakistan pact, as well as many other similar developments, can be fully understood only against the historical background.

The term 'cold war', as originated by the late Sir Winston Churchill, was used to identify a new historical phenomenon, an international conflict which was being fought with the implacability of war but without continual gunfire. Sir Winston applied the phrase to the non-shooting confrontation of 1946 between Soviet Russia and its satellites and their adversaries—the industrial West and the other existing and prospective independent nations of the non-communist world. He made it abundantly clear that he regarded the communists as the aggressors against powers, formerly complacent, which had to be aroused to assume even a proper defensive posture.

From this has grown one definition that, in essence, the conflict is solely a clash between the two super-powers, Russia and the United States, which is being waged somewhat on the pattern of eighteenth-century colonialism. Accordingly, the struggle began in 1946 with a race for position and influence in the new circumstances created by the Second World War, a race eventually joined, in the view of some nations, by Communist China. The newly-independent countries and others seeking to preserve their independence can best avoid involvement by non-alignment with either camp and by keeping the contenders at bay through political pressure. The definition, it appears, grew in part from the experiences and pre-dispositions of the released colonial powers. It was an essential premise for Nehru's philosophy of non-alignment.

But the cold war imbedded itself as a phrase in the global language not because it described a familiar phenomenon of big-power confrontation, but because no other term so succinctly portrays the unique characteristics of the conflict. It is, first of all, a struggle arising from confused and highly debatable sources. Communism and the motivations of Marxist-Leninists have many meanings for

H

different men, so diverse points of view govern the approach to the basic question: Is the struggle part of an 'inevitable' historical process of 'revolution', as the communists say, or is it a cloak for aggression? For purposes of this discussion, practical communism is regarded primarily as a power formula. While the ideology has great persuasiveness to some men, it is used entirely to gain local and international power for the leaders of the Communist Party. In its international phase, the philosophy justifies and prompts imperialistic expansion which, in the case of Soviet Russia and Red China, is also motivated by aggressive nationalism. Communism is a force that, by its nature and the nature of men it brings to command, will continue to be history's most relentless imperialism, until stopped by power or eroded by its internal inconsistencies.

'. . . nobody', says a former Soviet diplomat, 'knows better than the Russians that the Communist ideology does not play an important role in the present Communist system, whatever the Soviet leaders have persuaded the West to believe.' Writing in 1962, Aleksandr Kaznacheev, who defected to the West from a diplomatic post in Burma, added:

> The Russians know well that it is not the construction of the prosperous and classless Communist society which is the final goal of the Soviet rulers, but the perpetuation forever of their political power and their dictatorship. Everything else, including Marx's controversial theories, Soviet internal and external policies, the very Soviet system, are all put into service toward this goal. The Communist ideology is not the beginning and the end of the Soviet society, is not its driving force, as many Westerners believe, but a mere weapon, one of many, with the help of which the Soviet government carries on the thought-control and the massive indoctrination inside the country, and camouflages its expansionist aims abroad.[1]

In pursuit of their goals, the communists employ an arsenal of non-military weapons which have never before been used with such intensity or such primacy—propaganda, psychological manipulation, economic warfare, diplomatic and political interference in the affairs of sovereign nations, subversion, pervading military and industrial espionage, bribery, blackmail and the disloyalty of foreign-controlled domestic Communist Parties. These weapons are designed, by doctrine, to weaken and, it is hoped, to overthrow the 'bourgeois' enemy—a term that means all persons and groups not under Communist Party discipline. The bourgeoisie is to be supplanted in power by Communist Parties headed by pro-consuls who are absolutely controlled by foreign capitals. No clearer definition of war has been made. The attack, again by doctrine, is against every nation of the non-communist world, regardless of its revolutionary climate or its own desires. Therefore the conflict is theoretically the first truly world-wide war in history. Thus, while the absence of widespread shooting keeps it 'cold', it is, nevertheless, war in every sense of the word.

The conflict, however, is not as cold as it sometimes appears to be. Military power is the essence of communist strategy, and the effectiveness of non-military weapons depends primarily upon the armed strength behind them. When Sir Winston first warned the world of the cold war, Soviet Russia maintained history's largest standing military force in siege around Europe and parts of the Middle East and Asia, while the great Western armies of the Second World War were being reduced to a virtual shadow. The West would not rearm for another four years and would not complete the construction of deterrent power matching that of the communists until some time later. Meanwhile, Red China joined the global siege. The political and psychological manipulation of Europe, Asia and, through them, the rest of the world, depends upon the visible military force of the two communist giants and some of their more aggressively strong satellites.

Moreover, viewed globally instead of provincially, the conflict is far from cold. For nearly half a century, communist-instigated violence at some level of armed hostility—from war to back alley assassination—has been ceaseless. Since 1946, communist-sparked military operations have been conducted continually in some corner of the world; fluctuating, often, from Asia to the Middle East, to Africa and Latin America, as circumstances dictate. Although military power is decisive to the communists, they use it as inexpensively as possible, and therefore they have added another new concept to the standard belief that war is only nation-to-nation armed conflict. An insurrection in Caracas, Venezuela, while limited in range, may be more important to the world strategy of Moscow than a South Vietnamese war. Finally, the communists have confused many people with traditional opinions by inter-changing military power and war with diplomacy, used as an offensive weapon. Lenin, the 'father' of the Soviet Union, was an admirer of the German military philosopher, Clausewitz, and his axiom: 'War is merely the extension of politics by more violent means.' Lenin added his own principles to this, the most important being, in the words of a modern Soviet commentator, '. . . war is a continuation of politics by means of force'.[2]

In this sense, the cold war is world-wide, unorthodox, relentless and deadly. It began, obviously, in 1917, when the Soviet Communists took it upon themselves to lead and to expedite the 'world revolution' and turned their variegated weapons outward. Since then, revolutions as communists define them have been few and infrequent. But, in one form or another and with one weapon or another, communist pressure has been incessant upon every non-communist nation of strategic significance, and periodic upon every other nation. The Soviet Communists have not abandoned the attack any more than has Peking, but they have altered their tactics and have transferred their emphasis from the industrialised West to the underdeveloped world. As long as the Soviets maintain massive military power, pointed outward, there can be no solid reason for believing that they have ignored the lesson of recent history, that communist victory only comes through military power. As long as they adhere to a doctrine which specifies that communism is unsafe until the whole world is communised, there can be no reason to believe they can or will abandon 'revolution'. Although many influences govern Soviet and Chinese strategy at any particu-lar period, both nations have clearly demonstrated unremitting interest in areas of major strategic significance to them, for either communist or nationalist reasons. The subcontinent has been a primary military area for Russia and China for centuries. It occupies a position of particular importance for communist doctrine; there-fore it has never been able to escape the shadow of Russian and Chinese expansion.

The Russian tsars were envious of India's wealth for centuries and threatened to invade her for more than a hundred years. Although no actual invasion was attempted, several were planned; one of them through Kashmir. This threat was linked to the steady tsarist expansion southward across Central Asia in the nineteenth century.

In the 1890s, the Russians reached the Pamirs, which are separated from northern Kashmir by only a narrow strip of Afghanistan. India was further outflanked militarily by persistent Russian pressure on Turkey, Iran and Afghanistan, to the west, and in China's Sinkiang province, to the east. From the middle of the century, the British in India were preoccupied with the 'colossus of the north'. They shaped Indian military policy to anticipate an invasion along the traditional route through Afghanistan and the Khyber Pass into what is now West Pakistan. The Russians were halted along the rim of Eurasia, on the borders of Turkey, Iran and Afghanistan, primarily by the British presence and by intensive British diplomatic and military counter-pressure. In the east, meanwhile, Moscow continued to press forward. The Russians virtually controlled Manchuria, attempted to maintain a major position in China, and drove into southern Korea. Alerted, Japan fought two wars against the Russian penetration and in the second conflict, the Russo-Japanese war of 1904-5, aroused strong anti-westernism throughout Asia by humbling the tsarist power.

The Soviets instantly added to 'world revolution' all the imperialist dreams of the most vigorous Russian tsars, as well as their own specific military objectives, in particular reviving the age-old quest for a naval port that would be open all the year round. 'As applied to India,' says a historian, 'the plan of the world revolution meant nothing more nor less than the substitution of the British Raj by a disguised Russian Raj, ruled nominally by the Indian agents of the Soviet Union, operating as a radical Indian organisation, the Communist Party of India. The Russian line and that of the Communists often changed between November 1917 [when the Soviets came to power] and August 1947, as regards India, but those changes only reflected Russia's interests and not those of India.'[3] India lured the Soviets, as she had the tsars, by her wealth and strategic location. But she has also had for the communists a peculiarly significant dialectical meaning.

Karl Marx discussed the subcontinent rather extensively in seeking to establish the validity of the Marxist theory that a historical process would inevitably overthrow capitalism. Among other predictions, Marx insisted in the mid-nineteenth century that British 'bloodsucking' in India would lead to a 'serious complication if not a general insurrection' in Great Britain herself.[4] Lenin predicted the violent overthrow of the British in India as early as 1908. It was Lenin who said: 'In the last analysis, the outcome of the struggle [with capitalism] will be determined by the fact that Russia, India, China, etc., constitute the overwhelming majority of the population of the globe.' There is no documentary proof that Lenin actually originated the more familiar statement: 'The road to Paris lies through Hong Kong and Calcutta.' But a similar philosophy was preached in 1919 by his chief lieutenant, the now discredited Leon Trotsky.[5] India was a prime example among Lenin's disproved theses that the capitalists would inevitably fight each other in the quest for colonies and for vanishing raw materials; and that capitalism would collapse when it passed through the inevitable final phase of imperialism.[6]

In July 1920, Lenin and the late M. N. Roy, the one-time Indian Communist leader, first publicly debated the question forever dividing communists: how far to co-operate with non-communist elements in waging a 'revolution' in a colonial or former colonial area. The occasion was the Second Congress of the Communist International [Comintern], held in Petrograd and Moscow. Lenin, in his *Thesis on the National and Colonial Questions*, originally called for temporary alliances between the communists and all other anti-imperialist groups, regardless of their political views. This was the concept of 'revolution from above'. When using this strategy, the communists solicit help from any quarter in order to achieve their purposes. Roy, a determined and ruthless Brahmin from Bengal, opposed this tactic. He contended, no doubt with India in mind, that some 'bourgeoisie' were so opposed to communist aims that they could not be trusted under any conditions and no alignments should be made with them. The debate was unusual, for Lenin at that point was seldom challenged. As a result of this discussion, Congress adopted a somewhat contradictory programme which authorised tactical alignments between communists and other groups but did not require them.[7]

The dispute over how far to co-operate with 'bourgeois' elements in underdeveloped countries has never been resolved in the interminable hair-splitting debates which characterise the international Communist movement. Instead, it has become a major theoretical point in the current bitter controversy between Soviet Russia and Communist China. The question bluntly is how far the communists feel they can trust men like Nehru, Nasser and Sukarno to carry out their purposes. As in the beginning, India has become a major factor in the modern conflict over this issue. Since 1955, the Soviet Union has supported the non-communist Congress governments of India and has provided considerable economic aid. This is an adaptation of Lenin's 'revolution from above'. The evident strategy is to maintain the neutrality of this strategic country on Russia's flank until internal pressures can create a more favourable political situation for the communists. Peking has fought this policy as visionary and unproductive, for communist purposes. Both sides have sought to prove the validity of their divergent views by external pressure on India and by the manipulation of communist factions within the country. It is perhaps no exaggeration to say that this theoretical dispute was an important reason for the Chinese military attack in 1962. The hesitant and limited Soviet support for India in its conflict with China only intensified the struggle and heightened the pressures turned against India. Its strategic location between the communist giants makes India the primary proving ground for this theory, one of the major dogmatic points upon which Peking and Moscow are contending for control over the world movement.

The Russian Bolshevik leaders began their subversive attack on British India before they had won power in Russia. The first propaganda call for the Indians and their neighbours to overthrow 'Western imperialism in the East' was issued on October 13, 1917; a week later the Bolsheviks assumed power by overthrowing the provisional Russian government of Alexander Kerensky. From this beginning, the Soviets quickly established an elaborate organisation to direct propaganda and subversion throughout Asia. Its initial headquarters were in the ancient city of Tashkent. The Second Comintern Congress had established the Central Asiatic Bureau, with Roy holding a key position, and it became the first of several agencies to correlate Asian communist activities. The first of innumerable special communist meetings on Asia began in 1920 with the Congress of the Peoples of the East at Baku. The city, an oil centre, was in Azerbaijan, northern Iran, a former independent state which the communists had just taken over. The Indian Communist Party was formed a short time later, and the campaign of subversion, which continues, was soon launched, with the help of agents trained under Roy's apparatus.

At that time and during many subsequent periods, Soviet Russia's principal attention was directed towards Europe, but Asia, while often subordinated, was never neglected. The Far East, moreover, has served frequently as a diversionary front to which the Soviets could turn when halted in Europe. The precedent for this was established in 1919 by Leon Trotsky, the Bolshevik leader who later was driven from Russia and murdered in a classic struggle with Stalin. After winning power, the Bolsheviks quickly attempted to expedite revolutions in Germany and Hungary, while fighting their own civil war and holding off intervening forces from the West. The Soviet European adventures failed, and Western forces were soon pressing towards Moscow. Nevertheless, Trotsky, the commander of the Red army, urged the Party Central Committee in a secret memorandum to open a vigorous diversionary attack in Asia, where he believed revolutionary pressures were growing. He advocated the establishment of a separate Eastern command, backed up by its own logistics and industries, to expedite the attack. India would have been a major target, and Trotsky commented that it might be easier for Red troops to reach the subcontinent than to fight their way to nearby Hungary.[8] The plan was never implemented, but Moscow turned to the strategy of using Asia as a flank battleground when halted in Europe and the Middle East after the Second World War.

In the autumn of 1920, the Soviets launched an extensive campaign to isolate and invade British India. The plan, which was devised by Roy and approved by Soviet leaders, called for an expeditionary force, composed largely of dissident Indians, to cross the Khyber Pass from Afghanistan and to drive through the Punjab. Roy expected to overwhelm the war-weakened British with the aid of an internal insurrection. In preparation, the Soviets accelerated military operations to consolidate control over the nationalistic, semi-independent tribes of what is now southern Russia.[9] With Roy present, the Red Army established its authority in the Pamirs, after conquering the Khanate of Bukhara in mid-September 1920. Even under the expansionist tsars, Bukhara had been semi-independent, and Moscow had considered it beyond its sphere of influence.[10] The Soviet leaders had proclaimed in 1917 'the right of the nations of Russia to free self-determination, including the right to secede and form independent states . . .'[11] But Central Asia was one of their primary objectives, and there was no disposition in Moscow to permit freedom in this area. The proud tribesmen fought against absorption until 1924, and the rebellion smouldered for many years after. As a further outflanking move against India, the Soviets at this time also intensified their penetration of Persia and Sinkiang.

The invasion force for India arrived at Tashkent, its rear base, with two 27-car trains loaded with military stores, ranging from rifles to crated aeroplanes. They were escorted by two companies of crack Red Army soldiers and by Soviet airmen. Roy, the impulsive and energetic Indian 'commander', rode in a special saloon car. He immediately widened the scope of the propaganda centre at Tashkent, trained more subversive agents and began to raise a 'liberation' army. The plan depended upon the co-operation of Emir Amanullah of Afghanistan, who had lost an impulsive war against the British in 1919. The Emir at first co-operated completely. The Soviets obtained an important military position in Afghanistan and a virtual alliance with the Emir through a treaty signed in February 1921. The treaty alerted the British, however, and their stiffened opposition, among other factors, forced the Emir to change his mind. The expedition itself was cancelled primarily because of the new British posture. But the Soviets had also encountered other reverses, including the failure of an all-out attempt to capture the Persian capital of Tehran in 1921.[12]

Roy played a dangerous role in another Stalinist adventure of this period—the ill-fated Chinese revolution of 1927. The Soviets had manoeuvred Chiang Kai-shek into leadership of the Kuomintang Party and supported him from within the party. They depended upon him to accomplish their objectives of taking over the government and driving out Western influence. But the communists also wanted to make sure that Chiang remained under their control. Roy was sent to China to carry out this mission, while Chiang was leading an anti-government revolutionary movement. Chiang was able to turn on the communists and seize control of the revolution. Eventually, Chiang broke the communist influence in the Kuomintang. This constituted a defeat for 'revolution from above', as envisioned by Lenin; Peking cites it today as an example of the fruitlessness of Moscow's policies towards India. The Soviet role in the Chinese revolution was marked by incredible blundering, including that of Roy himself, and callous cynicism. Thousands were killed, for example, when the communists failed to capture the city of Canton through insurrection. The operation, ordered by Stalin, was designed primarily to bolster his position for a political show-down with Trotsky in Moscow.[13] In reaction to the disaster, Stalin discarded Lenin's tactics and turned to the right. This meant temporarily abandoning co-operation with non-communist elements, under the 'united front' philosophy which Lenin had inaugurated in the twenties. But Stalin was to return to it a few years later.

Meanwhile, Roy had swung to the Leninist position and, there-fore, was out of step with the new Comintern line as set by Stalin. For this reason and for his share of responsibility for the failure in China, Roy was expelled from the Comintern and the Indian Communist Party in 1927. He returned to India, where he continued active in socialist politics until his death in 1954. Roy has been ranked with Lenin and Mao Tse-tung as a theorist in developing fundamental communist policies for the underdeveloped nations. In particular, Roy urged violent agrarian revolution in emergent countries, a forerunner of the tactics now being advocated by the Chinese Communists.[14]

The British presence in India was the major deterrent against any revived communist invasion attempt during the period between the wars. In the twenties, the Soviets, seeking vitally needed trade with England, twice pledged that they would avoid 'revolutionary' activity in India and other British possessions. The Soviets had many other preoccupations, including the Spanish Civil War, their bloody internal purge and the threat created by the rise of Hitler. In Asia, they were primarily concerned with Japan's expanding power, and Soviet and Japanese troops had hundreds of clashes along the borders of Manchuria. Nevertheless, Stalin maintained his out-flanking pressure around India. In the west, the Soviets continued to press against Persia and Afghanistan. In the east, Stalin widened his foothold in Sinkiang: during a tribal war, 1930–4, he sent thousands of Chinese puppet troops and eventually Soviet regulars and Soviet aircraft into combat on behalf of the local governor. In gratitude, the governor welcomed Soviet influence. By mid-1934, when the fighting had ended, Sinkiang was 'a Soviet colony in all but name', in the words of Alexander Barmine, one of the thousands of Soviet officials involved. He later wrote that 'Sinkiang was to become a sphere of exclusive Russian influence and to serve as a bulwark of our power in the East'.[15]

Despite their revolutionary and anti-colonial propaganda, the Soviets remained conspicuously indifferent to the aspirations towards independence of Indian nationalists during the war years. The Congress Party publicly complained about this attitude. At the end of the war, with independence approaching, Nehru and other Congress leaders took the initiative in purging the communists who had infiltrated the party. Many Indian leaders were clearly concerned over Soviet intentions towards Free India, once the British presence was removed. The Congress official, Pattabhi Sitaramayya, who was historian of a special Nehru-Patel Congress committee investigating the communists, put it this way: 'Russia is knocking at our doors and is hardly forty miles from our frontier. If the Russians should invade the country—and this is not a fantastic proposition—on whose side will these Communists of India fight? This eccentric party whose centre of gravity is Leningrad, whose head is, however, in the Himalayas, is a dangerous party to be reckoned with.'[16]

But Stalin, who never used naked force when less expensive means seemed promising, quite clearly had a different plan in mind for Free India. As early as 1924, he had identified India as one of the most likely countries to fulfil Lenin's prediction that the weakest link in the imperialist chain would snap first and then the whole system would collapse. There were, Stalin said, promising revolutionary pressures in India and, no doubt, they seemed even more promising to him in 1945. His strategy was to allow the Indian nationalists to get rid of the British, then to overthrow the nationalists by a communist-led revolution. For more than twenty years, the Indian Communists had been burrowing deeply into every strata of Indian life, preparing to strike.

The Maoist 'peasant revolution' in Hyderabad, the urban insurrections and communal agitation were part of this campaign to set the subcontinent aflame. Moscow, which had been silent on Indian affairs during the war, revived its public discussion in 1945 and, typically, followed a double-edged policy designed to implement the work of its agents within the country. The Soviets insisted that Britain would never grant independence, as Moscow was required to claim by its rapidly outmoded colonial dogmas. It gave the communists and their sympathisers carte blanche to attack the Indian nationalists with every possible weapon by labelling the first interim government under Nehru in 1946 as a tool of imperialism. At the same time, the Soviets manoeuvred conspicuously to maintain a position with the Nehru government for possible future exploitation. Officially, Moscow opposed partition, winning the gratitude of Hindu leaders, while attempting within the country to fan separatism into a force that would fragment it. The Soviets gained more sympathy by generally opposing the Muslim League and delaying their recognition of Pakistan until 1948. This was consistent, because India was the more important target and the Indians, in general, were more receptive than the Pakistanis to Soviet penetration. In one of her first major moves at the new United Nations, Russia strongly supported an Indian resolution condemning South African treatment of Indian nationals. The solid vote of the Soviet bloc permitted passage of the resolution in October 1946, with Great Britain, by necessity, being opposed. The issue did not concern Moscow's political or security interests, and support for India, therefore, was cost-free. To New Delhi, however, the question had a strong emotional appeal, and it marked the beginning of the Indian effort to establish a political position of world significance. The Soviet gesture brought an official expression of gratitude from Nehru and strengthened his efforts to establish cordial relations with Moscow.

Stalin made his greatest bid for empire in the immediate post-war years. He expanded across eastern Europe, through the power of the Red Army and behind the screen of falsified 'revolution', to reclaim lands historically sought by tsarist Russia and to reach for more. He pressed forward, until stopped by political reverses in France and Italy and by the erection of western European military defences. In the Middle East, Soviet forces were pressing Persia [Iran] so strongly in 1946 that one of the first tasks of the United Nations was to secure their withdrawal from Azerbaijan. The communist guerrilla war in Greece and constant Soviet military pressure on Turkey compelled the United States in 1947 to abandon her peacetime isolationism and to aid the threatened countries. From this basic decision stemmed the subsequent world-wide American programme of economic aid and military support for more than a hundred nations.

In Asia, Stalin also outpaced the imperialist tsars. Joining the war at the last minute, he overran Manchuria in a one-week conflict with weakened Japanese forces. Despite formal pledges of withdrawal, Stalin held Manchuria until forced out in 1946 by strong American pressure. He had stripped the state of the Japanese industrial facilities sorely needed by Red China. Four years later, after the establishment of a communist government in China, the Soviets were actively trying to detach Manchuria and incorporate it into Russia.[17] Taking advantage of a temporary arrangement for the disarming of Japanese forces, the Soviets occupied North Korea and held it against concerted international and United Nations pressures. This conquest not only divided the nation, making the south vulnerable for further attack; it gave the Soviets in Rashin one of the warm-water ports that Moscow had sought for several centuries. The Soviets clung to a second such harbour, Port Arthur in China, for nearly a decade after they had promised their Chinese Communist 'brothers' that they would withdraw. Moscow took over Outer Mongolia, another area which Peking regarded as Chinese, shortly after the war. A second independent Mongol nation, Tannu Tuva, was incorporated virtually as a colony into the Soviet Union in 1944. During the war, the Soviets had lost their foothold in Sinkiang. But they returned promptly in 1945 and re-established themselves by subversion and by instigating tribal upheavals against the Chinese Nationalist government. Soviet planes again invaded Sinkiang in 1947, and a year later the province had been divided once more. Moscow continued to dominate its section and to seek further expansion long after the province came under Chinese Communist control.

With Stalin's dominance over the world movement unchallenged, the communists soon launched the Asian cycle of 'revolutions'. The Comintern, which had been officially abolished to please Russia's wartime allies, was re-established as the Communist Information Bureau [Cominform] in 1947. In September 1947, Andrei Zhdanov, then one of the leading Russian Communists, called on the first Cominform Congress to wage a total cold war around the globe. He established the policy that the world is divided irrevocably between the imperialist [non-communist] and democratic [communist] camps. He enunciated a policy for India that made it impossible for Indian Communists to support Nehru and still be loyal to Moscow.[18]

A conference of South-east Asian youth, held in Calcutta the following February, permitted Yugoslav agents of Moscow to transmit instructions for the ensuing upheavals in South-east Asia. This meeting was followed by a congress of the Indian Party, which made B. T. Ranadive the general secretary and led to a campaign of violence in India.

Guerrilla wars were fought in Malaya, Burma and the Philippines. In Indonesia, the Communist Party launched a bloody counter-revolution in 1948 against the nationalist regime of President Sukarno, which was simultaneously fighting for independence from the Dutch. In Korea, communist guerrillas invaded the south as early as 1948 and at one time controlled two provinces. Stalin struck South Korea with full armoured strength in mid-1950, primarily, it appeared, because a vacuum of power had developed with the withdrawal of American combat occupation forces and because statements in Washington implied that the United States would not defend the peninsula. In French Indo-China, the anti-colonial war against the French came openly under communist control. It had been led from the beginning by Ho Chi-minh, a co-founder of the French Communist Party and a Comintern agent of long standing who had served in the Soviet apparatus which guided the Chinese revolution of 1927.[19] Popular opposition to the communists, however, had forced him tactically to disband the Vietnamese Communist Party in 1945; but he felt sure enough of his position to revive the party openly in early 1951 under the name of the Dang Lao Dong Viet Nam [Vietnamese Workers' Party].[20]

By 1953, most of the South-east Asian wars had failed or were under control. The communists clearly had lost their gamble to capture South Korea, and with it the opportunity to encircle Japan, Stalin's main target in this campaign. The Soviets were blocked in Europe and halted in the Middle East. Only the war in Indo-China was proceeding favourably for the communist cause. It was building towards the climax that would come with the siege of Dien Bien Phu, the mountain fortress established by the French in the north-western part of the country.

By all these events history had proved that the Soviets were embarked on a communist-nationalist drive to build up Russian power by military domination of strategic territory. Neither ideology nor communist 'brotherhood' deflected or halted the advance. The

Soviets, for example, applied the same acquisitive policies against Mao Tse-tung that they had first used against the 'imperialist' Chiang Kai-shek. When Moscow halted it was only in face of superior military power. Furthermore, when checked in Europe, the Soviets had maintained the momentum of their forward thrust by striking in Asia. Finally, Stalin had demonstrated an unusual eagerness to rush into a vacuum of power by starting the Korean War, one of his biggest mistakes.

There was a possibility that policies would change after the death of Stalin, in March 1953. But there was no historical precedent for anticipating a permanent change, as distinct from a relatively temporary tactical readjustment. Stalin had implemented the dreams of the early Bolsheviks, with many detours, as fully as he had carried out the ambitions of the tsars. There was also a possibility that the Soviets would recognise their defeat in Korea and would resort to less costly methods of expansion in the future. This seemed to be the world's only chance of avoiding a whole series of fringe wars on the Korean pattern. But history had also demonstrated that the Kremlin had to be convinced, at all times, that it would meet superior power wherever it turned: that there were no undefended weak spots anywhere in the world. The United States policy of 'containment' was designed to produce these conditions. Washington had been endeavouring for several years to block all avenues of militant Soviet expansion by the creation of defensive alliances and bilateral defence agreements. The strategy was, first, to create local defence forces of sufficient strength to discourage a Korean-style attack or, if such an attack came, to hold defensive positions until American power could be applied. Hundreds of millions of dollars of 'defence support' funds were given in aid, so that these armies could be organised without wrecking the economies of the host countries. Under each treaty, the United States pledged her support against communist assault. This threat of American power was the major deterrent and, naturally, communist propagandists used every means to discredit it. As one result, the enormous historical significance of this pledge has not been generally recognised. For the first time, a nation so rich that it neither needed nor wanted more territory had offered to risk the destruction of its own cities by potential nuclear attack in order to shore up the defences of distant countries, many of which had no direct influence on American security.

The subcontinent at this time was unquestionably the most vulnerable area in the non-communist world. It was strategic, easily accessible to Russian power and virtually undefended against major attack. It presented a logical target for the continuation of the tsarist campaigns on which the Kremlin clearly had embarked. It also represented a logical battle area for a diversionary attack in response to stalemate elsewhere. If Stalin could assault South Korea with a North Korean army supported by more than 500 tanks, he could fight a similar campaign across Afghanistan and into India. It was possible that, behind the tight screen of Soviet censorship, he had organised another puppet army from the Turkish tribes of southern Russia. In short, there was compelling reason to believe in the possibility of attack and very little reason to doubt it. If war came, Pakistan as the guardian of the approaches to India would be the chief victim. But gigantic India was the main target, and Washington turned to Pakistan only after Nehru refused to discuss a defensive alliance.

Negotiations for the US-Pakistan treaty began under these circumstances early in 1953. Reports of a probable agreement were published in Washington in the spring, but the conversations were deliberately prolonged, and the agreement was not formally signed until May 1954. American officials made it clear that they preferred a defensive arrangement covering both nations. Barring this, they sought to minimise the repercussions in India from a final agreement with her neighbour. Nehru was sounded out at length in the summer of 1953 by at least two high-ranking visitors to New Delhi— former Vice-President Richard M. Nixon and the late Secretary of State John Foster Dulles. The author accompanied the Vice-President on this trip. Although Nixon was greeted by tremendous and friendly Indian crowds, Nehru went out of his way to darken the visit by publicly flattering a minor Soviet official who was in the capital at the same time. If this and a few similar incidents were designed to demonstrate independence, they were also singularly poor political tactics in dealing with a man who was to report directly to President Eisenhower. Dulles said nothing about the Indian attitudes in a speech on June 1 after his return to Washington; but he reported that he had found warm friendship in Karachi and that 'the strong spiritual faith and martial spirit of the [Pakistani] people make them a dependable bulwark against communism'.[21]

Nehru had a period of several months in which to seek an adjustment of the proposed American-Pakistani agreement through quiet
negotiation. There is no evidence that he made any counter-
proposals.

Nehru and apparently the vast majority of the Indian people were
dedicated to the policy of non-alignment and had no intention of
abandoning it. By this, Nehru explained, India would 'avoid
foreign entanglements by not joining one bloc or another' and
would reserve the freedom 'to act according to our own lights and
according to the merits of the dispute as they seemed to us.' He
insisted that it was a much more positive policy than neutralism,
because India would involve herself in world affairs and would
attempt to influence the super-powers. His disapproval helped to
eliminate the word neutralism as a suitable definition of the posture
adopted by India and, in time, by a large number of newly-independent nations. Non-alignment was, and remains, an eminently
suitable philosophy for young countries, jealous of their independence and suspicious of the great powers: new nations seeking an
international influence that would be impossible to achieve in
military weakness and passivity. In India, the philosophy also
reflected other deep currents, including an idealistic hope of a more
peaceful world, which run through some layers of society. Politically,
it was the one most suitable for the times, and Nehru might have
found it difficult at this period to adopt any other attitude. He explained in interviews that no other policy would give India the time
and the means for economic rehabilitation. Nehru was also motivated by his own strong internationalist, anti-colonial views. 'His
policy of neutralism', says a Western historian, 'was also a personal
one, but it arose more from calculation than principle or feeling.'[22]

All of these factors were well understood in Washington, despite a
considerable amount of undiplomatic public criticism of non-
alignment. Americans had not forgotten that the United States had
embraced freedom with precisely the same attitude and that one of
its manifestations, isolationism, had persisted until the outbreak of
the Second World War; but most American officials believed that
the circumstances of the 1950s had outmoded non-alignment as a
practicable concept for all but the most remote and unimportant
nations. President Eisenhower expressed this sentiment by saying,
in a letter to Nehru: 'No nation can stand alone today.'

I

As reports of the pending agreement circulated, the Indians became increasingly angry. During one week in January 1954, Nehru had to speak every night on the subject, and he attacked the proposed alignment with particular bitterness. He was supported fully by every Indian political faction. A virtual war psychosis developed in the country and lingered for a long time. Nehru insisted in his speeches that Pakistan only wanted American arms in order to assault India. In his correspondence with Mohammed Ali, Nehru raised three objections: (1) the agreement would bring the cold war to India's doorstep, disrupting the peace that India wanted to perpetuate; (2) it would sharply alter the military balance between Pakistan and India; (3) it was likely to re-introduce foreign domination in a disguised form.

Mohammed Ali denied these contentions. He also said that the military rebuilding of Pakistan would strengthen India as well by bulwarking its vulnerable northern frontiers. He wrote to Nehru:

> We have sought military aid from the USA so that, given this assistance to strengthen our defences, we may be able to devote our domestic resources increasingly to development of our economy. We believe that by doing so we can better serve the cause of peace in this area ... We do not have, we cannot possibly have, any intention of using this aid for the purpose of settling the Kashmir dispute by force.
>
> I know you hold a different view. You think that military aid will produce tension and a sense of insecurity. You also hold the view that there is a basic difference between the economic aid that you are getting and the military aid that we propose to receive, while in my view the difference is merely a matter of form and the resultant effect, that of strengthening the military and economic potential of a country, is the same in either case. While I do not share your views, I respect the sincerity with which you have expressed them. May I hope that you will credit us with the same sincerity in holding our views on this matter?[23]

General Ayub Khan, as Commander-in-Chief of the Pakistan army, conceived the idea of a military pact with the United States when faced with a concentration of Indian forces during the crisis of 1951. He took the initiative and the principal role in concluding the alliance.[24] Thus, from Pakistan's point of view, the military agreement sprang from the need to build strength against India. 'The ruling passion in Pakistan's foreign policy, a passion which has influenced its behaviour toward all other countries, has always been fear of India', says a modern commentator.[25] The alliance was explained domestically on this basis and perhaps would not have been acceptable without India's shadow. Pakistan shared the intense desire of other former colonial nations to establish and maintain complete independence. Only in extreme circumstances would it have become the first newly-independent nation to seek foreign alignment. But, with or without such intense fear of its neighbour, it is probable that Pakistan would have sought arms from the cheapest available source to build an army capable of defending the strategically weak nation.

It would be unrealistic, however, to conclude that Pakistan was not also influenced by fear of Soviet attack and concern over internal communism, particularly in the circumstances of 1954. During the weeks preceding the actual conclusion of the pact, officials in Karachi stressed the Soviet threat in conversations with visiting Americans. 'We may yet have to defend India', said Prime Minister Mohammed Ali Bogra during a generally anti-Indian conversation with the author. Perhaps this attitude was adopted for ulterior motives, but Pakistani officials at that time generally reflected a far more realistic appraisal of the Asian situation than was discernible in New Delhi. In later years, Ayub continued to point out the potentialities of Soviet military pressure. The Foreign Minister, Z. A. Bhutto, discounting any danger from Peking, said in 1962: '. . . given geography and the power realities of the nuclear age, the military threat to us, if there is one, would come more from the Soviet Union than from China.'[26]

The Pakistanis, moreover, carried out their part of the defence agreement faithfully, and in doing so invited strong Soviet counter-action and abuse. Accepting the pact required more courage than denouncing it. Internally, the Pakistanis in general were strongly anti-communist and had taken vigorous measures against the movement. Karachi had smashed what it officially called a communist conspiracy to overthrow the government. The plot was led by General Akbar Khan, the former army Chief of Staff and the commander of the tribal invasion of Kashmir. The general, a number of other officers, and communist civilians were convicted in the so-called Rawalpindi Conspiracy Case in January 1953. Six months later, the government banned the Pakistan Communist Party. Formed during the Calcutta conference of 1948, the party had grown in size and boldness until, particularly in East Pakistan, it constituted a serious subversive and disruptive force.

In addition to its own direct vulnerability, Pakistan was closer to the already inflamed Middle East and unquestionably more concerned over its problems than was India. The agreement with the United States was preluded, in fact, by a bilateral agreement between Pakistan and Turkey, which provoked sharp Soviet reaction. The Middle East was Soviet Russia's most favourable area of expansion, because it was closest to Red Army power. For more than 400 years, Russia had been striving to break into this region. It sought, among other objectives, a warm-water port closer to the homeland than those in Asia, and a position on the Mediterranean. This quest had been so significant that Molotov, the former Soviet Foreign Minister, had demanded in 1940 that Nazi Germany accept this area as a special Soviet sphere of aspiration. The United States, in December 1951, had officially reminded Moscow of Molotov's proposals, adding: 'In the light of the Soviet attitude toward the Middle East area since the end of World War II, the United States Government can only assume that the aims set forth by Mr. Molotov in 1940 remain the policy of the Soviet government.'[27] Washington had attempted for several years to create an adequate defence alliance for the area. With strategic Pakistan, the alignment was complete. She joined the Middle Eastern and South-east Asian defence groupings (CENTO and SEATO).

Nehru, in reply to Mohammed Ali's explanation, wrote: 'The total difference in our outlook is exemplified when you say that such aid given to Pakistan will add to the security of India. We think that we have nothing to fear from the attack of any country, but lining up with one of the Power blocs brings insecurity and danger, apart from this being a step away from peace.'[28]

But the issue manifestly involved much more than India's assessment of her own security position. It directly concerned Pakistan, Iran and Turkey, which were interlinked militarily and united in the desire to complete the Middle Eastern pact which Nehru was trying to block. Communist conquest of the Middle East, moreover, would gravely weaken the military security and economic well-being of western Europe; and this weakness, if it occurred, would be transmitted to many more nations dependent on Europe or linked to it. India's own security was deeply involved in the affairs of South-east Asia, although many Indians did not recognise the fact. The protection of this area was complicated, but patently no meaningful protection could be provided without legal justification for the introduction of American power.

Here was a primary test of the distinctions between non-alignment and neutralism, which Nehru himself had outlined. A neutral India perhaps would have complained, then would have withdrawn from the struggle. In accordance with neutralism, she would have refrained from direct interference in the affairs of another nation. A non-aligned nation in the generally accepted sense would have directed equal pressure against each of the super-powers to prevent expansion of the cold war. While India most certainly tried to prevent the United States from completing the arrangement, there is no evidence that she approached Russia or attempted to persuade her to abandon aggression. Instead, New Delhi, in response to what it regarded as an enlarged local threat from Pakistan, consciously widened the scope of the cold war on the subcontinent by immediately giving Russia a major foothold in India. Nehru had defined non-alignment as a policy of 'enlightened self-interest' which, as with all national policies, was designed first to serve Indian interests. His actions, therefore, could be regarded as consistent. But invisibly, and perhaps unconsciously, this crisis transformed non-alignment from a philosophy of peacefulness into a practical means of deep involvement in the affairs of other countries.

Nehru had sharply challenged Washington's right to act as the self-appointed policeman for the world and had bitterly disputed its tendency to insist that the American analysis of communism was the only correct one. Now he was demanding, in effect, that Pakistan, the nation in Russia's immediate pathway, repudiate the American umbrella and entrust its security to the hope that New Delhi's analysis of the situation was correct. When Pakistan refused to yield, Nehru invited its enemy to expand its position within India. The contradictions in this situation were readily apparent, and they became more so when Red China's attack destroyed Nehru's equally firm insistence on Peking's 'peaceableness'. The Pakistanis could not be persuaded thereafter that India had abandoned the desire to dominate them. They were more easily convinced that New Delhi opposed the military pact in order to prevent them from acquiring any significant armed force or to obtain the economic benefits of American help. The extent of Indian opposition, in fact, had helped to persuade some Pakistani nationalists to accept the alliance. On the other hand, the Indians clung so tenaciously to the thesis there was no Soviet threat that their interpretation of subsequent history was frequently distorted. This premise was necessary, however, to substantiate the persistent Indian contention that Pakistan wanted weapons only in order to strike India. That belief, in turn, helped to strengthen the Indian conviction that Russia wanted peace, despite considerable contrary evidence.

Nehru made it clear in private conversations at this time that he was acting from both idealism and practicality, as he saw it. The only alternative to the impairment of independence through alignment and the financial drain of building armies was to keep the world peaceful by political means. In time, he sought to act as 'honest broker' between East and West and to tie up the communist powers so completely in international commitments for peace that they would have difficulty in breaking them. This broad strategy, if it accurately portrays his policy, had a fatal weakness in the circumstances of the subcontinent. It depended very largely upon keeping Pakistan at roughly the military level of 1948. While Nehru played an increasingly active role internationally, he did not appear to make any consistent effort to reassure Pakistan that it would be safe without rearming. In the absence of such assurance and with the military insecurity created by its odd configuration, Pakistan inevitably would turn outward for arms. If the United States did not provide them, the search would continue; but, in any case, Nehru could not hope to enforce non-alignment on his neighbour without making concessions. As circumstances developed, India's most persistent concern over the US-Pakistan pact was its influence on the local military situation.

The United States built up the Pakistan army from comparative weakness into a compact fighting force. Washington supplied most of the weapons, particularly the key weapons, that were considered necessary to prepare the country for its dual role in two defence alignments. American officials, it appeared, seriously under-estimated the impact of these weapons on the situation of the subcontinent. But the assistance was relatively moderate as part of advance preparation to prevent another Korea.

The figures are classified, but the best available information is that the total US military investment was $1,500 million between 1954 and 1965. One reliable estimate, however, places the figure at $750 million. In one of the most controversial aspects of the build-up, the Pakistanis received just over 200 45-ton Patton tanks. They also received one squadron of supersonic F-104A fighters, four squadrons of older F-86F fighters and two squadrons of B-57B Canberra bombers.[29] The Indians were particularly worried by Pakistani heavy armour and supersonic aircraft. The Americans also supplied most of the additional basic arms, but Pakistan obtained some aircraft from Great Britain. India maintained a continual military expansion which gave her in 1965 an estimated two-to-one advantage in heavy and light tanks and numerical superiority in the air, except for supersonic planes.

Viewed in the limited context of the Indo-Pakistani conflict, as the Indians did, the Pakistani build-up was extensive indeed. But it was minimal in terms of Pakistan's position as the keystone of two alliances designed to contain the still undeterred Soviet drive. New Delhi also attempted to persuade the Americans, in secret talks, to insist that Pakistan meet any Soviet thrust in the mountains and to provide arms primarily for that purpose. This appeared to be a further effort to restrict Pakistani capability. The logical strategy, as Karachi pointed out, was to meet aggression with maximum power on the plains. The point was proved later in India, when Indian forces were unable to contain Chinese Communist troops pouring through the mountains.

Thus, military necessity dictated heavy tanks and supporting aircraft for Pakistan. The exact reasons for supplying 200 Pattons were obscured by military secrecy. It seems evident, however, that American authorities were seeking to avoid a costly mistake which had been made in Korea. For some time before the North Korean attack, American advisers had helped to build up the Republic of Korea (ROK) army to defend the country after the complete withdrawal of US troops. In doing so, the Americans decided to withhold all weapons that could be used for a major offensive attack. There were many reasons, but in particular Washington mistrusted the intentions of the late President Syngman Rhee, who had frequently threatened to invade the north. Accordingly, when the Korean War started, ROK troops had no tanks, no heavy artillery, no major airpower, and no heavy defensive equipment, such as anti-tank guns. The South Korean army was consequently no deterrent to Soviet-directed assault from the north; nor was it able to contain the advance of North Korean armoured columns. The heavy loss of life, both civilian and military, which characterised the communist drive southward was unquestionably higher because of this political decision. The peninsula was nearly lost before American troops halted the North Koreans.[30] The same mistake could have been made in Pakistan, if American officials had been deterred by Indian charges that Karachi only wanted to attack India. Korea had proved that half a deterrent force was no better than none.

The tank and air equipment allotted to Pakistan for anti-communist purposes apparently served also for several years to reassure Karachi of relative safety from any attack by India. The build-up, it would appear, actually provided a more feasible balance of power between the neighbours than had existed at the end of the Kashmiri war, when Indian supremacy was pronounced and had been proved by the fighting. The best proof of this is the fact that Pakistan did not turn its Patton tanks against India at the first opportunity, as many Indians had predicted, and did not use them until early 1965. Pakistan, in particular, avoided a major opportunity when India was deeply involved with China. On the other hand, India, by refraining from attack to prevent completion of the build-up, proved that it had no intention of launching the preventive war feared by Pakistanis. Thus, both nations disproved the generalities long preached by their fanatics, that aggression by the other side was a constant threat. Nevertheless, the fear of aggression has been a continual governmental characteristic, and each side is acutely sensitive to demonstrations of power by the other. Instead of maintaining an arms balance that was mutually acceptable, the two governments without consulting each other went their own ways militarily. The balance was periodically altered, or seemed to the adversaries to be altered, in response to outside pressures.

President Eisenhower told Nehru in a special message on February 24, 1954, that the pact was not directed against India and that Pakistan had agreed to that point. 'And I am confirming publicly', the President said, 'that if our aid to any country, including Pakistan, is misused and directed against another in aggression I will undertake immediately, in accordance with my constitutional authority, appropriate action both within and without the UN to thwart such aggression.' He added: 'If your Government should conclude that circumstances require military aid of a type contemplated by our mutual security legislation, please be assured that your request would receive my most sympathetic consideration.'[31]* The pact itself was somewhat ambiguous on the legitimate uses to which the arms could be put. It stated that: 'The Government of Pakistan will use this assistance exclusively to maintain its security, its legitimate self-defense, or to permit it to participate in the defense of the area, or in United Nations collective security arrangements and measures, and Pakistan will not undertake any act of aggression against any other nation. The Government of Pakistan will not, without the prior agreement of the Government of the United States, devote such assistance to purposes other than those for which it was furnished.'[32]

There would be bitter debate over the question whether Pakistan violated this agreement in the 1965 war, but the evidence clearly indicates that it did. New Delhi also sharply criticised the inability of American authorities to prevent Pakistan from employing US arms during the major fighting. It would appear from the available evidence that the Americans themselves were too easily persuaded that Pakistan would not use the weapons improperly and perhaps were too oblivious of the changing circumstances in the subcontinent. The Americans also apparently helped to engender false confidence in New Delhi by giving top Indian authorities the impression that they could control the Pakistanis more effectively than was possible. Manifestly, the inherent gamble in any military arrangement of this type is that the recipient nation will use the arms as it sees fit without regard for contrary commitments. The only significant pressure to prevent an initial blow is the possibility that it will cost the combatant nation future American aid. Pakistan

---

*An intimate of Nehru, the late Dr Sudhir Ghosh, says in his posthumous book, *Gandhi's Emissary*, that President Eisenhower volunteered to supply India with three weapons for every one furnished to Pakistan. The president further said he did not seek Indian guarantees that the arms would not be used against Pakistan, because he was confident Nehru had no such intention. 'But at that time', the author adds, 'Mr Nehru rejected the offer with contempt because the acceptance of such military equipment would do serious damage to his policy of non-alignment.'

quite evidently was willing to take that risk, so there was, in effect, no American deterrence. But there were other restraints on Pakistan. The supplies of American spare parts, ammunition and petroleum were so carefully controlled that American officers knew the Pakistanis could use their tanks for only about three weeks, the period of the main fighting in the Punjab. This circumstance obviously could not be advertised in advance. If there was no sure way for Washington to guarantee India against attack, she was protected against the use of American equipment for a prolonged war.

A three-week war, with all its consequences, clearly was a heavy price for India to pay for Pakistani rearmament. But as an event affecting history or governmental policy, the price has to be assessed realistically against the alternatives. The cost was far less than another Korea would have been, and no doubt considerably less than a war launched by Pakistan with weapons supplied from a communist source. In the circumstances India realistically had to choose between a Pakistani build-up under relatively effective American control or with no controls, as advertised by Moscow and Peking. There may have been mistakes along the way, but there is no serious reason to doubt that the pact was an absolute necessity for the entire area, dictated by the circumstances at the time.

Although the non-aligned nations have won acceptance of their philosophy by perseverance and political pressure, they have yet to prove the validity of the fundamental premise: that an area of strategic importance to the communists can be protected only by political means. The premise was weakened, not strengthened, by the developments following the military alliance.

7

SOVIET POLICY

PAKISTAN FITTED strategically into the heart of a defence line against communist expansion which stretched from western Europe to Japan. In key areas, the perimeter was solid around the Eurasian land mass, but there were notable gaps, in Afghanistan, India and South-east Asia. When this system was completed in 1955 by the formation of the Baghdad Pact in the Middle East, history's most formidable deterrence to an expansionist alliance had been erected. Local forces manned a front-line defence which was capable of containing the first communist land thrust. They were backed by the conventional and nuclear power of the United States, part of which was deployed in key positions blocking traditional Russian avenues of expansion.

The significance of this development is often overlooked. It constituted the first effective system of military alliances between sovereign states in an atmosphere of peace. Nations customarily come together under enemy attack, but never before had they united so strongly in advance of attack. And the ambiguities of expansionist communism had failed to obscure the threat; the alliances themselves demonstrated a unity of belief, among Western and non-Western peoples, in communist aggressiveness. The alliances have held solidly for more than a decade, unprecedentedly long for such agreements, despite many stresses and some serious disagreements. In that period, there has been no war and no overt military pressure against the nations unequivocally protected by American power. South-east Asia, where this protection is ambiguous, has been under almost continual attack, and non-aligned India was assaulted by Red China. The remainder of the uncommitted nations are removed from the areas of primary strategic significance to the communists and have been protected by distance from direct attack. The most important of them, however, have been involved in armed hostilities of varied intensity, precipitated or influenced by both Moscow and Peking.

The record substantiates the thesis that the communists were prevented only by the defence line and the Western nuclear threat from attempting to seize all objectives in Europe and Eurasia which are strategic to the nationalist as well as the communist aims of Russia and mainland China. The subcontinent obviously belongs to that sphere of operations, for both strategic and ideological reasons. The anti-communist perimeter halted the Soviet drive and forced Moscow into a number of outflanking operations, but it did not necessarily eliminate the possibility that the attack would be renewed at some more propitious future time. In the ambiguities of her area, Communist China has continued her strategic campaign with ceaseless persistence, from Tibet to India to South Vietnam. Although Sino-Soviet strategic operations are cloaked by the catch phrases of revolution and disguised by the techniques of communism, they are, basically, the policies of strategic expansion originated by the Russian tsars and the Chinese emperors. The pursuit of strategic rather than 'revolutionary' objectives is easy to justify by dogma. The defence of communist nations against inevitable 'counter-revolution' is primary in all types of communism. Peking has modified this tenet into authorisation for challenging Moscow and engaging in armed hostilities along the Soviet border. Among other factors, Peking claims that Russia herself is succumbing to 'bourgeois counter-revolutionary' trends against which it must protect itself. Finally, the distinction between old-fashioned imperialist expansion for tactical reasons and the extension of communism through 'inevitable' revolution has been virtually eliminated by another unilateral communist dogma: there are 'just' wars and 'unjust' wars. In practice, any armed conflict supported by the communist leadership is a just war, regardless of how it starts. Such action, if initiated by the communists, does not constitute a violation of peace, since it is covered by the 'holy writ'. Therefore, communists can proclaim themselves at peace with the world, while still employing every type of armed action to 'defend' themselves or to aid 'revolution'.

Soviet policies towards the subcontinent in the decade following 1954 were an indistinguishable and important part of modified world strategy which was designed to counter a number of new pressures. It was a decade of momentous developments. Internally, significant changes were apparent in Russia. They were reflected by the stresses which produced destalinisation and by those which followed this harsh denigration of the dictator. Within the Communist bloc, the Sino-Soviet cold war loosened Russian control over the world movement and weakened the *pax Sovietica* which had disciplined this half of the world. In the confrontation between communism and the industrial West, the Soviet recognition of the potentialities of nuclear war decreed an armed truce of indefinite duration. The underdeveloped world then emerged as the only feasible arena of expansion, for the Kremlin as well as for Peking. Using the up-to-date tactics of Nikita Khrushchev, the Soviets turned to this area with major concentration. The emergent nations represented a field through which communism could exhibit the momentum that it must maintain for survival; they constituted a route for outflanking the Western defence perimeter; they represented the major battleground between conflicting Sino-Soviet 'revolutionary' theories, on which the struggle for supremacy over the world movement was being waged, in large measure.

The strategic and 'revolutionary' goals of the Soviets remained unchanged. Some had to be postponed, others had to be approached obliquely, but none was abandoned. Khrushchev, who established the line that persisted long after his removal, did not introduce any new stratagems, for he followed Lenin's book closely; but he added a number of modern innovations which seemed new to a world forgetful of the past. Nor was there any concrete indication, by the start of 1968, that the changes perceptible within Soviet society had made Soviet communism any less expansionist than before, or any more disposed to compete for power solely by means of constitutional political methods. In foreign policy and in many aspects of domestic policy, Khrushchev attempted primarily to perpetuate the Stalinist system without the widespread use of internal Stalinist terror. Stalin, too, had gone many years between wars and 'revolutions', because circumstances were not promising, but he had unleashed the turmoil after the Second World War. Khrushchev had taken risks that the old dictator would have avoided.

It was Khrushchev who created the only really dangerous threat of world-wide nuclear war, through the Cuban missile crisis of 1962. And, again, it was Khrushchev who crushed the Hungarian revolt of 1956 with Soviet tanks. There were sharp distinctions between his internal and foreign policies and between his caution in Europe and Soviet aggressiveness in the underdeveloped world. The Khrushchev era in Soviet foreign policy, particularly the attitude towards emergent nations, is more understandable as a series of Soviet reactions to new challenges than as an indication of basic or permanent change in communist strategy or intentions. The two most significant external pressures were the creation of the Western defence perimeter and the increasing defiance of Peking.

Strengthened Western defences not only blocked major Soviet expansion but evidently created Kremlin fears for Russian security. With many deviations, many alterations, many mistakes, and evidently many quarrels within the Kremlin, Moscow followed a familiar central plan to overcome the problem. Lenin, when first faced by theoretical 'capitalist encirclement', had set the guidelines for a flexible counter-strategy. It was based primarily upon the belief that encirclement could be weakened and nullified by political manipulation, by playing upon the contradictions within the non-communist nations, and by creating such formidable Soviet power that no capitalist military attack would be attempted. Lenin first invoked the concept of 'peaceful coexistence' in the early twenties. It was, as Khrushchev later explained, a tactic to lull his adversaries and to give Russia a breathing spell. Behind it, Trotsky built up the Red Army, and communist agents throughout the world continually attempted to weaken the will of their adversaries or, in some cases, to overthrow them.[1]

Stalin periodically turned to Lenin's use of 'peaceful coexistence' and the 'popular front' to gain time. So did his first successors, headed by Georgi Malenkov, in 1953. Khrushchev followed the tradition implicitly, but eventually enlarged the concept. In his primary campaign to nullify nuclear deterrence and the Western defensive perimeter, Khrushchev used a three-phased attack. Like most communist strategy, it had a number of auxiliary aims, in addition to the principal purpose.

First, Khrushchev attempted to create allies and to prevent the further expansion of American influence, partly by helping to solidify the non-aligned nations into a Third World. Bitter Soviet denunciation of neutralism was changed swiftly into support for non-alignment. Moscow began to give economic assistance to nineteen non-communist nations, selected for their receptivity and strategic location. This was less of a change than is sometimes supposed. The Soviets had given limited economic help to key nations as early as the 1920s. The neutralisation of a force which can neither be assimilated nor ignored is a fundamental tenet of communist revolutionary strategy.

Secondly, Khrushchev attempted to weaken and, if possible, to destroy the defence perimeter. Communist parties in every aligned nation launched sustained campaigns, which still continue, to force their governments into repudiating the defence pacts. These activities have been reinforced by subversion, oblique pressures, political bribery and diversionary Soviet diplomacy. Throughout most of Khrushchev's reign, Moscow resounded with periodic threats to wipe out every important city with Soviet missiles, followed by appeals for peaceful coexistence. Through constant repetition of threat and promise, Moscow sought to implant the concept that, as Khrushchev said, peaceful coexistence is 'the only alternative to nuclear war'. Moscow propaganda was quite clearly designed to augment the internal actions of the Kremlin-dominated Communist Parties and of innumerable 'peace fronts', and so, at various times, was formal Soviet diplomacy. The constant mixture of bluster and cajolery was, it appeared, carefully calculated to confuse and mentally paralyse the majority of the people.

Thirdly, Khrushchev launched intensive efforts to outflank the defence perimeter. He succeeded, for example, in establishing an important new Soviet position on the Mediterranean by a massive arms deal with Egypt in 1955. The negotiations for this significant achievement were camouflaged by the first post-war Summit Meeting which created the short-lived 'spirit of Geneva'. Khrushchev had invoked 'peaceful coexistence', this time as a tactic, and had attended the Geneva meeting. The purpose was to settle the reunification of Germany, but a formal agreement to hold elections in the divided nation was never implemented. Less than three years later, Soviet attempts to establish a position in Syria, outflanking Turkey to the south, were so aggressive and so promising that non-communist Syrians annexed the country to Egypt to halt the tide.

The result was the first United Arab Republic, from which Syria eventually broke away. In 1958, a revolution broke out in Iraq, and Soviet involvement was deep and visible. The revolutionaries renounced Iraq's adherence to the Baghdad Pact, the anti-communist defence alliance in the Middle East. The pact was re-established, without Iraq, as the Central Treaty Organisation (CENTO). The Iraqi upheaval was partially responsible for the landing of British and American troops in Jordan and Lebanon, virtually on Russia's doorstep. Moscow avoided any direct retaliation. But Khrushchev, calling for a new type of peaceful coexistence, created a fresh crisis over Berlin by threatening to sign a separate peace treaty with East Germany. Tension lasted for several months.

This phase of the campaign had a more ominous aspect. Moscow gave virtually unlimited arms aid to Egypt, with no restrictions on the use of the weapons. A similar arrangement was concluded later with Indonesia, which provided an outflanking position in Asia for the Soviets. Each nation, in time, received equipment listed at more than one billion dollars. The prices were cut-rate, however, and the actual value was probably considerably higher. These arms, formidable in the areas to which they were assigned, included cast-off equipment from constantly modernised Soviet armies and weapons which could be made inexpensively in Russia.

The United Arab Republic eventually obtained some 1,200 Soviet tanks and assault guns, plus auxiliary equipment, and at least 100 heavy and light bombers and around 300 Soviet fighters and fighter-bombers, including 50 of the latest MIG-21s. This power, for a nation of 29 million people to meet purely local conditions, was many times greater than the United States supplied to Pakistan for its dual role in the defence perimeter. Indonesia received almost a complete Soviet-built coastal navy, headed by a heavy cruiser, more than 60 MIG interceptors, including 18 MIG-21s, and at least 50 heavy and light Soviet bombers. These arms were for an island nation which, while totalling 100 million people, was under no serious military threat at that time or later from any quarter.[2]

The arms were obviously far in excess of the legitimate defence needs of either the UAR or Indonesia. It seems evident that Moscow wanted to harness these strategic nations to itself by heavy debts and by Soviet control over primary weapons, ammunition and vital spare parts. These aims could have been accomplished, however, with smaller military build-ups. Therefore, the size of the rearmament programmes indicated that Moscow intended, and hoped, the weapons would be used offensively to fight local wars. It reinforced this probability by launching and maintaining a campaign to encourage war by these two aggressive nations, each centred in a particularly explosive environment. Soviet support for President Nasser was doubtless the decisive factor in the sequence of events in 1956 which led to nationalisation of the Suez Canal and the Israeli-French-British attack on Egypt.[3] This conflict was halted primarily by American intervention, after which Moscow threatened to attack London and Paris and offered 'volunteers' to Egypt. The Soviet reaction was carefully timed to avoid involvement, while obtaining maximum propaganda benefit.[4] Similarly, Soviet manipulation was a constant factor behind Indonesia's stormy preparations to go to war with the Netherlands over West Irian (western New Guinea) in 1962, a conflict averted by United Nations and American mediation. The Soviets gave strident propaganda support, as well as diplomatic encouragement, to Indonesia's guerrilla attack on the new state of Malaysia the next year.

'Proxy war' by puppet or third-power forces is also a long-standing communist strategy. Stalin deliberately helped to precipitate the Second World War by giving Germany a sanctuary in which to rearm, in defiance of the Versailles Treaty: so Khrushchev's use of this tactic was not necessarily dictated by the establishment of the Western perimeter; he could have adopted it in any case. As counter-strategy against Western defences, Moscow could have profited immensely by small but bitter wars between non-communist neighbours. Conflict could have pulled down the defence line. Most certainly, it would have created conditions favourable for communist penetration around and behind the Western wall. The use of this tactic in the mid-1950s underlines the point that the Soviets had no intention of abandoning war as an instrument of communist policy, when suitable for their purposes. And Khrushchev's successors have clearly carried over the policy of 'proxy war'. Among other indications, Moscow has continued her efforts to whip up war between Arabs and Israel, or among Arab nations, or by Arabs against the British. These activities have been reinforced by heavy new supplies of Soviet arms to the UAR.

K

Finally, Khrushchev through a variety of practices after 1955 sought to build up a position of Soviet bloc impregnability, despite the Western defence line. He enlarged his arsenal of intercontinental missiles aimed at the United States and the intermediate range missiles arrayed around Europe. But, perhaps for economic reasons, missile rearmament was neither as swift nor as extensive as Russian capabilities permitted. By 1966, the Soviets had an estimated 270 ICBMs, a fourth of the American total. The Soviets, however, had a total of 750 intermediate range missiles, capable of reaching targets around the rim of Asia, while the Western powers had none. Moscow maintained a fleet of 416 submarines, a three-to-one advantage, but possessed only about one-fifth of the American fleet missiles.[5] The Soviets had kept their long-range bomber force at a stationary level of around 1,200 planes. Thus they had substantial power but were far from parity in their striking capacity with the United States. The attempt to plant some of Russia's plentiful IRBM missiles on Cuba in 1962 was a gamble to alter the nuclear balance to Russia's advantage. The adventure forced the United States into further nuclear armament, which shifted the balance somewhat more against the Russians. Since the Kremlin evidently believed that grave risks were necessary to achieve a position of intimidation against the United States, this project remains potentially unconcluded. The Cuban crisis sharply altered the immediate course of the cold war, but it remains to be seen whether the Kremlin at some future date will attempt another Cuba.

Khrushchev sought to augment his nuclear position with intensive political warfare to convince the world that Russia was militarily unassailable. This, he explained to faithful members of the party, was the central purpose of peaceful coexistence; a condition in which, essentially, the West would not dare to retaliate against powerful Russia, regardless of communist provocations. In 1963, he claimed 'a victory for the policy of peaceful coexistence', because the United States had refrained from nuclear attack on Russia and from armed invasion of Cuba in response to the missile gamble.[6] Khrushchev's diplomacy, his propaganda, and such other activities as 'space spectaculars' were designed, among other purposes, to enhance this version of peaceful coexistence. The campaign has been continued by his successors. In the aftermath of Cuba, there were notable efforts to minimise East-West friction in

Europe. But the Kremlin had assumed a free hand to involve itself in other parts of the world where local hostilities would not threaten Soviet security. The Soviets, however, had not realised Lenin's dream of establishing such power that the 'capitalists' would be unable to retaliate, regardless of what Moscow did.

In 1954, the Soviet policies towards the subcontinent formed an important part of this over-all campaign and, tactically, paralleled it, except for deviations required by local conditions. Pakistan's new Western alignment provided a series of challenges for Russia. From bases in that country, American air power could dominate the strategic industrial heartland of the country. The Soviets protested against the bases long before they were built or their existence was acknowledged. United States military assistance to Pakistan, moreover, was preceded and originally justified by a military alliance between Turkey and Pakistan. This brought together two of the most vigorous Muslim nations bordering on Muslim-populated Central Asia, gateway to the industrial Urals. The Soviets possibly feared the potential threat of land invasion; more clearly, they feared the impact of a resurgent Pan-Islam movement on the still nationalistic Muslim tribes of Central Asia. The Turko-Pakistan alliance further undermined Moscow's determined efforts to dominate the Islamic world. The Soviets regarded it more seriously than earlier efforts to unite the quarrelsome Arabs into an anti-communist alliance.

The Soviets, accordingly, initiated a drastic programme in the spring of 1954 to eject Muslims from the strategic border areas within Russia, replacing them with more reliable Slavs. This 'genocidal' campaign, as it has been called, affected some 30 million people in the so-called 'autonomous' republics ranging eastward from the borders of Turkey to Soviet areas facing Chinese Sinkiang. The programme was justified as the agricultural development of virgin lands, and was widely advertised for that purpose by Khrushchev. But it began under the Malenkov regime as a massive effort to establish reliable fighting forces on the borders. The displaced Muslims were supplanted in the countryside by members of the highly-indoctrinated Communist League of Youth (Komsomol), whose reliability was accepted in Moscow. Further to maintain control, however, the Soviet authorities grouped most of the youths together in state farms, which were more strongly disciplined than collectives. Demobilised army regiments also were sent intact to the area, under their own officers, to serve as military-trained colonists. The Komsomol, says a historian of this area, 'will likewise provide the vanguard for future Soviet aggression in the direction of the Near East and India'.[7] The new programme extended to the countryside a Moscow campaign, begun after the Second World War, to water down nationalism by deporting tribal Muslims. Large numbers of Slavs had already been sent to the cities to replace Muslims sent elsewhere. This programme emphasised Soviet distrust of the willingness of subject Turkish tribesmen to defend the Soviet Union. It does not, however, necessarily prove that none of the tribes could be used for outward attack, even against Muslim countries. They have been employed extensively in Soviet border raids against predominantly Muslim regions of Red China. The heavy influx of trusted Slavs into the eastern territories of Central Asia, facing the Chinese, indicated that Moscow was preparing in the mid-1950s against resurgent pressure from Peking.

The Soviets also struck hard at Pakistan. Typically, they avoided any evidence of direct military action. But they took advantage of every opportunity to weaken Pakistani resolve by internal pressure and external flank attack. At this time, politics were particularly unsettled in East Pakistan, and the Muslim League was badly defeated there in the 1954 elections by a United Front opposition. The Front campaigned largely on a separatist platform, which included demands for East Pakistani independence in all matters except defence, foreign affairs and communications. Pro-Kremlin communists, said to be directed by Indians from Calcutta, intensified propaganda against the West on this and related grievances during and after the campaign. A series of strikes and labour riots, which the government blamed on the communists, soon erupted. The Chief Minister, the leader of the successful coalition, then demanded complete independence for East Pakistan and was dismissed for 'treasonable activities'. The Communist Party was banned in July. Although the communists did not originate separatism in East Pakistan, they played on it, and continue to play on it, so extensively that it has become a significant factor in the impasse over Kashmir. The crisis of 1954 was a particularly graphic illustration of the subsequent Pakistani claim that the loss of Azad Kashmir would inspire fresh pressures within East Pakistan for independence.

Moscow simultaneously attacked Pakistan through Afghanistan.

The Soviets had actually begun their limited foreign aid programme by advancing credits to Afghanistan in 1950. This move, part of a century-old effort to insure the friendship or, at least, the neutrality of the strategic country, was augmented five years later when Khrushchev advanced a $100 million loan. For a mountainous kingdom of 15 million people, this was proportionately a far larger gesture of Soviet help than Khrushchev made to India during this same period. The Soviets also took over the rearmament of the backward Afghan army, and by 1966 an army of between 80,000 and 90,000 men had been largely mechanised with Soviet equipment. In the first five years of the Soviet aid programme, Afghanistan was one of only five countries receiving Soviet arms. While the amount of money pledged for this purpose was only a modest $38 million by 1960, the purpose clearly was to create another area of friction or armed hostility for Soviet strategic purposes.

Moscow had another readily exploitable issue in Afghanistan. Sharing a 1,000-mile border with Pakistan, the kingdom has been defiantly apprehensive of its larger neighbour in somewhat the same way that Pakistan has been of India. The border, called the Durand line, artificially divides closely related tribesmen; the Pathans of West Pakistan and the Pakhtuns or Pushtuns, as they are called in Afghanistan. Before partition, the kingdom supported a proposal to allow these peoples a free choice to determine their future, including independence. The proposal was turned down on the grounds that the North West Frontier Province, containing the Pathans of West Pakistan, had decided to join that state. This election was somewhat ambiguous, because it had been boycotted by the Pathan 'Red Shirts'. Since then, the quest for the creation of an independent state of Pakhtunistan has been the cause of strong agitation among the Pathans. It is supported and fanned by Afghanistan, with the Soviet communists in the background. Maps of the proposed independent state show in it about three-quarters of West Pakistan, including the port of Karachi. This would provide land-locked Afghanistan with a sea outlet and may partially explain her interest in the project. But an independent Pakhtunistan would virtually destroy Pakistan.

In 1955, Afghanistan denounced a plan by Karachi for administrative consolidation of West Pakistan, claiming it would eliminate the special status given to the Pathans. With strong Soviet support and Soviet arms, the Afghans launched frequent armed clashes along the border and in the areas of Pakistan which Kabul calls 'occupied Pakhtunistan'. Moscow strengthened Afghan determination by providing free transit of goods across Russian territory, to break Afghan dependence upon communications running through Pakistan. The situation deteriorated so sharply late in the year that war threatened and could have resulted from less responsible Pakistani leadership. Another crisis arose in 1961, from the same interplay of nationalism, fear and Soviet manipulation. Pakistan levelled the charge that Afghan consulates were directing hostile activities against her and demanded that they be closed. Afghanistan broke off diplomatic relations. Once again, Russia provided the Afghan trade outlet and, among other results, American aid shipments were cut off. Diplomatic hostility and tension continued for another two years, until a political settlement was reached in May 1963. The inflammable issue of Pakhtunistan remains, however.

The Soviets have been able to maintain the Afghanistan gap in Western defences, partly by heavy pressure and by aid expenditures totalling an estimated $600 million since 1954. The kingdom also wants to preserve its traditional position as a buffer state. Despite Kabul's declared policy of 'positive neutralism', Moscow has established a significant military position, outflanking Pakistan. By manipulating the powerful symbol of Pakhtunistan, the Soviets have helped to produce near-war on two occasions and a semi-permanent state of tension between the two neighbours. It seems evident that Moscow hoped to promote small-scale 'proxy war' for its own benefit, even though both countries occupy strategic positions on Russian borders in which, theoretically, the Soviets might be expected to prefer peace. If they were worried by a possible spillover of Afghan-Pakistani hostilities, the Soviets clearly subordinated that danger to their more overriding purpose of destroying Pakistan's position in the defence alignments; possibly by destroying Pakistan herself. Yet, with consistent duality, the Soviets also maintained relations with Pakistan and made a number of small economic overtures, from 1956 onward. This kept the door open for some possible future rapprochement. At this same time, Moscow was attempting to drive Iran and Turkey from the Middle Eastern alliance by a sustained campaign of intermingled intimidation and offers of sizable economic aid.

The third major aspect of Soviet policy toward the subcontinent was rapprochement with India. Nehru, impressed by an earlier trip to Russia, had endeavoured to establish a strong relationship as early as 1946. Moscow recognised the interim Nehru regime the next year and maintained continuous relations with Free India, but originally Stalin made little effort to strengthen this association. India was dismissed diplomatically as an appendage of the Anglo-American 'imperialist' camp, despite non-alignment. The Soviets, like the Chinese, regarded as hostile any group not actively supporting them. The challenge of spreading non-alignment was reviewed in Moscow, however, during the Nineteenth Congress of the Soviet Communist Party in 1952. At that time, the first recognition was given to the potentialities of maintaining a separate Third World in which, at least, the communists could hope to bar 'capitalist' influence. After Stalin's death, the Soviets moved more quickly towards wooing the non-aligned nations. Nehru suddenly emerged, therefore, as a desirable ally, and the Soviets took the initiative to improve relations with India in the autumn of 1953. This policy obviously would have been implemented if there had been no US-Pakistan pact. Afterwards, a Soviet attempt to build up India as a counterweight to Pakistan was a logical reaction to the pact.

Indian leaders welcomed the change, but responded cautiously at first, awaiting a demonstration of Russia's post-Stalin goodwill. They were impressed, in particular, by Moscow's role in the Geneva Conference of 1954 which, on July 21, concluded a cease-fire in the long and bloody Indo-China war. India was not officially represented, but she took an important backstage part through the activities of V. K. Krishna Menon, Nehru's special envoy. Menon dropped the hint that vigorous Soviet efforts for peace would be interpreted in New Delhi as endorsement for *Panch Shila*, the five principles of peaceful coexistence which Nehru was actively promoting. Russia did take the initiative, and her pressure is credited with forcing the North Vietnamese and Red China, against their open disapproval, to accept terms more favourable to the French than they had expected. The battle for Dien Bien Phu had started before the conference assembled and was lost by the French on May 8. France, which had been seeking a way out of the increasingly unpopular war for a year, was then in an untenable bargaining position. The North Vietnamese, flushed with victory, were capable of striking farther south, perhaps to capture the whole of the peninsula. But they settled for division of the country at the Seventeenth Parallel, abandoning some territory to the southward, and for the prospect that they might win the entire peninsula through elections scheduled to be held within two years.[8]

New Delhi interpreted the Soviet position at the conference as evidence of Moscow's new peaceableness, and Indian satisfaction helped to expedite rapport between the two countries. This belief has had a strange durability in the Indian attitude toward Soviet motives, arising again in connection with the revived Vietnamese war of the 1960s. But there were other possible motives for the Soviet action which throw a somewhat different light around Moscow's subsequent policy. First, Moscow was fighting vigorously at the time against the formation of a proposed European Defence Community (EDC), to consolidate and strengthen new anti-communist defences in Europe. The Soviets evidently hoped to persuade Paris to veto EDC by producing a settlement at Geneva on more favourable face-saving terms than would be possible otherwise. The French did veto EDC, for a number of reasons, but European rearmament, although delayed, was expedited with French participation through the North Atlantic Treaty Organisation. Secondly, the Soviet Communists themselves suggest in official doctrine that they ended the fighting in Indo-China through fear of American nuclear retaliation. In the official manual for party members throughout the world, the Soviets later claimed: 'It is generally recognised that the fear of the anger of the [communist] nations prevented the imperialists from using the atomic bomb in Vietnam and forced them to conclude an armistice.'[9]

This is an obvious reference to the United States, the sole Western nuclear power at the time. Direct American involvement in the Indo-China war had been disapproved by Washington at the start of the Dien Bien Phu campaign, but Moscow could have believed that the Americans would be drawn into a conflict continuing after the fall of that fortress position. The Americans had already set the precedent in Korea of avoiding atomic attack from an active battlefield. Therefore it is probable that Moscow feared attack from one of the American bases outside Indo-China. It would seem, then, that Moscow's 'peaceableness' in this instance was dictated by the Western defence perimeter and the Soviet desire to weaken it, rather than by any change in attitude. The prospective importance of the new American position in Pakistan may have been a more powerful influence for peace than all Menon's lobbying. Moscow frequently jeopardises the interests of local Communist Parties for its own ends. But it had never done so for the sole purpose of winning a nation's friendship; a political emotion which communism does not recognise.

The Soviets inaugurated a fairly extensive economic aid programme to India by pledging funds in February 1954, for construction of the Bhilai steel mill, a cherished Indian project. The agreement was signed the next year. Since then, Soviet economic assistance has totalled somewhat less than one-fourth of the $6 billion which the United States has provided between 1951 and mid-1965. Soviet assistance, augmented by considerable technical help, has been a significant factor in India's development. It has provided the foundation for political relationships which, on the whole, have been smooth.

In mid-1955, Nehru received a warm welcome during a state visit to Russia. In November and December, Khrushchev and the former Premier, Bulganin, swept through India in an unprecedented foreign tour. They observed all the amenities, 'said the correct things', as Nehru later commented, and drew great crowds. Apart from the novelty of the event, India was receptive, in the words of a pro-Soviet Indian, because '. . . the people of India see in the Soviet Union a friend—and a friend who, to all appearances, demands nothing from them except friendship.'[10] This was, of course, the impression sought by the Soviet leaders. Khrushchev adopted Russia's strongest stand on Kashmir by fully endorsing the Indian position. 'The question of Kashmir', he told a rally in Srinagar, 'as one of the States of the Republic of India has already been decided by the people of Kashmir.' He kept his reservations to himself. Bulganin salved another Indian sore spot by proclaiming: '. . . there is no justification for the Portuguese colony of Goa to exist on the ancient soil of India.' These two statements provided the basis for surprisingly strong and durable Indian belief in the permanence and inflexibility of Soviet support.

The next year, Khrushchev offered to supply India with any and all arms she needed, with no restraints on their use, following the pattern of agreements with the UAR and Indonesia.[11] The Indians rejected the proposal, partly because of the United States guarantee that American weapons would not be used against them by Pakistan. The rejection was remarkable, under the prevailing circumstances, for India was smarting still from the US-Pakistan alliance and from continued frustration over Kashmir. By it, the Indians saved themselves serious problems, including heavy economic dependence on Moscow. They also illustrated the basic non-aggressiveness of the Indian government. The offer was kept secret, however, and from public appearances all that Pakistan might have seen was a subtle but definite stiffening of the Indian position thereafter. Soviet motives seemed clear, in the global context. India was being placed in a special category, along with the UAR and Indonesia, for unlimited rearmament. Not even Red China, it appears, has been given such support, and only Iraq, of the four other nations aided militarily by Moscow, had received substantial amounts of equipment. Moscow obviously expected, or hoped for, conflict in the subcontinent, and considered it the third promising area for 'proxy war'. No doubt, it believed that Kashmir was as inflammable as Israel and West Irian had been, particularly under Soviet manipulation. If India failed to attack with Soviet weapons, Pakistan might be goaded into preventive war against massive Indian rearmament. Arms also represented a quick and effective way of securing a dominant Soviet position. In offering them, Moscow again emphasised the strategic significance of India.

The Soviets evidently had a triple interest in war on the subcontinent. First, a conflict could precipitate a number of possible circumstances to drive Pakistan from her Western alignment, thus destroying the American position on the rim of Russia. The Pakistanis, for example, could lose so much equipment in battle and could find Washington so reluctant to rearm them that they might turn to Russia. This potentiality developed with a reverse twist after the conflict of 1965 when Rawalpindi turned to Peking, as well as Moscow, for military help after the Americans restricted arms shipments. Secondly, war could produce conditions which would permit Soviet puppets to intervene and occupy areas of prime strategic importance to Moscow. Any communist-sponsored struggle, even the overt aggression of Korea, is disguised as a 'revolutionary' or 'national liberation' war. The best cover is provided by a non-communist conflict. At least, such a war would permit Moscow to increase its influence over the belligerent government of its choice, in this case India, while expanding the underground influence of communism in the resultant unrest among the masses. Finally, failing its own expansion, the Kremlin had a primary interest in encouraging non-aligned India to capture Azad Kashmir.

Moscow has a vital strategic interest in all of Kashmir. But the region from Gilgit northward, now part of Pakistan-controlled Azad Kashmir, is particularly significant to it. During the nineteenth century, the rival ambitions of tsarist Russia and British India threatened a collision in this area. The two powers deliberately created a buffer zone by agreeing in 1898 to cede a narrow wedge of land, called Wakhan, to Afghanistan. The strip, some forty miles wide, still divides Soviet-controlled Pamir and northern Kashmir. The Anglo-Russian agreement also handed over the eastern portion of the buffer zone to Sinkiang, then only nominally controlled by the Chinese. Included were lands lying northward of Mintaka Pass, a main mountain gateway to northern Kashmir. For strategic reasons, the tsarist Russians and the Soviets have maintained military positions down to the northern reaches of the pass, through the co-operation of local tribes. Some 125 miles southward, at Gilgit, an airfield had been maintained for some time, and the Americans improved it after their 1954 agreement with Pakistan; but informed officials say it was not made into the major air base claimed by many Indians, though the position does have the potentiality for serving medium-range bombers. From Gilgit, says a knowledgeable Indian writer on this area, 'the whole of the Pamir region could be controlled and Soviet Central Asia threatened'. This writer, Dr Satyanarayan Sinha, is a former Comintern-trained communist and captain in the Soviet army who broke with the movement when he became convinced that Moscow wanted to dominate India. The air position at Gilgit has a further strategic significance: to counter military pressure from Sinkiang. When the Soviet Union virtually took over Sinkiang in the mid-1930s, for example, British Indian authorities quickly assumed administrative control over Gilgit.

Citing Gilgit, Dr Sinha says: 'Military considerations forced them [the Soviets] to join hands with India on the Kashmir question and proclaim Gilgit a part of India. She declared that Pakistan had no right to occupy Gilgit or to allow the Americans to build an anti-Soviet base there.'[12] This was, obviously, only one aspect of Moscow's strategic concern over the American presence in Pakistan, and the threat to Central Asia would exist even if there had been no American influence in that country. The Soviets could not tolerate the presence of a strong hostile power in Gilgit and its surroundings; nor, perhaps, in central Kashmir, from where long-range aircraft could harass the Central Asian territories.

There is strong evidence that the Soviets have consistently manoeuvred to insure communist domination over the whole of Kashmir, a strategy indicated by communist activities within the state. Dr Sinha gave to the Indian government a map drawn up in 1947 by the Soviet-dominated Comintern, showing a substantial portion of Ladakh, in eastern Kashmir, as a Chinese territory. Kashmir was designated as British, a label evidently designed to legitimise a Soviet effort to 'liberate' the territory, as a hostile base aimed at Russia. The same map also showed substantial portions of the North East Frontier Agency, in the vulnerable eastern sector of India, as being Chinese.[13]

For the first four years of the United Nations debate over Kashmir, the Soviets remained silent, probably awaiting the most opportune time to intervene. When Jacob Malik, the Soviet UN representative, broke the silence in 1952, he clearly indicated Moscow's strategic interest in the territory. As so often happens, he also outlined Soviet intentions by charging his adversaries with the same motives. He attacked UN proposals for Kashmir as 'annexationist, imperialist' plans of Great Britain and the United States. 'The purpose of these plans', he said, 'is interference by the United States and the United Kingdom in the internal affairs of Kashmir, the prolongation of the dispute between India and Pakistan on the question of Kashmir, and the conversion of Kashmir into a protectorate of the United States and the United Kingdom. . . . Finally, the purpose of these plans . . . is to secure the introduction of Anglo-American troops into the territory of Kashmir and convert Kashmir into an Anglo-American colony and a military and strategic base.'[14] Malik particularly attacked a Pakistani proposal to police Kashmir with Commonwealth troops, a plan that clearly would have interfered with Soviet intentions and would have placed foreign military power unacceptably close to Russia.

This line, which was good propaganda as well as basic strategy, was echoed repeatedly by communist and pro-communist leaders in Kashmir and India. The Indian Communists concentrated on Kashmir, after their defeat in Hyderabad, and soon were deeply involved in its affairs. Apart from blatant propaganda, they held Soviet-style 'peace' conferences, infiltrated political and labour unions and helped to create violent riots in Jammu in 1953. The Communists, under evident Moscow control, originally supported Sheikh Abdullah and his Soviet-style 'reform' government, into which they penetrated deeply. They also supported his dream of independence, probably in hopes of capitalising on it, until the crisis of mid-1953: then they jumped to the winner of the intra-cabinet fight, Bakshi Ghulam Mohammed. Josef Korbel, the former UN observer in Kashmir, writing at that time, says that in the Bakshi's India-backed government '. . . three out of five ministers . . . and heads of several important departments are now Communists or fellow-travellers.' And Abdullah, 'for six years their protector and protégé, was now branded as a traitor and a lackey of American imperialists.'[15]

In the mid-1950s, however, the possibility that the Soviets could co-operate with Red China in the division of Kashmir apparently ended. Instead, Moscow had to face the reality that Peking might be the hostile power it could not tolerate in Kashmir. Hidden tensions had existed for decades between the Soviet and Chinese Communists, and the Mao Tse-tung regime was profoundly distrusted by Moscow from the beginning. Mao's ambitions to make the Comintern plans for control of the Himalayas a purely Chinese project were clear by the mid-1950s. Border skirmishes had apparently already been fought before 1954, when the Soviets resettled areas of Central Asia opposite Sinkiang in the mass deportation of Muslims which followed the US-Pakistan military pact. A decade later, the Chinese had acquired control of lands south of Mintaka Pass, through agreement with Pakistan, and were in a position to dominate Gilgit.

By the time of Khrushchev's offer, therefore, the Soviets were probably interested in encouraging India to capture Azad Kashmir. They obviously had not abandoned their own long-range ambitions to dominate Kashmir and to profit, as fully as possible, from immediate tensions over it. Until Soviet control could be assured, Moscow's policy could best be served by placing the Gilgit region under Indian, instead of Pakistani, control. This evidently became increasingly important as Chinese encroachment continued.

Khrushchev therefore supported the Indian position on this vital question with considerable vigour. Yet he reserved the opportunity to accomplish his central purposes, neutralisation of American and, eventually, Chinese power in the centre of Asia, through diplomatic pressure and enticement of Pakistan. Consequently, he followed an ambivalent policy on Kashmir from the beginning.

When Khrushchev gave his verbal support to India in 1955, he carefully specified that the issue had been 'decided by the people of Kashmir'. This had been the Indian government's standpoint since the middle of the year and would continue to be its official position. It was based on the contention that the legal actions taken by Bakshi Ghulam Mohammed's government and the Constituent Assembly represented the freely-expressed electoral will of the people. The late Pandit Govind Ballabh Pant, then India's Home Minister, established the precedent by saying in a speech on July 7, 1955: 'Kashmir's accession was a reality which could not be changed because the people, through their representatives in the Constituent Assembly, had decided to remain with India.' The Assembly was controlled, however, by the Bakshi's National Conference Party. Only five of the seventy-five seats had been contested in the 1951 elections, mostly in Hindu Jammu. The freedom of this and the 1957 and 1962 elections in Indian Kashmir, where contested seats have not exceeded 50 per cent, has been questioned. The people of the Vale in particular, it was charged, had been dominated by the pro-Indian National Conference and intimidated by the presence of sizable Indian troop contingents. The troops were relatively inconspicuous, however, and wielded doubtful political influence. The ability of the illiterate Kashmiris to vote freely, under any conditions, is disputable, in view of their tendency to follow the most ruthless political force and the most demagogic leaders. Nevertheless, the charges have severely embarrassed New Delhi, for they strike at the basis of its legal case for integrating Kashmir.

Khrushchev's gratuitous support, therefore, was gratefully accepted in India and generally regarded as unequivocal. But three months later, on March 25, 1956, Anastas I. Mikoyan, then First Deputy Premier of Russia, gave a different version to the Pakistanis. He said in a speech at Karachi that the future of Kashmir was indefinite and ultimately would be determined by the people of the state. Thus, in the view of an Indian writer, Mikoyan provided 'a clear opening for a *volte-face*, should it become necessary in the Soviet interests'.[16]

During 1956, Nehru abandoned his talk of plebiscite and stressed that the Kashmiri situation had been changed by recent events. He made it clear that he was referring primarily to Pakistan's military pact with the United States and her association with Middle Eastern and South-east Asian defence alignments. But he also publicly welcomed the Khrushchev-Bulganin support. On March 29, he told the Lok Sabha: 'I have made it clear to the Pakistan Representatives that while I am prepared to discuss any aspect of the [Kashmir] question if they want to be realistic, they must accept and take into consideration all that has happened in the last seven or eight years and not talk in terms of eight or nine years ago. The only alternative is a continuing deadlock in our talks.' On April 2, he was asked in a press conference: 'An inference has been drawn that you do not want now any plebiscite to be held in Kashmir. Is it correct?' In reply, Nehru said: 'Largely so; I shall explain myself. What I have said was that we have tried and discussed the question of plebiscite for six or seven years, but the preconditions have not been fulfilled. Meanwhile, other things have taken place, like the military aid, etc., which have increased tremendously the difficulties of this problem.' Eleven days later, he proposed the partition of Kashmir along the cease-fire line, an idea which the Indians followed up in subsequent negotiations. 'I am willing', he said in a public speech, 'to accept that the question of the part of Kashmir which is under you should be settled by demarcating the border on the basis of the present cease-fire line. We have no desire to take it by fighting.'[17]

Pakistan brought Kashmir before the United Nations again in early 1957. On January 24, the Security Council passed a new resolution which specified that 'the final disposition of the State of Jammu and Kashmir will be made in accordance with the will of the people expressed through the democratic method of a free and impartial plebiscite conducted under the auspices of the United Nations . . .' In this first test of Soviet-Indian rapport, the Soviet delegate merely abstained. Two days later, India proceeded with the ceremony that finalised the accession of Kashmir as 'irrevocable'. Thus she formally assumed a position which, it has been charged, placed her in defiance of an official UN edict. The Soviets had been of no help to New Delhi. But they quickly used the veto on their own behalf in a subsequent instance. They killed a draft resolution of February 20, which provided for exploration of a Pakistani suggestion to station a temporary UN force in Kashmir, pending final solution. Soviet opposition resulted in a substitute plan which provided only that the Council President would re-survey the situation. In vetoing the possibility of raising a UN peace-keeping force for Kashmir, the Soviets aided India, which objected to the stationing of foreign troops on what she regarded as her own soil. More notably, this action prevented the prospect of placing a UN force near the Soviet border.

In 1962, the Soviets used the veto again on Kashmir under puzzling circumstances. The vetoed resolution, which was presented on June 22, was unusually innocuous. It merely offered the good offices of the UN and asked the two countries 'to solve the Kashmir problem by using the provisions of the UN charter by negotiations, mediation, arbitration or any other mode of choice'. This was a pronounced retreat from the organisation's insistence upon a plebiscite, as contained in the 1957 resolution, and its acceptance might have eliminated the question of plebiscite, which India has found so embarrassing. The late UN Secretary-General, Dag Hammarskjøld, had adopted the position regarding a plebiscite in Kashmir that '. . . the UN decision is valid until it has been invalidated by the organ which took it'.[18] Thus, the Soviet veto froze the Security Council in the hard-line 1957 position and prevented a softened attitude favourable to India. The *status quo* was preserved by another Soviet veto in 1963 and the threat of using it in 1964, through which new initiatives on Kashmir were prevented.

The Soviet vetoes on this question have been widely regarded, particularly in India, as an indication that Soviet opposition will continue to prevent any UN actions on Kashmir to which India objects. New Delhi relies very strongly upon this assessment. But the record indicates that the Soviets have been following a calculated strategy to obtain the maximum leverage for manipulating both India and Pakistan. Russia's decision to avoid the veto in 1957, at a decisive moment for India, appeared to be disciplinary. During the serious controversy over the Hungarian revolution, India had at first supported the Soviet bloc in opposing UN interference, but after November 15, 1956, Nehru had consistently called for the removal of Soviet troops. Other differences developed between Nehru and the Kremlin during the next year. The Soviet leaders sharply reminded Nehru of Kashmir, among other problems on which he sought Soviet support. By 1962, however, rapport was strong and apparently untroubled by major issues. India leaned more visibly towards the Soviets in reaction to growing pressures from Red China, and her leaders believed that Moscow relied increasingly on India as an anti-China bulwark. Nevertheless, the Soviet vetoes of 1962 and 1963 maintained the Security Council in a position over Kashmir that was more favourable to Pakistan's claims than those of India. Moscow could tell Pakistan at some future date: 'Look, all the time we were supposed to be supporting India, we kept your demand for a plebiscite alive at the United Nations.' India was placated, because the vetoes prevented any more embarrassing resolutions on Kashmir. Moscow had clearly demonstrated, however, that, far from being an unshakeable supporter of India on Kashmir, it would use the issue entirely for its own profit.

The development of the 1961 crisis over the Portuguese colony of Goa perhaps played a considerable part in the evolution of Moscow's Kashmir strategy. Goa, a port and community on India's west coast, was the most important of a few scattered possessions which the Portuguese had maintained for four and a half centuries. It totalled 1,301 square miles, with a population of some 600,000. Although France had negotiated the surrender of its small colonial stake in India, Portugal, the last colonist, refused to give up. Instead, she sought to hold her Indian possessions, possibly to avoid a precedent that might disintegrate her African empire, and declared them a 'province' of the mother country. Within Goa, sentiment for annexation to India was perceptible, but so was opposition, particularly from the Catholic Church and elements profiting from a considerable smuggling business. Acrimonious negotiations proved fruitless, and by the autumn of 1955 agitation was strong within India for 'peaceful invasion'. An unarmed Indian march on the colony in August resulted in gunfire with reported Indian losses of twenty-one dead and 120 wounded. India broke off remaining diplomatic relations on August 19, 1955.

Khrushchev and Bulganin promptly seized upon this situation. Bulganin's support for India was to be expected, for he was bound

L

to voice 'anti-colonialism' and Moscow wanted to embarrass Portugal, a member of NATO. The Indians sorely needed support, however, on an issue that had become a question of national honour. They were inclined to value the Soviet statement more highly than it deserved, particularly after the United States had allowed herself to be manoeuvred into an untenable retaliatory position. In a formal statement following a conference in early December, the US Secretary of State, Dulles, and the Portuguese Foreign Minister, Cunha, described the Indian possessions as a 'province' of Portugal, thus supporting Lisbon's legal point. This was, on the American side, primarily a political gesture, required by the fact that US aerial supply lines to NATO depended at the time upon Portuguese willingness to grant landing rights in the Azores. The Indians interpreted the statement as unqualified support for the Portuguese attempt to retain their colonies and reacted bitterly.

Portugal lost in an appeal to the World Court, which ruled in India's favour in 1960. The Portuguese were also condemned on several occasions by the UN General Assembly and its subcommittees for its general colonial policies, including those of Goa. Within India, political parties, the press, and other pressure groups demanded action, as did the pro-Indian faction within Goa. African nationalists attacked Nehru for inconsistent anti-colonialism, and New Delhi became sensitive to this rather blatant outside political interference in Indian affairs. Disorders within Goa, border incidents, and generalised reports about a Portuguese military build-up increased the tension. Portuguese fortifications fired on Indian vessels.

Nehru declared on December 11, 1961, that 'India's patience is exhausted'. A week later, well-organised Indian military forces invaded Goa and two other Portuguese enclaves, despite pleas from the West and the UN Secretary-General. The operation was completed in twenty-six hours. Official Indian casualty figures were: Indians, twenty-two dead, fifty-three injured; Portuguese, seventeen dead, thirty-eight injured.

This military action shocked the world and was sharply criticised; partly, it appears, on the familiar basis that it conflicted so dramatically with the ideals of non-violence. Many Indians several years later maintained an aggressive defensiveness about the incident. The Soviets, however, had no qualms in supporting New Delhi. On the eve of the assault, Leonid Brezhnev, then the Soviet President, said during a state visit to India that 'the Soviet people regard with full understanding and sympathy the desire of the Indian people to achieve the liberation of Goa, Daman and Diu'. A Soviet veto defeated a Portuguese-sponsored UN resolution condemning India. The Indians strongly believed they were entitled to eliminate a colonial remnant within the nation they were seeking to unify, and in this they were consistent with the immediate past. They also believed that they had suffered diplomatic impasse long enough and were justified in resorting to force. But this was incompatible with Nehru's insistence upon the establishment of rule by law, a principle that many believed should be applied particularly to international relations.

The Indians did not seem to see the parallel between Goa and Kashmir. They had resorted to force against Goa in frustration over a diplomatic impasse that had lasted for only one year following the World Court's ruling. But they bitterly condemned Pakistani threats to use force to end the stalemate over Kashmir, which then had lasted thirteen years. There were many differences between the two problems, but the neighbouring peoples apparently viewed their frustrations with the same intensity. Finally, the Indian military action itself raised unanswered questions. It was not clear whether the situation required the power assembled by India and, specifically, whether air action was justified. The attack was launched, to widespread domestic applause, two months before important elections for the Lok Sabha and local assemblies. The Defence Minister, Krishna Menon, faced a particularly difficult campaign in a district near Goa. The attack was so sudden that Indian diplomats were uninformed. On balance, it would appear that the Indians were entirely justified in demanding the elimination of the Portuguese colonies. The methods used, however, were too costly in terms of their international effect and their repercussions.

Pakistan reacted with particular sharpness, and thereafter the Goa invasion was cited among her arguments to prove 'Indian aggression'. Several newspapers emphasised the failure of NATO to aid Portugal and began to question the reliability of SEATO and CENTO to Pakistan in similar circumstances. The newspaper most closely reflecting the government's views, *Dawn*, stated bluntly on December 20, 1961, that Pakistan should pull out of the Western alliances and seek closer ties with Communist China. This was clearly a trial balloon, but it may have floated all the way to Moscow. Six months later, the Soviets cast the decisive UN veto on Kashmir which turned their apparent pro-Indian position completely around.

It is reasonable to conclude from the Soviet tactics that Moscow intended all along to establish a position for future rapprochement with Pakistan. In addition to Mikoyan's attempt to blunt Khrushchev's pro-Indian remarks on Kashmir, Moscow had maintained limited but enlarging contacts with Pakistan since concluding an oil exploration agreement in 1960. In that case, it would appear that the 1962 veto was part of careful planning to benefit from developments and turn more openly towards Karachi. But if the veto merely resulted from opportunist reaction to the suggestions that Pakistan might consider abdicating its Western alignment, the outcome hardly conformed to the Indian view of relations with Moscow. What India wanted and thought she had was a durable and dependable Soviet ally who would support her against most of the world on Kashmir and would ask only moderate political payment in return. But Russia had more complex goals. She wanted to drive Pakistan from the Western alliance and to establish a firm Soviet position in both Pakistan and India. In time, the need to forestall the potential thrust of Red China into the strategic Himalayas appeared also as a primary objective. Pakistan, in this situation, had perhaps a better bargaining position than India; not only because her Western orientation was one fundamental issue, but because the area north of Gilgit in Azad Kashmir represented a key point of Sino-Soviet strategic manoeuvring. This reality had been established by the beginning of 1962, nearly a year before the Chinese Communist attack would convince New Delhi that it had to depend even more strongly upon Moscow.

Soviet manipulation of Goa and Kashmir had contributed directly, if only invisibly, to a hardened and suspicion-encrusted impasse in the subcontinent. The Indian posture on Kashmir noticeably stiffened after Khrushchev's visit in 1955. Two years later, when it formally accepted 'irrevocable' accession, it became virtually impossible for it to establish a new status for Indian Kashmir and still save face, without great Pakistani concessions. Russia's subsequent veto at the United Nations, whatever the purpose, created the widespread impression that no anti-Indian actions could be expected there. To Soviet applause, the Indians had demonstrated in Goa a belligerency and comparative military efficiency which startled more chancellories than Rawalpindi.* The Indians had become tough and determined, a condition the Muslim Pakistanis had always feared; they had also temporarily isolated themselves from many of the industrial nations and could find public sympathy only from Russia. It is impossible to determine from the public record the direct Soviet influence behind this progression. Khrushchev's private remarks to Nehru are unknown, for example; so is the extent of Soviet manipulation behind the criticism by African nationalists which helped to precipitate the attack on Goa. The Soviet posture of friendship was itself a factor in such a situation. Soviet influence cannot be minimised, even though there is danger of over-emphasising it. India might have proceeded along the same path without Soviet support, although probably at a slower pace.

These developments, in any case, constituted a clear landmark on the road between 1947 and the war of 1965. The danger of an Indo-Pakistan war would, of course, have been far greater during this period if Nehru had accepted Soviet arms. On the other hand, it is quite possible that the Soviets would have armed Pakistan, after suitable political readjustments, if the Americans had not filled the void of 1954. Although they escaped these pitfalls, the two neighbours nevertheless continued policies that brought them to hostilities. The manipulation of this situation by Moscow and by the pro-Kremlin Indian Communists is detectable. It played a considerable role in the final outcome although, again, the exact extent is unmeasurable. The war of 1965, however, was in major aspects the same conflict that Khrushchev set out to precipitate a decade earlier.

On the surface, however, the Soviets have maintained politically correct and co-operative relations with India. The two countries, while not always agreeing, have given each other diplomatic support on important issues. The Soviets, notably, have refrained from attacking Indian leaders, and the Indian newspapers are remarkably free from criticism of Russia. The several hundred Soviet technicians working in India are circumspect and make only careful attempts to proselytise their hosts; while Indian students in Russia are spared the customary heavy dosages of political indoctrination which other

*The Pakistan capital was shifted in 1959 from Karachi to Rawalpindi.

foreign students are obliged to undergo. Soviet propaganda from inside and outside the country is constant but subtle. The weak Moscow-dominated branch of the Indian Communist Party has undertaken few actions in recent years calculated to frighten the Congress Party. Soviet economic aid has been significant to India both economically and politically. Among other results, it has helped to develop the state-owned enterprises which many Indian intellectuals believe are essential to national prestige. While American officials often frown upon the costly impact projects favoured by Russia, many of them welcome Soviet participation in the fantastically expensive task of modernising India.

Just beneath the surface, however, Soviet pressure and manipulation are constant. Soviet agents roam the country and a number of espionage cases have arisen in recent years, most of them with little publicity. At least one Soviet 'technician' attached to the Bhilai steel mill and a second assigned to a surgical instrument factory in Madras have been expelled for proselytising activities too bold for New Delhi to stomach. Moscow maintains absolute control over the pro-Kremlin faction of the CPI and dictates its policies. Control is exercised primarily through the 'reliable' chairman, S. A. Dange, a vice-president of the Communist-dominated World Federation of Trade Unions (WFTU). Soviet funds are channelled into India through the WFTU and other front organisations such as the World Council for Peace. Indian manufacturers doing business in Russia are required to pledge up to 30 per cent of their profits to the CPI, and Dange raises additional money by guaranteeing to keep labour peace in co-operating industries. The disciplined CPI handled Congress governments carefully for many years, because Moscow was able to influence India's policy through V. K. Krishna Menon and others in the Congress left wing. This policy was changed in April 1966, and Soviet leaders instructed Dange and other CPI officials at a Moscow meeting to get tougher with the government. Thereafter, the so-called 'friendly' Indian communists took an increasingly active role in Indian turmoil and, with a hard-core of 60,000–70,000, were able to create violence as well as unrest.

Further, the Soviet Union has established a multi-million dollar propaganda apparatus within India. With criticism of Russia stifled in legitimate newspapers, pro-Soviet propaganda is spread subtly in a number of the country's best known publications, which are financed and controlled by Moscow. These include the daily newspaper, *Patriot*, of New Delhi; the Bombay weekly, *Blitz*; the 'newsmagazine', *Link*; the weekly, *Mainstream*; and at least half a dozen other principal magazines. The CPI press is extensive and active. Overt Soviet propaganda is spread by a flood of cheap books and well-printed magazines, as well as constant radio broadcasts.[19]

The danger to India is not in accepting Soviet economic and political help; its danger is in becoming too reliant upon it. The concept that communists can be friends on a governmental level and enemies in every other respect is as difficult for the Indians to understand as for others who have been caught in this duality. Nevertheless, it is very clear that the Soviets are pursuing a careful long-range programme of benevolence, force, subversion and incitement to war for purposes that have nothing to do with the consolidation of a strong, independent, non-communist Indian government. For the present, the Soviets seem content to maintain a strong holding position in India. No doubt they would prefer to continue that position indefinitely, while devoting attention to a number of projects with greater priority than the communisation of India; but there are conceivable circumstances in which the Kremlin might be willing to jettison its Indian prestige. One of them might be the possibility of replacing the Americans and the ambitious Chinese in Pakistan. To the communists, all tactics are flexible, and they are ready quickly to abandon one line for something more promising. Those collaborating with the communists, either openly or implicity, must maintain equal flexibility.

This is one aspect of the strategy that Moscow claims Peking tried to wreck by attacking India in 1962.

8

PEKING'S POLICY

SINCE ASSUMING power over mainland China, the Chinese Communists have been waging what appears to be a sustained politico-military conflict on three broad fronts. The first and primary campaign is to dominate Asia and achieve world stature. On the second front, the Chinese, like Russia, are seeking to eliminate the major restraints to their expansion by driving Western power from Asia. The third campaign is against Russia. The Chinese have been fighting for decades against physical and political domination by the Soviets. The battle in recent years has developed into a concerted attempt by Peking to capture the world movement by leading a communist revolt against Moscow.

The triple attack has often been distorted by propaganda and by Chinese political dexterity, and the full details of the Sino-Soviet cold war have been hidden by censorship. But from all evidence Peking set out in 1950 on a sustained, relatively timeless effort to achieve these primary goals. There was no sign in early 1968 that anything had occurred to change the objectives. The internal 'cultural revolution' might temporarily weaken the country but, regardless of the outcome, it probably would not appreciably alter expansionism. The Chinese drive appears to be prompted by a complicated combination of ideology, Chinese arrogance and xenophobia and nationalistic imperialism. Each step is justified by the tenets of Marxism-Leninism and basically is designed to serve the 'world revolution'. But Peking, like Russia, has its own strategic considerations and expansionist ambitions which must be served, even if dogma has to be twisted. Communism is the spur and the authorisation for its effort to expand, but not the sole motivation.

Within a year after the Chinese People's Republic was established, the Chinese had illustrated the three-phased aspect of their foreign policies. They had begun their long, bloody effort to subdue Tibet, the first step in a campaign to recapture the old Chinese empire and, no doubt, to enlarge it. Peking was engaged simultaneously in a desperate if half-hidden struggle to free itself from Russian encroachment. Finally, a Chinese army a million strong fought on behalf of communism in the Korean War. Then, without pausing to recoup, the Chinese plunged into the interminable war in South-east Asia and have played a clearly major role in it since that time. Not all of these campaigns were planned by Peking in the way they occurred, and there is strong evidence the Chinese wanted to avoid involvement in Korea. But it was highly significant that the young government initiated extraordinarily militant action in its early days in response to ambition, communist pressures and opportunity. This combination of motivations is continually present and influential on Peking's policies.

Chinese troops invaded Tibet in October 1950, some time before Mao Tse-tung had established firm control over the Chinese mainland. He was preparing to consolidate his internal authority through the vicious purge of 'landlords' under the land reform programme. He needed time for this and for other pressing domestic affairs. Tibet nevertheless was given top priority, along with continued military pressure on Taiwan, the symbol of Mao's unfinished revolution. Otherwise, the evidence suggests that Mao had planned no immediate military projects; a reduction in the size of the militia had been announced. The importance attached to Tibet, under these circumstances, indicated at least that the new communist regime was implacably determined to revive the Chinese empire with the utmost possible speed. The mountain country had been conquered first by the emperors and then had been controlled periodically by pre-Communist China. It was upon this fact of conquest and imperial suzerainty that Peking based its claim to Tibet; not on geographical propinquity or any prior voluntary annexation by the anti-Chinese Tibetans. The Chinese thus made even less effort than Moscow to disguise their determination to establish a new empire on the foundations of the old one, despite the 'anti-colonialism' preached by communism. In reality, the Chinese attack constituted fresh imperialism, for the old Chinese sovereignty had been outdated legally by recognised periods of Tibetan independence.

The relative swiftness of the Tibetan operation demonstrated that the revival of empire was an urgent matter of face for Peking, and that it would therefore be prepared to pay a heavy price to restore the imperialist boundaries elsewhere in Asia. It also raised the question whether Peking could or would be satisfied merely with reviving the past or whether it would seek to exceed the power of the old emperors. These portents were largely ignored in 1950, even by those who recognised the Tibetan adventure as Chinese Communist aggression. But the possibilities suggest that, beyond the re-establishment of sovereignty, the Chinese had further long-range purposes behind their sudden thrust into Tibet. This country occupies particularly strategic terrain; it provided a major base in 1962 for the southward lunge into India; it also outflanked Sinkiang, which was half-owned by Russia in 1950. The evidence suggests, therefore, that a year after coming to power the Chinese Communists moved into Tibet in order to establish a firm position for some future assault against India and to strengthen its posture against the Soviets in Central Asia. The Chinese struck at the first possible moment, before the Tibetans could strengthen themsclves sufficiently to increase the cost of reconquest.

At this time, Mao was fighting his undercover battle to preserve Manchuria and Sinkiang from Soviet conquest. Moscow's efforts to detach these two key provinces from the new communist regime had been unabated. A personal feud between Stalin and Mao continued beneath the surface. Stalin had twice demoted Mao in the late 1920s for the Soviet dictator's own mistakes in China, and evidently had distrusted him since then. When Stalin started the Korean War in June 1950, the timing was suspiciously unfavourable to the Chinese, deeply involved in internal troubles and already concentrating troops around Tibet. While Stalin's motives for seeking quick victory over South Korea are clear, his simultaneous attempt to use the war against Mao has been less widely recognised. The Soviets virtually took over Manchuria as a supply base and flooded it with thousands of Russian advisers who directed the North Korean forces. Peking apparently knew of the Korean attack in advance but did not expect to participate. Yet by September 12, 1950, Mao had mobilised a force of 450,000 Chinese troops in Manchuria. These mobilisations were ordered some time earlier, when the prospects for a communist conquest of South Korea were still favourable. The tide did not turn until the United Nations landing at Inchon on September 15. The Chinese mobilisation, which has never been explained, could have been precautionary, to prepare for any eventuality in Korea. But it could also have been necessary to prevent the Soviets from physically detaching Manchuria under cover of the Korean conflict. The Chinese Communist military governor of Manchuria during this period, Kao Kang, was publicly disgraced and, no doubt, forced to commit suicide in 1954, after Stalin's death. He was charged with establishing an 'independent kingdom' in Manchuria during the war. The evidence behind this first major scandal of the Chinese Peoples' Republic suggests that Kao was Stalin's agent in an attempt to place Manchuria under Soviet control and was liquidated as soon as death removed Stalin's protection.

Massive Chinese involvement in the Korean War saved Russia's prestige, as Peking later claimed. The evidence indicates that Peking was motivated by the desire to prevent the extinction of Communist North Korea, because Marxism-Leninism cannot tolerate a setback of communism. The Chinese were notably indifferent to United Nations guarantees that Russian-dominated Manchuria would not be invaded. Despite the Chinese sacrifice, Stalin conspicuously attempted to prolong the Korean War artificially, probably in an effort to weaken Mao and to replace him with a more amenable Chinese leader. For its part, Peking exerted the greatest effort to make capital out of the war when it became involved. The Chinese tried desperately to humble Western power but completely failed. They also quickly and successfully fought Moscow for control over the Korean Communist Party, at the end of the military campaign. Yet a decade later, after the open Sino-Soviet break, Peking was still paying a remaining debt of some $500 million for the Soviet arms used in the war.[1]

Having failed to expel the United Nations forces from Korea, Peking settled for a stalemate armistice in July 1953. Within a few months, the Chinese were deeply involved in the Indo-China war. They supplied major arms to the Vietminh, and the climactic battle for Dien Bien Phu was tactically directed by a Chinese Communist general. Thousands of 'technicians' supported the anti-French forces.[2] Therefore the Chinese, as well as the North Vietnamese, were held back by the Soviet 'peace' efforts at the Geneva

Conference of 1954. Chou En-lai, then Foreign Minister, made a notable effort to dominate the conference by bombastic public statements, vowing to eliminate all Western influence from Asia. Thereafter, Peking more openly undertook to direct and expedite the communist campaign in Asia. The Chinese made it plain they considered themselves, not the Soviets, as the rightful leaders in this area.

Yet it took Mao until 1955 to break the Soviet hold over Manchuria and Sinkiang, which had been maintained through economic control of joint Sino-Soviet development companies. Khrushchev finally agreed at that time to liquidate these footholds and to return Port Arthur to full Peking control. In doing so, he may have demonstrated such weakness, in Chinese eyes, as to invite further pressure: a posture certain to be enhanced by the 'weakness' of his destalinisation programme which began the next year. In any case, the Chinese brought their feud with Moscow into the open in 1956. Among other tactics, they bitterly and publicly condemned the Soviet attempt to expunge Stalin and his control methods and strategies from the world movement. From that point, the Sino-Soviet split widened visibly. It grew into a complicated ideological discussion which illustrated that communist differences, as well as the conflict of nationalisms, were involved in a basic struggle between two of the world's giant nations.

By the mid-1950s, the strategic subcontinent had become the eventual target of two, rather than one, communist-nationalist imperialist drives. For both, it also exercised a unique attraction as a political testing ground for the rival tactical theories which became highly significant in the Sino-Soviet competition for control over the world movement. By this time, too, northern and western Kashmir had evidently assumed major strategic importance for both Moscow and Peking. Stalin's heirs did not abandon their efforts to conquer portions of Sinkiang with its rich mineral deposits, and Chinese Communist resistance was not long in becoming evident. Kashmir accordingly assumed new military significance.

The geopolitics of the communist cold war, therefore, were beginning to engulf the subcontinent at the period of the radical changes produced by the US-Pakistan military pact. The American presence sealed off the potential Soviet threat from the west, but India and Kashmir, on the east, were exposed to the Chinese drive.

In reaction to Pakistan's new alignment, New Delhi permitted Russia to establish a substantial political and economic position in India, together with a potential military position, which further invited Chinese attack and, perhaps, made it inevitable. It is likely that the Sino-Soviet power struggle would have involved the subcontinent, under any circumstances. Without American deterrence, the Soviets might have attacked India through Pakistan, if only to forestall the resurgent Chinese. At least, the Soviets could have been expected to seek a dominant political position in both countries, particularly in Pakistan, being the more strategic, through massive arms offers and economic aid; and Peking has its own peculiar reasons for seeking the downfall of India, if not her conquest. American involvement drastically altered the situation and probably saved both India and Pakistan from earlier and stronger pressures than they have undergone in subsequent years.

From the first invasion of Tibet in 1950, Peking gradually intensified pressure on India until the quick and massive blow of 1962. During this period, Chinese political and military actions often appeared to be dictated by opportunity, and some observers have concluded that opportunism was the primary factor behind them. It is always unwise, however, to ignore the continuity of Peking's long-range objectives and the relative timelessness with which they are pursued. The Chinese have quite clearly expressed their determination to expand and have advertised their immediate targets; but they also usually await the most favourable opportunity to strike and, whenever possible, choose the least expensive means. Thus there can be no doubt of Peking's determination to conquer Taiwan, a constant goal since 1949. After losing a sharp aerial war over the Taiwan Straits in 1958, however, Peking has avoided any further test of strength against American-supported power, but has concentrated upon political means. These include encouragement for the effort to humble and erode Taiwan politically by ejecting her from the United Nations. In the same way, Peking's assault on India has involved various and fluctuating methods of pressure, but the assault itself has never been abandoned.

Although in Tibet they claimed to be reoccupying an 'integral part of China', communist forces at first proceeded cautiously. Entering the eastern part of the country in late October 1950, they paused for nearly eleven months before marching to Lhasa, the capital. The delay was apparently due, in part, to Peking's desire to test the reaction of India, the United Nations and, particularly, the United States. No significant counter-action was taken: India protested officially, and Sardar Patel called the Chinese attack 'aggression'. Indian officials were worried but hesitated to intervene. Their influence helped to immobilise the United Nations and the United States on this issue.

The Chinese then proceeded to apply to Tibet one of the cruellest programmes in Asian history. They fought armed opposition in 1951–3; put down another revolt in 1955–6, led by the tough Khamba tribesmen, and in 1958–9 suppressed a more widespread insurrection which spread to Lhasa. The Dalai Lama, who escaped with thousands of Tibetans to sanctuary in India, reported that 90,000 of his countrymen were killed at this time. The International Commission of Jurists, after thorough investigation, charged the Chinese with planned genocide and other measures to break the Tibetan spirit. They included the familiar communist-style kidnapping of thousands of children.

With a ruthless and powerful army on the march just across its northern borders, India at this period, as Nehru later said, was 'out of touch with reality and living in an artificial atmosphere of our own creation'. The government, as well as the people, was blinded by the belief that Pakistan was the only enemy. Furthermore, Nehru had turned towards China in 1952–3 to demonstrate the validity of non-alignment based upon peaceful coexistence, in the non-communist meaning of the phrase. He sought to re-establish what he described as historic ties of friendship between India and China, although history shows, as one historian says, 'the ancient friendship between India and China was little more than a myth . . .'[3] In pursuing this objective, Nehru concluded a treaty with Peking in April 1954, through which, according to the official communiqué, India recognised Tibet as 'the Tibet region of China'. The treaty, concerning trade and other relations between India and the new Chinese territory, also enunciated the five principles of *Panch Shila*. The Chinese solemnly affirmed their belief in (1) mutual respect for each other's territorial integrity and sovereignty, (2) mutual non-aggression, (3) mutual non-interference in each other's internal affairs, (4) equality and mutual benefit, and (5) peaceful coexistence. This became the hallmark of what Nehru envisaged as an Asian 'peace zone', and the phrase was reiterated constantly. Spurred by the Bandung Conference of 1955, *Panch Shila* became a slogan of widespread appeal in Asia.

But in 1954, Peking published for the first time a map which delineated its expansionist ambitions clearly and unequivocably. The map showed the territories allegedly taken from China by the 'imperialist powers' between 1840 and 1919 and identified them as portions of China to be reclaimed. Included were all of the Russian Far East possessions in eastern Siberia, the Central Asian Soviet possessions, ringing Sinkiang and Afghanistan, and the Pamir region near northern Kashmir; Outer Mongolia; all of north-east India and Assam; Ladakh, in eastern Kashmir; the Sino-Indian border states of Nepal, Bhutan and Sikkim; all of Korea, all of Vietnam, Laos and Cambodia, Thailand, Malaya and Singapore; the Andaman Islands in the Indian Ocean, the Sulu Archipelago of the Philippines; Taiwan and adjacent offshore islands.[4] In this vast ring surrounding present-day China were lands once held by the old emperors, others conquered by the Manchus, who themselves were conquerors of the main Chinese tribes, and still more distant territories over which any historic Chinese claims were remote or confused. Thus, the map itself served as clear warning that Peking aspired to an empire greater than any in Chinese history.

The map was contained in a book entitled, *A Brief History of Modern China*, published for Chinese students. Far, therefore, from being mere propaganda or idle boasting, it constituted a serious reflection of Peking's ambitions. The urge to empire, for the Chinese as well as the Russians, is stimulated by the dogma of communism and justified by it. For both, certain strategic objectives for national defence are considered 'just' imperialist objectives, to be taken even at heavy cost. The Chinese also have other motives. They have economic and population pressures and the traditional ambitions of an organised state surrounded by disorganised, weaker and inherently richer neighbours. They have a historic sense of cultural superiority, the perpetuated belief that the 'Middle Kingdom' is the centre of the universe. They are driven by an implacable quest for irredentism. The Chinese 'urge to revolutionary empire', says a historian, 'is fortified by the feeling, drilled into all Chinese since the beginning of the Republic, that all territory ever included in the vast Manchu Empire belongs rightfully to China.'[5]

These forces drove the Chinese at an early stage of the Republic towards international stature, as well as regional empire. They sought global influence by defying the world and by dangerous meddling in Africa, Latin America and the Middle East. They have lost these first gambles and have demonstrated both unwillingness and inability to challenge the military strength of the industrial West or Russia. But the Chinese have quite plainly advertised their world-wide ambitions and no doubt will continue to implement them whenever possible.

The double quest for empire and international strength led Red China into the economically crippling effort to build up her own nuclear arsenal. The decision probably marked the final break with Russia, in terms of durable practical relations between the communist super-powers. Chinese irredentism involves nearly 600,000 square miles of Soviet territory. Peking has vowed obliquely but clearly, in the public quarrel with Moscow, to take back by force Soviet-held 'Chinese' territories which cannot be reclaimed through negotiation. In one of their attacks on Khrushchev in 1963, the Chinese specifically listed among the 'unequal treaties', needing revision, the main agreements by which tsarist Russia acquired Siberia and large tracts of territory bordering modern Sinkiang. '. . . we have always held', the Chinese said, that 'when conditions are ripe', these treaties 'should be settled peacefully through negotiations'. The Soviets replied crisply there were no territorial questions to be settled. When Khrushchev taunted Peking over its unwillingness to eliminate the colonial enclaves of Hong Kong and Macao, both profitable to the Chinese, Peking asked him: '. . . do you intend to raise all questions of unequal treaties and have a general settlement? Has it ever entered your heads what the consequences would be? Can you seriously believe this will do you any good?'[6]

In the mid-1950s, Peking's activities were centred in Asia for the practical reasons of opportunity and power limitations. The campaign in Asia was carefully confined to step-by-step expansion, but its eventual scope was limited only by the power raised against it. If irredentism demanded the eventual occupation of Ladakh, what would prevent a push into the whole of Kashmir? One Chinese map, in fact, showed all of Kashmir as being a part of China. Furthermore, Peking's drive into Tibet and her simultaneous deep but disguised involvement in Indo-China were regarded generally as separate developments. Were they? No one knows for sure, but the map of empire clearly identifies them as related, and so does the tactical situation. A Chinese thrust southward from Tibet into north-east India could cut off Assam, the eastern Indian state, thereby outflanking the whole of South-east Asia. And Assam also was identified as Chinese.

Nehru followed his dream of peace with China with such personal devotion that the Chinese attack on India, when it came, was, in the opinion of many Indians, the climactic factor causing his death. His logic was clear. 'It is a matter of importance to us, of course, as well as, I am sure, to China,' he told parliament in 1954, 'that these countries, which have now almost 1,800 miles of frontier, should live in terms of peace and friendliness and should respect each other's sovereignty and integrity, should agree not to interfere with each other in any way, and not to commit aggression on each other. By this agreement, we ensure peace to a very large extent in a certain area in Asia. I would earnestly wish that this area of peace could be spread over the rest of Asia and indeed over the rest of the world . . .'[7]

There was a fatal flaw in this reasoning. 'Peaceful coexistence' or *Panch Shila*, in the non-communist sense of mutual non-interference, cannot be established unilaterally; it exists and has existed for long periods during the cold war only because of a balance of power or by the mutual restraints of two or more participating nations. But communist dogma does not ascribe morality to dealings with 'imperialists' and therefore treaties between the two adversaries cannot and must not be honoured beyond the point of their usefulness to the communists. 'It is ridiculous . . .' said Lenin, 'not to know that a treaty is the means of gaining strength.' And again: 'The strictest loyalty to the ideals of Communism must be combined with the ability to make all the necessary practical compromises, to "tack", to make agreements, zigzags, retreats and so on, in order to accelerate the coming into [power] . . .' Lenin used 'peaceful coexistence' in the 1920s, said Khrushchev, in order 'to gain time and to secure a breathing space' to build up Soviet strength. The Chinese agree and applaud this use of 'coexistence' as a tactic or, in the communist sense, as a short-term expedient. They claim that they have 'unswervingly pursued Lenin's policy of peaceful coexistence with great success' and 'have enriched' the policy 'in the course of applying it'.

M

The Sino-Soviet Communists agree with Lenin's admonition that all tactics advancing the cause are justified, and they subscribe to the voluminous dogma that the 'capitalists' cannot be trusted under any circumstances. They also agree that capitalism 'will not yield power voluntarily' but must be forced to do so. How, then, can the Soviets practise 'peaceful coexistence' through trust in the West, as many appear to believe from a mere reading of the slogan? The Indians, for example, in reaction against the Chinese 'betrayal' turned more strongly toward Moscow and placed increased confidence in 'peaceful coexistence'. Although some other factors are involved, New Delhi transferred to Moscow somewhat the same faith that Nehru found so misused in China's case. It seems pertinent at this point to examine the question briefly to determine whether the Chinese use of 'peaceful coexistence' provides an example of or an exception to the meaning that the term now seems to have for the Kremlin.

Moscow-Peking polemics over this issue have been unusually bitter because, in part, the question permits each to blacken the other in the eyes of world communists; the Chinese are 'warlike' and the Soviets are 'weak'. In brief, the dogmatic issue involves the question of whether 'coexistence' should be a temporary tactic or, as the Kremlin has announced, long-range, semi-permanent strategy. Moscow arbitrarily applied this strategy to the entire world movement, and the Chinese accordingly were incensed, because they are fighting for independence from such ideological and political domination. Essentially, the current meaning of 'coexistence' is designed to modernise dogma as it relates primarily to Russia. It calls on the Party faithful to avoid starting a world war, because this would expose Russia to American nuclear arms. At the same time, the doctrine declares, the point has been reached where Soviet nuclear power is able to prevent non-communist retaliation against Russia for communist wars such as 'national liberation' struggles which do not appear openly as nation-to-nation conflicts but are disguised as internal struggles. Khrushchev, who set the pattern, indicated that it had become a strategy because nuclear power is here to stay. He stated bluntly that 'coexistence' is good politics because otherwise 'the masses of the people would not be attracted toward the communists, but would be repelled by them'. Khrushchev also advocated greater use of political and economic weapons in the quest for communist power, but made it plain repeatedly that armed hostilities—at a 'safe' level for Russia—were 'just' and therefore would be supported, when suited to Soviet purposes. Basic communist methods, he said, are unchanged from Lenin's day and involve 'mastery of all forms of struggle—the peaceful as well as the unpeaceful—[and] . . . the ability to replace one form in the speediest possible way with another'.[8] Khrushchev's policies have been followed in this respect so faithfully by his successors that Peking has termed the new regime 'Khrushchevism without Khrushchev'.

'The essence of the policy of peaceful coexistence of countries with different social systems', said Khrushchev, 'lies precisely in *compelling* the big Western powers to renounce war as an instrument of their policy and to adhere to peaceful, not military, methods of settling international problems *through the superiority of the peace-loving nations over the forces of militarism and aggression.*'[9]

On another occasion, he said: 'The policy of peaceful coexistence as regards its social content, is a form of intense economic, political and ideological struggle of the proletariat against the aggressive forces of imperialism in the international arena.' This was part of a highly significant and still valid strategy speech which Khrushchev delivered on January 6, 1961. He said, in essence, that communists should guard against involvement in 'local wars' between states, on the Korean pattern, because they threaten nuclear retaliation. But Khrushchev promised full Soviet support for 'national liberation' and civil wars, as well as smaller insurrections. Speaking of 'national liberation' conflicts, he said: 'These are revolutionary wars. Such wars are not only admissible but inevitable, since the colonialists do not grant independence voluntarily . . . The Communists fully support such just wars and march in the front rank with the peoples waging liberation struggles.'[10]

Nevertheless, the Chinese, in another phase of the feud, have accused Moscow of collaborating with the imperialists in an effort to suppress the 'world revolution'. This involves an issue which first split communism in 1925. The question is whether Russia, as the strongest communist power, should attempt to hasten revolution everywhere on the globe or should concentrate upon building her own strength. The Russia-first policy, expressed by Stalin's slogan of 'socialism in one country', won over the theory of 'permanent revolution' which was advanced by Trotsky. Since then the Soviets have attempted to use the world movement primarily to build up the economic strength and military defences of the Soviet Union. They support only those foreign armed struggles which contribute to Soviet purposes, as distinct from those of world communism, and only those which the Soviets control and which do not threaten Russian security. The Chinese claim they will support every 'revolution' in the world. This means every upheaval suitable for communist purposes and subject to Peking's control; not necessarily every revolution. Stalin's great purges of the 1930s were designed, in part, to hammer the world movement into permanent servitude to the Russia-first policies, which Moscow still follows.

The Chinese succeeded in splitting the movement partly because of the latent forces which opposed Soviet colonialism and which supported more vigorous 'world revolution' than Moscow wanted. It is clear, however, that Moscow has no desire to deprive itself of armed struggle as a source of expansion, and has no such purpose for advocating 'peace'. 'Some try', says a modern Rumanian commentator, 'to reduce the notion of peaceful coexistence to the renunciation of war. *But peace and peaceful coexistence are not one and the same thing*. Peaceful coexistence does not mean a temporary and unstable armistice between two wars, but something more complex.'[11]

Thus, it was 'peaceful coexistence' in the sense of restraining the West which permitted the Cuban crisis, the erection of the Berlin Wall and Khrushchev's attempt to spark 'proxy wars' on the subcontinent and elsewhere. It was 'peaceful coexistence' in the tactical sense of duplicity which disguised and justified Peking's steady encroachment upon India during the *Panch Shila* years, between 1954 and 1962. The parallelism of intent and amorality is obvious, and patently every action taken by the Chinese would have been applauded under Khrushchev's definition of 'coexistence'. The strategic parallelism which communism often imposes upon its faithful was also apparent. If Khrushchev wanted to create an Indo-Pakistan war for his purposes, so did Peking, for somewhat contrary reasons of its own. And the Chinese attack on India, whether intentionally or not, became the decisive factor in shifting the tide of events on the subcontinent definitely towards the war of 1965, if not irrevocably towards it. Finally, 'coexistence' means for communists of all sects the same essential premise: freedom from reprisal for any actions they take. Despite their criticism of Khrushchev, the Chinese have attempted for more than a decade to transform their massed armies, by deed and by propaganda, into a threat so overpowering that the Americans would not dare to become involved in another Asian 'national liberation' war on the mainland.

The spirit of 'coexistence' with India lasted only briefly on the Chinese side; in non-communist terms, it hardly existed at all. But the façade was carefully preserved. Previously, Nehru had helped Peking by championing its membership in the United Nations and opposing UN resolutions condemning Chinese aggression in Korea. On the Tibetan issue, Nehru continued to ignore the portent, as well as the content, of Chinese actions. Even after providing sanctuary for the Dalai Lama in 1958, the Indian leader successfully endeavoured, for a number of reasons, to block full-scale consideration of the question at the United Nations. This policy and Nehru's refusal to condemn the Soviet brutality in crushing the Hungarian rebellion seriously weakened Nehru's own prestige and led to future embarrassment of India, in the opinion of the Indian editor-author, Frank Moraes. 'Nehru's attitude seemed equivocal and even opportunist', Moraes says, 'and a great part of the world, including ironically a section of the Afro-Asian world, began to question India's implementation of her non-alignment policy. It almost seemed as if sometimes India wanted peace at the price of other people's security and freedom. Nothing tarnished the early shining splendour of Nehru's non-alignment policy more than these later developments.'[12] The Soviets and the Chinese accepted the Indian leader's services to them with parallel cynicism. While he fulfilled their expectations, they praised him: when he failed to do so, they condemned him bitterly. Khrushchev raised the Kashmir issue when Nehru supported measures to force the withdrawal of Soviet troops from Hungary. Peking bitterly attacked India for harbouring Tibetan refugees, and the Indians were so resentful that for a time even the façade was shaken.

Behind the screen, Peking relentlessly pursued its objectives. As early as 1954, it began to dominate a section of eastern Ladakh, Kashmir, called the Aksai Chin (white stone) desert. Although borders were imperfectly demarcated in this strategic back country, India claimed the area with considerably more authority than did Peking. Nevertheless, the Chinese built a military road to link Sinkiang with Tibet, across territory which India claimed. The project was started in 1954 and completed in 1956–7. Aksai Chin is a tableland of some 14,000 feet, forbidding, desolate and deserted. Once used by caravans for bypassing traditional mountain routes, the passageway had been long neglected because of blazing summers and scarcity of water. The Chinese made it into an all-the-year route between their two western territories, for the more familiar mountain passes are blocked by winter snows. Chinese troops crossed Aksai Chin in 1950 during their first invasion of Tibet. Five years later, they used the same route to move forces that suppressed the Khamba revolt. It was an invaluable passage at this time, because more direct access to Tibet from western China winds through extremely difficult terrain. Ambushes of the type used by the Khambas could be prepared easily.

By 1956, then, Aksai Chin, regardless of who owned it, was vital for Chinese control over Tibet. And the Chinese, both as communists and as Chinese, could not tolerate the successful severance of Tibet from Peking domination. They had come to Aksai Chin to stay and this terrain, as it turned out, was the chief immediate military objective of the 1962 fighting. Furthermore, the increased tension between the Soviets and the Chinese in the borderlands of Central Asia convinced the authors of one study that the Aksai Chin route, 'once essential for retaining Tibet, may now be equally essential for retaining Sinkiang'.[13] It is certainly possible that the Chinese, who had begun to defy Moscow in the early 1950s, initiated their encroachment on the Aksai Chin with the specific intention of preparing a defence against the Soviets, in addition to other motives.

The Indians did not discover the road until 1958. They had relied previously on the mighty Himalayas to protect their northern flank and had paid little military attention to the area. Military funds were relatively scarce and were used to strengthen defences elsewhere. After extensive exploration in the nineteenth century, the British had been convinced that the Karakoram Pass in north-east Kashmir was the best route between Sinkiang and Ladakh, but that the passage was too difficult for a dangerous invasion force. The Chinese, moreover, had obscured their operations in Aksai Chin by closing Sinkiang to the Indians and manipulating the Tibetan trade treaty to limit observation. When small Indian reconnaissance parties were sent there with the spring thaw of 1958, one detachment was captured, but another returned to New Delhi with reports that the Chinese had entrenched themselves. India protested and reaffirmed Indian sovereignty over the area in a strong note on October 18, 1958. The Chinese reply, on November 3, made the first positive and public Chinese claim to the Aksai Chin.[14] The Indians assert that the frontiers had been recognised by the Chinese in a treaty of 1842.

The Tibetan revolt of 1959 made the Aksai Chin route absolutely essential to the Chinese, for heavy fighting cut off access from eastern China. Peking's position hardened, particularly after the Dalai Lama reached India. Chinese forces moved more aggressively into Ladakh. On October 21, an Indian patrol ran into a fortified Chinese hill position near the Kongka Pass, almost fifty miles inside territory claimed by India and some thirty-two miles west of the Chinese road. The patrol was badly mauled. On the previous August 25, the Chinese had also struck far to the east, in the North East Frontier Agency, the eastern part of India. A Chinese force overran an Indian outpost at Longju, south of the McMahon Line in the centre of NEFA. This was the first demonstration of the diversionary pressure Peking would apply subsequently to this area. The Indian public, meanwhile, first learned of the seriousness of the situation that autumn through government statements. Strong defiance was aroused, and demands were raised in Parliament for the ejection of the Chinese. The government, realising the military odds against it, refused to take immediate action but quietly began to build up strength in the north. Nehru withheld from the public news of several subsequent border skirmishes with the Chinese. This action has been cited as evidence of his blind faith in 'coexistence', but it could also have been prompted by a desire to prevent undue pressures for precipitate Indian military action from excitable government critics.

In any case, the façade of *Panch Shila* remained in place, while serious sparring continued behind it. On November 7, 1959, Chou En-lai suggested the first of several Chinese diplomatic formulas, designed to trick or force the Indians into granting immediate concessions. He proposed demilitarisation of the entire Sino-Soviet border to a depth of twenty kilometres (twelve and a half miles). Troops would withdraw the correct distance from the line of actual control in Ladakh, while simultaneously falling back from the so-called McMahon Line on the east, in the North East Frontier Agency. This line had been established as the Tibetan-Indian border in 1913 by a conference, with Sir Henry McMahon as chairman, called to establish the status of Tibet and to adjust other relations between that country, China and British India. The Chinese government repudiated the final agreement, but it was ratified by the other two countries and served as an accepted boundary between them. Among other results, the Chinese rejection nullified a clause in the convention which recognised that Tibet was under Chinese sovereignty. The Chinese Communists have alternately repudiated the McMahon Line as imperialist dictation and tacitly accepted it as a boundary, when favourable to them. In this instance, however, they drew their own 'McMahon Line' some distance south of the actual boundary. Consequently, Chou's proposal in 1959, if accepted, 'would have seriously jeopardized Indian defense positions in the east and would have at the same time made a gift to the Chinese of the vital Aksai Chin area'.[15]

By the end of the year, Peking had abandoned evasion and subterfuge and openly challenged India's claims to the entire Sino-Indian border. The boundary includes not only the remote area of Ladakh in the north and the jungled obscurity of NEFA in the east; the two countries also meet at corners of two Indian states, Himachal Pradesh and Uttar Pradesh, along the mountains between Nepal and Kashmir. During all his conversations with Indian officials in New Delhi and Peking, Premier Chou En-lai made no mention of Chinese dissatisfaction with the borders until the claim to Aksai Chin was advanced in late 1958. In the absence of complaint, Indian officials were lulled into believing there would be no dispute. Chou later explained that the question was not raised 'because conditions were not yet ripe for its settlement'. On January 23, 1959, Chou in a letter to Nehru challenged the entire border. The following September 8, he advanced claims to 50,000 square miles of territory claimed by India. In November, he made the first attempt to establish significant Chinese military positions through diplomatic subterfuge. A month later, Peking brought the dispute into the open.

New Delhi has characterised Chou's explanation of his delayed border protest as 'one of the amazing admissions of dissimulation in modern history'. But the communists also have a specific meaning for the phrase 'when conditions are ripe', and Chou's suggestion that this stage had been reached in early 1959 appears significant. It shows that the establishment of a solid Chinese military position confronting India and protecting Tibet was a consistent Peking policy, to be followed and consolidated when all circumstances, external and internal, were favourable. Externally, the Chinese had been preoccupied with a number of major projects during the period of 'coexistence'. They included one high point of the feud with Moscow, when Peking demanded more aggressive 'revolutionary' action throughout the world, and the air war with Nationalist China over the Straits of Taiwan. Internally, the Chinese regime had passed through all the bloody and laborious process of establishing its control and building 'communism'. The suppression of dissident intellectuals under the 'hundred flowers blooming' campaign had occurred in 1957. The next year was the 'Great Leap Forward' and the forced regimentation of the commune system. With these projects under way and their failures still incompletely demonstrated, the Chinese were ready at the beginning of 1959 to increase their pressure on India. They preferred to retain *Panch Shila*, which had helped to disguise many of their machinations and had brought them considerable prestige in Asia as 'peaceful nationalists'; but they were ready to sacrifice this reputation, if necessary, for further advancement against India. By the end of 1959, the Tibetan revolt and grave domestic failures, with resultant world criticism, had hardened Peking's decision to encroach on India, but along predetermined lines. Thus India had become a primary and probably permanent Chinese target. The pressure of adverse world opinion, on which Nehru seemed to depend so much to restrain Chinese expansion, served only to accelerate their pressure and to harden their methods of advancement along the same path they would have taken if the world had remained indifferent.

It soon became clear that the Chinese had no intention of reaching an equitable border settlement. During an exchange of letters between Nehru and Chou, Peking rejected an apparently sincere proposal to avoid further clashes in the strategic Aksai Chin. Nehru suggested a mutual troop withdrawal to create a buffer no-man's zone and offered no impediment to the passage of civilian traffic along the Chinese road. The implication was that the use of the road for military traffic could be negotiated later. In his rejection, Chou clearly committed himself to acceptance of boundaries in this area contained in a 1956 Chinese map, but later the Chinese produced a new map claiming an additional 2,000 square miles of Indian territory. Under strong Chinese pressure, Nehru agreed to meet Chou in New Delhi. After six days of talks in April, arrangements were made to hold formal border negotiations in Peking. Chou in a press conference made it plain that the Chinese hoped to gain their objectives in Aksai Chin by agreeing temporarily to avoid inter-ference with the borders in NEFA. He said the McMahon Line was 'absolutely unacceptable to China', but it would be respected if the Indians accepted Chinese positions in Ladakh. This was the old Chinese and communist trick of agreeing to recognise an actual condition in return for major concessions. Nehru quickly saw through this suggestion and rejected it.

Indian and Chinese negotiators conducted protracted and fruitless border discussions throughout much of 1960, in Peking, New Delhi and Rangoon. They waded through interminable details, particularly concerning strategic eastern Kashmir, to present conflicting claims based upon geographical features, old treaties, customs and precedents. Boundaries would be difficult to define in that region under the most favourable circumstances, because of intersecting mountain ranges and other obscurities. The Indians argued with better logic and far better documentation that the proper boundary of Ladakh followed a series of mountain watersheds along the lines of their claims. The Chinese, according to an important study of the whole vast evidence, 'failed to demonstrate much knowledge of an area they claimed had been roughly surveyed by Chinese parties in 1941–42'. This study by American specialists, published as a book entitled *Himalayan Battleground*, documents the conclusion that 'the case the Chinese presented was a shoddy piece of work, betraying —if only to those in a position to consult the sources cited—a fundamental contempt for evidence'. In fact, the authors conclude that Peking could have presented a more plausible case but that 'the Chinese Government showed no interest in the substance of the talks, as their astonishingly careless presentation amply demon-strated'.[16] Instead, the Chinese appeared to use the negotiations primarily to overcome adverse international publicity and to lull apprehensions in Asia over their intentions. When a detailed report of the negotiations was unexpectedly published, Peking attempted to use it as propaganda to prove that it was willing to negotiate but India was obdurate. This image was strengthened by Peking's relative promptness and conciliation in settling other disputed borders at this time with smaller neighbours, such as Burma where, incidentally, Peking accepted the McMahon Line. 'The 1960 talks', says the American study, 'not only failed to provide a basis for negotiation but also had made it obvious that the Chinese had no genuine interest in negotiating.'

Instead, Peking sought to intimidate India into capitulation. Military power was concentrated at key points along the border, including a force reported to be 50,000 strong in Tibet. The Chinese nibbled deeper into Kashmir while 'negotiations' were under way. Against the nine-year Chinese build-up, the Indians began to militarise their side of the border for the first time in October 1959. Peking propagandists called for the 'liberation' of Ladakh, Sikkim and Bhutan, the usual prelude to intense Chinese interest or actual penetration. Sikkim, a small kingdom encompassing the key Chumbi Pass leading to West Bengal, became an Indian protectorate by treaty in December 1950. Neighbouring Bhutan, a princely state partially surrounded by Red China, has long been dependent on India. By a 1949 treaty, Bhutan yielded control over foreign affairs to India, and the next year Nehru guaranteed the security of the tiny territory. Peking had declared Bhutan a part of a greater Tibet and warned the Maharajah against permitting the entrance of Indian troops. The Chinese had been active for some time in both countries and in larger Nepal, with which it concluded a border treaty in October 1961. Peking propagandists also called for the creation of a Himalayan Federation of these states, together with NEFA, a recurrent political idea which India strongly opposes. By propaganda and, no doubt, through the talk of agents, Peking further attempted to turn the vital buffer states against India whom it labelled as 'expansionist', a theme emphasised after the Goa attack of 1961. On a world scale, the Chinese attempted to undermine India's cherished position among Afro-Asian nations. These pressures were augmented by a series of border clashes.

The Indians did not capitulate to pressure, but neither did they recognise its significance. 'Right up to the time of the Chinese aggression in October 1962,' says Frank Moraes, 'India's people were led to believe that the main threat to India's frontiers came from Pakistan.'[17] Yet the new Chinese posture had already become an influential and permanent element in the Indo-Pakistani confrontation; as Peking possibly anticipated. President Ayub evidently recognised the potentialities of the situation with far greater clarity than New Delhi; at the same time, he apparently tried to profit from India's embarrassment. These two conflicting reactions, complicated by the presence and frequent interference of Peking and Moscow, contributed to a further radical change in the geopolitics of the subcontinent.

Ayub made a series of statements analysing the military situation in 1959 which he correlated into a magazine article, published in *Foreign Affairs* in July 1960. His theses were supported fully by impartial military men. Ayub said in part:

> As a student of war and strategy, I can see quite clearly the inexorable push of the north in the direction of the warm waters of the Indian Ocean. This push is bound to increase if India and Pakistan go on squabbling with each other. If, on the other hand, we resolve our problems and disengage our armed forces from facing inwards as they do today, and face them outwards, I feel we shall have a good chance of preventing a recurrence of this history of the past, which was that whenever this sub-continent was divided—and often it was divided—someone or the other invited an outsider to step in.

The article suggests that, in 1960, Ayub was concerned about threats from both Russia and Red China. Although later he publicly ridiculed China's menace to India and acted as if there were none, Ayub nevertheless sent reinforcements to northern Azad Kashmir at the outset of Sino-Indian border troubles, because he was uncertain of Peking's motives.[18] Moreover, it was the Chinese build-up which prompted the Pakistani President to outline a basically sound military policy, whatever use he later made of the situation. In April 1959, Ayub first proposed a joint defence pact for the subcontinent, an idea which Nehru dismissed with the question: 'Against whom?' After the initial Chinese Communist thrust into NEFA, in August 1959, Nehru expressed his first anxiety to parliament over the situation. Ayub then requested a meeting with the Indian leader and visited New Delhi on September 1 to make the proposal formally.

Although it must be presumed that Ayub had sound military reasons for proposing joint defence, he made the pact contingent upon prior settlement of the Kashmir issue, presumably on terms favourable to Pakistan, and therefore the idea was foredoomed. Many Indians believed Pakistan was merely trying to use India's predicament for her own gain. Other differences over the idea were consequential. India objected to alliance as long as Pakistan continued membership of Western military pacts, arguing that it would affect non-alignment and would imply India's adherence to these pacts. Ayub and Pakistani officials contended that joint defence could be evolved separately from the foreign policies of the two nations, but Indian authorities were unconvinced. In return, India held out for a more informal arrangement, including a 'no war declaration' in relation to Kashmir and tacit agreement that common policies towards China would be followed. In October 1959, President Ayub further complicated the situation by announcing that an Indo-Pakistan defence system would be directed against the Soviet Union and Afghanistan, as well as China. This was a logical projection of Ayub's publicly stated views on the subject, but was unacceptable to India. She had already come to rely extensively upon Russia and made studied attempts to avoid arousing Moscow's anger. Moreover, Soviet-backed agitation over Pakhtunistan had created a fresh deterioration of relations between Afghanistan and Pakistan.[19] Indian suspicions over Ayub's motives were further aroused when Pakistan referred Kashmir to the United Nations again in December 1959, a critical period in the Sino-Indian dispute over Ladakh. The move produced no tangible result, except to exacerbate Indo-Pakistani relations again, after a brief period of goodwill during the defence discussions. Thus joint defence was scuttled by some of the principal factors which made it necessary—suspicion, opportunism and myopia.

After this sequence, Pakistan took the initiative in negotiating an agreement on the 300-mile border between Sinkiang and Azad Kashmir. President Ayub mentioned the subject publicly for the first time in a news conference of October 23, 1959. The foreign office, he said, had obtained a Chinese map which showed sections of Azad Kashmir as belonging to China. Pakistan intended to seek a peaceful solution of the issue. Actually, it was revealed later that Chinese maps claimed between 4,000 and 6,000 miles of Azad Kashmir, a point obscured by consistent Pakistani attempts to minimise border difficulties between the two countries. Pakistan's original overtures for negotiations, made in 1960, were not accepted by Peking until January 1961, less than a month after the abortive Sino-Indian talks. Peking agreed 'in principle' to discuss the question, but the nations sparred for another year without progress. The Chinese, originally cautious about the Pakistani move, turned eagerly towards negotiations in the spring of 1962, after India's attitude had stiffened. In May an agreement to negotiate was made known, and a provisional border treaty was announced on March 2, 1963.

Peking had carefully maintained a flexible position towards Pakistan. In contrast to India's bitter denunciation of Pakistan's Western alignment in 1954, the Chinese had accepted it mildly, although the threat to their purposes was evident. Chinese officials publicly accepted at face value Pakistan's contention that membership in SEATO would not prevent friendship with China. Official visits were exchanged in 1956, and Chou En-lai's appearance in Karachi was followed by a communiqué, published in *Dawn*, on December 25, saying in part: 'The two Prime Ministers are of the view that the difference between the political systems of Pakistan and China and the divergence of views on many problems should not prevent the strengthening of friendship between their two countries . . . They are happy to place on record that there is no real conflict of interest . . .' In 1959, Peking accepted with restraint the potential threat to its ambitions implied by Ayub's proposed joint defence agreement. The next year, during Sino-Indian border negotiations, the Chinese flatly refused to discuss the areas of Azad Kashmir west of the Karakoram Pass, on the grounds that negotiation should await solution of the Kashmir issue. The Indians reaffirmed their right to negotiate for these territories, which, however, were beyond their immediate control. Despite the public warmth of *Panch Shila*, in its early days, Peking never had supported the Indian position on Kashmir; but by border discussions with Pakistan, particularly on the strategic territory west of Karakoram Pass, the Chinese gave tacit recognition to Pakistani control over Azad Kashmir. In issuing their agreement to negotiate, moreover,

Red China and Pakistan specifically noted that they intended to reach only a provisional border settlement, to be renegotiated 'after the settlement of the dispute over Kashmir between Pakistan and India . . .' This was, for the first time, specific and public refusal by Peking to 'recognise Kashmir's accession to the Indian Union—a point it had previously been careful to obscure.'[20]

These manoeuvres suggest that Peking had made careful preparation for rapprochement with Pakistan. The two nations had co-operated before the American alliance, but Peking's new approach was first used when the Chinese failed to achieve initial concessions from India by negotiation or intimidation. Clearly, however, Peking had more long-range purposes in mind. It had earmarked India as a major enemy on the western flank, for both ideological and strategic reasons. To weaken India, at the proper time, the co-operation of Pakistan had probably long been contemplated—as a political ally and, no doubt, eventually as an agency through which to launch 'proxy war' on the original Soviet model. The domination of Asia would manifestly be impossible without control over India for it is too big to be ignored as a potential military factor. Moreover, India on two counts challenges Peking's attempt to initiate and consolidate its dominance through example: a primary route to political control for both the Soviets and the Chinese. First, India by its size and comparable economic circumstances represents a challenge to Peking's claims that underdeveloped nations can achieve swift modernity only through the Chinese Communist example. Japan, as a 'capitalist' and developed nation, is in a different category. Secondly, India is conducting its own revolution on a modified socialist pattern which competes directly with the Marxist-Leninist dogma that only the Communist Party can lead a successful revolution and that the development of communism is the only means of achieving the goals of revolution. Communist China cannot tolerate a prosperous and stable non-communist India: nor can the Soviet Union. The power structure of the entire communist movement would be destroyed. The Chinese, as India's nearest neighbours and self-appointed guardians of Asia, have clearly decided that, for political and ideological reasons as well as basic strategy, India must be periodically whittled down. The enlistment of Pakistan in this effort is as logical as Russia's use of India to outflank the American presence in Pakistan.

The Chinese, like Russia, were determined to eliminate American influence from Pakistan and to destroy the military alliances. They also wanted Gilgit and its surrounding areas as badly as Russia wanted to deprive them of this territory. It provides an outflanking position south of the Russian Pamirs, one of Peking's irredentist goals. The Chinese also sought absolute control over the Karakoram Pass, which would become an important military position in their hands. The southern edge of the pass is in the Pakistani section of Kashmir. There is strong evidence that Peking had pursued these goals for a number of years as part of their attempt to create a strong anti-Soviet position, as well as on account of their strategic significance in the subcontinent.

Dr Satyanarayan Sinha, on the basis of his contacts with a principal Soviet agent in Central Asia, reports that 'China had planned a full-scale attack on India as early as the spring of 1960'. The Chinese, he says, had assembled at least ten divisions in Sinkiang and were equipping them with Soviet arms in preparation for a limited assault on the northern Himalayas. The purpose was to link the fertile mountain regions with Sinkiang as a source of food to maintain a self-sufficient military force in the western Chinese province. The plan was wrecked when the Soviets, surmising Peking's intentions, cut off arms shipments in March 1960, and Soviet agents instigated an outbreak of guerrilla revolts in several parts of Sinkiang.[21] Moscow's own designs on Sinkiang would have been threatened by a successful Chinese build-up and expansion of its garrison, and so it would probably have acted to prevent an increase of Chinese power in the area, whether or not the purpose was to attack India.

There is, as Dr Sinha points out, considerable evidence to substantiate the belief that active Sino-Soviet border hostilities occurred in 1960. Soviet news agencies date Chinese border violations from that year; Peking, on the other hand, contends that Moscow unilaterally tore up its economic aid agreements with China and recalled thousands of Soviet experts in July 1960. In an official anti-Soviet statement, the Chinese added that the Soviet government then 'provoked troubles on the Sino-Soviet border'.[22] In 1962, the Soviets claimed that 5,000 provocative incidents occurred along the entire border. In one incident, the Soviets reported that 60,000 Kazakh tribesmen fled from Chinese Sinkiang and sought sanctuary across the Soviet border in the Ili Valley, opposite west-central Sinkiang. They demanded arms to fight the Chinese; instead the Russians allowed them to enter Soviet Kazakhstan and trained elements among them as guerrillas to be sent back into Sinkiang for anti-Chinese activities.[23] The Chinese version of this incident was as follows: 'In April and May 1962 the leaders of the CPSU (Soviet Communist Party) used their organs and personnel in Sinkiang, China, to carry out large-scale subversive activities in the Ili region and enticed and coerced several tens of thousands of Chinese citizens into going to the Soviet Union.' Moscow refused to repatriate them, Peking says, 'on the pretext of "the sense of Soviet legality" and "humanitarianism". . . . . This is indeed an astounding event, unheard of in the relations between socialist countries.'[24] In 1963, Peking allowed its tight censorship to reveal that heavy troop reinforcements had been sent to Sinkiang and Manchuria, and it charged Khrushchev with fomenting 'revolutions', 'border disputes' and 'subversive activities' against Chinese Communist rule.[25] In 1964, Peking claimed that Khrushchev had 'engineered border disputes between China and the Soviet Union and even conducted large-scale subversive activities in Sinkiang'.[26] Peking has let it be known that tens of thousands of Chinese have been sent as 'colonialists' to Sinkiang and Manchuria, presumably to shore up defences. At the same time, large numbers of Chinese technicians have been expelled for improper activities from Soviet-controlled Outer Mongolia.

The severity of the conflict between the two communist giants is emphasised by the importance it has assumed in their ideological dispute. The Soviets have admitted that they were fooled by the implications of Mao Tse-tung's statement in 1957 that: 'The wind from the East is beginning to prevail over the wind from the West'. At the time, Mao specifically said it meant that 'the strength of socialism exceeds the strength of imperialism'. However, the Soviet theoretician, Mikhail A. Suslov, told the CPSU Central Committee in a secret report on February 14, 1964: 'In the light of the practical activities of the Chinese leaders in recent years, the true political meaning of their slogan . . . has become all the clearer . . . In other words, that slogan is nothing but an ideological and political expression of the hegemonic aspirations of the Chinese leadership.'[27] No communist has ever given a more damning indictment of communist imperialism.

N

The Chinese so far have repressed most of the evidence of the physical aggression against Red China practised by Stalin, Khrushchev and apparently by their successors, except for their general charges. The long and sustained Soviet attempt to detach all or portions of Sinkiang and Manchuria from Red China lies in the background, however, of the central Chinese contention that Moscow is seeking to maintain and expand a communist empire for the sole purpose of serving Soviet interests. 'In the name of the "international division of labor",' an official Peking statement said on February 4, 1964, 'the leaders of the CPSU oppose the adoption by fraternal countries of the policy of building Socialism by their own efforts and developing their economies on an independent basis, and attempt to turn them into economic appendages. They have tried to force those fraternal countries which are comparatively backward economically to abandon industrialization and become their sources of raw materials and markets for surplus products.' Further, the Soviets, after the destalinisation campaign, have tried 'to change the leadership of other fraternal parties to conform to their will'. Again: '. . . the leaders of the CPSU regard fraternal parties as pawns on their diplomatic chessboard'. And, finally, the Chinese declare: 'Every remark and every word of Khrushchev's are imperial edicts, however wrong or absurd they may be. All the fraternal parties must submissively listen and obey and are absolutely forbidden to criticize or oppose them. This is outright tyranny. It is the ideology of feudal autocrats, pure and simple . . .'[28] Peking clearly has accused the Brezhnev-Kosygin regime of continuing all Khrushchev's policies.

The Chinese openly called for a communist revolt against the system of Soviet rule, as well as against Khrushchev, and this is one of the fundamental issues of the entire dispute. The call was aimed both at members of the Soviet Party and at dissidents throughout the world movement. In an official statement, Peking said:

Now is the time—now it is high time—to repudiate and liquidate Khrushchev's revisionism!*

Here, we would give the leading comrades of the CPSU a piece of advice: Since so many opportunists and revisionists have

---

* A 'revisionist' is one who seeks to change the 'pure' or fundamental tenets of Marxism-Leninism. The Chinese use the word against all who support Moscow.

been thrown on to the rubbish heap of history, why must you obdurately follow their example?

Here, too, we express the hope that those leading comrades of other fraternal Parties who have committed revisionist errors will think this over: What have they gained by following the revisionist line of the leaders of the CPSU?[29]

Thus, the full weight of a massive nation-to-nation clash made the Himalayas one strategic point of conflict, regardless of the wishes of those involved. The Sino-Soviet cold war is separate from the struggle between communism and non-communism and would probably have arisen regardless of the circumstances of the larger conflict. Frustration in their drive for 'world revolution', however, has heightened the communists' internal tension. The Western defence perimeter has contained outward Sino-Soviet expansion so effectively that the two powers probably turned to their inner conflicts more quickly than they otherwise would have done. Peking seems to confirm this thesis by constantly criticising Soviet 'weakness' in the face of Western power, by insisting that communists can take greater 'revolutionary' risks without fear of nuclear war, and by contending that 'revolutionary' momentum must be maintained or the masses will desert the movement.

From all the evidence, the Sino-Soviet hostilities are relatively small-scale border and guerrilla skirmishes, fought quite understandably with many of the same tactics that have been employed in the 'national liberation' struggles against non-communist targets. Soviet infiltrators into Sinkiang, for instance, are given large amounts of ammunition but few weapons; they depend for arms upon captured Soviet equipment which Moscow has supplied to the Chinese. The Sino-Soviet border, like many others throughout the world, is poorly defined. It cuts between territories occupied by men of the same or similar tribes who can be aroused to fight 'foreign' rule and for tribal reunification—on much the same pattern as the Pakhtunistan issue. The guerrilla war does not disturb the capitals or drain their finances and, in fact, most Soviets and Chinese probably know little about it. Regular army units, it is known, are also deployed on both sides of the border, and the possibility always exists that they will go into action. 'There is', says a Soviet diplomat who renounced communism, 'the general feeling

shared by Russians in all social strata that sooner or later there will
be a conflict between China and the Soviet Union, and that China's
alarming rate of economic and military growth, supported by the
nationalistic drive, makes it increasingly inevitable.'[30]

The evidence is clear that Moscow created this Sino-Soviet
struggle more than forty years ago by cynical misuse of Chinese
communism. The Soviets have prosecuted it as ruthlessly as the
Chinese. Peking, after freeing itself from much of Stalin's territorial
encroachment, has merged the fight for independence from the
Soviets with its own designs. Thus, the two communist powers seek
territorial expansion against each other as security or irredentism,
on the classical colonial model, without the camouflage of communist
dogma. When the Chinese grew strong enough to challenge Russia
openly, Khrushchev in fact, as Peking claims, 'applied a succession
of political, economic and military pressures against us and launched
attacks which became increasingly violent'.[31] Among other
measures, Khrushchev, as Stalin had done earlier, attempted to
bring Peking into line through a virtual economic blockade. He left
Chinese industrialisation suspended by tearing up 'hundreds of
contracts', as the Chinese say, and withdrawing thousands of
technicians. Soviet exports to China dropped from $817 million in
1960 to $367 million in 1961, with vital machinery cut by four-fifths.
The 1961 total was inflated by the Soviet export of $67 million worth
of consumer goods, including Cuban sugar, compared with $4·7
million the previous year. Red China, which had had an unfavourable
trade balance with Russia since 1956, exported $551 million to the
Soviets in 1961 compared with $848 million in 1960, partly to
continue repayment of Korean War debts. In 1965, Soviet exports
to China totalled $176 million.

Ironically, Khrushchev succeeded in establishing a 'peace'
image in some quarters of the world at the same time that he engaged
in hostilities with his major 'ally' and attempted to wreck it
economically. This, it appears, was due in part to the world's hope
for peace and in part to the welcome change in the Soviet propaganda line from missile threats to 'peaceful coexistence'. In any
case, some of Khrushchev's moves which were aimed specifically
at Red China were widely construed as evidence of Moscow's
peaceful intent. Diplomats are convinced, for example, that the
Kremlin's major reason for signing the limited nuclear test-ban

treaty of 1963 was to impede Peking's efforts to become a nuclear power. The Soviet-sponsored move to make Asia into an 'atom-free zone', from which nuclear arms would be banned, was clearly directed against both Peking and the United States. Khrushchev gained considerable propaganda benefit, if not tangible advantage, from a proposal to freeze all the boundaries of the world; an obvious reaction to China's claims against Soviet territory. Throughout the early and mid-1960s, as knowledgeable diplomats reported, Moscow's major preoccupation was the China threat, and Soviet policies in many cases were tailored to meet it.

Yet these two powers have demonstrated that they can fight the non-communist world while also fighting each other, as they did in Korea. And the aims and methods of communism as a power system are so much in line that many moves in this intramural conflict contribute at the same time to the central purposes of the world movement. The conflict over strategic military positions on the subcontinent had initiated that development by 1961. The Soviets were building up India as a counterweight to Pakistan and were endeavouring, in every discreet way, to precipitate war. Peking, applying increased pressure to India, was turning towards Pakistan, with results that would augment pressures for the war originally sought by Moscow.

It was against this general background that the Indians set out in late 1961 to drive the Chinese from Aksai Chin.

9

THE CHINESE ATTACK ON INDIA

INDIAN FORCES cautiously opened their 1961 counter-thrust against Chinese encroachment into Ladakh. The Indians completed an important but inadequate supply road from Srinagar to Leh, running through the Kargil sector of the northern cease-fire line. They built up their base in inhospitable Leh. Then they began to probe the Chinese outposts. The Chinese were deeply entrenched in advanced positions which were gradually being extended into Indian territory. They had built a second motor road west of their first supply line and had announced plans for a railway spur. By the end of the year, Nehru was carefully optimistic about the Indian advances, and the Chinese were worried. In November, they warned India to stop its current 'very erroneous and dangerous' strategy. If the Indians continued military operations in Ladakh, 'the Chinese Government would have every reason to send troops to cross the so-called "McMahon Line" and enter the vast area between the crest of the Himalayas and their southern foot'. This was a clear threat to initiate a diversionary flank attack in NEFA, and signalled the strategy Peking eventually used.

Nevertheless, in the spring of 1962, the Indian army continued with a series of operations in Aksai Chin which drastically changed the military situation. By the middle of the year, the Indians had established forty-three new positions in the border area, most of them within territory claimed by China. The new Indian outposts outflanked or leapfrogged Chinese positions, enabling the Indians to cut supply lines, to intensify patrolling and generally to harass the Chinese. This action, together with the stalwartness of Indian soldiers in facing up to the invaders, proved that the Chinese could not expect to penetrate farther into Ladakh without heavy fighting, nor could they intimidate New Delhi into accepting their demands.[1] In August, Nehru reported that the Indian *jawans* had reoccupied some 2,500 square miles of the 12,000 square miles which the Chinese had previously taken. Peking was faced with the fact that it would have to wage some form of war to obtain absolute control over its positions in Aksai Chin, and no doubt the decision to do so was made at about this time.

Meanwhile, diplomatic exchanges continued throughout the summer, and Peking made a final effort to win its aims politically. Tension heightened in May, with the Sino-Pakistan announcement of impending border negotiations. On June 2, the Sino-Indian trade agreement of 1954 on Tibet was allowed to lapse, India refusing to renew it until Chinese forces withdrew from her territory. This was the *ex post facto* demise of *Panch Shila*. The previous December, the month for re-negotiation, Peking had taken the official position that the 'peaceful coexistence' principles of the 1954 agreement applied only to 'questions relating to trade, cultural relations and friendly intercourse'; not to 'all the questions' between the two countries. The Five Principles 'did not even touch on the boundary question'.[2] With tension mounting higher, Peking notified New Delhi on August 27, 1962, that it might 'resort to self-defence, and the Indian side must bear the responsibility for all the consequences . . .' The Chinese again insisted upon negotiations, on the basis of long-standing Peking proposals. They delivered a virtual ultimatum on September 13, demanding that talks begin in Peking on October 15.[3] Nehru was prepared to conduct preliminary talks on the question of reducing tension and providing for troop withdrawals. New Delhi soon discovered, however, that Peking was manoeuvring to lure it into accepting a negotiated settlement on Chinese terms.[4]

Amid this diplomatic subterfuge and considerable propaganda, a Chinese detachment was sent across the McMahon Line into NEFA on September 8, 1962. It established a position near an Indian outpost at Dhola, two miles south of the border. When the Indian government ordered expulsion of the Chinese, a major incident occurred, and Peking immediately claimed 'an attack on China'. This incident, in addition to the previous offensive of Indian patrols in Ladakh, constitutes justification for the claims made by Peking and some others that the Indians started the conflict and the

Chinese fought back in self-defence. Actually, this is an old Chinese trick, which was used in the Korean War among other precedents. As pointed out in *Himalayan Battleground*:

> For political reasons, the Chinese were anxious to make it appear that their aggression—obviously under preparation for several months at least—had been provoked by Indian attacks on Chinese forces on their own side of the border . . . One can safely assume that if no firing had occurred at Dhola, the Chinese would have sought provocations elsewhere until they had an incident to 'justify' the 'self-defense' operations that immediately swept them deep within Indian territory. The success of the Chinese 'defensive' action is reminiscent of similar successful 'defensive' actions taken by the North Koreans at the beginning of the Korean War.[5]

The Chinese paused once more, to demand negotiations, while further skirmishing occurred in NEFA. New Delhi rejected any talks until Chinese forces were withdrawn from Dhola. The pause was clearly another attempt to gain control over all of Aksai Chin, the major immediate objective, by inexpensive political means. Peking evidently had decided already that the stiffening Indian resistance meant it could take Aksai Chin only at heavy cost through a single-front campaign. The diversionary thrust into NEFA was the result. But the combination of intimidation, mounting pressure and diplomatic subterfuge failed again.

Then, on October 20, 1962, the Chinese struck in force. One army hit at Ladakh. A second plunged southward from Tibet into NEFA, crossing the McMahon Line at four separate points. The middle sector of the Sino-Indian border, north-west of Nepal, remained quiet. The Chinese caught the Indian army woefully unprepared in both battle sectors. Primary units had been deployed against Pakistan and generally remained in that position. The army's expansion since 1961 had been slow and irregular, handicapped by shortages of equipment, a scarcity of officers and completely inadequate roads in the remote, mountainous areas under immediate Chinese threat. Nehru's confidant, V. K. Krishna Menon, serving as Defence Minister amid numerous other duties, had been the most insistent among the Indian officials in minimising any danger from Peking. He was widely blamed for the unpreparedness and was removed on October 31. He was replaced by Y. B. Chavan, an aggressive politician from Bombay, who soon became popular with the military, particularly since he avoided interference in military matters. Chavan had to rebuild an establishment that, from all appearances, was not only disorganised by improper management but had rusted through the long lull created by India's faith in Chinese 'coexistence'.*

Chinese forces attacked in Ladakh with a six-to-one superiority in numbers and firepower. Until mid-September, the Indians had deployed only an under-armed brigade to cover a front of nearly 400 miles. Road communications were defective, and supplies were carried across a hazardous air lane. The Indians had only inadequate means of reinforcing threatened points on this battleground of the moon, which soared to 16,000 feet. The Chinese used artillery and heavy mortars, employing armour in one instance, against Indian forces whose heaviest guns were infantry mortars. During some of the fiercest fighting of the limited war, the Chinese made substantial but irregular gains against stubborn resistance in Ladakh. At their deepest penetration, they more than doubled the westward advances they had made during the nibbling encroachment between 1959-62. But the campaign proved definitely that the conquest of Aksai Chin would be formidable.[6]

In NEFA, where in general the Indians were even less prepared, the Chinese gains were more spectacular. Deploying an estimated 110,000 men on this front,[7] the attackers probed for weak spots in an evident search for an area capable of quick exploitation. They found it at Thag La ridge, in the tangle of mountains on the north-west corner of the Kameng Frontier Division of NEFA, near the borders of Bhutan, Tibet and India. The Chinese had struck this area in their first southward penetration of September 8. Now, they poured over the Thag La slopes in a massive dawn attack which New Delhi learned about through a rebroadcast of a Peking announcement. Indian forces, in the midst of reorganisation, had built up a defensive strength of only one brigade, to meet an enemy with at least a

---

*Lieutenant-General B. M. Kaul, the corps commander for the NEFA operations, shocked India in early 1967 by charging in his book, *The Untold Story*, that the military establishment was woefully unprepared for the Chinese attack because top leaders had underestimated the danger and had withheld necessary funds.

five-to-one advantage. The Indians were supplied by a 120-mile mountain road, barely capable of holding up under trucks carrying one ton of supplies.

The first Chinese offensive in this area, October 20–24, forced the Indians to fall back to positions south of the Namka Chu river, and gave the attackers control of the monastery town of Tawang and surrounding territory, substantially inside India. The second offensive, beginning November 17 after another diplomatic lull, was a massive penetration backed by six Chinese brigades. The Chinese outflanked the strategic Se La Pass and plunged past Bomdila to the plains of Assam. The advance threatened Tezpur on the Brahmaputra river, some ninety-six miles, on a straight line, south of the border. The offensive also threatened the conquest of Assam, a state rich in oil and rice and the tea and jute which provide nearly one-third of India's export income. This campaign was fought largely in altitudes ranging from 14,000 to 17,000 feet, and Indian soldiers from the plains were critically affected by the heights. The Chinese also used tactics and tricks familiar in the Korean War but new to the Indians, who had inadequately studied that conflict. Weak points were overrun by 'human wave' tactics. Indian military authorities concluded, as had those of the United Nations, 'that the Chinese placed higher value on weapons than on the human material which they freely expended'.[8] Strong points were outflanked by troops clambering across mountains that were sometimes considered militarily impassable. Chinese infiltrators, wearing tribal dress or captured Indian uniforms, penetrated Indian positions close enough to open deadly fire with concealed weapons. The Chinese intercepted Indian radio communications and issued false orders in local dialects.

The breakthrough at Se La Pass and the advance to the plains took only four days. The fighting in this area, says the Indian official account, produced the only 'really serious setback' of the war. It was also the campaign most widely reported in the world press. A third major front, however, was also involved. It was in the Lohit Division of NEFA, to the far east, near the Burmese border. Here the Chinese fought bitterly in mid-November for Walong, launching sixteen separate attacks. The action was broken off, says the Indian account, when the remnants of the Indian brigade were withdrawn on orders of November 16. The Chinese followed the main force for some forty miles deeper into Indian territory and continued to fire at stragglers until December 3.

The Chinese, however, had announced a spectacular unilateral cease-fire on November 21. They promised to withdraw north of the McMahon Line by December 1, a deadline that they largely met. India did not formally accept the cease-fire, but the Chinese had bound her to it by announcing the move with great propaganda effect. Thus Peking had broken off the action at the moment of India's deepest humiliation, and had created world-wide political pressures against an Indian counter-attack.

India was thrown into turmoil by the suddenness of the attack and the swiftness of the advance. On one hand, there arose a near-panic fear of major invasion and, particularly, of air attacks against India's crowded cities. It was sufficient to bend non-alignment to the degree whereby Nehru unhesitatingly accepted prompt offers of Anglo-American help. The late Dr Sudhir Ghosh, an intimate of Gandhi and Nehru, says in his posthumously published book, *Gandhi's Emissary*, that a special appeal by Nehru for American air protection was delivered to President Kennedy on the night of November 19, 1962, by Ambassador B. K. Nehru. The communication, which long was kept in the prime minister's private files, mentioned sixteen squadrons of fighter planes, presumably to be manned by American pilots. An American aircraft carrier was immediately dispatched toward the Bay of Bengal. This support and rapid shipments of emergency arms had significant influence. On the other hand, the emergency created an unexpected sense of national unity, a nationalism which was expressed unmistakably for the first time in Free India. From volunteer labour and militia training to the donation of gold ornaments for the national cause, Indians of all strata responded to the emergency with a dedication of purpose that was unforeseen by New Delhi. The national reaction was portentous. It would return in 1965. Its immediate effect, however, was to reinforce the government's determination to defend the nation's territory as fully as possible. New Delhi had made that decision, without an expression of national support, in attempting to block Chinese encroachment in Ladakh and in a formal policy determination to defend NEFA, despite military liabilities.

The nation instantly turned as fervently against the Chinese Communists as it had welcomed their friendship during the period of coexistence when the cry was: 'Hindi–Chini Bhai Bhai!' (Indians and Chinese are brothers). Nehru thereafter sharply distinguished between Chinese and Soviet communism. 'We believe and many countries agree with us', he told Parliament, 'that China as constituted today is an aggressive and expansionist country, possibly with vast designs for the future . . . China has become a menace and a danger to the world. It has been our misfortune that we have been the victims of this aggression. This aggression has made not only us but other countries realise the nature of the problem that faces the world.'[9] His own personal feelings were revealed most strongly when he wrote to Chou En-lai in the midst of the campaign, on October 27, 1962: 'Nothing in my long political career has hurt and grieved me more than the fact that the hopes and aspirations for peaceful and friendly neighborly relations which we entertained and to promote which my colleagues in the Government of India and myself worked so hard . . . have been shattered by the hostile and unfriendly twist given on India–China relations during the past two years.'[10] The Indian leader had just declared a state of national emergency under which, among other effects, leaders of a Communist Party faction which supported and applauded the Chinese attack were imprisoned indefinitely without charge or trial under 'Defence of India Rules'. Rule by decree continued thereafter and principal pro-Chinese communist leaders were detained for several years. The nation was hurt, humiliated, frightened, angry and worried. Its dominating impulse, reflected long afterwards, was voiced by the mild and soft-spoken Dr Radhakrishnan, the President: 'The Indian reverses in NEFA should be regarded as a matter of sorrow, shame and humiliation. Such a thing should not be repeated. Our army has to be re-oriented and refashioned according to the latest canons of military science. We have to retrieve our lost prestige.'[11]

Peking no doubt was surprised and angered by this reaction. The whole course of its intermingled military-diplomatic pressure appeared to betray the belief, or the hope, that India would capitulate under the October 20 assault, granting the minimum Chinese concessions. And these minimum demands, quite clearly, were control over an unassailable military position in Aksai Chin, if not over the entire plateau, plus a cease-fire position that would weaken Indian defensive capabilities in NEFA. This was the purpose behind a rather confused debate over the dates involved in establishing a truce line. Peking insisted in a note of October 26 and again in its armistice announcement that both sides should withdraw twenty kilometres behind the 'line of actual control' as of November 7, 1959. The Indians countered by suggesting a return to the line of September 8, 1962. The differences were substantial, because the Chinese sought to include in their definition of the earlier line some of the advances they had made during their offensive. This amounted to some 2,500 square miles in Ladakh, Nehru told Parliament. 'Under these deceptively worded proposals,' says *Himalayan Battleground*, 'the Indians would have been forced to give the Chinese everything needed for a secure military grip on the part of Ladakh where their roads were constructed' and would have lost other important positions, including control of the Karakoram Pass. 'In the eastern part of the frontier, the Indians would have had to accept the Chinese version of the McMahon Line (which runs considerably south of the original Line) as the "line of actual control"—which was not only far from the actual situation of 1959, but would also, in effect, surrender Assam (and Bhutan) to Chinese control.' Elsewhere, the Indian military position 'would have been equally hopeless' and Sikkim and Nepal would be completely exposed to a new Chinese offensive.[12]

An alternative proposal—a rough compromise between the Indian and Peking versions of the 'control line'—was offered in December 1962, by six Afro-Asian nations meeting at Colombo, Ceylon. The Colombo Proposal was adverse to Indian interests, but Nehru accepted it; quietly, at first, to avoid arousing his own jingoists. The Chinese initially attempted to attach modifications that, in one respect, would have meant that Indian military forces would be barred from the twenty-kilometre demilitarised zone in NEFA, which would be patrolled only by police. Nehru went so far as to give local commanders authority to use police instead of troops if conditions warranted. But he could not accept this *de facto* erosion of the Indian defence position. Peking rejected the Colombo Plan on another point, and the boundary dispute remains unsettled.

These are the terms and the machinations of a conqueror. They reinforce the evidence that Peking had no intention of adjudicating the border, and that one of its primary political purposes was to humiliate and intimidate India and to tarnish its world reputation.

In fact, Peking escaped from this episode without major condemnation in the non-aligned world, where the political stakes were highest, and without being branded for aggression. '. . . the Indian people and government', says Frank Moraes, 'were genuinely taken aback when the non-aligned Afro-Asian countries continued to be non-aligned in the Sino-Indian conflict.'[13]

Moraes, among others, makes the suggestion that India, by a more flexible policy towards Chinese border problems, might have obtained a settlement with Peking, as did Burma, Nepal and Pakistan. This is rejected today by the Chinese experts of the Indian government. They believe that Peking has set out on a deliberate campaign to reduce India in political, economic and geographic size, through diplomatic and military nibbling. The thesis appears to be sound, and the attack of 1962 quite logically marked the opening phase of such a long-range effort. Chou En-lai partially confirmed this after the Sino-Pakistan agreement by suggesting the age-old oriental tradition that large powers can grant concessions to smaller ones without losing face, but to do so to a nation of comparable size would be the gravest sign of weakness. Explaining the settlements with nations around India, Chou said: 'Since the boundary questions left over by history are settled through friendly negotiations, and since China is bigger than these neighbouring countries and the border areas are mostly sparsely populated, China always made more concessions to the opposite party in the process of mutual accommodation in order to seek a settlement of the question.'[14] The Indian government experts believe Communist China may be willing to coexist legitimately, on Western terms, only with a recognisably second-rate India; one that is economically weak, politically unimportant and shorn of the Himalayan buffers now surrounding it—Kashmir, Nepal, Sikkim, Bhutan and NEFA.[15]

Militarily, the Chinese broke off the attack, particularly in NEFA, at the point where they might have encountered stronger and more effective resistance on the plains. The Indian army had assembled reinforcements and armour to meet the attackers on more favourable terrain, and the odds would doubtless have shifted considerably; while the Chinese would have been under the handicap of lengthy supply lines and the exhaustion of long campaigning. The Indian Defence Ministry suggests that a combination of factors caused the withdrawal: Peking quickly achieved the political objectives of isolating India and impressing her neighbours with Chinese power; the prompt Anglo-American arms aid altered the military situation; the Chinese were short of supplies and were desperately searching the world for food for the mainland; India's resistance was unexpected.

Further, the campaign was a classic example of limited war. The attacker maintained control at all times and accomplished a number of objectives with minimum loss and little fear of significant retaliation. It is probable, therefore, that the assault was planned as a hit-and-run guerrilla use of large conventional forces, a pre-timed cease-fire being an integral tactic. Even under this strategy, however, local commanders may have been given the option of striking for further targets in strategic Ladakh and rich Assam, if circumstances were favourable. An Indian collapse, therefore, or the failure of New Delhi to ask or to receive Western help could have produced much more fighting. As it happened, the Defence Ministry reports with justification: 'There was no major engagement; the main forces of the Indian Army were never committed.'[16]

The Soviet Union, on which Nehru since 1957 had relied increasingly to restrain Peking, took up an ambiguous position. The Soviets had given India cautious and limited support during the Sino-Indian incidents of 1959. Through Tass, the Kremlin called for a settlement in September 1959, and said: 'This incident on the Chinese-Indian border is certainly deplorable. . . . The Chinese and Soviet peoples are linked by the unbreakable bonds of fraternal friendship. . . . Friendly co-operation between the USSR and India is successfully developing in keeping with the ideas of peaceful coexistence.'[17] This was interpreted as a clear warning to Peking to avoid interfering in Soviet strategy for India. In October, Khrushchev told the Supreme Soviet, 'We would be happy if there were no incidents on the Sino-Indian border'. Two years later, the governments announced that India had purchased eight ANI2 Soviet transport planes for use in the Ladakh area, with more transports and helicopters to be purchased later. The Soviets had agreed, in May 1962, to supply some supersonic MIG jets to India and to build a factory for Indian-made jets. This deal, although deplored by the Indian Air Force which wanted American planes, was explained by Indian diplomats as necessary to conserve foreign exchange, since Moscow had agreed to accept rupees. These moves, cautious as they were, generally inspired confidence in New Delhi, particularly since they were accompanied by a rising chorus of criticism from Peking of the help Moscow was giving to a 'reactionary' government. The MIG deal established a public Soviet military position in India, which appeared to be much exaggerated by propaganda. It may have helped to time the Chinese assault.

When the Chinese attack came, however, the Soviets waited silently for weeks before voicing lukewarm support for India. The Kremlin had been unable to prevent the offensive, which coincided with the Cuban missile crisis, and doubtless had no prior knowledge that it would occur. Its original silence has been interpreted as disapproval of the Chinese action, but it was no help to a sorely pressed and politically isolated India. On October 25, *Pravda* and *Izvestia*, the party and government newspapers in Moscow, in their editorials supported Peking's demand for negotiations on terms unfavourable to India. The papers carefully avoided 'choosing right and wrong' and named no aggressors, a subtle warning to pro-Soviet Indian elements to avoid supporting anti-Chinese sentiment.[18] The Soviet statements, moreover, applauded the Chinese proposals as demonstrating a sincere 'desire to put an end to the conflict'. By mid-November, Nehru was able to tell Parliament only that the Soviet Ambassador had expressed 'good wishes' on behalf of Moscow, although a special emissary from the External Affairs Ministry had gone to Moscow and Warsaw specifically to obtain stronger Russian condemnation of the Chinese.[19] The Soviets did agree shortly afterwards to continue the MIG project, including the sale of fighter planes, but the Peking truce followed quickly and the first four MIGs did not reach Bombay until February 1963. It was not until December 12, 1962, with the Cuban crisis over, that Khrushchev contended that the Himalayan conflict benefited only the 'imperialists' and strengthened the 'reactionary' while weakening the 'progressive' forces in India.

The Chinese have revealed, moreover, that Khrushchev told Peking in mid-October, 1962, that the Soviets were convinced India planned to attack Red China and fully approved any punitive measures the Chinese wanted to take. 'On October 13 and 14, 1962,' says an unrefuted official Chinese document, 'Khrushchev told the Chinese Ambassador the following: Their information on Indian preparations to attack China was similar to China's. If they were in

China's position, they would have taken the same measures. A neutral attitude on the Sino-Indian boundary question was impossible. If anyone attacked China and said they were neutral, it would be an act of betrayal.'[20] When Khrushchev later changed his public posture, the Chinese made it clear that they regarded the shift as opportunism.

The weakest aspect of the Chinese offensive was the possibility that a flank attack somewhere along the supply lines stretching ultimately to Sinkiang would cut off the advancing forces and isolate them deep in India. The Soviets were in the best position to apply this flank pressure and would have had a military motive for doing so, if they feared erosion of their own position through prospective Chinese dominance over part of India. If the Soviets prevented a Chinese assault on India through guerrilla action in 1960, however, there was no evidence that they made any hostile gesture during Sino-Indian hostilities in 1962. Three years later, Vice-Premier Ho Lung charged Moscow with having sponsored a revolt in 1962 against Peking rule over Sinkiang, but he did not give the month of this occurrence; nor did he complain that it interfered with Peking's 'defensive war' against India. This complaint undoubtedly would have been made if the 'revolt' had occurred at the end of the year. Most probably, Ho referred to the already publicised incident of the Kazakh migrations and Soviet-instigated guerrilla action in the Ili district in April and May. This suggests that the Soviets were quite prepared to launch limited guerrilla attacks for their own purposes in the spring, but were unwilling to revive them to aid India during the winter. Although Moscow was evidently worried by Chinese successes in Assam, its policies were determined by analysis of the probable impact on the Sino-Soviet power balance, not by what was happening to India.

The Soviets, it is true, were deeply involved in the Cuban affair, but so were the United States and Great Britain. By rushing arms to India, despite their own troubles, the Anglo-American powers took the risk that they might ultimately be drawn deeper into a conflict on the subcontinent, far distant from their capitals. This was, proportionately, a graver gamble than the theoretical prospect that the massed regular Soviet armies in Central Asia might have to beat off Chinese reprisal attacks from Central Asia. Politically, the Soviets were clearly embarrassed by the necessity of choosing sides between

O

an expensive non-aligned supporter and a communist 'ally'. Among other aspects, the embarrassment emphasises the point that hard-line elements are strong in the world movement and that, regardless of the Sino-Soviet quarrel, Moscow would find it difficult to maintain discipline while actually taking measures to preserve peace. The Soviets continued to call the Indians their 'friends', but the Chinese remained their 'brothers'.

Pakistan held the second major military flank position to the long Chinese columns. From the airfield at Gilgit, it is possible to destroy the main Chinese base at Kashgar, Sinkiang, the centre for all troops and supplies moving southward.[21] Thus, in theory, the power controlling Gilgit could seriously cripple Peking's southward expansionist plans against India; at least until a more remote Sinkiang base and a network of alternate communications could be developed. This was a second important reason why the Chinese wanted to establish themselves in the Hunza district of Azad Kashmir, south of Mintaka Pass, and why they were evidently prepared to pay a high price for this position. If President Ayub had been genuinely interested in defending the subcontinent against all outside intrusion, he could have made a gesture towards using Gilgit as a deterrent base during the height of the Chinese offensive. Although potentially dangerous to Pakistan, such a move might have persuaded the Indians to join with her. There is no evidence, however, that any step of this sort was contemplated; certainly it was not initiated. Ayub had wisely pointed out that the divided subcontinent invited attack, but he had neglected to emphasise a second axiom of equal validity: an attack on one nation of a divided subcontinent constituted a threat to both nations.

Instead, Pakistan quite evidently sought to obtain all the profit it could from India's embarrassment. Although Ayub made no effort to exploit the military situation by attacking Kashmir, he did follow a political line that was certain to exacerbate Indo-Pakistan relations. With India violently anti-Chinese, the Pakistanis continued border negotiations with Peking during the fighting and followed these with a number of other steps constituting a moderate rapprochement with the Chinese. India protested against the border discussion on the grounds that all of Kashmir was 'legally' hers, and Pakistan had no authority to discuss questions relating to the 'occupied' sections; but the Indians were more affronted because Pakistan so ostentatiously dealt with the enemy at the moment of their great ordeal. They did not acknowledge that, in less serious circumstances, they had adopted the same practice of treating as a friend the 'enemy of my enemy', by embracing Soviet Russia in reaction to the US–Pakistan pact.

Announcement of the provisional Sino-Pakistan border agreement on March 2, 1963, intensified the clamour and created Indian apprehensions that multiplied for the next three years. The details were obscured by discrepancies in the maps published by Pakistan and Red China and by the vagueness of public announcements. It appeared, however, that despite prolonged bargaining the Pakistanis had made a deal of doubtful value to themselves and of considerable potential danger. In the main transfer of territory, the status of which had previously been uncertain, Peking obtained some 2,500 square miles of Hunza lying in Kashmir south of Mintaka Pass and pointing towards Gilgit. Pakistan acquired 750 square miles of grazing land and salt mines in terrain previously occupied and developed by the Chinese. The Foreign Minister, Zulfikar Ali Bhutto, particularly lauded this Chinese cession. He added, in reference to a second main element of the agreement, that Pakistan also obtained access to all the passes in the Karakoram range and three-quarters of the famed mountain climbers' peak, K-2, which had never been considered Chinese. The Pakistanis had never maintained actual control over the southern exit of strategic Karakoram Pass, but they had a claim to the territory stretching westward from the pass to the terrain they did control; this title, however, appeared to be watered down by the acceptance of access, rather than control, over the passes and by the rephrasing of Sino-Pakistan statements on the question. Although the Chinese did not obtain legal control over the southern exit of Karakoram Pass, they hold its northern entrance, and the use of this gateway during an emergency will obviously depend upon power. 'Foregoing a claim to 12,050 square miles in order to clinch a deal', noted one commentator, 'may have been realistic, but such concessions did not represent a first-rate achievement.'[22] For the settlement, the Pakistanis also relinquished the claims made by published but disputable Pakistani maps to part of Sinkiang: a potential bargaining point, at least.

The border agreement in general follows the principle of delineating boundaries by mountain watersheds, as demanded by India.

Thus New Delhi, it has been said, should have no objection to the terms. The legalisms were further observed by specifying renegotiation if India's claims to Azad Kashmir were recognised. This point clearly rested, however, upon Peking's willingness to abandon territory to a rival of equal size—an unlikely contingency, since Peking now had a vested interest in making sure India did not secure that portion of Azad Kashmir. The argument in defence of the pact further states that Peking withdrew from Chinese-held territory to fulfil its terms, whereas Pakistan was not obliged to abandon terrain under its control.[23] But a portion of Hunza which went to China had apparently been evacuated by Pakistani police in the mid-1950s to avoid a potential clash with the Chinese.[24] Finally, Pakistani fear or respect for newly demonstrated Chinese military power seemed implicit in another argument on behalf of the treaty. The Pakistanis contend that peaceable agreement on the border helped the West, because it reduced the possibility that Peking would attempt to redefine the boundary by force, a move that would threaten Western involvement. The Foreign Minister, Ali Bhutto, more explicitly suggested that the government was concerned over the possibility of a Chinese attack similar to that on India. 'Surely,' he said in a speech at Dacca on April 8, 1963, 'as a Government it is our responsibility to see that such a situation, God forbid, is not repeated for our people in which we are unnecessarily involved in a misunderstanding with a neighbour and a great power. Surely we would not like to see the tantrums and all the crisis that has been created as a result of misunderstanding over the boundary between People's Republic of China and India.'

What made the pact particularly dangerous was the fact that it altered the geopolitical situation still further. In the east, the Chinese increased their influence over Karakoram Pass, one of their strategic objectives in Kashmir. In the north-west, they acquired a beachhead within Kashmir through the Pakistani cession of lands in Hunza, south of Mintaka Pass. This is extremely rough country, but no worse than that which the trained Chinese guerrillas have conquered in Korea and Ladakh; therefore it must be considered as terrain which the Chinese can and will exploit militarily.

In Hunza, the Chinese have a position deep within Kashmir from which to exert significant military pressure on the rest of the mountain state. The concession apparently brought them close to the

Gilgit airfield. It was from this area that a Pakistani column moved overland in the war of 1947–8 to threaten Srinagar. The possibility cannot be excluded that, at some propitious time, the Chinese themselves might use their own forces for guerrilla or infantry attack along a similar route. Theoretically, they have the capability of also assaulting Kashmir by land from the Karakoram Pass and from Ladakh. In the light of the 1962 conflict, these possibilities constitute a grave and permanent menace to Indian Kashmir. In addition, Chinese officials have ostentatiously visited the Gilgit airfield, giving rise to belief in some Indian military circles that Peking has acquired the use of this landing ground. Gilgit directly threatens the Indian position in the Vale of Kashmir, but it was not used for aerial action in the war of 1965. Nevertheless, the new Chinese influence in Kashmir, and heightened Sino-Pakistani co-operation, intensified Indian apprehensions between 1963 and 1965 and contributed to the atmosphere of war.

The new position in Hunza also constituted a spring board for potential Chinese outflanking movements against the Soviet Pamirs, to the north, one of Peking's irredenta. Dr Sinha reports that the Chinese started to exploit this potentiality in 1963, but had to give way to the Soviets in an attempt to secure a further outflanking foothold in Afghanistan. This phase of the Sino-Soviet cold war, which doubtless remains unfinished, directly concerned Pakistan. One of Moscow's chief weapons in securing Kabul's favour is the capacity and evident willingness to step up Afghan-backed claims for the establishment of Pakhtunistan. Moreover, the Pakistanis had apparently placed themselves at a further disadvantage: they had allowed the Chinese to come within military striking distance of Gilgit. Peking wants the airfield as a pressure point against the Pamirs and needs to eliminate its possible use as a deterrent against further Chinese attack on the subcontinent. It was probably prepared to take it if necessary. Although Sino-Pakistan relations were cordial on the surface during the years immediately following the agreement, they were almost identical with the early phase of the Sino-Indian period of 'friendship'. The possibility that Peking might find it advantageous to turn against Pakistan in the future could not be excluded by national planners; but a primary means of holding the Chinese in check had evidently been bargained away by Rawalpindi. In the meantime, Pakistan quite evidently has placed itself in a position inviting stronger Chinese and Russian pressures over Gilgit. It is conceivable that it might be threatened by Chinese attack unless Gilgit were made available for anti-Soviet pressure; while simultaneously it might be threatened by Russia, through Afghanistan, to prevent this.

Peking, no doubt by design, had completely changed the strategic situation in the Himalayas and in Kashmir, by assault and by diplomacy. The Chinese military positions in eastern Ladakh and Hunza vetoed all the laborious plans by which the United Nations had striven for fifteen years to obtain a Kashmir settlement. Each of these proposals had been based upon the maximum withdrawal of Indian and Pakistani military forces, an obvious impossibility with expansionist China entrenched in the state. The same pressure from Peking nullified any prospect of independence for Kashmir and seriously clouded the practicability of such alternative suggestions as a confederation. It also weakened the possibility of holding a fair plebiscite, even with Indian agreement.

Further, the new geopolitics emphasised:

> . . . the great strategic importance of the mountainous regions of Kashmir to the security of both Pakistan and India. Neither of the governments can safely afford to allow Kashmir to come entirely under the control of the other. Gilgit and Baltistan [the territory lying eastward of Gilgit] are certainly vital to Pakistan, while the Indian defense system would be gravely weakened by the loss of Ladakh. The best—indeed only suitable—access routes to both Baltistan and Ladakh run through the Kashmir valley. No proposed solution ignoring these fundamental security considerations can possibly form the basis for agreement between Pakistan and India, or between either of them and China.[25]

Yet this reality was almost entirely overlooked. '. . . India and Pakistan,' says a historian, 'which were both threatened by China and should have been joined in defending the subcontinent, were pursuing opposite courses, a sad consequence of their own quarrel over Kashmir.'[26] The arguments at the United Nations and parallel diplomatic and political initiatives over Kashmir followed the same old pattern. Pakistan contended, in essence, that nothing had changed since 1947; India insisted upon the 'legal' right to absorb Indian Kashmir. Pakistan seemed to be obsessed by the drive to secure the whole state, or at least the Vale and surrounding territory. There were strong and understandable internal pressures for this, but Pakistan's main argument of self-defence was not necessarily convincing. '. . . the present cease-fire line', President Ayub said of Kashmir, 'is just like a grip around our neck. That is the military meaning of the present situation.' He referred to the threat of Indian aggression but Indian aggressiveness had been proved neither by events nor logic. To make his point, Ayub had to ignore the proven aggressiveness of Peking.

In the strategic situation India was somewhat more realistic, even though legalistic politicians continued to berate her for refusing to accept a plebiscite. Nehru's early offer of formal partition along the *de facto* borders of the cease-fire line still held. Indian officials subsequently offered to make some adjustments militarily favourable to Pakistan. This was, of course, insufficient to satisfy either the political or strategic demands of Pakistan, but it went further than any proposal from Rawalpindi. After all, the Indians had discovered a new enemy on their borders—and a real enemy, despite Pakistani efforts to blame the attack on Indian provocation. New Delhi was preoccupied with preparations to meet any subsequent Chinese threat, and Kashmir was a secondary issue; certainly, it was subordinate for the country as a whole. In this atmosphere, the willingness to recognise Azad Kashmir was a considerable conces- sion, for many Indian military officials were genuinely concerned over the new Chinese position around Gilgit.

Through the swift and shrewd application of limited warfare, the Chinese had accomplished a number of objectives. Militarily, they held strong positions in Aksai Chin with little chance that the Indians would again try to dislodge them. They had strengthened their strategic position in the Himalayas against Russia, India and Pakistan. Reports that an old caravan route between Hunza and Kashgar was being renewed indicated further attempts to exploit this advantage. Politically, Peking had humbled and discredited India and had demonstrated its own power to a watching world. The Chinese carefully timed their 'armistice' to prevent any Indian counter-attacks that might alter the picture of Chinese superiority over its giant rival. Indian prestige fell, particularly in the Afro-Asian sphere, where New Delhi had placed particular diplomatic emphasis. Pakistan was emboldened. The events leading to 1965 were strongly influenced by Pakistani belief that India had been revealed as weak and blundering; a sudden shift from its efficient aggressiveness in the Goa incident. The Pakistanis also thought they would have got more help from Peking in anti-Indian hostilities than they did.

Economically, the Chinese had set back Indian rehabilitation to a substantial if unmeasured degree. The Indians were forced to prepare for the worst possible threat from China and this entailed the expensive army outlay which Nehru had sought to avoid. India's foreign exchange holdings dropped by approximately $100 million to a disturbingly low average of around $500 million, with most of the drain going for arms, and many economic goals of the Third Plan were unfulfilled, partly because of rearmament. Most of these results, no doubt, were carefully anticipated by the Chinese. It is possible that they finally decided to launch the offensive primarily to prevent Indian erosion of their position in Aksai Chin, but they planned for more extensive objectives. If the Indians had not begun their attack in Ladakh, the Chinese would have taken the strategic territory they wanted, until stopped by power; and, most probably, they would have opened the political offensive anyway at a propitious time. This was deliberate counter-revolution, to slow down Indian progress.

The Chinese failed, however, to accomplish a number of other apparently primary objectives. India did not capitulate nor did the country fall apart into quarrelling factions; rather, it was united with surprising universality behind the determination to resist further Chinese pressure. The government, instead of collapsing, turned more to the right, contrary to the desires of both Peking and Moscow, as Khrushchev noted. Despite considerable economic distress, the country's rehabilitation was far from crippled. Instead of breaking the spirit of the Indian army, the Chinese had aroused it to the point where the recovery of military, as well as national prestige was a prime motivation during subsequent years. Finally, Peking had alerted its adversary into preparedness, committing the same mistake Stalin had made by launching the Korean War and reminding the West of its weakness. The Chinese, therefore, lost as much, in terms of long-range objectives, as they gained in short-term advantage. Yet Peking did not abandon the tactics which had proved so unproductive; instead, typically, it relied more than ever upon them. The incomplete results of the first military attack only increased the Chinese stake in another war on the subcontinent. There is strong evidence that they set out quickly to encourage the Pakistanis to start it.

In its first mood of humiliation and frustration, India had little left from the shambles of the brief war except pride and a fierce sense of independence. When it set out, therefore, to rebuild its strength against China, it clung doggedly to that independence. After accepting emergency shipments of Anglo-American arms valued at $60 million, Nehru restored non-alignment as the central policy. This was a matter of international and domestic politics, as well as pride. The government's Chinese experts believed that one of Peking's intentions was to drive New Delhi into Western alignment, in order further to injure its standing among uncommitted nations. From this point of view the Indian policy was wise.

But the government also insisted upon a practically all-India arms build-up with moderate foreign support. Among other measures, India immediately increased the defence budget by 12 per cent. In 1964, Chavan the Defence Minister announced a five-year rearmament programme designed to prepare the country for any type of Chinese aggression. Obviously, to defend itself adequately, India needed arms that could resist the greatest possible conventional attack from Red China, as well as the means to fight a limited or guerrilla war. In pursuing this programme, however, Indian officials apparently overlooked the necessity of maintaining a suitable arms balance on the subcontinent. They made no adequate effort to quiet Pakistani fears.

Pakistan reacted with predictable anger to every Indian move towards rearmament. President Ayub and other leading officials frequently attacked what they called 'massive' foreign arms shipment to India. Ayub absented himself on a hunting trip to avoid accepting prior American notification of the plan to provide emergency weapons to New Delhi. Later, he told Washington and London bluntly that they must abandon the aid-India programme to keep Pakistan's friendship. At various times, the Pakistanis insisted publicly that the Western arms should be furnished only on condition that India settle the Kashmir problem, presumably on Pakistan's terms. Ayub declared that India was in no danger from Red China, and Bhutto insisted the Indians would not fight again. 'India,' he said during a Washington visit, 'at the appropriate time, will negotiate a settlement with China on her border dispute. India has no intention whatsoever of allowing another conflict with the Chinese.'[27]

Far from being massive, Anglo-American help was moderate and was limited to non-offensive equipment of primary value to mountain divisions. It was carefully allotted for the deliberate purpose of maintaining a practicable arms balance. Washington and London also made it absolutely clear that they had no intention of forcing Indian capitulation on Kashmir in return for this help. Former US Ambassador J. K. Galbraith underlined the point in a New Delhi press conference on December 28, 1962. 'The American assistance is in no way contingent on an India-Pakistan agreement on the Kashmir problem', he said. 'The USA will not put a price on its aid and it is not out for a bargain. When our friends are in trouble, we are not doing business that way.'[28] The Anglo-American powers strengthened their assistance by implicit promises of active air support against any Chinese bombing attacks on India's crowded cities.

Soviet military assistance was of only marginal value in meeting a new Chinese attack, but MIG planes and anti-aircraft missiles were of more consequence in terms of Pakistani fears. Pakistan clearly included Soviet arms in its condemnations and sometimes mentioned them, but subordinated the point to stronger criticism of Anglo-American efforts. This distortion was due possibly to the fact that Pakistan was beginning to move somewhat closer to Russia. The Indians supplied much of their new equipment from their own resources. The rearmament programme, as a whole, was modest in relation to the threat posed against India; but it did alter the balance on the subcontinent, giving Pakistan cause for complaint.

It was during this time that Pakistan and Red China concluded a trade agreement in January 1963, a barter economic arrangement and a cultural accord later in the year. They also reached an agreement in August which permitted Pakistan International Airlines to fly to Canton and Shanghai, and which was described by the US State Department as 'an unfortunate breach of free world solidarity'. Pakistanis claimed it was made necessary by the refusal of landing rights in other Asian countries, but the agreement permitted an increased volume of Chinese Communist travel to points as distant as troubled Africa. Ostentatious state visits were resumed. When Chou En-lai and Ch'en Yi, the Foreign Minister, were invited to Pakistan in February 1964, the State Department declared: 'We consider it unfortunate that the leaders of the Chinese regime should be accorded an opportunity to pay a "friendly visit" to Pakistan, a country allied with us against communist aggression.' Influential segments of the Pakistani press quickly adopted a pro-Peking line that eventually reached fulsome proportions, and on occasion Chinese Communist propaganda was openly preached. The leading newspapers again publicly questioned the value to Pakistan of its Western alliances, because they had failed to break the Kashmir impasse.

Many Indians and most government officials read into these developments the threat of close Sino-Pakistan collaboration on some future attack against Kashmir or India herself. Despite official denials, some authorities believed the border agreement contained secret military clauses. Bhutto, the Pakistani Foreign Minister, added to this concern by telling the National Assembly, on July 17, 1963, that:

> . . . if India were in her frustration to turn her guns against Pakistan the international situation is such today that Pakistan would not be alone in that conflict.
>
> A conflict does not involve Pakistan alone. Attack from India on Pakistan today is no longer confined to the security and territorial integrity of Pakistan. An attack by India on Pakistan involves the territorial integrity and security of the largest state in Asia and, therefore, this new element and this new factor which has been brought into the situation is a very important element and a very important factor.

Communist China is Asia's largest state. Bhutto's statement' accordingly, was widely interpreted to mean Peking would support Pakistan in event of an Indian attack on her. This inference was strengthened by further Chinese statements which, however, skilfully avoided making any definite commitment. It was also possible that a fully rearmed India could be a threat to both Pakistan and China—in the view of those who believed that India started the war of 1962. While this was a remote possibility, one commentator points out, 'an India reinforced by unlimited supplies of Anglo-American defensive equipment would be a very different India, and it was the latter picture that deeply alarmed the Pakistanis.'[29] Further, Bhutto could have meant that the Sino-Pakistan border treaty had given Peking reason and justification to intervene militarily to protect the *status quo* of Azad Kashmir. Any Indian attack on north-west Azad Kashmir might be construed as a threat to the new Chinese military position in Hunza; and any Indian military effort to alter the situation might undermine Peking's legal claim to strategically important territory in Kashmir.

Meanwhile, Kashmir again became a live issue. It had been automatically revived by the Chinese attack and the Sino-Pakistan border agreement. A new search for a solution resulted, with Anglo-American encouragement, in fresh Indo-Pakistan negotiations. Six separate meetings were held between December 27, 1962, and May 16, 1963, but they were fruitless. India formally proposed partition of the state, roughly along the borders established by the cease-fire line, a no-war pact and military disengagement. Pakistan proposed a division which would give it 85,000 square miles of Jammu and Kashmir, including the Vale, leaving India with 3,000 square miles. Pakistani negotiators also suggested internationalising the valley under foreign troops, with a plebiscite to be held within six months.[30] In May, President Kennedy sent Dean Rusk, the Secretary of State, to New Delhi to win Nehru's agreement to mediation. During the following weeks, the search for a suitable mediator was conducted. While it was still under way in August, Nehru, in a parliamentary speech, unexpectedly withdrew all the concessions he had offered Pakistan. Dr Sudhir Ghosh called this action a unilateral cancellation of mediation and said it shocked Washington and ended chances for Nehru-Kennedy co-operation on international affairs.[31]

In 1964, Peking abandoned its ambiguous position and gave its support to Pakistan. During a visit, Premier Chou En-lai signed a joint communiqué which 'expressed hope that the Kashmir dispute would be resolved in accordance with the wishes of the people as pledged to them by India and Pakistan'. This led to a new round of Pakistani agitation. Peking thus pointedly ignored a peace gesture from New Delhi. Prime Minister Shastri suggested that peace talks could be held, if China as a gesture of good faith withdrew from the seven civilian posts it had established in the demilitarised zone of Ladakh.

By all their activities, the Pakistanis were taking a serious risk over their invaluable military and economic aid relationships with the United States: particularly in view of the known fickleness of the American Congress. Clearly, they were playing for major stakes. Their willingness to continue the game stressed the fact that they had embarked upon a desperate gamble for Kashmir—prodded, no doubt, by genuine and deep distress over the Indian build-up. The wheel had come full circle; the Pakistanis were attempting to block what appeared to be legitimate Indian defence objectives, just as Nehru had tried a decade earlier to keep Pakistan perpetually weak by opposing the US defence alliance.

Tensions were strong and the failure of the latest negotiations over Kashmir resulted in so much feeling during the autumn of 1963 that diplomats were expelled from both countries. Pakistan had won stronger international support for her position, and India reacted by making another move towards full integration of Indian Kashmir into the Union. Then, on December 27, Srinagar erupted into riotous turmoil over reports that a sacred Muslim relic had been stolen. The relic was a Hair of the Prophet which reputedly had been kept for three centuries in a tiny glass tube within a silver casket in Hazratbal mosque, on the edge of the city. Although protected by hereditary Muslim family guards, it was said to have been stolen by thieves who crept back into the mosque and restored it a week later. In the meantime, wailing throngs of 100,000 swirled through the icy streets of Srinagar, and the city and its authorities were virtually paralysed. The turmoil provoked further riots in East Pakistan, which were put down by troops. Unrest soon spread to the Calcutta tinderbox, and in the first six days of upheaval, an estimated 163 persons were killed and 636 injured. The situation was not under control until April 1964, when the respective Home Ministers met and agreed on common security measures. The atmosphere was exacerbated by Pakistani charges that India had expelled large numbers of Muslims from West Bengal on the grounds that they were infiltrators. A two-way flight of refugees began again, and an estimated 700,000 crossed from Pakistan to India during the first nine months of 1964.

The old enmities had fused with the new geopolitics, and the mixture was more explosive than before.

IO

NATIONS STRIVING TO BE BORN

AT THE beginning of 1965, both India and Pakistan faced formidable problems in their separate but parallel processes of nation-building. Each had made considerable economic progress, but the immediate challenges were immense. Both had survived the first test of political viability, yet they still had to experience much more growth before reaching complete national unity. The future was promising but precarious. After nearly twenty years of independence, the two nations in reality were striving to be born. War was the last luxury they could afford.

For India, the year opened in an atmosphere of deep uncertainty. The nation had not recovered from its two recent grievous losses—the loss of face during the Chinese attack, and the loss of Nehru's commanding personality. The death of the disillusioned and saddened Indian leader, on May 27, 1964, had sobered the sub-continent and, for a brief period, had brought the two neighbours together in one of their memorable periods of goodwill. The mood soon vanished, however, leaving deeper uncertainty over Kashmir; for it was generally recognised, by that time, that a settlement would be possible only if Nehru used his vast authority to win domestic acceptance of a compromise. The passing of Nehru, moreover, constituted more than the end of one remarkable man's leadership. It was the end of an epoch which had been singularly unique in the history of emergent nations. For nearly fifty years, as Frank Moraes points out, India had lived under the pervasive influence of Gandhi and Nehru, an influence of continuity, despite the differences between the two men. Now, the second of these two towering personalities was removed, at a moment of national frustration when most Indians instinctively searched for personal guidance from another political giant.

The new Prime Minister, Lal Bahadur Shastri, had not established such a position for himself, nor had he attempted to do so. He was well known nationally, but had yet to create a popular public image. He was virtually unknown internationally. The Shastri government attempted, in general, to perpetuate Nehru's policies on major foreign and domestic affairs, and this created the illusion that India was marking time. The economy was expanding, but too slowly to match the population increase or to absorb the sacrifices of rearmament. India had to depend upon the importation of some 6 million tons of American wheat to sustain her; a depressing statistic for many independent-minded Indians. The country's influence in foreign affairs, which once had been impressive under Nehru, was diminishing; partly, the Indians believed, because they had been deprived of a chance to strike back at Communist China. The politicians and the army burned with the desire to re-establish the nation's prestige. The Indians, with their tendency towards introspective moroseness, allowed these and other trends to convince them that circumstances were worse than they actually were.

In reality, the Indians had successfully completed a most important phase in their development towards nationhood. The transfer of authority had been accomplished without internal dislocation or upheaval, despite numerous predictions that Nehru's death would set off a power struggle threatening to break up the Union. The process by which leaders of the Congress Party designated Shastri as Prime Minister was accomplished so smoothly, in fact, that its importance was often overlooked. India had not been forged into a single, solid nation by such customary pressures as common danger or a common heritage. Rather, she was an amalgamation of diverse races and regions, grouped under a strong central government. The constitution recognised fourteen principal languages, and many others were regionally important. Regional ambitions and enmities remained strongly divisive. Innumerable tribes were unassimilated and periodically restive; Naga tribesmen in the southeast have been in rebellion for years against central authority. The fear of 'Balkanisation', which Nehru had expressed at the beginning of independence, was strong and legitimate. Although Hinduism provides a measure of cohesiveness for many of these divergent elements, it is insufficient by itself to hold the nation together. The greatly varied country was bound into a whole by more subtle forces, the most important of which, in general Indian opinion, was the strength of Nehru himself. His death without a clearly designated political heir had been dreaded, as the signal for powerful separatist forces. Some feared that ambitious men manipulating strong regionalism might tear the nation apart.

Shastri's unchallenged assumption of authority was due in large measure to the unique political impact of the Congress Party. Congress, which began as a social organisation and evolved into a revolutionary movement, has become one of the world's most unusual political parties. The party has maintained itself in continuous power since independence, and has developed what, for all practical purposes, is one-party control of a democratic political system. In 1955, the Congress Party was represented by 378 out of the 498 elected members of the 510-seat Lower House, the Lok Sabha. Congress then was so powerful and its village-by-village organisation so widespread that men ambitious for power preferred, for practical political benefit, to operate within its ranks, regardless of their differences with the leadership. Consequently, when Shastri was selected by a small group of Congress leaders, there was no political organisation capable of thwarting the decision by such parliamentary methods as splitting the cabinet or obtaining a vote of non-confidence. Regional leaders with separatist tendencies generally belonged to Congress, were beholden to it and accepted its discipline on important national matters.

This system, developed under Nehru's leadership, exercised a stabilising influence on the nation's political life during the most critical post-independence years. Under Indian conditions, the adoption of democracy was a gigantic gamble, however strongly the leaders were dedicated to it. The massive electorate, beginning independent life with a literacy rate of 16 per cent, was inexperienced and easily misled. Politicians not only lacked a strong sense of loyalty to central authority as a restraint on ambitions for power; they were, in general, the products of the political amorality produced by years of revolutionary activity. The democratic gamble might well have failed without a strong and imperious Congress Party.

The result, however, was the creation of an amorphous political organisation. The real conflicts over Indian political policy occurred within the party, quite often in secret; and the principal influences on governmental policy resulted from the same source, the leadership making adjustments to meet these internal pressures. One consequence in the post-Nehru period has been a marked tendency to conduct government by compromise, sometimes with stultifying results. The internal pressures have forced Congress to choose the least controversial candidates as Nehru's two successors.

Shastri, at first sight, was such a man. Standing only 5 feet, 2 inches, he was doll-like in appearance, invariably wearing an immaculate *dhoti* and a Gandhi cap. Indian associates towered over him and seemed to overshadow him, for Shastri was mild and subdued in public. When he first went abroad, Shastri appeared to be so self-effacing, by contrast with the bustling, confident world leaders he met, that many Indians were embarrassed to have him represent them. He came from the shadows of provincial Hinduism, to replace the urbane Nehru. Shastri was educated entirely within India and travelled to power in semi-obscurity, serving Gandhi and Nehru faithfully but often facelessly. To some, he was the epitome of the 'meek and mild Hindu', a generalisation which many Indians bitterly resented. Reacting to their double loss, the people unconsciously, and sometimes consciously, sought a bold, aggressive, internationalist leader who was capable of restoring their world prestige; they wanted a man on horseback. Shastri disappointed them—in the beginning. At his appointment, one quip circulating in New Delhi was: 'Can you imagine him at an international conference? President Johnson might pick him up by the ears', a reference to the President's practice of lifting his beagle hounds that way. The applause that usually greeted Nehru's filmed appearance on motion picture screens turned to silence or stealthy departure when Shastri was shown. It did not matter, then, that Shastri's face bore a a look of such beatific gentleness that it reminded many of Gandhi.

Congress has remained in power through an elaborate nation-wide political organisation which was highly sensitive to public opinion. The perpetuation of power was and remains its dominating impulse and its constant preoccupation. In the estimation of party leaders, the circumstances required selection of a new prime minister who would least disrupt national unity and public order. Shastri fulfilled this and other requirements and was selected by the consensus of those in control of party machinery. As Michael Brecher

P

points out in his penetrating study, *Nehru's Mantle*, Shastri won majority support from the principal institutions within the party which, operating largely in secret, determined the issue. These are: the Congress Working Committee, the body which directs party affairs; the Congress Parliamentary Party, composed of elected legislators; the political machines in principal states and the Syndicate or Caucus of the four or five most powerful party leaders at that time.

In addition to these influences on government, New Delhi is strongly sensitive to powerful pressures from another source. Protest by demonstration, by violence and by dramatic sacrifice has become an established aspect of Indian political life. To those with legitimate complaints, demonstrations often seem the only way to be heard. To the less scrupulous, the volatile emotions released by mass protest provide a means of pursuing power or prestige or seeking political disruption. Mass demonstrations are organised periodically by extremists of both Right and Left, and sometimes by Congress members. Many build into violence under agitators, working on the combustibility of the populace and the inflammability of its many frustrations. Gandhi turned the hunger strike into a potent weapon against the British and once against the first Indian government. It has been used periodically since then, often with success. Suicide by self-burning was employed in the southern state of Madras during violent protests over plans to supersede local languages with Hindi, the tongue of the mistrusted northerners. Governmental policies are often changed or suspended in reaction to these outbreaks, even though the majority of protests are quickly taken over and exploited by the *goonda* thugs.

The Shastri government, in this atmosphere, moved cautiously throughout its first eight months of life. It undertook few initiatives, either internationally or at home. Instead, the emphasis was on the continuation of Nehruism: international non-alignment, coupled with an attempt to lead the Afro-Asian nations towards moderation; independent rearmament against the Chinese; a modified form of domestic economic socialism. 'The government', said one Indian critic, 'is afraid to get out of Big Brother's shadow.' This policy appeared to be dictated not only by practical politics, but by Shastri's own preference. Throughout his career he had been known as a conciliator, a man with the rare talent for settling seemingly insoluble issues by bringing the main disputants together. He had demonstrated this capacity most recently by calming down the explosiveness in Kashmir created by the theft of the Hair of the Prophet. As Home Minister, Shastri went to Srinagar at the height of the tension, and somehow talked the excitable Muslim leaders into accepting the fact that the genuine relic had been recovered after its mysterious disappearance.

But caution did not necessarily mean weakness, on the part of either Shastri or India. The Prime Minister was known in public for the genuine simplicity of his living and for his often quoted self-appraisal: 'I am a mediocre person.' To those who dealt with him he revealed another facet, as Ambassador Galbraith noted: 'There is more iron in his soul than appears on the surface. He listens to every point of view, he makes up his mind firmly and his decisions stick. He is the kind of man who is trusted.' Shastri revealed that trait most vividly under the stress of military hostilities. He grew with leadership and was reaching the height of influence when he died at Tashkent. During his brief tenure, he made it particularly clear that he was no more disposed to relinquish Kashmir than was Nehru in his most defiant period. Further, Shastri was the first home-grown ruler of free India, a devout Hindu who appeared in some respects to be wedded to the Hindu past. Born on October 2, 1904, of a poor family, Shastri obtained his intermittent education in the sacred city of Banaras; his surname was actually the degree he finally received. At seventeen he left school to join Gandhi's anti-British movement. He was sent to prison seven times for terms exceeding nine years. Beginning his public career and his association with Nehru in Allahabad, Nehru's home town, Shastri devoted himself to local and regional affairs until 1951. Then Nehru called him to New Delhi to organise the party's campaign for the first general elections, as General Secretary of Congress. Thereafter, Shastri was a principal figure in party politics, in parliament and in the cabinet; once resigning as Minister for Transport and Railways in order to take responsibility for a train crash. He became Home Minister in 1961, a post responsible for internal order which required a firm mixture of strength and conciliation. Nehru relied increasingly in his later years upon Shastri's political skills.

Economically, India was merely holding the dykes against the population flood. Total economic growth barely exceeded the annual average population increase of 2·4 per cent. During the decade preceding the 1961 census, India had added 78 million to its underfed hordes; the equivalent of a new nation more than one and a half times the size of France. Although industrial production had increased since 1956 at an annual rate of 7·7 per cent, agricultural output lagged. During 1964, grain harvests increased from the previous year, but they totalled less than during the 1960–1 period.

Yet much progress had been made during independence; far more, perhaps, than the average Indian realised. Industrial production had increased 110 per cent since 1951 and over-all agricultural production expanded by 40 per cent. The country produced 4·3 million tons of finished steel from its own mills, a fivefold increase, and six giant irrigation dams had been constructed. Installed electrical generating capacity had quadrupled. Under the late Dr Homi Baba, Indian scientists had achieved unusual efficiency in nuclear production, and the country was a leading exporter of radioactive isotopes. It was generally recognised that India had the capacity to manufacture nuclear weapons from her own resources within one year. Other technicians had produced an Indian-built fighter plane of considerable capacity. Indian domestic and international commercial airlines had an enviable safety record.

The perennial food shortage was due to many factors, including low productivity, but one of the most revealing was the fact that millions were eating two meals a day, instead of one. The average daily intake of 2,100 calories was still below recommended world levels, but it represented a steady improvement in mass well-being; so did greater increases in the use of cotton goods and electricity. The number of school pupils had tripled, and the literacy rate increased to 26 per cent. Hospital beds also doubled, and major progress was made towards controlling disease. A birth-control movement, to curtail the rise in population, was expanding. There was, in short, much progress and much activity, beneath a deceptive air of unchangeability. The conservative farmers, for example, had demonstrated, in selected village projects, that proper incentives and training could demolish the age-old apathy which had made the Indian farmer one of the lowest producers in the world. Industrialists and scientists had demonstrated great capacity for both work and accomplishment.

A spark might have set off an explosive rate of progress in the atmosphere of strong nationalism. The country needed a new emphasis and new impetus. Shastri recognised the first of these requirements and gave belated, but essential, priority to agricultural production. India had concentrated upon industrial expansion during its early five-year plans, but while the results were impressive, they led to dangerous agricultural stultification. Instead of the independence and prestige which many planners sought through steel mills, India was forced into indefinite dependence upon American grain shipments to keep alive. It discovered after 1962 that international prestige, particularly in the Afro-Asian world, was measured more by military power than steel mills.

The new impetus, however, was lacking. The government did not mobilise the newly-awakened sense of nationalism into a mass attack on internal problems, both social and economic. There was no organised effort, for example, to expand rural production or to build more roads, or to clean up city slums. With unemployment at the high rate of 9 per cent and under-employment endemic, public projects of this order could have yielded direct economic benefit. They could also have expedited an essential step in nation-building, the diversion of an aroused sense of nationhood towards the vital if sometimes mundane task of building up the country. The first widespread sense of pride in country was left dangling as merely a sense of humbled military honour.

Instead, Shastri kept in place the economic and social system he had inherited. The social revolution was the primary responsibility of a large, conservative and generally cautious bureaucracy in the central government and in the various states. Under this leadership, the revolution itself proceeded unevenly, for it fluctuated with individual leadership and with regional political factors. After the urgent sense of emergency, the states returned to their customary quest for economic semi-independence. For instance, they competed to obtain new prestige steel mills, some of them unnecessary. A few states hoarded foodstuffs and refused to export their surpluses to under-supplied neighbours. Separatism revived, on language and regional lines. At the outset of the 1965 hostilities, New Delhi faced a major crisis from Sikh leaders demanding redivision of the Punjab on linguistic lines, behind the threat of a new hunger strike. The nation's economy followed the somewhat diluted and vague principles of Fabian socialism bequeathed by Nehru. Most Indian planners had abandoned the extreme Marxist view that capitalism is the source of all evil, but they remained strongly suspicious of Indian business men and apprehensive of untrammelled free enterprise. In general, the goal was to create a mixed economy between private and public enterprises. Bombay business men insisted, however, that governmental controls and uncertainties were stifling expansion. They contended that, if given relatively free rein, the country's industrialists could create an expansionist era rivalling the spectacular development of Japan; that, in the process, some industrialists would build up fortunes, but the inequalities could be levelled by such governmental measures as penalty taxation. The bureaucrats, in general, were unconvinced or unwilling to take the gamble.

On the surface, then, the major change created by the Chinese attack was the new Indian rearmament programme. Otherwise, it appeared, the country had returned to normal. But Indian nationalism had merely gone underground. Deprived of adequate outlet, it merged with other frustrations and manifested itself in obscure ways. One of its most pronounced expressions, perhaps, was an accelerated revival of traditional Hinduism, with its emphasis upon ancient ritual and its powerful belief in Mother India. The revival resulted in a great increase in religious meetings in certain parts of the country, particularly in southern Madras. It was also reflected by the growth in stature and public explosiveness of the Bharatiya Jana Sangh political party, dedicated to a vigorous pro-India policy with no compromise on the question of Hindu greatness. 'If there are people in this country outside the pale of Hinduism,' said one of the party's early campaign statements, 'it is their duty in the interest of nationalism to emulate, and subscribe to the Hindu way of life.'[1] The Jana Sangh, as it is popularly called, was formed in 1951 on the nucleus of the old fanatical RSS, which had been officially disbanded after one of its members assassinated Gandhi. Following numerous vicissitudes and internal quarrels, the party reached a position of strong public influence in 1965, although it was represented by only thirteen members in the Lok Sabha.

Pakistan, judging by her consistent propaganda, misjudged this situation on two basic counts. She evidently underestimated the strength of latent nationalism within Indian society and concluded that her neighbour was irreparably weak and divided on national terms. The quick reunification of India during the hostilities of 1965 was a significant factor behind the government's willingness to wage large-scale war, if only briefly. Secondly, Pakistan apparently misinterpreted the political influence of the Jana Sangh and like-minded Indian organisations. Pakistani newspapers consistently accused the Indian government of plotting or practising 'aggression', largely, it seemed, on the basis of statements by the irresponsible leaders of such Hindu groups. With their monolithic outlook, it was perhaps inevitable that Muslims should discount the Hindu tendency to speak with many voices; the loudest of which is not necessarily the most influential. There is no evidence that the Jana Sangh at any time could have forced the Indian government into aggressive military action which it opposed. Thus it was improper and misleading to couple rearmament and flamboyant political speeches as evidence of aggressive intent, as Rawalpindi did publicly. On the other hand, the Jana Sangh had a disproportionate veto authority over the politically sensitive Shastri government, in the manner of government by dramatics which has become part of Indian political life. On August 16, 1965, with fighting active in Kashmir and a critical session of the Lok Sabha opening, the Jana Sangh organised a protest march of an estimated 100,000 persons through the hot streets of New Delhi. The demonstrators, who came from many parts of the country, peaceably but firmly demanded the repudiation of a previous agreement to settle the Rann of Kutch conflict; a 'surrender' the party called it. Although the protest concerned the Rann settlement, the portent was clear: the party would not tolerate a second withdrawal in the new hostilities over Kashmir. Mingled with the general atmosphere of reviving national-ism, stimulated by the Kashmir hostilities, the party's dramatics meant that New Delhi could halt the conflict unilaterally in its early stages only at grave, perhaps impossible, risk of internal upheaval. Thus Pakistan, by attacking, had not forestalled any predictable Indian assault as the result of Jana Sangh pressure, but had helped to mobilise that pressure so as to make any sudden Indian retreat impossible.

For Pakistan, 1965 opened as a year of great promise and challenge. The country had achieved considerable success in a newly-invigor-ated economic development programme. At birth, the nation had virtually no industrial facilities and woefully inadequate supplies of electric power and raw materials. During the 1950s, it had reached the world's highest rate of industrial growth in order to establish the industrial equipment of nationhood. Even with that base secured, the output of industrial goods increased in the 1960s at an annual average rate of 14 per cent, a level ranking among the highest in the world and rivalling Japan's expansion. Moreover, Pakistan after a slow start increased agricultural production by 5 to 6 per cent annually, thus becoming one of the few underdeveloped countries to boost food production faster than the population growth. These developments did not bring agricultural self-sufficiency nor did they make Pakistan an industrial nation; it remains 85 per cent rural, compared with 82 per cent for India. But the expansion had been remarkable by comparison with nearly every other emergent country.

This growth was due in large measure to the rise of a powerful, sometimes ruthless, business community which was permitted, under certain governmental controls, to pursue profits that at one time reached 100 per cent of investment. Protected against foreign competition by import quotas, the business leaders developed and broadened the industrial base with considerable swiftness; then, because import controls left little for them to buy, they reinvested their profits in further expansion at the remarkable rate of between 60 and 80 per cent. In general, the government did not compete with private industry, although it provided capital for enterprises with a potential profit too low to attract private investment. The profit motive was allowed to operate even in rural areas, down to the sale of essential fertilisers. The government augmented this stimulant by increasing agricultural prices, instead of depressing them, and by a Rural Works Programme which pumped funds into rural development.

The system operated somewhat like an adaptation of the vigorous free enterprise which built up the United States in a remarkably short period during the nineteenth century. In both countries, the system worked in roughly the same way: private initiative spurred the economy faster and more vigorously than would have been possible under tight government control or with government interference. In the process, however, huge private fortunes were amassed. The United States eliminated this inequality, to a considerable extent, through strong legislative and tax measures in the twentieth century. In Pakistan, the discrepancy was greater, because the contrast between the very rich and the woefully poor is so marked, but the government possessed the means and had taken the first steps to equate society more nearly.

Despite the complications, this release of private initiative was essential for full capitalisation of the two primary factors behind Pakistan's phenomenal growth. First, the nation was freed from massive expenditures for defence through its military pact with the United States; as Mohammed Ali had told Nehru, the savings were ploughed into the civilian economy. Secondly, Pakistan received a high level of economic assistance from the United States. By the end of 1965, this totalled $3 billion, half the amount given to India but for about one-fifth the number of people. As a result, Pakistan, starting from bedrock, had approached, without completely equalling, the general standard of living which India had achieved on the foundation of its inherited economic structure.

After completing an extensive survey of the Pakistani economy, Dr Gustav F. Papanek, Acting Director of the Development Advisory Service, the Center for International Affairs, Harvard University, summarised the situation in this way in mid-1965:

> I would say that a major reason for the success of Pakistan, and I think there is little doubt now that it is a success story, is that, unlike many countries in Asia and Africa, Pakistan decentralised decisions. It relied on private investment and management not only in industry but also in the distribution of fertilisers, the development of wells, in agriculture, and of course in trade. It used, again unlike many countries in Asia and in Africa, private incentives to efficiency and accumulation. Unlike, however, many countries in Latin America, it had a Government that was sufficiently effective, sufficiently committed to development, to prevent capital flight, to prevent consumption, and to plan and guide the economy as a whole . . .

> For another decade anyway, Pakistan's continued growth will depend on a very substantial inflow of foreign resources, and on rather sharp limits on the expenditure for defense. If either of these changes markedly, either because of something that Pakistan does, or something the United States or other aid-givers do, if defense

expenditures go up and foreign aid goes down, it could still be disastrous over the next decade.[2]

Politically, Pakistan was groping toward a new national identity and an all-Pakistani political system. The first enthusiasm with which young Pakistani leaders had begun to build their nation in 1947 had disintegrated into corruption and inefficiency. On October 7, 1958, a military coup led by General Iskander Mirza swept away civilian rule and established a military autocracy. Twenty days later, power was seized by General Ayub Khan, the Commander-in-Chief of the Pakistan army and one of the organisers of the coup. Mirza was sent into exile 'to stop the rot'. Ayub instituted a revolution within a revolution: extensive land reforms, stern governmental reorganisation, strong measures against corruption. Ayub also decreed that democracy had failed in Pakistan and experimented with a new electoral method, by which the people expressed themselves through a relatively small core of elected representatives who actually voted for national and local officials.

Beginning in 1962, Ayub turned his country with increasing vigour towards fierce internal jingoism and an active search for international freedom of action. The Pakistani press launched a 'hate India' campaign which was pursued daily, relentlessly and vehemently for at least two years before 1965. It featured, among other elements, the constant cry that Pakistan was threatened by Indian aggression, continual demands for Pakistani control over Kashmir and periodic reports of revolt against Indian rule in Kashmir. Pakistani leaders themselves matched the vehemence of the strongly controlled press. By contrast, Indian officials were remarkably restrained, if coldly defiant on Kashmir, and the press was moderate.

Internationally, Pakistan accelerated attempts to establish firm relations with both Peking and Moscow, as well as with Eastern Europe. Ayub sought to rally a Muslim bloc around Pakistan's leadership and tried to replace India in a position of influence among Afro-Asian countries. He actively courted such nations as Nepal on India's borders. Ayub had clearly set out to reduce his dependence upon the United States, while simultaneously attempting to reactivate Kashmir as a live world issue. This shift began before the Chinese attack of 1962 changed the geopolitics of the subcontinent, and consequently it appeared as part of a comprehensive long-range readjustment. The shift became more pronounced after Chinese propagandists bitterly attacked the shipment of Anglo-American arms to India. Many Pakistanis then believed that the West was determined to build up India as the main anti-communist bulwark in that area, that Pakistan could no longer depend upon them for protection against Indian attack and therefore was obliged to woo her communist neighbours in self-defence.[3] Ayub was clearly angered that India was not forced to give up Kashmir in exchange for Anglo-American support, although it was a misreading of Western psychology to expect this to be done.

The Pakistani government left little doubt that its principal purpose was to increase national solidarity and strength against India. In this respect, the final cycle that led to the war of 1965 can be traced to this Pakistani initiative, which created a significant series of repercussions. As usual in such comprehensive political changes, however, there appeared to be other motives. A posture of international flexibility, for example, was more suited to the Pakistani temperament than strong alignment. The pressures to establish such a position were bound to increase as visible evidence of a Soviet threat decreased. They were bound to accelerate, as they did, after India's success in obtaining arms from both East and West while remaining officially uncommitted.

Domestically, Pakistan was restless, uneasy and divided beneath her economic progress and outward air of confidence. There is some evidence that Ayub revived anti-Indian propaganda in an attempt to create cohesiveness, just as Jinnah and his immediate predecessors invoked fear of Hindu aggression for the same purpose. One of Ayub's most persistent and influential critics, Miss Fatima Jinnah, the white-haired sister of Pakistan's founder, emphasised this point. 'Today in Pakistan', she said in a message published in *Dawn* on April 13, 1965, 'we are passing through a critical time. There is a lot of talk of economic development, but the impact of such development is nowhere perceptible. People are groaning under the heavy load of poverty. Propaganda machinery will never succeed in brainwashing carried out by the self-imposed .... One cannot but express anxiety at a manner in which the people's voice has been throttled under the banners and bayonet.'

Ayub evidently tried to create a powerful new nationalism to expedite his internal revolution. President Charles de Gaulle of France, with whom Ayub has been compared, did this by deliberately invoking past French glories to bind his diverse people together. But Ayub had no national memories to evoke and no past glories of Pakistan, as a nation, to resurrect. The symbols of a rather fundamentalist form of Islam and the tarnished glories of Muslim rule over India were substituted. Moreover, Pakistan herself had yet to become a nation. Her people did not know a nationalism built around the concept of a nation to which all people owed allegiance. There had been inadequate time and attention for the creation of one Pakistan under respected central authority, as distinct from West Pakistan and East Pakistan and further regional groups resistant to central authority. Nationalism on behalf of a recognised national government is new and relatively unassimilated throughout the emergent world, even in countries with a national past. What passes as nationalism in most instances, in reality, is the temporary unifying effect of strong hatreds: anti-colonialism, anti-foreignism, racial and religious prejudices and, in countries with direct experience, anti-communism. Men are brought together for varying periods *against* something, but they have yet to be united on any universal and lasting scale *for* service to their countries. Even the relative unity of India degenerated into pronounced separatism when the emergency ended, although nationalism on behalf of the nation had been exhibited briefly.

Through 'nationalism', therefore, Ayub and his confederates rekindled virulent hatred against India. It turned into jingoism and became a volatile element in the life of West Pakistan. Instead of reuniting the truncated country, however, it increased divisiveness by repelling the East Pakistanis. Thus the campaign failed as a means of expediting internal progress, but developed into an influential force for war. As hate nationalism grew in West Pakistan, it contributed new pressures to such other policies as rapid rapprochement with Peking which produced strong reactions in India and led to Indian initiatives that further aroused Pakistan. Thus, in the circumstances of the subcontinent, the deliberate and systematic invocation of hate nationalism would have had dangerous consequences, even if there were no violent quarrel over Kashmir and the purpose had been solely for domestic unity.

Ayub had won the reputation in the West of being a firm, dedicated soldier who was inflexibly anti-communist and personally pro-American: the assets by which, unfortunately, many foreign leaders are most frequently judged in Washington. He looks the role. A 200-pound 6-footer, he moves and talks with military precision and bluntness. Born in 1907 in Rehanna, a village in the North West Frontier Province, he was the son of a Pathan bugler in the Indian army. Ayub studied at the Muslim Aligarh University in preparation for Sandhurst and was selected, in 1926, for military training in England as one of the first Indians not from a maharajah's family. Ayub rose slowly during the Second World War, command-ing troops only briefly, a battalion on the Burma front. Several of his classmates from the subcontinent were of higher rank at the end of the war. Ayub is a devout Muslim.

The extent of Pakistan's shift on major foreign policy has been outlined by Ayub himself. In July 1961, he evoked cheers from a joint session of the US Congress in Washington by saying bluntly that America must never tire of giving aid to Pakistan. '. . . If there is real trouble, there is no other country in Asia where you will be able to even put your foot in. The only people who still stand by you are the people of Pakistan.' Less than four years later, he said in Peking on March 3, 1965, that, in addition to history and proxim-ity, Pakistan and China were united 'by a common determination to eradicate the last vestiges of imperialism in all their forms'. As quoted by *Dawn* the next day, Ayub added: '. . . friendship with China is for us a long-term policy and not a matter of expediency'.

In Indian government circles, Ayub has the reputation of being a man with shrewd native wit but with the tendency to let important matters pile up without action until he is forced to solve them quickly, and largely by intuition. From this has come a rather prevalent Indian belief that many of Pakistan's recent policies, particularly rapprochement with Peking, were principally the handiwork of the flamboyant Foreign Minister, Zulfikar Ali Bhutto. Some Indian authorities contend that Bhutto formulated the Red China programme and forced Ayub to pursue it; others insist that the two men were fighting for power. It is notable, however, that Bhutto owed his position to Ayub and was quiet and subdued when with him publicly. Whatever the precise circumstances, Bhutto was closely identified with the pro-Peking policy and had become a figure of some personal mystery in the diplomacy of Pakistan's new line. He was among the leading officials who consistently preached friendship for China. As Minister of Industries, he advocated closer relations with Peking as early as November 1962. At first, he was virtually alone, but a year later this same position had been adopted by many leading officials. Bhutto became Foreign Minister in 1963, after most of the preliminary work on the Sino-Pakistan treaty had been completed. The joint communiqué of May 1962, which announced the agreement of the two countries to negotiate their border, gave primary credit to S. K. Dehlavi, the Pakistan Foreign Secretary (permanent under-secretary).[4]

Nevertheless, on the subcontinent the pro-China policy generally is attributed to Bhutto. He has been sharply attacked for it, even in pro-Pakistan circles in Kashmir. The mystery is whether Bhutto is primarily a bold diplomatic gambler or whether, as some critics contend, he is personally sympathetic to Chinese communism. Bhutto's biography provides little clarification. Tall, dashing and well-dressed, he looks like a playboy and acts like a man of dedicated inflexibility. Bhutto was born in 1928 into a prosperous Muslim family. His intellectual brilliance first attracted attention at the University of California, where in 1950 he graduated with honours in political science. Returning to Pakistan some years later, with a law degree from Oxford, Bhutto practised law and was a lecturer on international law at the Muslim Law College in Sind, his home province. There he impressed Ayub, then the Pakistan Commander-in-Chief, and the two often hunted together. Ayub brought the young man into the government in 1957 testing him as a member of the Pakistan delegation to the United Nations. The next year, Bhutto was taken into the cabinet and successfully filled a number of posts until he became Foreign Minister. He was considered the key man in implementing Ayub's land reform programme, although Bhutto's own holdings were affected. The story is told that a friend once jokingly reported to Bhutto in 1959 that everyone was involved in black marketeering. Bhutto, then Minister of Commerce, promptly summoned his bodyguard and ordered his friend's arrest; releasing him only after being convinced finally that the remark was a jest.[5] As Foreign Minister, Bhutto inevitably became the principal spokesman for a new attitude of defiance against the West which characterised the new Pakistani line. He carried this aspect of the campaign to one logical conclusion by threatening the withdrawal of Pakistan from the United Nations, unless it was supported on Kashmir. Simultaneously, Bhutto also became the principal figure in the widening effort to win more support from Russia, as well as Peking. These activities increased his personal mystery in Asia and to many made him a man to watch. There was little doubt that the Foreign Minister enjoyed the intrigue and personally welcomed Sino-Soviet rapport. Bhutto resigned for 'health' reasons in July 1966, in what appeared to be a gesture by Ayub to regain some of Washington's confidence. But the possibility that the fiery ex-Foreign Minister could return to power was a constant factor in the politics of the area.

On January 2, 1965, Ayub was re-elected President by a comparatively narrow margin over Miss Jinnah, candidate of the Combined Opposition. The balloting, conducted by 80,000 'basic democrats' as the representatives of the country's total population, gave Ayub 49,647 votes and Miss Jinnah 28,343. The figures in West Pakistan were 28,927 for Ayub and 10,263 for Miss Jinnah; but in more critical East Pakistan, the results were 20,720 to 18,080. This first presidential election in the nation's history, said *Dawn* on January 4, 'entitles Pakistan to claim its rightful place as an adult member of the brotherhood of democratic nations'. It was, the newspaper added, 'an overwhelming vote of confidence', in Ayub's foreign and domestic policies, and 'the people have given him a clear mandate to pursue these policies more vigorously and fearlessly'.

The election was highly significant, indeed, for a country seeking a new political identity, but it was more of a warning than an endorsement of Ayub and his policies. Emerging from a military dictatorship towards an approach to elected government, the rulers no doubt were frightened and disturbed by the strength of the opposition. It had been a bruising, bitter campaign, dominated to a considerable extent by the ghost of Jinnah, who had been watched over in his later years by his devoted sister. Miss Jinnah and her supporters campaigned primarily on the broad demand for more political freedom and on controversial local issues. The government lost in urban areas, where the need for more rapid internal reform created its own series of pressures. The closeness of the vote in East Pakistan was serious. When he learned that he had won,

Ayub said: 'God has saved Pakistan.' Later, he urged the people in a nation-wide broadcast to forget the 'campaign of misrepresentation, vilification and hatred whipped up in the recent election. They have no place in a civilised society, least of all in an Islamic society.'

For all its promising aspects, the election served to emphasise the differences between West and East Pakistan which had persisted through the years. East Pakistan or East Bengal, as it is also called, contains 55,800,235 people—55 per cent of the nation's population—crammed into 55,126 square miles. The 47,080,378 West Pakistanis live in an area totalling 310,403 square miles. The Bengalis are small, rice-eating men from humid river and jungle areas who speak one common language and remain linked ethnically to the Indians of West Bengal and their other neighbours of South-east Asia. The West Pakistanis speak many languages, to which Bengali is foreign. They are big-boned wheat eaters from the dry plains and deserts. The two wings remain as separate as they were at partition, and, in general, time has only exacerbated the antagonisms and the insecurity on which Jinnah's state was formed.

In early 1965, the Bengalis simmered over a number of accumulated grievances. They contended, in essence, that East Pakistan, despite its size, was dominated by the West and treated as an economic stepchild. Many insisted that the military revolution, which changed Pakistan's history, was actually launched because West Pakistani generals feared they would come under Bengali rule. The revolt forestalled the nation's first scheduled general elections which, the easterners contend, would have selected a parliament dominated by Bengalis. Throughout the years, the nation's government has been drawn primarily from West Pakistan, as have the armed forces, and industry is owned largely by westerners. The easterners further complain that, while their jute produced most of Pakistan's foreign exchange, the government spent a disproportionate share of the proceeds in the West. Finally, the easterners regarded themselves as inadequately defended from encircling India by the one Pakistani division on duty in their area; cut off, as it is, from adequate support by the West.

'The exploitation of East Pakistan by West Pakistan', said the *Pakistan Times* of Lahore on July 20, 1965, 'can be judged from the fact that one can see West Pakistan officials in every village of East Pakistan.' Another critic complained: 'East Pakistan had been earning two-thirds of the country's foreign exchange and if the central rulers of Pakistan had a mind to play fair with the eastern wing they would have spent the foreign exchange earned by this region on its industrialization.' A local legislator declared in the East Pakistan Assembly: 'Today there is disparity not only in the economic sphere, but also in the administrative services, in executive power and in the legislative field, because any legislation is subject to the veto of the President. There is great disparity in the defence services . . . The East Pakistanis are not anybody's chicken-feed, and do not intend to be . . . Policy making in many spheres is being laid down without the opinion and interests of this province being consciously and strongly kept in view . . .'[6]

These and parallel emotions kept Pakistan in a perpetual condition of semi-divided uncertainty. The feeling was so pronounced that Indian military leaders made no plans to attack East Pakistan during the 1965 hostilities because, as one prominent general said: 'Why kill the East Pakistanis who hate the West Pakistanis anyway?' The failure to heal the breach had perpetuated the sense of separatism which had precipitated the crisis of 1954 over East Pakistani demands for a semi-independent status. There had been neither the spark nor the leadership to precipitate a new crisis over this question in the ensuing years, but neither had the situation been alleviated by Rawalpindi's various tactics of nation-building. In particular, as a *New York Times* correspondent reported, 'Bengalis generally make no secret of their lukewarm interest in the Kashmiri dispute . . .' And fear of India served more to increase the divisiveness than to cement the two sections, for it intensified the Bengali sense of insecurity and inaccessibility. After the Indo-Pakistan conflict, separatism returned more strongly to East Pakistan than for many years, and 'many are now expressing bitter resentment over the war which left them feeling exposed and helpless'.[7]

These cross-currents presented the Ayub regime, in the aftermath of the 1965 election, with a last-minute choice between pursuing a dangerous independent jingoism or of reducing foreign adventurism in order to concentrate upon internal rehabilitation. The stakes were enormous. In continuing rapprochement with Peking, to the open disapproval of Washington, Pakistan was dangerously trifling with American affections. Her entire armed strength depended on the United States, which also supplied an estimated 40 per cent of

Q

Pakistan's annual budget. War with India could be militarily disastrous and, at the very least, would disrupt or cripple the dazzling programme of economic rehabilitation. It could intensify the pressures dividing Pakistan by alienating East Pakistan, and this actually happened. The fear of a national break-up has been reflected consistently in Pakistani policy and has served to justify such self-defeating measures as the controversy over Kashmir. It is questionable whether West Pakistan could survive economically by itself; the prospects are better for an independent East Pakistan, if supported by foreign help.

There is no public evidence that these alternatives were considered in the light of the election or that this was a period of review. Pakistan continued on the same course, without visible deflection. The decision, however, to accept the massive risks, realistically represented a quest for security and power for West Pakistan alone, rather than for the country as a whole. The West would benefit most from the prospective gains, particularly from any conquest of Kashmir, and as the seat of the government it would also obtain most of the value of added international stature. If the arms balance were altered more favourably for Pakistan, the profit again would go mostly to the West. East Pakistan was not involved in the 1965 fighting, but the war heightened its insecurity; and it would lose most from disruption of economic rehabilitation, for it was just beginning to reap some of the benefits. Thus a policy leading to war was adopted by, and largely on behalf of, the minority section of Pakistan.

The minimum goals of the Pakistani campaign of diplomatic power politics, as the government saw them, appeared to be clearly outlined by a commentary in *Dawn* on March 23, 1965. The article, by K. M. Siddqi, contended that the Pakistani administrations preceding General Mirza's revolution in 1958 'gave the country a foreign policy that dismally failed to serve the interests of our nation. It won us few friends but many enemies. At some places, people took us for granted, at others we were regarded, not without resentment, as a camp follower of certain Western powers . . .' But Ayub has maintained a 'foreign policy that has raised our prestige high in the capitals of the world'. He did this, Siddqi said, by 'normalising' relations with China, initiating co-operation with the Soviets and trade with Eastern Europe and by establishing closer relations with Muslim countries. 'Above all, the Kashmir issue, long dormant, has been reactivated.'

From Pakistan's standpoint, Kashmir needed reactivation, to prevent disappearance of the issue. But this was necessary only as an offensive measure, to keep alive the claims to Indian Kashmir. The possibility of Indian military action to occupy all or a substantial portion of Azad Kashmir, held by Pakistan, was never very strong, and it had been virtually eliminated by the Sino-Pakistan border agreement and the establishment of a Chinese bridge-head in Hunza. The probability of Chinese involvement through any Indian attack in the strategic territories near the Chinese positions was logically a sufficiently strong deterrent to quiet legitimate Pakistani military fears of any but the most limited Indian military action against Azad Kashmir. The Pakistanis, of course, could not afford to lose any of Azad Kashmir, for internal political reasons, any more than the Indians could afford to give up any part of Indian Kashmir. There was, however, no perceptible pressure on Rawalpindi to take over the entire state as a necessary measure to preserve the cohesion of Pakistan. The tacit division of Kashmir along the cease-fire line had persisted without significant domestic difficulties in either country. It probably could have been formalised, as India frequently suggested, without undue trouble.

There was, therefore, a subtle change in the real nature of the controversy at this time. Pakistan, basically, was seeking territory which its westerners in particular considered rightfully theirs and which they believed they were unlawfully prevented from acquiring. The desire to free Kashmir Muslims from unwelcome Indian rule was an important justification for further action but not, it would appear, the dominant motive. West Pakistanis were seeking to change the *de facto* border alignment created by the first Kashmiri war under circumstances which had now altered, so that this goal in the mid-1960s amounted to little more than another form of expansion. The Pakistani campaign logically raised the question, which many Indians asked, whether Pakistani control of all Kashmir would lead to other territorial demands against India.

India followed the Sino-Pakistan provisional border agreement and the failure of bilateral Indo-Pakistan talks in 1963 with further political moves to place Kashmir completely under the shadow of the Union. On October 4, 1963, Bakshi Ghulam Mohammed, as Kashmiri Prime Minister, announced a series of 'policy directives' to his party which were designed to integrate the state further. They aroused Pakistani protest, although they were not adopted by the legislature. The Indian Home Minister, Gulzarilal Nanda, announced in the Indian parliament on November 27 that Kashmir had been 'fully integrated into India'. Nehru also told the legislators there had been a 'gradual erosion' of Kashmir's special status which would be allowed to continue.

These statements were cited by Pakistan, early in 1964, in demanding another immediate meeting of the United Nations Security Council on the question. The statements proved, said an official Pakistani letter, that India was 'deliberately set on defying the Security Council and on "integrating" the Indian-occupied part of Jammu and Kashmir with the Indian Union'. In reply, during the subsequent debate, the Indian representative, Mahomedali Currim Chagla, said: '. . . Jammu and Kashmir became an integral part of India when the Instrument of Accession was signed and accepted, and from that day till today it continues to occupy the same position *vis-à-vis* the Indian Union and no question can possibly arise of annexing Kashmir or further integrating it into the Indian Union. You cannot make more complete what is already complete.' Further, said Chagla, the two basic UN resolutions of 1948 and 1949 'were conditional and contingent on Pakistan vacating its aggression and the condition has not been complied with. . . . The condition not having been complied with and the basis having disappeared, these resolutions are no longer binding on us.' Consideration of the issue, which continued intermittently for several weeks, coincided with the tensions created by the Hair of the Prophet incident in Kashmir and subsequent communal disturbances in India and Pakistan. Z. A. Bhutto, representing Pakistan, described the turmoil in this way: 'The present rebellion', in Kashmir, '. . . has led to communal riots in the two countries.'

The debate ended inconclusively, under threat of another Soviet veto, but it established more firmly than before the support of the big powers for bilateral conversations as the only possible solution for the impasse. The United States, Great Britain and Russia particularly backed this approach, thus apparently eliminating any final possibility that Pakistan could expect the United Nations to force India into a plebiscite. The late Adlai Stevenson, the United States representative, again supported self-determination as a principle but called for a 'fresh attempt . . . in the light of today's realities to see how the basic principles can be applied to achieve such a political settlement' in Kashmir. Stevenson added that 'India, and indeed part of the very area in dispute, is under threat of Chinese Communist military attack. For this reason, as well as because of our long-standing concern that the Kashmir question be peacefully resolved, we urged bilateral talks between the parties last year. . . . An agreement cannot be imposed from outside.'[8]

Further efforts by the two nations to reach a settlement appeared promising in early 1964, until extinguished suddenly by Nehru's death. The belief persists strongly in New Delhi that Nehru regarded the failure to settle Kashmir as the greatest blight of his career and that he was prepared to move vigorously in his final weeks of life to remove it. Sheikh Abdullah and many of his confederates were released from their long imprisonment, and the Sheikh conferred at length with Nehru in New Delhi. The releases, which were apparently arranged by Shastri during his trip to Srinagar, helped to calm the explosive situation in the Vale and perhaps were designed partly for this purpose. But Abdullah himself reported that his conferences in New Delhi were seriously concerned with a Kashmiri settlement. Speaking of Nehru, the Sheikh said later: 'My talks with him convinced me of his genuine desire to find a solution of the problem.' At Nehru's request, Abdullah went to Pakistan and arranged a personal meeting between Ayub and Nehru. 'I was heartened to find', the Sheikh said, 'that President Ayub Khan fully shared the desire for such a settlement.'[9] Nehru died before the two leaders could meet, and the prospects for an early political solution died with him. Some of the Indians personally involved in arrangements for the scheduled 'summit meeting' on Kashmir said later they were confident that it would have broken the impasse. But the evidence is by no means clear that the situation was so promising.

The indications are that, as Selig Harrison has written, 'the Kashmir settlement envisaged by Nehru presupposed a larger Indo-Pakistan accommodation based on confederal relation between the two countries'.[10] This basis for settlement was consistent with Nehru's constant assertion that Kashmir was only part of the wider problems between the two countries. But obviously it required great readjustments and concessions which appeared extremely difficult in view of the political encrustations of nearly two decades. Some in New Delhi believe that the plan, which was never announced, was to create a confederation between India, Pakistan and a semi-autonomous Kashmir. This proposal was made by Nehru's successors and rejected on May 31 by President Ayub. The rejection, it is believed, was based upon Ayub's concern that granting semi-autonomy to Kashmir would stimulate irresistible separatism in East Pakistan.[11] India also had her own separatist problems which, while possibly less serious than those of Pakistan, convinced many Indians at this time that the loss of Indian Kashmir would threaten the stability of the Union. Whether confederation or any parallel solution would be workable, with the reality of the Chinese presence in Kashmir, was extremely doubtful.

In any case, this latest period of optimism, as so often happened, was followed relatively quickly by a further initiative which hardened the impasse. India acted in this instance. The Home Minister Nanda, a determined Hindu fundamentalist, reported to the Lok Sabha on December 4, 1964, that new legal steps would make 'empty and redundant' the special status granted Kashmir under the 1950 constitution. India extended two previously inapplicable articles of the constitution to Jammu and Kashmir. The result, in the words of one observer, was to make 'the political integration of Indian-occupied Kashmir . . . a reality . . .'[12] One article (356) empowered the Indian President to extend his rule to Kashmir, as previously applicable to other Indian states. Under this authority, the President can take control of any state and administer it directly, through an appointed representative, whenever in his opinion and that of the Governor the state leadership is unable to maintain an adequate or peaceful administration. The second article (357) abolished the terms 'chief of state' and 'prime minister' which had been retained specifically to designate the two leading officials of Jammu and Kashmir. They became 'governor' and 'chief minister', as was the practice elsewhere in India. This ended the legalistic distinction of Kashmir which had been implied by its authority to maintain its own Prime Minister.

The Pakistanis cite this move as a specific factor in precipitating military hostilities, as no doubt it was. The legalisms removed the last fiction that Indian Kashmir had a special or undetermined status and placed it on the same level as other Indian states. Pakistan, therefore, had to take dramatic action, lest the entire issue disappear from international debate and world attention. Theoretically, this required more drastic measures than the legal manoeuvres which Pakistan had used fruitlessly for so many years. In that light and in view of the background, it is possible to conclude that Pakistan had decided on military action in some form and was making preparations by early 1965. A rather significant hint of the underlying basic strategy, moreover, was given by Bhutto before the United Nations in February 1964, when he referred to the Kashmiri religious unrest as 'rebellion'.

Meanwhile, a number of significant trends had been growing within Indian Kashmir itself. Militarily, the cease-fire line had become through the years an increasingly significant barometer of the political climate between the two nations. The line was originally established in 1949 relatively quickly and through local adjustments made by military men of both sides who had much in common with each other. They maintained good working relations with the small but active United Nations peace-keeping force. By providing battle plans and other secret information to the UN observers, the opposing commanders in the beginning made it possible to eliminate military suspicions and to reduce the possibility of surprise attack. Consequently, the long front was relatively quiet during the early years and the annual number of incidents averaged around twenty. This situation changed in 1954, states an authoritative study of UN activities, and military pressures steadily increased.[13]

'The increase in incidents between 1954 and 1961', says the study, 'stemmed from the policy of Krishna Menon, then the Indian Defence Minister, that the cease-fire line should become a fixed international boundary.' Apparently concluding that Indian control of the Vale could not be assured in any other way, Menon evacuated civilians from the 500-yard demilitarised zone on the Indian side of the line and encouraged Pakistan to do the same on its front. 'The Pakistanis did not follow a similar policy . . . since they have always contended that the cease-fire line is not a boundary.

Most of the incidents arose when Pakistani civilians approached or crossed the line.' The annual average of incidents rose to around 2,000 during this period.[14]

The number of incidents declined in late 1962 and early 1963, after Menon's removal and India's involvement with Communist China. However, pressures intensified along the line in the middle of the year, this time on Pakistan's initiative, and the number of incidents continued to mount. 'Beginning in June, 1963,' the study continues, 'General Mohammed Ayub Khan concluded that despite India's fear of the Chinese Communists, the Indian Government was unlikely to take any steps to solve the Kashmir question in the absence of continuous pressure from Pakistan.' Therefore, he stepped up military action along the front to augment the pressures Pakistan was already applying through rapprochement with Red China and her vigorous effort to win support over Kashmir from Afro-Asian nations.[15]

Official Indian figures differ considerably. They list 62 incidents as the highest annual total for the years between 1954 and 1961. After that, action intensified, according to the Indian version, and the number of engagements totalled 468 in 1962, 354 the next year, and 1,522 during critical 1964 with Pakistan taking the initiative. By the end of May, the Indians had reported 1,345 incidents for tense 1965. Part of the discrepancy may be due to different interpretations of what constitutes an incident. Indian authorities say three-quarters of those reported by them consisted of fighting between military units or firing across the cease-fire line. Indian statistics for the Menon period are not necessarily reliable, for New Delhi is highly sensitive to charges that it initiates action along the line. The foreign study says the annual number of engagements reached 2,000 by 1961 'and there has been little change since that time'. Presumably it based its conclusions upon information from United Nations sources. The report was written by researchers of the Washington Center of Foreign Policy Research of the Johns Hopkins University School of Advanced International Studies under the auspices of the US Arms Control and Disarmament Agency. The study, of which Kashmir constituted only one part, was published as a book entitled *International Peace Observation, A History and Forecast*. Pro-Pakistani 'revolutionary' leaders in Kashmir, notably, agree in general with Indian statistics on the number of incidents

in recent years. They say, however, that the majority were precipitated by India to 'create turmoil'. But the logic of the situation
would imply that India wanted to prevent turmoil, as much as
possible, to support her contentions that Kashmir is quiet and
happy, and Pakistan needed continuous tension. The United Nations
in general withholds such information.

Despite this confusion of detail and the practice of each side to
blame the other entirely for all friction, the evidence supports the
conclusion that India and Pakistan have both used military pressure along the line at various times as part of deliberate policy. This
is hardly surprising, in view of the intensity of the quarrel over
Kashmir. Moreover, considerable action without conscious political
intent doubtless resulted from continual patrol and probing activities which are standard among armies arrayed against each other.
The UN observers exercised skilful on-the-spot diplomacy to curb
sometimes excitable armed military men. It is quite probable that,
although they were helpless to prevent planned hostilities as governmental policy, the UN officials over the years did prevent war by
accidental explosion.

The turmoil precipitated by the Hair of the Prophet incident
added a new dimension to this military situation. It demonstrated,
first, that the Kashmiri were not as supine as generally supposed
and that they could be stimulated into violence. The mobs defied the
police and intimidated the government. Priests and political leaders
quickly turned the agitation into shouted demands for the release of
Sheikh Abdullah. The clamour revealed considerably more hostility
to Indian rule and to local Kashmiri authorities than had appeared
publicly before. Finally, the upheaval created a semi-permanent
organisation capable of manipulating these emotions. Various political and religious bodies joined to organise what was called a Holy
Relic Action Committee, to demand restoration of the relic and
punishment of the thieves. When the religious crisis had passed, the
front continued. Representing three political associations and four
religious groups, with a claimed total membership of 700,000, the
Action Committee maintained a continual political campaign in support of Sheikh Abdullah and for a plebiscite on Kashmir's future.

The potentialities for using this newly-arisen force for disruption
or actual revolt were recognised by Pakistan, who, with or without
the encouragement or assistance of Peking, attempted to harness it.

There is little doubt that close ties had been maintained for a long period between leaders of the Action Committee and Muslims in Azad Kashmir; one of the most influential young priests, in fact, told me he was merely occupying the position temporarily for his uncle, who had been 'exiled' to Azad Kashmir and once served as its President. Contacts were obviously increased in the new atmosphere, and it is logical to presume that Pakistan supplied some of the funds for the Committee's rather expensive activities.

The opportunities were so obvious that some observers on the spot expected Ayub to abandon his military action in preference for this subversive method of harassing Indian Kashmir. But pressures continued along the cease-fire line, and three particularly serious incidents occurred amid the rising number of minor episodes during 1964. In one, Pakistani irregulars ambushed twenty-six Indians and took a number of them prisoner. The second involved an exchange of mortar fire in a graveyard along the international border in south-western Jammu and Kashmir. The third apparently resulted when Indian forces killed or captured twenty-four Pakistanis who wandered across the cease-fire line. Both sides, it appeared, were responsible for these and lesser incidents, for part of the tension was attributed to Indian objections to a political move in Azad Kashmir which tightened Pakistani control. Further, all of the incidents in the mid-1960s occurred in 'relatively well-populated areas and not along the cease-fire line in the sparsely settled mountain regions. This eliminates any implication that the uncontrollable tribes from the north-west province of Pakistan were responsible for the violence as they had been in 1948.'[16]

In early July 1965, a month before the outbreak of Indo-Pakistani hostilities, the city of Srinagar, beneath the clamorous surface, was uneasy, restless and apprehensive. There was no sure way to measure the extent of discontent or to assess its potentialities. An Indian correspondent called the situation 'explosive'. The Muslim guide, who assaulted me upon arrival, dogged my days to demand, alternately, that I tell the world of the 'terrible' conditions in the Vale and that I buy souvenirs from his friends. The mood of uncertainty was easily detectable, even without this testimony. Yet, outwardly, Srinagar seemed preoccupied with its normal activity of attempting to fleece every available tourist in preparation for the long, snow-blocked winter.

Srinagar, a city of 300,000, lies in faded grandeur in the heart of the Vale, surrounded by awesome beauty. Bisected by the Jhelum river and a series of canals and flanked by the sparkling waters of Lake Dal, it is a city of boats, known as the Venice of Asia. Thousands live in cluttered intimacy aboard *donghas*—long, unpainted houseboats with thatched roofs which sprout flowers in spring and weeds in summer. The British adapted the houseboat principle when denied the right to purchase land, and lived afloat during lazy vacations. Dozens of these craft, awaiting the tourists who flock to Kashmir between crises, dot the lake, breathing of British days. The old city, however, is a crowded Byzantine bazaar, dominated by alert merchants ready to sell anything from sheep's eyes to modern canned goods. Faded Persian houses lean wearily against each other and peer through cracked glasses into the Jhelum. From a steep nearby hill, an eighteenth-century fort stands guard over the sprawling city. Farther away, on the edges of lakes looping away from the town, the magnificent Mogul gardens attract thousands of Hindus and Muslims on a balmy Sunday; the Kashmiris carrying live coals in a pan to heat their afternoon tea. In the distance, on all sides, the Himalayas rise in sculptured rock and snow.

Near the centre of the old city, the Action Committee maintained an office in a riverfront building and advertised its location with a huge banner flapping over the Jhelum. A short distance away, down narrow streets choked with swirling humanity, an ancient Muslim mosque, the Mujahid Manzil, squats behind a heavy stone wall. Here, in what might be called the conspiratorial headquarters of the organisation, the leaders had gathered one day in advance of another anti-Indian rally—this one permitted by the authorities—in the mosque grounds. I had been directed to the rally by my Muslim guide, who covertly slipped a note into my hand and told me to read it in private. He claimed I was being tailed by two Indian policemen —whom I never detected—and advised me shake them off by travelling to the Committee headquarters in a *shikara*, one of the sharp-prowed boats plying on the waterways. When I had done so and had stumbled on the strategy meeting of the 'revolutionary' leaders, they greeted me affably, poured tea and talked interminably.

All the principal leaders were present; men whose names were meaningful in that area, including Maulana Masoodi, the scholarly spiritual leader; Maulana Noor-u-din, a Falstaffian activist; and the articulate lawyer, G. M. Karra. They were moderates, in the sense that they opposed demands for dramatic armed action, while being willing themselves to arouse violent mob protest. At the time the moderates were in complete control of the anti-Indian movement. They were strange men; determined and articulate, but singularly restrained in conversation. As they sat on the floor of a small and dusty room, sipping tea, puffing a *hookah* and talking affably, they resembled a group of middle-aged professional men enjoying a coffee-house discussion. But all had been anti-Indian agitators for years, all had been jailed several times and frequently beaten by police; all were rearrested after the outbreak of the Indo-Pakistan fighting.

During several hours' conversation and in subsequent interviews, they voiced parallel views. Their fundamental objective, of course, was to obtain a plebiscite on the principle, as Sheikh Abdullah once phrased it, of the 'right of the people in Jammu and Kashmir state to be masters of their own destiny'. This sounds like a demand for independence, and the mood of the 'revolutionaries' clearly favoured this solution, although, like Karra, they had decided it was impossible to achieve. Under present circumstances, they said, a free vote would mean merger with Pakistan, because of the Muslim majority in the Valley. The leaders, all Muslims, said simply, 'they are our brothers'. Some contended that Kashmiri economic conditions would improve under Pakistan, but otherwise offered no arguments on its behalf. They appeared to be dominated primarily by the desire to escape Indian rule. Many of them were outspokenly critical of the Sino-Pakistan rapprochement, and one called Bhutto, the Foreign Minister, a communist.

Apart from their obvious dislike for what they termed foreign rule, the 'revolutionaries' bitterly objected to Indian control methods. 'India', said one, 'is ruling Kashmir exactly as Great Britain ruled India, with repression mixed with economic benevolence.' They claimed that five separate Indian intelligence and security organisations operated within Kashmir to keep the populace under surveillance. 'Foreign' police from other Indian states had been imported to keep order with more toughness than might be expected from Kashmiri police. At the time of Sheikh Abdullah's rearrest, in May 1965, the Committee had brought the mobs back on to the streets, shouting for his release. In subsequent disorders, the leaders claimed, 36 were killed and 478 injured by police gunfire. Arrests were prompt and soon 1,000 were in jail, 60 per cent of them remaining in custody for at least two months, uncharged, under the Defence of India Rules. The Committee, by vigorous petitioning, had succeeded in improving the diet provided for the prisoners but had failed to change the government's policy of sending men accustomed to Kashmir's cool climate to prisons located in hot Jammu. After the May turmoil, newspapers and radio stations hostile to India were shut down and all demonstrations banned, except those specifically authorised and closely supervised by the authorities.

Control measures were maintained ostensibly by the state government, but Indian authorities were not particularly careful about hiding their ultimate authority. The 'foreign' police, for example, were present and visible; so were Hindu Indian security agents. Army units were bivouacked in Srinagar but at that time were relatively inconspicuous. Nevertheless, the 'revolutionaries' considered Kashmir as an 'occupied' country. What, apparently, had developed was a double control system which operated with certain regional peculiarities. Under the government of Bakshi Gulam Mohammed, in particular, the state authorities maintained discipline on behalf of India, and in the process evidently settled their own scores or imprisoned those who opposed their control as well as that of India. This, together with widespread corruption, gave the Bakshi regime its unsavoury reputation for what Sheikh Abdullah later called 'a policy of repression and oppression from which thousands of my followers and sympathisers heavily suffered'. But the Sheikh himself had utilised the same principle of imprisoning political opponents following internal Kashmiri quarrels. The lawyer, Karra, recounted, for instance, that the Sheikh had once jailed him for turning against his regime; Karra then welcomed the Sheikh and his followers when they arrived at the same prison in 1953 after losing power to the Bakshi. Now Karra was again campaigning vigorously for Abdullah. The Bakshi government was removed in 1964, no doubt under Indian pressure, and conditions improved somewhat under Gulam Mohammed Sadiq, the current leftist Chief Minister, a man strongly pro-India in public. In the troubles of May 1965, the 'revolutionary' leaders were not arrested at the outset. Two of them said they were caught by 'foreign' police leaving the Mujahid Manzil and were beaten up 'by mistake'. They were 'rescued' by Kashmiri police and given sanctuary in the Prime Minister's official residence.

In this confused situation, statistics on political arrests tend to become somewhat meaningless. The circumstances were further clouded by a curious reluctance of Kashmiri and Indian authorities to discuss the question and by their insistence that conditions were normal. But it was quite evident that political arrests were frequent and that the practice would be used without restraint to remove objectionable agitators when Kashmiri leaders, and the Indians behind them, considered their activities to be threatening. The Action Committee had begun a civil disobedience campaign, modelled on Gandhian tactics, in June. Groups of five volunteers paraded peaceably with anti-Indian signs once each week, in defiance of the continued ban on unauthorised protest marches. While the purpose was to cause India loss of face, the authorities freely admitted that the demonstrators were arrested as soon as they took to the streets; the government was quite evidently prepared to arrest as many volunteers as the Committee produced. Subsequently, the authorities took quick measures to break up another Gandhian tactic, the *hartal* or work stoppage, which had also proved effective against the British. In July, the Indian police were obviously worried about the underlying current of uneasiness; they mobilised at least a hundred police outside the walls of the Mujahid Manzil on the day of the authorised rally called by the Committee, but the police did not interfere with the meeting.

These practices constitute the basis for Pakistan's constant charges that India is maintaining a 'repressed colony' in Kashmir from which Muslim 'brothers' must be rescued. India has been embarrassed and angered by critical news stories and intemperate diplomatic speeches on the subject. The record is far from favourable for India. On the whole, however, the Indians were governing Kashmir as they governed themselves. They had learned that the absence of a sense of nationhood provided the climate within India for powerful and ruthless anti-government elements which could only be controlled, along with the mobs behind them, through vigorous police measures. The Defence of India Rules, providing blanket authority for political arrests, were unpopular with India, as well as Kashmir, but they appear to have been necessary at this stage of India's development. In Kashmir, the Indians were more lenient in some respects than with their own dissidents. They allowed the Action Committee to operate at full strength in July 1965, for example, yet it is now clear that Pakistan's plans to use the Committee as the spearhead for anti-India 'revolt' were well advanced by then. There are also notable debits. By tolerating the corruption of the Bakshi regime for a decade, in the interest of perpetuating a submissive government, New Delhi further complicated the task of winning the confidence and co-operation of the Kashmiri people. Political liberties, it appears, have also been restricted beyond normal security requirements. The local government political party, the National Conference, was theoretically absorbed into the Congress Party under pressure. The purpose, Nanda announced in mid-1966, was 'to combat all anti-national influences and the few people . . . who are making some noise'. Most Kashmiris believed the widespread report, repeated by Sheikh Abdullah, that those refusing to join Congress were arrested.[18]

Economically, the 'revolutionary' leaders charged, India had tried to buy off the Kashmiris by pouring money into the state. They acknowledged that roads, schools, power plants and small factories had been built and some improvements made, particularly in education. They claimed, however, that conditions were deteriorating, and that living had become more difficult for the average man. Annexation with booming Pakistan might improve the situation. Reliable comparative statistics on living conditions were unavailable, but circumstances in Srinagar were certainly no worse than in India or in Pakistan. The Indian government has obviously spent more money in Kashmir than its economic situation warrants, but some has been wasted and much has gone into basic development projects which are invisible to the average city worker. New Delhi reports that allotments for Kashmir under the first three five-year plans totalled 1,216 million rupees (more than $200 million at the 1965 exchange rate). This coincides with the figure used by the Action Committee in a petition protesting against the acceptance of large loans from India. 'Revenue receipts of the State from its own resources are not enough to pay the annual interest incurred on the loans taken' from India, the resolution stated. 'In fact, the State is proving a white elephant on the already weak financial position of the Government of India . . .'

There was a mixture of revolutionary zeal, restless dissatisfaction and political protest in the attitudes and words of these Kashmiri leaders. But they did not appear to be fired with the desire to lay down their lives or to expose their fellow-men to armed counter-action. They were settled and ageing men to whom protest or 'revolution' was a way of life and a source of satisfying political endeavour and intrigue; not a blind motivation. They were idealists, to be sure, for they had all undergone prison, deprivation and physical danger; but they had no vivid or fresh political philosophy and expressed no desire to eliminate the existing form of government. Their ideal seemed to be the separate identity of the Kashmiri people, a dream as old as Kashmir itself. They were revolutionaries to the extent that they had dedicated themselves to the elimination of 'foreign rule'; most of them had joined the Sheikh in opposing the Maharajah in the 1930s. Like all revolutionaries, however, they did not see beyond this dominating goal; nor did they see the inconsistency of demanding freedom from one 'foreign' neighbour in order to come under the control of another neighbour, nearly as alien. While as Muslims these men doubtless would be more comfortable as part of an Islamic state, they had no guarantee that annexation to Pakistan would remedy their major grievances. Pakistan, like India, had discovered the need of controlling the mobs and had her own system of arresting dissidents without charge under Defence of Pakistan Rules. If East Pakistan complained of being unfairly treated in the allocation of development funds, there was little assurance that Pakistan could or would match India's expenditures in less important Kashmir. In other respects, the moderate leaders had clearly become self-styled revolutionaries because, throughout their careers, there had been no other way in Kashmir to voice political protest. The majority of the innumerable resolutions passed by the Action Committee concerned political questions which in other localities are decided by electoral means.

Within the Action Committee and its member organisations, however, younger men were pressing for more forceful action. The moderates themselves said they had to maintain a tight rein on students and other youths, some of whom had demanded arms to fight India. 'What good would that do?' asked one of the moderates. 'The Indian police and the army are too strong to challenge, and our people would only be killed.' Nevertheless, there had been internal bickering on this question, and only the age and authority of the moderate leadership had prevented more violent anti-Indian expression up to mid-1965. State authorities insisted, without independent confirmation, that the tension had created open fighting within the movement which had resulted in at least one death. This was an exploitable field for communist agitators who long had worked in Kashmir. The moderate leaders said they recognised the threat and were on guard against it. At the time of the Chinese attack, one added, 'there was some pro-Chinese sentiment among the youth; not on ideological grounds but because they wanted support to escape from Indian control'. The Home Minister D. P. Dhar told me that both pro-Peking and pro-Moscow communist organisations operated in the Valley but with very little influence. As in the rest of India, the four chief leaders of the Chinese wing of the party had been jailed. 'Chinese agents', he said, 'have been known to operate in Ladakh and some time ago two of them were apprehended.'

In many respects, this situation was more promising for the strategy of communist-style 'national liberation war' than was South Vietnam at the outset of the phase of the war which developed there in 1961. The essence of this strategy, as applied particularly by Peking, is that active warfare can create the conditions for revolt in any part of the underdeveloped world. The application of military power and the turmoil of war create proper 'political consciousness'. Thus, Peking says: 'Today, more than 90 per cent of the world's population desire revolution, *including those who are not yet but will become politically conscious.*'[19] In South Vietnam, the communists built up active warfare, from rural bases, into a major pressure which helped to set off subsequent political and religious turmoil in the cities. In Kashmir at this time, the political and religious emotions were already present in the one city. Mobs had twice been driven into defying the government with violence unprecedented in Kashmir's history: once over the Hair of the Prophet episode and again on the rearrest of Sheikh Abdullah. A 'revolutionary' organisation was in being and in active control of the mobs. If its leaders were relatively non-violent, younger men were pressing for action.

The potentialities behind the force of the mobs were outlined to me bluntly by one of these young men, the twenty-one-year-old

R

Grand Priest, Maulana Farooq, the nephew of the former Azad Kashmir President. He defined a Grand Priest as a 'sort of Pope for the Valley'. At one point in our conversation, he said quietly: 'My congregation will obey me.' The thin, intense young man then proved this, up to a point, by strolling through the streets to the reverent greetings of innumerable passers-by. During the religious riots of 1963, he said, great throngs came to hear him one wintry day; he placed the total at 300,000. 'At that moment, I was the government.' From all the evidence, he was.

II

DIPLOMATIC PRELUDES TO WAR

THE TAUT atmosphere of late 1964 and early 1965 created new political challenges for the subcontinent. It was a period, possibly the last one, for a sober review of the pressures which were driving the neighbours towards a collision: the time to suspend the most dangerous contributing policies. In essence, the two nations confronted a common fundamental problem: how to prepare against possible attack from the outside without increasing the dangers of intramural war. The problem had arisen in 1954, and Pakistan's resultant alignment had produced a series of dangerous repercussions. The same issue had been revived by the Chinese attack on India, and the impact was still visible and strong three years later. Neither Pakistan nor India had attempted to separate the external and internal threats, but deliberately merged them. Instead of trying to minimise the influence of the cold war on the subcontinent, both nations had sought to expand it for their own advantage in pursuing local objectives.

The growing antagonism between Indian rearmament and Pakistani apprehension, however, required a separation of the two conflicts in which the adversaries were involved. If Indo-Pakistan problems could not be solved or suspended, they could with wise diplomacy be kept apart from India's preparations against the enlarging threat of Peking. But apparently there was no effort by either side to consider doing so during this period at the end of 1964 when a change could have been made. On the contrary, both nations deliberately used the Chinese threat as another weapon in their confrontation.

Throughout 1965, therefore, India and Pakistan waged a diplomatic and political war of nerves. Once more, inflammable initiative produced sharp counter-action. Pakistan generally maintained the offensive, seeking to exert pressure on India by every means, ranging from the steady drumfire of the internal 'hate India' propaganda campaign to persistent diplomatic attempts to isolate India internationally. The Indians responded with sufficient spirit to give warning against precipitate action, but the evidence suggests that Pakistan was in no mood to be warned. It appeared implacably determined to force a showdown over the twin issues of Kashmir and Indian rearmament.

For this policy, Rawalpindi quite evidently placed great reliance upon the support of Red China. President Ayub paid an eight-day state visit to Peking in March 1965, during which the foundations were completed for a two-phased use of the Chinese presence. Firstly, Ayub emphasised in several speeches the 'friendship' and 'peaceful' aspirations of the Chinese Communists. This theme was elaborated and repeated at length in international Pakistani propaganda in terms rivalling the warmest phases of the Sino-Indian period of 'friendship'. The extent of this internal campaign suggested there were many Pakistani doubters, despite the fulsomeness with which Pakistan leaders sought to embrace Peking. Secondly, the Chinese lent themselves to a limited and possibly intentionally obscure position of support behind Pakistan and her claims on Kashmir. During the Ayub visit, Peking subscribed for a second time to a communiqué supporting a plebiscite. Marshal Ch'en Yi, the Chinese Foreign Minister, used this occasion to make the first of several equivocal statements implying Chinese military support for Pakistan without pledging it. The evident purpose was to intimidate India.

In Peking, Ch'en Yi told Pakistani newsmen, as reported by *Dawn*, that 'China would go to the assistance of every friend if asked for against an aggressor'. Later, during a speech on a visit to Karachi, he said that 'the friendship and co-operation of the two big Asian nations—China and Pakistan—are a positive factor in the present international situation. The solidarity of the 750 million people of China and Pakistan constitutes an important force for the defence of world peace.'

These statements were conspicuously non-committal. The communist definition of the 'defence of world peace', for example, means in both Soviet and Chinese jargon a condition preventing counter-action against the 'peace bloc' regardless of provocation. Ch'en Yi seemed to be saying that Red China and Pakistan together had sufficient military power to discourage military action against them; not necessarily that the power would be used. Although both Moscow and Peking have pledged military support for certain selected 'friends', there is no precedent for either communist nation coming openly and actively to the defence of a non-communist power. For Peking to defend Pakistan while she remained aligned with the United States would be a complete violation of Chinese doctrine. These factors would not prevent Communist China from intervening in a war on the subcontinent for its own advantage. They meant that the Chinese would do so only when they stood to gain thereby, and when there were no great dangers from involvement. In this instance, the 'pledges' were suspect on more than ideological grounds. Red China was visibly concerned by the war in South Vietnam and was unlikely to open a second front that might expose it to Western power.

Nevertheless, the possibility of Chinese involvement was used extensively by Pakistani leaders in the drumfire of threats which characterised 1965. The signing of the Sino-Pakistan border protocol and a cultural pact in Rawalpindi on March 27 was turned into a major propaganda event. *Dawn* devoted half of its front page to the ceremony. The newspaper quoted the Foreign Minister, Bhutto, in paraphrase, as saying that 'Asian leadership had found its destiny and had to be respected. If the rest of the world is not reconciled to it, world peace could not be maintained.' The next day, Bhutto said in a press conference, as reported by *Dawn*, that 'by rushing military assistance to India, a country hostile to Pakistan, the United States of America has not merely jeopardised the concept of alliances but has shattered it.' This was clearly a bid for offers from Moscow, as well as Peking.

Although Bhutto admitted that Pakistan had grown closer to Peking, he insisted that this was in the interests of peace. In *Dawn*'s paraphrase, he contended:

Particularly since the independence of the country, we have been victims of aggression from India. On each and every occasion India has wronged us. Even today India holds in her hands the soul of Pakistan, the people of Jammu and Kashmir. Pakistan without Jammu and Kashmir is like a body without a head. There is no conceivable reason or justification for India to do such a wrong to Pakistan. It is not correct to say that other countries will ensure that India will not commit aggression against Pakistan. We are already victims of perpetual aggression. India is in perpetual aggression against Pakistan.

This was an old Pakistani theme, which had a strong emotional appeal, even though its accuracy was disputable.

Indian authorities, understandably, were concerned by signs of closer Sino-Pakistan collaboration. Red China had exploded her first nuclear device on October 16, 1964, and her military shadow had grown larger over Asia. In essence, the circumstances created the first test of Peking's ability to use its new power for intimidation. The experimental explosion had been predicted well beforehand and had been expected to coincide with the Conference of Non-Aligned Nations at Cairo in early October. The Chinese evidently tried and failed to set off the blast in time to influence the conference. Nevertheless, Prime Minister Shastri, in his first important initiative in international affairs, had attempted to rally these powers into a force to halt the proliferation of nuclear weapons. Addressing the Cairo Conference on October 7, he proposed that a delegation of non-aligned nations visit Peking 'to persuade China to desist from making nuclear weapons'. Peking replied three days later with a sharp anti-Indian propaganda attack which clearly indicated that the attempt to halt nuclear armament had become another reason for increased Chinese pressure on India. In a lengthy statement the Chinese repeated a number of old charges, in an attempt to belittle India before the conference, and accused the country of 'double alignment' in accepting arms from both Russia and the United States. Peking again claimed the disputed 50,000 square miles of territory south of the McMahon Line in NEFA. The effect of this attack on the Cairo deliberations was unmeasured, but Shastri's proposal was rejected, and he dropped the idea.

Within India, the explosion created renewed pressures for the development of an independent Indian nuclear device. Shastri firmly clung to Nehru's policy of avoiding nuclear armament, a decision which he announced at Cairo. The fact that the issue had been raised again, in the new atmosphere of the subcontinent, was highly significant. In view of its known nuclear capacity, India was capable of sharply tipping the balance of military power against Pakistan, if not Red China, within a comparatively short time. Shastri refrained from doing so apparently for moral reasons, not because of decisive economic or political considerations. On the day of the Chinese explosion, he enunciated this philosophy, which continued to govern his administration: 'China has been trying to build herself a mighty war machine. The atom bomb is the latest type of weapon which cuts across the general desire of humanity to live in peace. It is a danger and a menace to mankind. I do hope that the voice of the peace-loving people in all countries will be raised against it and the world conscience awakened to fight this aggression on peace and security.'

On the ground, Chinese troops remained massed behind the passes through which they had poured into India. On December 8, 1964, Chavan, the Defence Minister, told the Indian parliament that fourteen to fifteen Chinese divisions were in position along the Sino-Indian border. This total equalled or perhaps exceeded the size of the 1962 attacking force. Despite Pakistan's expressed fears of growing Indian strength, the Indians knew that their build-up was incomplete. It was insufficient to meet a new Chinese massed attack, even by the assembled Chinese armies, without the reinforcements that Peking was capable of pouring in. Although the possibility of another massive Chinese thrust was generally discounted, Indian military authorities obviously had to plan for the worst possible contingency. The potentialities included a two-front war against the land armies of Pakistan and Red China: a prospect that does not seem to have been taken with complete seriousness in New Delhi, although it was an element in the psychology of the period.

In addition to these factors, the Sino-Pakistan rapprochement was regarded in New Delhi as a threat of new guerrilla attacks on India. Pakistan, the Indians believed, deliberately used a tribal guerrilla assault in 1947 to prelude the war over Kashmir. Nehru had predicted that Pakistan would follow the same strategy in a second attempt to conquer the state. Now, the danger was intensified by the possibility that Rawalpindi would receive Chinese support and arms and active help in training guerrillas and planning tactics. Thus, to many Indians, the Sino-Pakistani agreement was more than a diplomatic double cross by which a neighbour joined the enemy.

It opened the prospect that India would be plunged into a new type of long, suppurating conflict, both in Kashmir and in the areas of West Bengal adjoining East Pakistan.

For an influential minority of military and civilian officials, this development also meant that Peking had acquired new strength for what they regarded as a long-range war against South-east Asia, with India as the ultimate target. This group had taken a new look at communist tactics in South Vietnam and had concluded that 'national liberation' warfare had become a disguised form of creeping communist aggression.[1] These men believed that the Chinese had already launched a campaign to conquer South-east Asia through the intermingled military and political weapons of 'liberation' war; and, indeed, Peking had publicly named Thailand as its next target. India was already involved and could not extricate itself. This viewpoint was expressed by the Indian army officer, Major General P. S. Bhagat, VC, in his book *Forging the Shield*, 'A Study of the Defence of India and South East Asia', published in 1965. 'In the context of today,' he writes, 'the countries of South East Asia, particularly their border regions, are vulnerable to guerrilla warfare. A guerrilla movement, communist inspired and abetted by China, can be much more of a menace than open war with all its international complications.' He adds: 'India being the only possible comparable power to China must of necessity play a pivotal role. Peking's strategy therefore must include the neutralising of India, without which consolidation of any gains cannot be permanent.'[2]

The Vietnamese conflict created great controversy within India. Many Indians regarded it as a spontaneous anti-government mass movement in which communist involvement was limited to helping South Vietnamese revolutionaries. A minority of government officials and a rather surprising number of non-official Indians, however, considered the war as a calculated campaign by North Vietnam, guided and supported by Peking, to conquer the southern part of the peninsula. Many sharing this viewpoint remained publicly silent, because their position opposed official government policy. Still others sought peace on moral grounds or because they believed any Asian war threatened India, and most of them were only secondarily concerned by the issues. At the other extreme, the Swatantra Party, among other minority factions, attacked the government publicly for taking a variety of diplomatic initiatives and for not openly supporting Saigon and the United States. 'The Americans are fighting India's battle in Vietnam', tartly observed C. Rajagopalachari, the party's elder statesman. He contended that American forces and their allies were actively helping to defend India by keeping Peking preoccupied so that it could not revive meaningful pressures against India. The defenders were also successfully challenging the 'national liberation' tactics which, he said, doubtless would be used against India at some future time.

Apart from its political complications, the Vietnamese war impressed certain Indian military and civilian officials by the applicability of its tactics to the subcontinent. The essential strategy of 'national liberation war' is to fight a protracted conflict, as Mao Tse-tung has advised, with political and military weapons designed to isolate and wear down the target government. Militarily, well-trained guerrillas, with great mobility and the will to avoid decisive engagements, can oppose a conventional army ten times its size. If the guerrillas can win the active or tacit support of the people in their operational areas, defence against them is extremely difficult. To secure this support, political agents seek to woo the people through the propaganda of promise, playing upon their aspirations and grievances in the hope of enlarging them into an effective anti-government force. The techniques include the promise of farms for land-hungry peasants, but inevitably the land is taken back by the state for the establishment of collective farms, as was done in Communist China and Sheikh Abdullah's Kashmir. Terrorism also is a major weapon, designed to intimidate the people and, by systematic assassination, to weaken and discredit government administration.

Thus, military tactics are directly linked to the political strategy used in key villages and particularly in the cities where, under war-time stress, religious and political emotions can be whipped into violent anti-government demonstrations. The purpose is to confuse the people and to undermine the government so that it will capitulate. Consequently a bloody urban student riot may be correlated with a guerrilla attack on a government outpost in the countryside. Meanwhile, every attempt is made to isolate the target government internationally, so that foreign support is minimised and hopelessness intensified. If the government capitulates to these combined pressures, the guerrillas can win without achieving a military decision; if not, Mao Tse-tung says they must build up conventional armies strong enough to capture the principal cities.

The fundamentals of this strategy were developed by Soviet, Chinese and Vietnamese communists during internal civil wars. It was designed to permit weaker forces to battle successfully against stronger armies—the function of guerrillas for generations. The communists added political and terrorist methods to previously recognised irregular military tactics. In South Korea during the late 1940s and in South Vietnam in the early 1960s, however, the same tactics were used to spearhead aggressive attack across recognised borders by organised military forces which were more powerful than those they opposed. The use of guerrillas thus became an offensive technique. The intent was to disguise the fact of aggression and to keep hostilities at a level below the threshold for Western nuclear retaliation. Further subterfuge was maintained by the creation of foreign-controlled 'liberation front' proxy governments, by intensive propaganda from freedom radios and by consistently portraying the conflict as an internal revolution.

There is ample documentation that the North Vietnam Lao Dong (communist) Party decided in September 1960, if not earlier, to initiate the present phase of the war in South Vietnam. The North possessed the larger and more powerful army, but it turned deliberately to low-scale guerrilla action for deception. Three months after deciding on war, the Lao Dong Party established the 'National Front for the Liberation of South Vietnam'. This added further camouflage. The Front, the South Vietnamese Viet Cong guerrillas and regular North Vietnamese troops fighting in the south, often as guerrillas, remain under Hanoi's tight control.[3] These communist tactics were quickly adapted by others. The technique of masking military expansion behind guerrilla warfare was purposefully initiated by President Sukarno of Indonesia in his 1963 confrontation with Malaysia, although the Indonesian military force was many times stronger.

Many Indians clearly saw the threat to them of 'national liberation' warfare, practised either directly by Peking or by Pakistan, or by the two acting together. India, in essence, contained on a massive scale all the major elements which the Viet Cong had detonated into devastating war in South Vietnam. There was a direct parallel to the situation in Kashmir where the Indians believed the Action Committee was already acting as a front for Pakistani penetration. In the north-east, India is bordered by small and inherently unstable buffer states, Nepal, Sikkim and Bhutan. Chinese pressure has been incessant for many years in these regions, where illiterate tribesmen in remote valleys are potentially susceptible to subversive manipulation. Within India, numerous borderland tribes have been periodically restive, including the rebellious Nagas and several groups in Assam, in the south-east, who had already been contacted by suspected Chinese agents. Assam, the target of the eastern Chinese assaulting force in 1962, is connected to the rest of India by a thin corridor skirting its neighbour, East Pakistan. The Indians, doubtless with good reason, regard East Pakistan as a continual source of trouble to them. Officials contend that Pakistani agents constantly infiltrate into West Bengal, the centre of some of India's worst communal riots. Many other sections of India had been swept periodically by violent food riots and by bloody upheavals created over language and other regional issues. Indian Communists, particularly the pro-Peking faction, had been instrumental in originating or inflaming many of these demonstrations.

Consequently, the enlarging concept of 'national liberation' war exercised its own influence on the progression of Indo-Pakistan suspicions. To the Indian officials alert to this danger, the Sino-Pakistan rapprochement represented a specific threat, in addition to the political hostility aroused by this apparent union of two enemies of India. The more Pakistan flaunted the presumed military backing of Peking, the more these Indians stiffened their defiance. Some military officers of high rank, in particular, were doubly alert against subversion in Kashmir, which they seemed to regard as a more valid potentiality than another overt Chinese attack. Thus India was geared to react strongly to any move threatening to upset the delicate *status quo* in the northern state. Far from intimidating New Delhi by invoking Peking's shadow, Pakistan heightened the tensions and made Indian response inevitable.

The Vietnamese conflict had another significant impact. It drove the Indian government into a more open rapprochement with Russia and this produced its own chain of events. New Delhi based its Vietnamese policies upon a conscious attempt to prevent the war from becoming a pressure to reunite Russia and Red China, in fear that this would seriously endanger India. As a leading cabinet minister explained, the government believed that India's national salvation depended upon perpetuating the Sino-Soviet split. While the split lasted, Russia would maintain India as a bulwark against Chinese expansion and, the Indians hoped, would supply weapons for defence against any further Chinese assault. This protection would end, however, if there were a reunion between Moscow and Peking, and India might then become a principal target for the two communist powers, acting in concert. New Delhi saw the possibility that continued enlargement of the Vietnamese struggle could force Peking and Moscow to repair their differences and come together in common support for a threatened Asian 'revolution'.

This was the principal reasoning, though not the sole impetus, behind persistent Indian attempts to suppress the Vietnamese conflict, often on terms strongly opposed by the South Vietnamese and most Americans. As the struggle intensified in 1965, Prime Minister Shastri condemned the bombing of North Vietnam and, originally, the continued infiltration of North Vietnamese into the south. He demanded the suspension of both activities as the prelude to negotiations. Later, he limited himself to condemnation of the bombings as an impediment to peace. The inference was that he was responding to Moscow pressure. Consequently, Indian officials were forced into the position of protesting against the counter-action of American forces and their allies in face of provocations which New Delhi never mentioned. Similarly, many Indians insisted upon negotiations, long after Hanoi and Peking had repudiated them, with the implication that Washington's overtures for a diplomatic settlement were unsuitable. When India later adopted many of the same military measures, on a relatively smaller scale, to meet the guerrilla threat in Kashmir, it was again accused of hypocrisy. No doubt, New Delhi would have advocated quick peace in Vietnam, even without an ulterior purpose, for this position coincided with Nehru's past policies and was popular among articulate Indians. New Delhi had a further responsibility to seek an early end to hostilities as chairman of the International Control Commission. Nevertheless, the Indian arguments clearly favoured the Soviet position and were quickly responsive to Moscow influence. In 1966, Prime Minister Indira Gandhi advocated reconvening the 1954 Geneva Conference, which Russia as co-chairman had blocked, but she dropped the demand after a visit to Moscow.

The basic assumptions behind the Indian policy were subject to serious question, on at least three major points. First, as the record shows, Moscow's support for India in the 1962 border conflict with Peking was by no means as unequivocal as most Indians assumed. Secondly, the ability of third parties to influence the Sino-Soviet controversy is doubtful. American authorities in Indonesia, for example, urged the Soviets to join them in opposing a Chinese Communist takeover of the Indonesian Party and through it, possibly, the country, during developments preceding the Chinese-directed insurrection of 1965. The Soviets refused, even though their massive arms investment in Indonesia was directly threatened. Thirdly, as events proved, the two communist powers were capable of continuing their bitter feud while becoming deeply involved in Vietnam.

By pursuing this policy, New Delhi enlarged the Soviet presence in India. This position appeared more solid, possibly greater than it was, because apparently smooth Indo-Soviet relations contrasted with frequent public US-Indian differences over Vietnam and other issues. At the same time, Moscow undertook a firm, almost overt, effort to build a stronger position in Pakistan, while maintaining its Indian foothold. It is possible that Moscow believed the Indians were so dependent upon Russian military help that a double rapprochement on the subcontinent could be attempted with minimum political risk. In any case, Moscow had responded cautiously but definitely to repeated Pakistani overtures for closer relations. Since 1962, a series of barter economic arrangements and cultural agreements had been concluded by Pakistan with Russia, Poland, Hungary and Czechoslovakia. In 1963, Pakistan received the first foreign landing rights in Russia for commercial aircraft.

On April 4, 1965, President Ayub and Foreign Minister Bhutto began a six-day state visit to Moscow. Soviet officials clearly went out of their way to impress the Pakistani leaders and, particularly, to praise them for their new 'independent' foreign policy. This was the first top-level contact between officials from the subcontinent and the Soviet successors to the ousted Khrushchev—Premier Alexei Kosygin and Party Leader Leonid Brezhnev. Since assuming power the previous October, the Soviet leaders had moved slowly and had given no precise indication of their prospective foreign policies—the customary procedure following each shift of power in Soviet Russia.

In the final communiqué, issued on April 10, the Soviets clearly moved a step towards the Pakistan position on Kashmir. *Dawn* reported that the two countries declared their 'resolute support' for 'peoples fighting for their right of self-determination'. Both further agreed that 'in order to promote universal peace and harmony, international agreements should be implemented'. This was vague language indeed, and doubtless weaker than Ayub desired, although he was portrayed at home as being satisfied. But the Soviets had given strong new support for two of Pakistan's principal arguments over Kashmir: that the people were entitled to self-determination and that India should be forced to implement its old—and in Indian eyes outmoded—pledge to hold a plebiscite.

When Shastri, the Indian Prime Minister, made his own visit to Moscow in June, he failed to get any mention of Kashmir into the communiqué. Despite another display of Soviet hospitality, Moscow also refrained from giving any public indication that it would support India with any vigour in future disputes over Kashmir. This omission was glossed over in the Indian press but, as later events confirmed, it was highly important. Shastri returned to New Delhi with fulsome praise for the Soviets; as, indeed, he would be obliged to do under any circumstances. India had based too much of its foreign policy upon Soviet support against Red China and Pakistan to allow any suspicion to appear publicly. Indian authorities suppressed the concern that some of them felt over the Soviet shift; nor did they reveal that they had found the Soviets to be hard, tough bargainers on economic aid and uncomfortably slow providers of promised military assistance. It was not until later in the year that Frank Moraes warned the country as a whole that the changed geopolitics of the subcontinent made closer Soviet-Pakistan co-operation inevitable. Until then, most Indians appeared to regard Soviet backing on Kashmir as inflexible.

From this dual position, Russia exercised what proved to be the decisive influence on the military situation in the subcontinent. Pakistan's primary anxiety over the growing Indian military potential concerned the supersonic aircraft and other modern arms pledged or delivered by Moscow to New Delhi.[4] This reality was obscured generally, and particularly within Pakistan, by the heavier propaganda emphasis given to blaming the United States and Great Britain for supplying 'massive' arms aid. The emphasis, in part, reflected Pakistani disillusionment with their Western alliance and its failure to deliver Kashmir. The Pakistanis, like the Indians, also had learned the necessity of subordinating criticism of Russia while courting her. Nevertheless, direct Soviet intervention provided the impetus to upset a military balance which had helped to preserve peace between the neighbours for eleven years under frequently uncertain conditions. It can be argued that Pakistan was driven to war in 1965 only by the combination of her military fears and India's further integration of Kashmir, and that the legal action over Kashmir would not have been sufficient by itself to precipitate hostilities. If so, the Soviet presence was the vital spark for war.

The Indian decision after 1962 to undertake unilateral rearmament, with limited Western help, was risky enough by itself, in terms of the probable effect upon suspicious Pakistan. The Indians did not seem to recognise this risk; in fact, they have long ridiculed as unnecessary the attempt to maintain an arms balance. The Indians argued that Pakistan had already been disproportionately strengthened by American weapons, and India, therefore, was entitled to replenish her arsenal without regard for the consequences. Moreover, the argument ran, since India had no intention of attacking Pakistan, there was no need to maintain a balance. New Delhi, however, apparently made no attempt whatsoever to convince Pakistan that she would not be attacked. And in the general Indian attitude to this question, as late as the spring of 1965, there was the same unpractical dismissal of Pakistan's legitimate security considerations as there had been a decade earlier when the quest for arms led to the US alliance.

The Western powers, however, clearly recognised the dilemma created by the Chinese attack. The late President Kennedy had outlined the problem at a press conference on September 12, 1963, in terms that remained valid two years later: 'The fact, of course, is we want to sustain India, which may be attacked . . . by China. So we don't want India to be helpless with half a billion people. Of course, if that country becomes fragmented and defeated . . . that would be a most disastrous blow to the balance of power. On the other hand, everything we give to India adversely affects the balance of power with Pakistan which is a much smaller country. So we are dealing with a very, very complicated problem, because the hostility between them is so deep.'

During the Chinese campaign, the emergency Anglo-American arms programme totalled $120 million. The two nations, sharing the total, provided equipment of primary usefulness in the mountain terrain where the Sino-Indian confrontation was concentrated. General Robert J. Wood, the director of US Military Assistance, told a US congressional committee in April 1965, that the American assistance consisted of 'transport aircraft and spare parts, light infantry weapons for mountain divisions, ammunition, communications equipment and engineer and medical equipment to meet this emergency'. The same general type of equipment formed the basis of subsequent American assistance, totalling around $80 million by the autumn of 1965. The American effort, said General Wood, was 'to assist that part of the Indian armed forces which would bear the brunt of any future Chinese Communist incursion either through the Himalayan mountains or from the east through Burma.' In addition, India was able to purchase an unspecified amount of American equipment 'primarily for modernization and expansion of defense production facilities'.[5] This assistance included a factory for the production of ammunition for small arms and the promise of a second such facility, which was suspended during the military conflict.

'The objective of the United States', General Wood continued, 'is to minimize tensions between Pakistan and India and ultimately to secure their co-operation on the matter of defense of the subcontinent. We recognize that their disputes stem from old and violent antagonisms which are not easily overcome. Our military aid programs to these nations, however, are in no way intended to aggravate those old problems. Instead, their purpose is to prevent the incursion of communism on their borders from the north.' Further, the American authorities obtained stronger guarantees from India on the use of American-supplied equipment than they had secured a decade earlier when arming Pakistan. An exchange of notes at the time of the first emergency shipment 'stated that the assistance will be furnished for the purpose of defense against outright Chinese Communist aggression now facing India'. Washington gave Pakistan the customary guarantee that it would employ all legal methods to prevent misuse of the arms.[6] Great Britain followed similar policies.

The Indian Defence Minister, Chavan, confirmed this outline of Anglo-American assistance in a speech before the Lok Sabha on November 29, 1965. He said American assistance between October 1962 and September 1965 had totalled about $76 million (Rs 36·13 crores). Deliveries amounted to about 45 per cent of US pledges. The British, he said, had delivered arms amounting to about $47 million, or slightly less than two-thirds of their commitments (Rs 22·41 crores in deliveries, out of a total commitment of Rs 36 crores). The Anglo-American equipment provided limited support for a number of mountain divisions, he said, plus some transport and trainer aircraft and aircraft spares, signal and road-building equipment.[7]

This relatively modest assistance, when added to the equipment India obtained through her own resources, disrupted the Indo-Pakistani balance to some extent. The newly-raised and Western-armed mountain divisions expanded the total Indian military establishment and permitted the actual or potential use of other divisions on Pakistani fronts. Yet it was possible that, with forbearance and better diplomacy on all sides, the Indians could have established adequate anti-Chinese defences without unduly alarming Pakistan or without drastically altering the real military situation.

The Indians, however, had begun rearming against Pakistan before the Chinese assault and continued this phase of their programme along with the construction of distinctly anti-Chinese defences. In particular, the Indians had sought supersonic military aircraft to match those supplied by the United States to Pakistan. New Delhi was disturbed when the Pakistanis received relatively slow F-86 Sabre jet fighters and aroused when modern F-104A Starfighters were delivered. While Pakistan demanded more of this equipment, the Indians sought unsuccessfully to obtain a matching force from Washington. The controversy over this weapon illustrated the political as well as the military complications of the American position. In the military thinking which underlay the US-Pakistan alliance, there was a defensible need for supersonic aircraft as protection against a Korean-style attack which would presumably be supported from the air. The Soviet industrial establishment enabled Moscow to equip any puppet army as fully as it desired:

S

a point underlined by the equipment supplied to North Korean forces.

On the other hand, supersonic planes were of limited military value in India's anti-Chinese build-up; they were unsuitable for combat in the mountains. India had no serious intention of launching air attacks against China and depended upon Anglo-American protection against any Chinese air war. Since American assistance had been provided solely against Peking's threat, jet planes were considered unnecessary. The same considerations applied to tanks, for the Chinese were considered incapable of reaching the Indian plains with any substantial armoured force. Terrain elements in the two potential battle areas constituted one fundamental difference in the defensive arms considered necessary. Furthermore, American officials appeared to be more alert after 1963 to the impact of their arms on internal conditions of the subcontinent than they had been nine years earlier when they armed the Pakistanis originally. They had learned the inability of both Pakistanis and Indians to dissociate their intramural conflict from the exterior communist challenges.

But supersonic planes and heavy tanks were essential to both sides in the Indo-Pakistan confrontation. These were the weapons by which military officials, politicians and large numbers of commoners judged the prestige of their country and the honour of their army. In the emergent world, modern arms were presumed to demonstrate military maturity, just as steel mills represented industrial maturity, regardless of practical value. The aircraft proved to be of only marginal value in subcontinental warfare, but the tanks were of major significance. For military as well as political reasons, then, India sought modernised equipment with increased intensity. The army quite possibly would have demanded these weapons under any circumstances in the effort to revitalise itself after the shock of the Chinese attack.

The Soviets capitalised on this situation. Of the $500 million in military assistance which they are believed to have promised India by the end of 1965, some $300 million were earmarked for the construction of an Indian-manned factory to build MIG fighters. The project was pledged in May 1962, and reaffirmed after the Chinese attack. On paper, the Indians were permitted to pay for this help in rupees and would acquire complete control over the factory upon completion. Thus a vital weapon for use against

Pakistan would be obtained without depleting scarce foreign exchange. The United States had demanded payment in dollars for comparable American fighters; a condition that apparently was applied in order to discourage New Delhi from upsetting the balance. Moreover, the Indians believed they would have the complete independence which they cherish over the production and use of the MIGS.

Whether the factory project develops this favourably for India is uncertain. Progress was slow during the critical period preceding Indo-Pakistan hostilities, but the plant began production on schedule in 1967. Senior Indian officials said they were 'reasonably satisfied' with progress in 1965. They seemed to realise, however, that a good many political, as well as mechanical, complications could arise before the factory becomes fully operable. Moscow in other respects had manipulated its military aid with apparent care. It installed two surface-to-air missile (SAM) facilities to protect major Indian cities, a purely defensive measure which, of course, produced considerable effect. But it took the Soviets two years to supply the first of the MIG-21 fighters they promised India in 1962. By the autumn of 1965, India had twelve of these planes. They were comparable to the latest American-built fighters in the Pakistani air force.

The Soviets supplied an unknown quantity of additional arms to India, including some helicopters and transports suitable for mountain operations. Soviet assistance was provided under unusual secrecy, and it is known that New Delhi was warned all aid would be stopped if its extent were publicised. When Chavan was asked in the Lok Sabha about Russian assistance, he replied: 'The USSR had supplied military equipment on suitable credit terms both before and after 1962. It would not be in the public interest to give more details.'

Despite this secrecy, the Soviets had permitted advertisement of the fact they they were helping India achieve a breakthrough in air power. The inference was clear that Russia might also provide India with tanks and other modern weapons of primary significance in the struggle with Pakistan and, as usual, without restrictions on their use. Whether the Soviet performance fulfilled the advertising was unknown. The visible evidence indicates that by 1965 the Soviets had created a potential rather than an actual military position of major proportions, yet their military aid to India far outstripped that of the Anglo-American powers. Thus the arms balance was disrupted primarily by Russia through apparently careful design, either by clever propaganda or by actual performance. Pakistan's concern over the potential was stressed by a commentator in the *Pakistan Times* of July 15, 1965, who said: 'Foreign powers are pumping arms and ammunition into India. Five years hence the Indians will be very strong.' The Pakistanis readily believed reports circulating in early 1966 that Moscow had promised offensive arms, including armour, to New Delhi.

It may be noted that the Soviet military reputation rested primarily upon modern weapons that were of great significance in the Indo-Pakistani confrontation but of little importance to India's build-up against Peking. This was clearly intentional. There is little evidence that, after an initial deal in helicopters and transports, Moscow provided any suitable equipment for the Indo-Chinese frontier. Apart from their reluctance to furnish strength for use against their Chinese 'brothers', the Soviets were evidently more interested in making capital out of Indian fears of Pakistan. By pledging arms to India, the Soviets were also waving a potential promise to Pakistan, and were quite willing to risk war on the sub-continent in order to pursue this double policy. By 1965, it was evident that many Indian officials felt dependent upon Moscow for anti-Pakistani strength. There was less evidence to support the governmental thesis that the Soviets would supply weapons to repel another Chinese attack.

Sino-Soviet pressures, administered separately and contrarily, thus provided the catalyst for intensified mistrust between the neighbours which grew rapidly throughout 1965. Pakistan maintained a rising crescendo of propaganda against the 'massive' arms aid to India and against Indian 'aggression'. The Indians responded in better temper and with remarkable restraint. Nevertheless, both publicly and privately, the Indians re-emphasised their concern over the American-built Pakistani army. There was genuine fear that the Patton tanks were capable of smashing down the Grand Trunk Road to New Delhi.

The best available foreign information indicates that the statistics used to bolster these mutual fears were grossly exaggerated. In the autumn of 1965, India did not have the overwhelming superiority that was claimed and was not in a position to launch physical aggression against Pakistan. On the other hand, Pakistan had neither the equipment nor the skill to mount an irresistible air-tank attack against India.

At the outbreak of hostilities, the Indian army was estimated at slightly more than 800,000 men, plus an estimated 47,000 reserves. They were grouped in seventeen operational divisions of between 16,000 and 18,000 men. The regular Pakistani army totalled about 230,000 men, in eight divisions. In addition, Pakistan had in being a lightly armed militia of around 250,000 men and an Azad Kashmir force of some 30,000. These figures, contained in a Reuters news agency report from the field, were regarded in Washington as the most reliable of several somewhat conflicting compilations by foreign sources and are used hereafter. The Institute for Strategic Studies (ISS) of London, in its report for 1965–6, placed Indian regular authorised strength at 825,000, in sixteen divisions, but said this had not been fully realised. Pakistan's regular army was set at between 188,000 and 208,000 men, in six infantry divisions, with only 70,000 irregulars in addition.

In terms of manpower, one of the criteria used in debate over the arms balance, this gave India an 8–1·8 or 8–2·3 advantage in regular army forces. This was misleading, however, because the type of terrain along the Kashmir front and the type of action characterising any armed conflict in this area placed a premium upon so-called irregular operations, so that Pakistan's militia becomes more significant. Moreover, the militia was incorporated into the regular army and came under its operational control in July 1965. The more realistic maximum figures for the two sides, then, were 8·47–5·1, in terms of manpower. Some of the Indian reserves and most of the Pakistani irregulars probably were improperly trained and inadequately armed for conventional combat.

Pakistani military officers claim that a division-to-division comparison of the two armies is misleading, because Indian units organisationally contain more troops. They say, for example, that an Indian brigade totals from 900 to 3,600 more men than a Pakistani brigade. By early 1965, these sources contend, India had reached a 4·5–1 manpower superiority, but this figure apparently did not include Pakistan's para-military forces. The Pakistani government, through its publications, has said that it would be 'happy' with a 3–1 superiority for India and would accept 4–1.

The disposition of these forces in mid-1965 was another essential consideration in measuring intent and the balance of strength. India maintained an estimated garrison of 150,000 men, at least three divisions, in Kashmir. They were required to guard the Ladakh front against Communist China and the 470-mile cease-fire line with Pakistan. Part of this force may also have been used to cover the northern edge of the 800-mile border between India and West Pakistan. Another six Indian divisions were positioned in the Himalayas and near East Pakistan. A portion of this garrison was expected to contain the one Pakistani division stationed in East Pakistan; New Delhi sources said a maximum of two or three divisions would be sufficient. The balance of this Indian force was required to protect the 1,800-mile border with China, less the Ladakh section. This means the Indians had eight divisions left from their known standing strength for use on the Indian-West Pakistan border, for strategic reserve and other purposes. Of the seven divisions stationed in West Pakistan, four or five were believed to be in the Kashmir-Lahore section, with three in reserve.

If these figures are correct, or close enough to be indicative, they suggest that India was not in a condition or a position to launch an aggressive attack that could be expected to precipitate major fighting. Half of the regular army was pinned down to defensive commitments and could not feasibly be used for action elsewhere as long as there was a valid threat of a two-front war, with Red China and Pakistan. Some of the best units were located in Kashmir where, theoretically at least, they could be occupied and immobilised by the efficient use of Pakistani irregulars. The half of the army available for action in the critical Punjab, the most feasible area for opening offensive action, was not large enough to launch an offensive attack and still maintain the necessary reserve. In general a three-to-one advantage in manpower is considered necessary for attack, particularly over the fortified terrain in the crucial Punjab areas. When the possibility of a two-front war subsided, the Indians used one or two mountain divisions in the Punjab, but even so their manpower superiority was minimal for offensive purposes. Thus the Indian army was not logically positioned to initiate major hostilities, although it was capable of responding vigorously to a single-front attack with limited offensive action.

Pakistan was in a more favourable position for a quick, limited offensive. The bulk of her regular forces was concentrated in the Kashmir-Lahore section of the Punjab, the main battle area. Her supply lines were shorter and more effective. She had no worries about a second front and no long border with a third power to guard by herself; her aid pact gave her assurances of support against communist assault. In terms of over-all manpower and, particularly, in industrial capacity, the Pakistanis could not match India's potential staying power in a long war. But it was far more feasible for them to initiate a quick attack.

Nevertheless, the size of the Indian army as well as the size of the Indian nation obviously worried the Pakistanis. So the relative firepower of the two forces was a third critical factor in the balance between them. In this respect, both sides tended to consider the tank with undue awe and to assign disproportionate significance to the supersonic plane. India at this time possessed an estimated total of 1,450 heavy and light tanks and Pakistan had around 1,100. These totals demonstrated a relative balance in numbers, considering India's wider defence commitments. It was credited with a division of British Centurion heavy tanks and a brigade of lighter American-built Shermans, as well as two regiments of light tanks. Pakistan had a division of Pattons and an incompleted second division, along with other forces of Shermans and the French light tank, the Chaffée. This gave Pakistan a slightly more favourable position, particularly in striking power. Although the Patton and the Centurion were each about 45 tons, the American weapon was more modern, faster and better equipped. It had almost a two-to-one range of gunfire, more manoeuvrability and a capacity, through infra-red equipment, to operate at night, which Indian tanks lacked. The Pakistanis misused the Patton in combat, but until then it gave them theoretical battle superiority. In addition, heavy American artillery, supplied as part of the basic build-up, surpassed the best in the Indian Army by a range of 25,000 yards to 18,000 yards, according to Indian accounts. If properly used and properly evaluated, these two weapons should have given Pakistan assurance that it had superior firepower to offset any numerical superiority of an attacking Indian force. Instead of being content, however, with this relative land balance of guns and men, the Pakistanis flaunted their Pattons and thereby helped to drive the Indians into efforts to increase their own armoured power. President Ayub openly taunted Shastri with the boast that his tanks could reach New Delhi along the Grand Trunk Road in a matter of hours, and the refrain was printed in the press. The distance from the border to the Indian capital is some 200 miles.

In the air, India had numerical superiority with what she regarded as tactical inferiority. The Indian air force included more than 500 fighters and bombers, compared with about 200 Pakistani combat aircraft. Pakistani equipment again was more modern and the F-104s were more powerful than the limited numbers of supersonic aircraft, mostly Soviet-supplied, possessed by India. This should have meant further reassurance for the Pakistanis against Indian offensive action, in view of the pronounced tendency to exaggerate the dangers of air assault and to exalt the importance of speed in the military context of the subcontinent. The Indians were grimly determined to acquire their own supersonic aircraft. In addition to closer reliance upon Russia for this weapon, they were expediting the development of their own models. But supersonic planes were primarily valuable in a war of up-to-date aircraft, and preferably against their own type. The F-104s were of little military value when the war actually came, although airpower had a marginal role. The Indian-produced subsonic interceptor, the Gnat, a highly manoeuvrable battlefront aircraft, proved of considerable importance under combat conditions. The Indians, seeking to expand their airpower, had put at least 100 of them in service by the autumn of 1965.

The balance of power, then, was delicate, variable and partly psychological. India had a legitimate requirement for a much larger army to man the China front. But the increase in numbers worried Pakistan, for the same divisions could be used against that country. Pakistan had reason to maintain heavy armour and fast fighters, but they directly threatened New Delhi. The balance had doubtless been effective for as long as it had because superior firepower reassured Pakistan in the face of perpetually increasing Indian forces. But by early 1965, at the latest, it seemed clear that the Indians would not consider themselves secure until they had matched, in relative terms, the potential manpower of a Chinese attack and the potential firepower of a Pakistani attack. The Indian military budget therefore rose steadily. It was estimated at $1·8 billion for the 1964–5 year and $2·1 billion, including war costs, for the following twelve months; compared, in the latter year, to $289 million for Pakistan. When the build-up was completed, some time in 1968 by foreign estimates, it was conceivable that India would have an unassailable superiority in both men and firepower.

Of these two main elements, the potential increase in firepower was unquestionably more important to Pakistani officials, as their constant emphasis on 'massive' foreign arms aid indicates. It is possible they would have accepted, with only political retaliation, an Indian build-up limited primarily to arms and divisions for meeting another Chinese attack in the mountains, as Anglo-American officials had advised. The balance, however, was changed drastically enough to contribute to war when heavy weapons of primary value against Pakistan became a more dominating aspect of the Indian programme. Although India had undertaken some initiatives of its own to increase this modern arsenal, notably in Indian-built aircraft, the firepower balance could not have been altered significantly without Russian intervention.

The only restrictions placed on India's use of foreign weapons applied to the light equipment furnished by Washington and London. These Anglo-American arms were supplied from the beginning without demand for a change in India's policy of non-alignment. Nehru told a mass meeting that one Western leader, presumably President Kennedy, had written him to this effect.[8] This permissive gesture by the Western powers enabled the Indians to maintain their traditional posture, which they clearly wished to do. The comparative freedom of non-alignment thus became an integral part of a relatively unrestricted unilateral rearmament programme. However, the competitive machinations of the Sino-Soviet powers had made non-alignment virtually mandatory for India, regardless of what might have been its own desire to change. Moscow had supplied enough economic aid and had promised enough military assistance by the end of 1962 to make New Delhi dependent upon the continuation of both programmes. The Soviets could hardly maintain this assistance to an openly pro-Western 'third' country in the face of strident criticism from Peking.

Pakistan, on the other hand, was hobbled by alignment to a single source of arms which were supplied under strict limitations on their use against India. Its quest for international 'independence' had begun before the Chinese attack on India. It was accelerated inevitably as soon as India proved it could obtain more diversified and unfettered arms through non-alignment. The Pakistanis made no secret of their belief that they had been penalised for stoutly contributing to the defences of the non-communist world, while India had gained strength, for the intramural conflict on the sub-continent, by bargaining with both camps. Accordingly, the Pakistanis moved closer to Red China, their only immediate potential source of additional arms, despite the evidence that Peking was feared and mistrusted in some quarters of Rawalpindi. When Ayub became convinced in mid-1963 that the Anglo-American powers would not require India to bargain over Kashmir in ex-change for arms and that New Delhi would not otherwise alter its stand, he tightened his military and political pressures.

Thus the neighbours undertook a series of inter-acting initiatives which placed them on a collision course before 1965, and which required resolute diplomacy in order to prevent an explosion. The fatal cycle probably began in early 1962, when India achieved an ostensible breakthrough in supersonic planes through the Soviet MIG deal and Pakistan turned to 'normalisation' of relations with Peking. The cycle quickened in the aftermath of the Indo-Chinese conflict and with new tensions in and over Kashmir. By the end of 1964, the situation was delicate. Both nations quite clearly attempted to use political and military pressures to intimidate the other into inaction. This is an old tactic, which seldom works when the participants have reason to believe they have relatively equal power. In this instance, neither the Indians nor the Pakistanis backed down. Instead, the seemingly unrestrained Indian build-up and the apparently unrestricted aggressiveness of Pakistan's 'hate India' campaign merely solidified the other's determination and led to a renewed search for fresh power to counteract it. Neither capital seemed to comprehend the potential consequences of their escalating conflict of power politics. Certainly neither one, after mid-1963, made any effort to curtail or alter the trend of events.

The lesson was clear. The circumstances of the subcontinent would not permit India to construct adequate defences against a two-war threat, on its own, without increasing the danger of war. One alternative was to soften the impact of rearmament with political or diplomatic reassurances. All evidence indicates that India had no intention of attacking Pakistan, even when the military programme was complete. Therefore, its best interests lay in reassuring Pakistan of this reality to the fullest practicable extent, particularly after Pakistani suspicions became clearly discernible. The responsibility for such a move rested on New Delhi, because the Indians had taken the initiative in upsetting the prevailing arms balance.

Time and events had outmoded two methods of providing India and Pakistan with diplomatic reassurance against attack. One of these, the possible conclusion of a no-war pact, remained diplomatically alive and was discussed fruitlessly after the military conflict. Efforts to establish such an agreement failed then, as they had before, primarily because each side sought to use non-aggression proposals to strengthen its position over Kashmir. Further, the political and strategic significance of this issue in the total range of Indo-Pakistani hostilities made each nation reluctant to surrender its full right to the use of military power until the Kashmir question was settled. Thus India would not agree to forswear war against the Punjab until assured that this theatre was no longer necessary as a flank pressure point against any possible Pakistani aggression in Kashmir proper. Although both capitals at various times have proposed no-war pacts and both long have needed to conclude one, the chances of achieving this relationship have decreased over the years. Secondly, the possibility of increasing and extending the activities of the United Nations observer group to prevent military action anywhere on the Indo-Pakistani borders, while logical, was impracticable. Even if the UN were willing, such a move would be opposed by India, pridefully determined to minimise even a peacekeeping foreign presence on territory it claims. More significantly, the Soviet Union would have vetoed any such suggestion, in her own interests, with or without India's concurrence.

What the situation required was not an overt and politically vulnerable method of guaranteeing peace on the subcontinent, but an avenue for private reassurances which might at least prevent war by miscalculation. Anglo-American diplomats, in a way, had attempted to fulfil that function by seeking to calm the neighbours and, particularly, by attempting to maintain an arms balance. Assuming London-Washington willingness to become more deeply involved, it is conceivable that their diplomats could have acted as intermediaries to assure each side against attack by the other. If given enough information and trust, they might have performed a role similar to that of the UN observers who, through knowledge of battle plans, prevented major incidents along the Kashmir cease-fire line prior to 1954. To accept this degree of advance mediation would have required extensive, but not impossible, psychological changes in both governments. In particular, each would have been obliged to discard the belief that attack by the other was always imminent and inevitable. Even though Pakistan's subsequent offensive has convinced most Indians that its government was always bent on hostilities, there is no convincing evidence that this was true through most of 1964. While it is manifestly impossible to say that advance mediation would have prevented hostilities, the point is that no efforts to do so were initiated by the prospective belligerents.

Instead, both India and Pakistan attempted to use the Anglo-American powers primarily as a means of reducing the other's strength. Pakistan consistently attempted to get Kashmir in return for Anglo-American arms aid to India. New Delhi sought to wreck the US-Pakistan alliance, on the grounds that it had been abrogated by Sino-Pakistani rapprochement. The governments and informed officials who knew better encouraged the growth of two myths among their people which were particularly harmful to popular understanding of events swirling around the subcontinent. Pakistan's constant complaints against 'massive' Anglo-American arms created disproportionate fear of Indian strength and intent. The Indians, for their part, continued to foster the misconception that, without American weapons, Pakistan would have remained militarily weak and, therefore, inoffensive from the Indian point of view.

Nevertheless, as tension increased on the subcontinent, sharp questions about the continued validity of the US-Pakistan alliance circulated not only in India but in many Western circles. There was considerable belief that Russia had become less aggressive and less 'revolutionary' and that, therefore, the anti-communist defence line had lost much of its significance. This belief was based upon a misreading of both the record and the doubletalk of the Sino-Soviet dialogue. The record had demonstrated that, while there were no further Soviet-sponsored Korean wars and Europe was quiet, there had been a tremendous upsurge in the Soviet attempt to use arms for creating 'proxy wars' by third powers in sensitive under-developed areas. The Soviets, furthermore, had demonstrated and proclaimed their consistent support for 'wars of national liberation' under conditions suitable to them. Both Moscow and Peking, said the US Secretary of State, Dean Rusk, have put increasing emphasis on this disguised form of warfare 'as the risks of overt aggression, whether nuclear or with conventional forces, have become in-creasingly evident . . .'. If these risks decreased, however, there is, in the prevalent American view, every possibility that the com-munists of both camps will revert, when practicable, to the more efficient tactics of thinly-disguised aggression by conventional forces. Khrushchev had outlawed wars on the Korean scale only because of the risks; the tactic could be revived as quickly. In their debate with Peking, moreover, the Soviets have not turned away from militant expansion, as the Chinese have charged; they have merely reiterated the doctrine of supporting 'revolution' for the primary benefit of the Soviet Union. This is the same dogma of 'socialism in one country' under which Stalin justified all his conquests and his excesses. Under these circumstances, American authorities believed that the global defence line was as essential in 1965 for the protection of the non-communist world as when it was first erected. Despite the severe strains of the US-Pakistan relationship, Pakistan occupied a key position in these defences and continued to contribute to them. General Wood assured Congress in April 1965, that 'thus far, Pakistan has not, by any particular action, affected the essentials of our alliance relationship'.[9] Washing-ton was no more disposed to abandon an ally or begin unravelling the global defence system in response to Indian complaints than it was to take Kashmir from India in response to Pakistani com-plaints.

The outbreak of Indo-Pakistan fighting, however, revived criticism in several quarters, particularly India, over the extent to which Pakistan's heavy striking power had been increased. The argument ran like this: Moscow was less openly belligerent in the mid-1960s than a decade earlier, therefore the need for heavy tanks and supersonic aircraft was less pressing; yet Washington supplied even more of these weapons to Pakistan. Actually, the United States never fulfilled the arms commitment she had undertaken in 1954. Washington agreed then to arm five and a half divisions with modern weapons. In tanks, the light Shermans were first supplied and were to be replaced by the heavy Pattons when they became available. Under the schedule being followed, this process would not have been completed until 1967. As a result, the second American-equipped Pakistani armoured division, the Sixth, was incompletely organised in 1965 when it was thrown into action around Sialkot.

The build-up had been unusually prolonged for a number of reasons. Primarily, considerable time was needed to train the Pakistanis to utilise and absorb sophisticated equipment. But there were also political considerations. The international situation had eased sufficiently to eliminate need for a 'crash' build-up, but not enough in Washington's opinion to cancel the need for the continual display of organised power in sensitive Pakistan. Nevertheless, American officials were wary of Pakistan's propensity for flaunting its armour against India and for merging its international commitments into subcontinental pressures. They anticipated prompt demands from Rawalpindi for immediate modernisation, as soon as all the promised Second World War Pattons were delivered, and postponed that probability as a means of maintaining the subcontinental arms balance. In short, the situation required careful handling of Indo-Pakistan tempers, but the international climate had not been sufficiently altered to renounce the commitments of 1954. Although there was a tendency to believe that the presence of arms, particularly foreign arms, was the sole factor causing war in 1965, it was notable that the great Hindu-Muslim civil conflict of 1947 occurred without the influence of foreign weapons.

American officials explained these and other aspects of the global situation privately to leaders of both countries, but for a variety of reasons the explanations were never made public. In India, this was true partly because most Indian officials did not accept the American position but primarily because, even if they had, their freedom of speech was curtailed by Moscow's well-known instantly aroused anger. Moreover, as the tensions and frustrations created by their own policies intensified, both nations turned for relief to public criticism of the United States and Great Britain. Throughout much of 1965, this attitude was enlarged by simmering resentment in both countries over one of Washington's errors. In the spring of the year, President Johnson abruptly postponed a scheduled visit by President Ayub, to stress his disapproval of the Sino-Pakistani rapprochement; disapproval which had previously been expressed in many ways, including postponement of the consideration of new foreign development loans. As an afterthought, the postponement was applied also to Prime Minister Shastri, who was due to visit Washington at about the same time. The blunt announcement shocked both countries, and they cancelled the visits. As events developed, this probably helped India. Pakistan, despite her new posture, had influential friends in the American Congress who valued Pakistani military co-operation in the past and wanted the alliance to continue as firmly as possible. India, on the other hand, had infuriated these same Congressmen and others by publicly opposing American policies in Vietnam at a critical phase of the war. If Shastri alone had been welcomed in Washington, it was highly possible, as the Johnson administration explained, that pro-Pakistani congressional elements would have retaliated by reducing foreign aid appropriations for India: a precedent for such action had been established. Nevertheless, the Indians were as angry over the incident as was Rawalpindi.

The consequence, however, was that India and Pakistan cut themselves off from the two major powers most interested in preventing armed conflict on the subcontinent, as distinct from the Soviet role of encouraging hostilities, then helping to stop them after they had begun. In the mood of the subcontinent, Anglo-American diplomats were obliged to move discreetly and to concentrate upon private efforts to warn the leaders of the two nations of the dangers they were creating for themselves. Far from encouraging or instigating the conflict, as some angry newspapers charged, the Western officials found that most of their advice was rejected. Throughout the preludes to war, when it still might have been prevented, politicians on both sides responded to events and provocations with uninhibited emotionalism and little statesmanship.

With the United Nations discredited and the Anglo-American capitals rebuffed, the available channels for restraining diplomacy shifted to the Commonwealth, the Afro-Asian nations and small countries bordering the subcontinent. No serious effort was made to enlist their good offices, either separately or collectively. It is probable no one thought of doing so, for Indo-Pakistani misunderstandings were too implacable to invite outside participation. Yet one of the new concepts emerging from this progression towards war is that the established peace-keeping machinery is too easily immobilised and that other methods of supplying restraint and advice have become increasingly necessary in a quarrelsome world.

In the major diplomatic arena of the Afro-Asian nations, India and Pakistan competed openly for influence and for backing behind their respective positions regarding Kashmir. Both were rather conspicuously involved in the quarrels and factionalism which rose to the surface during late 1964 and early the next year, and which came to a climax in a bitter Sino-Soviet battle for dominance. Chinese efforts to prevent Soviet participation, on the grounds that Russia was not an Asian nation, paralysed and to some extent discredited the effectiveness of this loose alliance of the emergent nations. At the Cairo Conference of 1964, India preached moderation and 'coexistence' and was prepared to follow the same general policy at the scheduled Algiers Conference of mid-1965, which was never held. These broad policies coincided with New Delhi's beliefs, but in Afro-Asian politics they also constituted support for Russia; as, indeed, might have been expected, since one aspect of the Sino-Soviet quarrel concerned Moscow's role in the Sino-Indian border struggle.

Pakistan, taking the offensive, aligned herself with the radical wing of the Afro-Asian countries. This political shift was clearly reflected in internal propaganda. *Dawn*, in an editorial on February 9, 1965, claimed, for instance, that the Western powers were backing India in neo-colonialist schemes on the subcontinent. They wanted to use the Indians as a means of 'shifting the focus of the cold war from the white man's continent of Europe to the coloured peoples' continents of Asia and Africa'. On May 2, *Dawn* again proclaimed that India was 'deliberately stepping up provocations against Pakistan' as part of a calculated campaign. The campaign began in late 1963, the paper said, 'when she [India] realised that Western arms aid would not even be slowed down for the sake of bringing about a Kashmir settlement'. President Ayub, in a press conference on June 29, publicly endorsed the thesis enunciated by President Sukarno of Indonesia that a showdown was imminent between the have and have-not nations. Sukarno had been rebuffed at Cairo in an attempt to win endorsement for this thesis and for the parallel contention that coexistence is impossible as long as this situation is maintained.

India had emerged from the crisis of 1962 with a profound sense of international isolation. She had been rebuffed, says an Indian writer, in a global search for adequate arms. 'Indian diplomacy met with scant respect abroad. We slumped in the esteem of Afro-Asian opinion. It looked as though we had not a friend in the world.' The 'efforts for a breakthrough resembled those of a caged animal desperately trying to break out'.[10] It is evident that this sense of isolation also contributed substantially to a hardened Indian response to Pakistani initiatives.

Although Indian diplomats diligently attempted to regain a strong position among the Afro-Asian powers, they did not change established policies in order to appeal to the predominant radical nations. India had been out of step with this increasingly left 'revolutionary line' and its strong anti-colonialism since Nehru told the Belgrade Conference of 1961 that colonialism was outworn as a valid issue and that nuclear weapons and development problems were more important. In his maiden speech to the bloc, delivered at Cairo on October 7, 1964, Prime Minister Shastri outlined a Nehruist 'positive programme in furtherance of peace'. The speech stressed these points: nuclear disarmament, peaceful settlement of border disputes, freedom from foreign domination, aggression and subversion and racial discrimination, the acceleration of economic development through international co-operation, and full support for the United Nations. In particular, he advocated direct negotiations for the settlement of border disputes, but insisted that the basis for negotiations must be 'customary or traditional boundaries which may be in existence and not any new boundaries that may have been created by force of any kind'. He further urged the conference to adopt as part of its final communiqué this principle: '. . . self-determination is the right of any country that is dominated by another. But there can be no self-determination for different areas and regions within a sovereign and independent country, for this would lead only to fragmentation and disruption and no country's integrity would be safe.'[11]

This amounted to a careful restatement of one aspect of the Indian case on Kashmir and a bid for Afro-Asian support. The Indians consistently maintained that the Kashmiris were no more

T

different from the remainder of Indians than other regional groups and, therefore, self-determination in the accepted sense did not apply to them. After a reputedly stormy backstage controversy, the conference rejected Shastri's proposal. It restored the old principle of supporting the self-determination of 'peoples'. This outcome was to be expected, for the Cairo meeting was dominated by excessive concentration upon colonialism. The principle of self-determination in its broadest meaning was too potent as a political concept for the non-aligned extremists to think of diluting it.

What Shastri had proposed, however, was more than the mere repetition of an Indian argument on Kashmir. He was suggesting that the non-aligned powers should take the initiative to codify the loose principle of self-determination to conform to practical reality. All nations with urgent tribal problems, including most of those represented at Cairo, had separatist movements, and all suppressed them. Some of the most vocal supporters of this principle had built their nations by subduing minority peoples in recent times. Pakistan, for example, rigorously controlled her Pushtu separatist movement on the valid grounds that it threatened her national unity. She invoked the same principle to justify the retention of Azad Kashmir. Shastri's proposal was important, because the turmoil of regionalism and tribalism threatens to become increasingly significant in emergent nations. Kashmir had proved that the loose application of self-determination created its own political complications.

Pakistan and India also competed assiduously for support among their neighbours and in other parts of the world. When hostilities broke out, however, most of this diplomatic spadework proved useless. The Afro-Asian nations and the neighbours of the combatants remained passive. Pakistan won non-communist support almost exclusively from a handful of nations with whom she had the ties of Islam and, on the whole, a common Middle Eastern outlook. Turkey reciprocated Pakistan's past favour in permitting the creation of a Middle Eastern anti-Soviet defence alignment; Indonesia returned Pakistani support over the confrontation with Malaysia. India fought alone primarily because she had no substantial links of religion or political belief with any nation likely to come to her support purely in 'friendship'. She had done few favours for non-communist nations. Malaysia became her most vocal supporter partly because of previous Indian backing against

Indonesia's militancy. This isolation was a concomitant of Nehru's philosophy that a non-aligned nation would determine its position, and therefore its compatriots, on the merits of each international episode. As with individuals, the nation practising this independence has considerable freedom but few friends. Thus, both of the belligerents devoted considerable attention to the attempt to establish power positions which quickly fell apart, without exercising the same diplomatic initiative towards preserving peace.

If there was no tendency by either side to use diplomacy for reducing tensions, there were, however, two broad methods of accomplishing somewhat the same result through bilateral contacts. One was the familiar and rather unpromising possibility of reviving talks on Kashmir or on some other aspects of accumulated Indo-Pakistan problems. The second was to reduce or to minimise political actions within the subcontinent which might raise tempers and produce a clash.

On his return to New Delhi from Cairo in October 1964, Shastri stopped in Karachi for his first brief personal meeting with President Ayub. They discussed Kashmir, and Shastri evidently voiced a sincere desire to solve the problem, but made no commitment. His position at Cairo had underlined the fact, however, that there was no change in the fundamental Indian position; neither had there been any softening of the Pakistani demands. After the war had been fought indecisively, Ayub told Shastri that, without a settlement of Kashmir, 'there could be no peace between India and Pakistan'.[12] Nevertheless, in their first conference, the two leaders discussed some of their other problems, and Shastri later reported: '. . . I must say it did create some impression on me. For when we talked amongst ourselves we felt some of the burning problems should be resolved and settled.' As a result, New Delhi fixed two dates for meetings of the two Home Ministers to discuss refugee problems, as Ayub had suggested, but Pakistan avoided attending either of them. They also discussed growing military tensions in Kashmir, and Ayub stressed the necessity of halting the skirmishes between the two armies. Shastri said this could be arranged through the local commanders, but apparently no effective action was taken. There was no indication that the two leaders discussed broader military problems or that Shastri undertook to reassure the Pakistani leader about the Indian build-up.

Recapitulating this meeting in a parliamentary speech on November 16, 1965, after the military conflict had been fought, Shastri made it clear that he believed Ayub's relatively conciliatory attitude was merely a façade. 'It was far from my imagination', said Shastri, 'that Pakistan was then preparing for something entirely different' from the peaceful relations which he contended India sought. Even while this discussion was held, the Indian leader maintained, Pakistan was preparing to force India to surrender on 'certain points with regard to the Rann of Kutch and Jammu and Kashmir'.[13]

Pakistan's strident anti-India propaganda campaign constituted the most consistently explosive element in the political preludes to war. Indian officials responded to this constant uninhibited criticism with asperity and a sharpness they might not otherwise have displayed. So did the Indian people, when some of the propaganda found its way into their newspapers. At the beginning of 1964, the Indian representative told the United Nations Security Council that 'the threats of violence which have emanated from Pakistan from time to time ... must cease'. Then he added, 'Once a better atmosphere prevails, it will be possible—and we are prepared—to discuss with Pakistan all our outstanding differences.'[14] But the atmosphere, far from clearing, had grown darker by the time of the Shastri-Ayub meeting, and thereafter the Pakistani press campaign grew more thunderously anti-Indian. There was no doubt that it was encouraged and controlled by the Pakistani government and that, accordingly, it represented a conscious means of pressure on India. It should have been clear in Rawalpindi, however, that this pressure was counter-productive and made any political solution of Kashmir, through Indian agreement, even more remote.

In these circumstances, Nanda announced the political measures of December 1964, which equalised Kashmir with other Indian states, under the constitution, and thereby completed integration. The timing was not explained. It could have been dictated by impatience with the unflagging Pakistani press campaign, thereby constituting a deliberate form of Indian pressure. It could also have been timed merely by bureaucratic processes. On the surface, the move appeared to be the inevitable culmination of a legal annexation which had begun a decade earlier. Its practical value was to give New Delhi the legal means of directly intervening in state affairs through the application of President's rule. As a result,

India could exercise more direct authority over Kashmir without the foreign criticism to which New Delhi was sensitive. This may have been considered desirable as a result of the Hair of the Prophet incident.

Symbolically, however, the new legal measures were momentous. They meant, in effect, that New Delhi had no further intention of seriously negotiating a new status for Kashmir. Obviously, it would not bargain away a totally assimilated part of the Union. This did not appreciably change the apparent reality of the situation. But it eliminated the last prospect of a diplomatic settlement, a face-saving possibility that quite probably was essential for the Pakistan government. As long as leaders of the two sides could promise to discuss Kashmir, the issue would remain alive. The Pakistanis could nurture hopes of a favourable settlement in the future, and Pakistan's international prestige on this issue would be unchanged. The new Indian measure threatened to upset this delicate situation by removing Kashmir from domestic and international debate, unless Pakistan kept it open through overt pressure.

What New Delhi had done, in essence, was to place Pakistan in an untenable legal position over Kashmir at a moment when its official and popular fears about Indian rearmament had reached a zenith. Thus two powerful forces merged to press Rawalpindi into a new and more impressive initiative over Kashmir than all of its past assortment of measures. On a national level, this move paralleled the circumstances under which, nearly twenty years earlier, Jinnah in political frustration had turned to the policy of 'direct action' which created the Calcutta riots and led to the civil war. Once more, it seemed, the Hindu Indians had misunderstood their troublesome Muslim neighbours and had impatiently washed their hands of them. Ayub had responded, as had Jinnah, by abandoning political means for force.

Under the circumstances, it was to India's advantage to cushion the impact of her rearmament by avoiding unnecessary political incitement. Since Kashmir was by far the most explosive area of confrontation, prudence would have dictated the maintenance of the *status quo*. India was under no great pressure to complete the absorption of her portion of the state, and neither was Pakistan under immediate compulsion to acquire Indian Kashmir. The situation might have been contained indefinitely on a level of political acrimony and low-level military pressure—annoying enough for the Indians but better than active war. By adding the new policy over Kashmir to the accumulated concern over rearmament, New Delhi made military action almost inevitable. It is not clear whether, as Shastri suggested, Ayub had definitely decided on military measures by October 1964. But the circumstances indicate that this policy was determined relatively soon after Nanda's Kashmir moves and that the military episodes of early 1965 were in preparation for war.

12

MILITARY PRELUDES

THE STRANGE conflict in the Rann of Kutch provided the first test of Pakistan's revived course of 'direct action'. The Rann, lying on the north-western Indian boundary with Pakistan is a virtually uninhabited region of mudflats and wasteland. It is 320 miles long and 50 miles wide. During half the year, the area is covered with water, whipped in from the Arabian Sea by the western monsoon, beginning in May. Oil deposits have been reported but never exploited; unless they exist, the Rann is economically and strategically useless. Nevertheless, the neighbours have quarrelled periodically over the status of an irregularly-shaped portion of the wasteland totalling about 3,500 square miles. India contends that its right to the entire Rann was established clearly by pre-partition gazetteers and agreements, and that there is no territorial dispute. Using other documents, Pakistan claims nearly half of the Rann, the territory extending southward to the Twenty-fourth Parallel. The area under controversy lies north of this parallel.

Fighting broke out accidentally in January 1965. Indian police discovered belatedly that Pakistani border guards had been patrolling for some time along a track or rough road which enabled them to avoid the sand dunes. The track, in the north-western part of the disputed zone, lies about one and a half miles south of the boundary claimed by India but within the territory claimed by Pakistan. Indian police expelled the Pakistani guards, then erected a series of outposts to secure the territory. They were wiped out by reinforced Pakistani guards. In early April, according to the Pakistani account, the Indians struck at a Pakistan position near Ding at the extreme northern tip of the western portion of the disputed area. Ding lies some ten miles north-west of the ruined fort of Kanjarkot, one of the landmarks near the disputed desert road which started the skirmishing. Both sides had been reinforced, but still relied upon police and border guards, without regular army troops.

On April 9, units of the regular Pakistani army attacked Indian positions at Sardar Post, near Kanjarkot, and initially drove back the defenders. The attack was made in force—India claims that two battalions of about 1,400 men were involved—and swiftly extended the fighting. India quickly dispatched army forces to take over the front and announced this move the next day. Pakistan claims the Indian army had supplanted the police before the attack. A Pakistani proposal for negotiations was made at this point, but Rawalpindi refused to accept Indian demands to withdraw from Kanjarkot, and no talks were held. On April 24, Pakistan simultaneously attacked four Indian positions, using Patton tanks and 100-pound guns for the first time. Before this flare-up ended on April 29, the Indian army also apparently brought up some heavy equipment, and Pakistan claimed that tanks were used. But the Indian writer, D. R. Mankekar, who is close to the army, says the ground in Indian-held territory was unsuitable for tanks and none was employed.[1] This point has been confirmed by impartial sources. Both nations established the precedent at this time of preventing foreign diplomats and newsmen from witnessing the battle and this practice was followed later in their larger clash.

Nevertheless, it was clear that Pakistan used the conflict as a low-cost test of Indian will and capabilities. The 'war' was fought against time before the battlefield became flooded, and the time element alone might have prevented major Indian retaliation against the initial heavy Pakistani attack. This assault, moreover, was aimed at an area where Indian forces, for logistic reasons, could not assume the offensive and where senior Indian military officials did not wish to fight.[2] Their supply lines were long and difficult, while Pakistan had relatively favourable communications. Under these circumstances, the Pakistanis, profiting from the striking power of their Patton tanks, penetrated at least seven miles into India-claimed territory. Casualties apparently were light; Mankekar reported the total Indian dead and wounded as 93, with an estimated 350 casualties for Pakistan.[3]

On the whole, the hostilities appeared to compare with the initial Chinese campaigns in Ladakh, as Indian officers contended. The

Pakistanis tested arms and intention, for the first time since the war of 1948, in a remote battle area, under a brief timetable, where the chances for effective Indian retaliation were of the slightest. This has become the hallmark of Chinese tactics, but it was not necessarily the proof of close Sino-Pakistan co-operation that many Indians assumed; for the concept is standard in general military strategy for probing actions. Ironically, the parallel went further than the Indians admitted. Both the Indian and Pakistani official versions indicate the fighting was touched off by the initial attempts of Indian police to eject the Pakistan border guards. Whether this constituted aggression or defence against aggression depends upon which border is accepted. As in Ladakh, however, the Indians evidently implemented what from their point of view were legitimate measures to repel an 'invader' without building up adequate defences against a counter-blow. Although the Pakistanis apparently did not originate the January crisis, they took the opportunity three months later to strike at inferior forces with power that was clearly greater than required by the tactical situation and for no possible strategic gain. This was a military decision that, it would appear, could only have been valid if further military action were already contemplated.

'Pakistan's manoeuvres in Kutch', the Indian government charged, 'were only a perfidious smoke-screen for her pre-planned intrusions in Kashmir.'⁴ Shastri contended later that Ayub was not only planning this campaign during their meeting in October 1964, but that success in the Rann encouraged Pakistan to continue her aggression. Mankekar, writing from the Indian military standpoint, calls the brief wasteland conflict a 'test to gauge the mood of the Indian army. It was the precursor of, and preliminary to, the more ambitious operation scheduled some four months later' when the Kashmir conflict opened.⁵ In the light of developments, these charges were far more convincing than Pakistan's claim that she was defending herself against aggression, and the Indian version was generally accepted by foreign experts. On that basis, the real significance of the Rann of Kutch episode was that Pakistan turned to military power to implement 'direct action' to combat her frustration over Kashmir. This was a further step in the move away from dependence upon a political solution, and set Pakistan upon a course which events proved her leaders were reluctant to change.

Pakistani officials were clearly encouraged by the tactical results in the Rann and by the international political climate. Their equipment had fulfilled their expectations. *Dawn* asserted on May 19 that 'Pakistani commanders, both on the front and on the base, generally subscribed to the view that the battles against the Indians by and large had been "easy victories" for Pakistan. The trouble with the Indians was that they would hardly ever allow themselves to get too close to the Pakistanis. Even at the sight of the Pakistanis they fled the field in much disorder. They "vanished" without looking back.'[6] And later, in London, President Ayub told a group of his countrymen that a full Indian division would have been destroyed in the Rann battle except for his express orders restraining pursuing Pakistani troops. 'We had to shake off the Indians somehow', he added. 'But I did not want the rift to get wider. Even so, they are squealing like they did after their conflict with China. We want peaceful relations with India but we want peace with honour and do not want to be a satellite. In view of her chauvinistic attitude, we shall have to watch India. If war is forced on us, it will have to be one that seeks a decision. We shall go full out, and smaller though we are than India, we shall hurt India beyond repair.'[7] Pakistan was obviously encouraged also by the international political climate. The United States protested against the use of American arms in violation of the mutual defence agreement, but was unable to prevent the fighting. The rest of the world was not unduly concerned.

The Indian army, however, had fought primarily a holding action in the Rann. In view of logistical difficulties and the oncoming monsoon, major reinforcements were withheld. Instead, India built up forces in the vulnerable Punjab, some 600 miles to the north-east, and reinforced them with more tanks. This was designed as a flank pressure to cool off the Pakistanis.[8] The build-up followed on the heels of a statement by Prime Minister Shastri before the Lok Sabha on April 28 in which he said: 'If Pakistan continues to discard reason and persists in its aggressive activities, our Army will defend the country, and it will decide its own strategy and the employment of its manpower and equipment in the manner which seems best.' Ayub responded on May 1, in his regular monthly broadcast to the people, that: 'India has now threatened us with further aggression in a battleground of her own choice.' Then he asked: 'Does she realise that this will mean a general and total war between India and

Pakistan with all its unpredictable consequences?' After reiterating his willingness to negotiate the Rann issue, Ayub said, 'We have been accused of naked aggression. If we had wanted to commit aggression, we would have chosen a better area than the mudflats of the Rann of Kutch, but our desire to maintain peace restrained us in spite of frequent and grave provocations.'[9] With the Punjab movement apparently in mind, Pakistan sent a letter to the United Nations in early May protesting that India was moving troops in 'hostile deployment'. The protest stated that 'the bulk of the Indian armed forces have been moved close to Pakistan's borders and are now poised in offensive formations, apparently ready for an armed attack on Pakistan'.* *Dawn* and Pakistani officials repeatedly referred to Shastri's remarks as proof that aggression was being planned in New Delhi, without noting that Ayub had dismissed the military importance of the Rann in almost identical terms. Shastri, in essence, had repeated Nehru's warning of 1952, that India would activate the sensitive Punjab front, rather than submit to unacceptable pressure on the flank border of Kashmir; or, in later years, the Rann of Kutch.

Pakistan built her entire case against Indian 'aggression' from this type of material. Officials and the press added the Rann of Kutch to the old examples of aggression—Hyderabad, Junagadh and Kashmir. Another minor incident during 1965, which raised tempers but failed to demonstrate Indian aggressiveness, also became prominent in internal propaganda. The episode, beginning March 16, involved the movement of Indian forces into the Pakistani enclave of Dahagram in south-east India. This was one of several small areas in this section of India which remained Muslim after partition and which, by agreement, were to be exchanged eventually for similar Hindu districts in East Pakistan. The exchange was never completed, and some of the enclaves have caused periodic trouble since then. Dahagram lies about 150 yards from East Pakistan

---

*Impartial sources say India positioned its First Armoured Division and four infantry and mountain divisions in the Punjab. The armour was nearly 1,000 miles from its regular base. Pakistan also maintained the bulk of its army in West Punjab, the home station for all but two of its divisions. When a settlement was reached in the Rann of Kutch affair, both forces withdrew from the immediate border area, but remained within striking distance of the border. Neither army was disposed to return to the deployment it had maintained before the emergency.

within the Indian territory of Cooch Behar. Indian officials said their military forces moved into the district to expel troublesome Pakistani infiltrators; the Pakistanis retorted with a charge of aggression. The incident was quickly settled, but not before the Pakistani press had asserted that 10,000 of India's best troops had gone into Dahagram to drive out all Pakistanis and that many were killed.

With all its constant repetition of the 'threat' from India, the Pakistani press also retained the conspicuous undertone of defiance which stemmed from Jinnah's days. Speaking of Dahagram in an editorial, *Dawn* concluded: 'By itself, the Indian threat is not much of a threat at all, and if Pakistan makes up her mind to punish instead of protest, better sense will dawn on Delhi. After all it was not so very long ago that the call of the Muezzin to prayer used to produce devastating effects on the households of the Indian braves.' Moreover, the Pakistanis, while constantly repeating these doubtful examples of Indian aggression, did not dwell inordinately upon the build-up in the Punjab, nor did they charge India with any specific plans for invading West Pakistan or conquering Azad Kashmir.

These circumstances suggested that the constant cry of 'aggression' was designed primarily for propaganda effect, and that Rawalpindi carefully tried to create general fear of India without turning it into a weakness. This might explain the periodic defiance inserted into the campaign, along with the fact that the press minimised the vulnerability of such areas as the Punjab. But it also seemed evident that the Pakistanis had several meanings for the word 'aggression'. It meant the threat of military invasion, of course, but it was also used to define Indian refusal to abandon Kashmir and other pieces of territory demanded by Pakistan. Rearmament was further aggression. The Indians had employed the term in precisely the same way for many years, so the neighbours were talking a common language. This usage is considerably broader, however, than the general understanding of the word. One standard dictionary defines it as: 'An unprovoked attack'. A more practical working definition, in this age of camouflaged warfare, might be this: 'Aggression is the overt or covert invasion, without similar provocation, of territory controlled by one government by organised groups of armed men under the control of another government'. Discounting reciprocal violations of the Kashmir cease-fire line, India in this sense had not committed aggression in recent years and was not likely to do so. But it would respond to what it regarded as provocation with a temporary concentration of power that might be regarded as aggressive by an apprehensive neighbour. Pakistani officials consistently maintained that India could force its will on Pakistan without a physical invasion by maintaining heavy military pressure on the borders. They regarded the Indian concentration in the Punjab in this light, because it required a matching mobilisation which they said Pakistan could not continue for practical and economic reasons.

It was impossible to determine from the public record and from individual conversations how much of the universally expressed Pakistani fear of India was due to genuine emotion and how much resulted from fairly consistent anti-Indian propaganda since before partition. Certainly, the 'hate India' campaign since 1963 abnormally aroused the emotions of men willing to regard Hyderabad as aggression against Pakistan. Pakistani officials were equally ambiguous about their true feelings. They constantly gave the impression of being genuinely fearful, yet they were evidently confident after the Rann of Kutch, even while continuing to warn against the Indian 'threat' with increasing intemperance. It is probably safe to conclude that Rawalpindi, up to mid-1965, had no immediate fear of Indian aggression or undue concern over the level of rearmament. The potentialities after completion of Indian rearmament, however, were obviously compelling enough to force them into deciding to embark on what amounted to preventive war. From early 1965, it appears, propaganda, diplomatic negotiations and peace offers were used to camouflage preparations for conflict.

The mood within India had been growing increasingly explosive since the Chinese conflict. 'An impatient nation demanded that the Government and the Army stop shilly shallying, act and wipe out the humiliations heaped upon the country and avenge themselves against a perfidious neighbour', says Mankekar.

'Resentment and frustration were heaping up. Indian leadership gritted its teeth. The Indian army strained at the leash.'[10]

This public attitude was not necessarily a pressure on the ever sensitive government to initiate aggression against Pakistan, in the sense of launching a planned campaign to conquer territory. Among other reasons, the Indians were too involved with their multitudinous internal affairs. But the mood did reinforce the same determination to avoid further insult or encroachment which had been perceptible in 1962 and which had lingered beneath the surface thereafter in Indian society. The fighting in the Rann of Kutch intensified these emotions, particularly after New Delhi acknowledged that Indian forces, under severe pressure, had withdrawn from Biar-bet, a worthless but disputed position seven miles inside Indian-claimed territory. The mood was reflected by the normally inoffensive upper house of parliament, the Rajya Sabha, which on May 3 endorsed a statement voicing the people's resolve 'to drive the Pakistani invaders from the sacred soil of India'.

Shastri defied this public mood to accept a settlement of the Rann of Kutch which brought jingoists marching into the streets in protest. In Britain, Harold Wilson had instituted early peace efforts, but no progress was made until Shastri and Ayub had their second face-to-face meeting during the Commonwealth Conference in London in June. The Indian version of this meeting is that Ayub, when handed the diplomatic papers on the controversy, said: 'I can't understand all this writing; bring me a map.' Then he accepted a settlement which gave both sides a face-saving solution. The agreement, signed on June 30, generally restored Indian police control over the disputed area by reviving the *status quo ante* and obliging Pakistani troops to evacuate the areas they had occupied, before the monsoon forced them out. However, Pakistani border guards were permitted to continue patrolling the disputed road near Kanjarkot, over which the fighting had started. Shastri also accepted a provision to submit the dispute to eventual binding arbitration by a three-man tribunal. Pakistan and India would each name one member and would jointly determine the chairman; this selection would be made by the UN Secretary-General, if the two countries disagreed. The Jana Sangh and similar Indian groups attacked the agreement as 'surrender' and contended that the principle of arbitration would work against India in Kashmir. Shastri denied this contention. But it seemed probable that the successful application of arbitration to one area of Indo-Pakistan controversy would create pressures for its use in Kashmir. At least, Indian refusal to do so would doubtless strengthen Pakistan's political position. Ayub hailed the agreement with the expressed hope it would 'constitute a turning point in Indo-Pak relations . . . It was a victory for common sense and it constituted a model for the manner in which all Indian–Pakistan disputes could be settled, should other peaceful means of settling them prove unavailing.'

After a series of meetings at lower levels, the two Foreign Ministers were scheduled to confer in New Delhi on August 20 to consider final demarcation of the border in the Rann. The meeting was cancelled on August 18 by mutual agreement, on India's initiative, because of the guerrilla fighting in Kashmir and, probably, because of the mammoth Jana Sangh protest demonstration two days earlier. Thereafter, implementation of the agreement was suspended, and no test of arbitration was made. In the rising tensions of the period, the practicability of arbitration, even over the worthless Rann, was doubtful. Yet it was significant that Ayub did not give this principle a chance to operate. Its acceptance by India constituted the first political breakthrough in many years that might have helped Pakistan in Kashmir. Without waiting, Pakistan opened her guerrilla attack against Kashmir on August 5, no doubt realising that suspension of the Rann agreement and of arbitration would be one result. This impatience was another sign that Ayub had turned irrevocably towards a military solution before the conclusion of the Rann agreement.

Indian authorities read further confirmation of this probability into the sequence of events. They say that India originally suggested early August for the Foreign Ministers' meeting. Bhutto replied that he could not make the trip before August 20. 'This showed', said one influential Indian, 'that he either expected to have the whole Kashmir problem settled by then or that the area would be in such an uproar India would be willing to talk about Kashmir along with the Rann.' Shastri contended the Rann agreement was regarded by Pakistan as 'a means to achieve something else'. Speaking to parliament on November 15, he added: 'They thought they can force us to agree to either separation of Jammu and Kashmir or to its merger with Pakistan or to whatever they had in mind. They felt that through force they could compel us to agree to their demands. Therefore, even before the ink was dry on the Kutch agreement, Pakistan made a further attack on Kashmir.'

After the flare-up in the Rann of Kutch, political and military attention quickly returned to Kashmir. In the progression towards a final test, May became a particularly critical month. Concurrent tensions along the borders of East Pakistan appeared to be largely diversionary. On May 8, Sheikh Abdullah and his principal lieutenant, Mirza Afzal Beg, were taken into custody upon their return to New Delhi from a wide-ranging trip abroad, which had begun on February 22. They were hustled into house arrest at a comfortable former British hill station in southern India on general charges, under the Defence of India Rules, of conducting political operations hostile to India. The arrests set off a new and climactic wave of agitation in Srinagar.

Since the death of Nehru and the collapse of last-minute hopes for a Kashmir settlement, Abdullah had reverted to the political erraticism which New Delhi had previously found unacceptable. In August 1964, for example, he had again declared that independence was the only solution of Kashmir's problem, and a month later he publicly backed the use of force to achieve it. On another occasion, he accused India of atrocities in Kashmir. Still the predominant political figure in the Valley, the Sheikh secured international publicity from these and parallel statements, to New Delhi's evident discomfort. After going abroad, he wrote to Prime Minister Shastri from London on March 17, 1965, detailing some generalised charges of Indian misrule in Kashmir and appealing for a halt or a reversal of the Indian takeover. With the inauguration of a new Indian government, he said, 'it was in the interest of the parties concerned to refrain from doing anything that would vitiate the atmosphere and make a settlement difficult'. While giving Shastri time to consolidate his rule before undertaking any further initiative, Abdullah added: 'I, therefore, hoped that the Indian Government would, at least, help in maintaining the *status quo*, until the task that we had taken in hand during Panditji's life was resumed. Nothing, it was expected, will be done in Kashmir which may create tension or give a set-back to the hope that the people still entertained for an amicable settlement. Unfortunately, this was not to be. . . .' The constitutional changes announced in December 1964, 'clearly showed,' he said, 'that the Government of India, far from going ahead to pursue the revised Kashmir policy initiated by Panditji, was actually moving in the reverse direction, and, in fact, undoing what had been done.'[11] While merely asking Shastri to review the situation, the letter was tough and could be interpreted, as New Delhi obviously did, to mean that Abdullah was planning further steps on his own, unless India quickly backed down.

In this atmosphere, Abdullah went to Algiers during preparatory meetings for the abortive Conference of Non-aligned Nations, which was scheduled for June. On March 30, he called on Chou En-lai, the Chinese Communist Prime Minister, and they conferred at some length. Abdullah told a news conference that the Chinese leader assured him of China's support for the 'right of self-determination of the people of Kashmir' and invited him to visit Peking. The Kashmir firebrand added that he intended to go to Red China at the earliest opportunity. Unless India changed her policy toward Kashmir, he said, every effort would be made to bring the problem before the Algiers Conference, which he might personally attend. Indian authorities said this contact was dangerous collusion with the 'enemy' which warranted Abdullah's arrest upon his return to India. He had visited Mecca during his tour, and Muslims claimed the arrest violated the state of grace which the pilgrimage had given him; but, in view of this political machination, the claim of religious inviolability was hardly justified.

The Indians were legitimately concerned that Abdullah's flirtation with Peking could become a serious threat to them. The prospect of being charged before a non-aligned conference with suppressing a 'revolutionary' movement in Kashmir was unsettling; even though it can be argued that New Delhi placed undue emphasis upon the fluctuating opinions of these nations. Moreover, to those Indian officials recognising the 'national liberation' strategy, the situation was ready-made for deep Peking involvement. Sheikh Abdullah, whose tongue commanded thousands, could whip up far more turmoil within Indian Kashmir on the issue of independence than could the existing pro-Pakistan movement. The Indians moved, as had the British in the past, to remove the threat by silencing the man. It is doubtful if the Sheikh was surprised.

The result, however, was predictable. Protest demonstrations erupted in Kashmir and, in a week of unrest, were put down only by Indian police gunfire. Estimates of the death toll varied widely. Pro-Indian sources say seven were killed, and the Pakistan press claimed forty died in the first two days. The Sheikh's arrest reinvigorated the passions which had gripped Srinagar since the theft of the Holy Relic and created the explosiveness which lasted until

U

the outbreak of hostilities. The incident apparently constituted the final proof desired by Rawalpindi that the 'revolutionary' potential in the Valley was exploitable. The Pakistan press responded instantly, and *Dawn* devoted almost its entire front page to first reports of the revolt which it claimed was sweeping Kashmir. The Foreign Minister, Bhutto, was quoted in paraphrase as calling 'upon the people to ponder afresh the teachings of Islam which made it incumbent on every Muslim to wage war against tyranny and oppression'. Pakistani spokesmen of various types talked repeatedly of liberating Kashmir. Propaganda pamphlets featured a statement made by Sheikh Abdullah in mid-1964: 'No sacrifice would be considered too great for securing the right of self-determination. Like the people of Algeria, the Kashmiris would never recoil from the struggle to attain their goal.' An 'Algerian settlement' became the watchword.

Military pressures along the cease-fire line (CFL) simultaneously intensified, with both sides ready for quick action. New Delhi reported a total of 339 incidents during May, a new monthly record. U Thant, the United Nations Secretary-General, noted that, since the first of the year, there had been a disturbing increase in violations of the cease-fire boundary. In mid-June, the late General R. H. Nimmo, chief of the UN observer group, reported an aggregate of 2,231 complaints from both sides for the preceding five months. 'Most of these involved firing across the CFL, although some concerned crossings of the Line by armed men', U Thant stated in a report on September 3 to the Security Council. As of mid-June, '377 violations in all categories had been confirmed by investigations of the Observers, 218 of which were committed by Pakistan and 159 by India. Some of these violations took the form of "heavy and prolonged firing" from weapons up to the calibre of field artillery.'[12]

One of the most serious, the Secretary-General noted, involved an Indian attack on commanding heights at Kargil, on the north-central CFL. On May 17, 1965, several hundred Indian troops, in battalion strength, crossed the line and occupied three Pakistani observation posts on a crenellated mountain overlooking the vital Srinagar-Leh road. It was a difficult military operation, for the attackers had to scramble through a huge upswept rock wasteland, commanded by Pakistani guns. One of the captured posts was perched at 13,600 feet on a barren rock ledge; the others were nearly as inaccessible. The positions looked down on the long mountain road which constitutes the main supply route, during favourable weather, for Indian troops facing the Chinese in Ladakh. The Indians contended that Pakistanis had harassed the movement of supplies with gunfire and had attempted to cut the road by armed assault across the CFL. They claimed that Pakistani infantry units had attacked in force on May 16, and the Indian assault was a counter-attack. In all, New Delhi maintained that twenty-eight incidents occurred in this sector between January 1, 1965 and June 7, half of them after May 16; compared with a total of thirteen incidents for the three previous years. The Indians withdrew from the captured Kargil positions at the end of June under a formula for the stationing of UN observers on both sides of the line to prevent further incidents. U Thant, who made no mention of Pakistani assaults on the road prior to the Indian operation, reported that after the Indian withdrawal '. . . there were some military attacks on the road by armed elements from the Pakistani side'.

The limited Indian offensive was more significant than generally recognised at the time. Although the temporarily captured Kargil positions were tactically important in relation to the Srinagar-Leh road, Indian military leaders were confident they could keep the road open, despite Pakistani harassment. The primary significance of the mountain outposts was that they provided a point for offensive action into Azad Kashmir. Despite the ruggedness of the terrain, Indian forces with air-dropped supplies could have mounted a limited attack farther into Pakistani territory in the north-west where Pakistani-controlled tribal forces were weak and ineffective. As in the earlier movement of Indian armour to the Punjab front, the evident purpose was to persuade Rawalpindi to avoid aggressiveness. In general, senior Indian commanders at this period appeared to be convinced that Pakistan would not launch a general assault because it could not hope to defeat India. They believed, however, that the best way of perpetuating that situation was to make sure Pakistani officials constantly recognised the odds against them.

Perhaps in recognition of this factor, Pakistani officials thereafter listed the Kargil operation among evidences of Indian aggression and among the immediate causes of the war. Otherwise, the operation apparently did not have any deterrent effect. On the other hand, India was more sharply criticised for this attack than was Pakistan for clearly initiating the majority of incidents along the CFL at this time. This was due in large measure, no doubt, to the fact that India made a relatively open assault whereas Pakistan's infractions were hidden behind vague, sometimes suppressed, and always disputed statistics. Apart from its broader implications, the Indian operation could be justified by the tactical situation around Kargil. It relieved serious pressure on a vital road, a military objective of undoubted validity. The CFL had already been breached in this area, as it had to be breached to threaten the road; so a counter-thrust, while technically illegal, was no more so than the original Pakistani assaults. The fact that the Indians refrained from exploiting the advantage they had gained indicated the attack was not designed to prelude a larger offensive. The Indians were in no mood to accept the argument that the CFL should not be crossed before Pakistan did so more overtly; nor would they accept the argument that military necessity was an insufficient reason for occupying the Kargil positions. Yet New Delhi had taken this position in the case of the South Vietnamese war. It had opposed American and South Vietnamese bombing across the Seventeenth Parallel, another cease-fire line, to counter intensified violation of the parallel by infiltrating regular troops from North Vietnam. Once again, the inconsistency of the Indian position helped to augment the criticism from a world opinion based largely upon headlines and propaganda.

Politically, the Kargil episode was also significant. News of the attack electrified India and raised the country's spirits. It softened but did not eliminate the drumfire of bitter criticism directed at the Shastri government by opposition leaders for the 'surrender' over the Rann of Kutch. There was an unmistakable atmosphere of vibrancy and new confidence in New Delhi and even in normally more unconcerned sections of India. Yet the withdrawal of Indian forces from Kargil under the UN agreement was accomplished easily and without important internal friction. This certainly would have been impossible if, as the Pakistani press charged, Indian leaders had attempted to create an aggressive war hysteria.

Kargil had demonstrated the alertness and sensitivity of the proud and eager Indian army. It had also indicated that military thinking had become predominant in the reaction to Pakistani moves and that India would not be unduly restrained by political considerations. International criticism of the Kargil operation was clearly predictable. But, judging by appearances in one crucial sector of the Kashmir front, the army was not deployed for major and concerted offensive action, as implied in Western thinking by Pakistan's constant charge of aggression. Along the Uri-Baramula road leading to Srinagar, for example, the author observed Indian units in a state of readiness but in general they occupied primarily defensive positions. This road, the invasion route in 1947, became another important segment of the early 1965 hostilities. The Indian forces were prepared for limited offensive action, and their officers seemed anxious for a provocation that would enable them to demonstrate their strength. For an army that felt compelled to redeem the honour lost in 1962, this was an understandable attitude. But it was far different from the mood of an army determined to take the sustained offensive and conquer an enemy's territory.

The Indian government has charged that final plans to attack Kashmir were completed by Pakistan before the end of May, a month before the cease-fire agreement governing the Rann of Kutch was signed. 'Reliable evidence from various sources, including interrogation of captured infiltrators, has established the fact that plans for the Kashmir attack had been finalised by the third week of May, 1965', said an official statement.[13] By the end of the month, compulsory military training was established for youths in Azad Kashmir between the ages of sixteen and twenty-five. In June, Pakistan created a special 'Mujahid [crusader] force' of lightly-trained civilian reserves. This organisation, with a total strength of 150,000, was part of the Pakistan army. After two weeks' guerrilla training, these men returned to their jobs. A special ordinance required employers to take them back. These trainees were expected to serve primarily in their home areas. Later an additional semi-military volunteer force of lightly-armed Razakars, totalling around 8,500, was placed under army control, along with other militia units.

The main assault force for the Kashmir guerrilla campaign was organised in Murree, West Pakistan, on May 26, 1965. It was composed of some 30,000 men, and was known as 'Gibraltar Forces', in commemoration of an early Muslim conquest of the Mediterranean outpost. General Akhtar Husain Malik, commander of Pakistan's 12th Division, was in supreme command, and component units of the new group were commanded by officers of the

regular Pakistan army. The group was composed of eight to ten
'Forces', each comprising six units of five companies (110 men to
each company). Each company contained regular troops of the
Azad Kashmir army, which was part of the Pakistan army, along
with Mujahid and Razakar irregulars. The men were equipped with
standard automatic weapons, including light machine guns, as well
as hand-grenades and other explosives. They were trained compre-
hensively for six weeks at four camps in Pakistan, learning guerrilla ‚
and sabotage techniques, as well as basic military conditioning.
'Their instructions', Shastri informed the United Nations, 'were
to destroy bridges and vital roads, attack police stations, supply
dumps, Army headquarters and important installations, inflict
casualties on Indian forces, and attack VIPs in Jammu and Kashmir.'
Interrogation and captured equipment, Shastri added, 'prove
beyond a shadow of doubt that the infiltrators were armed and
equipped by the Pakistan Government and have operated under
their instructions.'[14] President Ayub visited the Murree headquarters and addressed a special conference of Force commanders
during the second week of July.[15]

This outline of Pakistan's build-up for guerrilla assault is
generally confirmed by informed but impartial foreign sources. The
Indians also claimed that Chinese Communist instructors had been
sent to the camps to give specialised training, but there is no
independent confirmation. The evidence indicates that the Pakistanis
handled these preparations by themselves but were influenced by
Chinese methods and probably encouraged by Chinese agents.
Captured arms and ammunition, New Delhi contended, were all
supplied by the Pakistan government. Many bore the stamp of the
Pakistan Ordnance Factory.[16] In addition, certain non-military
items, such as matches, flashlight batteries and incendiary materials,
were of Chinese Communist manufacture.

Pakistan has consistently denied any connection with the 'uprising' in Kashmir. It contends there never were any infiltrators
but that the guerrillas fighting the government were 'the sons of the
Kashmiri soil who have risen to defend themselves against Indian
repression'. One spokesman, who said the rebels all originated
within Indian Kashmir, reported that the Azad Kashmir government had refused a request for troops but did supply arms.[17]
Bhutto, the Foreign Minister, contended on August 10, five days

after hostilities began: 'The responsibility of whatever is happening in Kashmir could not by any stretch of imagination be attributed to Pakistan.' President Ayub later maintained that 'the uprising in Kashmir was merely a pretext for India to embark on a long-planned course of aggression'. The earliest date for direct Pakistan involvement admitted by any official is September 1, the date of the first armoured attack on the south-western front, in the Chhamb area. Bhutto told the United Nations that Pakistan was forced to defend itself in a war which he said began on September 6 with the Indian assault toward Lahore, West Pakistan.

Nevertheless, the evidence is convincing that Pakistan prepared and launched the guerrilla attack and carefully deployed her mechanised army to give it maximum support. Indian authorities were alert to the guerrilla threat, if incompletely prepared to meet it, but generally they were oblivious of the potentialities for conventional attack. In July, officials of the New Delhi Home Ministry met with state authorities in Srinagar and decided that guerrilla sabotage was possible but that Pakistan was unprepared for major conventional war against India. On August 2 a senior Indian army commander told officers in Srinagar that the next phase of the Kashmir struggle would not be overt organised power but murder and terrorism.[18] On the other hand, a variety of intelligence agencies received solid information during this period about a build-up of conventional Pakistani power. In July, a European official of a specialised UN agency returned from the Punjab with this information: 'The Pakistanis', he said, 'are assembling a massive tank force in the Punjab. The Indians are asleep, and they won't know what hit them.' Some foreign observers with access to unpublished information had concluded at this same time that Pakistan had decided to attack in a desperate attempt to change the course of history.

13

THE HOSTILITIES

THE PAKISTAN-CONTROLLED guerrillas slipped into Indian Kashmir at widely separated points during August 1965. They crossed apparently in four main areas along the 470-mile cease-fire line, chosen for the concealment of the terrain and the accessibility of military objectives. By Indian accounts, the attackers were engaged in eight primary battle areas along almost the entire stretch of the CFL, and isolated bands were located at six other points. Travelling on foot and at night across steep rocky peaks or through a remote jungle the invaders penetrated deeply before being discovered, and some units reached Srinagar. They were nondescript men, mostly wearing the baggy trousers and shirts of the region, with a scattering of identifiable Pakistan military uniforms. They carried rifles and light automatic weapons, light bombs, grenades, plastic charges and other equipment which could be easily concealed, and maintained radio contact with their headquarters in Azad Kashmir.

This outline of what Shastri, the Indian Prime Minister, called a 'thinly disguised armed attack' on Kashmir has been confirmed by impartial foreign sources. The United Nations Secretary-General, U Thant, told the Security Council on September 3 that the then chief of the UN observer group, the Australian General R. H. Nimmo,

> has indicated to me that the series of violations that began on August 5 were to a considerable extent in subsequent days in the form of armed men, generally not in uniform, crossing the CFL from the Pakistan side for the purpose of armed action on the

Indian side. This is a conclusion reached by General Nimmo on the basis of investigations by the United Nations Observers, in the light of the extensiveness and character of the raiding activities and their proximity to the CFL, even though in most cases the actual identity of those engaging in the armed attacks on the Indian side of the Line and their actual crossing of it could not be verified by direct observation or evidence.

The Secretary-General made public at that time a report on a number of investigated incidents up to September 2. In discussing those occurring during the initial phases of the guerrilla invasion, between August 5 and August 10, General Nimmo established several basic facts. He demonstrated, for example, that a number of attacks were made, that they occurred over 400 miles apart along the CFL and that, in at least one incident, a soldier of the regular Azad Kashmir infantry was involved. One of the most serious attacks, on the night of August 7–8, resulted in the capture of the town of Mandi, near Poonch in the west-central area, by raiders, who held it for four days. 'UN Observers confirmed most of the reported fighting', General Nimmo's report said. 'The number of raiders was estimated to exceed 1,000. The available evidence indicated that some of the raiders must have come from across the CFL. As of August 24, the raiders were still holding some Indian pickets [outposts] north of Mandi. . . .' Another attack in the Kargil sector, on the northern stretch of the CFL, was verified and the dress of one dead raider, the report said, 'was similar to the uniform of Pakistan frontier corps of scouts', a unit controlled by the Pakistan army. At another point near Baramula, on the road to Srinagar, attacks on the night of August 7–8 were confirmed. 'The observers interviewed one of the captured raiders, who stated that he was a soldier of the 16 Azad Kashmir infantry battalion and that the raiding party was composed of about 300 soldiers of his battalion and 100 "mujahids" [armed civilians trained in guerrilla tactics]. United Nations Observers noted that some of the materials said to have been abandoned by the raiders were manufactured in Pakistan.'

Other foreign sources agree that the attackers were under complete Pakistan military control and that they were engaged in operations which showed considerable detailed pre-planning. In general, these sources confirm the outline of Pakistan's strategy which has been reported by the Indians. The guerrillas, by this account, were expected to set off a 'revolt' within Indian Kashmir to create maximum turmoil and, hopefully, to produce a pro-Pakistani regime. Pakistani conventional forces were in support. It is not clear, however, whether there was a pre-arranged intention to use them for intervention in a Kashmiri civil war, as the Indians charge. Some foreign observers believe Rawalpindi had not developed a precise battle plan. The guerrillas depended on Pakistan for arms, a point not seriously contested by Rawalpindi. The fact that they carried some Chinese-made non-military equipment has been established.

Some details of the Indian story, particularly the numbers of guerrillas and the effectiveness of their operations, remain unclear. New Delhi contends that 3,000 invaders had crossed the CFL by August 9, and that another 2,000 infiltrated subsequently. There is no independent confirmation of precise numbers but impartial experts agree the invasion was sizable. The Indians say the majority of the attackers were killed, captured or dispersed before they could do significant damage, but small groups remained in the area as late as mid-October. Although eye witnesses agree that there was little sign of combat action in Srinagar, the operation at Mandi, among others, indicated that the guerrillas represented a greater potential military threat than the Indian public version implies. There is no doubt, however, that the 'revolt' failed to occur and that the guerrilla operation was a failure. Yet a significant number of irregulars seriously interfered with life in the valley during the following four weeks.

The main guerrilla force headed for Srinagar. The plan, say the Indians, was to reach the capital on August 8, when crowds were celebrating the festival of a Kashmiri saint. With arms concealed beneath baggy clothes, the guerrillas hoped to enter the city undetected, and elements did penetrate four suburbs. The next day, a well-advertised political rally had been scheduled by the Action Committee. The occasion was the anniversary of Sheikh Abdullah's first arrest and dismissal twelve years previously. The armed raiders were to participate in the demonstration, to seize control of it and to arouse the crowds into overthrowing the Sadiq government in the name of the people. Adjacent forces were ordered to capture the airfield and the nearby radio station. More distant units were detailed for such operations as bridge demolitions to isolate the Valley and to impede the movement of reinforcing Indian troops.

These objectives were to be secured during the morning of August 9. When this phase was completed, a pro-Pakistan revolutionary council would be established to take over political control, backed by propaganda from the captured radio station.[1] The new regime would then call upon Pakistan for help. With the probability of widespread fighting and concerted Indian counter-action, regular Pakistan forces would intervene to support the 'liberation'. The plan failed because there was no uprising on the required scale, but the details of the failure were obscured by Indian press censorship.

Elsewhere in Kashmir, sizable guerrilla forces were evidently originally employed in direct support of the proposed rebellion. One main force operated in the Jammu section of the state, for the apparent double purpose of creating turmoil and cutting Indian communications. It was supported on occasion by heavy Pakistan artillery fire from across the CPR. In other areas, guerrilla units were involved in operations evidently designed to sever Indian military roads. If successful, these operations conceivably could have cut the Indian garrison into about five different elements, isolated from each other, thus reducing the effectiveness of the Indian numerical superiority. The United Nations confirmed a sufficient number of incidents to substantiate the outlines of this broad strategy. During the period between August 5 and 8, in particular, the UN findings indicate a concerted attempt by raiders to clear the way for comparatively large infiltrations, while other units attempted to carry out the isolation of Srinagar. The guerrillas were supplied by air-lifts.

Impartial eye witnesses who were in Srinagar during this period confirm Shastri's contention that 'The whole world knows there was no revolt'. The witnesses reported that the city was relatively calm, without sign of armed combat, and life was proceeding normally. Maulana Masoodi told Richard Critchfield of the *Washington Star*, however, that attempts to trigger the revolt had been made for three days, but that Indian security forces were too strong. This is possible, although the extent of Indian precautions, apart from customary control arrangements, appears uncertain. Few additional security preparations had evidently been made in the four days since August 5, the date when the infiltrations were first discovered. In fact, one Indian reporter complained about the inadequacy of preparations throughout Kashmir, after exposure of the guerrilla invasion. '. . . everyone in Srinagar knows that the first reports were underestimated if not altogether dismissed by those responsible for the defence of the [cease-fire] line.' After the failure of the 'revolt', security was quickly tightened in Srinagar. The garrison was reinforced, roadblocks and a curfew were established, public buildings were sandbagged, bridges made more secure and police even staked out ambushes in canoes, hidden in lake willows, to intercept infiltrators who might arrive by boat.[2] Armed Jammu and Kashmir police initially attempted to handle the guerrillas, but regular Indian army forces took over this task on August 9.

The indications are that the operation failed because the Kashmiris were in no mood to revolt. This was not necessarily due to strong loyalty to India or to a determination to resist Pakistani attack, as the Indians claimed. It was probably due primarily to the fact that relatively sterile political issues were insufficient to rouse the people into risking their lives. As a correspondent for *The Times* of London put it: 'Experience has shown, however, that it is only when the religious emotions of the Kashmiris are deeply stirred that they will come out in mass and defiant support of their political leaders.'[3] The results might have been far different if the upheaval of August 9 had been linked with the emotions aroused by the theft of the Hair of the Prophet. As it was, the failure underlined the point that the imprisonment of Sheikh Abdullah and the generalised concept of joining Pakistan were not sufficient to arouse the people to an attempt to overthrow a government which had military backing. To a degree, this substantiated Shastri's comment: 'In my judgment,' he said, 'it was a great blow to Pakistan that a territory which they had imagined would join Pakistan within two or three days did not do anything of the kind.' General J. N. Chaudhuri, the Army Chief of Staff during the hostilities, said in his post-war book, *Arms, Aims and Aspects*, that the guerrilla movement failed in the Valley because 'none of the infiltrators were Kashmiris. This broke a first principle for guerrillas. South of the Pir Panjal it was a little more successful as the ethnic groups were similar and some of the infiltrators came from the area itself. But the movement failed because it was not of the State but imposed.' Other Indian sources maintain that Pakistani Punjabis were sent into the Valley and were easily identifiable by their race and the fact that they wore sufficiently distinctive Punjabi civilian dress to be identified by their commanders. It seems evident, however, that Pakistani Kashmiris also were involved. This was indicated by UN reports, by the tone of official Pakistani propaganda, and by the fact that some of the infiltrators were given refuge in Srinagar.

It has also been demonstrated that the guerrillas were not altogether successful in establishing the necessary rapport with the local populace for securing supplies and safety. Some were turned over or revealed to the Indian army, and many others were rejected. Indian authorities say many of the guerrillas, supplied with relatively generous sums of money, were treated well as long as they could buy food, but were repulsed by local citizens when they tried to steal it. The favourite story of how the infiltrations were first betrayed is that a Muslim shepherd boy ran to the authorities when he became suspicious of a stranger who offered him too much money for a packet of cigarettes. On the other hand, a number of infiltrators apparently received sanctuary in Srinagar and some other towns, for Indian reprisals were stern. In one incident several hundred houses were burned down in a section of Srinagar, after the inhabitants had been ordered to leave. This was done by the Indian army, despite New Delhi denials, but evidently for the defensible military reason of denying to the guerrillas sharp-shooter positions overlooking the Secretariat, the offices of the state government—one of the avowed objectives of the attack. In Srinagar, the task of rooting out sheltered infiltrators could have been extremely difficult, and there were potentialities for prolonged turmoil. Although news censorship obscured day-to-day developments, foreign newsmen made periodic trips to the capital and confirmed that no major guerrilla action occurred in the city during the Indo-Pakistan war.

The failure of the 'revolt' marked the end of the first phase of the conflict, but the guerrilla threat continued throughout the war. By the end of August, the main irregular forces were confined in an area ten miles deep along the south and central CFL. Considerable numbers of infiltrators remained in the Valley, and others were active on the northern front and in Jammu.[4] United Nations observers confirmed a guerrilla ambush on an Indian convoy on September 1 at a point twenty-four miles within Indian Kashmir along the Srinagar-Leh road. A prisoner told the observers that he belonged to the Karakoram Scouts, a mountain force controlled by the Pakistan army. Shastri informed the nation on September 3 that 'some bands of raiders are, however, still attempting to come in with full backing of the Pakistan army'. In general, the raiders incompetently carried out paper plans that, with efficiency, could have seriously threatened the Indian position.

The Pakistani press covered the Srinagar 'uprising' in detail, reporting among other developments the establishment of the Revolutionary Council of Patriots as the new state government. This 'government' issued a proclamation appealing for world support for 'this freedom movement' and announced the abrogation of 'all alleged treaties and agreements between Imperialist Government of India and Kashmir'. Proclamations and instructions were broadcast over a freedom radio, the supposedly captured station near Srinagar. Actually, the evidence is convincing that the Revolutionary Council and the freedom radio were established and maintained in Azad Kashmir, when the Srinagar operation failed. The radio station, Sada-i-Kashmir (Voice of Kashmir), broadcast long enough to be definitely located near Muzaffarabad. Pakistani newspapers reported a number of other details about the operation which appeared obtainable only through prior knowledge.

'Pakistan', said Shastri, 'has, on the one hand, sought to deny its complicity and, on the other, she has put herself forward as the chief spokesman for the infiltrators. The world will recall that Pakistan had created a similar situation in 1947 and then also she had initially pleaded innocence. Later, she had to admit that her own regular forces were involved in the fighting.'[5] The parallel between the two conflicts, in this respect, was remarkable. In 1947, Pakistan insisted that the tribesmen invading Kashmir rose spontaneoulsy to help their 'brothers', and Pakistan originally supplied no help, except for individual 'volunteers'. In 1965, the position was that individuals from Azad Kashmir participated in a 'vigorous war of liberation against the Indian forces in Kashmir' which was proclaimed by the Revolutionary Council established in Srinagar. Those assisting the rebellion included 'the police and civilian officers and also armed civilians. . . .' They were legally entitled to cross the CFL, since Kashmir 'forms one unit' divided only by an artificial military boundary. Others moved into action from villages under Azad Kashmir control which lie on the Indian side of the

CFL. 'To describe these liberators as infiltrators is thus absurd, both morally and legally', says Professor M. A. Aziz, who is identified as Spokesman of the Revolutionary Council of the People of Jammu and Kashmir: Accredited to the Azad Kashmir Government. In a pamphlet distributed by the Pakistan government, Aziz further claims: 'In the struggle for liberation, Azad Kashmir is justified in helping all resistance fighters.' But he adds that a request for troops by Kashmiris living in the neutral belt on both sides of the CFL was turned down. 'The Azad Kashmir Government could not provide troops to help these people in the neutral zone but it did provide them with arms to defend themselves.'[6]

Pakistan maintained that, until September 1, only 'freedom fighters' were involved in the struggle, and this remains the official position. In this contention, Pakistani officials placed considerable emphasis upon the fact that General Nimmo's report did not specifically identify Pakistanis in the guerrilla action, made no estimate of the numbers involved and did not positively assert that the raiders came from Pakistan territory. The UN observers, however, were never by numbers or mission in a position to witness events as they occurred. They could only undertake *ex post facto* investigation of complaints lodged with them. U Thant noted the problems confronting the observer group of forty-five members charged with surveillance of a CFL totalling 'almost 500 miles, about half of which is in high mountains and is very difficult of access. UNMOGIP (the UN Group) exercises the quite limited function of observing and reporting, investigating complaints from either party of violations of the CFL and the Cease-Fire and submitting the resultant findings on those investigations to each party and to the Secretary-General, and keeping the Secretary-General informed in general on the way in which the Cease-Fire Agreement is being kept. Because the role of UNMOGIP appears frequently to be misunderstood, it bears emphasis that the operation has no authority or function entitling it to enforce or prevent anything, or to try to ensure that the Cease-Fire is respected.' U Thant further noted, in his September 3 report to the Security Council, that the UN group preferred to report its conclusions in secret, and consequently the majority of investigated incidents during the Indo-Pakistan conflict were not disclosed publicly. 'The procedure that has been followed is for General Nimmo to submit the reports of the investigations of each incident and the Observers' findings fixing blame, to each party, confidentially, and to send copies to me without any public disclosure', U Thant said. 'This procedure, which has been found to be in the best interest of the effective functioning of UNMOGIP is being continued.'

With these qualifications, the official UN reports, together with other circumstantial evidence, constituted a strong case proving Pakistani involvement in the guerrilla action; a case strengthened by the subsequent corroborating information of impartial investigators. The Nimmo reports did not fully support Prime Minister Shastri's contention that the UN had established 'beyond doubt' that 'the infiltrators were well armed with modern weapons and the whole operation was conceived, planned and executed by Pakistan'. But the field investigations of UN observers did prove Pakistani involvement in a greatly accelerated military action in widely-separated sectors of the CFL.

This involved a confirmed increase in Pakistani artillery fire, as well as convincing evidence that the line was crossed at several points. The presence of men in the uniforms of military units controlled by the Pakistan army in areas deep within Indian Kashmir suggested the extent of organisation behind the operation. Moreover, the range of incidents and the variety of tactics and weapons used were clearly beyond the capacity of the closely-guarded Action Committee in Srinagar to organise or to direct. The movement of men from Azad Kashmir, a region under strong Pakistani military and political control, would have been impossible, on the face of the evidence, without the approval of Rawalpindi. The Pakistan press itself confirmed the outlines of the 'revolution' plot by its prompt reporting of the details. The establishment and maintenance of the Revolutionary Council and the freedom radio in Azad Kashmir—further actions requiring Pakistani approval—provided a definite confirmation of the extent and probable durability of the plot. Pakistani officials openly supported these actions and intensified their complicity by reviving a number of discredited propaganda charges, including fresh accounts of Indian genocide against Muslims.

The Secretary-General sounded out both governments in August on the advisability of publishing the reports available up to that time. India voiced no objection, although the UN observers condemned some Indian actions. But India, said U Thant, 'at first wished certain modifications which, in part at least, I regarded as unacceptable.' The belief in New Delhi at the time was that the Indians wanted clearer condemnation of Pakistan for aggression. U Thant added: 'The Government of Pakistan was strongly negative about the statement in general on the grounds that it favoured India in that it dealt only with the current cease-fire situation without presenting the political background of the broad issue and thus was lacking in balance, since a cease-fire supports the *status quo* to India's benefit.' After careful consideration, U Thant decided to withhold publication, and the reports did not become public until September. The Secretary-General said he concluded 'that a public statement by the Secretary-General at that time would serve no constructive purpose and might well do more harm than good. My first and primary objective has to be to see the fighting end rather than indicating or denouncing any party for starting and continuing it. I thought it might be helpful to make another quiet effort toward achieving observance of the Cease-Fire through a new approach to the two Governments.'

As a result, the nature of the conflict was obscured during the important early phase. By the time the reports became public, they were overtaken by more dramatic battle events, and their impact was soon obliterated by the outbreak of heavy fighting in the Punjab. Pakistan generally escaped blame by inflexible denial of any direct involvement. But the denials also served to strengthen the circumstantial evidence proving the Pakistani role in the tribal invasions of 1947.

In reviving this technique nearly twenty years later, Rawalpindi added a sophisticated refinement. It sought to establish a fall-back position in which it would appear merely as a friendly supporter for the attempt of a semi-independent Azad Kashmir to reunify the state through 'legal' hostilities. Professor Aziz, the propaganda spokesman on these matters, contends that the 'resistance fighters' were legally entitled to cross the CFL and that India, as 'a foreign occupying country' had no legal right to take action against them. 'It is only the local authority in Occupied [Indian] Kashmir which can do so.'[7] Thus, if necessary, the legal position was to be that the well-trained Pakistani-controlled Azad Kashmir army was entitled to attack the government of Indian Kashmir, which had no army of

X

its own and was dependent on Indian forces who, however, had no legal right to participate in the struggle. This position was untenable when open warfare broke out between Indian and Pakistani units. But the careful contrivance of the legal structure tends to confirm Indian claims that the Azad Kashmir army was maintained and prepared to spearhead such an action. It is probable that the bulk of the guerrillas were Kashmiris, under Pakistan officers, but they were from Azad Kashmir, a part of Pakistan. The essential point in fixing responsibility was not the nationality of the soldiers but the identity of those who controlled them. Pakistani newspapers have left no doubt of the subservience of Azad Kashmir. The *Civil and Military Gazette* of Lahore reported on June 5, 1965, for example, that all but two government departments 'are entirely manned by non-Kashmiris'. Noting that no popular elections had been held in the area, the publication added, it is 'no use glossing over the unpalatable fact that during our stay in Azad Kashmir we have made ourselves thoroughly unpopular'.

Prompt publication of the UN findings obviously would have helped to clarify the situation at a particularly critical period. The result might have been an entirely different global picture of the conflict and less criticism of India for her share in extending it. In this respect, the UN failed again to serve as an impartial fact-finding body at a time when these services were urgently needed. Another consequence was further encouragement for disguised warfare. India was unsuccessful in subsequent attempts to induce the United Nations to brand Pakistan as an aggressor.

But U Thant clearly gave greater priority to peace-keeping. In mid-August, he was faced with a localised struggle which had not yet assumed major significance but which would be easily accelerated. One element in the situation was the possibility that Pakistan might be driven into a heavier attack with conventional forces, if she lost face through open condemnation for aggression. It is possible that U Thant withheld the report to avoid this contingency precisely because he was convinced of Pakistan's responsibility. If the operation had, in fact, been launched by a semi-independent Azad Kashmir government with only minimal support from Pakistan, disclosure of the UN findings would have involved no loss of face for Rawalpindi. The Indians, however, were infuriated by the Secretary-General's decision to withhold the Nimmo reports. Many contended, as one Indian correspondent wrote, that suppression of the reports 'encouraged Pakistan to embark on war'. In retrospect, it appears unlikely that the temporary withholding of the UN investigations had any effect, one way or the other, on battle developments.

The Indian government also missed a prime opportunity to establish a convincing case for itself. There was sufficient indisputable proof of Pakistan's disguised aggression for Indian authorities to enlist world support by inviting foreign newsmen and diplomatic officials to inspect the evidence in Kashmir. New Delhi resisted pressures to do so, however, and hampered adequate observation at this period. As a result, India moved into offensive-defensive action before there was general conviction that she was, in fact, the victim of attack.

The strategy of the guerrilla campaign, as indirectly confirmed by the Pakistan press, clearly conformed to a type of communist-patented national liberation war. The Indians were fully convinced on this point. Shastri said the techniques and methods were of 'the Chinese pattern' and claimed that Chinese officers, located in Azad Kashmir, were instructing the Pakistanis. D. R. Mankekar, in his book *Twenty-two Fateful Days*, directly compares the Kashmir struggle with the war in South Vietnam. Presumably reflecting the viewpoint of the Indian army, Mankekar says that Ayub's mujahids played the central role in attempting to carry out 'the famous three-step formula of General Vo Nguyên Giap, Ho Chi Minh's guerrilla expert'. In this strategy, he says, 'The launching phase is accompanied by a wild, no-holds-barred propaganda barrage against the chosen victim, to be followed by the infiltration of armed guerrillas into that country who would engineer an internal rebellion and stage a *coup d'état* to overthrow the disapproved regime, and install in its place a stooge Government. In the final phase, the regular army of the "liberating" country steps in to protect the newly-installed puppet government.'[8] Another Indian commentator maintained: 'The present plot is to convert Kashmir into another Vietnam, with Pakistan playing the role of the Hanoi regime, and to introduce further Vietnam-type struggles in other sectors of India's frontier. . . . It is useful to remember that the Viet Cong guerrillas and the Pakistani bands plaguing Kashmir are, in all probability, disciples of the same master [Peking].'[9]

The strategy in Kashmir was more properly a blend of Soviet and Asian communist 'revolutionary' philosophies. The tactic of seeking control over a state or nation by capturing the capital through swift urban insurrection is basically Soviet; so are such techniques as attempting to isolate the stricken city from reinforcing government forces. These methods failed in a number of attempted Soviet-directed revolutions, which cost thousands of lives, notably in Hamburg in 1923, and in Canton, China, four years later. Nevertheless, the strategy of urban insurrection was codified and remains valid for pro-Kremlin communists.[10] The Soviets have also used the open power of the Red Army to establish or to support a puppet regime, notably in Eastern Europe after the Second World War. Lenin originated this tactic with the invasion of Poland in 1920. The strategies of Red China and North Vietnam, which are parallel, emphasise the use of guerrillas to weaken the adversary through patient 'protracted war'. The essential tactic, as Marshal Lin Piao, Peking's Defence Minister, repeated in his 1965 thesis, is 'the establishment of rural revolutionary base areas and the encirclement of cities from the countryside. . . .' In the detailed Chinese-Vietnamese strategy, one essential is to attack weaker cities first, working up to encirclement of the most powerful. Puppet regimes are established in the 'revolutionary base areas' ready to move into the capital, as the National Liberation Front has been maintained in South Vietnam. These regimes are protected by regular armies of the supporting state but usually not openly. The million-man Chinese army which defended North Korea, for example, was composed entirely of 'volunteers'. Hanoi has not admitted that thousands of its regular army troops are fighting in South Vietnam, both as organised units and as Viet Cong guerrillas, complete with forged identification cards. According to Mao Tse-tung's theories, the guerrillas themselves, including infiltrated regulars, must organise on the battlefield into conventional forces in order to win final military victory.

The communists are the world's only professionals in the art of winning power through 'revolution'. Any army seeking to avoid responsibility for aggression by using these methods is obliged, therefore, to study their tactics, if not to accept their direct instruction. The Kashmir situation theoretically called for a mixture of Sino-Soviet techniques. Srinagar is the only city of consequence in the mountains. The assembled Indian power and the weakness of the guerrillas made open conventional intervention a tactical consideration, if Pakistan intended to seek control. This suggests that Rawalpindi did not depend directly upon Chinese instructors, for they certainly would have demanded the avoidance of any Soviet tactics. Furthermore, the Chinese as well as the Russians, if given authority, presumably would have insisted upon much more standard preparatory work to ensure the success of the operation. Both communist nations, for example, attempt to paralyse the opposing army and military forces by infiltrating and subverting them; a technique which, if tried in Kashmir, was evidently unsuccessful. The Chinese and Vietnamese depend heavily upon the intimidation of local officials through terrorism, as was done in Hyderabad nearly twenty years earlier. In South Vietnam, the Viet Cong have killed or kidnapped more than 18,000 local government officials since 1957; 2,800 of them between January 1964 and mid-1966.[11] No organised activities of this type were reported in Kashmir, although the Indians claimed the infiltrators had orders to kill the principal Kashmiri leaders.

The Indian army was convinced, as Mankekar says, that 'the defence against paramilitary invaders is an attack on their bases far inside the enemy territory from which he launched his paramilitary assaults'.[12] This has been the lesson of the Vietnamese war, as it was in earlier guerrilla conflicts. Mao Tse-tung places primary reliance upon the maintenance of a secure base area. In South Vietnam, the communists have sought to establish this position by such tactics as militarising the demilitarised zone between North and South Vietnam, by maintaining base areas in Laos and Cambodia and by virulent propaganda efforts to restrict or eliminate the bombing of North Vietnam. In Kashmir, the Indian army was instantly ready and, no doubt, anxious to strike at the guerrillas' bases, or at least at their entrance routes into the Indian portion of the state. Shastri defined the attitude by telling the nation on August 13 that '. . . force will be met with force and aggression against us will never be allowed to succeed'. Although Indian units clearly were capable of crossing the CFL at any time after the discovery of the first guerrillas on August 5, they waited another ten days for a major operation, apparently hoping for a Pakistani provocation that would justify in world opinion a thrust across the line.

The provocation, in Indian eyes, was provided by a series of developments beginning on August 14. On that day, a considerable force crossed from the Pakistani side of the CFL into Jammu in the area to the east of the Azad Kashmir town of Bhimbar, on the south-western sector of the CFL. The Indian Defence Ministry said this marked the first commitment of the regular Pakistani army and claimed that the attacking force totalled a battalion of about 1,000 men. The next night Indian positions in this sector were heavily shelled by Pakistani heavy artillery and mortars. The attackers, who had penetrated a mile in their first thrust, moved out under the covering fire and captured nine Indian positions, which they held for another ten days. United Nations observers confirmed the shelling and the fact that considerable fighting occurred, but were unable to identify the attackers. Continuing hostilities prevented further investigation at the time, but the observers saw sixty-two Indian casualties in one hospital. General Chaudhuri later told a news conference that this was a 'big attack' and said a UN observer told him the Pakistanis had gathered together an unusual array of artillery for use against Indian positions in that sector. The main supply road from Jammu for Indian forces farther north in the Poonch and Uri sections of the CFL runs through this combat area: the same road over which the two sides fought bitterly in 1947–8.

On August 15, after a preliminary artillery barrage, Indian forces crossed the cease-fire line and reoccupied the three lofty mountain positions they had previously held in Kargil, on the northern sector. This was the first significant crossing of the CFL by Indian forces since the start of the guerrilla attack. It was the twelfth confirmed incident listed by General Nimmo in his initial report; all the others, except one Indian artillery attack, being attributed to anti-Indian forces. At Kargil, the attacking troops found the positions empty, and the Pakistanis had apparently not reoccupied them since the withdrawal of the previous May. The purpose of this thrust was evidently the same as before: to warn Pakistan that the Indian army would strike back promptly against further provocation.[13]

Four days later, a large force of Pakistani artillery moved close to the CFL and began shelling villages and Indian troop concentrations near Tithwal, Uri and Poonch. The Indians responded with two more limited attacks into Azad Kashmir. On August 24, they struck into the Tithwal sector, on the north-western bulge of the line, and captured two strategic Pakistani positions, including the important peak, Pir Saheba. Eventually, the Indians consolidated points dominating a key road in Azad Kashmir, enabling them to seal off the main invasion route to Kargil and to Gurais, another important northern gateway. Other Indian units on August 25 advanced across the line in the Uri sector, on the west-central front. They captured a number of strategic Pakistani mountain positions and finally took the important 8,600-foot Haji Pir Pass, five miles on the Pakistan side of the line. The pass was taken from the rear against light opposition by an outflanking movement across steep mountains. A link-up of these forces with another Indian column from the south on September 10 enabled the Indians to cut off a bulge of some 150 square miles which had been left protruding into Indian Kashmir when the cease-fire line was accepted. The bulge provided the main springboard for infiltrators bound for the Srinagar area. The link-up also permitted reuse of a road valuable for the Indians which had been immobilised since the cease-fire in Kashmir.[14] Indian military officials long resented the loss of the Haji Pir bulge through the 1949 armistice and were anxious to retain it. The captured positions were eventually evacuated, however.

These were justifiable operations from a purely military standpoint. Shastri had heralded them by his series of warnings and by a statement to parliament on the day of the Tithwal advance. He said bluntly that India considered herself free to attack the bases serving the infiltration movement, which was continuing. Nevertheless, the Indian offensives dangerously tightened the pressure on Pakistan. The Indians later claimed that they had captured documents from General Malik, the commander of the Gibraltar Forces, expressing concern over the 'offensive capability' of the Indian forces in the Tithwal sector. This operation in some respects duplicated the 1948 manoeuvre which threatened the Azad Kashmir capital of Muzaffarabad, eighteen miles distant, and which was instrumental in prompting the Pakistani army to intervene openly in the first Kashmiri war. Malik's documents, dated August 29, also showed that he was concerned by the Indian flank threat to his road communications serving infiltration routes into northern Kashmir. He ordered one of his forces to create diversionary action to push back the forward Indian units, but this manoeuvre failed.[15]

Pakistan then struck in force on September 1 far to the south in the Bhimbar-Chhamb area of the south-western front. After heavy preparatory artillery fire and three infantry probing attacks, Pakistani forces drove into Indian territory with a column of seventy tanks and two brigades of between 3,000 and 4,000 infantry troops. United Nations observers had warned the Indians of preparations that signalled such an assault, but Indian officers evidently did not expect the strength that was used. They had only about 1,000 men and an outnumbered tank force in defensive positions. Foreign military sources reported that the defensive forces consisted primarily of lightly-armed police. Elements of two Indian divisions were in the vicinity but did not move into the battle zone until after the Pakistani attack was under way. The terrain favoured an armoured Pakistan thrust and was somewhat disadvantageous to the Indians. The Pakistanis had short lines of communication to Pakistan proper and suitable tank country up to the main area of conflict. The Indians had to move their armour along a single road through generally unfavourable country, establishing longer lines of communication. While Pakistan could assemble a striking force without legal complications in its own nearby territory, the battle area was in Kashmir, where the disposition of Indian troops was curtailed by the Cease-Fire Agreement. For this reason and because of a relative scarcity of armour, General Chaudhuri later told a news conference, the Indians lacked the heavy firepower to oppose the atack.

In other words, the Bhimbar-Chhamb area was the most suitable front in Kashmir for the application of Pakistan's heavy striking power; in fact, it was the only sector along the CFL where offensive tanks could be used with comparative effectiveness. It was, therefore, a vital pressure point to be exploited by Pakistan, either as a diversionary thrust to ease pressure elsewhere or as a further offensive to capture Kashmir. Moreover, the tank column drove towards the town of Akhnur, some twenty miles inside India, where a key bridge spans the Chenab river. This is the same bridge that figured prominently in the campaigns of 1948, for its preservation is vital to communications along the main supply road serving Indian forces in the north-west. The Indians believed that the initial objective of the attacking column was to capture or destroy the Akhnur bridge, thus cutting off Indian forces in the north-western sectors of the front. If that objective were achieved, the Indians expected a second thrust by fresh Pakistani tank forces, headed for Jammu, south-east of the battle area. The conquest of Jammu would have severed the second main road into northern Kashmir, thus cutting land communications and isolating the Indian Kashmir garrison. This would have prevented a substantial portion of the Indian army from participating effectively in further campaigns during the war.[16] Pakistan gave the operation the code name 'Operation Grand Slam'.

The war at this point assumed an air of excitability that caused some knowledgeable foreign observers to conclude that successive operations were begun in unprepared haste for purposes of quick and sometimes desperate reprisal. Each offensive attack by the rival armies appeared on the surface as a well-planned and calculated manoeuvre to offset the previous action of the adversary. They were predictable military reactions. But operations on both sides were marred by grave mistakes and by a certain amount of battlefield hysteria. Neither side appeared to have detailed over-all contingency plans. Instead, they launched each action without contemplating the next step. Thus, it was never clear whether Pakistan intended by the Bhimbar-Chhamb thrust to cut off Kashmir, as New Delhi feared, or whether the offensive was originally designed only to relieve the pressure on Azad Kashmir created by the Indian advance in the Tithwal area, as Rawalpindi claimed. There is reason to believe that Pakistani forces ultimately hoped to cut the western road at Akhnur, and this clearly became their objective. If they could do so, the logic of the situation indicated that they might later have attempted to conquer Jammu. When the offensive began, however, there was no convincing evidence that these were the objectives. Consequently, it is not certain whether the Pakistanis turned to conventional warfare as a pre-arranged second stage of the struggle for Kashmir. They may simply have stumbled into it.

Indian officials were convinced that the Bhimbar-Chhamb attack was part of a co-ordinated campaign to sever Kashmir. 'When this scheme of sending infiltrators into Kashmir to create a "revolution" did not succeed,' Shastri said, 'Pakistan resorted to the method of attacking with regular armed forces.'[17] This phase of the conflict, in the Indian view, began with the attack across the CFL in the Bhimbar area on August 14—the assault that produced the Indian thrust at Kargil. The Pakistani purpose at that time evidently was to test Indian strength, although there is some indication that the limited offensive was designed also to rescue a group of beleaguered infiltrators.[18] Pakistan did not acknowledge the action, which was powerful enough to support India's contention that regular army forces were used. As to the ultimate goal of a Kashmir encirclement, B. G. Verghese, then a correspondent for the *Times of India* with close governmental contacts, provides this explanation: 'Pakistan calculated that the political shock of such a military disaster would break the Indian will to resist, sow confusion, panic and discord in Delhi and enable Pakistan to absorb Kashmir with whatever minimal international formalities might be decently required.'[19]

The Pakistani command acknowledged to UN observers that it had launched the offensive of September 1, but the government long attempted to hide or disguise that fact. On September 2, the Pakistan command said its troops had crossed the CFL in the Bhimbar sector, adding, 'this was a purely defensive measure to forestall Indian action in the area'. The command gave no particulars, but the Pakistani government later claimed that it was threatened by a reported Indian military buildup in this general area and that the Chhamb offensive eliminated the threat. With the offensive proceeding favourably for Pakistan, General Nimmo on September 4 made an 'official protest and urgent request' for the withdrawal of Pakistan troops from the Chhamb area. The Pakistani Chief of Staff replied that the attack was being pressed to force Indian troops from the positions they had taken in Azad Kashmir. '. . . having seen the hopelessness' of UN efforts to produce an Indian withdrawal, the Pakistani commander said, 'we were forced to take action to stop the Indians from annexing Azad Kashmir. Our action was taken after repeated requests to you to convey to Indians that their failure to vacate positions on our side of CFL will have very serious consequences. Indians apparently refused to heed our warning. They are maintaining their occupation of posts on our side of CFL in Kargil, Tithwal and Uri-Punch sectors and have now crossed the CFL in yet another sector. Under these circumstances how can you expect us to unilaterally halt our purely defensive operations which are designed to forestall Indian aggressions?'[20] Meanwhile, the Pakistan government labelled the operation as an offensive by Azad Kashmir forces 'backed by the Pakistani army', despite the fact that Azad units had no tanks and obviously could not lead an armoured assault. Nevertheless, this designation was used in Rawalpindi throughout the major fighting. While some Pakistani officials have subsequently stated that the Pakistani army undertook the operation to save Azad Kashmir, prominent leaders generally continued to obscure the army's role. Foreign newsmen, permitted near the front by Rawalpindi, called this a Pakistani operation, without qualification.

The Pakistani attack clearly marked the first major escalation of the conflict, a shift from limited infantry action across the CFL to tank operations across new and more vulnerable terrain. The Indians immediately charged that Pakistan also had crossed an international border for the first time and cited this as legal justification for their own subsequent violation of the Punjabi border. The charge became a factor in the long diplomatic effort by each side to blame the other for aggression.

Two basic points were involved in the question of whether Pakistan was responsible for the initial step in what might be called multiplication of the type of borders which could be crossed during the fighting. The first was whether Pakistani forces crossed any demarcation line except the CFL; secondly, if so, did they violate an international border. In the general area of Chhamb, the Kashmir cease-fire line, straggling from the north, joins the recognised partition boundary between West Pakistan and Jammu, since in this area Pakistani troops held no territory east of the border at the 1949 cease-fire. Chhamb lies north-eastward of this juncture. Thereafter, the Pakistan-Jammu border serves as the CFL for roughly another 120 miles before the territory of Jammu ends. At that point, the West Pakistan-Punjab border begins.

The Indians claim that Pakistani guerrillas first crossed the Pakistan-Jammu line in a village raid on August 15, and that Pakistani regulars later crossed the border during preparatory attacks for the September 1 offensive and in some actions connected with that offensive. Pakistan vigorously denied violating any boundary except the CFL. Pakistani officials, on the occasions when they have admitted the involvement of the Pakistani army in the September 1 offensive, contend that it set out from Bhimbar, a point opposite the CFL more than twenty miles north of Chhamb. The Indians reply that a second column struck through the Chhamb area over the Pakistan-Jammu border on the shortest axis to Akhnur. Indian military maps show three Pakistani crossings over the CFL opposite Bhimbar, while five crossings were made in the Chhamb region, four of them across the border.

In his public reports on the Bhimbar-Chhamb offensive, General Nimmo acknowledged Indian complaints that the border had been violated and seemed to provide some confirmation. India, he noted, 'claimed that Pakistan troops had crossed the border with approximately 90 tanks and that by the afternoon of 2 September, 16 of those tanks had been destroyed.' On this and several other Indian and Pakistani complaints, the general noted: 'UN Observers confirmed most of the reported actions had taken place.' But the observers had been confined by the hostilities behind the Munawarwali river 'since the beginning of the Pakistan thrust', he continued, and were dependent upon the information they could gather from that position. The river lay several miles east of the border and the CFL. By September 2, available information was 'that the Pakistan troops have managed to occupy an area of approximately 30 square miles, roughly extending 5 miles east of the CFL up to the Munawarwali river and 6 miles north of the border up to the Chhamb village area'. This description suggests that the general accepted the fact that a Pakistani drive northward towards Chhamb village would by necessity involve some crossing of the border, in addition to the CFL.

The available evidence is confused; however, it indicates that the main thrust did, in fact, come from Bhimbar but that the Pakistanis used outflanking tactics that probably involved a crossing of the border. The main road along the route taken by the attackers runs from Bhimbar to a point south of Chhamb. The Indians say that it was vulnerable under combat conditions, because access is blocked by a range of easily-defended hills. The roads proceeding northward from Pakistan across the border towards Chhamb are secondary and less usable for such a campaign. Qualified foreign observers who visited the area shortly after the attack saw no evidence of heavy tank traffic along the roads traversing the Pakistan-Jammu border, as would have been left by heavy treads on light surfaces, although there were signs of some vehicular traffic. An article in the *Pakistan Army Journal* in June 1966 reported, however, that Chhamb was taken from the right, or the east, by a wide outflanking movement that surprised the Indians. Logically such a manoeuvre would have been launched northward across the Pakistan-Jammu border, but it did not necessarily have to include armour. Competent Indian sources say the defenders were surprised by the border crossing and had not prepared for it, holding positions instead along the ceasefire line to the west.

In any case, the Pakistan-Jammu border occupied a political position midway between that occupied by the CFL and the clearly recognised international border in the Punjab. Secretary-General U Thant seemed to give this connotation by telling the Security Council that the northernmost tip of the Indo-Pakistan battle line from the Arabian Sea to the Punjab 'is not directly connected with the southernmost end of the Cease-fire Line in Kashmir; between them there is a stretch, roughly 120 miles long, between Pakistan and Jammu.'[21] The Indian claim that this stretch constitutes an international border is based primarily upon New Delhi's unilateral designation of Jammu and Kashmir as an integral Indian state. This position has not been accepted by the United Nations or by any individual government on a legal basis.

Whatever the legalism or the precise objectives, the Pakistani attack moved swiftly. The weight of the offensive quickly pushed back the Indians. On the afternoon of September 1, General Chaudhuri decided that the attack could only be halted with air support. Approximately an hour and a half later, the first Indian fighters were airborne.[22] Pakistan retaliated with its own aerial operations the next day. This was the beginning of a rather limited sky war. Thereafter, fighter aircraft and a small number of bombers were involved regularly in hostilities, mostly in or near the front lines. Until then, both sides had refrained from hostile air action, although the Indians claimed that Pakistan planes had been used over Indian territory since August 23 for air-lifts to the guerrillas and for reconnaissance.

On September 5, the Pakistanis captured the village of Jaurian, which lies fourteen miles east of the CFL and five miles north of the Pakistan-Jammu border. It is linked by road to Akhnur, and soon the head of the armoured column was six miles from the strategic bridge city. The column eventually reached a point four miles distant. Independent sources say the Pakistanis should have been able to capture Akhnur, if their surprise attack against inadequate defences had been adequately exploited. The drive was slowed, however, by the small Munawarwali river and by dilatory tactics. The Indians quickly established new reinforced defensive positions.

Meanwhile, New Delhi had been stirred by parallel developments. The Pakistani Commander-in-Chief, General Mahommed Musa, on September 5 sent his troops the oft-quoted message: 'You have got your teeth into him. Bite deeper and deeper until he is destroyed. And destroy him you will, God willing.' Three days earlier, Pakistan had rejected U Thant's first appeal for peace. On September 3, the Secretary-General stated in his first report to the Security Council: 'I have not obtained from the Government of Pakistan any assurance that the Cease-Fire and the CFL will be respected henceforth or that efforts would be exerted to restore conditions to normal along that line. I did receive assurance from the Government of India, conveyed orally by their Representative at the United Nations, that India would act with restraint with regard to any retaliatory acts and will respect the Cease-Fire Agreement and the CFL if Pakistan does likewise.' These developments were interpreted in New Delhi as evidence of Pakistani intransigence and confidence, in face of what the Indians believed was their own conciliatory attitude.

On September 4, Peking's Foreign Minister Ch'en Yi stretched a brief stop in Karachi into a six-hour conference with Bhutto. The Chinese official gave oblique support but no concrete reassurance to Pakistan in a statement backing the 'just action taken by Pakistan to repel the Indian armed provocation'. Some circles in New Delhi interpreted the statement as evidence that Peking had formally labelled this a 'just' war from Pakistan's point of view, meaning that it should be supported by communists, and they feared Peking might take suitable action. Finally, Indian military leaders were aroused by an attack on September 5, by a single Pakistani F86-F Sabre jet, on anti-aircraft installations near Amritsar. Although the attack was limited, it was regarded as the opening of a new front in the Punjab. Amritsar, the Sikh stronghold, was far distant from previous areas of action.

'This sequence of events', says Mankekar, 'was enough to make up New Delhi's mind. The Army HQ in New Delhi now decided that serious diversionary moves directed at Pakistani territory itself was the only remedy for the dangerous military situation developing around' Akhnur.[23] Referring later to the circumstances, Shastri said: 'It is not customary to let out State secrets, but I can tell you that when our Generals consulted the Government about the situation,

I told them firmly that there was no room for indecision, that they must go ahead and not flinch.'[24] One logical Indian response was a thrust into Pakistani Punjab, where Pakistan would be forced to consolidate its forces to defend vital objectives. This was the counter-attack that Nehru and Shastri had warned Rawalpindi to expect as the result of unacceptable pressure on Kashmir.

There is considerable evidence, however, that India long had relied on a thrust into the Punjab to counter any Pakistani attack as serious as the Chhamb offensive. Well-qualified Indian sources say the army had decided that the Chhamb-Akhnur sector was inde-fensible against major assault, because of terrain difficulties. This is why defensive forces were light and initially ineffective. The only defence was to invade the Punjab, and contingency plans were based upon that strategy. New Delhi expected a Pakistani reaction to Tithwal, and, when it came at Chhamb, preparations were made to attack the Punjab. Indian forces began to deploy along the border on September 4, occupying the same positions they had established after the Rann of Kutch episode. The positions were generally considered defensive at the time of that episode but were quickly exploited for offensive action.

The Indians launched a major attack on September 6 across the international border towards Lahore, the fabled city of religion and history, lying fifteen miles from India. A second offensive began the next day against Sialkot, an important railway and road centre, fifty miles to the north. In the effort to reduce the pressure against Akhnur, Sialkot was militarily the more vital target. It was a main supply and staging centre for that area of the front and, in Indian hands, would have seriously threatened West Pakistan. The Lahore offensive started first only because the troops involved in it were better prepared to meet the need for swift movement.[25] The diver-sionary effort worked, and Pakistan withdrew the bulk of her armoured strength from the Akhnur sector to meet the new challenge. As a result, the threat to Kashmir quickly subsided and it became a secondary theatre for the remainder of the conflict. Pakistan's offensive in this quarter had been serious enough to change the entire context of the war. Some competent observers believed it could have captured Akhnur, even after the start of India's Punjab offensive, if Pakistani armour had not been rede-ployed to West Pakistan. Although the Indians claimed heavy damage to Pakistani tanks during this withdrawal, it was accomplished with considerable logistical skill. Pakistani forces continued to occupy a substantial stretch of Indian territory.

The Lahore offensive was a three-pronged attack across a thirty-mile front. The northern column drove towards Lahore along the Grand Trunk Road across the Wagah border crossing. The southern force struck from Khem Karam in India, towards Kasur, in Pakistan. Roughly in the centre, a third column advanced from the Indian village of Khalra on a north-westward axis towards the fortified Pakistani village of Burki. The immediate military objective, say the Indians, was to establish control over the east bank of a long irrigation canal which also serves as a defensive moat for Lahore. This feature is known both as the Bambansala-Ravi-Bedian (BRB) Canal and the Ichhogil Canal. It runs for forty-seven miles west of the border and parallel to it, at distances of between three and nine miles from India. The canal is 140 feet wide and 15 feet deep. Built several years ago, it serves as a tank trap facing eastward, and heavy fortifications and gun emplacements, many disguised as mud huts, reinforce it. The Indians claim the canal was designed deliberately for military purposes, and say that approaches from the western side were prepared so as to facilitate better movement of vehicles across the water than is possible from the east.

In staging their offensive, Indian officials said one of its chief purposes was to prevent an anticipated Pakistani attack across the same border into India. The Indians feared a Pakistani attempt to drive to New Delhi behind an armoured column—a threat that was emphasised, they claimed, by what they identified as captured Pakistani documents. Subsequently, it was confirmed that the Indians did secure Pakistani field plans for an armoured attack along a stretch of Indian Punjab, which was apparently designed to trap Indian forces in a narrow wedge of land along the border. The plans, however, were merely routine operational orders of the type customary in all such actions; they were implemented, but failed. Whether the Pakistanis intended to attempt a drive to the Indian capital is doubtful, yet the potentialities were strong and Indian apprehensions were great. Under the circumstances, the most aggressive Indian counter-action was to be expected.

The question of whether India intended to capture Lahore

remains unclarified by the available evidence. Pakistani officials made this claim during the fighting. A year later, the Pakistan government said in a pamphlet, *Indo-Pakistan War, A Flash-back*, that the city was to be taken on D-Day and that India previously had designated the officials and police to administer the city. Indian newspapers first gave the impression that Lahore would be occupied, and so did some officials. But the Defence Minister, Chavan, and other officials soon emphasised that conquest of Pakistan's queen city was never an objective.

Circumstantial evidence supports Chavan. The city of 1,300,000 persons would have been both a military and a political liability. Although the Pakistanis claimed the Indians expected to produce a collapse by taking Lahore, there seemed to be considerable feeling within New Delhi that this would only intensify Pakistani resistance. There is no convincing data, moreover, that India intended any permanent territorial conquest, as distinct from temporary occupation, or that it had the capacity for conquest. 'What India sought', says B. G. Verghese, 'was not conquest of territory in Pakistan proper from which it would in any case retire at some point, but the destruction or attrition of the enemy's war potential and military machine. This was the real objective and in the subsequent battles was substantially achieved.'[26] Mankekar says the Indian army employed six and a half divisions in the Lahore and Sialkot operations and points out that larger forces would be necessary against Pakistan's six available divisions to hold conquered terrain while continuing the battle. Other sources state that India employed somewhat more than nine divisions—or more than 150,000 men in the two operations. This was perhaps a two-to-one manpower advantage, a superiority still too small for conquest, particularly against Pakistan's paramilitary reserves.

Nevertheless, the Indian offensive was severely condemned in many parts of the world and India was accused of aggression across an international border. The UN Security Council two days earlier had unanimously adopted a resolution demanding a cease-fire and a return to the 1949 CFL. The Indian action appeared to demonstrate blunt defiance of the international organisation, but the truth was that UN activities at that time appeared on the subcontinent as unreal and insubstantial. Neither nation was willing to call off the hostilities at the indecisive stage they had reached. If India had been

Y

disposed to heed the UN, battle circumstances gave her little time to do so.

The Prime Minister, Shastri, explained the situation clearly from the Indian standpoint. The Pakistani attack on Chhamb of September 1, he said,

> was no border incident, and they crossed not only the cease-fire line but also the international border and entered the Chhamb territory of Jammu. Time was of the essence and we had to act quickly. Although Pakistan's attack on India was first launched in Chhamb, they had an eye on our territory of Punjab also. As you know, they made a rocket attack on Amritsar and tried to destroy the airport near Wagah.
>
> President Ayub had been talking a great deal about the tanks and other military equipment Pakistan had acquired and had on many occasions boasted that if they decided to march on Delhi, it would be a walkover. The military situation created by Pakistan was such that our Forces had no choice but to advance in the Lahore sector.
>
> The British Government criticised India bitterly for her action and accused her of attacking Pakistan but did not say that India had been attacked by Pakistan when thousands of armed infiltrators from Pakistan entered Kashmir. Nor did they say a word when Pakistan crossed the international border, or even when Pakistan launched her massive attack on Chhamb with heavy armour.*
>
> Pakistan's attack was so formidable and so swift that we could not afford merely to talk of defending ourselves. We had to take decisive, effective action without losing time. The needs of the situation could no longer be answered by local action. We could not afford to endanger the freedom of our country; no country in the world would have allowed its freedom to be threatened as ours was. We have always held fast to the principle of peace, but in the situation that was created, not to act would have been cowardice and sloth. The display of armed might we saw within our territory could be resisted only with arms.[27]

Militarily, the Indians had another alternative. It would have been

---

*The British government later denied it had intended any unilateral condemnation of India.

possible to reinforce the Akhnur area and, most probably, to defend Akhnur successfully. The war would then have been confined to Kashmir, as Pakistan evidently desired. Assuming that Pakistan was unprepared for a subsequent invasion of Indian Punjab, the conflict might have spent itself in contained, relatively low-key combat. This policy would have had certain definite political advantages. In particular, India would have received far less world criticism, and the task of post-war reconciliation would have been less complicated. From the Indian military point of view, however, the assignment of sufficient armour to defend Akhnur would have risked weakening the forces in the Punjab where even the high command apparently expected a violent Pakistani attack with the feared Pattons. The Indians kept their best armour in the Punjab area, protecting the route to Delhi, and the progress of the war gave them no assurance that Pakistan would avoid the opportunity of striking in this sector. In fact, the swift progress from irregular war in Kashmir to the tank attack towards Akhnur convinced the Indians, as Shastri noted, that Pakistan was following a strategy to be culminated by a thrust towards the Indian capital. If Rawalpindi had no such intention, it had nevertheless intensified the probability of an Indian offensive-defensive assault in the Punjab by boasting of Pakistani armoured power. By shifting the main battle axis to this region, the Indians made sure that they did not expose themselves to a frontal attack by becoming over committed on the Akhnur flank. The crisis also illustrated one significant facet of Indian psychology. Although clearly unwilling to launch aggressive war, the Indians, once attacked, were ferociously determined to inflict the maximum punishment on Pakistan. They were not deterred by moral or political considerations from any actions they deemed justifiable for this purpose.

Pakistan's version of the immediate events leading to the Lahore thrust is less clear and is clouded by the unconvincing insistence that the Bhimbar-Chhamb offensive was undertaken primarily by Azad Kashmir forces. The minimum objective for this attack, which most certainly was made by the Pakistani army, appeared obvious from General Musa's note to the UN group, that counter-pressure was invoked through fear that India would occupy Azad Kashmir and destroy Pakistan's hold on the territory. This point was emphasised by well-informed Pakistani sources during conversations with the author in Rawalpindi in 1967. There was no evidence that Indian forces intended to strike for Muzaffarabad or to seek further permanent territorial conquests in Azad Kashmir; neither was there any guarantee that they would not do so. Obviously, the loss of Azad Kashmir was unacceptable to Rawalpindi, and age-old fears that India intended conquering this area inevitably prompted the most vigorous counter-action. President Ayub, in contending that India used the Kashmir 'uprising' as the pretext for opening 'a long-planned course of aggression', added: 'Abandoning all principles and dishonouring all agreements, the enemy first crossed the cease-fire line, and when his designs were forestalled in the Bhimbar sector, he invaded Pakistan in the Lahore area.' He gave no details. 'The enemy plans', Ayub continued, 'were to occupy Lahore in one swift move and then launch a major offensive from the direction of Sialkot, cutting down to Gujranwala and Wazirabad.'[28]

The possibility that Rawalpindi intended the Bhimbar-Chhamb offensive as a drive to cut off Kashmir and its garrison cannot be excluded. If so, the authorities would hardly admit it. Although the war was not always fought logically, it would appear that Pakistan's objectives would have been served best by confining hostilities to Kashmir and seeking to destroy the maximum amount of Indian equipment on nearby battlefields with the minimum risk to Pakistani Pattons. This consideration tends to support the Indian contention that Pakistan expected an easy tank victory in the Akhnur drive and believed India would not dare to retaliate outside Kashmir. It also tends to discount the possibility that pre-planned Pakistani strategy included a tank drive to New Delhi, as distinct from a militarily crippling effort to trap and destroy Indian forces in the Punjab. The careful political position of obscurity, which Pakistan had constructed around her operations in Kashmir, would have been destroyed by an open thrust to the Indian capital. Such a drive, moreover, would have been productive only if it brought prompt and thorough Indian collapse. Nevertheless, the Indian fears were real and constituted a vital element in the psychology of the conflict.

What happened was deliberate escalation of the war by both sides, with each step calculated to place additional pressure on the adversary but without, however, any apparent consideration of the probable consequences. In retrospect, it also appears evident that the long accumulation of mutual fears and animosities meant that, once fighting broke out between the neighbours, they could not be parted until one side had won or both were exhausted.

Under these circumstances, world reaction was lamentably unrealistic. Shastri was quite right in suggesting that India received almost universal blame for crossing the international border from political leaders, diplomats and editorial writers who avoided condemning Pakistan's previous initiatives. The principal reason was probably that India carried out her operations with relative openness while Pakistan employed subterfuge with considerable success. India's thrust towards Lahore was unmistakable and so was the crossing of a recognised international border. The evidence to support India's contention that Pakistan had previously violated an accepted border was confused and obscure; her insistence that the Pakistan-Jammu line constituted an international border, even more controversial. But it was manifestly inadequate to blame India most vigorously for violating an international border while avoiding condemnation of Pakistan for starting the war and for the Bhimbar-Akhnur attack, because the evidence was hazy. Diplomats and leaders of opinion had the responsibility of investigating the available facts more fully than they did. Moreover, it was impossible to discount the military circumstances. Pakistan opened armoured warfare in a new battle area far distant from current guerrilla hostilities in response to counter-action that did not directly threaten her security. But the Indians believed, with justification, that this offensive did threaten their security, and they retaliated with the most logical response possible. It is doubtful if any nation would have respected the international border in similar circumstances. To insist, therefore, upon the inviolate sanctity of the border was pedantry, even though this principle by necessity must be preached as an essential of peacetime diplomacy. In this age of disguised warfare, the cause of peace might have been served better if Anglo-American statesmen, in particular, had properly blamed both sides for their transgressions.

Foreign criticism hurt the Indians, infuriated them and intensified their determination. Newspapers accurately characterised the national reaction to the Lahore offensive as 'proud'. Announcement of the attack was loudly applauded in the Lok Sabha. This was not necessarily due to chauvinism. As Mankekar explains it: 'The applause . . .

expressed the people's sense of relief that their Government had, at last, given up what they considered a policy of "offering the other cheek" and had stood up to Pakistani bullying.'[29] A newspaper columnist wrote that 'the latest confrontation with Pakistan destroys as much the myth of the meek and mild Hindu as it has the legend of American-built and American-supplied Patton tanks and Sabre jets.' Newspapers, reacting to India's relative diplomatic isolation, spoke of 'going it alone'.

Pakistan responded to the assault with predictable vigour. 'We are at war', President Ayub announced in a nation-wide broadcast, adding that he was invoking the self-defence provisions of the United Nations charter. 'Our soldiers have gone forward to repel the enemy,' and the Pakistan people 'will not rest until India's guns are silenced forever'. Ayub again insisted: 'The Indian rulers were never reconciled to the establishment of an independent Pakistan homeland of our own. All their military preparations during the past eighteen years have been against us. They exploited the Chinese bogey to secure massive arms assistance from some of our friends in the West who never understood the mind of the Indian rulers, and permitted themselves to be taken in by India's profession that once they were fully armed they would fight the Chinese. We always knew these arms would be raised against us. Time has proved this so.'[30]

The Pakistanis also became more defiant. Those in West Pakistan, who felt themselves under long-feared, all-out Indian assault, expressed this attitude most particularly by turning against the Americans. Individuals and some newspapers accused the Americans of helping the Indians, even to the extent of deliberately violating blackout regulations. Behind the scenes, relations between the government and the 100-member US military mission cooled quickly, as they had when the Americans had tried to curtail the fighting in the Rann of Kutch. After the Lahore operation, government authorities prevented official American visits to battle areas, although the military agreement specifically authorised the US officials to supervise the use of American equipment. The Americans were told that they could read the government statements (which were biased) if they wanted to know about the progress of hostilities. Pakistani diplomats quite understandably attempted to make capital out of the relatively favourable world attitude resulting from the reaction against the Indian attack. In doing so, however, they attempted to convince the world that the war began for Pakistan on September 6, the date of the Indian offensive. Bhutto made this claim solemnly before the UN Security Council. This contention obviously weakened Pakistan's entire case, for there was little inclination to accept the Chhamb offensive as an initiative by an independent Azad Kashmir army. If this was not precisely a further sign of Pakistani defiance of world opinion, it was an example of the diplomatic legerdemain of the period.

The war soon spread over a front described as 1,200 miles long and even longer, if the extreme flank areas of periodic confrontation were included. The main fighting, however, remained in the Punjab. On September 8, India began to advance westward in the desert along the border between Pakistani Sind and Rajasthan, some 400 miles south-west of the central combat area. General Chaudhuri later explained that this was a diversionary thrust. Indian commentators concluded the purpose was to keep Pakistani forces pinned down in the principal city of Karachi, west of the area of the desert advance. The origins of this diversion were somewhat different, however, and they illustrate the atmosphere of the moment. Well-informed sources say that the drive began in this way: a local Indian politician visited the headquarters of the Indian commander on the edge of the desert and demanded to know what he was doing in the war. 'Well,' the commander replied, 'I sent some patrols out this morning.' The politician thereupon announced to waiting newspapermen that a massive new offensive had begun, and New Delhi had to support the story. Nevertheless, Pakistani sources insist that Rajasthan was an active war front.

On the Lahore front, Indian forces achieved initial tactical surprise when they moved forward at 5.30 a.m., September 6. The Pakistanis had deployed their Tenth Division in defensive positions forward of the city only a few hours before the attack, and there was no Pakistani armour east of the BRB canal. At this point, say competent sources, the Pakistanis still doubted that India would dare to cross an international border. They were also startled by the vigour of the Indian attack, for the vision of Indian ineptness remained strong, nurtured by the relatively feeble response in the Rann of Kutch crisis. The Indian offensive involved three armour-supported divisions, by Indian account, but it is known that eventually five divisions were involved. Initially, the assault proceeded with relative speed. By nightfall, the centre column had captured two key villages. Infantry units of the northern column, proceeding along the Grand Trunk Road, reached the outskirts of Lahore and were driven back by heavy opposition. This particular advance created a belief that the Indians intended to capture the city and were prevented from doing so by stout defences. The Indian version is that the infantry outraced its armour in an unplanned over-extension and was recalled. Thereafter, the campaign in this sector settled down to hard and continuous fighting for strategic waterways, bridges and fortified villages. Combat was continual from D-day until the cease-fire on September 23, swirling from the border to the canal and involving all types of heavy weapons. Eventually, the Pakistanis blew up some seventy bridges across the BRB Canal, and it served as a defensive moat for both sides against further armoured assault in this salient.

In one of the key battles, Indian forces captured the village of Burki on September 10, after a full day's battle. The objective of the central advancing column, Burki was situated in a dominating position on the east bank of the canal and had been made into a major fortified position, guarded, the Indians say, by eleven concrete pill-boxes, camouflaged to resemble rural mud huts, with three-foot walls, steel-shuttered gun openings and ample supplies for a three-man garrison. The battle, which began at night, involved tanks on both sides and unusually heavy fire from Pakistani artillery, ranging up to 150-millimetre guns. Control of the village and supporting operations by other units gave the Indians command of a considerable stretch of the Ichhogil Canal in the central area, although they remained under Pakistani artillery fire. This position was some twelve miles from the centre of Lahore but only about five miles from its airport; so the Indians reported, with some pride, that American authorities asked for their co-operation in suspending fire while American residents of the Pakistani city were evacuated by air.

Farther north, a second major battle was waged continually for Dograi village, another fortified position on the east bank of the canal. The village, seven miles inside Pakistan due west of Amritsar along the Grand Trunk Road, was part of the outer defences of Lahore, eight miles distant. Dograi changed hands at least three times, in some of the fiercest fighting of this campaign, before the Indians captured it a few hours in advance of the cease-fire. In one of the first eye-witness stories of the war from the Indian side by a foreign newsman, Thomas F. Brady of the *New York Times* reported that the Grand Trunk Road had been fought over, yard by yard, from the border to the canal. Near Dograi he saw extensive debris of war and at least a dozen immobilised tanks, many destroyed by fire or explosives. Dograi itself was badly damaged after the final battle, but Pakistani troops were positioned near it in deep trenches, supported by Sherman tanks and a line of recoilless rifles. Brady's dispatch, filed September 23, was never published, because of the New York newspaper strike at that time.[31]

Pakistani military sources confirm this account of the Dograi campaign but contend that the Indians succeeded only in capturing the western outskirts of the village just before the armistice. They failed, however, to capture the Batapur bridge across the canal in this region, an objective the Pakistanis claim was the primary Indian objective. Control of the bridge conceivably could have allowed the Indians to send an armoured thrust deeper toward Lahore along the Grand Trunk Road. Farther northward along the canal, the Indians launched a flanking movement toward another key objective, the Bhiani bridge, but failed to capture it, the Pakistanis say, after making fifteen attacks to clear a path for tanks. The ferocity of the fighting around Burki is reflected in Pakistani accounts which, however, claim this campaign was a major Indian mistake because of its intensity.

The fighting in this area was waged almost continuously and involved weapons from tanks and heavy artillery to bayonet charges. Competent foreign sources report that the Pakistani counter-offensive at one point drove the Indians back almost to their line of departure, seven miles from Dograi, before some of the territory could be regained. The Pakistanis, contending they were out-numbered four-to-one, regard this campaign as a heroic defence of Lahore during which the Indians were unable to penetrate their main defences.

By the end of the campaign, the Indians claimed control over more than thirty miles of the east bank of the canal. The implication is that they held positions on the canal itself, but Pakistani sources say the actual line of control ran irregularly to the eastward of the waterway. In any case, the canal in this sector had become a barrier against the movement of armour either eastward or westward, because all the principal bridges were destroyed. Indian forces held a wedge of land on the Pakistani side of the border totalling around 140 square miles, a figure generally confirmed by independent sources. If the purpose was an offensive-defensive attack to destroy the enemy's striking power without attempting to penetrate deeper into Pakistan, as the Indians say, the major objective seems to have been accomplished. But the Pakistanis insist that the occupation or encirclement of Lahore was the primary objective and that the Indians launched thirteen major attacks of brigade strength or greater without breaking Pakistani defences. This 'victory' continues to be extolled in Pakistan and a monument to the battle is being erected in Lahore.

Pakistan launched its major counter-thrust on the Indian left flank to the south. The Indian column, advancing from Ferozpore through Khem Karan towards Pakistani Kasur, took its initial objectives easily. But the opposition was so slight that the commanding officer, fearing a trap, halted the advance and withdrew to the west bank of the Sutlej river. The Pakistani armoured attack, beginning on September 7, forced the Indians back to their starting point. Indian intelligence had reported that the main Pakistani tank force, the First Armoured Division, was in the Sialkot sector. But the Pakistanis had concentrated it around Kasur to prevent a feared encirclement movement towards Lahore. The division, created and trained by Americans, was equipped with heavy American Patton tanks, light American Shermans and medium French Chaffées. This column of clanking land warcraft, with its artillery and infantry, constituted the principal threat to New Delhi if such a threat existed, for a second American-organised armoured division was incomplete. India's pre-war concern over the American equipment was perhaps reflected by the fact that an official citation commending a non-commissioned officer for heroism noted his action against 'several of the supposedly invulnerable Patton tanks. . . .'

The Pakistan First Armoured and a supporting infantry division opened a major offensive on the night of September 8, choosing darkness because Pattons are equipped with infra-red 'eyes' for night-fighting, whereas the heavy Centurion tanks, India's best, were blind after sunset. Indian accounts say that more than 225

Pakistani tanks were involved, but the active strength for such a division is between 125 and 150 tanks; further, the Pakistani commander is said to have held substantial forces in reserve. In any case, Pakistan threw a heavy concentration of armour into the battle, outnumbering the Indian Centurions and Shermans by a substantial ratio, if somewhat less than the Indian figure of four-to-one. In this most decisive engagement of the war, Pakistan launched five separate attacks at Indian positions during the next day and a half, seeking a breakthrough which was never achieved. At one point, the attackers penetrated fifteen miles into Indian territory, but were beaten back.[32] Originally, the assault exceeded expectations; then it was stopped. The attackers were able to send such an extensive force across the BRB canal, the Indians say, because they secretly built a tunnel beneath the waterway. New Delhi had incomplete prior knowledge of this installation.

The Pakistanis sought unsuccessfully to implement an operational plan to trap Indian forces—the plan which the Indians later obtained. It called for the armoured conquest of a substantial segment of territory between the border and the Beas river, extending north-west from Khem Karan to the Grand Trunk Road. At the road, the Beas and its vital bridge lie twenty-seven miles east of Amritsar. One armoured column was to take this position after a thrust roughly parallel with the river. The western attacking column was to capture Amritsar, or at least to put it out of action. A third column, in the centre, was ordered also to reach the Grand Trunk Road. If successful, this operation would have cut off Indian forces between the Beas and the border, exposing them to piecemeal destruction.[33] 'If it had succeeded', says Mankekar, 'east of that point, up to Delhi, the Grand Trunk Road lay open, practically undefended, with all our forces on the other side of the Beas—thus bringing within an ace of realisation Ayub's dream of "strolling up" to Delhi!'[34]

The battle plan was a logical manoeuvre, designed to circumvent major terrain liabilities. In that area, numerous canals and drains run roughly north-eastward from the area of the border. The Pakistani columns were ordered to advance along the waterways, instead of attempting to cross them, until they reached the more manoeuvrable Grand Trunk Road. The Indian defence also was logical; it blocked the approaches to the road by utilising the terrain as fully as possible. These defensive plans were formulated by field commanders before the Pakistani battle order was captured. The evidence as confirmed by post-battle investigation is that the Indians won the engagement by superior use of territory and equipment against a potentially stronger attacking force.

Indian armour and infantry, by the Indian account, fell back from Khem Karan in order to draw the Pakistanis into a huge horseshoe-shaped trap near the village of Assal Uttar, a short distance away. Entrenched infantry and concentrated artillery beat off preliminary attacks piecemeal. On the morning of September 10, the Pakistanis threw the main force of their armoured division, with supporting infantry, into vigorous outflanking efforts to get behind Indian positions. The manoeuvrability of the armour was hampered by irrigation ditches and by flooded areas created when the Indians cut key dykes. The principal tank attacks were then diverted into fields of sugar-cane, left standing some nine feet high, behind which a force of Indian Centurions crouched in ambush. The narrow terrain and the newly created marshlands cut down the superior speed and mobility of the Pattons. The high cane-fields reduced the attackers' visibility and thereby helped to curtail the superior gunnery range of the Pattons, which the Indians say is 1,800 yards to around 1,000 yards for the Centurions. Moreover, the Indian tanks were hidden, while the waving sugar-cane exposed the position of the Pakistani Pattons.

When the Pakistani armour rounded a corner of the fields and exposed itself, dug-in Indian tanks, mostly old American-designed Shermans, opened fire. The Indians profitably used Canadian-designed 76 mm high velocity tank guns. The tanks were supported by jeep-mounted 106 mm recoilless rifles, which were American-designed but were being manufactured in Indian factories. Two Pakistani outflanking attempts were blocked on this general pattern by Indian tanks, artillery, aircraft and infantry. The offensive was halted. Pakistani forces fell back to Khem Karan, where they dug in and, at the cease-fire, held a strip of Indian territory three miles deep and ten miles long. Indian officers in the battle area said they had destroyed sixty Pakistani tanks and captured another ten intact; later Indian estimates were a total of ninety-seven destroyed or captured. Independent sources say Pakistan lost perhaps forty tanks in this engagement. There is no doubt that the Indians won a significant victory in what was probably the most important single battle of the conflict, as Indian military sources say. These sources, however, do not claim that the Pakistani offensive was aimed at New Delhi, nor do they reveal any indication that the Defence Ministry believed Pakistan had the military capability of threatening the capital.

The Pakistani version of this battle is that a headstrong commander led a tank regiment beyond the line of advance required by his orders and this 'mistake' resulted in serious losses. But this was a local action which was not strategically significant to the campaign as a whole. Pakistani tank officers contend they have no plans for attacking New Delhi, because they could not support the necessary long supply lines through hostile territory.

Meanwhile, the battle for Sialkot, fifty miles north-east of Lahore, was developing into what was described as the biggest tank engagement since the Second World War. The Indians attacked on September 7, and both sides quickly rushed heavy concentrations of armour into action. During a fifteen-day battle, with armoured action relatively continuous, the Indians say 400 tanks were involved, while President Ayub placed the number at around 600. Again, the figures are unconfirmed, but impartial sources reported during the engagement that there was no doubt of its extensiveness or ferocity. The two sides fought across flat land at close range in overpowering dust, and when it had settled both claimed exorbitant successes. This was, nevertheless, the biggest engagement of the war.

The exact outcome remains unclear, because the precise Indian objective is uncertain. The question is whether the purpose was to immobilise or capture Sialkot or whether the Indians intended only diversionary pressure and more attrition. The city was, as Mankekar suggests, a primary pressure point for New Delhi's diversionary attack.[35] Another Indian writer says the central purpose was to destroy Pakistani equipment and to forestall another Pakistani thrust into India which had been expected on September 10.[36] The capture of Sialkot, a major communications centre, would have cut in half Pakistan's ability to supply the Chhamb front and the capital of Rawalpindi, lying to the north-west. Some Indian sources report that the supply line to Chhamb was cut when Indian forces advancing from Jammu secured control of the main road. These informants contend that neither capture nor encirclement of Sialkot was contemplated. Yet a highly-qualified Indian source said that Indian troops attempted to surround the city; they were unable to do so before the cease-fire. Pakistani sources give equally conflicting versions. Some adhere to President Ayub's contention that Sialkot was among the cities that India intended to capture. A different version is contained in *Seventeen September Days*, one of several Pakistani books on the conflict. Jehangir A. Khan, one of the contributors, says the Indians made only a diversionary thrust at Sialkot and the main offensive deliberately bypassed the city in an attempt to cut the Grand Trunk Road and cut off Rawalpindi. Then Sialkot and Lahore were to be encircled 'in a fatal pincer calculated to paralyse all resistance'. Pakistani sources generally agree that the attack in this area was India's main offensive. Military officials say it involved fifteen major tank-infantry attacks.

Ayub maintained that 'as the enemy withdrew from the Lahore sector, he hastened to build up an offensive in the direction of Sialkot. It is here that the enemy exhausted all his offensive power.'[37] The Indians did not withdraw to this extent from the Lahore front, but their pressure on it was lessened by the Pakistani armoured attack to the south at Khem Karan and by the destruction of bridges which turned the Ichhogil Canal into a moat. The Indians moved large quantities of armour from the Punjab to reinforce the Sialkot offensive, an operation apparently giving credence to Ayub's contention of 'withdrawal'. The movement also convinced some foreign observers that Indian forces intended to drive beyond the Ichhogil Canal and that, when stopped there, they sought further penetration of West Pakistan through Sialkot.[38]

What happened, however, was that General Chaudhuri daringly manoeuvred his armour to mount the Sialkot offensive. He left one force in the Lahore sector and sent the other, mainly the newest equipment, into action around Sialkot. This required the movement of some 3,000 vehicles along a single road and into enemy terrain under potential aerial threat of considerable proportions. The gamble was twofold; first, that the forces defending the road to Delhi would not be disproportionately weakened and, secondly, that the movement toward Sialkot could be accomplished without devastating loss to enemy action. The gamble succeeded to the extent that the Indians were able to inflict heavy punishment on Pakistan's armoured striking force on two fronts.

Major fighting occurred along the main line of the Indian advance, on a southward axis from the Indian village of Samba, midway between Jammu and Pathankot. Heavy tank and infantry battles were fought around the Pakistani villages of Phillora and Chawnda, south-east of Sialkot. The immediate objective was the Lahore-Sialkot railroad, which runs through Chawnda. A second railway parallels the Grand Trunk Road some thirty-five miles west of Chawnda. The action around Phillora was a tank-to-tank conflict, with little air participation, involving India's First Armoured Division and elements of Pakistan's newly-formed Sixth Armoured Division. Pakistani sources say the Indians opened the Sialkot offensive with a four-to-one advantage. After two days of heavy armoured attack and counter-attack, Indian forces captured Phillora on September 12. Both sides then regrouped, and a third major battle was fought between September 14 and 17. On September 15, the Indians cut the railroad at Chawnda, but the Pakistanis fought back to secure and maintain control over part of the station. At the cease-fire, the opposing armies held positions only thirty yards apart at some points along the railroad track.

In the north of the city, where the Indians launched their initial two-pronged attack on Sialkot, further heavy tank-infantry battles were fought. The Indians reported slow gains towards the heavily-fortified city which, at the cease-fire, left them entrenched 4,000 yards away. They also cut a northern branch of the railway. This position, however, meant that Sialkot was only partially encircled, and a main railway and road running due westward were apparently unaffected. When the fighting ended, the Indians claimed possession of 180 square miles of Pakistani territory in this area, most of it lying between the border and the principal battle zone of Phillora. Pakistan agreed generally with the depth of penetration claimed by India.

In the unvarying Pakistani version of the conflict, numerically superior Indian forces were stopped by small but determined Pakistani defenders on both the Lahore and Sialkot sectors. The people seemed as firmly convinced in 1967 as two years earlier that they had won major victories over the Indian giant and had gallantly repulsed a concerted attempt to conquer them. Pakistanis of all types demonstrated a total rejection of all responsibility for events preceding September 1 or, in many instances, September 6.

Consequently there was in their account of the hostilities no relation between the guerrilla attack on Kashmir and India's Lahore offensive. Instead, they regarded themselves as the victims of 'unprovoked aggression'. This is the only version of the conflict known by the general public. It constitutes the background against which Pakistanis generally interpret contemporary relations with India.

Another Indian offensive was thwarted at a point between the Sialkot and Lahore battle areas when Pakistani sappers succeeded in blowing a key bridge across the Ravi river at the village of Dera Baba Nanak. The attack at this point, say the Indians, was to support the Lahore offensive. Pakistani sources say it was to have constituted a third major prong of the Sialkot campaign.

These land battles constituted the principal and most significant operations of the conflict and, because of mutual fears, the outcome of the tank engagements was of prime importance. Although both sides claimed victory, the consensus of informed foreign opinion was that the conflict resulted in a draw. In terms of equipment, military circles in Washington concluded, on the basis of post-war information, that Pakistan lost 200 tanks, with another 150 put out of action but recoverable. India by this assessment, lost between 175 and 190, with another 200 temporarily out of commission.[39] These are admittedly only rough figures, but they indicate that, during the fighting, India was deprived of 27 per cent of her tank force of 1,450, while Pakistan lost 32 per cent of her 1,100 tanks. Some foreign assessments place Indian losses at the lower figure of 100 to 125.

The statistics do not reveal the ratio between light and heavy tanks in these losses. Neither do the figures announced by the combatants; India claimed 471 Pakistan tanks destroyed, and Pakistan claimed 516 Indian tanks. These totals are considered artificially high and misleading; the Indians, for example, announced the immobilisation of more Pattons than the Pakistani army possessed. Nevertheless, the nature of the fighting indicated that Pakistan employed a maximum number of her Pattons and therefore suffered proportionately high losses in this category. Foreign experts generally agree that the striking power of Pakistan's armoured forces was blunted at least temporarily on the battlefield. This assessment appeared to be confirmed indirectly by the fact that Pakistan did not mount another flank attack to ease the pressure against Sialkot during that intensive battle.

Tactically, the judgment of impartial experts is that the Indians demonstrated somewhat greater skill and better strategy in the use of armour. The Patton tanks did not prove to be failures, as some Indians thought, or less powerful than expected: they were misused. The Indian writer, Dewan Berindranath, made one basic point in his book, *The War With Pakistan*. Attributing his assessment to Lieutenant General O. P. Dunn, Commander of I Corps in the Sialkot engagement, Berindranath says: it was '. . . the total dependence of the enemy on its superior weapons which helped in its undoing. Pattons perhaps proved too much of a sophisticated organism for an ordinary Pakistani "Sawar" who is as rustic a peasant as our own men are. This proves the age old dictum that it is not the machine, but the man behind the machine, who has always the last say.'[40]

The Pakistanis encountered difficulties with both the complexity of their primary weapon and the organisation required to maintain it. In the thrust at Khem Karan, for example, the tanks were brought from some distance within Pakistan, then sent into the offensive without replenishing half-empty petrol tanks. At the battle of Assal Uttar, some ran out of fuel and were abandoned intact; others became bogged down in the terrain. The Pakistanis stumbled into the cane-field ambush in this sector because they neglected the fundamental principle of sending forward an adequate scouting force. In other areas, tanks were committed in units that were too small for strategic purposes or, as in Phillora, too closely grouped for effectiveness. The necessary collaboration between infantry and armour sometimes broke down. After the war, Ayub reportedly retired eleven generals and thirty-nine colonels.

The Indians, for their part, also encountered battlefield deficiencies which handicapped their offensives and resulted in a less effective campaign than many foreign observers believed they could have conducted. A general, for instance, was court-martialled for the failure which permitted Pakistani destruction of the Dera Baba Nanak bridge. A number of other officers were reportedly relieved of their posts, but there has been no official announcement. Yet both sides demonstrated moments of tactical efficiency, as in the Pakistani withdrawal from Akhnur and the Indian movement of armour

z

toward Sialkot. There was, in general, little to distinguish between the individual fighting man and the individual junior officer of each army; each was brave and long-suffering.

The even score was further indicated, in general terms, by the positions held by the two armies at the cease-fire. India claimed control over 720 square miles of Pakistani territory, including an area of 150 square miles of relatively worthless desert in Sind around Gadra. These figures have been generally accepted. Pakistan claimed 1,617 square miles of Indian territory, of which 1,200 were in the desert of Rajasthan. India acknowledged that Pakistan dominated 220 square miles of her territory, and Washington placed the figure at 310–20 square miles. Tactically, the positions were clearer. India held the Uri-Poonch bulge and territory around Tithwal, as well as positions around Sialkot and a strip of land in the Punjab between the BRB Canal and the border. Pakistan controlled the territory taken in her Chhamb-Akhnur offensive and, farther south, a narrow wedge around Khem Karan.

These dispositions indicated that each side was able to consolidate control over terrain taken during the first thrust of offensives initiated with a certain amount of tactical surprise. Neither army had been dislodged from these bridge-heads, possibly because the war had shifted quickly to other fronts soon after they were established. But Pakistan was unable to drive closer to Akhnur and India was unable to complete the encirclement of Sialkot, as each undoubtedly attempted and would have done with sufficient power. Therefore, neither side was capable of fully exploiting a major offensive while simultaneously resisting the outflanking attacks of the opponent. In the Akhnur area and on the Lahore front, this situation apparently resulted in a military draw.

In Rawalpindi and in some quarters of New Delhi, however, there was considerable surprise that the Indians did not succeed in greater penetration around the Sialkot area, with the heightened pressure that this would have produced on Pakistan. By the closing phases of this campaign, the Pakistanis 'were hurting', in the words of well-informed sources, and senior officers were frightened. The Pakistan army was short of supplies, it was running out of ammunition and had lost heavily in equipment and trained men and officers, particularly junior officers. The Indians were expected to take advantage of this situation and press for more decisive gains.

General Chaudhuri's gamble in sending a powerful armoured force toward Sialkot strengthened the belief that the intention was to drive as deeply as possible on this front, an area threatening much of West Pakistan.

The exact reasons for India's failure to extract a greater toll are unclear. There are indications that the Indians were stopped at Sialkot by rugged Pakistani defences which were assembled with relative speed. Some observers believe the Indians failed to achieve their objectives in this battle area because their offensive began twenty-four hours too late—a delay apparently imposed by the inadequate organisation of the attacking force—yet at this point the Indians were in a far better over-all military position than the Pakistanis. There is also evidence that Indian military authorities came under increasing control from political leaders who were responding to fresh UN appeals for peace. As a result, the army was given sufficient time to inflict more attrition upon Pakistani forces but not enough to launch a more punishing offensive.* It is possible that Pakistan was saved from further devastation by a political decision.

Farther north, in Kashmir, military parity was less certain. The large Indian garrison was not appreciably drained by the fighting in the Punjab. While required to maintain strong defensive positions against guerrillas and the possibility of a flank Pakistani offensive, Indian Kashmiri forces appeared capable of exploiting the positions gained in their first thrusts across the CFL. In particular, they did not use their offensive capability in the Tithwal region for an attack on the highly sensitive capital of Azad Kashmir, Muzaffarabad. For the second time in nearly twenty years, Indian troops had reached within striking distance of Pakistan Kashmir's nerve centre and had been restrained, apparently by political decision in New Delhi. A combination of factors was probably involved. An attack on Muzaffarabad or deeper into Azad Kashmir would certainly have stimulated vigorous Pakistani counter-action elsewhere. In certain areas, an Indian offensive might have aroused vigorous retaliation from Peking, and India would undoubtedly have been further condemned for aggression. Nevertheless, the opportunity was present and the fact that India failed to take it was clear proof that she was not intent on blind aggression against Azad Kashmir, as Pakistan had claimed

* See pages 366–9 below.

for so long. These circumstances tended to negate Rawalpindi's claim that it had captured Indian orders which called for the conquest of all Azad Kashmir.

In general, the air war was limited to objectives in or near the battlefield. Despite innumerable rumours, civilian areas in the chief cities were not bombed, probably because indiscriminate air war was feared and consciously avoided by both sides. Pakistani students caused more damage in one anti-American riot in Karachi than all the Indian aerial sorties over that principal city.[41] Pakistan's feared F-104s were used sparingly, and India's MIGs apparently did not appear; most of them were inoperable. Under prevailing battle conditions, the Indian-built subsonic fighter plane, the Gnat, proved its versatility and effectiveness. One of the weapons supplied by the United States to Pakistan which had troubled many Indian officials, the Sidewinder missile, played a secondary part in the conflict. Mankekar, presumably giving the Indian air force explanation, says the missiles were affected by the comparatively low altitudes of between 15,000 and 20,000 feet to which the Gnats forced the air-to-air combat. The missiles, which find their targets by the heat expulsion of jet aircraft, are designed for much higher altitudes. They were deflected by radiation from the earth.[42] In all, India lost an estimated sixty-five to seventy planes; Pakistan, up to twenty. Pakistan claimed the destruction of 115 Indian planes; New Delhi claimed seventy-three Pakistani aircraft. At sea, the war was extremely limited and relatively ineffectual.

The battlefield draw should eventually have convinced both sides that many of their principal long-standing fears were erroneous. The Patton tank did not constitute an irresistible weapon with which Pakistan could reach Delhi. The tanks were contained by stout defences, and a dash to the Indian capital, even if planned, never became a realistic possibility. Neither the superior manpower of the Indian army nor its 'massive' imports of weaponry were decisive or even very discernible. The Indians did use some of their US arms, when American-equipped mountain divisions entered combat, after Pakistan's heavy employment of American equipment made the question of foreign weapons irrelevant. The supersonic planes, which were literally worshipped in the military thinking of both sides, were largely neutralised by battlefield conditions and by the mutual vulnerability of crowded cities. India gave substantial proof that she was not determined to conquer Azad Kashmir and was not attempting to destroy Pakistan. To this extent, a sober reappraisal of the conflict provided convincing evidence that for many years both countries had been living under fears artificially magnified by the deliberate or mistaken manipulation of political leaders. The fact that no such conclusions were drawn with clarity on the subcontinent indicates to some extent that these apprehensions, while basic, were not the sole, or perhaps even primary, motivations for conflict. This factor, in turn, was a consequential element in the psychology of the war and the post-war periods.

Throughout the fighting, both capitals were dominated by the deep and persistent fear that the conflict would set off new waves of internal communal troubles, reviving the first civil war. 'Your foremost duty at the present moment', the Indian Prime Minister, Shastri, told his people on September 3, 'is to do everything possible to ensure that peace is not disturbed and that communal harmony is maintained. There are no Hindus, no Muslims, no Christians, no Sikhs, but only Indians.' This communal danger was a potential Trojan Horse which each side feared the other would exploit as a drain on its internal strength. Moreover, communalism had its own peculiar influence on the conduct of hostilities. The most convincing reason for believing that India had no intention of capturing or heavily damaging Lahore, for instance, was the fact that the Pakistani city contained some of Sikhdom's sacred shrines. Their destruction would not only have aroused Pakistani Sikhs but might have caused serious repercussions among Indian Sikhs. This community provided the Indian army with some of its best fighting men and more than 30 per cent of its commissioned and non-commissioned officers. In the end, the bitter conflict was waged without significant communal disturbances in either country. Some provocations occurred and were promptly suppressed, usually without publicity. In India, the authenticated story was told that a political leader helped to maintain quiet by warning his followers that he wanted no communal disorders.

But India, in particular, suffered until the start of the September 6 offensive from bitter and sometimes bloody internal quarrels. In late July, Shastri was insulted personally during a demonstration at Bangalore staged to coincide with the opening of a convention of the All-India Congress Committee. The issue, which created a certain amount of turmoil, was a rather artificial demand for the annexation of Goa to the state of Mysore. During August, twelve major incidents and many minor ones erupted throughout the country, their frequency and violence unaffected by the start of the guerrilla war. A particularly violent riot broke out on August 9 in the northern city of Patna, where students besieged the headquarters of the local government and set it on fire. The disturbances, in which at least thirty-five persons were injured, resulted from protests over food problems, rising prices and over the Rann of Kutch crisis. This usual catch-all collection consisting of volatile issues was assembled for a joint anti-government demonstration staged cooperatively by communists of both factions, the opposition Revolutionary Socialist Party and some trade unions. By mid-August, Indian officials had gathered sufficient information to report that communists were behind a series of upheavals occurring at the same time in West Bengal, Mysore, Hyderabad, Uttar Pradesh, Kerala and several other states.[43] A Punjabi leader named Sant Fateh Singh threatened on August 8 to go on hunger strike to the death unless demands for separate political and language status were met. This was an old complaint and an old tactic, but the government promised concessions which were later implemented. The 86-year-old Master Tara Singh, whose actions had helped trigger the bloodshed in the Punjab in 1947, was again a principal figure in this campaign of defiance of central authority. At one point, the Sikhs massed religious fighters to defend their Golden Temple at Amritsar. Master Tara Singh told the author that the community's demands had been pressed with particular vigour at that time because of the threat from Pakistan. The strategy, he said, was to strike 'while the government is in trouble' over Kashmir and needed the Sikhs; 'we control the army.' This separatist threat did not end until early September.

In New Delhi, these troubles were viewed, at the least, as encouragement to Pakistan to increase her pressure. Shastri told the Congress Party Parliamentary Executive, the influential group of the party's parliamentary leaders, on August 14, that Pakistan evidently thought India was weak and divided and that a push would oust the central government.[44] At the most, influential circles in the Indian capital regarded the most violent demonstrations as a deliberate attempt by Peking to aid Pakistan by ordering pro-Chinese Indian communists into the streets. It was generally taken for granted that communists were involved in all the major disturbances they could join, with the pro-Peking faction most active, despite the continued imprisonment of many of its principal leaders. The tactic of attempting to weaken the government under armed attack through internal turmoil was accepted as an integral part of the strategy of 'national liberation' warfare.

Yet the war had a profoundly unifying effect on India, as had the Chinese attack of 1962, particularly after the start of the Punjab offensive. The incidence of anti-government demonstrations appeared to decline, and manifestations of significant separatism disappeared. Ayub, says an Indian writer, 'failed to reckon . . . with the peculiar complex that independent India carries with her like a branded guilt. A thousand years' history, replete with foreign invasions and conquests, underscored the scorching moral: that India's undoing all along the line was her political disunity, which had repeatedly led to her defeat in battle, conquest and political humiliation.'[45] There was also the very strong feeling that national honour was being re-established. It was strong enough to reach South India, which never was in danger of major hostilities; strong enough to prompt Dr Radhakrishnan, the Indian President, to tell the country on September 11: 'We are proud of our soldiers, our airmen, our naval ratings, their achievements and their valour, but above all, we are proud of their nobility, which is a great part of the gift of India.' The emotions which the conflict aroused, however, were fleeting and potentially volatile. They demanded success, would not tolerate admitted failure and repudiated concession. The popular mood, as well as the latent power of separatists, forced New Delhi into a position of rigidity. This posture suited the leaders themselves, but it was another factor making retreat over Kashmir impossible. This attitude was reflected in the fact that New Delhi did not reveal its great tank victory in the battle of Assal Uttar until some time later, probably to avoid admitting that Pakistan still held a section of Indian territory.[46]

Within West Pakistan, similar deep and powerful emotions swept the people and their government. If the Indians believed they were defending themselves, so did the Pakistanis, with somewhat more visible reason. Yet the conflict was not unifying but divisive, on a national level. East Pakistan drew apart, partly because the conflict had exposed its vulnerability to Indian counter-action, partly through conviction that Kashmir did not justify this danger. Accordingly, Rawalpindi was under double pressure to fight for a victory. It shared New Delhi's need for a face-saving solution that would convince the West Pakistanis that they had won, while simultaneously it needed, if possible, a victory of such visible consequence that East Pakistan would consider it worth the effort.

This was the broad background for the diplomacy of the war.

14

WAR DIPLOMACY

MILITARY HOSTILITIES between the armies of 600 million people in the sensitive subcontinent instantly became a world problem, and, with rare unanimity, the world sought to impose a quick peace. Contrary to Indian belief, the United Nations and leading foreign capitals were deeply concerned over the outbreak of guerrilla warfare and made immediate attempts to end it. World opinion was aroused by the Pakistan attack of September 1 and supported strong public demands for peace. Pressures for a truce grew stronger after the Indian offensive in the Punjab, and peace efforts from several major sources were constant from that time.

Only three nations opposed this trend with any vigour—the two belligerents and Communist China. For all practical purposes, India and Pakistan fought in isolation. President Ayub paid tribute to Peking's 'moral support' and the diplomatic backing of Indonesia and five Middle Eastern nations. Turkey pledged a symbolic amount of arms, and Iran promised petroleum. Ayub failed in an effort to create an Islamic bloc capable of supplying the military material he needed to continue fighting. He made a futile and foredoomed attempt to invoke the CENTO and SEATO pacts in Pakistan's defence. On the other hand, India had no active supporters and few sympathisers. One of the latter, Malaysia, became the target of bitter criticism in New Delhi for sponsoring the United Nations armistice resolution.

'It is worth . . . considering why such unusual efforts on a world scale have been made to end this conflict', U Thant wrote to Shastri and Ayub in mid-September. 'Clearly it is because there is almost universal recognition that war between India and Pakistan can lead only to disaster for the two countries themselves and for the world at large.'[1] There were other, lesser reasons. The issues were uncertain, and the principles as the belligerents saw them were obscure. There was little acceptance of the Indian contention that the conflict was between democracy and dictatorship. There was less acceptance, among the knowledgeable, of Pakistan's assertion that she was fighting for her life against 'aggressive' India. The tendency, rather, was to regard the war as a great danger imposed on the world by two nations which were both wrong. The *New York Times* phrased one prevalent American attitude in an editorial on September 6:

> India refused to permit a plebiscite [in Kashmir] and in the last year she made clear that her portion of Kashmir was to be considered an integral part of India. President Ayub Khan evidently decided that it was a case of accepting defeat or of fighting. That these were his only choices is doubtful and, in any circumstances, to wage war over Kashmir was to risk far more for his own country and for peace in South Asia than Kashmir was worth. Two wrongs never added up to a right. . . . The plain fact is that the only power taking comfort in the Kashmir conflict is Communist China.

In essence, the world as a whole applied to the subcontinent the same pressure for peace, regardless of the issues, which India frequently and Pakistan on occasion had urged in other conflicts remote from their interests. Shastri noted this point himself by telling parliament that India had taken the same position on past wars. There is, he said, nothing wrong 'if we do not get direct support from different countries'.[2] But both principals bitterly resented this policy when it was turned against them. Obsessed by the struggle and convinced that their security was at stake, each sharply condemned peace overtures and, in fact, defied the world to stop the fighting. '. . . For one reason or another, including our own sins of commission and omission,' said the Indian *Express*, 'we do not seem to have many friends abroad. Yet, as the last war [1962] proved, a country is sometimes strongest when it stands alone.' It quickly became apparent that world opinion by itself was insufficiently powerful to deter the peoples of the two nations from continuing the struggle.

The record of the persistent diplomatic quest for a truce further demonstrated that it was not produced and could not have been produced by negotiations. India generally was more amenable than Pakistan to an early cease-fire, but New Delhi insisted upon restoring the *status quo ante* with no change. India did not waver from the consistent position that Kashmir was non-negotiable and that the only possible give-and-take in an armistice settlement was withdrawal from territory won during the recent fighting. This stand was maintained successfully, and the truce became possible when Pakistan eventually accepted it, although with a public face-saving promise that the United Nations would seek a future 'political' settlement.

Thus the fighting was halted without significant influence from the two pressures—world opinion and 'negotiations'—upon which India and other non-aligned nations had relied heavily to suppress other conflicts. The armistice was imposed through the backstage pressure of the big powers, working through the United Nations. In this instance, Russia and the United States co-operated, both at the UN and in less conspicuous diplomacy. Their interests in restoring peace to the subcontinent at that moment coincided. In essence, the absence of Soviet opposition permitted the United Nations Security Council to function.

The Soviets, however, played only a negative role throughout the decisive period when the warring armies were parted. The main pressures were applied by Great Britain and the United States. Both nations promptly suspended economic assistance to the two belligerents. Washington halted military aid to both sides on September 7; London, the next day. The military embargo, made so effective that two freighters bound for Karachi were turned back to the United States, primarily affected Pakistan, which was almost completely dependent upon American arms. 'The aid that we had given to India', the US Secretary of Defence, Robert S. McNamara, told Congress, 'was very, very small in relation to its total military budget or to the total force and the value of military equipment they had available at the start of the conflict with Pakistan. . . .'[3] The embargo meant, however, that India would lose replacement parts for her British arms, particularly the Centurion tanks. The suspension of economic assistance would also force India to use a proportionately larger share of available assets for arms. These measures served primarily to restrict the weapons the two belligerents could expect to use in a matter of weeks or longer, since they cut off future deliveries, not available equipment. Consequently, the most decisive influence undoubtedly was the fact that American authorities had only permitted Pakistan to stockpile enough supplies of such essentials as ammunition and spare parts to hold off the first thrust of a possible communist attack; not to wage prolonged war with India.

This point has been confirmed indirectly by extremely knowledgeable Indian sources. They say that Pakistan hoarded as a reserve for war ammunition and other supplies provided by the United States for normal training. This permitted the Pakistanis to fight as long as they did but it also meant that their troops were inadequately trained.

From all the evidence, the armistice became possible and the major threat of more dangerous war was averted when these factors began to restrict military operations, particularly those of Pakistan. That moment evidently coincided with a number of other significant influences. Pakistan had lost her chance for a quick or decisive victory, and the war had reached a relative battlefront stalemate. Thereafter, India's greater size and larger industrial capacity would assume increasing significance. Pakistan's striking power had been crippled, but not destroyed.[4] To continue the struggle under these circumstances and with the principal fighting concentrated in Pakistan would bring the risk of further heavy losses without immediate hope of gain. At a disadvantage and deprived of future arms from her one important source, Pakistan, with much bluster and defiance, finally had to accept India's condition for a truce which settled none of the issues which had precipitated war. For her part, India in a sense had won an initial victory by successfully preventing Pakistan from encircling Kashmir or sending armour deeply into India. But the war of attrition had reached the point where New Delhi also had to consider its future losses against immediate gain. 'I do think', said McNamara, 'that the cessation of our aid, and the pressure we thereby put on India and Pakistan, had much to do with terminating the conflict.'

Under these circumstances, the practical function of diplomacy was to provide the atmosphere in which the two fiery adversaries could end the fight. The United Nations gradually assumed this role, and its intervention permitted the operation of the more influential backstage pressures. The Secretary-General, U Thant, had taken the first initiative to produce peace as a humanitarian gesture, and he worked assiduously for this purpose; but the UN had neither moral nor political force to apply against the combatants. In the outpouring of the subcontinent's emotion, the international organisation was helpless by itself to do more than provide counsel and admonition. Without the Anglo-American pressure, it is doubtful whether the war could have been stopped at or near the point when the armistice was declared, even if some of the belligerent leaders had desired it. But without the UN as a medium through which to work, it is also doubtful whether the influence of the big powers could have been exercised so swiftly or with such relatively moderate domestic repercussions in the neighbouring countries. The two agencies complemented each other, with the UN providing a face-saving escape from a conflict which the leaders of both countries had decided to end.

U Thant initiated efforts to halt the fighting before the Pakistani and the Indian people themselves realised they were in conflict. In his September 3 report to the Security Council, the Secretary-General recounted that General Nimmo had advised him on the morning of August 9, 'the situation was deteriorating along the CFL'. On the basis of that information, U Thant a few hours later summoned the Pakistani representative and asked him to inform his government of 'my very serious concern about the situation that was developing in Kashmir, involving the crossing of the CFL from the Pakistan side by numbers of armed men and their attacks on Indian military positions on the Indian side of the Line, and also my strong appeal that the CFL be observed.' In the afternoon, U Thant told the Indian representative of this démarche and 'asked him to convey to his Government my urgent appeal for restraint as regards any retaliatory action from their side'. At this time, the Indians had learned from their press only fragmentary details of the guerrilla attacks. The first comprehensive story was published on August 10. Three days later, Shastri in a nation-wide broadcast first indicated the severity of the 'thinly disguised armed attack on our country organised by Pakistan . . .' The Pakistanis were told throughout August that the 'revolt' in Kashmir was succeeding. It was not until September 1 that Ayub warned of the 'threat of war in Kashmir which is being forced on us by India'.

The UN Secretary-General repeated his oral representations during subsequent days. On the basis of the reaction, he reported that he was unable to obtain assurance from Pakistan that the cease-fire or the CFL would be respected, but received the oral assurance of the Indian representative that Delhi would retaliate with restraint and would respect the CFL, if Pakistan did so. U Thant considered, and discarded, the idea of publishing a summary of the CFL infractions. He indicated in his report to the Security Council his belief that such a summary would clearly place the blame on Pakistan. The Secretary-General also abandoned a plan to send Dr Ralph J. Bunche, Nobel prize winner and Under-Secretary for Special Political Affairs, to the subcontinent as a special mediator. The idea was discarded when both governments were consulted on August 20 and attached conditions which U Thant believed would make the mission unfeasible. By this time, Indian officials had seen a copy of General Nimmo's first reports and were privately urging publication on the grounds that they would arouse unfavourable world opinion against Pakistan and would restrain her from further action. The reports also blamed India for violating the CFL, particularly in the reconquest of the Kargil outposts.

The Secretary-General publicly called for peace in a communication to the leaders of the warring nations on September 1. The appeal, which was also circulated to the Security Council, was prompted, U Thant said, by 'alarming reports indicating a steady escalation of the fighting in the air and on the ground, involving regular army forces on both sides'. Pakistan had launched the attack with a whole battalion on August 14 in the Chhamb area, India had captured Kargil, the Tithwal area and the Uri-Poonch bulge; then Pakistan had opened the September 1 tank attack at Chhamb, and India had initiated the air war. This sequence of events had attracted increasing world interest and concern, and the Secretary-General's appeal stimulated pressures for peace which had already been growing. One of the first responses disappointed both India and Pakistan. The two leaders on whom each had depended to swing the Afro-Asian world to its side of the controversy, Presidents Nasser of the UAR and Tito of Yugoslavia, met in Belgrade and promptly adopted a neutral position. They called on September 3 for a cease-fire and offered their good offices, a proposal soon repeated by other capitals. Efforts by the British

Commonwealth to separate its two warring members had failed already. The issue was then passed to the United Nations.

The six elected members of the Security Council co-sponsored a resolution on September 4, requesting a cessation of hostilities and re-establishment of the 1949 CFL. The Council, in adopting it unanimously, requested the Secretary-General to report back within three days on the implementation. Two days later, after the Indian attack in the Punjab, a second stronger resolution was again passed unanimously. It specifically called for a withdrawal of 'all armed personnel back to the positions held by them before 5 August 1965'. The resolution also gave the Secretary-General broad authority to 'exert every possible effort' to make the two UN resolutions effective. The atmosphere of crisis during these tense sessions in New York was emphasised by the fact that Russia and the United States voted together, for the first time since the UN was formed, on a question involving war and peace in a major area of the world. The atmosphere was further enhanced by the delegates' words of concern and by the fact that the Secretary-General broke precedent to deliver his report in person to the Security Council. 'There can be little doubt', said U Thant, 'that the Kashmir problem has again become acute and is now dangerously serious. Implicit in it, in my view, is a potential threat to peace not only between India and Pakistan, but to the broader peace.'

The belligerents, however, demonstrated fully at this time that they were in no mood for peace, regardless of the consequences. They also demonstrated that their attitude towards the revitalised Kashmir question was completely unchanged from the long un-yielding past. During the initial UN debate, when the conflict was temporarily going against them, the Indians sought to shore up the position of Indian Kashmir. Gopalswami Parthasarathi, the permanent Indian delegate, made it clear that India was inflexible on the political status of Kashmir. He said the issue had remained alive 'because the Council has refused to face the fact of aggression by Pakistan', and unsuccessfully attempted to have Pakistan identified as the aggressor in the fighting then under way. Shastri laid down two primary conditions for a truce in a message, replying to the September 1 peace appeal, which was received by U Thant less than three hours before the opening of the Council meeting. The Indian leader outlined these 'essential' pre-conditions for a truce:

(1) acceptable guarantees from Pakistan that all infiltrators and military personnel would be withdrawn from Indian Kashmir and (2) acceptable guarantees that no further attack will be made. 'We cannot be expected to wait for Pakistan to violate the cease-fire line and attack us at will', Shastri wrote. 'And we cannot go from one cease-fire to another without our being satisfied that Pakistan will not repeat its acts of violation and aggression in the future.'[5]

Pakistan officially ignored the first Council resolution and neglected to provide sufficient instructions to her permanent UN representative for a formal policy statement. The representative, Ambassador Amjad Ali, spoke only long enough to deny as 'deliberate fiction' every point of Parthasarathi's detailed indictment of Pakistan for planning, controlling and instigating the guerrilla war. President Ayub clearly outlined his government's position, however, in a telegram of September 5 and a letter of September 8 to U Thant. He repeated his government's official contention that 'the people of Kashmir, finding all avenues of peaceful realization of the right of self-determination barred to them, have taken to arms against Indian tyranny. Who can blame them? The freedom fighters who have challenged the might of the Indian Army are not raiders but sons of the soil of Jammu and Kashmir, ready to make the supreme sacrifice for their cause.' On September 1, the 'Azad Kashmir forces backed by the Pakistan Army were forced, in the exercise of the inherent right of self-defence, to cross the Cease-Fire Line in the Bhimbar sector for the first time since the Cease-Fire Agreement was reached seventeen years ago, and after repeated Indian armed attacks and occupation of Azad Kashmir territories by the Indian Army.' This situation was influenced, Ayub suggested, by the fact that: 'The Security Council, faced with India's bad faith, intransigence and growing power, chose practically to wash its hands of the responsibility for a peaceful and honourable settlement.' The latest two Council resolutions were unsatisfactory because they lacked 'any assurances that you [U Thant] and the Security Council will strive to implement' the UN resolutions of 1948 and 1949 calling for a plebiscite in Kashmir.[6]

The internal emotionalism of the warring countries made public intransigence by government leaders obligatory at that moment. Even so, there was little room for bargaining between the positions initially adopted by the two governments, because, in essence, they represented the minimum goals for which their people believed they were fighting. For Pakistan, the war had been so well symbolised as a campaign for the 'liberation' of Kashmir that it was notable Ayub did not emphasise the need for any guarantees against Indian 'aggression' on Pakistan proper. The Indians were convinced that they were defending themselves against direct, if originally camouflaged, attack from Pakistan, and they considered the demand for guarantees against a repetition to be reasonable. 'What is at stake in the present conflict', Shastri told his people on September 3, 'is a point of principle. Has any country the right to send its armed personnel to another with the vowed object of overthrowing a democratically-elected Government?' The answer is obvious. But Pakistan had placed its national reputation at stake in denying any role in the Kashmiri 'revolt'. It could not now admit responsibility nor offer guarantees against a future 'revolt', in order to obtain a cease-fire. New Delhi knew this and, in advancing the demand, seemed to expect its abrupt rejection. This factor tended to confirm the general impression within India that the Indian leaders were as anxious as those of Pakistan to continue fighting until a more clear-cut decision had been reached.

In world opinion, however, the nature of the war had been changed drastically by India's invasion of West Pakistan on September 6. Until that point, the struggle had involved a single, remote state. Warfare had been localised, camouflaged and relatively small-scale. It could be ignored, except by the specialists. But the Indian attack had enlarged the scope of battle and had turned the conflict from localised action into a nation-to-nation struggle which could not be ignored. Although the operation was defensible militarily and was regarded by the Indians as the logical response to aggression, it was generally viewed abroad as a totally new war. A number of concepts which had become part of the carefully inculcated diplomatic environment were swiftly invoked. They included the sanctity of international borders and the favourite Afro-Asian theme that a large nation is always wrong when it fights a smaller country. The Indians soon discovered also that, in the headline atmosphere of world reaction, the larger or latest 'wrong' tends to obscure or eliminate the smaller or original wrong. These factors were responsible for much of the criticism directed against

2A

New Delhi: criticism the Indians believed to be predominantly or completely one-sided. They made it virtually impossible for any statesmen openly to support India, particularly after September 6. For the remainder of the conflict, the Indians believed they were fighting alone, and they reacted with bitterness and asperity. Yet the reality of the situation was that, while public diplomacy was adverse to India, she was being aided by private diplomacy; for the arms embargo, which primarily affected Pakistan, was then established.

Peking shouldered its way into this situation. On September 8, when the Pakistani armoured counter-offensive was beginning in the Punjab, the Chinese communists made the first of a series of border threats against India. The Chinese sent a formal note to India accusing her of violating the Sikkim border on several occasions during July and August, demanding a halt to further 'provocations' and warning that 'India must bear the responsibility for all consequences arising therefrom'. The Chinese had established the foundation for this intervention by charging the previous day that India's 'naked aggression' into the Punjab 'constituted a grave threat to peace in this part of Asia'. The statement contended that India had continued to intrude on Chinese territory since 1962 and that 'Indian aggression against any one of its neighbors concerns all of its neighbors'.[7] These were strong statements which were taken seriously, in the atmosphere of the moment. Pakistani diplomats previously had spread the word that they expected direct Chinese assistance in the form of diversionary action.[8] The threat to Sikkim particularly concerned New Delhi. A full Indian division was said to be maintained in this Indian protectorate, where the Chumbi Valley provided one of the most vulnerable gateways to eastern India from the north.

From the beginning of the conflict, Indian authorities had sought strong and preferably public Soviet support, particularly as an antidote to Peking. As in 1962, they failed to receive unequivocal backing at a time when New Delhi felt this was most necessary. Moscow, instead, quickly adopted a policy of neutrality towards the Indo-Pakistan struggle. An Indian government spokesman later told the press that Soviet officials had advised the government they would remain neutral. Nevertheless, this position served to benefit Pakistan, in the context of Russia's presumed strong support for

India on Kashmir, and was adopted, as the Indians themselves realised, to facilitate future good relations with Rawalpindi. The deep disappointment over this posture, felt in some Indian government circles, was not allowed to appear publicly. The Indian press generally gave the impression that Soviet support for India on the Kashmir issue was strong and unchanged.

The Soviet Communist Party newspaper, *Pravda*, called for a quick settlement of the conflict in the first Russian response on August 24. At the same time Premier Kosygin, in an unpublished letter to Shastri, was reported to have advised India to avoid any actions that would lead to major conflict with Pakistan. 'Observers [in New Delhi] consider the Soviet reluctance to blame Pakistan publicly for the present situation in Kashmir', said an Indian news agency on August 25, 'as stemming out of her desire to continue her efforts to improve her relations with Pakistan and to wean her away from Chinese influence.'[9] The same effort was continued at the initial UN Security Council meeting on the war. The Soviet delegate, Platon Morozov, said that Russia was maintaining 'traditional friendship' with India and added: 'The strengthening of bonds between the Soviet Union and Pakistan is part of the general policy of the Soviet State towards the securing of peace in Asia and throughout the world.'[10]

After the Indian attack in the Punjab, the Soviet news agency, Tass, reflecting official policy, urged the two nations to halt the conflict and offered the good offices of Russia. The agency on September 7 called on the leaders of the subcontinent to 'display realism, restraint and understanding of the grave consequence of the development of an armed conflict'. Whereas Morozov had blamed the outbreak of fighting in Kashmir on 'imperialists', the official Soviet attitude now was that unidentified 'outside forces' were responsible for the expanded hostilities. The Soviets again carefully avoided taking sides and within Russia news of the conflict was reserved and confined to official statements. The hostilities were causing serious concern in Russia, Tass added, especially because the battle area was adjacent to Soviet frontiers. 'The armed Kashmir conflict cannot benefit either side. Present developments in that region play only into the hands of those outside forces that seek to disunite and to set at loggerheads those states that have cast off their colonial yoke.'[11]

The Soviets had made two additional appeals for a cease-fire by September 11, the second of these during an unusual press conference which, the *New York Times* remarked, 'indicated that the purpose was to publicize their efforts as an antidote to Communist China'. At that time, Moscow released the text of letters sent the previous week by Kosygin to Shastri and Ayub. They contained the same phrases concerning the involvement of 'outside forces' which had been used in relation to Kashmir by Tass and which had been employed earlier to condemn Peking involvement in affairs on the subcontinent. Continued Indo-Pakistan hostilities, the letters said, 'can only be welcomed by those outside forces which are trying to divide and oppose to one another states freed from the colonial yoke and which are interested in weakening the unity of the Afro-Asian Countries.'[12] The significance attached to this particular phraseology emphasised that one of Moscow's primary concerns was to block further Chinese inroads into Pakistan under the guise of war. Ideologically, the Soviets were seeking to defend their strategy of maintaining the Afro-Asian nations as friendly neutrals, against Peking's charges that the 'bourgeois' leaders of these nations could not be trusted and should be opposed. The official Chinese news agency, Hsinhua, had asserted the previous night that 'it is universal knowledge that the Soviet leaders have always supported the Indian expansionist stand in Kashmir'. It referred to Khrushchev's 1955 statement that Kashmir was 'an integral part' of India.

Moscow, in fact, had moved far from Khrushchev's position on Kashmir. Now, with war providing the climactic test of Soviet support, Moscow's studied neutrality amounted to severe reversal for the Indians. It was made worse, for those aware of the situation, by the fact that the Soviets were using the war to approach Pakistan, the enemy. Yet the shift was accepted without public complaint by knowledgeable Indians who at the same time were prompted by their trials bitterly to criticise the United States and to attack Great Britain so strongly that demands for withdrawal from the Commonwealth were made in parliament. This silence was only partially due to the tendency of articulate left-wingers to ignore the possibility that Russia would threaten India and to conclude, therefore, that none of her policies is dangerous.

Moscow had followed a careful strategic line to make sure that the

Indian government did not react adversely to the Soviet overtures towards Pakistan. While calling publicly for peace and avoiding use of the veto at the United Nations, Moscow had refused to join the embargo which actually brought peace to the subcontinent. No effort was made to interrupt the flow of Soviet economic assistance or to restrict arms aid to India. Work proceeded on the MIG factory, the military pipeline continued in operation, and the machinery was in place to expand arms assistance. Moreover, an Indian military mission was in Moscow during the early part of the conflict, negotiating for a Soviet submarine, destroyers and coastal naval craft and, possibly, other weapons. The Soviets did not permit news of the progress of these negotiations to be published during the fighting, and thereby deprived India of an anti-Pakistan psychological weapon. From this mission, however, came the promise of four submarines and hints of greater Soviet military assistance, including armour, in the future.[13]

As a consequence, Russia expanded her military position in India, even though Soviet weapons do not appear to have been involved in the fighting. Faced by the Anglo-American embargo and the threat of Red China, New Delhi was more dependent than ever upon Moscow. If Peking struck, top Indian officials expected Moscow to provide arms and support to defend India's independence. If the war with Pakistan dragged on, it was possible the Indians might have to seek more Soviet weapons. In any case, the Indo-Soviet rapprochement gave New Delhi a potential arms source, in defiance of the Western embargo, which was of far more consequence than any supplies Pakistan could expect from Peking or from Islamic nations. From past experience, however, Indian authorities knew this position could be maintained only through the utmost discretion and the complete elimination of all Soviet criticism.

Meanwhile U Thant, in pursuing the Security Council resolution of September 6, had undertaken a personal peace mission to the subcontinent. He arrived in Rawalpindi on September 9 and reached New Delhi three days later. During his visits he conducted intense and sustained peace negotiations through personal conversations and correspondence. The public mood in both countries was strongly opposed to concession and emotionally aroused for further war. It was also evident that the leaders of both sides were split on the advisability of continuing the struggle or of accepting UN peacemaking efforts. In this situation, U Thant directed his efforts toward obtaining an immediate and unconditional cease-fire, leaving further questions for future action.

On the day of his arrival in Pakistan, the government admitted for the first time that its forces had crossed into Indian territory. This announcement was coupled with claims of heavy successes in the counter-offensive on the Lahore front. Two days later, the Pakistan government announced these conditions for a cease-fire: (1) the complete withdrawal of all Indian and Pakistani forces from Kashmir; (2) establishment of a United Nations force, drawn from the Afro-Asian nations, to maintain security in the state, pending a plebiscite; (3) a plebiscite to be held within three months. A Foreign Office spokesman said Chinese forces in Kashmir would not be expected to withdraw, but Indian troops facing the Chinese in Ladakh would have to pull out. Pakistan, he added, found the Chinese claims to Ladakh just and therefore there was no need for a change in Chinese dispositions. These terms were obviously excessive and it was no surprise when Shastri told Parliament on September 16 that 'Not one of these conditions is acceptable to India'. The Prime Minister had specifically given his answer to the general question of a Kashmiri plebiscite by telling the nation on September 3 that Pakistan 'talks glibly of a plebiscite in Kashmir, while it is not prepared to have a free election in its own country. . . . How would Pakistan like a plebiscite in the Pakhtoon area to find out whether it wishes to remain a part of Pakistan? How would Pakistan like a plebiscite in East Bengal to find out whether the people of East Bengal want to be ruled from Rawalpindi?'

Pakistan could win nothing from the war, however, unless she could attach the strongest possible political qualifications to a cease-fire. The Foreign Minister, Bhutto, is said to have told U Thant that Pakistan was extremely disappointed by the fact that all the UN efforts to restore peace had started from the premise that the 1949 CFL should be re-established. If the line could not be changed to Pakistan's advantage, its minimum terms, it would appear, required a clear guarantee of future political readjustments in the status of Kashmir as the price of a truce. On the other hand, India's advantage lay in the fact that its minimum requirement was an unconditional, non-political cease-fire which restored the *status quo ante*. U Thant, seeking such an immediate solution, found the

Indians more amenable than the Pakistanis, who temporarily clung to their demands.

Nevertheless, Indian military circles strongly opposed acceptance of a premature cease-fire, because they wanted to cripple Pakistani armour sufficiently to reduce the possibility of another major attack in the immediate future. The usually well-informed American correspondent, Selig S. Harrison, reported that the Indian cabinet was divided over the timing of a truce during U Thant's visit. General Chaudhuri reputedly urged the cabinet, on September 13, to avoid a cessation of hostilities at that point. The army, he said, was on the verge of a decisive victory in the Punjab and should be allowed to inflict the maximum damage on Pakistani power. He was supported strongly by the Defence Minister, Chavan. In this account, Shastri held out for acceptance of the UN resolution of September 6. The Prime Minister, who had proved to be a political leader of considerable force, was supported by the Finance Minister, T. T. Krishnamachari and the Food Minister, C. Subramaniam. Both were deeply concerned over the effect of hostilities on India's economy. During cabinet debates, the argument was advanced that Pakistan would probably reject a cease-fire at that time and India, by accepting one, would have the chance to stigmatise her adversary in world opinion for continuing the war. On this basis, the army accepted Shastri's position.[15] This version of the prevailing cross-winds appeared to be confirmed by developments.

U Thant, in New Delhi, sounded out Indian leaders on the basis of his talks with those in Pakistan, then quickly initiated correspondence with Shastri and Ayub seeking a prompt cease-fire. He wrote to both leaders on September 12, urging a suspension of fighting at 6.30 p.m. (New Delhi time) on September 14. He requested a reply by 7.30 a.m., September 14, at the latest. At 5 p.m. the previous day, however, India requested an extension of time, lending credence to the reported intensity of the cabinet discussions. This was accepted, and the Secretary-General notified both capitals that the proposed cease-fire was postponed to 6.30 p.m., September 15. After the Indian cabinet meeting, in which, Shastri later told parliament, 'we went into the pros and cons of the cease-fire in some detail', the Indian Prime Minister expressed willingness for a truce. 'In deference to the wishes of the Security Council and to the appeals which we have received from many friendly countries, we accept your proposal for an immediate cease-fire', he told U Thant in a letter of September 14. 'We would, therefore, be prepared to order a cease-fire effective from 6.30 a.m., Indian standard time, on Thursday 16 September 1965, provided you confirm to me by 9 a.m. tomorrow that Pakistan is also agreeable to do so.'

Shastri then pointed out, however, that such a truce would apply only to uniformed soldiers; he went on:

The problem of thousands of armed infiltrators who have crossed over into our State of Jammu and Kashmir, from the Pakistan side, will, I am afraid, continue to remain on our hands. Armed as they are with dangerous weapons of destruction such as machine-guns and hand-grenades, they do even now, as I write this letter, make sudden depredations in an effort to damage vital installations and other property and harass the people of the State of Jammu and Kashmir. . . . Let me make it perfectly clear, Mr Secretary-General, that when, consequent upon the cease-fire becoming effective, further details are considered, we shall not agree to any disposition which will leave the door open for further infiltrators or prevent us from dealing with the victims of aggression, or the chances of peace will fade out.

Apparently, U Thant considered the Indian Prime Minister's comments as qualifications to his request for 'a cease-fire without condition'. He told the two leaders in a letter of September 14 that, despite their 'positive attitude' towards his suggestion, 'both governments have added to their replies . . . conditions and qualifications upon which I have no right under the Security Council resolution to give undertakings. . . .' Shastri replied the next day that he understood the Secretary-General 'cannot give any undertakings . . . and in fact I did not ask you for any . . . I reaffirm my willingness, as communicated yesterday, to order a simple cease-fire and cessation of hostilities as proposed by you, as soon as you are able to confirm to me that the Government of Pakistan has agreed to do so as well.'

If the Indian leaders expected Pakistan to reject a cease-fire at that time and permit New Delhi to continue fighting without losing face, they were not disappointed. Ayub replied on September 13 to U Thant's original letter that Pakistan agreed to a cease-fire in principle but that 'if the conflict is to be resolved and this subcontinent spared the horror of an even wider war, the Cease-Fire must be accompanied by action which would resolve the real cause of this conflict.' He then reiterated Pakistan's three-point demand to demilitarise Kashmir and hold a plebiscite.[16]

The Secretary-General had accepted Shastri's proposal for an armistice at 6.30 a.m., September 16, and had forwarded it to Pakistan. He delayed his departure from New Delhi, awaiting a reply. Shastri informed Parliament that U Thant had told him 'that if by the evening of September 15, 1965, Pakistan did not give a reply agreeing to a cease-fire, we should take it that an agreement on this question has not been possible. Since no such acceptance was received by the stipulated time, an announcement was made that our defence forces would have to continue the operations with unabated vigour.' Ayub's answer to U Thant reached New York in the late morning of September 16, several hours after expiration of the proposed truce deadline. In it, the Pakistani President said a cease-fire could be 'meaningful' only if followed by steps 'to evolve an effective machinery and procedure that would lead to a final settlement of the Kashmir dispute'.

During these diplomatic exchanges, the climactic tank battle raged around the village of Phillora on the Sialkot front. The Indians had captured the village on September 12, the day of U Thant's arrival. They regrouped during the first round of diplomacy and attacked again on the morning of September 14. During the three-day battle which followed, Indian sources claimed to have destroyed as many as 240 Pakistani tanks. On their part, the Pakistanis fought bitterly for control of the railway line leading northward to Sialkot, and when it was cut on September 15 followed with heavy counter-attacks to regain the lost position. During the last phase of this battle, Indian officers reported that Pakistani armour made such massive frontal attacks, in an attempted breakthrough, that they became vulnerable to counter-fire by grouping themselves too closely together. The intensity of the fighting gave evidence of the Indian intention, on this front, of inflicting maximum punishment before hostilities ended. Pakistani military sources confirm the intensity of the fighting and say maximum power was necessary to defend their country.

Ayub had confused the diplomatic situation by calling for direct American peace efforts during a press conference on September 15.

The United States, he said, could and should 'play a very definite role by telling India and Pakistan she will not stand for this struggle' which he said was doing the two countries 'no good'. The Pakistani leader was explicit, however, that he was thinking of a peace which included a plebiscite on Kashmir. During the news conference, he softened his position on this point somewhat by saying that the proposed three months' deadline for such a vote was negotiable. Indian opposition to the consideration of a plebiscite had been re-emphasised repeatedly and was, of course, well known to Ayub. Shastri told parliament on September 16 that the Indian leaders, in their talks with U Thant, 'made it clear that we were fully determined to maintain the sovereignty and territorial integrity of India of which the State of Jammu and Kashmir was an integral part. From this resolve we could never be deflected, no matter what the pressure or the threat. These were not conditions attached to our acceptance of the cease-fire, but were meant to be a clear and unequivocal reiteration of our stand in regard to these matters.'

Consequently, Ayub's gesture was interpreted at the time as an effort to enlist American support for a settlement favourable to Pakistan. The air on the subcontinent had been agitated by a remark attributed to the US Secretary of State, Dean Rusk, that a Kashmir plebiscite should be part of an over-all settlement of the war. Bhutto, Pakistan's Foreign Minister, had praised the statement. But the supposed remark, which strongly aroused the Indians, had been reported incorrectly. 'Rusk did not actually say that, however,' the *Washington Post* reported on September 16. 'After he testified at a closed session of the Senate Foreign Relations Committee Monday (September 13) a reporter asked him, "What is the United States' view of Pakistan's demand for a UN-supervised plebiscite in Kashmir?" Rusk replied, "We have expressed our views on that subject over the years. That is part of a general problem of a political solution of outstanding issues between India and Pakistan. We believe that these matters should be taken up and resolved by peaceful means. We do not think they should be resolved by force."'

Although it was possible Ayub was encouraged by news reports of Rusk's misquoted statement, it appears in retrospect that the Pakistani President had another motive, if his remarks to the press were pre-planned. It is likely he was manoeuvring for a fresh, face-saving way of accepting a cease-fire. With the major offensive around Phillora and Chawnda under way and his arms reserves receding, Ayub may have decided that he would need peace shortly after the tank battle ended, regardless of how it turned out. Under the circumstances, it would be preferable to back down before public American pressure on both adversaries than to accept previously rejected UN terms. Military sources in Rawalpindi predicted at this time that both sides would soon exhaust their military resources at the rate of battle then in progress.[17] Notably, U Thant suggested on his return to New York on September 17 that the remaining problem was to find a way for Pakistan to quit gracefully. He decried news reports that his mission had failed and said both governments wanted to stop fighting. With Shastri's acceptance of unconditional cease-fire, the truce now depended upon Ayub. In these circumstances, Washington publicly threw its support behind UN peace efforts, but kept open avenues of approach to Pakistan. American authorities considered a settlement of the Indo-Pakistani conflict as a vital interest, but strengthening the United Nations was vital too.

Peking intervened again at this point. In a note delivered to the Indian chargé d'affaires at 1 a.m., September 17, Peking time, the Chinese accused India of maintaining fifty-six military installations on the Tibetan side of the Sikkim-Tibetan border. The Chinese demanded that 'the Indian government dismantle all its military works for aggression on the Chinese side of the China-Sikkim boundary or the boundary itself within three days...' otherwise, the 'Indian government must bear full responsibility for all the grave consequences arising therefrom'.[18] The Chinese note further accused India of more than 300 incursions into Chinese territory in this area, by ground or air, in recent years. It said thirteen separate representations to the Indian government had been ignored. Finally, the Chinese demanded the return of four Tibetans, 800 sheep and fifty-nine yaks allegedly abducted from Tibet.

In reply, India said she was satisfied that strict instructions against border transgressions had been fully observed by the Indian army. 'As regards China's stand on Kashmir and on the present unfortunate conflict between India and Pakistan,' the Indian note continued, 'it is nothing but interference on the part of China calculated to prolong and to enlarge the conflict.' Shastri further told parliament that a number of Indian defence structures, built on the Sikkim side of the border in September 1962, had been abandoned the following November. He said India would accept joint inspection of the border facilities; a procedure which the Peking note claimed New Delhi had rejected four times previously, and which the Chinese themselves rejected on this occasion.

'I know', said Shastri, 'that the House would feel concerned about the intentions of the Chinese Government'. The Peking note coincided with reports of ominous Chinese troop concentrations in Sikkim and in the Ladakh area. 'We do hope that China would not take advantage of the present situation and attack India', the Prime Minister continued. 'The House may rest assured that we are fully vigilant and that if we are attacked, we shall fight for our freedom with grim determination. The might of China will not deter us from defending our territorial integrity.'[19]

In New Delhi and in Washington, the possibility of a large overt Chinese attack, on the 1962 pattern, was discounted, but diplomats and military officials were concerned over possible diversionary action. The Chinese, it was believed, were anxious to prolong the subcontinent's war and to obtain the maximum gains for themselves at minimum risk. Shastri is reported to have told Chester Bowles, the US Ambassador in New Delhi that, for these reasons, the Indians expected limited military hostilities on the Indo-Chinese borders. Indian military officials went further. In private conversations with American officials, they said a Chinese attack in division strength would necessitate prompt intervention by US combat aircraft.[20]

Washington's policy was to give Peking clear warning that it could not attack bleeding India without risking American retaliation, but simultaneously to conserve the common front with Russia on Asian peace as fully as possible. Soviet willingness to co-operate in United Nations efforts to end the Indo-Pakistan conflict had encouraged some hope that Moscow would participate more fully in efforts to reduce Asian tensions that served primarily to advance the interests of Chinese Communists. For that reason, unilateral US response to Peking's threat against India was deliberately subordinated, and Washington operated primarily through the United Nations. The strongest American warning to Peking was made secretly, before the Chinese publicly menaced Sikkim. Direct contacts between Washington and Peking have long been maintained through periodic ambassadorial meetings in Warsaw. On September 14, at one of these brief sessions, the American Ambassador, John M. Cabot, told the Chinese representative bluntly to stay out of the Indo-Pakistan conflict; otherwise, he implied that the United States and other UN nations would retaliate against China. This private word reinforced Secretary Rusk's public admonition the previous day that Peking was dangerously meddling in the conflict.[21] There is little doubt that the message was clear to Chinese officials.

The United Nations Security Council, meanwhile, had undertaken the long, tense and exacting backstage diplomacy necessary to formulate a new resolution for peace on the subcontinent. Delegates began their work upon U Thant's return to New York, holding public sessions and sometimes more important private negotiations. In the newly-inflamed circumstances, the Council sought a means of dissuading China while also attempting to devise a solution for the Indo-Pakistan conflict that would give Pakistan a face-saving escape and would be enforceable. Many points of dispute developed in private and in public as a consensus was sought on an acceptable new resolution. France and Russia objected to a marked increase in the UN supervisory power to oversee the proposed withdrawal of the contending forces. Jordan, rising to Pakistan's support, insisted upon inclusion of a mandatory plebiscite. Malaysia contended that the resolution should appeal to Pakistan to end the fighting, since the Indians had already agreed. In one of the most controversial proposals, U Thant suggested on September 16 that the Council could invoke Chapter VII of the UN charter permitting the Council to use military and economic force, if necessary, to insure an end of the fighting.[22] These powers have been used only once, to end the Arab-Israeli conflict in 1948, and the Council rejected U Thant's suggestion. In making it, the Secretary-General indicated belief that extraordinary pressure was necessary to wring compliance from Pakistan. There was no indication that he doubted Shastri's willingness to implement the previous Indian acceptance of a cease-fire.

The Security Council adopted a third resolution unanimously, with Jordan abstaining, on September 20. This time, the Council demanded a cease-fire on the morning of September 22 and a subsequent withdrawal of all armed personnel to the positions of August 5. After this was done, the Council promised to consider 'what steps could be taken to assist towards a settlement of the political problem underlying the present conflict'. In view of the UN record of failure on a political solution for Kashmir, this provision was generally regarded as a concession to the sensibilities of Pakistan and her supporters. The Council more specifically placed major emphasis again upon a bilateral solution of the subcontinent's problems by urging the two governments to use all peaceful means of settling them. U Thant, on September 15, had proposed a summit meeting between the two leaders, and pressures for such a conference were growing. On September 19, Russia invited Shastri and Ayub to confer on Soviet soil, and the Central Asian city of Tashkent was first mentioned as the rendezvous. The most unusual aspect of the UN resolution was an unprecedented warning to Peking. The Council, it said, 'calls on all States to refrain from any action which might aggravate the situation in the area'.

India accepted the cease-fire and the demand for withdrawal the next day, but made it clear that she did not accept proposals to reconsider a political settlement. On subsequent days, speaker after speaker emphasised in the Indian parliament that they supported only a cessation of fighting and warned against a precipitate withdrawal. Shastri reiterated that Kashmir is 'an integral part of India, a constituent unit of the Federal Union of India . . .' and '. . . there is hardly any case for the exercise of self-determination again', because the Kashmiris had joined India through three general elections. The Indian leader is reported to have had trouble in winning support for the general principle of withdrawal, facing strong opposition from some members of his own party as well as nationalist groups. For some time, he hinted that India would continue to hold such positions as the Haji Pir Pass which were generally considered essential to its security.[23]

In Pakistan, riots against the resolution erupted in Karachi, where a mob of thousands set fire to the US Information Service library; and in Lahore, where students stoned the US consulate. The official government response remained in doubt for hours. Bhutto hastily departed for New York and appeared in the early morning of September 22 before the haggard members of the Security Council, who had been in almost continual session. The Foreign Minister launched into an impassioned speech; then at the precise moment when the original UN deadline expired, 3 a.m.,

New York time, he drew out a telegram from Ayub reporting that a cease-fire had been ordered, in the 'interest of international peace', even though the Council's resolution was 'unsatisfactory'. Before then, Bhutto had detailed Pakistan's grievances, while the delegates fidgeted, and had threatened, 'We will wage a war for 1,000 years . . .' After announcing acceptance of the truce, Bhutto said Pakistan would withdraw from the international organisation if the Security Council failed in its 'last chance' to 'put its full force, full moral responsibility and full weight behind an equitable and honourable settlement of the Jammu and Kashmir dispute.'[24] At 3.30 a.m., September 23, South Asian time, the guns were silenced and hostile troops stared curiously at each other across their narrow battlefields.

Bhutto's last-minute dramatics underlined Pakistan's unwillingness to abandon the struggle without tangible gain. There were, obviously, strong pressures requiring her to do so, but they were not implicit in the latest UN resolution. Clearly, Pakistan was compelled by the military situation to accept India's insistence upon restoring the *status quo ante*, with only minimum face-saving provisions in the UN resolution for some future consideration of the problems for which the country had embarked on war. This was, perhaps, the strongest indication that, for all practical purposes, Pakistan had lost the conflict. Amid the jubilation over the restoration of peace, however, the question immediately arose whether Pakistan had lost the will to fight for Kashmir.

During this finale, Peking manoeuvred to extract the last ounce of profit from the situation. Although their original ultimatum sent a shiver throughout the world, the Chinese quickly weakened it and the threat died down within five days. On September 19, before expiration of the original three-day deadline, Peking in an un-Chinese gesture extended it by seventy-two hours, with a statement implying that India had provided a conciliatory reply. The Indians, however, were anything but conciliatory. An exchange of shots between outpost forces, both in Sikkim and Ladakh, prompted Shastri to tell Parliament, amid cheers: 'If China persists in aggression, we shall defend ourselves by all means at our disposal.' In response to the demand for the return of 'abducted' livestock, the Indians paraded a flock of 800 sheep before the Chinese Communist embassy in New Delhi. Some of the animals carried signs around their necks: 'Eat us but save the world'; 'Don't start a war: we are here'. On September 22, Peking announced that the Indians had complied with its demands for dismantling the disputed military structures. If any were destroyed, said a spokesman in New Delhi, the Chinese 'must have done it themselves'. The crisis promptly receded, amid a muttering of Chinese propaganda.

The exact motives behind the Chinese performance were obscure. Shastri told Parliament that 'what China is looking for is not redress of grievances, real or imaginary, but some excuse to start its aggressive activities again, this time acting in collusion with its ally, Pakistan.' Others have theorised that Peking was attempting to stiffen Pakistani resolve to continue the conflict with India. Shastri added that the extension of the time limit for 'dismantling' the Sikkim military posts 'was, in our view, no more than a device to gain time to watch what comes out of the discussions in the Security Council'. This unusual development has been interpreted as meaning that Peking was prepared for more vigorous action if Pakistan rejected the UN resolution, but did not want to carry out warfare on its own if the Pakistanis accepted a cease-fire.

It is equally possible, however, that China felt obliged to make some non-committal gesture at the last minute to compensate for the fact that, despite her apparent pledges of support for Pakistan, she had been conspicuously inactive during the military hostilities. Apart from propaganda, the Chinese had done nothing to aid Pakistan significantly except, perhaps, to pin down otherwise useful Indian forces along the Sino-Indian frontier. A bolder demonstration was required to maintain Peking's reputation for military invincibility. In this regard, Sikkim was a logical crisis point. It is one of the most sensitive areas along the border but also one of the best defended by Indian forces. Therefore, it was useful for political pressure but unsuitable for limited military assault, since more vulnerable terrain was also available. The threat over Sikkim created the headlines anticipated by Peking and raised the appropriate fears, at no cost to the Chinese. Having created the crisis, Peking then extended its ultimatum to make sure that Pakistan would not reject the UN resolution and place the Chinese under an obligation to provide further 'help'. Notably, the Chinese further minimised their involvement by waiting until the closing days of the conflict to intrude.

The cumulative evidence indicates that this is as far as Peking intended to go, unless more favourable circumstances arose. 'It is doubtful', says Professor William E. Griffith of Massachusetts Institute of Technology, 'that Peking ever intended to use serious military force against India, the more so because Pakistan was too fearful of US intervention against Peking (and therefore in support of New Delhi) to accept major Chinese assistance.'[25] This factor, however, would not prevent the Chinese from launching limited hostilities on their own, with or without the concurrence of Pakistan. The principal deterrent was the presence of American power and the possibility it would be involved in Sino-Indian hostilities. While implementing their expansionist plans with determination and persistence, the Chinese since the Korean War have consistently avoided a direct confrontation with the United States. They were told clearly at Warsaw on September 14 that the Americans would come into a Sino-Indian war, and three days later the careful drama over Sikkim was staged. The fact that the US warning was unmistakable and that, in this instance, Moscow approved was indicated by a Prague radio comment: 'It appears that a warning delivered to Peking by the US government stated that a large-scale action against India could result in extensive US retaliation . . . Damage that the US army and, above all, the US air force could inflict on China would be very considerable and severe.'[26] Peking was forced to consider that the Americans, in an expanded war, might strike China not only from India but from the warfronts of Vietnam, far closer to vulnerable targets. The risk for the belligerent but cautious Chinese was far greater than the probable gains. 'While Peking's threat had again brought home to India that it could not do without American military power in case of a Chinese attack,' Professor Griffith continues, 'the lack of Chinese military action indicated that Peking was probably effectively deterred by Washington from attack on India.'[27] Professor Griffith, a recognised authority on communist affairs, is Director of the International Communism Project at the MIT Center for International Studies. The fact that many other nations, including Russia, voted for the UN warning was significant but not decisive. Only Great Britain could be expected to join the United States in actively supporting a threatened India. While the Chinese consequently avoided the best possible opportunity to weaken India further, their restraint in this instance does not by any means end the threat that they will strike again at some more

2B

propitious time. Nor does it necessarily exclude the possibility that Peking might have considered the risk acceptable in 1965, if it had not already become deeply involved by the threat of expanding warfare in Vietnam.

The Chinese themselves revealed their respect for American power in this situation by the intensity of their propaganda. As the United Nations resolution of September 20 was being adopted, for example, Peking claimed without confirmation that it had shot down an American-piloted F-104 over Hainan Island, the first such contention since the Korean War. The incident was used for a new attack on 'United States imperialists' who, an official in Peking's defence ministry stated, were 'expanding their war of aggression against Vietnam, backing the Indian reactionaries' invasion of Pakistan and instigating Indian troops to carry out repeated provocations along the Sino-Indian border.'[28] A week later, the Foreign Minister Ch'en Yi, bristling with anger, said in a Peking news conference that the United States and her allies could attack the Chinese mainland but they could not send enough troops to conquer it. 'The Chinese people are ready to make the supreme sacrifice', he said, in a half-shout. 'We welcome them to come—to let the Indians come with them—to let the British imperialists come with them—to let the Japanese militarists come with them—and to let those [Soviet] revisionist leaders co-ordinate the attack.'[29] This emotional outburst was similar to previous occasions when the Chinese have let it be known that American power has thwarted their ambitions. Further, the fear of American 'invasion' has been invoked repeatedly as a method of driving the Chinese people into greater unity or extracting more sacrifices from them.

Ch'en Yi's outburst typically served two principal purposes. It was clearly a calculated part of a sustained anti-American, anti-Soviet and anti-Indian propaganda campaign, intensified by Chinese frustration over their inability to manipulate the subcontinent more completely. Thereafter, Peking maintained an intensive, if fruitless, effort to thwart further peaceful negotiations, particularly the Soviet-sponsored meeting at Tashkent. The Chinese leadership also was opening a new internal drive against 'anti-party' elements who were accused of opposing the vigorous 'revolutionary' posture of the leadership. This campaign lashed the mainland during 1966 and resulted in the removal of several key officials and numerous minor party functionaries. Peking obviously did not want to embark on a new foreign war while undergoing this domestic turmoil, but as usual it used the threat of foreign aggression as a slogan to whip the masses into greater obedience.

There was some belief in Washington at the time that, as well as its obvious self-serving purposes, the last-minute Chinese campaign resulted from appeals from Pakistan for diversionary pressure. In this version, the two nations closely co-ordinated their activities during the climactic stages of cease-fire diplomacy. Bhutto appeared to confirm this theory in part, by contending later that the Chinese pressure was responsible for including in the United Nations resolution of September 20 the clause pledging future consideration of a political solution for the Kashmir problem. This was, he told a news conference, 'China's resolution'. As reported by the London *Times* on October 6, he added: 'The Chinese ultimatum to India had shaken the United Nations and the great powers into realizing the danger of war on the sub-continent, and that only a political settlement could allow permanent peace.' The evidence is more convincing, however, that the clause was inserted because UN diplomats recognised that a cease-fire depended upon Pakistan's acceptance of the inflexible Indian position and that a face-saving provision was necessary to permit Rawalpindi to do so. President Ayub, announcing the cease-fire to his people, said: 'The moral support which the Chinese Government extended to us so willingly and so generously will for ever remain enshrined in our hearts. We are grateful for this.'[30] Nevertheless, the circumstances indicated that Peking, for questions of its own prestige, would have intervened to the extent that it did whether or not invited by Pakistan.

Ayub conspicuously attempted to maintain a flexible diplomatic position in such a way that it tended to support the belief that he was embarrassed by the fact that Pakistan had obtained its primary support from Peking, and seemed to be heavily dependent upon it. Ayub, for example, publicly pledged his willingness to co-operate with U Thant, as a 'great Asian'. Peking had sharply castigated the Secretary-General for allegedly favouring India in the Kashmir dispute. The Pakistani President further wrote to the Soviet Premier Kosygin before the UN cease-fire, saying that Russia, as the 'most powerful' member of the Security Council, could exercise considerable influence in framing a 'meaningful' UN resolution that could lead to an 'honourable' settlement in Kashmir. This initiative was also interpreted in Rawalpindi as evidence that Pakistan had detected a shift in Soviet policy away from firm support for India on Kashmir and hoped to exploit it.[31] The text of the letter was published on September 25, two days after Peking had accused Kosygin of fostering 'Indian expansionism'. The Chinese identified the Soviet Premier by name for the first time since the expulsion of Khrushchev the previous year.[32] Nevertheless, it was clear that Pakistan benefited by the Chinese manoeuvres and, no doubt, welcomed them. Peking, notably, became the strongest foreign propaganda supporter thereafter of the discredited Kashmiri Revolutionary Council and its reiterated pledges to continue the fight for 'freedom'.

These activities served to confuse the extent of Sino-Pakistan collaboration during the actual fighting phases of the war. No substantial evidence of close and co-operative operations and strategy was revealed. If the Pakistanis adopted some Chinese tactics in the guerrilla phase of the war, they also grossly violated Chinese strategy in improperly extending the struggle. Peking never would have opened the armoured offensive in the Chhamb salient on September 1, for example, because it was uncalled for by the previous failure of the guerrillas and, more particularly, because it gave India an opportunity to retaliate with conventional power. One of the intriguing questions left by the hostilities, therefore, was how the conflict would have developed if Pakistan had confined itself to the basic strategy of 'national liberation' warfare. The Chinese method would have been to withdraw after the failure of the 'revolt', to reorganise the guerrillas, to intensify political agitation and the intimidation of local officials and to strike again with irregular forces at a more propitious time. Conventional military power would have been used only when victory was certain or, at least, when the odds for victory became overwhelming.

During the succeeding months, when the cease-fire was applied, violated, then consolidated, one of the principal undertones of the situation was an apparent attempt to reapply the patient 'national liberation' strategy to the subcontinent. The effort was frequently obscured by more dramatic developments, but it was maintained with apparent continuity. Pakistan was openly accused by India of fostering these activities, with or without the help of Peking. The Pakistanis frequently appeared in the forefront. But this strategy, while sometimes beneficial in a minor way for Pakistani purposes, did not appear to suit the impulsive Pakistani desire for a quick solution of the problems with India. Rather, it bore suspicious Chinese overtones. Peking had established a position, through its last-minute involvement in the war, to press its influence further on the restless tribes surrounding India and was determined to do so, regardless of Pakistan. For the present, Sino-Pakistan co-operation was apparently strong and durable. But it was probable that the Chinese were using Pakistan for the early stages of a long-range, low-level pressure campaign against India from which the Pakistanis could withdraw, if they desired, only with difficulty. From all the evidence, the Chinese were, in fact, involved deeply in the effort to keep India off balance through continual internal disorders. In reality, then, the cease-fire applied to two inter-related wars, the Indo-Pakistan confrontation with massive power, and the Sino-Pakistan 'national liberation' weakening process.

The first of these conflicts, the Indo-Pakistan confrontation, produced continual tension and brisk, if limited, fighting during the first several weeks of the cease-fire. The situation quieted towards the end of 1965 and was controlled, in all outward respects, by the Indo-Pakistan agreement at Tashkent on January 10, and the subsequent withdrawal of opposing forces to their pre-war positions by the deadline of February 25, 1966. The second struggle, the 'national liberation' attack on India, clearly has not ended. It flamed into new Kashmiri tensions in October 1965, and fresh Indian charges that more Pakistani infiltrators were being trained. It was detectable in new outbursts of the rebellious Naga tribesmen and an unprecedented uprising of Mizo tribesmen, in India's unconsolidated south-east, during March 1966. This strategy was also reflected in an unusual level of violent demonstrations within India in the spring of 1966 and in 1967. It was quite evident by that time that India was involved in a long struggle against the efforts of its neighbours to weaken its solvency, in addition to more open military pressures.

15

MILITARY AFTERMATH

AFTER THE main fighting ended on September 23, both India and Pakistan quickly embarked upon a campaign, within the cease-fire, to expand their territorial holdings and to consolidate current military positions. Both nations, it appeared, were manoeuvring for advantage in anticipation of long political bargaining, the next inevitable step in their unfinished struggle. Within hours of the formal truce, India lodged the first complaint of an infraction by Pakistan. But in the ensuing weeks both sides were charged in official UN reports with a variety of military actions, some of them considerable, which violated the armistice and threatened to destroy it.

Again, an undermanned and handicapped international force of UN observers attempted to preserve the peace and to sort out hundreds of complaints. The truce line along the battle areas of the 1965 conflict extended for more than 1,000 miles, from the Arabian Sea to the foothills of the Himalayas. Another 120 miles of border separated Pakistan and Jammu, then the 470-mile CFL of 1949 began. To supervise the 1965 lines, U Thant created a United Nations India-Pakistan Observer Mission (UNIPOM) with an eventual strength of 150 observers under Major General B. F. MacDonald. The observer group for the Kashmir CFL, UNMOGIP, was strengthened to ninety-two members. Both forces were equipped with better transport for faster movement. The designation of two separate groups was solely for administrative purposes, U Thant explained, and did not mean acceptance of Pakistan's contention that the Punjab and Kashmir constituted two separate wars. India had strongly protested against this administrative arrangement, with the contention that the two battle areas were part of the same conflict. A third temporary UN mission later supervised arrangements for troop withdrawals. It was headed by Brigadier General Tulio Marambio of Chile.

In 1949, the procedures for maintaining the cease-fire in Kashmir were set out in some detail by the Karachi Agreement of July 29 which established the line. Through the years, precedent and mutually accepted interpretation of the agreement established six broad categories of violation. They include: crossing the line or firing across it, firing within five miles of the line, new wiring or mining of any positions, reinforcing existing positions or strengthening certain defences, reinforcement of troops or supplies from outside the state and flying aircraft over the other country's territory. The new observer group supervising the more explosive Rajasthan-Punjab front, however, had no agreed list of violations as a guide; it was governed merely by the Security Council injunction to supervise the cease-fire and the withdrawal of troops. As U Thant suggested in a special report, the ground rules had to be formulated and adopted amid all the other complications of the battle areas.[1] The Karachi Agreement, for example, specified that the opposing forces generally would remain at least 500 yards from the CFL. In the Punjab, however, the observers found rival forces dug in within thirty yards of each other, and they regarded it as a small triumph when in some instances they managed to persuade them to take up new positions 100 yards apart.

These circumstances helped to precipitate an outpouring of complaints to the UN Secretariat over truce violations. They ranged from the refusal of small outposts to move back to organised attack and counter-attack by both sides, with large numbers of men, artillery support and, in some instances, tanks. Dozens of infractions were confirmed, but many more were made and not confirmed. Each side, of course, was attempting to discredit the other. The early situation was so serious, however, that the Security Council passed its fourth resolution on September 27, noting that the cease-fire 'is not holding' and demanding that the commitment be honoured. U Thant reported on that day that 'complaints about positions on the wrong side of the line are reported by United Nations Military Observers to be "continuous", and they emanate from both sides.' In a further clarification, he said later 'there was some forward movement at various places along the line and from both sides of it, with the apparent purpose of tactical improvement of military positions . . .' No progress had been made either on the withdrawal of forces. U Thant wrote to Shastri and Ayub on October 14 that the withdrawals 'have not taken place and there is no present indication that they are likely to take place any time soon under present circumstances unless some new effort is made.' This was, he added, 'a matter of great concern to me and, I believe, to the members of the Security Council.' On November 5, the Security Council adopted its fifth resolution, demanding 'the prompt and unconditional' implementation of the Indo-Pakistan agreement to meet with a representative of the Secretary-General to formulate a plan and a schedule, under an accepted timetable, for troop withdrawals.[2]

The record of confirmed major battlefront incidents during this period suggests that some actions were initiated by local commanders but that both armies also carried out detailed plans to establish stronger post-war military and political positions. Pakistan, for example, quickly launched an attack in the desert wastes of Rajasthan which, from all evidence, gained it most of the 1,600 square miles of Indian territory which it claimed. India repeatedly protested. The Foreign Minister, Swaran Singh, claimed in a letter dated October 26 that 'Indian forces have intercepted Pakistani signals to their troops including the Indus Rangers, operating on the Rajasthan border, after the cease-fire was announced, asking them to capture the maximum possible territory of India.' He said Pakistani Rangers and Mujahids, supported on occasion by Pakistani troops, captured eleven remote villages after the cease-fire, between September 23 and October 3.[3] Pakistan claimed control of this territory before the cease-fire. The UN observers apparently lacked the manpower to determine the precise troop dispositions on this long, isolated front at the time of the cease-fire. Although U Thant reported the respective battle positions with some precision in other areas he was forced to rely solely upon Pakistani claims in outlining the situation in Rajasthan.[4]

UN observers in that region reported on October 6 'that the cease-fire was not yet fully effective in their sector'. As late as November 13, UN observers saw fighting in Rajasthan and observed Pakistani tanks. Pakistan claimed India had counter-attacked to regain territory lost during the war and that these latest hostilities were part of the action set off by the Indian initiative.[5] Nevertheless, the evidence indicates that Pakistan set out to acquire territory which could be used as a pressure to force Indian withdrawal from much more important and strategic positions in the Uri-Poonch bulge and Tithwal. A stretch of worthless but 'sacred' Indian soil could have significant bargaining value, and in this sense the Pakistani offensive appeared to be a logical development under the prevailing uncertainties of the truce. The Rajasthan campaign, however, again excited India and fortified her resolve.

On the other hand, Indian forces apparently took the stronger initiative to strengthen military positions in more strategic areas, but Pakistan also was active. In one major incident, as they reported on October 25, the Pakistanis captured Indian field orders for the occupation of a bulge in the Tithwal area that would give India command of territory in the north-west up to the strategic Kishenganga river. The orders also called for the destruction of a bridge at Jura. This plan was carried out with a brigade of troops. Pakistan contended the action was a deliberately prepared violation of the cease-fire. The Indian Foreign Minister, Swaran Singh, confirmed the engagement but maintained that it was a defensive counteraction against a Pakistani attack by a whole battalion. The bulge, he claimed, had been occupied by Indian forces during the war but after the cease-fire Pakistan had used the Jura bridge and another one 'to make intrusions across the Cease-Fire Line. . .'.[6]

Both armies on the strategic central front actively expanded their forward positions and attempted to strengthen those which had been established prior to the cease-fire. In general, the confirmed engagements indicated strong Indian attempts to reduce the Chhamb-Akhnur bulge and to establish or to improve defensive positions on the east bank of the Ichhogil Canal. Pakistani forces not only resisted these efforts, but sought to enlarge their own holdings. The action ranged from vigorous patrolling to heavy artillery and infantry attacks. In one sector, the Indians captured two villages which they did not hold at the time of the cease-fire. In another, the Indians launched an attack of three infantry battalions against Pakistani positions on the Indian side of the CFL. At one point, Indian troops, under heavy protective artillery and mortar fire, crossed the CFL and attacked Pakistani positions as deep as one mile west of the line.[7] The Pakistanis, on the other hand, launched one attack with

1,100 men and others of lesser size.[8] In one quarrel over illegal Pakistan occupation of bunkers on the east bank of the Ichhogil or BRB Canal, firing commenced and became so hot that the United Nations observers themselves had to take cover.[9]

Pakistan maintained a vigorous political offensive at the United Nations, as, indeed, the situation required if Kashmir were to remain an active issue demanding future political consideration. Ambassador Amjad Ali sent innumerable complaints and arguments to the Secretariat, many of which Ambassador Parthasarathi answered on India's behalf. In this correspondence, which became part of the UN record, and in debate before the Security Council, the two nations again restated with vigour their classic arguments over Kashmir. The exchanges demonstrated once more that the conflict had tightened the impasse by 'bolting the door' on the Kashmir question, as one Indian writer put it. 'Indeed, never before in the eighteen-year history of this Indo-Pak dispute,' he says, 'has New Delhi been so categorical and unequivocal in its declaration that Kashmir is an integral part of India and that it is a closed chapter, never to be reopened. In the present mood and temper of the country, no Government in New Delhi dare agree to negotiate with Pakistan on the status of Kashmir.'[10]

One new element of the debate involved a protracted review of the origins of the 1965 hostilities. Pakistan continued to insist that it had no responsibility for the infiltrators and contended that the international war started on September 6 when 'India attacked Pakistan'. India argued that the Security Council had tacitly confirmed its contention that hostilities began with Pakistan-directed infiltrations by twice demanding, in official resolutions, a withdrawal of all armed personnel 'back to the positions held by them before 5 August 1965'. A somewhat heated dispute then arose over the exact significance of that date as used in the resolutions.

Ambassador Rifa'i of Jordan, one of the sponsors of the September 4 resolution in which the date was used for the first time, contended it had no significance. He told the Security Council on September 17: 'The date 5 August was intended merely to be an indication regarding the lines behind which the armed forces of both India and Pakistan were asked to withdraw. It was not meant to pass judgement on the claim of infiltration or to establish a fact in this regard.'[11]

The representative of Malaysia, Radakhrishna Ramani, defended the Indian position and contended the date was basic. '. . . we, the co-sponsors of that resolution, did not invent it for fun or choose it arbitrarily because we liked the look of it on a calendar. The date of August 5, 1965 is the vital date in this debate. It is in fact and in truth the starting point in the long and sorry train of tragic events narrated by the Secretary-General in his report of the initial incidents.' He noted that U Thant had used the date seven times in his report of September 3 and that the annotated list of incidents reported by UN observers showed the first and second episodes as occurring on August 5 and 6. In studying this list, Ramani added, 'one finds that not until after the first eleven incidents, spaced within August 5 and August 14, had occurred, each with increasing intensity and severity, did the Indian troops for the first time cross the cease-fire line and reoccupy the position north-east of Kargil. . . .' He continued:

I would venture to suggest that from the Secretary-General's report, supported by the careful findings of General Nimmo as a part of it, one can only—and I say this with the deepest regret—reach the conclusion that the highly armed, well-trained and well-led infiltrators came from Pakistan's side of the cease-fire line.

We in our part of the world have been facing for over two years this kind of war—infiltration, subversion, sabotage—and we may speak with some large knowledge, learnt in the hard school of experience. It is an exhausting, exasperating war where the initiative is forever with the aggressor, where the real casualties are not so much human bodies or valuable material, but the slow erosion of the steel, the determination, the will to fight, the will to stand firm in the face of odds, possessed by the passion to give one's all to save one's country.

Military pundits have calculated the defensive human costs of such operations in the ratio of at least ten to one. The art and science of this wearing, wearying, wasteful war have now been perfected in Asia. The peril of our times is the expansion, export and propagation of this kind of war into regions farther beyond, regions which are judged to be ripe for revolution. Today, however, Asia is its testing ground.

When the truth with regard to these infiltrations became known, Pakistan answered with vague denials and claims that these are but the symptoms of an ancient malignancy and the Security Council should direct its mind and employ its energies in exterminating the root cause of all: the denial by India of a plebiscite in Kashmir, agreed to by India as long ago as 1948. This was repeated this morning by the Minister of Law of Pakistan. This has been a time-honoured refrain.[12]

Pakistan initiated the effort to force the Security Council into a political consideration of Kashmir by demanding, on October 22, an urgent session to consider the 'virtual collapse of the cease-fire and the total disregard by India of the letter and spirit . . .' of the September 20 resolution. The occasion brought the two Foreign Ministers to New York and created further acrimonious debate. The Indian delegation underlined New Delhi's strengthened determination on Kashmir by refusing to participate in discussions related to any change in Indian Kashmir's political status. The final result of this session was the Council's resolution of November 4, demanding swift action on troop withdrawals and reaffirming its support for all aspects of the September 20 resolution, including the promise to consider future political solutions.

The solidarity of the big powers ended at this time. Russia abstained on the November 4 resolution. The action probably suited India, but Russia was evidently motivated primarily by its own interests. The Soviet delegation had proposed a time limit of three months on the presence of UN observers on the subcontinent, a revival of Moscow's traditional opposition to the stationing of foreign peace-keeping forces so near its borders. When the United States refused to support the time limit, the Soviets withdrew it and their support for the resolution.[13] Indian officials promptly raised the subtle suggestion that a Soviet veto might be revived to protect their Kashmir interests at the UN. Returning to New Delhi, Swaran Singh, the Foreign Minister, told newsmen the episode demonstrated that the Security Council could only suggest ways for disputing nations to settle their disputes. 'Once this limiting factor is fully comprehended, it should be clear to us that no international body, not even the Security Council, can give any decision which may not be acceptable to us. They can suggest means by which disputes can be resolved and it is for us to say whether they are acceptable or not.'[14]

Meanwhile, the situation was darkened by new Pakistani threats of a 'second round'. President Ayub had warned that, if the United Nations 'wish to bring about lasting peace in this area, they must address themselves urgently to the need of evolving an honourable solution of the Kashmir dispute. If they fail in this, this continent will again be engulfed in a much wider conflict.'[15] By mid-November, the Indian Defence Minister, Chavan, considered it necessary to assert that his country was prepared for further conflict 'in case the enemy is itching for it'. The revived Pakistani warnings and the accumulated apprehensions of Indian officials themselves had no doubt prompted the army's aggressiveness during the first few weeks of the cease-fire. Chavan noted that India could be caught napping once by Red China and by Pakistan but not a second time.[16] The mood of the country had been further reflected by President Radhakrishnan. 'We have today', he said in a nation-wide broadcast, 'retrieved our prestige and it is my hope that our army, air force, and navy will continue to function with daring heroism and skill and be treated as a force to be reckoned with.'

New Delhi appeared confident of withstanding another conventional attack but revealed concern over the possibility of revived guerrilla warfare in Kashmir. The Indians had found irregular conflict difficult to control and even more difficult to 'sell' to the world. Shastri had revealed this concern by originally insisting upon guarantees against further infiltrations as an essential precondition for a cease-fire. He had backed down from that position with evident reluctance, when the UN avoided placing responsibility on Pakistan for initiating guerrilla hostilities. During the height of the conventional war, signs also appeared that further efforts to stimulate a new round of irregular harassment might be made. U Thant noted on September 16, in a report on the military situation, that 'A sizable number of infiltrators continues to operate on the Indian side of the Cease-Fire Line. Also, in addition to the regular forces engaged, tribesmen from the North-West Frontier are becoming increasingly involved in the conflict, arriving at the front for the most part through Rawalpindi.'[17]

Ambassador Parthasarathi informed the Secretary-General on October 14 of 'the continued recruitment and training of irregulars in Pakistan-occupied Kashmir and in the tribal areas of Pakistan and the preparations for fresh armed infiltrations across the Cease-Fire Line in Jammu and Kashmir'. He said the Indian government had learned that '14,000 raiders from the North-West Frontier have been recruited and dispatched to Pakistan-occupied Kashmir by the Pakistan Government.' The North West Frontier provided the tribesmen who invaded Kashmir in 1947. In addition, the Indian representative said, the Pakistan government made efforts at the end of September to recruit twenty new platoons of irregulars in one sector of Azad Kashmir. In another area, one group of 400 guerrillas completed training, and it was said that another 1,000 youths were being recruited in another district. The Ambassador described other 'preparations for much more intensified attacks in Kashmir', which he claimed New Delhi had discovered. They included the recall of all ex-servicemen in Azad Kashmir. Fresh infiltrations, he added, would violate the cease-fire and 'India would be free to take suitable action in self-defence.' He concluded by pointing out that 'only two of the major infiltration routes were closed during the last operations, namely those in Tithwal and Uri-Poonch areas, and that several other routes still remain open to the infiltrators.' Swaran Singh, the Foreign Minister, added the charge twelve days later that Pakistani leaders had given a 'clear directive' to the armed infiltrators in Indian Kashmir that the cease-fire 'did not apply to them'.[18]

Although still disclaiming responsibility for the irregulars, Pakistan had indirectly confirmed its involvement. The government issued a press release at the end of September announcing the opening of a training camp for guerrillas in Azad Kashmir. The Indians, of course, maintained that several camps had been operated since May. The Pakistanis obviously expected to win general acceptance for going into the guerrilla business openly on the pretext of providing 'sympathetic' support for a 'spontaneous revolt'. But it was clear that Pakistan was deeply involved in the irregular war and took few pains to hide the fact, except at the United Nations. An American reporter, who had sharply criticised many Indian actions in Kashmir, made this observation in October: 'That Pakistan has been fomenting strife in Kashmir, including the training of guerrillas, is accepted without question in both countries' (India and Pakistan).[19] The evidence supported the Indian Foreign Minister Swaran

Singh's comments: 'All efforts of Pakistan, military, political, and diplomatic, are intended to maintain and heighten tension in the sub-continent, particularly in the Indian State of Jammu and Kashmir. The design still is to force India, by all means, to surrender its sovereignty over the State of Jammu and Kashmir.'[20] From the Pakistan standpoint, however, this was a justifiable effort. 'It is obvious', said Ambassador Amjad Ali, 'that when a country bars all avenues for peaceful settlement of a problem, it does nothing but provoke war. That is what India is doing today.'[21]

In early October, a series of disturbances broke out in Srinagar. They were put down with swift and evidently stern action by the government, with Indian authority quite apparent. The details were obscured by heavy press censorship and by the customary wide divergence between the accounts of pro-Indian and anti-Indian sources. A number of foreign correspondents, nevertheless, attested to the unrest in a series of stories that generally paralleled each other. From their accounts, it is clear that several anti-Indian demonstrations were staged, with students in the vanguard. Rocks were thrown at the police who, in turn, charged the demonstrators with their iron-tipped staves, the *lathi*. Gunfire was also involved, and by October 12 the government acknowledged that five persons had been killed. Anti-Indian sources gave the total as ten or twelve. A *hartal*, or Gandhian work stoppage, was also attempted, and demands for an immediate plebiscite were raised during public meetings. Demonstrators were arrested and on October 21 the last leaders of the Action Committee who were still free were jailed. The government said twenty-six leaders and five or six students were involved; anti-Indian sources claimed that more than 250 were in prison. The *hartal* was broken up, it is said, by threats to participating merchants that they would lose their ration cards, essential for all personal necessities, or would lose their business licences. In some instances, shuttered and padlocked stores were stated to have been pried open by police. Other reported counter-measures included heavy troop concentrations in the city and strong security checks; a regular curfew, and a curfew over the entire city on one occasion for twenty-four hours; temporary refusal of permission for Muslims to visit a favourite mosque for the first time in 250 years.[22]

'Even the overtly pro-Pakistan in Srinagar lay low while India and Pakistan were at war over Kashmir last month', *The Times* of

London reported on October 25. 'After the cease-fire they stirred, however, and, carrying the moderates with them, attempted belatedly to begin a popular agitation to voice the constant and general demand for self-determination. But they immediately met the Government's unyielding determination to keep Srinagar and other towns in the Valley quiet and it was the intended agitation, not authority or order, which was broken.' James S. Keat of the *Baltimore Sun* reported on November 5: 'Officials in Kashmir have explained the arrests by saying those detained have been stirring up trouble in a state which remains on a war footing. The state remained relatively quiet during the guerrilla war in August and subsequent full scale conflict between India and Pakistan, but has been rocked by sporadically violent demonstrations for the past month.' Haynes Johnson reported in the *Washington Star* on October 17 that censorship had hidden the story but added: '. . . this reporter has been in Srinagar and can report it is a fact that rocks have been thrown at troops, that civilians have been struck with long poles topped with pieces of iron, that Srinagar is an armed camp with soldiers every few feet, that crowds of young Kashmiris shout "Indian dogs go home", and that a deliberate policy of suppression of these facts exists.' J. Anthony Lukas said in the *New York Times* of October 16: 'The Indian guns and lathis are now needed to control Srinagar's own people, many of whom are now openly anti-Indian. This does not necessarily mean that they are pro-Pakistan. Srinagar's Moslems did not rise last August to support the infiltrators as Pakistan had expected them to do.' Lukas added that the capital was more restive than four months earlier but that there was little of the pre-war hope among Action Committee leaders that India could be moved by such measures as non-violence to grant them more autonomy. 'Today there is little hope left. Last month's war seems to have convinced many Kashmiris that India means to hold on to the state at all costs.'

The origin of this cycle of unrest is not clear. It was apparently increased, however, by the arrest on October 10 of Maulana Farooq, the young pro-Pakistan Muslim Grand Priest who had boasted of his hold over the crowds during the 1964 religious riots. On October 18, a group of students stoned the police, then retreated for sanctuary to the Hazratbal mosque, from which the Hair of the Prophet was reputedly stolen in 1963. Police followed them into the mosque and did some minor damage—enough, anyway, to add a religious spur to the political agitation. Perhaps fifty persons were injured in the mêlée. D. P. Dhar, the Hindu Home Minister and strong man of the Kashmiri government, was quoted by a Canadian newspaper as saying that 'the Holy Relic Action Committee wanted to re-enact the days when the holy relic was stolen. The Koran was exhibited in processions as a façade for hooliganism and paid Pakistani agents.' During this episode, Dhar added, Maulana Masoodi again called for a plebiscite.[23] Three days later, the Maulana, along with G. M. Karra, were among the arrested leaders of the Action Committee. These two moderate 'revolutionary' leaders evidently had been left free during much, if not all, of the war and post-war crisis, possibly in the hope they would restrain more radical elements.

Dhar, together with other Kashmiri officials, claimed that Pakistani infiltrators gave arms to the students and incited them to violence. The students said they were acting on their own, and no infiltrators were involved.[24] On the face of the evidence, Pakistani agents might have been on the scene but there was less likelihood that guerrillas had any role. Dhar estimated on October 16 that about forty infiltrators remained in the Valley, out of between 300 and 400 who were still in Kashmir. Officials of the Defence Ministry in New Delhi gave the same estimate for the Valley, with the total for the entire state at between 500 and 600. They claimed that 1,500 infiltrators had been killed and several hundred captured. The survivors began withdrawing after the cease-fire.[25]

In any case, the agitation during October failed to generate great strife or to approximate the religious turmoil of 1964. If attempts were made to turn it into a second 'revolt', it clearly had less chance of success than the first one. India responded, however, with the suspicion and nervousness of a nation for whom the war was not ended. The measures taken to suppress the unrest were harsh and decisive, at least temporarily. But those which have been confirmed by reliable independent sources, while perhaps unusually repressive for a well-developed society in peacetime, were not conspicuously excessive in what amounted to wartime conditions in an Asian nation. Pakistan officially charged the Indians with genocide again in its October 22 demand for an urgent Security Council meeting, but the charge was not seriously considered. In a further series of

2C

communications, the Pakistani representative claimed a revival of incidents on the pattern of the 1947–8 civil war, with the Jana Sangh launching terror raids, refugee trains being attacked and Kashmiris being burned alive when Indian authorities set fire to whole villages. There was no independent confirmation.[26]

The Indians were far more concerned over their international image from these developments than they were over what might be the more important result: if resentment had built up during the war to the extent that elements of the Kashmiri populace were willing to take bolder anti-Indian action in October than they had been in August, a severe crisis of leadership had developed. 'At the very least,' said Haynes Johnson in his dispatch to the *Washington Star*, 'it is clear that a large number of Kashmiris do not favor the continued rule of India. Whether they want an independent Kashmir or to be a part of Pakistan is unanswerable. But they do desire a change. For that reason a tenuous form of order is being maintained by armed force. How long it will last no one can say.' The Indian determination to hold Indian Kashmir was understandable. The Pakistanis, by turning to war, had strengthened that determination and so, as in 1947, had done a distinct disservice to the Kashmiris they proposed to 'rescue'. But the Indians themselves had long made the point that no armed force, no matter how powerful, could rule indefinitely without popular support. As long as dissatisfaction was suppressed and not remedied, Kashmir would be a potential Achilles heel for India in the 'national liberation' war which was being waged against it. Curiously, no one accused the communists of being involved in these disorders, although the tactics and the purpose more clearly fit the communist design than that of Pakistan. The moderate 'revolutionary' leaders themselves had attested to the communist influence on Kashmiri students. The emergence of the radicals at this time, when they had been relatively quiescent in August, was highly suspicious, to say the least. In general, Indian and Kashmiri authorities seem to overlook the possibility that an exploitable communist hard core exists in the state, despite the impetus given to its creation by the Sheikh Abdullah regime. It would be surprising, indeed, if there were no communist links with the students and with the volatile anti-Indian sentiment they reflected. These are basic conditions for 'national liberation' agitation, as favoured by Peking.

The first few weeks of the cease-fire thus became a sort of twilight war between the unreconciled and undefeated neighbours. There was little prospect that the UN could force a change, and less chance that the belligerents themselves could agree on peace. In fact, both nations went out of their way to exacerbate tensions during the 'peace'. Apart from battlefront and diplomatic hostility, they maintained various forms of pressure on each other within their national boundaries. The two High Commissioners or ambassadors were withdrawn in October as the result of fresh quarrels, although the war was fought without severing diplomatic relations. Most of the diplomatic staffs returned home the next month, amid mutual complaints of improper treatment. Each nation accused the other of stimulating a new two-way movement of refugees and of refusing entrance to persons ejected from the other state. Pakistan formally complained that India was withholding irrigation water from rivers covered by the Indus treaty. India denied the accusation, but did not formally reconfirm her intention of abiding by the treaty until November 10, after some nationalist legislators had demanded that the water be cut off until Pakistan yielded on Kashmir.

In early November, Pakistan reported with apparent accuracy that India had received two new squadrons of Soviet MIG-21 fighters, and Pakistani emotions accordingly were rekindled. The Indian government, moreover, openly sought more Russian arms while simultaneously making strenuous efforts to prevent any further American assistance to Pakistan. Prime Minister Shastri later emphasised in an interview that it would be 'palpably wrong' for the United States to resume military aid to Pakistan. Such a step, he said, 'could impose a very severe strain on our relations'. But he did not propose any method of quieting Pakistan's legitimate security fears. On November 15, President Ayub announced, in effect, that he would search the world for weapons—and there was no doubt that a new arms race had begun. 'In obtaining military assistance from foreign sources,' Ayub told the National Assembly, 'we have to be on our guard against the danger of relying too heavily on any single source of supply. Already we have suffered on this account.' The statement seemed to confirm the significant role of US restrictions in limiting the war : first, the restrictions against stockpiling supplies for a long anti-Indian conflict and, secondly, the arms embargo.

Russia stepped into this unpromising position on November 21 with a renewed suggestion that the two leaders meet together at Tashkent. Shastri announced India's acceptance two days later, and Pakistan soon agreed. The move was supported by American officials on the grounds that any effort to restore peace to the subcontinent was eminently worth while. The Soviets, it appeared, were risking much international prestige by sponsoring an apparently hopeless new attempt to settle the impasse, but they also would gain immeasurably from success. Moscow had made it clear that it intended to take this gamble alone. The Soviets had previously turned down a Pakistan proposal for the creation of a special four-nation UN task force to explore Kashmir and other Indo-Pakistan problems. The members would be France, Great Britain, the United States and Russia. India had objected to the inclusion of France and Great Britain in lingering anger over their supposed lack of neutrality during the war. But New Delhi had suggested a joint US-Russia initiative, a proposal met in Moscow with silence and inaction.

The Soviet Union quickly brought its controlled press in India behind a concerted propaganda campaign to popularise and, in fact, to over-sell Tashkent. The CPI newspaper, *New Age*, as well as surreptitious Kremlin-controlled publications, had followed the popular jingoistic line of fully supporting the war and vigorously attacking Pakistan. It is known, however, that shortly before the Kremlin's renewed attempts to popularise Tashkent, Chairman Dange and N. K. Krishnan, a member of the central secretariat, were in Moscow and were ordered to change the line. Mikhail A. Suslov, a member of the CPSU presidium and the party theoretician, told the Indian leaders that peace on the subcontinent was in Russia's interest. He demanded the elimination of all anti-Pakistan propaganda and a dilution of chauvinism. The new line, although conspicuously out of place in India's atmosphere, was soon followed by *New Age*, *Link*, *Blitz*, *Mainstream* and other publications. All of these then turned promptly to exuberant support for the pending Tashkent meeting, with *Blitz* notably in the forefront.

Red China became active again at this time. After their retirement from the September 'crisis', the Chinese had maintained low-level pressure on Sikkim and on the north-western front in Ladakh through patrolling action and occasional gunfire. An Indian note of October 2 protested against a number of small incidents in Ladakh and new intrusions in Sikkim. It said, 'Chinese troops still remain poised in strength across the Sikkim-Tibet border.'[27] The Indians reported 'intensive' Chinese firing on November 13 in the Dongchui La area of Sikkim where Peking had applied pressure in September. This was followed by three other brief but open 'intrusions' into Sikkim by units of forty to fifty Chinese soldiers between November 19 and November 24 when the question of new Soviet peace overtures was raised. Chavan the Defence Minister told Parliament that the Chinese purpose, while not entirely clear, could have been to probe Indian defences. 'But we must be careful not to be provoked by the intrusions', he said. Since September, a total of twenty-five other intrusions had been reported along the entire Sino-Soviet border, Chavan added.[28]

The attacks became stronger and more militarily significant in late November. Chinese troops 'in strength' occupied positions along the Thag La ridge in NEFA on November 26, the Indians alleged in an official note. On December 1, a unit of some 250 Chinese penetrated to the Namka Chu river, and about 100 of them crossed to the south bank where they took up positions. This line of attack was the principal route used in 1962 by Chinese forces, who advanced to the plains of Assam and so changed India's history. The Indian note, delivered on December 4, said, 'This is nothing but a deliberate act of provocation and a calculated attempt to raise tension and create incidents on the Indo-China border.' It contended that the Chinese attack violated the 20-kilometre demilitarised zone established in this area on the suggestion of the Colombo powers and specifically accepted by Peking. The Chinese withdrew voluntarily from Namka Chu a few days later, but continued to hold their positions on the critical Thag La ridge within the supposedly demilitarised zone. On December 9, small Chinese forces probed Indian positions in Ladakh. The next day, a half battalion of some 400 men turned the action back to NEFA, capturing the border village of Longju. This point had been the first target when the Chinese opened their border campaign against India by taking the village on August 25, 1959. On December 12, complained the Indians officially, action moved westward to Sikkim. There, a force of 250 to 300 Chinese started an encounter inside the Indian protectorate which produced the sharpest Sino-Indian action since 1962. It resulted in thirty Chinese dead.[29]

Shastri the Prime Minister and other Indian officials, expressing their concern over the Chinese pressures, regarded them as part of a campaign to sabotage the Tashkent meeting. This would undermine the Soviet initiative, while keeping the subcontinent's war situation alive, to Peking's potential advantage. New Delhi believed that the Chinese hoped to create a sufficient threat so that Shastri, by this time doubtful of the forthcoming talks, would be unable to leave his capital. At the least, the purpose seemed to be to enhance Ayub's position and to strengthen his determination to avoid the concessions that seemed essential for a successful summit meeting. The principal Chinese attacks in NEFA coincided, apparently by design, with the Pakistani President's visit to Washington, where he was told unequivocally that the restoration of US aid depended upon reviving peace. This theory was strengthened by the fact that Peking delivered a series of sharp notes to India during the Tashkent talks. But if Peking expected the pressures to weaken Indian resolve, it had sorely miscalculated the country's mood.

Peking evidently had a second motive for penetrating as deeply as three miles into NEFA at this time. As reported by Warren Unna in the *Washington Post* on December 19, 'Indian officials confide that they fear China has begun a long-term harassment of the eastern border with the specific objective of penetrating India's tribally unstable Northeast Frontier Agency (NEFA). This would permit China to break loose from the geographical confines of the Himalayas and begin to mix with the peoples of the sub-continent. Then China would dispense with military action and infiltrate and subvert in the respectable revolutionary way.' The Chinese had supplied a number of indications that they had a long-range programme in view. For one thing, they abandoned their pledge to respect the demilitarised zone in NEFA and another pledge to leave open key passes in the area, regardless of the possible damage to their political reputation among Afro-Asian nations. Chinese agents were believed to be active in politically unstable Bhutan, where Indian troops are barred. The attacks on Sikkim, where the border has not been specifically disputed by Peking, were made with the apparent intention of demonstrating Chinese power to adjacent tribesmen with complaints against India. The presence of nearby military power is an essential ingredient in creating 'national liberation' unrest, and the Chinese had reinforced their positions along the rim of India with several key road-building projects. As a result of the December thrusts, Chinese troops and the political agents invariably accompanying them had acquired a better physical and political base from which to propagandise and infiltrate the areas of some fifteen or more tribes which New Delhi controlled only loosely. Peking clearly signified its intention of arousing anti-Indian elements by its vigorous propaganda campaign on behalf of the Kashmiri 'rebels'. Recruitment of agents and supporters in the remote and restless south-eastern sections of India might take time but, in the Chinese view, would be relatively easy. Mao Tse-tung once philosophised that the party wanted people to serve it and could always get them 'through greed, through fear, inferiority, vengeance, what have you. . . .'

Thus, the Chinese at the end of 1965 strengthened their own posture against India amid their greater failure to wield decisive influence on the subcontinent. They had been conspicuously unable to help Pakistan or to prevent either the UN cease-fire or the ultimate Tashkent peace. These were major defeats which coincided with parallel grave setbacks for Peking in Indonesia, in Africa and particularly in South Vietnam, where 'national liberation' invincibility was being disproved. The failures made it all the more likely that Peking would be obliged, at some future propitious time, to undertake a new initiative, if only to regain face. This gave added significance to the fact that the Chinese appeared well placed to implement their own 'national liberation' struggle on the vulnerable borders of India more effectively than before. For this, they could use their own agents without necessarily relying on the Pakistanis.

Peking's anger at being thwarted by American power in profitable exploitation of the Indo-Pakistan conflict had been sharp and clear. The Chinese were equally vitriolic when they suspected that temporary Soviet-American co-operation would block their diplomatic efforts. 'Who', asked *Jen-min Jih-pao*, the Peking party newspaper, 'are their [the Indian reactionaries'] backers? One is US imperialism, the other the revisionist leadership of the Soviet Union . . . [which] is not one whit inferior to US imperialism . . .' In an editorial on September 18, the paper added: 'The Soviet leaders are pursuing Khrushchev revisionism without Khrushchev. In order to carry out their general line of US-Soviet co-operation to dominate the world, they always oppose the revolutionary struggles and wars of the peoples and thereby help US imperialism and its flunkeys. They brazenly supported the Indian reactionaries in attacking socialist China and are now brazenly supporting them in committing aggression against Pakistan.' The polemics intensified. By mid-October, the Soviets had abandoned the restraint first shown by the Kosygin-Brezhnev regime in this public feud and were responding in kind to Peking. But the Soviets quickly made it clear that their co-operation with the United States on peace was only a temporary measure to pursue major objectives in the subcontinent. They had no intention of creating a working arrangement to contain Communist China, as some Washington officials hoped would be possible. While the Soviet delegation was still voting with the United States on UN resolutions concerning the subcontinent, Andrei Gromyko, the Soviet Foreign Minister, revived an unremitting Soviet attack on the American role in South Vietnam.

The Soviets were pursuing specific objectives in their complex and bold diplomacy over the Indo-Pakistan war. In the words of Professor Griffith:

> Moscow wanted: to increase its influence in India; to maintain at the least its newly won rapprochement with Pakistan; to prevent China from profiting from the conflict; to prevent or at least limit Washington from profiting as well; and, finally, to maintain good relations with China's neighbors and former allies, but now increasingly 'neutralist,' North Korea and North Vietnam. Moscow's minimal objective was the containment of both Peking and Washington; its maximum aim was to detach India from Washington and Pakistan from Peking while moving both closer to Moscow, and, finally, to improve relations between the Indians and Pakistanis so that together they might devote their energies to containing China rather than to fighting each other. This final objective is shared by Moscow and Washington, and it is sufficiently important for both to make each willing to settle for Indian and Pakistani neutrality vis-à-vis themselves—the more so because this is what India and Pakistan want.[30]

These purposes were clearly of sufficient importance for Moscow to underwrite the gamble of sponsoring the Tashkent Conference.

16

THE TASHKENT CONFERENCE

THE SOVIETS carefully chose Tashkent as the site for their first attempt to settle a dispute between two non-communist adversaries. The city, the capital of the Soviet Republic of Uzbekistan, was the most accessible major city in Central Asia, a two-hour flight from New Delhi. It combined bustling modernity with a past that was familiar to both Indians and Pakistanis. They remembered Tashkent as the place from which the great Emperor Babar came to India to create the Mogul dynasty. The Soviets, with their penchant for symbolism, no doubt also remembered Tashkent as the base for the ill-fated communist expedition against British India in the 1920s.

The city of one million was presented as a showcase of communism. In welcoming the delegates, Premier Kosygin noted that Soviet Uzbekistan 'has achieved great successes in the fraternal family of the peoples of the Soviet Union. The peoples of my country and in particular of the Central Asian Republics have long-standing close trade and cultural ties with the peoples living in Pakistan and India.' Restoring normal Indo-Pakistan relations, he added, 'will be conducive to still greater development of friendly ties of the Soviet Union with Pakistan and India and will lead to the further expansion of economic and cultural co-operation aimed at the strengthening of their national independence and the rise in the welfare of their people.'[1]

But the conference opened on January 4, 1966, amid growing doubts that a peaceful Indo-Pakistan accommodation was possible. The battle areas were still unpacified, economic relations were suspended and diplomatic contacts were negligible. For several weeks beforehand, Ayub and Shastri had maintained public attitudes of rigidity, with no sign of compromise. Shastri originally insisted that Kashmir could not be discussed at all, then relented to say that the question could be talked about but not negotiated. Ayub insisted that a political settlement of Kashmir was the fundamental necessity and made this a prerequisite to a 'no-war' agreement, which the Indians greatly hoped to obtain. In short, India's hope from the meeting was to clean up the aftermath of the war, by agreeing on such matters as the withdrawal of forces, without touching the central problem. Pakistan's purpose was the unchanged desire to keep the Kashmir question alive.

The pressures for peace were growing. The belligerents quite obviously could not afford to maintain indefinitely even the half-war which characterised the cease-fire. Pakistan had invoked a drastic austerity programme to shore up the war-weakened economy. In late October, a $217 million cut in the government's development expenditures was announced. This was followed a week later by a sharp reduction in private investment opportunities, and then by a 25 per cent increase in excise, customs and sales taxes. These measures reflected the country's uncertainty over the future of foreign aid and the possibility of renewed hostilities with India. Ayub had visited Washington in mid-December and afterwards reported that he did not ask for a resumption of the life-giving American aid programme. He was told, however, that President Johnson regarded peace on the subcontinent as an essential prerequisite for reviving assistance. India, suffering her worst drought of the century and facing near-famine, had requested heavy emergency American food grain shipments in early December. Officials stated that a minimum of 10 million tons, or some 4 million more than previous annual shipments, might be necessary to ameliorate the situation. Throughout the war, US food shipments had continued, but Indians were worried by Washington's insistence upon short-term agreements. This policy had been established to prevent excessive Indian dependence upon imported food and to encourage increased domestic production. Shastri, who planned to visit Washington early in 1966, had been given a definite indication that he also would be told that peace was essential for resumption of direct economic assistance, and that self-help was needed for long-term food commitments.

Nevertheless, both leaders went to Tashkent under severe

domestic pressures which they believed required implacability, as had been true so often in the past. 'Neither Mr. Shastri nor President Ayub', said Krishan Bhatia in the *Hindustan Times* on November 26, 'have the political strength to sell in their respective countries any solution which may even remotely look like a compromise.' The mood within India, for example, strongly favoured permanent Indian occupation of the territories in Kashmir which had been won during the fighting, and this had been an impediment against re-establishment of the August 5 positions. 'The coveted valley apart,' Bhatia continued, 'should the Pakistani leader demand the return of the Tithwal and Haji Pir posts, Mr. Shastri would have no option but to reject it immediately.' Finally, the new fears created by the war remained strong. 'At present, the two countries are glaring at each other with hatred and deep suspicion. Each side expects the other to begin another round of hostilities at a time of its choosing. This is a dangerous situation because even if neither side has any desire for further fighting their suspicious fear—in fact hysteria— might drive them to war again.'

The Soviets had advised the two governments beforehand to avoid discussing major issues at Tashkent and to regard the meeting as the first of a series of bilateral discussions. These, the Soviets suggested, should be continued within the subcontinent.[2] Nevertheless, Pakistan quickly raised the question of Kashmir. The conference came to a standstill for two days while officials wrangled over the inclusion of Kashmir in the formal agenda for serious Ayub-Shastri talks. Kosygin was forced to mediate. He had attended the conference as host with the understanding he would participate only to the extent requested by the principals. On the third working day, however, he spent eight hours travelling between the widely-separated villas assigned to Shastri and Ayub and holding separate meetings with them. In the end, the first impasse was broken by eliminating a formal agendum. On Friday, January 7, the two leaders resumed their personal discussions, which had been suspended for a day, and met twice. They did not confer the next day, and an Indian spokesman said 'the positions on both sides are far apart'. By Sunday, January 9, the conference came to a deadlock again over the question of including Kashmir in any final joint statement to be issued. The Indian delegation made plans to leave on Tuesday, January 11, and it appeared possible that the meeting would end with no formal communiqué. 'Unless a miracle happens,' reported an Indian correspondent, 'the Tashkent conference should end . . . on an unmistakable note of disagreement . . . A détente on any basic issue is considered impossible.'[3]

Kosygin initiated last-minute rescue operations. For fourteen hours, he shuttled back and forth between Ayub and Shastri, carrying messages and doubtless making his own overtures. It was an unprecedented role for the head of a powerful state. Showing the strain himself, the sombre-faced Soviet leader concluded his talks shortly after midnight on Monday, January 10, after a final meeting with Shastri. Word was quickly passed to officials that a concluding statement might be made. In the forenoon, conference authorities announced that the Tashkent Conference would end at 4 p.m., but said the two delegations were deadlocked on basic issues. At 1.30 p.m., Shastri invited Ayub to confer again, and agreement was reached on the text of what became the Tashkent Declaration. It was signed that afternoon.

The Declaration in its most important aspect announced the agreement of the two leaders that 'all armed personnel of the two countries shall be withdrawn not later than 25 February 1966 to the positions they held prior to 5 August 1965, and both sides shall observe the cease-fire terms on the cease-fire line.' Prisoners of war would be repatriated promptly. They also agreed to re-establish normal diplomatic relations, to consider measures for restoring economic and cultural relations and to discuss the refugee problem further. The two leaders also 'have agreed that the sides will continue meetings both at the highest and at other levels on matters of direct concern to both countries. Both sides have recognized the need to set up joint Indian-Pakistani bodies which will report to their Governments in order to decide what further steps should be taken.'

On principles, the leaders agreed to abandon the use of force in accordance with the United Nations charter, to base their relations 'on the principle of non-interference in the internal affairs of each other' and to 'discourage any propaganda directed against the other country', while encouraging propaganda contributing to friendly relations. They agreed, the Declaration said,

> . . . that both sides will exert all efforts to create good neighbourly relations between India and Pakistan in accordance with the

United Nations Charter. They reaffirm their obligation under the Charter not to have recourse to force and to settle their disputes through peaceful means. They considered that the interests of peace in their region and particularly in the Indo-Pakistan Sub-Continent and, indeed, the interests of the peoples of India and Pakistan were not served by the continuance of tensions between the two countries. It was against this background that Jammu and Kashmir was discussed, and each of the sides set forth its respective position.

The Declaration served primarily as a means of permitting the belligerents to implement the UN Security Council resolution demanding the withdrawal of forces. The indications were that both sides wanted to end their half-war but needed a new justification to do so without arousing unacceptable internal opposition. The UN had exhausted its credit for this purpose. To withdraw their forces, the belligerent leaders had to recede from strong public positions. They could do so only under cover of a fresh declaration that protected, or appeared to protect, each nation's interests. The overriding necessity at that time, at least in India's mind, was to prevent the war from exploding again into major hostilities; or hostilities within the arms levels of the opponents. Shastri, in one of his last statements, told newsmen that the Tashkent meeting was held 'in order to see that there is no escalation of conflict between India and Pakistan. If there had been no agreement here, tension would have become more acute and it would have led to further conflagration.'

To create this situation, both sides had to compromise. On the surface and in the view of some Indians, Shastri made the greater concessions in order to reach agreement on the Tashkent Declaration. By deciding to carry out the withdrawals, he gave up the Haji Pir and Tithwal positions. Many Indians believed these outposts were necessary to prevent further infiltrations and a resumption of the guerrilla war. Shastri further abandoned his demand that Pakistan should acknowledge its responsibility for the infiltrators and agree to prevent any new guerrilla attack: a position Pakistan was unlikely to take under any circumstances. But this was not a complete retraction. Shastri's original demands had been unrealistic and probably were made for bargaining purposes. What India evidently wanted was to establish a political position enabling it to seal off the invasion routes in Azad Kashmir, without world disapproval, in any new guerrilla conflict. Swaran Singh, the Foreign Minister, later told parliament, in effect, that this had been achieved. He said India's objectives were secured through new Pakistani pledges to avoid interfering in internal affairs, to observe the cease-fire line and to abjure force. 'If they [the Pakistanis] send infiltrators [again], it will be a violation of the agreement and we will be within our right to take the sternest possible steps. The real guarantee is our capacity to deal with such a situation.' Military counter-action, as the Soviets are reported to have told the Indians at Tashkent, is the only effective defence against guerrillas. Swaran Singh said the government had definite information that Pakistan had asked the infiltrators remaining in Kashmir to withdraw and that by February 21 many had left the area.[4]

Pakistan, on the other hand, had failed to establish any sure procedure guaranteeing the future political consideration of Kashmir's status or, in fact, insuring that it would remain a global issue. Under Soviet auspices, as well as that of the United Nations, the question had been returned to bilateral negotiations, probably because the Soviets also regard it as insoluble. Consequently, one of Pakistan's basic war objectives was unfulfilled. Ayub himself made it clear that he regarded the Tashkent Declaration as inadequate. He was left only with the general statement that Jammu and Kashmir had been discussed in the context of the subcontinent's need for peace and the promise that the UN would try again. Although Ayub and the Pakistani press attempted to make the best of these circumstances, their dissatisfaction was evident. Ayub found it necessary to emphasise his intransigence on Kashmir and to ask his people to disregard critics of the Declaration. 'We also impressed on the Indian Prime Minister', the President said in a nation-wide broadcast, 'that the future of the people of the two countries depended on peace in the subcontinent and that this peace could not be lasting unless the Kashmir dispute was amicably settled. If this dispute was not settled both the countries would continue with warlike preparations and their resources, instead of being dedicated to the welfare of their people, would be diverted to the purposes of war.' Much of the controversy over discussing Kashmir and over including a reference to it in the final Declaration revolved around Pakistan's attempt to force India into admitting that the territory was still in dispute. 'Pakistan', said Ayub, 'was not prepared to consider Jammu and Kashmir as part of India or that it was their internal affair. The people of Jammu and Kashmir had a right to decide their own future and we will continue to support their inalienable right.'[5]

Regarding a no-war pact, on which, said an Indian correspondent, 'India had set her heart', Ayub commented: 'The Indian Prime Minister wanted us to sign a no war pact, but we made it clear to him that we would never be signatory to such a pact unless the Jammu and Kashmir dispute was settled honourably and equitably. We, however, offered to reaffirm our obligation under the UN Charter. This obligation means that nations will not resort to force unless they have explored all avenues of peaceful settlement.' The qualification was significant, in view of the pre-war Pakistani claim that UN inaction and Indian opposition meant closing the door to political action on Kashmir. Even under post-war circumstances, it seemed, neither side would abandon its traditional attempt to use no-war proposals to consolidate the Kashmir situation to its advantage. This evidently was Shastri's intention in reviving the suggestion at Tashkent, for the effect would be to prohibit renewed Pakistani military action against Kashmir. It was also Ayub's apparent purpose in suggesting during the conference a proportionate reduction in defence expenditures by the two nations, after machinery had been established for a political solution in Kashmir.

The record indicates that Shastri broke the impasse over troop withdrawals by agreeing to evacuate Indian positions in Azad Kashmir, in return for the vague guarantees of future peaceableness which he received. This enabled Pakistan to contemplate withdrawing from territory it held in India primarily as pressure to force Indian troops out of Pakistan Kashmir. The impasse over a final declaration, which permitted the appearance of harmony in the newly-created 'spirit of Tashkent', evidently ended when Ayub backed down from efforts to force India into a position of re-examining Kashmir. Since this meant abandoning a war aim, it probably signified that Ayub had made the greater concession and was under greater pressure to do so. The Pakistanis gave the appearance, at least, of expecting much benefit from Tashkent. Shastri's concession, while of consequence in terms of domestic politics, was, in effect, a repetition of his previous pledge to carry out the with-drawal section of the UN resolution of September 20.

This final solution and the agreement on the Tashkent Declaration were kept so secret, even from those at the conference, that the announcement constituted, in the words of a Pakistani correspon-dent, 'one of diplomacy's big surprises'. There was little doubt that, as Krishan Bhatia phrased it in the *Hindustan Times* of January 11, 'the surprise agreement is unmistakably the result of what is euphemistically described as "friendly persuasion" on the part of Soviet leaders.' The question of how much force was behind this persuasion immediately arose.

The parties to the conference had been under heavy international pressure, both public and private, to reach an accord since the early days of the conflict. Further pressures were supplied by mutual military and economic exhaustion and the growing necessity for both nations to re-establish vitalising American assistance. They had assumed a tacit obligation, in going to Tashkent, to avoid embarras-sing their Soviet hosts, whom both nations carefully refrained from irritating. Unless it is assumed that the whole performance was a charade, none of these pressures, nor indeed the probable fact that both sides wanted peace, was sufficient by the night of January 9 to avert the impending collapse of the conference. It could have ended in a more drastic failure had the principals been unable even to agree upon a final statement.

Kosygin undertook his unusual last-minute mediation in this atmosphere. The stakes were vital for him. The failure of the con-ference at that point would have meant a severe loss of prestige for the Soviets, in their first peace-making endeavour of this sort. Peking's reputation accordingly would have been enhanced—a highly distasteful prospect for Moscow. These odds were clear beforehand and, in undertaking to sponsor the meeting, the Soviets unquestionably believed they could produce an accord. This mood had been reflected throughout the meeting by the generally more optimistic tone of the Soviet spokesman, than of the Indian and Pakistani delegates. But the Soviets seldom depend upon persuasion as the principal method of winning a point; they prefer hard, secret bargaining. It is unlikely they would have undertaken the gamble of Tashkent unless they felt they had a bargaining point that would be more influential on the principals, in an emergency, than the other international pressures to which they were subjected.

So Kosygin spent much of his final fourteen-hour non-stop mediation effort in realistic negotiations which, at that point, were as much on Russia's behalf as on that of the belligerents. He suggested to Shastri that Russia might not always be on India's side on the Kashmir problem at the UN if India failed to reciprocate for the political risk taken by Moscow in sponsoring the Tashkent meeting. This hint was enough to secure Shastri's co-operation, say well-qualified Indian sources. At the same time, Pakistani newsmen say, Kosygin reminded Ayub it was to his advantage to disengage, because India held the most strategic military terrain. Developments indicated this was an influential, if not decisive, argument.

Kosygin's most persuasive talking point was the fact that he had arms and was willing to supply them to the two mutually suspicious neighbours. Whether he used this argument, or was obliged to do so, remains unclear. But it is evident that the availability of Soviet weapons, without restrictions on their use, soon became a basic factor in the geopolitics of the subcontinent. India already had intensified its pursuit of Soviet arms, and received new shipments in 1966. Pakistan sent a military mission to Moscow in July. Thus, at least, there were compelling reasons at Tashkent for both participants to avoid alienating their Soviet hosts, and this in turn became a subtle but significant pressure for a successful finale. The Tashkent meeting quite clearly established stronger relations between Russia and both India and Pakistan. Ayub predicted that the conference would result in closer Soviet-Pakistan ties and hinted that he expected more Soviet help in solving the Kashmir question on terms acceptable to Pakistan. '. . . the interest shown by the Soviet Government in the settlement of the dispute will also facilitate the task', Ayub told the nation on January 14.

The strain of the conference and, particularly, the final negotiations showed on all the participants. Shastri, who had suffered two previous heart attacks, apparently bore up well and in public demonstrated remarkable physical fitness. He appeared in good spirits when he attended the final banquet on the night of January 10. Leaving at about 10 p.m., he returned to his villa and remained alone. At 1.20 a.m., he awoke with severe coughing and died ten minutes later from a third heart attack, despite the efforts of his

2D

personal physician and a team of Soviet doctors who quickly arrived. His death saddened the diplomats and brought genuine condolences from President Ayub, one of the pallbearers at Tashkent. The two men, so dissimilar, seemed to understand each other, and both remarked frequently that they could discuss their problems together with friendliness. The Prime Minister's body, returned to New Delhi, was cremated on January 12, with a million mourners in the streets. War had brought Shastri from the shadows, had made him a popular public figure and a backstage political leader of such toughness and determination that the government soon missed his firm control. Shastri, who had never travelled abroad before reaching power, once predicted that he would die in a foreign land. When he did, his passing sobered the subcontinent and, perhaps, contributed directly to the smoothness with which many elements of the Tashkent Declaration were carried out.

The circumstances, nevertheless, forced Indian officials to deny repeatedly that Shastri was under strong Soviet pressure to sign the Declaration. The issue arose again on February 21, when the Lok Sabha endorsed the Declaration with little strong opposition. The Foreign Minister categorically denied that the Soviet Union had exercised any direct or indirect pressure on the Indian leader. 'It is wrong to suggest this', Swaran Singh said. 'The Soviet attitude was of full understanding and objective. We are grateful to them.'[6]

In any event, the Tashkent agreement was followed by a quick end to the military phases of the half-war. Military commanders, who had previously been deadlocked over the procedures for disengaging their forces, met promptly. They quickly agreed on the complex details of separating their troops by 1,000 yards, destroying defence positions, and similar activities. Disengagement was completed according to schedule on January 30. Four days later, the exchange of prisoners began. U Thant reported to the United Nations that the withdrawal of all forces to pre-war positions had been completed on time by February 25. Meanwhile, a start had been made towards implementing the political aspects of the Declaration, but it soon came to a standstill amid mutual recriminations.

Tashkent, as Kosygin pointed out, provided an atmosphere in which the leaders of the two warring nations could meet and, with or without Soviet pressure, end their military confrontation, at least temporarily. The Soviets provided a notable service in creating this atmosphere. But they made it clear they were primarily interested in staging this single conference and were not willing to become more deeply involved in peace-keeping or in the political ramifications of Kashmir. Kosygin said plainly that the implementation of the Declaration would depend upon the skill of the political leaders in the subcontinent itself. He made no additional offer to mediate. By continuing to furnish arms, Moscow obviously helped to stimulate the pressures for a 'second round', instead of seeking to reduce them. The United States had made it evident they would not contribute further to an arms race in the area. Although British arms restrictions were lessened somewhat in November 1965, the complete American embargo was maintained. It was relaxed only slightly on March 2, after the troop withdrawal.

Thus the Soviets ignored an opportunity to assume a new peace-making role in the emergent world. They also avoided a further chance to co-operate with the United States, if only tacitly, in containing Communist China. Instead, the Brezhnev-Kosygin strategy, it soon became clear, was to acquire a series of satellites, placed so as to bolster Soviet influence and to counteract Peking. This strategy has led to heavy supplies of arms for the United Arab Republic and a new Soviet attempt to establish a strong relationship with Japan. Whereas Khrushchev withdrew from South-east Asia to a considerable extent, the successor regime has increased its activities there, in an apparent effort to contain Peking largely by itself, among other purposes. As one consequence, the Soviets have moved back into influence in North Vietnam by supplying the anti-aircraft weapons and other sophisticated arms needed in that expanding war and which Peking cannot provide.

In this light, it appears that Moscow desires to establish the greatest possible military competence in both Pakistan and India, using both strategic nations as an anti-Chinese barrier. To do so, Moscow is willing to encourage a new arms race on the subcontinent; in fact, if a major build-up by the two neighbours does result, Moscow will probably have to supply much of the power, under present circumstances. Apart from the quest for temporary diplomatic prestige, the Soviets were obviously following this strategy at Tashkent. They were anxious for peace at the time, because war would profit only Peking, but they were willing to play with further war on the subcontinent for Soviet purposes.

The Tashkent Conference, therefore, became another phase in the complex struggle in which the subcontinent is involved.

17

THE 'SPIRIT OF TASHKENT'

THE TASHKENT CONFERENCE, while deciding nothing itself, created the atmosphere in which the belligerent nations could alter the pressures driving them towards further war. First, it provided an avenue for them to implement the disengagement and withdrawal provisions of the United Nations resolution. Secondly, as with all top-level conferences, however stormy, the meeting produced a 'spirit of Tashkent', a momentary period of calm and hope during which, theoretically, a new start could be made. Tashkent was a lid put on a boiling kettle. The problem was to turn off the fire.

The revitalised pressures and suspicions which had been built up over the years, however, were strengthened by the outcome of the war. Despite claims of great victories in both countries, major hostilities were broken off before there was a vital decision. The governments knew this at once, of course, and the people soon realised it; so that the talk of a 'second round' became almost automatic. The indecisiveness of the first Kashmir war had perpetuated the unsettled position of that state, making it a magnet for an almost continual Pakistani political offensive that finally led to war. The indecisiveness of the second, greater conflict left open a broad new range of problems and objectives, with both belligerents still strong enough to pursue them. If there had been no climate in which to negotiate Indo-Pakistan differences before hostilities, the relative parity of battlefield strength made negotiations even more impossible after the conflict.

The war had disproved some of the primary fears which irresponsible leaders in both countries had spread continuously, yet to those involved it had at the same time proved beyond doubt the validity of the one predominant anxiety which had overshadowed both nations since partition. The Indians were convinced that Pakistan had at last launched the long-predicted aggressive war and could not be halted except by superior force. Nothing was likely to shake them from the conviction that they must acquire maximum military strength. To the West Pakistanis, India had in fact invaded their territory and given confirmation to their conviction that the Hindus were determined to eliminate Pakistan as an independent nation. The East Pakistanis had escaped invasion but not the overwhelming sense of helplessness and isolation created by the shadow of powerful India.

At the moment of peace, then, each side saw a still powerful enemy reorganising for a renewal of the attack. Military leaders quite obviously shared this view and regarded the war merely as an inconclusive though serious test. Consequently, the new arms race was begun openly by both nations, even before they were able to agree on the disengagement of their forces. All the potentialities raised by the 'spirit of Tashkent' and the diplomatic steps that were taken afterwards were based upon the fundamental reality that the principals were building up new military strength as rapidly as possible. If the conflict of 1965 constituted a military interlude in an endless political war over Indo-Pakistan differences, the armistice threatened to become merely a political interlude in what had been transformed into a politico-military campaign.

With the Anglo-American embargo in effect, the two neighbours had turned to Moscow and Peking in November 1955 for more arms. In addition to the apparently accurate report of fresh Soviet MIG arrivals in India, a contract was signed in New Delhi for the purchase of four Soviet submarines and other craft. The Indian Finance Minister, T. T. Krishnamachari, led a mission to Moscow in the middle of the month for the declared purpose of seeking military as well as economic help. He said that in particular he hoped to obtain Soviet backing for a second small arms factory which had been suspended with the American embargo. The Moscow conference pleased the Indians and produced public promises of doubled economic aid and trade. After the Finance Minister reached Moscow, further news of military negotiations was curtailed, but it seemed likely he had discussed weapons requirements, for he announced satisfaction with progress on the MIG factory on his return to New Delhi. The Pakistani Foreign

Minister, Bhutto, went to Moscow late in November for the purpose, it was proclaimed, of discussing Soviet aid to India and to advance Pakistan's request for military help. In the same period, President Ayub announced the establishment of a special organisation to expedite the maximum defence production from Pakistani resources, in order to augment military strength drawn from abroad.

On March 23, 1966, Pakistan displayed five Chinese-made T-59 medium tanks and four Chinese MIG-19 fighters among American equipment assembled for a national day parade. Foreign sources stated that the Pakistanis had begun receiving unspecified shipments of Chinese Communist arms during the autumn of 1965, after major Indo-Pakistan hostilities ended.[1] Ayub gave warning in a speech that the arms race with India would continue unless the two nations settled their differences on 'just and honourable terms', a phrase generally interpreted as meaning a Kashmir solution favourable to Pakistan. Three days later, the Chinese Communist Chief of State, Liu Shao-ch'i, arrived to a thunderous welcome for an unprecedented state visit to both sections of Pakistan. The 'Chinese people', he said on the conclusion of the visit, 'unswervingly stand on the side of the Pakistani people in their struggle to defend the nation's independence and sovereignty and to oppose aggression.'

By August, 1966, officials of the two countries were ready with detailed lists of the new equipment they accused each other of acquiring. The Indians contended that Pakistan had doubled its strength in Azad Kashmir since the war, by organising new Kashmiri forces, stationing more regular Pakistani troops in the area and by concentrating in strategic offensive territory. They said Peking had promised 270 tanks and 125 MIG-19 planes and had delivered roughly half of them. The Pakistani army of five or six divisions was to be augmented by the creation of five new divisions. The Indian sources said India also had increased her strength, but the build-up amounted to less than two new divisions and did not exceed the plans adopted after 1962.[2] Pakistan, it was reported, also purchased fifty F-86 jet fighters from world sources. By rearming 'at a frantic rate', said the Indian Defence Minister, Chavan, Pakistan posed a 'long-term and grave threat' to India's security. 'It may suit China to try to attack India through the agency of Pakistani forces. We have to and are taking the necessary steps for the defence of our country.'

Pakistan's new Foreign Minister, Syed Sharifuddin Pirzada, charged in his turn that India had purchased 600 tanks from East European countries, as well as 400 heavy guns and more than 200 tank transporters. The Indians had also acquired 200 supersonic missile-carrying fighters and fifty naval craft, he said. Further, he maintained that India intended to build up an army of twenty-one divisions facing Pakistan, and another group of nine divisions. India soon will have 'a formidable array of armed forces'.[3]

Both claims were regarded as excessive in Washington. Without discounting the fact that major arms competition was under way, American authorities said there was no independent evidence to confirm the size of the build-up attributed to the other by each side. Soviet arms shipments to India, begun early in 1962, continued steadily, but there was said to be no sign of an unduly heavy increase. On the other hand, it was believed that Peking was in no condition to supply heavy equipment to Pakistan in any quantity, at least not while obliged to furnish arms for a hot war in South Vietnam.[4] The tanks and aircraft displayed by Pakistan were primarily intended to impress the Indians, as they did. The Soviet-designed MIG-19 planes are still serviceable and effective, although the Soviets have withdrawn them from front-line duty in their forces. The Chinese have shown that they can build this model, though their ability to produce large numbers of more sophisticated fighters is more doubtful. Medium tanks of the T-59 class probably would not be a decisive weapon, unless Pakistan were able to obtain large numbers of them.

Behind these charges, both nations maintained heavy pressure on the Western powers, particularly the United States, over arms. India resumed her traditional effort to block any renewal of American assistance to Pakistan. The resumption of aid or the supply of spare parts for war-disabled equipment, said Foreign Minister Swaran Singh, 'will only encourage Pakistan in its aggressive and hostile designs against India'. The Pakistanis exerted equal pressure for an end to the embargo, as it affected them. Ayub is believed to have dismissed Bhutto from the cabinet in an attempt to placate Washington, while also removing his pro-Western Finance Minister, Mohammed Shoaib, in an effort to demonstrate national 'independence'. Pakistan closed some American intelligence channels in the northern part of the country in April 1966. The move, which deprived the non-communist world of some of its facilities for gathering information of Soviet military activities, was regarded as an implicit warning that Ayub was prepared to take stronger anti-American measures, if necessary, in order to obtain arms. If the United States did not respond, the inference was he would turn more openly to Moscow. A high-level Pakistani military mission went to the Soviet capital in July, but the results were not announced.

Amid these overt pressures and considerable backstage diplomatic activity, the US maintained its embargo throughout 1966. The restrictions prohibited sales of 'lethal' weapons to Pakistan, but carefully restricted sales of 'non-lethal' equipment had been resumed in February. 'By lethal equipment', said one expert, 'we mean spare parts for tanks, combat aircraft, artillery, ammunition, bayonets and so forth. By non-lethal equipment, we mean radios, parts for trucks, training aircraft, electronics, medical equipment and some types of defence production machinery.'[5] American diplomats consistently attempted to relax the tensions and to create a workable formula for guaranteed peace. One proposal was to make it a condition of resuming economic aid that the two countries should agree to limit their military spending. But the pressure of urgent economic requirements forced a resumption of full economic assistance to both countries in June, without any such qualification. India had already announced a 1966–7 military budget which was about 15 per cent higher than her war budget.

In this atmosphere, the 'spirit of Tashkent' quickly disappeared. A two-day ministerial conference was held in Rawalpindi at the beginning of March to discuss mutual problems, but it turned into a miniature Tashkent meeting, without Soviet intervention. Pakistan insisted upon a solution of Kashmir before undertaking other questions, and India refused to budge from its previous position that Kashmir was non-negotiable although other problems could be solved. The meeting, which nearly reached the breaking point, adjourned with the public promise to reconvene, but the prospects were unpromising.

By the autumn of 1966, the two nations had failed to make tangible progress in restoring normal business and trade relations, despite strong pressures to do so. The flow of Pakistani visitors into India had dropped from 1,000 a day to less than five, and these were carefully screened by Rawalpindi beforehand. Pakistan had observed her pledge to end the 'hate India' propaganda campaign with considerable scrupulousness during the early part of the year. Later, the same suspicions and fears of India were planted in the press through the statements of public figures, but on the whole the campaign was less thunderous than before. *Dawn* indicated the mood, however, in an editorial of April 4, by saying that India had not changed under her new Prime Minister, Mrs Indira Gandhi, who was duplicating the policies of Nehru, her father. 'The moral to be drawn from all this is that Pakistan should quickly get rid of whatever remains of the post-Tashkent euphoria, brush up on its realism once again and continue to prepare—internally and through the strengthening of tested and dependable foreign relations—for whatever the future holds.'

The stalemated war, in essence, had accelerated the same pressures which produced it, while creating others, and political leaders in both countries were unable or unwilling to change them. Pakistan, having turned to military action to break the Kashmir impasse, was committed to further use of power as the impasse hardened under the impact of hostilities. India, faced with this challenge and Peking's continual threat, sought protection by keeping Pakistan as weak as possible while rebuilding her own strength, this time by concentrating more openly upon weapons of primary usefulness against Pakistan. Ayub asserted in August that India's new arms were 'most sophisticated and meant for use in fighting on the plains and not on the hills against the Chinese'. Mrs Gandhi seemed to confirm the primary anti-Pakistan nature of the build-up by reputedly advising Washington that India did not desire a resumption of American equipment for use against China, if this would also mean resumed shipments to Pakistan.

Once again, India was faced with the problem of increasing its security without increasing the danger. The need and right to rearm were unquestioned; Pakistan was clearly on the attack. But if India had no intention of initiating further military hostilities, as all evidence indicates, its best interests lay in reducing the possibility that Pakistan would do so. The Indians, in general, seemed to regard Pakistan as a typical aggressor, to be contained through quarantine and superior defences. But the Pakistani drive appeared to be more complicated. The assault of 1965 was partly an aggressive desire to solve the Kashmir question by force; partly, it appears, a preventive war against India's prospective strength. In attacking a nation five times their size, the Pakistanis demonstrated that a whole people can be driven into *jehad* or holy war under the Islamic injunction to fight when it appears necessary, even if the cause is hopeless. The mere threat of a strongly militarised India had served as an incitement, not a deterrent.

India's policy of attempting to keep Pakistan weak by exerting pressure on her prospective allies had failed before, and it would clearly fail in 1966. The American arms embargo, which had been maintained largely at India's insistence, had driven Pakistan into greater dependence upon Red China. While Peking's capacity to supply adequate armaments during the Vietnamese war was questionable, its ability to strengthen Pakistan in certain areas of weaponry was recognised. At the same time, India revived consistent efforts to procure peace in Vietnam. These initiatives were unpromising but they were clearly threatening India's interests, for a Vietnamese truce would permit Peking to give Pakistan more help. New Delhi appeared to be gambling, however, on the possibility that it could keep Pakistan's war-destroyed equipment immobilised by preventing Washington from supplying the necessary replacement parts, and that Peking could not make up the difference under any circumstances. If so, this strategy would leave Pakistan wide open for stronger rapprochement with Russia, even at the cost of the American alliance, a possibility that could not be underestimated. The danger to India from a Soviet-armed Pakistan, with no restraint on the use of the equipment, was clear.

It was notable, in these circumstances, that the trends which had increased the subcontinent's significance to both Moscow and Peking had also accelerated in the post-war period. The two countries continued their implacable battle for control over the world communist movement. Periodic tensions arose along their extensive borders. In January, Peking transferred some 60,000 troops, in division formations, to the Sinkiang front and Russia had steadily built up her forces in this region for several months, withdrawing armoured and motorised divisions from Eastern Europe and northern Russia. The Chinese had heavily colonised Sinkiang and had begun to industrialise it; it was the source of uranium and other resources and Peking's major nuclear-testing site. Troop movements in this critical area were often timed to political events and apparently designed for political purposes, but they also had a fundamental military basis. By the middle of the year, the Sino-Soviet border region was sufficiently alive to prompt the Soviet Chairman Podgorny and Premier Kosygin to make separate 'inspection' trips, an unprecedented sign of top-level attention.

This strategic situation was reflected in the priority given by both communist capitals to expanding their mobility in critical areas of the subcontinent. After winning a foothold in Hunza, northern Kashmir, through the Sino-Pakistan border agreement, Peking promptly expanded it. In May 1966, an old caravan route running across Sinkiang and through Hunza was reopened, after being closed for eighteen years. It had also been extended. *Dawn* reported on April 19 that 'now the caravan can move to Gilgit', the key airbase in north-west Kashmir. The paper described this development as a boon to tribesmen living in the border regions, without mentioning its military potentialities. One of Russia's first projects, following closer rapport with Pakistan, was to begin construction of a trunk road from Russia through Afghanistan to Karachi. This project was likewise a civilian enterprise with military overtones. Similarly, Red China had been involved for some time in road-building activities in the sensitive kingdom of Nepal. Manoeuvred out of a key project which would have come close to the Indian border, the Chinese nevertheless were awarded a contract to build an east-west highway farther north, between Katmandu and the Tibetan border. The Chinese purpose in foreign road-building had been made amply clear in the kingdom of Laos. At the request of the neutralist government, they constructed a highway in the north-western part of the country which, as intended, gave access to isolated farmlands. But it also permitted conquest of the area by the communist-dominated Pathet Lao, under Chinese and North Vietnamese supervision. In Nepal, the Soviets attempted to counter the Chinese so vigorously that, among other projects, they financed a 'capitalist' cigarette factory and paid skimpy newspapers to publish large quantities of Soviet propaganda.

Within the subcontinent, the Soviets maintained their careful attempt to enlarge their foothold in both India and Pakistan. They avoided precipitate action and unmanageable publicity which might upset either of the target countries. These nations, in turn, carefully avoided criticising Moscow, even while voicing concern over the shipment of Soviet arms to the adversary. The primary Soviet objectives of containing and eventually expelling the Western powers and Communist China remained intact. There was a short-term objective, however, which softened their anti-American policies. As in other parts of the world, the Soviets wanted to keep the billions of dollars of American aid continually flowing, so that they would not have to assume the entire heavy burden of rehabilitating Pakistan and India. Moscow could be expected to refrain from any abrupt move that might end American help to Pakistan, edging more stealthily towards influence, as it had in India. Consequently, if the Soviets intended to help rearm Pakistan, as the Pakistanis obviously hoped, they would do so as covertly as possible. This strategy could be reversed, however, by any requirement to act swiftly and forcefully to prevent China from establishing a dominant position in Pakistan. Therefore the more India contributed to Pakistani reliance upon Peking, the more she helped to intensify the pressures requiring deeper Soviet involvement with her enemy.

For Peking, the importance of the Sino-Soviet border regions, particularly Sinkiang, and the strategic nearby territories, including northern Kashmir, had intensified. The Chinese had placed primary emphasis upon nuclear arms as a method of dominating Asia, attaining world stature and challenging Soviet control over world communism. Great sacrifices had been made to expedite a nuclear programme which had proceeded more swiftly than many experts anticipated. The us Secretary of Defense, McNamara, warned NATO in late 1965 that Peking could develop a medium-range nuclear ballistic missile by 1967 and might be able to deploy several launchers for these weapons by 1969.[6]

This is a primary threat to Asia, but it is also a threat to Russia. The Soviets could not tolerate the loss of territories in Central Asia claimed by Peking. Soviet officials have freely discussed the possibility that they might have to fight China eventually. The Chinese fully recognise this attitude and have defied it, to continue their anti-Soviet policies. Peking, less sanguine about Soviet methods than most other capitals, knows that, if the Soviets could attempt to strangle their 'brothers' economically in order to enforce communist discipline, they could seek to destroy China's nuclear capability by direct military assault. In such a situation, the old Soviet target, Sinkiang, would be a primary objective, as one of China's major nuclear areas. The Chinese quite obviously are seeking to build up their defences, not only by colonisation and troop deployment, but by establishing such key outflanking positions as that afforded by Pakistan.

Meanwhile, Kosygin, emerging as a tough and resolute leader, had initiated a new offensive in the Middle East. His policies not only reinforced the old strategy of 'proxy war' but seemed to outline current Soviet tactics towards the underdeveloped world. During an official visit to the United Arab Republic in the spring, he laid the foundation for what became an intensive and active campaign of renewed hostility between the Arab states and Israel and between the leftist Arab states and the monarchies. The key to this effort was heavy new shipments of modernised arms to the UAR which had been under way for months. On July 23, President Nasser paraded his large Soviet-equipped army. He unveiled at least 120 new radar-equipped Soviet tanks, two squadrons of new MIG-21D jet fighters, furnished with air-to-air missiles, new bomber missiles and heavy artillery.[7] This massive armed strength, the largest Soviet 'proxy' army in the world, provided the power behind both of the campaigns which the Soviets fostered in an obvious effort to catapult the Middle East into new turmoil. It was generally believed, however, that Moscow did not want war there on a scale to attract Western power, so it was apparently encouraging Syria's constant demands for a 'people's war' against Israel.

Peking, meanwhile, reacted to a series of grave defeats, notably in Ghana and Indonesia, by intensified dedication to its own parallel strategy of encouraging 'people's war' or 'national liberation war'. British experts predicted at the start of 1966 that the Chinese would turn to more aggressive support for 'revolution' and subversion and that they would back such further hard-line tactics as strikes, small rebellions, civilian disturbances, riots and demonstrations. Red China's intensive internal purge turned the country back toward communist fundamentalism. One result could be more vigorous foreign 'revolutionary' activity. By the autumn, Marshal Lin Piao, the present-day spokesman for stepped up subversive warfare, had been identified as Mao Tse-tung's heir apparent. The war in South Vietnam expanded, with both the Soviets and the Chinese becoming more deeply involved on a competitive basis.

Some specialists believed, for example, that Peking hampered Soviet arms shipments on Chinese railways in an attempt to force Moscow into supplying Hanoi entirely by sea, thus risking destruction by American bombing and the possible threat of Soviet-American hostilities. The attempt by the Soviets further to isolate Peking by enlarging their own presence in neighbouring countries appeared initially successful in Japan and North Korea. The Communist Parties in both countries turned against the Chinese. Peking's reaction evidently was mirrored by further hard-line activities, including encouragement for increased communist guerrilla activity in Thailand, its next announced target.

Most Asians regarded Communist China as a rapidly growing menace to them. They were concerned by the Chinese nuclear potential, by the size and historic implacability of the country and by the modern manipulation of 'people's war' as disguised aggression. The concern was expressed officially by the Council of Ministers of the South-east Asia Treaty Organisation in a communiqué issued on June 29. Noting communist setbacks during the previous year, the communiqué added: 'Nevertheless Communist aggression and efforts at subversion remain a major threat to the peace and security of the area. The Council considered that the situation in the treaty area is at present the most dangerous in the world and that efforts to meet the Communist challenge there must not fail.' The statement further noted that Lin Piao and other Chinese leaders clearly 'have reiterated their belief that the assault on the Republic of Vietnam is a critical test of the concept of what they call a "war of national liberation" but which is in reality a technique of aggression to impose Communist domination.' The communiqué, which further accused the North Vietnamese of violating the sovereignty of Laos, was not fully acceptable to all the members; Pakistan disassociated itself from sections opposing the communists and their activities in Laos and South Vietnam.[8] But it mirrored the apprehensions expressed to the author by large numbers of Asians in the Treaty countries and elsewhere. The essential point was that they believed China's threat was growing, not receding, and that co-operative efforts to contain it were necessary. From this base emerged several attempts to create regional organisations for mutual strength.

The position of India as an impediment to Chinese aspirations had correspondingly increased. Apart from her strategic location and competitive political philosophy, India had fought an armed conflict without collapse and was growing militarily stronger in the aftermath. Since the funds for rearmament came from the resources needed for general economic rehabilitation, the Chinese by their encouragement to Pakistan were able to apply a form of counter-revolution against India. But the pressures were growing for more direct Chinese efforts to impede India's progress and to disrupt her attempts to establish national unity. This reality was not refuted by the insistence of Bhutto, the ex-Foreign Minister, that 'Communist China does not pose any threat to the Indo-Pakistan sub-continent'. New Delhi was convinced that the Chinese threat was constant.

During the spring of 1966, India was swept by an unusual series of upheavals under circumstances suggesting strong Chinese Communist influence. In one category, riots and demonstrations in three major areas created a period of violence greater than at any time since partition, with the exception of the religious outbreaks of 1964. In the Punjab and in New Delhi, Sikhs and old-line Hindus fought bitterly over the government's promise to create a Punjabi-speaking state, as the Sikhs had long demanded. While this was basically communal, Indian communists, particularly those of the pro-Peking faction, were deeply involved in other bloody riots at this time in West Bengal and Kerala. The issue here was food short-ages, unemployment and allied ills, the type of complaints which the communists and other opposition groups have long turned into anti-government violence. Mrs Gandhi attributed the upheavals mainly to India's customary turbulence in advance of the general election, scheduled for February 1967. It was significant, however, that the Kerala disturbances forced the government to arrest E. M. S. Namboodiripad, the leader of the pro-Peking Party in India and a man long left free because officials believed he would act as a restraining influence on that communist wing. Whether Peking ordered disturbances at that period or whether Indian leaders merely seized upon a promising opportunity was less important than the fact that serious disruption could be produced. In May, most of the pro-Chinese communist leaders who had been jailed under the Defence of India Rules were released. They opened negotiations with pro-Kremlin leaders for a temporary working agreement to participate in the elections. Although the two factions had battled against each other bitterly and street fights between them were not uncommon, their party tactics were parallel.

The second category of outbreaks involved small, but possibly significant, tribal disturbances. In early March, an element of Mizo tribesmen rebelled and fought police and army troops for several days in the south-eastern corner of India. The uprising occurred in the Mizo Hills district of Assam, a wedge of land bordered by East Pakistan and Burma. The Mizos have long demanded independence but without resorting to serious violence. A sudden offensive by an estimated 800 to 1,300 tribesmen on February 28 caught the government by surprise. The rebels attacked five villages, overwhelmed the police and held the administrative centre, the town of Aijal, until driven out by the army on March 6. Armed with automatic weapons and hand grenades, the attackers used a number of standard guerrilla-communist tactics, including bank robbery and kidnapping. Indian officials said the offensive showed considerable planning and charged Pakistan with arming and training the rebels. The Pakistan radio called the brief uprising a 'war of liberation'. Meanwhile, a small group of underground Naga tribesmen were accused of several terrorist actions, brought to a climax by a train explosion which killed ninety-five people in August. The Nagas, who live farther north in Assam, also on the Burmese border, have fought Indian troops for a decade in search of independence. A cease-fire has been in effect since September 1964, while negotiations for a settlement continue sporadically. The activities of the underground, which also was accused of links with Pakistan, threatened at one time to upset the cease-fire and the negotiations.

These incidents were as significant for their potential as for their immediate results. The Mizos and the Nagas constituted only two of the unassimilated tribes inhabiting Assam in various degrees of dissatisfaction and independence. The terrain is highly suitable for the new-style disguised war, remote and isolated with few roads for counter-attacking troops. Indian soldiers had to march eighty miles to reach the centre of Mizo resistance. The probability of constant hostile pressure in this and similar areas along the long Indian perimeter is great; if, in fact, the Mizo outbreak was not actually a signal that intensified 'people's war' had begun. The Mizo rebellion had become a chronic and complex security problem by October

2E

1966.[9] India's urban unrest is endemic and its misuse constant.

All of the basic postwar trends continued through the first eleven months of 1967, but they were often obscured by compelling internal problems. Pakistan had revived its interrupted economic expansion with notable success, but still struggled with the effort to create national unity. India was engrossed in the battle for food and economic development. The Indian General Elections of February 1967 had created profound political readjustments; the once-dominant Congress Party lost control of nine state governments and its majority in the Lok Sabha dwindled from 133 to 47 over the combined opposition. Preoccupation with these affairs absorbed the energies of both countries, and no doubt helped to maintain peace between them. Two notable flare-ups along the generally quiet cease-fire lines were settled quickly enough to indicate that neither side wanted immediate hostilities. Yet no progress was made towards restoring commercial relations or communications between the two nations. Still less had been done to revive confidence in each other.

The arms race continued at what must have been the maximum possible speed. Pakistan had a defence budget for 1966–67 of $473 million, 19 per cent of government revenues and 3·1 per cent of the Gross National Product. India had reduced expenditures but its buildup was costing $1,171 million, some 17 per cent of revenues and 3·8 per cent of the Gross National Product.

By early 1967, independent sources estimated that the Indian army totalled 890,000 men, plus para-military auxiliaries, grouped into twenty to thirty divisions. Indian officers themselves talked of a 'million-man army'. The Institute of Strategic Studies had placed the manpower total in late 1966 at 807,000, plus approximately 41,000 in the Territorial Army and in para-military forces. The Institute credited India with nine infantry divisions, eleven mountain divisions, one division of heavy tanks and a brigade of light tanks. This represented an increase of three infantry and two mountain divisions over the Institute's estimates of the previous year—although these figures showed total military manpower as being less than the 825,000 men authorised by the pre-1965 buildup. In the same report, the Institute estimated the Pakistan regular army at 250,000, including 25,000 Azad Kashmiri, an increase of at least 70,000 over the previous year's figures. The Pakistanis had eight infantry divisions, an increase of two, and two complete armoured divisions.[10]

Both sides were replenishing heavy weapons at an equally rapid rate. Competent foreign sources said substantial numbers of Soviet tanks had been delivered to India, although the exact total was unknown. These deliveries began in late 1965, probably after the major Indo-Pakistani fighting. India also had produced at least a hundred of its own tank, the Vijayanta, a good reproduction of the British Centurion, for which it depended upon some imported components, such as heavy guns. The Soviet-supported MIG factory also was in production, on an unknown scale. India continued to produce the versatile Gnat and, early in 1967, reportedly went into production with an Indian-designed jet engine, HJE-2500. The Institute reported that the Indian army was equipped with 2,500 artillery pieces, mostly British-originated. Indian officers said artillery, particularly long-range guns, was one area of critical Indian weakness revealed by the war.

Pakistan, according to the Institute, had incorporated an unspecified number of Chinese Communist T-59 tanks into her second armoured division. Unconfirmed Indian press reports placed this total at 215, plus thirty lighter T-34 tanks. The Pakistanis had about 900 heavy field guns, ranging from 125 mm to 175 mm. In the air, Pakistan was credited with 200 planes, including the Chinese-built MIG-19, compared to India's 750 aircraft, including two interceptor squadrons of MIG-21s and some Soviet-built helicopters. Pakistan was rebuilding only against an Indian 'threat', but the Indians planned their defences for a potential two-front war.

In late January 1967, President Ayub said: 'Both Pakistan and India have squandered vast sums on armament, diverting resources which could be better utilised for feeding their people. We now stand perhaps at a turning point and may find ourselves engaged in an even fiercer arms race. This will be an act of the greatest folly.' Ayub said India had forced Pakistan into the arms race, but he continued to insist that a settlement in Kashmir was a prerequisite for peace. In April, India made tentative proposals to reduce troop strength down to a 4–1 ratio, but these overtures were received in Rawalpindi with qualifications which New Delhi considered a rejection.

In mid-April, the United States took steps to disengage from the arms race. Washington announced that it would provide no new equipment to either nation and that it would withdraw American military missions in July. This meant that Pakistan no longer could expect the US to modernise its armour and aircraft or to supply the weapons necessary to meet the original force goals of the United States-Pakistan military agreement. But Washington softened the blow by relaxing previous restrictions to permit the purchase of 'lethal' spare parts for existing equipment. The evident purpose was to restore a semblance of the pre-1965 balance of power by permitting Pakistan to rejuvenate some of its war-disabled arms. Nevertheless, both capitals bitterly condemned the new American policy. 'We strongly hope', said the official Washington announcement, 'that [India and Pakistan] will give increasing priority in the allocation of their resources to agricultural and industrial development.'

The American decision was made with the realisation that it would open wider potentialities for Moscow to enter a partial vacuum by rearming Pakistan.[11] But this did not materially change a situation which had existed at least since the Tashkent Conference. Throughout early 1967, there were conflicting reports on the amount of Soviet arms assistance, if any, given or pledged to Pakistan. No firm evidence had been made public, but knowledgeable sources concluded that Moscow had supplied some assistance and was likely to provide more. Rawalpindi continued to appear receptive, while simultaneously attempting to maintain strong relations with Peking.

For Moscow, Pakistan had become the key to an intensified effort to detach Muslim nations along its borders from their strong pro-Western positions. With the precedent of Pakistani friendship, Premier Kosygin was able to make an unprecedented visit to Turkey in late 1966. In February 1967, the Soviet Union reportedly agreed to sell Iran $110 million worth of sophisticated arms for defences against its southern neighbour, Iraq, also a recipient of Soviet weapons. This deal heightened Indian fears of a Russo-Pakistan military agreement and probably made one more likely. At least, the apparent importance of this new Soviet campaign in Muslim nations made it unlikely that Moscow would risk offending an arms-seeking Pakistan.

Sino-Soviet hostilities continued unabated in 1967, both in public debate and, evidently, in half-secret border pressures. Soviet officials charged that the Chinese were suppressing local tribes in Sinkiang, that they had established their own 'Berlin Wall' of minefields and watch towers to prevent escapes and that Russia had given refuge to 70,000 Kazakhs and Uighurs.[12] On the other hand, a Turkish defector reported that the Soviet Union had created a guerrilla army from 60,000 refugees from Sinkiang and was using it to raid Chinese territory.[13] The 'cultural revolution', still sweeping the Chinese mainland, created reports of revolt and counter-revolution in Sinkiang. Despite their domestic turmoil, however, the Chinese maintained heavy troop concentrations around India and applied periodic pressure through threats, propaganda and accusatory notes. Peking's foreign adventurism apparently had been temporarily curtailed by events at home and in Vietnam, but there was no evidence that expansionism would be permanently affected.

Consequently, the simmering 'national liberation' war against India's unstable south-eastern region continued to be potentially serious. The Mizo and Naga rebellions were active, if small-scale, in 1967, and Indian army efforts to suppress them were not completely successful. Well-informed sources said the situation in these two districts presented India with the same problems encountered by Washington and Saigon in South Vietnam towards the middle of 1965. With easy accessibility to both Burma and East Pakistan, the anti-Indian rebels apparently had sufficient arms to conduct disruptive operations indefinitely. The degree of direct Sino-Pakistan involvement was uncertain in 1967, but little outside influence was necessary.

Indian authorities responded to the Mizo threat with a 'pacification' programme very similar to the one in South Vietnam for which Indian critics had bitterly assailed Washington and Saigon. In a surprise military operation, which was announced on January 3, only one day in advance, the army resettled some 60,000 Mizo villagers in quickly-constructed new security villages in less than two months. About one-fifth of the region's population, the residents of 195 villages, were regrouped into seventeen large settlements along the Silchar-Aijal-Lungleh road, which runs for 190 miles through the centre of the district. The purpose was to bring them within the army's defensive power. This strategy worked in Malaya but failed in its original application to South Vietnam, because adequate military security was not provided. By the time New

Delhi made this move, the Mizo rebels had established a consequential political base. The rebel National Front dominated 140 of 531 elected village councils.

In an effort to prevent similar unrest among other hill peoples of the south-east, New Delhi agreed to the creation of a federal system within the state of Assam to establish partial political separation between the mountain tribes and the plainsmen. The six hill regions would be allowed their own legislature and council of ministers, with unspecified authority to handle their own affairs. The All-Party Hill Leaders' Conference, representing the region, had demanded a separate state for the tribesmen. The Conference was formed in 1960 to oppose the application of Assamese as the official language for the hillmen, and came in time to reflect other disagreements between the state's two geographic entities. The compromise was accepted by all concerned with some hesitancy. Its effectiveness depended upon the implementation.

Kashmir remained quiet, even through a particularly disputed election campaign. In Jammu and Kashmir, the Congress Party won 60 of the 73 seats in the state assembly. It gained half of the 42 seats in the Vale without contest, when a total of 118 opposition candidates was disqualified before the election by methods which have been challenged in Indian courts. Congress won 12 of the 21 contested seats in the Vale against its principal rival, the revived National Conference, also strongly pro-India. With his name only partially cleared of past malfeasance, Bakshi Ghulam Mohammed, the former Chief Minister, led the National Conference and scored a substantial personal victory. His return to politics split the anti-Indian 'revolutionaries', and the Karra faction boycotted the election in protest. The voting, consequently, provided inadequate evidence of post-war opinion and failed to clearly reveal the position of the 'revolutionaries'. In the Bakshi's district, the son of the pro-Pakistan leader, the Maulana Masoodi, trailed behind the runner-up, a candidate of the Jan Sangh.

Pakistan took the opportunity to protest in the UN Security Council against the 'farcical' election, but this was clearly a single propaganda exercise. The Kashmir voting did not necessarily prove the contention of some Indian papers that the people had demonstrated their support of the Congress or their acceptance of India. The results did indicate that anti-Indian sentiment, as a continuing political emotion, was not sufficiently strong in the valley to over-come the charism of well-known names and the practical mechanics of political machines. There was little violence, and the boycott resulted from personalities, not issues. Whether the Congress had minimised opposition by excessively illegal means could not be determined by independent sources. Notably, the National Conference, which was the chief complainant, had used the same methods to eliminate all opposition in thirty-four constituencies during the 1962 election.

The election results in Kashmir seemed to constitute another phase in consolidating the status quo. The nationwide losses sustained by Congress furthermore made its leadership more cautious than before and increased its intransigence over Kashmir. Nevertheless, through the party's efforts, India elected its first Muslim president in May. Dr Zakir Husain, the scholarly vice-president, won the prestigious ceremonial office over a candidate of the combined opposition by a substantial majority of votes cast by members of Parliament and state assemblies. This result did not necessarily prove the full acceptance of secularism in India, as the *Hindustan Times* pointed out, but it could have deep significance in the nation's slow development out of communalism.

Turmoil and periodic violence continued to dominate Indian political life. Communists of both factions were more aggressive, and their activities were potentially more significant. Moscow had dramatically abandoned its ten-year-old policy of seeking influence by manipulating the Congress left wing and had ordered the CPI into open attack on the government party, while maintaining 'friendly' state-to-state relations. Soviet secret agents had failed to heal the CPI breach, through the attempted bribery of outstanding leftists, and the two factions fought each other openly in many constituencies during the election. Nevertheless, the pro-Moscow CPI won 23 seats in the Lok Sabha and the pro-Peking party won 20. The total of 43 compared with 14 for the then united party in the previous house; the popular vote was relatively unchanged. A coalition dominated by left-wing communists won control of the state of Kerala for the second time. Left communists were influential in an anti-Congress coalition which briefly ruled West Bengal. In mid-1967, a peasant outbreak in the Naxalbari district of Bengal, near Darjeeling, was hailed as 'revolution' by Peking.

India's political problems forced it to turn inward. Those arising in Pakistan tended to point it outward. The continuing effort to revitalise Kashmir, for example, stimulated new diplomatic efforts to create stronger unity among Muslim nations behind Pakistan. Economic progress was geared to expanded exports, including an 85 per cent increase in trade with communist nations. At home, Ayub was coming under increasingly open criticism. Young intellectuals sharply attacked the unhealed inequities between rich and poor in the cities. Political opponents condemned his 'dictatorship' and critical religious leaders were so active that the president had to resort to preventive measures. National unity between the country's two wings had not been achieved, although Rawalpindi had devoted an increased amount of economic resources to this effort. Dissident tribal elements within West Pakistan were unassimilated; in the past, they had been quieted by creating tensions with India. These trends might compel Ayub to turn again to jingoistic 'nationalism', with all its dangerous potentialities. This possibility was strengthened by the re-emergence of Bhutto as a political opponent of undoubted ambition.

There was peace on the subcontinent in the autumn of 1967 and there was strong hope in both belligerent nations that it would continue. But the underlying trends were for more war at some time and at some level of military action. Nothing was being done to halt or reverse these trends.

18

WAR OR PEACE?

IF THERE is a predominant theme in the story of Indo-Pakistan relations, it is the pervading influence of mutual insecurities. Each nation has fed itself throughout independence on fear of invasion and conquest by the other. Pakistan's apprehension is understandable, if unacceptable, because of her size and configuration. Giant India has mesmerised herself into believing that Pakistan has the power, as distinct from the intent, to wage successful aggression. Neither country has been developed into a unified nation or has completely controlled separatism. The leaders are deeply troubled and greatly influenced by internal political insecurity. Religious fanaticism has been nurtured by doubt and uncertainty. Economic and social insecurity are endemic. They help perpetuate internal turbulence in both countries, and this turbulence, in turn, increases self-doubt.

These insecurities were built into the two nations by the history of communal discord, by the nature of their birth and by the alchemy of independence. Every newly-freed country in history has lived through doubts and apprehension basically similar to those of the subcontinent, although frequently less complicated. Each of the newly-independent nations today is reacting in various ways to its own uncertainties; many with bombast, some with melancholia. One manifestation may be the stridency of 'anti-colonialism', when Western colonisation has virtually ended: as much the product of fear that independence may still be lost as the heritage of unpleasant memory. Historically, these insecurities have been diminished only by time and by the creation of domestic unity and national self-confidence. They do not begin to recede until the governments are relieved of unwarranted fears of their neighbours and themselves. On that basis, it is probable that Indo-Pakistan hostilities and suspicion will persist on some level for a prolonged and indefinite period, until nation-building creates two sound and assured neighbours.

It is notable, however, that twenty years of independence have produced no fundamental changes in the outlook of the two countries towards each other. On the contrary, the leaders on both sides responded to the crisis of 1965 very much as their predecessors did to the crisis of 1946. Jinnah sought Muslim separateness with ruthless determination to press every advantage and to exploit every weakness. He turned to 'direct action', regardless of cost, to achieve his purposes. Now Ayub, on an infinitely more dangerous level, has revived 'direct action' under circumstances that make it difficult for him or his successors conveniently to abandon the threat of further military initiatives. Pakistan continues to insist, without a single piece of solid evidence, that India intends to invade and obliterate her as a nation. This may have been a dream of some Hindu leaders two decades ago, but it apparently soon died, and Patton tanks outmoded it. The Indians again have reacted with disdain, incredulity and anger. They have alternately underestimated and overrated the power and potentialities of this drive. Their fear over Ayub's threats to send his tanks to Delhi was very real to people obsessed by their loss of face in 1962, yet no responsible Indian leader seems to have pointed out the military liabilities of such an attack by a woefully outnumbered adversary.

Perhaps twenty years is too short a span for the deep Indo-Pakistan emotions and suspicions to have healed themselves. Yet the conclusion is inescapable that religious prejudices would have been greatly reduced without periodic manipulation during this period, and that national apprehensions would have receded before the logic of events if unrecalled by propaganda. Pakistan may feel incomplete and unfulfilled because without Kashmir she has failed to insert the 'K' in her name. Yet this does not negate the fact that a new and thriving Islamic state has been successfully established and so the Pakistani dream has proved itself. Nehru's thesis that the loss of Kashmir would threaten India's concept of a secular state has been widely accepted by Indians, but it would appear valid only if Pakistan succeeded in conquering much more of the country.

Manifestly, it was to the advantage of each country to encourage in its neighbour the fullest development towards nationhood and security as a means of reducing suspicion. On the whole, however, the opposite policy has been followed, despite some moments of friendship and co-existence. Pakistan, maintaining the offensive over Kashmir in accordance with Jinnah's tenets, has frequently attempted to offset its inferior size with bombast. But the tactics which Jinnah found useful against the uneasy British and the impatient Hindus were less suited to the purpose of wresting territory from a sovereign nation. India never yielded on Kashmir, and increasing pressure only made it more stubborn. Pakistani threats helped to perpetuate Indian uncertainty, and the Indian response, in turn, aroused fresh Pakistani fears, for New Delhi sought to meet the challenge by keeping its neighbour militarily weak.

As one result, there has been little positive initiative in two decades to adjust the fundamental differences between the two nations. To share the subcontinent in peace, each nation needs convincing assurance that the other is not intent upon armed aggression. When that point is resolved, if there is mutual disposition to resolve it, such subsidiary problems as the treatment of refugees become tractable. But it is questionable whether an essential basic sense of security can be established as long as Pakistan threatens India and India holds a physical stranglehold on Pakistan. Judging by official statements, the Pakistani pressure on Kashmir has been motivated through the years largely by the uncertainties of the nation's impossible configuration. Pakistan's fear of Indian suppression may persist until there is some adjustment of this situation: at least by the establishment of a corridor across India linking the two wings of the country and guaranteed against all interference. Yet in 1967 the Indians were unprepared to allow even uninterrupted rail service across India from West to East Pakistan. They were unlikely to make concessions on this problem as long as Pakistan continued her pressure over Kashmir. But Pakistan seemed to believe that, if the Kashmir question were allowed to die, so would her chances of altering the disadvantages of her divided nation.

In this confused situation, the importance of Kashmir has been frequently exaggerated. Quite obviously, it is of only secondary military significance in the Indo-Pakistani confrontation, for the military threat to each nation lies across the endless plains of the Punjab, not the narrow valleys of Kashmir. The annexation of Indian Kashmir by Pakistan would not automatically make Pakistan secure, nor would it increase her strength, in relation to her neighbour, by any but the most infinitesimal degree. Indian control over the entire territory would accomplish little more in regard to Pakistan than to cut off some potential invasion routes into the Valley. Politically, both capitals argue that Kashmir is essential for national unity. But Pakistan's drive for the mountain state has increased the country's disunity by alienating East Pakistan; and there is no evidence that the central Indian government is too weak to survive the separatist pressures that might follow relinquishment of Indian Kashmir. Rather, Kashmir is a symbol of the broader military, political and religious insecurities of the two adversaries; it has become a convenient peg on which to anchor world attention and to base internal propaganda. An equitable solution would not affect the wider Indo-Pakistan problems, except to create an atmosphere of goodwill. But progress toward easing basic Indo-Pakistan differences might well relegate Kashmir to the secondary position it deserves.

It can be argued that Kashmir, as an Indo-Pakistan issue, has been insoluble since 1949. At that time, it was clear that the tribal invasions had transformed the state into a symbol of military face for the uncertain new nations, that neither would voluntarily withdraw from territories won in combat and that there would be no compensating concession by one side to persuade the other to evacuate its occupied territory. Therefore the resultant legalisms and Indian promises of plebiscite may have been well meant but were unrealistic. As this situation stabilised, Pakistan's argument for the 1949 settlement lost validity, and it became irrelevant after 1962. It was a disservice to a confused world that this point was never made clear at the United Nations. Yet Pakistan has gone back to 1949 in her insistence, after the 1965 conflict, that Kashmir must be settled before other problems are considered. This has raised an impassable barrier against even a modest start towards an over-all solution of the subcontinent's problems.

In the long struggle over Kashmir, the evidence makes it difficult to identify either side as wholly right or entirely wrong. It is notable, however, that the years have reinforced the probability that there would have been no controversy over Pakistani control of Kashmir if Karachi had not instigated the tribal invasions of 1947. In that case, the rights of the Kashmiris probably would not have been respected any more than they have been under Indian rule. It also seems probable that an independent Kashmir would have been eliminated long ago, if left to stand alone against Red China. A number of other equally valid realities have been obscured by the moral tone of the international debate over the Kashmir issue, although morality has been a minor consideration for the two principals. Both, like history and geography, have ignored the rights of the Kashmiris. They have found that national interest and, in India's case, national security have forced them to encroach on weaker neighbours with tactics almost identical with those for which their intellectuals condemn Western 'imperialists'; and Kashmir has become such an obsession in both Pakistan and India that it has distorted their foreign policies and poisoned their politics. In particular, the struggle for Kashmir has itself created a major barrier against efforts to solve broader problems and lessen the greater insecurities on which peace depends. For many years, Kashmir was approached as the obstruction which prevented the settlement of these larger issues, and which had to be removed before further progress could be made. This remains the Pakistani position. In reality, Kashmir is the peak of the differences and, as India now argues, must be approached by clearing away the undergrowth at its base.

Ironically, the belligerents reached a significant landmark in their quest for security from each other in the stalemate of 1965. The most important lesson of that conflict was that neither country seriously threatened the welfare or stability of the other with the armaments at hand. Here was proof that the fear of conquest was invalid, under such conditions. There is reason to believe that Pakistani leaders, if not the people, realised they could not topple the Indian government with a swift armoured thrust and that guerrilla warfare against Kashmir was risky and uncertain. The Indian leaders clearly saw their capability of containing the whole mobilised power of Pakistan within an isolated battle area, so long as that power was hobbled by the American restrictions on ammunition and other essentials. This could have been a starting point for a concerted attempt by both sides to reduce mutual military insecurity.

The logic of the situation gave India the responsibility for the initiative. 'If we are really serious when we invoke the spirit of Tashkent,' wrote the Indian editor, S. Mulgaoeker, in the *Hindustan Times* on February 2, 1966, 'we must constantly produce positive ideas for the improvement of relations between the two countries to the point where in a climate of understanding and good neighbourliness the dispute in Kashmir is seen in its proper perspective. In this field the initiative must come from India, firstly because we are the larger country and have a great responsibility for and interest in the stability of the region.' Further, India had the most to give in the way of low-risk concessions that might ease Pakistan's uncertainty and therefore reduce the possibility of a second attack prompted by fear of India. New Delhi dominated its neighbour's misshapen borders, controlled the sources of many of its vital rivers, cast a larger shadow.

Mulgaoeker suggested among conciliatory gestures open to India: (1) a suspension of the practice of expelling Muslims from Assam, (2) the removal of barriers to the 'flow of people and information', (3) restored commercial relations, and (4) positive moves by India to permit Pakistan to maintain uninterrupted rail transportation between her two wings. Another possibility would have been a unilateral guarantee of the free flow of river waters originating in India and vital to Pakistan, regardless of other complications between the two countries. This would remove a pressure which has seriously concerned Pakistan but which, apart from verbal manipulation by zealous politicians, has been of only secondary value to India.

Militarily, India as the defender had a vital stake in perpetuating all the conditions of the arms balance which had produced the stalemate. The balance had two vital aspects. One was mobilised Pakistani power of sufficient size to reassure Rawalpindi against the possibility of Indian attack. The second aspect was effective restraints against the use of that power for sustained aggression against India. Both of these factors had operated to preserve peace for eleven years, when all of the pressures that created the conflict of 1965 were present, except the disproportionate Indian arms build-up. When Pakistan turned her American arms against India, the whole concept of a military balance on the subcontinent was sharply criticised. But the balance was at best only a crude substitute for wise political policies which both nations should have taken during the period of peace, and which they failed to do. Instead, consciously or unconsciously, both leaned on the superimposed balance as a crutch. When it broke, no one drew attention to the political failure during the wasted years of peace.

Unless India intended to assume a political initiative of greater impact than ever before, it seriously needed a restored arms balance in the aftermath of 1965. Pakistan, with its armoured power crippled, was bound to search desperately for replacement. Ayub had clearly stated that he did not want to place himself again under the restraints imposed by the American control over spare parts and ammunition. The Pakistanis had already proved that their sense of insecurity could drive them into preventive war. Now, insecurity had multiplied and restraints were greatly weakened. It was a moment of perhaps decisive importance. India with a bold gesture might have reduced Pakistani insecurity to controllable proportions. By accepting a limited easing of the American arms embargo, for example, it could have magnanimously allowed Pakistan to revitalise a portion of its armour, under reapplied American controls. This would have been a tangible overture toward assuring Pakistan against attack and might have had considerable influence on its rearmament. There was, to be sure, risk that the restored weapons would be used again against India, but this was less threatening than the uninhibited arms race which resulted from India's insistence upon maintenance of the American embargo.

The Indians saw only that they had been attacked twice, and turned to the discredited tactic of preventing a repetition by building their own strength and attempting to suppress Pakistan. This attitude was to be expected in the superheated atmosphere of the war and, if the government had believed otherwise, it would have encountered political difficulty in enforcing any contrary policy. But many other large nations faced with a reckless and aggressive neighbour have found it necessary to temper the use of their power, because their preponderant size places upon them the greater responsibility for seeking peace. As the Secretary of State, Dean Rusk, said of the United States: 'We are too powerful to be infuriated.' In a somewhat comparable position on the subcontinent,

India allowed itself to be infuriated by the anticipated tendency of Pakistan to pursue 'direct action' with implacability. The Indians tend to ignore their size and to justify their actions if they correspond to those of the weaker neighbour. But adequate military deterrence, particularly on the subcontinent, depends not only upon strong defences but upon convincing the adversary that the defensive arms will not be used to attack him. No such assurance was given by deed or, apparently, by private word, and the arms race which followed the stalemate was inevitable.

Pakistan also desperately needed a new posture, if only for self-defence. Its strategy of political and military attack had failed in every aspect; with it, Pakistanis only saw Kashmir recede farther from their grasp and Indian power grow greater. They evidently believed they had demonstrated temperance by suspending the 'hate India' press campaign, but this was only a negative gesture which was soon nullified by diplomatic intransigence. The time was long overdue to reach a practical *modus vivendi* on Kashmir, even if agreement had to be kept secret from mob passions. Pakistan, as the attacker, had to make the first meaningful overture in this respect. But, like the Indians, the Pakistanis merely perpetuated the tactics which had brought war.

This was a particularly dangerous policy for both nations under the circumstances. It gave to Moscow and Peking the initiative for war and peace on the subcontinent. It seemed evident by late 1966 that either communist capital, or both of them, could set off renewed hostilities by delivering adequate arms to Pakistan. This basic reality created wide opportunities for Sino-Soviet manipulation of both countries. Moscow as the chief potential armourer, for example, can secure absolute obedience from New Delhi by regulating the flow of arms to the two belligerents. Peking has already demonstrated its ability to intimidate India with pressure which has little risk to itself, and to dominate Pakistan through promises. This Sino-Soviet advantage has been further increased by India's attempt to reduce the US presence in Pakistan, thereby diminishing the American counterweight. Strengthened by this position, the communist nations quite obviously will pursue their own objectives on the subcontinent, as time and events dictate, regardless of the wishes of the occupants, as Peking already has proved.

Thus, Pakistan and India have become the perfect 'proxies' for communist purposes, because the intensity of their enmity creates permanent instability and because it has led each of them to barter away independence of action. The subcontinent has the potential of becoming another strategic storm centre like the Middle East. Although the problems of Kashmir and Israel are vastly different, each is a symbol capable of driving men into blind passion to settle by force an issue that is otherwise insoluble. The Soviets have manipulated this emotion for twenty years in the Middle East, for the consistent purpose of creating perpetual turmoil and eventually a 'proxy war', under conditions favourable to Moscow. These Soviet machinations clearly helped to precipitate war between Israel and her Arab neighbours in June 1967.

One hope for peace on the subcontinent under these circumstances is that astute leaders in both nations will eventually realise their common danger from the communist world and will retreat from it. This is, however, a distant possibility. Anglo-American diplomats have tried for many years to persuade the neighbours that their welfare depends upon subordinating their differences and joining in common defence against expansionist Red China. The advice has been rejected, and the diplomats have lost influence by offering it instead of taking sides on Kashmir. India's belated recognition of the Peking challenge was not enough to prevent its leaders from attaching priority to a dangerous arms build-up against Pakistan. In turn, Pakistan refused to believe the realities as stubbornly as India rejected them before 1962 and turned to Nehru's disastrous tactic of wooing Peking for use against the nearest adversary.

In general, both countries accept Soviet Russia as a benign neighbour. This appears to be due largely to the fact that the Soviets have given no bloody example of their power in the immediate neighbourhood, as did Peking, and to a distortion of past history as evidence of Moscow's non-imperialist intentions. India on the whole credits the Soviets with a desire to help in its total economic rehabilitation, apparently without realising that they have given no significant aid to agriculture, the most critical and decisive area of essential improvement. Instead, by performance and promise the Soviet Union has attempted to encourage the maximum development of state farms in India. The apparent purpose is to create conditions by which agricultural failure will drive the Indians into embracing the Soviet system as the only alternative. Industrially,

2F

the Soviets have concentrated upon prestige industrial projects capable of spawning the rioting workers of tomorrow. Obviously, Moscow can no more tolerate the successful completion of a non-communist social revolution than can Peking. This would repudiate the basic tenet of Marxism-Leninism, that 'revolution' can be led only by the Communist Party and can succeed only with the achievement of communist socialism. Therefore, Moscow's strategy is not to help to rehabilitate India but to contribute to the economic sphere most useful for future exploitation. This purpose requires the occasional practice of counter-revolution, to prevent the development of a rounded and wholesome economy, as would the emergence of a self-sufficient agricultural sector. Through arms, which withdraw funds from rural development, Moscow can practise counter-revolution in both countries as effectively as can Peking in its relations with Pakistan or its military pressure on India.

It is notable that throughout the long Sino-Soviet debate over the Chinese attack on India, Moscow has never criticised the Chinese for assaulting an unprepared neighbour. Soviet criticism has been based upon the charge that the campaign 'aided the imperialists'; in other words, it disrupted communist strategy, particularly Soviet strategy, for India and therefore was unwise. Frank N. Trager, Professor of International Affairs at New York University, presented the issue in this way in the American intellectual magazine, *Orbis*, in the Fall, 1965, issue: 'Perhaps the United States will eventually persuade India and Pakistan to accept the view that neither Peking nor Moscow can be trusted; that though they may employ different methods, each represents dangers against which defense insurance is required.'

In the meantime, peace on the subcontinent may well depend, in the absence of local initiative, on further unwelcome foreign interference. By late 1966, the belief was strong in Washington that Pakistan, as well as India, recognised that another campaign was economically impossible, because it would cut off life-giving US aid. Internal conditions required both countries to seek the greatest possible assistance in economic rehabilitation. In this sense, the aid programme served or could serve as another balance of power which perhaps might be as influential as the military balance.

Foreign influences can precipitate war in the subcontinent and can impose temporary peace, but they cannot solve the area's underlying problems. The best that can be expected is that India and Pakistan will gain more time to advance their own evolution and revolution, so that domestic security, national maturity and economic improvement can begin to erode the suspicions and fears perpetuated by a past that is best forgotten. The people themselves, as well as their leaders, must recognise or be taught that they are engaged in an antiquated internecine struggle that has proved to be self-defeating —politically, economically and militarily. The issues, while momentous and dominant to those involved, are overshadowed by the challenges of the modern world. Many Indians and Pakistanis recognise this fact, of course, but on the whole they have been submerged by recurrent floods of popular passion and by the persistent tendency of both governments to align themselves with the mobs. Yet there are signs that time has begun to shape the two nations. Individual Muslims and Hindus in India, for example, have adopted their own fairly successful neighbourhood coexistence. In the aftermath of the war, one of the most encouraging developments was the military agreement, in late 1966, by which each side undertook to inform the other of troop deployments, in order to prevent attack through misinformation or miscalculation.

It is probable that the potentiality for major conventional hostilities or for disguised guerrilla attack will exist in the subcontinent for many more years, until the neighbours achieve a far higher level of nation-building. Its exploitation or attempted exploitation by both internal and external forces may eventually make this one of the world's most critical areas. The lessons of the war of 1965, as well as those of the future, are crucial for the rest of the underdeveloped world, for India and Pakistan are the largest and in many ways the most sophisticated of the emerging nations. The challenges are multiple; among them is the fundamental, unanswered question raised by Nehru: 'Can the newborn nations escape the cycle of wars which plagued the old nations?'

BIBLIOGRAPHICAL COMMENTS

For material on the Indo-Pakistan military hostilities of 1965, the author has depended primarily upon sources which must remain anonymous; military and civilian officials in both countries and competent foreign informants. Little of substance has been published on the actual fighting. The war is described best from the Indian viewpoint by D. R. Mankekar in his book, *Twenty-two Fateful Days: Pakistan Cut to Size*, Manaktalas, Bombay 1966. Mankekar is close to the Indian army and apparently had access to all of the information the army wished to be published at that time. A second Indian account, which is non-official but sufficiently acceptable to New Delhi to be circulated by the government, is contained in a series of articles by B. G. Verghese, a *Times of India* correspondent who later joined the government, and reprinted as a pamphlet, *India Answers Pakistan*, Bombay 1965. Another Indian newsman, Dewan Berindranath, published a parallel account in the book, *The War With Pakistan*, Asia Press, New Delhi 1966. The basic details of Indian operations contained in all three summaries have been confirmed by impartial sources, but not such specifics as claimed Pakistani losses. General J. N. Chaudhuri, Chief of the Army Staff during the hostilities, added some comments of pertinence to this engagement in updating a series of dispatches he wrote as the anonymous military correspondent for the *Statesman*, published in the book, *Arms, Aims and Aspects*, Manaktalas, Bombay 1966.

The Pakistani version of the conflict, which omits all reference to Pakistani responsibility for guerrilla fighting in Kashmir, is outlined most succinctly by Major A. R. Siddiqi in 'The 17-Day War: A Pro's Account', *Pakistan Army Journal*, June 1966. See also: *Seventeen September Days*, edited by Aziz Beg, Babur and Amer

Publications, Lahore 1966; *Pakistan's Finest Hour*, edited by Rahman A. Syed and Wing-Commander M. Syed (Retd.), The Printers, Chittagong 1965; *Pak-India 17-day War of 1965*, edited by Nek Alam, Guidance Publishing House, Karachi 1965.

For contemporary coverage of the fighting, see: the *New York Times*, particularly the summary of October 12, 1965, by Anthony J. Lukas, Jacques Nevard and Paul Grimes, and battle area stories by Thomas F. Brady during September, some of them unpublished but contained in the newspaper's permanent supplemental file; the *Washington Post*, particularly John Norris's story of October 17, 1965, which was compiled from available non-classified information to that time; the *Baltimore Sun*; the *Washington Star*; *The Times*, London.

Some of the political ramifications of the conflict are outlined by Louis Dupree in 'First Reflections on the Second Kashmir War' and 'Further Reflections on the Second Kashmir War', Universities Field Staff, South Asia Series, Vol. IX, No. 5, December 1965, and Vol. X, No. 3, May 1966.

Official publications by the Indian and Pakistani governments were openly propagandistic and added little to factual information on the hostilities. The most useful are: *Indo-Pakistan War, A Flashback*, Department of Films and Publications, Government of Pakistan, Rawalpindi, September 1966; and *Pakistan's New Attempt to Grab Kashmir*, Publications Division, Ministry of Information and Broadcasting, Government of India, New Delhi, September 1965. Pakistan's official views were expressed most vigorously by President Ayub Khan in an address to the nation on September 22, 1965, and by the former foreign minister, Z. A. Bhutto, in his speech of September 28, 1965, to the United Nations General Assembly, 'Kashmir, Last Chance for the United Nations', both published by the Department of Films and Publications, Government of Pakistan. See also G. Ahmed, Pakistan Ambassador to the United States, *The Indian War*, Pakistan Embassy, Washington DC, and Mohammad Ayub Khan, *Pakistan Perspective*, a collection of important articles and addresses, Embassy of Pakistan, Washington DC, 1965. A further outline of the Pakistan position on the guerrilla fighting in Kashmir is contained in a pamphlet by Professor M. A. Aziz, *Struggle for the Liberation of Kashmir*, produced by the Revolutionary Council of the People of Jammu and Kashmir, and distributed by the Pakistan Embassy, Washington DC. Prime Minister Shastri revealed some political background, as well as India's views, in a series of speeches contained in a pamphlet, *When Freedom Is Menaced*, Publications Division, Ministry of Information and Broadcasting, Government of India, New Delhi, October 2, 1965, covering the period August 13–September 26, 1965; and in an additional speech to Parliament on November 16, summarised the next day in the *Hindustan Times*.

United Nations documentation is extensive. It includes Security Council resolutions, special reports by the Secretary-General, U Thant, official communications from the leaders of the two nations, special reports from UN observers containing portions of their investigations into violations of ceasefire restrictions, and a host of charges and counter-charges by the Permanent Representatives of the two nations. The most pertinent documents are: Security Council Resolutions Nos. 209, 210, 211, 214, 215; Security Council Documents S6651, S6661, S6666, S6672, S6683, S6686, S6687, S6688, S6699, S6710, S6719. The text of the Tashkent Declaration is contained in S7221.

The literature on the broad subject of Indo-Pakistan differences is so extensive that only a few books need be noted, for the general reader. Two readable histories adequately set the scene: T. C. Percival Spear, *India, A Modern History*, University of Michigan Press, Ann Arbor 1961; W. Norman Brown, *The United States and India and Pakistan*, revised and enlarged edn., Harvard University Press, Cambridge, Mass., 1963. A thorough review of the subject is contained in Dr Jyoti Bhusan das Gupta, *Indo-Pakistan Relations, 1947–1955*, Lounz, New York 1958; Djambatan, Amsterdam 1958; Sisir Gupta, *Kashmir, A Study in India-Pakistan Relations*, Asia Publishing House, New York 1966, London 1967. Two other recent Indian accounts: K. C. Saxena, *Pakistan, Her Relations With India, 1947–1966*, Vir Publishing House, New Delhi 1966; a special double issue of the quarterly, *International Studies*, 'India's Relations with Pakistan', Vol. 8, Nos. 1–2, July–October 1966.

The problems of partition and the civil war are described, somewhat controversially, in Leonard Mosley, *The Last Days of the British Raj*, Weidenfeld and Nicolson, London 1961; Harcourt, New York 1962. V. P. Menon, one of the principals, recounts the political history of this period convincingly in *The Story of the*

Integration of the Indian States, Longmans, London 1956; Macmillan, New York 1956; *The Transfer of Power in India*, Longmans, London 1957; Princeton University Press, Princeton 1957; and *An Outline of Indian Constitutional History*, Bharatiya Vidya Bhavan, Bombay 1965. For British accounts of this period see: Alan Campbell-Johnson, *Mission with Mountbatten*, Robert Hale, London 1951; Dutton, New York 1953; Lieutenant-General Sir Francis Tucker, *While Memory Serves*, Casswell, London 1950; Lord Birdwood, *A Continent Decides*, Robert Hale, London 1953. The development of Pakistan is described by Ian Stephens, *Pakistan*, Benn, London 1963; Frederick A. Praeger, New York 1963. For sketches of the leading personalities, see Michael Brecher, *Nehru, A Political Biography* (abridged edn.), Oxford Paperbacks, London 1961; Beacon Press, Boston 1962; and Hector Bolitho, *Jinnah: Creator of Pakistan*, John Murray, London 1954; Macmillan, New York 1955. On the revolutionary movement, see Maulana Abul Kalam Azad, *India Wins Freedom*, Orient Longmans, Bombay 1959, and Sasadhar Sinha, *Indian Independence in Perspective*, Asia Publishing House, Bombay 1965.

For the early struggle over Kashmir, see: Josef Korbel, *Danger in Kashmir*, Princeton University Press, Princeton 1954; Oxford University Press, London 1955; Lord Birdwood, *Two Nations and Kashmir*, Hale, London 1956; Michael Brecher, *The Struggle for Kashmir*, Oxford University Press, New York and Toronto 1953; James P. Ferguson, *Kashmir, An Historical Introduction*, Centaur Press, London 1961; International Publications, New York 1961; Walter Leifer, *Himalaya, Mountains of Destiny*, trans. Ursula Prideaux, Galley Press, London 1962; and Aziz Beg, *Captive Kashmir*, Allied Business Corp., Lahore. See also Lord Louis Mountbatten, *Time to Look Forward, Speeches as Viceroy of India and Governor-General of the Dominion of India, 1947–48, including related addresses*, N. Kaye, London 1949. The official Indian account of the first Kashmiri war is contained in *Defending Kashmir*, publication of Ministry of Information and Broadcasting, Government of India, New Delhi 1949. The Pakistani side of this campaign is contained in Major-General Fazal Muqeem Khan, SQA, *The Story of the Pakistan Army*, Oxford University Press, Lahore 1963, particularly pp. 83–122. Nehru revealed his political philosophy in many of his writings, particularly in *The Discovery of India*, Asian

Publishing House, Bombay 1947. See also *Jawaharlal Nehru's Speeches, 1945–59*, Ministry of Information and Broadcasting, New Delhi 1959. For an Indian evaluation of Nehru's leadership, see Frank Moraes, *Nehru, Sunlight and Shadow*, Jaico Publishing House, Bombay 1964; and a foreign assessment, Geoffrey Tyson, *Nehru, The Years of Power*, Pall Mall, London 1966; Frederick A. Praeger, New York 1966.

Some diplomatic problems of Kashmir are discussed by A. G. Noorani in *The Kashmir Question*, Manaktalas, Bombay 1964. A concise updated review is contained in Alastair Lamb, *Crisis in Kashmir, 1947–1966*, Routledge and Kegan Paul, London 1966. A brief review of military problems along the Kashmir cease-fire line is included in David W. Wainhouse, et al., *International Peace Observation, A History and Forecast*, Johns Hopkins Press, Baltimore 1966.

For an extensive and well-documented survey of the background to the Chinese attack on India in 1962, see Margaret W. Fisher, Leo E. Rose and Robert A. Huttenback, *Himalayan Battleground, Sino-Indian Rivalry in Ladakh*, Frederick A. Praeger, New York 1963; Pall Mall, London 1963. For an account of the fighting and some aspects of Sino-Soviet competition in the subcontinent, see Dr Satyanarayan Sinha, *China Strikes*, Rama Krishna and Sons, New Delhi 1964. The official Indian version of the campaign and Peking's political attack is summarised in two pamphlets: *Treachery in the Himalayas*, Ministry of Defence, New Delhi 1963; and *India-China Conflict*, Ministry of External Affairs, New Delhi. For detailed documentation, see *Report of the Officials of the Governments of India and the People's Republic of China on the Boundary Question*, Ministry of External Affairs, New Delhi, February 1961. See also N. J. Nanporia, *The Sino-Indian Dispute*, a *Times of India* publication, Bombay, July 1963, and A. G. Noorani, *Our Credulity and Negligence*, Ramdas G. Bhatkal, Bombay 1963. The Indian corps commander who was directly involved, Lieutenant-General B. M. Kaul, makes a somewhat controversial delayed report in *The Untold Story*, Manaktalas, Bombay 1967. For a foreign assessment, see George N. Patterson, *Peking Versus Delhi*, Frederick A. Praeger, New York 1964; Faber, London 1964.

Among numerous books on Soviet Russia's ambitions and activities in Central Asia and the Far East, see: John H. Kautsky, *Moscow and the Communist Party of India*, Massachusetts Institute of

Technology Press, Cambridge, Mass., 1956; Alexander Barmine, *One Who Survived*, G. P. Putnam's Sons, New York 1945; David J. Dallin, *Soviet Russia and the Far East*, Yale University Press, New Haven 1948; Max Beloff, *Soviet Policy in the Far East*, Oxford University Press, London 1953; Olaf Caroe, *Soviet Empire: The Turks of Central Asia and Stalinism*, Macmillan, London 1953; St Martin's Press, New York 1953; David N. Druhe, *Soviet Russia and Indian Communism*, Bookman Associates, New York 1959; Ivar Spector, *The Soviet Union and the Muslim World, 1917–1958*, University of Washington Press, Seattle 1959; Gunther Nollau, *International Communism and World Revolution, History & Methods*, Frederick A. Praeger, New York 1961; *Communism and Revolution, The Strategic Uses of Political Violence*, edited by Cyril E. Black and Thomas P. Thornton, Princeton University Press, Princeton 1965; Kermit McKenzie, *Comintern and World Revolution, 1928–1943*, Columbia University Press, New York and London 1964; and a wide range of exposés by defecting Soviet officials, ranging from W. G. Krivitsky, *In Stalin's Secret Service*, Harper and Bros., New York and London 1939, on the Stalinist era, to Aleksandr Kaznacheev, *Inside a Soviet Embassy, Experiences of a Russian Diplomat in Burma*, J. B. Lippincott, New York 1962, on the post-Stalinist period. For an evaluation of the continued influence of Stalinist psychology, see Milovan Djilas, *Conversations with Stalin*, Harcourt, Brace & World, Inc., New York 1962, and Djilas's *The New Class* (revised edition), Frederick A. Praeger, New York 1963.

The creation of competitive power systems underlying the Sino-Soviet feud are described in many works. Among the most useful general books: Leonard Schapiro, *The Communist Party of the Soviet Union*, Eyre and Spottiswoode, London 1960; Random House, New York 1960; and Peter S. H. Tang, *Communist China Today*, Vol. 1 (second edn., revised and enlarged), Research Institute on the Sino-Soviet Bloc, Washington DC, 1961. The history of early conflicts is outlined, inter alia, in Harold R. Isaacs, *The Tragedy of the Chinese Revolution* (second revised edn.), Stanford University Press, Palo Alto 1951; Robert C. North, *Moscow and Chinese Communists*, Stanford University Press, Palo Alto 1953; Oxford University Press, London, Bombay and Karachi 1953; Robert C. North and Xenia J. Eudin, *M. N. Roy's Mission to China: The Communist-Kuomintang Split of 1927*, University of California

Press, Berkeley 1963; Cambridge University Press, London 1963; Conrad Brandt, *Stalin's Failure in China, 1924–1927*, Harvard University Press, Cambridge, Mass., 1958; Benjamin I. Schwartz, *Chinese Communism and the Rise of Mao*, Harvard University Press, Cambridge, Mass., 1951.

For general works on the Sino-Soviet controversy, see: Edward Crankshaw, *The New Cold War, Moscow vs Pekin*, Penguin Books, London 1963; Klaus Mehnert, *Peking and Moscow*, G. P. Putnam's Sons, New York 1963; George Paloczi-Horvath, *Mao Tse-tung: Emperor of the Blue Ants*, Doubleday, Garden City, New York 1963. For more detailed documentation, see: C. F. Hudson, Richard Lowenthal and Roderick MacFaquhar, *The Sino-Soviet Dispute*, Frederick A. Praeger, New York 1961; Donald S. Zagoria, *The Sino-Soviet Conflict, 1956–1961*, Princeton University Press, Princeton 1962; Oxford University Press, London 1962; Zbigniew K. Brzezinski, *The Soviet Bloc, Unity and Conflict* (revised edn.), Frederick A. Praeger, New York 1961; Pall Mall Press, London 1963; William E. Griffith, 'Sino-Soviet Relations, 1964–65', *The China Quarterly*, No. 25, January–March 1966; Alexander Dallin, Jonathan Harris and Grey Hodnett, *Diversity in International Communism, A Documentary Record, 1961–1963*, Columbia University Press, New York and London 1963; and periodic official statements published in pamphlet form by Moscow and Peking, particularly a series of editorials published in 1963 and 1964 by the editorial departments of *Renmin Ribao and Hongqi* under the general title, *Comment on the Open Letter of the Central Committee of the CPSU*, Foreign Language Press, Peking. For the territorial issues, see Dennis J. Doolin, *Territorial Claims in the Sino-Soviet Conflict, Documents and Analysis*, The Hoover Institution on War, Revolution and Peace Studies, No. 7, Palo Alto 1965.

Among numerous books on Sino-Soviet strategies in Asia and the wars of the past two decades are: *The Communist Revolution in Asia*, edited by Robert A. Scalapino, Prentice-Hall, Inc., Englewood Cliffs 1965; *Communist Strategies in Asia*, edited by A. Doak Barnett, Frederick A. Praeger, New York 1963; Pall Mall Press, London 1963; *Modern Guerrilla Warfare, Fighting Communist Guerrilla Movements, 1941–1961*, edited by Franklin Mark Osanka, The Free Press of Glencoe, New York 1962; Arnold C. Brackman *Indonesian Communism, A History*, Frederick A. Praeger, New York and London 1963; and Brackman's *Southeast Asia's Second Front: The Power Struggle in the Malay Archipelago*, Pall Mall Press, London 1966; Frederick A. Praeger, New York 1966; Valentin Chu, *Ta Ta, Tan Tan*, W. W. Norton, New York 1963; Chiang Kai-chek, *Soviet Russia in China*, Farrar, Straus & Cudahy, New York 1957; David Rees, *Korea: The Limited War*, St Martin's Press, New York 1964; Macmillan, London 1964; Bernard B. Fall, *The Two Viet-Nams: A Political and Military Analysis*, Frederick A. Praeger, New York 1963; Pall Mall Press, London 1966; and Fall's *Viet-Nam Witness, 1953-66*, Frederick A. Praeger, New York 1966; Pall Mall Press, London 1966; Robert Strausz-Hupé, William R. Kintner, James E. Dougherty, Alvin J. Cottrell, *Protracted Conflict*, Harper, New York 1959; *The Strategy of Deception: A Study in World-Wide Communist Tactics*, edited by Jeane J. Kirkpatrick, Farrar, Straus and Company, New York 1963; P. J. Honey, *Communism in North Viet Nam: Its Role in the Sino-Soviet Dispute*, Massachusetts Institute of Technology Press, Cambridge 1963; Ampersand, London 1965; Major-General P. S. Bhagat, VC, *Forging the Shield*, published by the *Statesman*, Calcutta 1965; George K. Tanham, *Communist Revolutionary Warfare, The Vietminh in Indochina*, Frederick A. Praeger, New York 1961; Methuen, London 1961. For Asian tactics, as outlined by Communist leaders, see *Selected Works of Mao Tse-tung*, Vol. II, People's Publishing House, Bombay 1954, particularly the essays: 'Strategic Problems in the anti-Japanese Guerrilla War' and 'On the Protracted War'; Vo Nguyen Giap, *La Guerre de Libération et l'armée populaire*, Hanoi 1950; in English, *People's War, People's Army*, Frederick A. Praeger, New York and London 1963; Truong Chinh, *Primer for Revolt, the Communist Takeover in Viet-Nam*, Frederick A. Praeger, New York and London 1963; Marshal Lin Piao, 'A Declaration Urging World "People's War" to Destroy U.S.', *New York Times*, September 4, 1965. An authorised Soviet outline of urban insurrectionary tactics was published by the Comintern in the 1930s and has not been repudiated; see A. Neuberg, *Le Plan Communiste d'Insurrection Armée*, abridgements and comments by Leon de Poncins, Les Libertés Françaises, Paris 1931. A former Soviet intelligence chief, Alexander Orlov, has duplicated in the *Handbook of Intelligence and Guerrilla Warfare*, University of Michigan Press, Ann Arbor, 1963, the tactics still taught in the Soviet Union. The continuing Soviet

452 *Bibliographical Comments*

attitude toward 'national liberation' warfare and Moscow's role in it was outlined by the former Chairman, Khrushchev, in his speech of January 6, 1961, 'For the New Victories of the World Communist Movement', *Kommunist*, No. 1, Moscow, January 1961. See also the handbook for pro-Kremlin communists, *Fundamentals of Marxism-Leninism* (second impression), Foreign Languages Publishing House, Moscow 1961.

Other books which help to illuminate various ramifications of Indo-Pakistan relations include: Selig S. Harrison, *India: The Most Dangerous Decade*, Princeton University Press, Princeton 1960; Frank Moraes, *India Today*, Macmillan, New York 1960; Ronald Segal, *The Crisis of India*, Penguin Books, London 1965, an exhaustive survey with disputable conclusions; Mohammed Ahmed, *My Chief*, Longmans, Green, Pakistan Branch 1960; Aslam Siddiqi, *Pakistan Seeks Security*, Longmans, Green, Pakistan Branch 1960; and Siddiqi's *A Path for Pakistan*, Pakistan Publishing House, Karachi 1964; *A Study of Lal Bahadur Shastri*, edited by B. S. Gujrati, Sterling Publishers, Jullundur 1965; *Policies Toward China: Views from Six Continents*, edited by A. M. Halpern, McGraw-Hill, New York 1965; Michael Brecher, *Nehru's Mantle, The Politics of Succession in India*, Frederick A. Praeger, New York 1966; Oxford University Press, London 1966.

A number of magazine articles, particularly useful in sketching the background of the 1965 conflict, include: Frank N. Trager, 'The United States and Pakistan: A Failure of Diplomacy', *Orbis*, Fall 1965; Arthur Stein, 'India's Relations with the USSR, 1953–1963', *Orbis*, Summer 1964; S. M. Burke, 'Sino-Pakistani Relations', ibid; C. N. Satyapalan, 'The Sino-Indian Border Conflict', ibid; Selig S. Harrison, 'Troubled India and her Neighbors', *Foreign Affairs*, January 1965; W. M. Dobell, 'Ramifications of the China-Pakistan Border Treaty', *Pacific Affairs*, Autumn 1964; Cecil V. Crabb, Jr., 'The Testing of Non-Alignment', *Western Political Quarterly*, September 1964; Warren Unna, 'Pakistan, Friend of Our Enemies', *The Atlantic*, March 1964; Arnon Bernon Tourtellot, 'Kashmir: Dilemma of a People Adrift', *Saturday Review*, March 6, 1965; Khushwant Singh, 'Why Hindu and Moslem Speak Hate', *New York Times Sunday Magazine*, September 19, 1965; Richard Critchfield, 'Background to Conflict', *Reporter Magazine*, November 11, 1965.

Further documentation: *American Foreign Policy, 1950–1955, Basic Documents*, Vol. ii, US State Department Publication 6446, Washington DC, released December 1957, for aspects of the US-Pakistan Mutual Security Agreement, particularly pp. 2172, 2192; *Notes, Memoranda and Letters Exchanged and Agreements Signed Between the Governments of India and China, 1959–1962*, Ministry of External Affairs, New Delhi, for diplomatic exchanges during the first Sino-Indian crisis; UN Documents S/6763 and S/6776, for principal Indian notes to Peking during the Sino-Indian crisis of October 1965; see also *Hindustan Times* during this same period for details of Peking's official communications; *The Military Balance, 1965–1966* and *1966–1967*, Institute of Strategic Studies, London, for analysis of world military forces, including those of India and Pakistan; 'Foreign Assistance and Related Agencies Appropriations for 1966', Hearings before a Subcommittee of the Committee on Appropriations, House of Representatives, Eighty-Ninth Congress, First Session, US Government Printing Office, Washington DC, 1965, for outline of US arms assistance to India since 1962; *Aggression From The North: The Record of North Viet-Nam's Campaign to Conquer South Viet-Nam*, Department of State Publication 7839, Washington DC, February 1965; *A Threat to the Peace, North Viet-Nam's Effort to Conquer South Viet-Nam*, Parts I and II, Department of State Publication 7308, Washington DC, December 1961.

NOTES AND REFERENCES

(For full publication details of works cited, see the Bibliographical Comments.)

1: THE GLOBAL SETTING
1. *The Military Balance, 1965–1966*, pp. 28–34.
2. *Hindustan Times*, New Delhi, November 24, 1965.
3. David Rees, *Korea: The Limited War*, pp. 440–1, 460–1.
4. Nehru, *Report to The All-India Congress Committee*, July 6, 1951, *The Hindustan Times*, July 7, 1951.
5. G. Ahmed, *The Indian War*, p. 8.
6. *New York Times*, September 7, 1965.
7. *The Military Balance, 1965–1966*, p. 34.
8. *New York Times*, September 7, 1965.
9. New Year's Message, *The Hindu*, Madras, January 2, 1952.
10. Drew Middleton, *New York Times*, May 5, 1966.

2: THE PARTITION OF INDIA
1. For a description of the riot, see Leonard Mosley, *The Last Days of the British Raj*, pp. 31–9.
2. W. Norman Brown, *The United States and India and Pakistan*, p. 134. See also Mosley, pp. 129–46; Percival Spear, *India: A Modern History*, pp. 94–101; James F. Drane, "Kashmir, A Religious War", *Catholic World*, January 1966; Khushwant Singh, "Why Hindu and Moslem Speak Hate", *New York Times Sunday Magazine*, September 19, 1965.
3. Brown, p. 141.
4. Spear, p. 327.
5. V. P. Menon, *An Outline of Indian Constitutional History*, p. 34.
6. Spear, p. 394.
7. Mosley, p. 67.
8. Brown, p. 151.
9. Mosley, p. 68: statement by Jawaharlal Nehru.
10. Statement made in 1939; quoted in Ian Stephens, *Pakistan*, p. 27.
11. Undated interview, quoted in Stephens, p. 27.
12. Quoted in ibid., p. 83.
13. Brown, p. 148.
14. Menon, *Constitutional History*, p. 56.

15. Mosley, p. 68.
16. Stephens, pp. 96–107.
17. Statement to the British Viceroy and Congress, quoted at more length in Mosley, pp. 22–3.
18. Menon, *Constitutional History*, pp. 65–6.
19. Michael Brecher, *Nehru, A Political Biography*, abridged edn., p. 121.
20. Quoted in Mosley, p. 30.
21. For further details see A. Doak Barnett, ed., *Communist Strategies in Asia, A Comparative Analysis of Governments and Parties*, Chapter 4, "The Communist Party of India: Sino-Soviet Battleground", by Harry Gelman, particularly pp. 101–4.
22. For details see Selig S. Harrison, *India: The Most Dangerous Decades*.
23. Menon, *Constitutional History*, pp. 68–71; Mosley, pp. 109–27.
24. Lord Louis Mountbatten in Foreword to Menon, *Constitutional History*.
25. Menon, *Constitutional History*, pp. 72–3.
26. Mosley, p. 248.
27. An opinion shared by many historians; see Spear, p. 417; Jyoti Bhusan das Gupta, *Indo-Pakistan Relations, 1947–1955*, p. 34.
28. Spear, p. 416.
29. Menon, p. 56.
30. Mosley, pp. 102–5; Brecher, p. 161.
31. Quoted in Mosley, p. 99.
32. Quoted in ibid., p. 116.
33. Quoted in ibid., p. 23.

3: THE HERITAGE OF CIVIL WAR
1. Jinnah to Lord Ismay, Chief of the Governor-General's General Staff, quoted in Alan Campbell-Johnson, *Mission with Mountbatten*, p. 190.
2. Quoted in das Gupta, p. 44.
3. See Brown, p. 162; Stephens, pp. 182 and 188.
4. Brecher, p. 152.
5. Ibid., p. 155.
6. das Gupta, p. 58.
7. Quoted in ibid., p. 59.
8. An opinion shared by, among others, Brown, p. 175 and Mosley, p. 183.
9. Brown, p. 179.
10. Author's interviews in Hyderabad.

4: KASHMIR: THE FIRST WAR
1. James P. Ferguson, *Kashmir, An Historical Introduction*, p. 27.
2. Ibid., pp. 57–8.
3. Lord Birdwood, *Two Nations and Kashmir*, p. 34.
4. Ibid., p. 43.
5. Mosley, pp. 186–7.
6. Campbell-Johnson, p. 120.

7. Lord Louis Mountbatten, *Time to Look Forward, Speeches of Rear Admiral, the Earl Mountbatten of Burma*, pp. 268–9.
8. Stephens, p. 199.
9. das Gupta, p. 95.
10. Birdwood, p. 50.
11. Ibid., p. 129.
12. Stephens, p. 200.
13. V. P. Menon, *The Story of the Integration of the Indian States*, p. 381.
14. Ibid., pp. 381–2.
15. Indian Ministry of Information and Broadcasting, *Defending Kashmir*, pp. 26–7.
16. Birdwood, p. 61.
17. Stephens, p. 202.
18. Birdwood, pp. 54–5.
19. Menon, *Integration*, p. 384.
20. Josef Korbel, *Danger in Kashmir*, p. 147.
21. Menon, *Integration*, p. 386.
22. Ibid., p. 383.
23. Birdwood, p. 59; Stephens, p. 205.
24. *Defending Kashmir*, pp. 26, 73 and 83; Birdwood, pp. 71–2.
25. *Defending Kashmir*, p. 42.
26. Birdwood, pp. 67–9.
27. *Defending Kashmir*, p. 62.
28. Birdwood, p. 70.
29. *Defending Kashmir*, pp. 73 and 83; Birdwood, pp. 71–2.
30. Birdwood, p. 70.
31. Ibid., p. 73; Menon, *Integration*, p. 393.
32. Menon, *Integration*, p. 394.
33. Ibid., p. 391.
34. Brown, p. 187.
35. Letter from Lord Mountbatten to the Maharajah of Jammu and Kashmir; text in Birdwood, appendix.
36. das Gupta, p. 229.
37. Brecher, p. 154; personal interviews by the author in New Delhi.

5: Kashmir: The Political Struggle

1. For a discussion of this phase of UN efforts to settle Kashmir, see Brown, pp. 188–94.
2. Quoted in das Gupta, p. 138.
3. Indian Government Pamphlet, *ABC of the Kashmir Question*, p. 17.
4. Richard Critchfield, "Background to Conflict," *Reporter Magazine*, November 11, 1965.
5. Dr. Dunga Das Basu, *Commentary on the Constitution of India*, quoted in Birdwood, pp. 179–80.
6. Quoted in Korbel, pp. 206–7.
7. Ibid., p. 207.

8. Quoted in Birdwood, p. 176.
9. Korbel, pp. 213 and 261.
10. Lieutenant-General B. M. Kaul, *The Untold Story*, pp. 143–6.
11. See, for example, Brown, p. 195.

6: THE COLD WAR
1. Aleksandr Kaznacheev, *Inside A Soviet Embassy: Experiences of a Russian Diplomat in Burma*, p. 125.
2. N. A. Lomov, *Soviet Military Doctrine*, p. 5.
3. David N. Druhe, *Soviet Russia and Indian Communism*, pp. 12–13.
4. Quoted in ibid., p. 17.
5. V. I. Lenin, "Better Few, But Better" (1923), in *Selected Works*, International Publishers, New York 1943, Vol. IX, p. 400. For Trotsky, see Isaac Deutscher, *The Prophet Armed: Trotsky, 1879–1921*, Oxford University Press, London and New York 1954, p. 457.
6. For a discussion of Lenin's theses, see Louis Fischer, *The Life of Lenin*, Harper, New York 1964; Weidenfeld and Nicolson, London 1965; pp. 95–107.
7. For a discussion of the Lenin-Roy debate at the Second Congress of the Communist International, see Robert C. North and Xenia J. Eudin, *M. N. Roy's Mission to China: The Communist-Kuomintang Split of 1927*, pp. 12–29.
8. Deutscher, pp. 456–8.
9. Druhe, p. 35.
10. Olaf Caroe, *Soviet Empire, The Turks of Central Asia and Stalinism*, p. 115.
11. The *Declaration of the Council of People's Commissars*, signed by Lenin, Stalin and others on November 15, 1917; quoted in Caroe, p. 105.
12. For an account of the expedition, see Druhe, pp. 30–45.
13. For an account of this episode, see Harold R. Isaacs, *The Tragedy of the Chinese Revolution*.
14. North and Eudin, pp. 1 and 7.
15. Alexander Barmine, *One Who Survived*, quoted in David J. Dallin, *Soviet Russia and The Far East*, pp. 98–101.
16. Quoted in Druhe, p. 246.
17. US State Department Background Paper, quoted in Max Beloff, *Soviet Policy in The Far East*, p. 72.
18. Druhe, p. 285.
19. Bernard B. Fall, *The Two Viet-Nams: A Political and Military Analysis*, pp. 81–103.
20. P. J. Honey, *Communism in North Vietnam: Its Role in the Sino-Soviet Dispute*, pp. 12–13, fn 4.
21. *American Foreign Policy, 1950–1955, Basic Documents*, Vol. II, US State Department Publication 6446, released December 1957, p. 2172.
22. Spear, p. 433.
23. Quoted in Birdwood, p. 141.
24. Mohammed Ahmed, *My Chief*, pp. 73–6.

2G

25. Khalid B. Sayeed in A. M. Halpern, ed., *Policies Toward China: Views From Six Continents*, p. 229.
26. *Washington Post*, March 10, 1963.
27. *American Foreign Policy, 1950–1955, Basic Documents*, p. 2192.
28. Quoted in Birdwood, p. 140.
29. Diplomatic sources in Washington; air figures from *The Military Balance*, *1965–1966*.
30. The author, as a newspaper correspondent, covered the Korean War and its preludes.
31. *American Foreign Policy, 1950–1955, Basic Documents*, p. 2192.
32. Ibid., p. 2195.

7: Soviet Policy

1. For a discussion of the initial Soviet uses of 'coexistence,' see George F. Kennan, *Russia and the West under Lenin and Stalin*, Little, Brown, Boston 1961; Hutchinson, London 1961; pp. 165–6 and 216 *ff.*
2. *The Military Balance, 1965–1966*, pp. 38 and 34.
3. Ivar Spector, *The Soviet Union and the Muslim World, 1917–1958*, p. 230.
4. Robert Strausz-Hupé, et al, *Protracted Conflict*, pp. 88–9.
5. iss, p. 40.
6. Nikita Khrushchev, speech to the Sixth Congress of the East German Communist Party, January 16, 1963.
7. Spector, p. 213; see also, ibid., pp. 211 *ff*, 214 and 217.
8. For a discussion of the Geneva Conference, see Bernard B. Fall, *Viet-Nam Witness, 1943–66*, pp. 69–83.
9. *Fundamentals of Marxism-Leninism*, p. 583.
10. K. P. S. Menon, *The Flying Troika*, Oxford University Press, London and New York 1963, p. 131.
11. Unimpeachable personal sources.
12. Dr Satyanarayan Sinha, *China Strikes*, p. 151.
13. Ibid., p. 41.
14. Quoted in Korbel, p. 260.
15. Ibid., p. 267; for Communist activities in Kashmir, see ibid., pp. 249–71.
16. A. G. Noorani, *The Kashmir Question*, p. 71.
17. Quoted in ibid., pp. 71–2.
18. Quoted in ibid., p. 73.
19. Author's sources in India.

8: Peking's Policy

1. For further historical background on these developments see, inter alia, Peter S. H. Tang, *Communist China Today*, Vol. 1; Max Beloff, *Soviet Policy in the Far East*; George Paloczi-Horvath, *Mao Tse-Tung: Emperor of the Blue Ants*; Allen S. Whiting, *China Crosses the Yalu, The Decision to Enter the Korean War*, Macmillan, New York and London 1960; Klaus Mehnert, *Peking and Moscow*.
2. Diplomatic sources in Saigon and Washington.

3. Brown, p. 347.
4. Sinha, pp. 145–7; Frank Moraes, *Nehru, Sunlight and Shadow*, p. 106; Dennis J. Doolin, *Territorial Claims in the Sino-Soviet Conflict*.
5. O. Edmund Clubb, *20th Century China*, Columbia University Press, New York and London 1964, p. 417.
6. *A Comment on the Statement of the CP of the USA*, and editorial in *Renmin Ribao* of March 8, 1963; published in *Peking Review*, Nos. 10–11, March 15, 1963.
7. Quoted in George N. Patterson, *Peking Versus Delhi*, pp. 121–2.
8. Khrushchev speech to the Sixth SED Congress.
9. Khrushchev message to the 9th International Conference at Hiroshima, Japan, for the Banning of Atomic and Hydrogen Weapons, August 19, 1963 (italics added).
10. Khrushchev speech of January 6, 1961, "For the New Victories of the World Communist Movement", *Kommunist*, No. 1, January, 1961.
11. H. Dona, *Peaceful Coexistence: A Basic Principle of the Foreign Policy of the Rumanian People's Republic*, State Publishing House, Bucharest 1963, p. 2 (italics added).
12. Moraes, p. 95.
13. Margaret W. Fisher, et al, *Himalayan Battleground, Sino-Indian Rivalry in Ladakh*, p. 146.
14. Ibid., p. 86.
15. Ibid., p. 89.
16. Ibid., pp. 91–128.
17. Moraes, p. 118.
18. Nasim Ahmad, "China's Himalayan Frontiers: Pakistan's Attitude", *International Affairs*, October 1962, p. 428; quoted in *Orbis*, Summer 1964, p. 395, fn 11.
19. Fisher, pp. 139–40.
20. Ibid., p. 142.
21. Sinha, pp. 131–7.
22. *The Origin and Development of the Differences Between the Leadership of CPSU and Ourselves, Comment on the Open Letter of The Central Committee of the CPSU*, Foreign Languages Press, Peking 1963, p. 32 (hereafter identified as *Origin*).
23. Sinha, p. 148.
24. *Origin*, p. 47.
25. *Christian Science Monitor*, August 29, 1963.
26. Red Flag (*Hongqi*) editorial, November 21, 1964, "Why Khrushchev Fell", published in *Peking Review*, No. 45, November 27, 1964.
27. Summary of report by Mikhail A. Suslov, distributed by Tass News Agency, *New York Times*, April 4, 1965.
28. *Renmin Ribao-Hongqi* editorial of February 4, 1964; *New York Times*, February 7, 1964.
29. *The Proletarian Revolution and Khrushchev's Revisionism, Comment on the Open Letter of The Central Committee of the CPSU* (VIII), Foreign Languages Press, Peking 1964, pp. 87–8.

30. Kaznacheev, pp. 123–4.
31. *Origin*, pp. 54–5.

9: THE CHINESE ATTACK ON INDIA
1. Fisher, pp. 131–2.
2. Ibid., p. 134.
3. *Notes, Memoranda and Letters Exchanged and Agreements Signed Between the Governments of India and China*, Vols. VI and VII. See also C. N. Satyapalan, "The Sino-Indian Border Conflict", *Orbis*, Vol. VIII, No. 2, Summer 1964, pp. 374–90.
4. Fisher, p. 135.
5. Ibid., pp. 135–6.
6. Ibid., p. 135.
7. Sinha, p. 85.
8. *Treachery in the Himalayas*, p. 19 (hereafter identified as *Treachery*).
9. Quoted by Sinha, pp. 155–6.
10. Quoted in *India-China Conflict*, p. 1.
11. Quoted by Sinha, p. 83.
12. Fisher, pp. 137–8.
13. Moraes, p. 117.
14. Interview with the Associated Press of Pakistan, April 10, 1963; *Dawn*, April 11, 1963.
15. Author's interviews in New Delhi.
16. *Treachery*, pp. 21; 25.
17. Quoted in Arthur Stein, "India's Relations with the USSR, 1953–1963", *Orbis*, Summer 1964, p. 363.
18. Alexander Dallin, et al, *Diversity in International Communism, A Documentary Record, 1961–1963*, p. 660.
19. Stein, p. 366, fn 23.
20. *The Truth About How the Leaders of the CPSU Have Allied Themselves With India Against China*, Foreign Languages Press, Peking 1963, p. 6.
21. Sinha, p. 151.
22. W. M. Dobell, "Ramifications of the China-Pakistan Border Treaty", *Pacific Affairs*, Autumn 1964, p. 290.
23. For a discussion of the Pakistani position, see S. M. Burke, "Sino-Pakistani Relations", *Orbis*, Summer 1964; pp. 391–404.
24. Dobell, p. 289.
25. Fisher, p. 143.
26. Brown, p. 349.
27. Quoted by Warren Unna, "Pakistan, Friend of Our Enemies", *The Atlantic*, March 1964.
28. Quoted by Dobell, p. 292.
29. Ibid.
30. Sisir Gupta, *Kashmir, A Study in India-Pakistan Relations*, pp. 352–5.
31. Dr Sudhir Ghosh, *Gandhi's Emissary*, pre-publication excerpts, No. III, *The Statesman*, February 16, 1967.

10: NATIONS STRIVING TO BE BORN

1. General Secretary Upadhyaya of the Jana Sangh, quoted in H. D. Malaviya, *The Danger of Right Reaction*, p. 30.
2. Speech in New York, May 4, 1965, under joint auspices of Pakistani-American Chamber of Commerce and The Asian Society.
3. Khalid B. Sayeed, p. 239.
4. W. M. Dobell, pp. 286 and 292.
5. *New York Times*, September 12, 1965.
6. *Daily Ittefaq*, Dacca, June 24, 1965; Nurul Amin in the East Pakistan Assembly, quoted in *Pakistan Observer*, Dacca, July 6, 1965.
7. Jacques Nevard, *New York Times*, April 24, 1965.
8. *US Participation in The UN, Report by the President to the Congress for The Year 1964*, State Department Publication 7943, released February 1966, pp. 63–70.
9. Letter from Sheikh Abdullah to Prime Minister Shastri, March 17, 1965 (hereafter identified as Abdullah Letter). Distributed by The Action Committee, Srinagar.
10. Selig S. Harrison, "Troubled India and Her Neighbors", *Foreign Affairs*, Vol. XLV, January 1965, p. 321.
11. Ibid.
12. Louis Dupree, "First Reflections on The Second Kashmir War", *American University Field Staff, South Asia Series*, Vol. 9, No. 5, December 1965, p. 4.
13. David W. Wainhouse, et al, *International Peace Observation, A History and Forecast*, pp. 357–73.
14. Ibid., p. 368.
15. Ibid., pp. 368–9.
16. Ibid., pp. 369, 370–1.
17. Abdullah Letter.
18. Ibid.
19. *Renmin Ribao-Hongqi* editorial, February 4, 1964 (italics added).

11: DIPLOMATIC PRELUDES TO WAR

1. Based upon the author's interviews in New Delhi, Saigon and Washington DC, 1965.
2. Maj. Gen. P. S. Bhagat, *Forging the Shield*, pp. 90–1.
3. P. J. Honey, *Communism in North Viet Nam, Its Role in the Sino-Soviet Dispute*, pp. 67–8, 111; US State Department, *Aggression from the North*, Department of State Publication 7839, released February 1965, pp. 20–1.
4. Frank N. Trager, "The United States and Pakistan: A Failure of Diplomacy", *Orbis*, Fall 1965, p. 629. (In possible confirmation of its major points, the Pakistani government widely distributed reprints of this article.)
5. "Foreign Assistance and Related Agencies Appropriations for 1966", *Hearings before A Subcommittee of the Committee on Appropriations, House of Representatives, Eighty-Ninth Congress, First Session*, US Government Printing Office, Washington 1965, p. 266 (hereafter: *Hearings*).

6. Department of State Press Release 679, November 17, 1962.
7. *Hindustan Times*, November 30, 1965.
8. Cecil V. Crabb, Jr., "The Testing of Non-Alignment", *Western Political Quarterly*, September 1964, pp. 528–32.
9. *Hearings*, p. 267.
10. D. R. Mankekar, *Twenty-two Fateful Days: Pakistan Cut to Size*, pp. 13–14.
11. *Indian Express*, October 8, 1964.
12. Ayub broadcast to the nation, *Dawn*, January 15, 1966.
13. *Hindustan Times*, November 17, 1965.
14. *US Participation in the UN*, p. 66.

12: MILITARY PRELUDES
1. Mankekar, p. 30.
2. Author's interviews, New Delhi.
3. Mankekar, p. 33.
4. *Pakistan's New Attempt to Grab Kashmir*, p. 13 (hereafter: *New Attempt*).
5. Mankekar, p. 17.
6. Quoted in Dewan Berindranath, *The War With Pakistan*, p. 111.
7. *Dawn*, June 20, 1965.
8. Mankekar, pp. 28 and 31.
9. Quoted in ibid., pp. 28–30.
10. Ibid., p. 14.
11. Abdullah Letter.
12. S/6651, *Report by UN Secretary-General U Thant to the Security Council*, September 3, 1965
13. *New Attempt*, pp. 12–13.
14. S/6672, *Prime Minister Shastri's message to UN Secretary-General, September 4, 1965*, September 8, 1965.
15. *New Attempt*, p. 19.
16. Mankekar, p. 58.
17. Prof. M. A. Aziz, *Struggle for the Liberation of Kashmir*.
18. Author's interviews, New Delhi.

13: THE HOSTILITIES
1. Mankekar, p. 61; Berindranath, p. 7.
2. Panyapriya Dasgupta in *Indian Express*, August 31, 1965. For the fact there was no uprising see, inter alia, *New York Times*, October 12, 1965, a point confirmed by the author's investigations in New Delhi and Washington.
3. *The Times*, London, October 25, 1965.
4. Mankekar, p. 63.
5. Prime Minister Shastri's broadcast to the nation, August 13, 1965.
6. Aziz, p. 8.
7. Ibid., p. 7.
8. Mankekar, pp. 76–7.
9. M. Swaram, *Indian Express*, September 4, 1965.
10. For a discussion of the Hamburg revolution, see Werner T. Angress,

Stillborn Revolution: The Communist Bid For Power in Germany, 1921–1923, Princeton University Press, Princeton, 1963; for Canton, see, in addition to Isaacs, Robert C. North, *Moscow and Chinese Communists*; for an official outline of Soviet revolutionary tactics, see A. Neuberg, *Le Plan Communiste d'Insurrection Armée*. (The original document was published by the Communist International and has not been rescinded. Neuberg, it is widely believed, was the pseudonym of Heinz Neumann, a principal strategist in the Canton revolution of 1927 and once a Stalinist favourite, until he was liquidated in the Great Purges.) See also: Gunther Nollau, *International Communism & World Revolution, History and Methods*. For the basic principles of Asian tactics, see inter alia, *Selected Works of Mao Tse-tung*, Vol. II, particularly: "Strategic Problems in the anti-Japanese Guerrilla War" and "On the Protracted War"; Vo Nguyên Giap, *La guerre de libération et l'armée populaire*; George K. Tanham, *Communist Revolutionary Warfare, The Vietminh in Indochina*.

11. *Washington Post*, July 3, 1966, and September 18, 1966.

12. Mankekar, p. 77.

13. Berindranath, p. 10.

14. Mankekar, pp. 71–4.

15. B. G. Verghese, *India Answers Pakistan*, p. 7.

16. Mankekar, pp. 93–5; Berindranath, p. 17 *ff*; Verghese, p. 9.

17. Prime Minister Shastri, speech in Hindi at Ramila grounds, New Delhi, September 26, 1965; contained in publication, *When Freedom is Menaced*, p. 54. The publication includes selected speeches of the Prime Minister from August 13 to September 26, 1965. Hereafter, in referring to these particular addresses, the pamphlet, identified as *Freedom*, will be cited, with page numbers.

18. Mankekar, p. 92.

19. Verghese, p. 9.

20. S/6661, *Report by the UN Secretary-General on the situation in Kashmir*, September 6, 1965.

21. S/6699, *Report by the Secretary-General*, September 21, 1965.

22. Mankekar, p. 95.

23. Ibid., pp. 98–9.

24. *Freedom*, p. 55.

25. Mankekar, p. 99; see also ibid., pp. 102–30 for the most detailed account of the Punjab campaign, on which the author has drawn heavily.

26. Verghese, p. 11.

27. *Freedom*, pp. 54–5.

28. Broadcast to the nation by President Ayub Khan, September 22, 1965, published by Department of Films and Publication, Pakistan government, Karachi, September 1965, p. 4.

29. Mankekar, p. 102.

30. *New York Times*, September 7, 1965.

31. Brady's story is contained in *New York Times* file of supplemental material.

32. Brady interview with Indian field commander, *New York Times* supplemental file, September 23, 1965.

33. Brady, on basis of interview with Indian brigade commander, *New York Times* supplemental file.
34. Mankekar, p. 118; for further details of this battle see ibid., pp. 112–19; Verghese, pp. 11–13; Berindranath, pp. 51–8; *New York Times* supplemental file, September 23, 1965.
35. Mankekar, p. 98.
36. Berindranath, p. 60.
37. President Ayub, broadcast speech of September 22, p. 5. For more on the Pakistani version of the hostilities, see also Rahman A. Syed and Wing-Commander M. Syed (Retd.), eds., *Pakistan's Finest Hour*.
38. John Norris, *Washington Post*, October 17, 1695.
39. Ibid.
40. Berindranath, p. 70.
41. *Washington Post*, October 17, 1965.
42. Mankekar, p. 136.
43. *The Hindu*, Madras, August 10, 1965; *The Statesman*, New Delhi, August 17, 1965.
44. *Hindustan Times*, New Delhi, August 15, 1965.
45. Mankekar, p. 15.
46. Brady dispatch of September 23, 1965.

14: WAR DIPLOMACY

1. S/6683, *Preliminary Report by the Secretary-General on His Visits to the Governments of India and Pakistan*, September 16, 1965.
2. Speech of Prime Minister Shastri to Lok Sabha, November 16, 1965, PTI report.
3. *Hearings*, p. 671.
4. Mankekar, p. 165; Brady, frontline interview with Indian commanders, September 23, 1965, *New York Times* supplemental file.
5. Louis B. Fleming, *Los Angeles Times*, in dispatch dated September 4, 1965; AP and Reuter dispatches, same date; S/6672.
6. *New York Times*, September 9, 1965; S/6666, *Telegram from President Ayub to UN Secretary-General*, dated September 5.
7. *New York Times*, September 8 and 9, 1965.
8. Ibid, September 7, 1965.
9. PTI dispatch, August 25, 1965.
10. *The Statesman*, New Delhi, September 6, 1965.
11. *New York Times*, September 8, 1965.
12. Ibid., September 12, 1965.
13. *Washington Post*, September 16, 1965.
14. *New York Times*, September 10 and 12, 1965.
15. Harrison in *Washington Post*, September 14 and 15, 1965.
16. S/6683.
17. Reuters dispatch, *Washington Post*, September 17, 1965.
18. *Washington Post*, September 17, 1965.
19. Statement by Prime Minister Shastri to Lok Sabha, September 17, 1965.

20. *Washington Post*, September 19, 1965.
21. Ibid.; *Washington Star*, September 22, 1965.
22. S/6686, *Second Report by the Secretary-General on His Mission to India and Pakistan*; *Washington Post*, September 19, 1965.
23. *New York Times*, International Edition, September 22, 25 and 26, 1965.
24. Z. A. Bhutto, "Kashmir, Last Chance for the United Nations", speech at The General Assembly, September 22, 1965, published by Department of Films and Publications, Government of Pakistan, October 1965.
25. William E. Griffith, "Sino-Soviet Relations, 1964–65", *China Quarterly*, No. 25, January–March 1966, p. 116.
26. Quoted in ibid., p. 115, fn 378.
27. Ibid., p. 117.
28. *New York Times*, dispatch from Hong Kong, September 21, 1965.
29. Charles Taylor, *Toronto Globe and Mail*, published in *Washington Post*, September 30, 1965.
30. President Ayub's speech of September 22, 1965.
31. *New York Times*, supplemental file, September 26, 1965.
32. *New York Times*, International Edn., September 23, 1965.

15: MILITARY AFTERMATH

1. S/6888, *Report by the Secretary-General Relating to an Aspect of the Procedures Employed in Observing and Reporting on the Cease-Fire*, November 9, 1965.
2. S/6719, *Report by the Secretary-General on Compliance With The Withdrawal Provision of Security Council Resolution 211 of 20 September 1965*, September 27, 1965; S/6782, *Letters from the Secretary-General to the Permanent Representatives of Pakistan and India*, October 13, 1965; *New York Times*, December 15, 1965.
3. S/6836, *Letter Dated 26 October 1965 from the Minister for External Affairs of India Addressed to the President of the Security Council*, October 27, 1965, pp. 4–5 and 8.
4. S/6719, p. 3.
5. S/6710, *Report by the Secretary-General on the Observance of the Cease-Fire under Security Council Resolution 211 of 20 September 1965*, November 13, 1965, add. 9, p. 14; S/6865, *Letter Dated November 2, 1965, from the Permanent Representative of Pakistan Addressed to the President of the Security Council*, November 3, 1965, pp. 9–10.
6. S/6828, *Letter of October 25, 1965, from the Permanent Representative of Pakistan*; S/6836, pp. 5–6.
7. S/6710, add. 9, pp. 13 and 3–4.
8. S/6836, pp. 6 ff.
9. S/6710, add. 8, p. 6.
10. Mankekar, p. 163.
11. Quoted in S/6858, *Letter of November 1, 1965, from the Permanent Representative of Pakistan*, p. 3.
12. A/6100, pp. 3–4.

13. *New York Times*, November 6, 1965.
14. PTI report in *Hindustan Times*, November 8, 1965.
15. President Ayub, speech of September 22, 1965, p. 3.
16. Speech in Hyderabad, November 14, 1965; *Hindustan Times*, November 15, 1965.
17. S/6687, *Report by the Secretary-General on the Military Situation in the Area of Conflict Between India and Pakistan*, September 16, 1965, p. 1.
18. S/6790, *Letter of October 14 from the Permanent Representative of India;* S/6836, p. 11.
19. Haynes Johnson, *Washington Sunday Star*, October 17, 1965.
20. S/6836, p. 11.
21. S/6865, p. 11.
22. See inter alia, *Washington Star*, October 17, 1965; *The Times*, October 25 *Toronto Globe and Mail*, October 27; *New York Times*, October 25.
23. David Van Praagh, *Toronto Globe and Mail*, October 27, 1965.
24. Ibid.
25. *New York Times*, October 17, 1965.
26. S/6821, S/6879, S/6950, *Letters from the Permanent Representative of Pakistan dated October 22, November 5 and 18, 1965.*
27. S/6783, *Note Delivered by the Indian Government to the Embassy of China in New Delhi*, October 2, 1965.
28. *Hindustan Times*, November 25, 1965.
29. Ibid., December 5 and 15, 1965.
30. Griffith, p. 117.

16. THE TASHKENT CONFERENCE

1. *Hindustan Times*, January 5, 1966.
2. *Hindustan Times*, December 3, 1966.
3. *Hindustan Times*, January 10, 1966.
4. *Hindustan Times*, February 22, 1966.
5. *Dawn*, January 15, 1966.
6. *Hindustan Times*, February 22, 1966.

17: THE 'SPIRIT OF TASHKENT'

1. *Washington Post*, Rawalpindi dateline, March 24, 1966.
2. Lukas, *New York Times*, July 3, 1966.
3. *New York Times*, Karachi dateline, August 11, 1966.
4. *New York Times*, Washington dateline, August 12, 1966.
5. Ibid.
6. *New York Times*, December 16, 1965.
7. *New York Times*, July 24, 1966.
8. *New York Times*, June 30, 1966.
9. *New York Times*, October 2, 1966.
10. *The Military Balance, 1966–1967*, pp. 66–7.
11. George Sherman, *Washington Star*, April 13, 1967.
12. *Hindustan Times*, February 6, 1967.
13. *New York Times*, January 30, 1967.

INDEX

2H

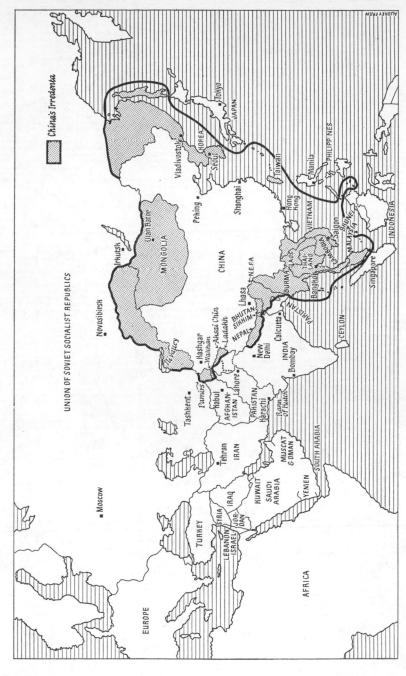

AUDREY FRAEW

UNION OF SOVIET SOCIALIST REPUBLICS

☐ Chinas Irredenta

1 : Eurasia

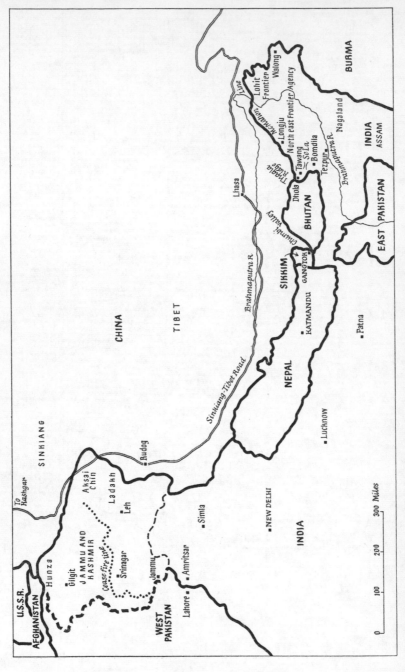

2: Sino-Indian Border

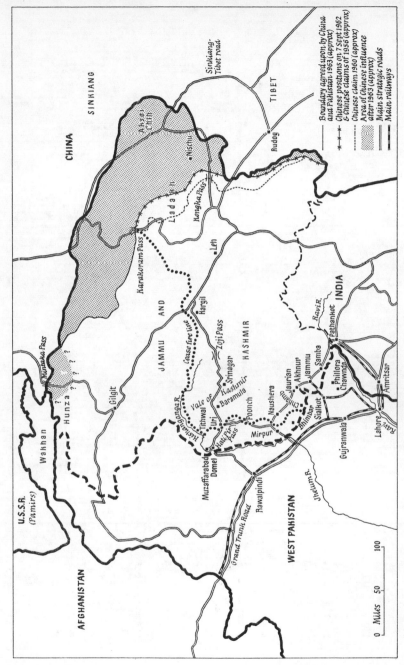

3: Jammu and Kashmir: main strategic features

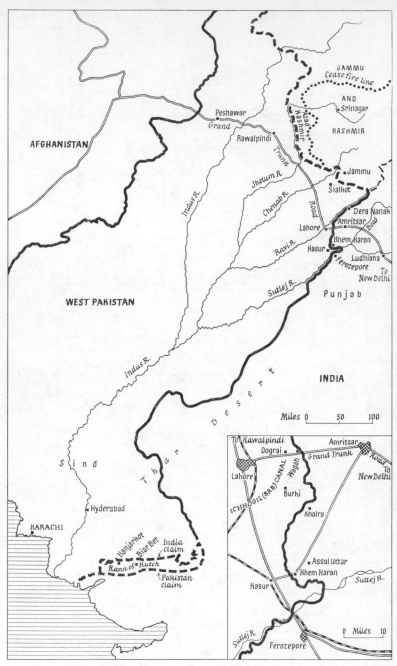

4: Indo-Pakistan Border